HMRC Investigations
Enquiries 2011–12

HMRC Investigations and Enquiries 2011–12

General Editor
Graham Funnell
Indpendent tax journalist

Bloomsbury Professional

Bloomsbury Professional Ltd
Maxwelton House
41–43 Boltro Road
Haywards Heath
West Sussex
RH16 1BJ

© Bloomsbury Professional Ltd 2011

Bloomsbury Professional is an imprint of Bloomsbury Publishing plc

All rights reserved. No part of this publication may be reproduced in any material form (including photocopying or storing it in any medium by electronic means and whether or not transiently or incidentally to some other use of this publication) without the written permission of the copyright owner except in accordance with the provisions of the Copyright, Designs and Patents Act 1988 or under the terms of a licence issued by the Copyright Licensing Agency Ltd, Saffron House, 6–10 Kirby Street, London, EC1N 8TS, England. Applications for the copyright owner's written permission to reproduce any part of this publication should be addressed to the publisher.
Warning: The doing of an unauthorised act in relation to a copyright work may result in both a civil claim for damages and criminal prosecution.
Crown copyright material is reproduced with the permission of the Controller of HMSO and the Queen's Printer for Scotland. Parliamentary copyright material is reproduced with the permission of the Controller of Her Majesty's Stationery Office on behalf of Parliament. Any European material in this work which has been reproduced from EUR-lex, the official European Communities legislation website, is European Communities copyright.

British Library Cataloguing-in-Publication Data
A CIP Catalogue record for this book is available from the British Library.

ISBN 978 1 84766 532 4

Typeset by Columns Design XML Ltd, Reading, Berkshire
Printed and bound by CPI Group (UK) Ltd, Croydon, CR0 4YY

Preface

Since the second edition of this book we have witnessed a change of Government and two Finance Acts, as well as further redundancies amongst mainly the clerical staff at HMRC. However, the new Coalition government is committed to closing the 'tax gap' and unearthing as much as possible of the Hidden Economy.

It is evident from several highly-significant recent events that HMRC have not only increasingly harnessed modern technology as part of their information-gathering and dissemination process, they have partially changed direction. Following the various offshore Disclosure Opportunities, more of the same have been promised as soon as time and resources permit. However a bold and decisive move, in January 2010, was to offer a similar disclosure opportunity to various segments of the medical profession, with the promise of lighter penalties for those who made a voluntary disclosure by 30 June 2010. HMRC subsequently announced that some of the early disclosures revealed several sources of sundry income in that profession of which even they were not previously aware!

It has also been established, as a result of *HMRC v Glenn & Co (Essex) Ltd*, that HMRC can legally remove computers from business premises when making an inspection visit, to copy the hard-drives, as long as they return them promptly.

Against the above backdrop there has also been the HMRC 'raid' in June 2010 on the offices of media accountants Christopher Lunn & Co, where the files of up to 7,000 clients were removed by HMRC for perusal. This was quickly followed by letters from HMRC to most of the clients of that practice stating that Christopher Lunn & Co was subject to an HMRC *criminal* investigation, with all affected clients being given a Disclosure Opportunity, offering lighter penalties, providing they disclose tax irregularities by 28 February 2011. Whilst the offices of some small firms of accountants and tax-avoidance specialists have been raided by HMRC in the past, this is the first time one with so many clients has been tackled in this way. It should be noted that no formal criminal charges have yet been brought by HMRC against Christopher Lunn & Co, who have proclaimed themselves to be completely innocent, and hired a top law firm to represent them.

Preface

Finally, we have seen an increasing trend for politicians *and* HMRC to group together their objectives of 'tackling tax-avoidance, evasion and fraud' in the public perception. A prominent example of this was at the Liberal Democrat party conference, when Chief Secretary to the Treasury, the Rt Hon Danny Alexander MP, announced extra £900m HMRC spending for that same purpose.

All these issues are discussed in detail within this book, with many chapters having been completely re-written this year. Practitioners who deal with HMRC investigations on a regular basis will find this book an invaluable reference and resource, as will those for whom such client-investigations are only a rarity.

Graham J Funnell

Graham Funnell is an accountant and tax specialist whose chosen area of expertise is countering HMRC investigations.

Contents

Table of statutes	xiii
Table of statutory instruments	xix
Table of cases	xxiii

Chapter 1 Enquiries under self-assessment — 1
Introduction — 1
Disclosure — 2
Handling an enquiry — 3
The start of an enquiry — 5
Meetings — 9
Books and records — 14
Section 19A and para 27 notices issued prior to 1 April 2009 — 15
The section 19A procedure — 21
Information powers from 1 April 2009: FA 2008 Sch 36 — 23
Completion of enquiry — 27
Discovery — 29

Chapter 2 Special Investigations — 31
The role of Special Investigations Office (SI) — 31
Structure of Special Investigations Office — 32
Criminal investigations — 33
Definition of fraud — 34
The Fraud Act 2006 — 36
Code of Practice 9 — 36
Civil Investigation of Fraud procedures — 38
Civil Investigation of Fraud thresholds — 42
Code of Practice 8 – cases other than suspected serious fraud — 42
Handling SI/CIF investigations — 43
HMRC compliance projects — 44
Offshore disclosure campaigns — 45
Professional campaigns — 50
Trade campaigns — 51

Contents

Chapter 3 VAT and Revenue & Customs visits   53
Overall concept   53
Assurance visits   54
Credibility visits   60
Intrastat visits   61
Mutual assistance through exchange of information   62
Other visits   63
Preparing for visits   63
Search and entry   66
Surveillance operations   68
Investigations   69
Role of the professional adviser   70

**Chapter 4 National Insurance visits
and investigations**   73
Inspectorate powers   73
Record keeping   79
Errors and omissions   80
Inspection report   81
Future visits   81
Conclusion   82

**Chapter 5 National Insurance: fines, penalties
and appeals**   83
Offences and penalties   83
Interest   90
Appeals   92

Chapter 6 NIC investigation trigger points   103
Introduction   103
Reasons for investigations   105
Conclusion   112

Chapter 7 Criminal investigations in relation to direct tax 115
Background   115
Investigation statistics   115
The new regime   118
Prosecution policy   120
Factors suggesting the likelihood of criminal investigation 121
The organisation of criminal investigation in HMRC   123
HMRC's criminal investigation powers   124
Search warrants and production orders   125
Order for the delivery of documents under TMA 1970, s 20BA   128
Dealing with a dawn raid   132
Intrusive surveillance   134
Legal privilege   134
Interviews   135
The trial   136

Chapter 8 The nexus between tax evasion and money laundering   139
Introduction   139
A brief history of tax evasion   140
The money laundering legislation   142
The view of the government   146
Guidance for financial intermediaries and professional advisers   148
The role of the fiscal authorities   154
The risk to financial intermediaries and professionals   157
Conclusion   161

Chapter 9 Meetings with HMRC   163
Introduction   163
Purpose of the meeting   164
Preparing for the meeting   167
What the compliance officer wants   170
Checklist for preparing for a meeting   170
The meeting itself   171
Pre-planning checklist   180
During the visit itself   181
Checklist for areas the compliance officers are likely to review   181
Conclusions   182

Chapter 10 The information powers of HMRC   183
Introduction   183

Finance Act 2008, Sch 36   187
The criminal investigatory powers of HMRC   210

Appendix The pre-1 April 2009 direct tax powers   219
Introduction   219
Overview of TMA 1970, s 20   220
The indirect tax powers   235

Chapter 11 Tax appeals   241
Introduction   241
Section one – introduction of the new tribunal system   243
The overriding objective   247
Alternative Dispute Resolution   248
Section 2   248
Indirect taxes   249
Direct taxes   250
Section three – the First-tier Tribunal   256
The position before the predecessor tribunals   263
Approach of the High Court   264
Section four – the Upper Tribunal   270

Contents

Jurisdiction of the First-tier Tribunal in respect of public law matters	273
Section five – the tax courts	277

Chapter 12 Settlement negotiations — 281

Introduction	281
Start the negotiating groundwork early	282
Are interest and penalties due?	282
Calculation of interest	282
Penalty negotiation	282
Payments on account	284
VAT disclosure	285
Professional costs	285
Why negotiate?	286
Consideration of grey areas	287
Litigation and settlements strategy	288
The art of negotiation	288
Claims, allowances and reliefs	291
Remittances by non-domiciled individuals	291
Innocent error and reasonable excuse	291
Advantages for the officer	292
Workload	293
When agreement cannot be reached	293
The settlement package	293
Funding the settlement and time to pay	294
The letter of offer	296
Making sub-standard offers	296
Settlement meetings	297
Relationship with the officer	297
Relationship with the client	298

Chapter 13 Employees and directors — 301

Scope of chapter	301
Introduction	302
PAYE compliance issues	303
Directors	321
Schedule E benefits and reimbursed expenses	321
Liability for tax arising	345

Chapter 14 The new penalty regime — 347

Consultation documents	347
New legislation	348
HMRC material	349
Defaults and errors	349
Potential lost revenue	350
Documents subject to the new regime	350
Degrees of culpability	351
Quality of disclosure	354
New penalty concepts	358

Amount of the penalty	359
Time limit	359
Appeals	359
The previous penalty regime	360
Transitional rules	361
Computer records	361
Information and inspection powers	361
Failure to notify	362
Senior accounting officers	365
Naming and shaming	365
Powers to obtain contact details for debtors	366
Time limits for assessments	366
Penalties for failure to make returns	366
Multiple penalties	367
Amount of penalty	367
Reductions for disclosure	368
Failure to pay tax	369
Suspension of penalties: deferred payment	372
Offshore disclosures	372
Breach of minimum wage legislation	374
Consequences and action	374
Chapter 15 Tax avoidance investigations	**375**
Introduction	375
What is tax avoidance?	376
The current avoidance environment	377
The evolution of avoidance case law	388
HMRC approach to working avoidance enquiries	398
Key implications and considerations for the advisor	407
Appendix 1: Supplementary Anti-Money Laundering Guidance for the Tax Practitioner	**414**
Contents	414
Glossary and interpretation	414
1. About this supplementary guidance	415
2. How to use this supplementary guidance	415
3. Tax practitioners, MLR 2007 and POCA	416
4. Overview of the tax sector	416
5. What are the money laundering risks in the tax sector?	417
6. Tax offences	417
7. Reluctance to correct past errors	418
8. Intention to underpay tax	419
9. Tax evasion	420
10. Failure to obtain Treasury consent – s765 ICTA	421
11. Indirect tax	422
12. The privilege reporting exemption	424
13. Customer due diligence (CDD)	425

Contents

Appendix 1: Money Laundering and disclosures to HMRC: A Questions and Answers guidance note	426
Appendix 2: Examples of when the privilege reporting exemption *might* apply	428
Appendix 3: Examples of when the privilege reporting exemption is *unlikely* to apply	429

Appendix 2: An Anti-Money Laundering Strategy for the Inland Revenue — 431

1. Background	431
2. Roles and Responsibilities within Government	433
3. The Inland Revenue's prosecution policy	434
4. Strategic Themes	437

Appendix 3: Criminal Finances Strategic Framework — 441

Contents page	441
Purpose	441
Cross-Government Working	442
HMRC's Objectives	444
Business Areas	448
Powers	449
Cash Seizures and Forfeiture	451
Restraint and Confiscation	452
Civil Recovery and taxation (ARA)	454
Money Laundering	454
Money Service Businesses and High Value Dealers	456
Taxing Crime and the Criminal Taxes Unit	458
Next Steps	459
Abbreviations	460

Index — 461

Table of Statutes

	PARA
Access to Justice Act 1999	11.120
s 54(4)	11.122
55(1)	11.121
Capital Allowances Act 2001	
s 45	11.41
Sch 2, para 51(1)(a)	13.133
Children Act 1989	
Pt IV	10.95
Commissioners for Revenue and Customs Act 2005	12.02
s 35	10.04
Companies Act 1976	1.49
Constitutional Reform Act 2005	11.111
Criminal Justice Act 1988	8.43
Criminal Justice Act 1993	8.20, 8.21, 8.53
Criminal Justice (International Cooperation) Act 1990	
s 4	8.37
Criminal Justice and Police Act 2001	7.21
s 50	10.122, 10A.45
52	10.123
Criminal Justice and Public Order Act 1994	
s 34	7.44
Criminal Procedures and Investigation Act 1996	7.16
Customs and Excise Management Act 1979	3.64
Employment Act 2002	
s 11	5.03
12	5.03
Sch 1	5.03
Finance Act 1988	
s 126	10A.29, 10A.31
127(1)	10A.51
172(2)	10A.19

	PARA
Finance Act 1989	5.13
s 144	10A.11
178	5.39
Finance Act 1995	
s 106(9)(b)	13.163
Finance Act 1996	
s 54	11.30
Finance Act 1998	
s 58	13.38
127(1)	1.57
Sch 18	9.40, 9.62, 11.36
para 2	14.98
3	14.24, 14.27
3–35	1.10
17	14.88
18	14.88
21(1)	1.39
21(2)	1.40
21(3)	1.40
21(6)	1.40
22	1.78–1.80
24	1.15, 1.77, 10.22, 10A.50
24(1)	1.52
27	1.19, 1.48, 1.49, 1.58, 1.59, 1.63–1.69, 1.100, 10.21, 10.22, 10.83, 10A.48
27(1)(b)	1.48
28	1.63
28(4)	1.66
28(5)	1.67
28(6)	1.66
29	10A.57
31A–31D	11.43
32(1)	1.91
33	1.92
34	1.91
34(3)	1.94

Table of Statutes

	PARA
Finance Act 1998 – *contd*	
s 127(1) – *contd*	
Sch 18 – *contd*	
para 46	1.99
48	11.35
64	1.74
Finance Act 1999	13.147
Finance Act 2000	
s 38	13.59, 13.60
149(1)	10.138
Sch 10	13.145
Finance Act 2003	
Sch 10	11.35
Finance Act 2007	7.15, 10.01, 10.08
s 97	14.07
Sch 24	5.19, 5.25, 5.27, 10.09, 10.11, 10.109, 14.07, 14.11
para 1	12.10, 14.21
5	14.17
9(1)	14.42
Finance Act 2008	
Pt 1	1.73
Pts 4–9	1.73
s 36	3.67
113	14.07, 14.90
114	14.07
115	14.07
116	14.07
118	14.07
119	14.07
122	14.07
123	14.07, 14.97
Sch 36	1.18–1.23, 1.46, 1.84, 1.100, 3.64, 4.03, 9.62, 9.69, 10.03, 10.13–10.71, 10A.14, 10A.60, 13.10, 14.07, 14.90, 14.123, 14.187
Pt 1	1.74
2	1.29, 1.35, 1.86–1.89, 10.51
5	1.82, 2.77, 2.85
6	1.83
para 1	10.21–10.28
2	10.29–10.37
5	10.41–10.51
10	10.52–10.55
10A	10.67
11	10.64–10.66
12	10.60, 10.62
12A	10.69
12B	10.71
13	10.57, 10.71
18	10.73
19(1)(a)	10.103

	PARA
Finance Act 2008 – *contd*	
Pt 1 – *contd*	
Pt 6 – *contd*	
23	10.87
24	10.104
25	10.105
26	10.106, 10.107
28	10.56
34A	10.38–10.40
39	10.58, 10.101, 10.110
40	10.58, 10.110
40A	10.113
44	10.111
45	10.58, 10.101
50	10.110, 11.100
61A	10.68
84	4.03
Sch 37	1.39, 1.44, 3.64, 14.07
Sch 39	3.64, 14.07
Sch 40	14.07
para 3	14.70
Sch 41	14.07, 14.97
para 2	14.101
12	14.102
13	14.102
14	14.106
21	14.109
22	14.107
Finance Act 2009	3.59, 14.07
s 93	14.07, 14.114
94	14.07, 14.119
95	10.12, 14.07
96	10.12, 14.07
97	14.122
97–109	14.07
106	14.126
107	14.151
108	14.1676u
Sch 46	14.07, 14.114
Sch 47	10.12, 10.55, 10.65, 10A.14, 14.07
Sch 48	0.12, 10.20, 10.67, 10.68, 14.07
Sch 49	14.122
Schs 49–56	14.07
Sch 51, para 16	14.124
Sch 55	5.13, 5.17, 14.07, 14.126
Sch 56	14.151
Sch 57, para 6	14.77
Finance (No 3) Act 2010	10.01
Finance Act 2011	10.01
Fraud Act 2006	2.21–2.23, 8.15
Human Rights Act 1998	7.10

Table of Statutes

	PARA
Income and Corporation Taxes Act 1988	
s 419	1.52
Income Tax (Earnings and Pensions) Act 2003	5.11
s 6	13.05
7	13.05, 13.98, 13.126
7(5)	13.145
10	13.49
10(2)	13.05
44	13.79
62(2)	13.05
66(4)	13.103
71	13.107, 13.144
97–113	13.115
99(1)	13.115
105	13.115
125	13.121
126	13.121
132	13.121
167(1)	13.121
174(1)	13.145
180	13.145
180(5)	13.145
188	13.41
188(2)	13.145
203	13.41
203(2)	13.110
203(3)	13.118
204	13.110
216(3)	13.121
223(7)	13.172
225	13.34
237(2)	13.121
240	13.149
264	13.157
288(4)	13.155
315	13.115
316(1)	13.147
320	13.118
321	13.160
328	13.159
328(1)	13.118, 13.136, 13.140, 13.145, 13.147
336	13.94, 13.97
337	13.165, 13.168
356(1)	13.133
357	13.133
394	13.36
403	13.30, 13.33, 13.35, 13.38, 13.41
413	13.43
684	5.11, 13.61

	PARA
Income Tax (Earnings and Pensions) Act 2003 – *contd*	
s 721(5)	13.108, 13.132
Inheritance Tax Act 1984	
s 222(3)	11.128
Jobseekers Act 1995	
s 27	5.51
National Insurance Contributions Act 2011	
s 8(6)	5.51
National Insurance Contributions and Statutory Payments Act 2004	4.02
Pension Schemes Act 1993	
s 170(1)	5.86
Police Act 1997	7.39
Police and Criminal Evidence Act 1984	2.31, 10.01
s 8	7.14, 7.17–7.21, 7.38, 10.07, 10.120, 10.122, 10.125, 10.127, 10.138, 10A.44, 10A.60
10	7.20, 7.40
11(1)	7.20
14	10.128
14(2)	7.21
14A	10.131
14B	10.131
16	7.38
18	7.22
21	7.22
23	7.17
66	7.06
67	10.132
67(11)	10.132
82–87	7.18
Sch 1	7.14, 7.17, 7.21, 10.120, 10.130, 10A.60
Sch 1, para 12	10.129
Code B	7.35, 10.125, 10.129, 10.132
Proceeds of Crime Act 2002	7.10, 7.49
Pt 7	8.21
s 327	8.22
327–329	8.35
328	8.23
329	8.24
330	8.29
337	8.56
340	8.25
340(2)(b)	8.32, 8.35, 8.36
340(11)	8.31

Table of Statutes

	PARA
Regulation of Investigatory Powers Act 2000	7.39
Serious Organised Crime and Police Act 2005	
ss 60–70	10.133
s 62	7.35
62(3)	10.134
66	7.14, 7.35, 7.36
66(2)	10.136
Social Security Act 1998	
s 12	5.87
49	13.53
59	5.43
60	5.03
61	5.05
62	5.10
63	5.10
64	5.15, 5.69
Social Security Administration Act 1992	
s 113A	5.03
113B	5.03
115	5.07
(1)	5.06
(2)	5.06
118(1)	5.10
(3)	5.10
121B	5.10
C	5.15
D	5.69
Social Security Contributions and Benefits Act 1992	
s 15	5.89
16	5.33
17	5.91
18	5.91
110ZA	4.02, 4.03
113	5.03
114	5.05
121C	5.51
Sch 1, para 6	5.39
7	5.13, 5.14, 5.20
Sch 2, para 6	5.42, 5.43
8	5.89
Social Security Contributions (Transfer of Functions, etc) Act 1999	5.48
s 8	5.56, 5.92, 5.94, 5.96
(1)	5.51
(1)(c)	5.61
(2)	5.52
(3)	5.53
9	5.55

	PARA
Social Security Contributions (Transfer of Functions, etc) Act 1999 – contd	
s 10	5.56
11	5.69
12(1)	5.71
(2)	5.71
(3)	5.73
16(1)	5.86
(6)	5.86
Taxes Act 1988	
s 148	13.38
167–168	13.106
202B(6)	13.51
203A(1)(c)	13.51
419(4A)	14.18
577	13.136
(1)(a)	13.137
(b)	13.137
577(3)	13.135, 13.137
(5)	13.136
Sch 6, para 6	13.121
9	13.121
Sch 11A	13.153
Taxes Management Act 1964	
s 5(6)	11.125
29(6)	11.125
Taxes Management Act 1970	
s 1(1)	12.02
7	14.84, 14.88, 14.98
8	9.40, 14.23
A	14.23
8–28B	1.10
9A	1.46, 1.77, 9.35, 9.40
(1)	1.15, 1.52
12AA	14.23
AB	14.23
AC	1.77, 10A.50
B	1.42, 1.43
(1)	1.39
(b)	1.40
(b)	1.40
(6)	1.40
13–19	10A.02
19A	1.16, 1.19, 1.46, 1.54, 1.57–1.70, 1.100, 10.11, 10.22, 10.25, 10.72, 10A.03, 10A.47–10A.53
(2)	1.48
(a)	1.48, 10A.20
(b)	10A.20
(9)	1.66
(11)	1.66

Table of Statutes

	PARA
Taxes Management Act 1970 – *contd*	
s 20	1.19, 1.49, 1.70–1.72, 10.11, 10.25, 10.72, 10.108, 10A.04–10A.46
(1)	10.21, 10A.04, 10A.07–10A.46
(2)	10.21, 10A.05
(3)	1.71, 10.29, 10.50, 10A.04–10A.12
(4)(b)	10A.29
(7)	10.43, 10A.13
(8A)	2.77, 2.85, 7.07, 10.41–10.40, 10.84, 10A.04, 10A.08, 10A.20, 10A.29–10A.36
(8B)	10.50, 10A.36
(8C)	10A.16
A	1.49, 10.114–10.119
B	4.02, 10.25, 10.31, 10A.08
(1)	10A.08
(2)	10.103, 10A.23
(4)	10A.18
(5)	10A.37
(6)	10.27
(9)	10A.23–10A.27
(11)	10A.26, 10A.27
(12)	10A.26, 10A.27
(13)	10A.27
BA	7.04, 7.14, 7.22, 7.24–7.36, 7.40, 10.03, 10.130, 10.131, 10.138, 10.140, 10.145, 10A.11, 10A.46
BA(2)	10.139
B	4.02, 10A.10
C	7.14, 7.18, 7.22, 10.05, 10.122, 10.127, 10.138, 10A.05, 10A.44–10A.46
(1)	10.127
(1AA)	10.138
(4)	10.126, 10.134
C	10.144, 10A.45
20D(1)	10.138
(3)	10A.15
ss 20–20D	10A.02
23–28	10A.02, 10A.03
s 25(6)	1.08
28A	1.46, 11.35–11.38
(1)	1.91
(3)	1.91
(5)	12.93
(4)–(6)	1.92
B	11.35
ss 28ZA–28ZE	11.43
s 29(3)	12.76

	PARA
Taxes Management Act 1970 – *contd*	
s 29(5)	1.08
(6)	1.08
30B(1)	11.35
31	1.94
(1)	11.35
(b)	1.96
34	1.99
46(2)	11.47
49	5.76
49A–49I	11.53
50(7)	12.76
54	11.47, 12.04
55	11.45, 11.59
(5)	11.46
56A	11.105, 12.21
59C	11.56, 12.21
(4)	12.21
65(3)	5.12
86	5.42, 12.09
88	5.42, 5.43
93	14.88
(2)	11.56
(4)	11.56
95	12.64, 14.01, 14.88
97	12.68
97AA	10A.57
98	10.11, 10.109, 10A.42
A	5.13
(4)	5.20
100B	10A.43, 10A.58
C	10A.42, 10A.57
118(2)	12.65
Sch 1A, para 5	1.77
AA	7.24, 7.25, 7.28, 7.40, 10.138, 10.141, 10.143, 10.144
Theft Act 1968	8.15
s 17	8.35, 8.98
Theft Act 1978	8.15
s 17	10.133
Tribunals, Courts and Enforcement Act 2007	11.02
Pt 1 (ss 1–49)	11.17
s 9	5.84
11(1)	11.105
(4)	11.106
12	11.105
(4)	11.109
14(3)	11.109
18	11.111
29	11.91
29(4)	11.93

Table of Statutes

	PARA
Tribunals, Courts and Enforcement Act 2007 – *contd*	
Pt 2 (ss 50–61)	11.17
Sch 2	11.18
3	11.18
Value Added Tax Act 1994	3.64
s 72(1)–(8)	10A.71
(11)	7.04
73(1)	10A.60

	PARA
Value Added Tax Act 1994 – *contd*	
s 82(2)	10.07
83	11.30
(2)	10.07
Sch 11	3.66, 10.07 10A.59
para 7	3.67, 10.29, 10A.61
10	10.65, 10A.68, 10A.69
10(3)	10A.70, 10A.71

Statutory Instruments

	PARA
Appeals (Excluded Decisions) Order 2009, SI 2009/275	11.104
Civil Procedure Rules 1998, SI 1998/3132	10.76
r 1	11.24
Finance Act 2007, Sch 24 (Commencement and Transitional Provisions) Order 2008, SI 2008/568	10.09
Finance Act 2008, Schedule 36 (Appointed Day and Savings) Order 2009, SI 2009/404)	10.10, 10.11
General Commissioners (Jurisdiction and Procedure) Regulations 1994, SI 1994/1812	7.43
Income Tax (Employments) Regulations 1993, SI 1993/774	
reg 3	13.27
5	13.27
49	5.34
Income Tax (Incentive Payments for Voluntary Electronic Communication of PAYE Returns) Regulations 2003, SI 2003/2495	
reg 97	9.63
Information Notice: Resolution of Disputes as to Privileged Communications Regulations 2009, SI 2009/1916	10.99
Money Laundering Regulations 2003, SI 2003/3075	

	PARA
Money Laundering Regulations 2007, SI 2007/2157	8.02, 8.19
reg 14	8.39
Money Laundering Regulations 2003 (Amendment) Order 2006, SI 2006/308	8.54
Order for the Delivery of Documents (Procedure) Regulations 2000, SI 2000/2875	7.25
reg 4(2)	7.25
5	7.30
6	7.32
7	7.41, 10.143
Police and Criminal Evidence Act 1984 (Application to Revenue and Customs) Order 2007, SI 2007/3175	10.07, 10.118
art 4	10.117
7	10.131, 10.138
Rules of the Supreme Court, SI 1965/1776	10.76
Ord 24, r 2	10.79
7(1)	1.49
Social Security (Adjudication) Regulations 1986, SI 1986/2218	
reg 16(1)	5.98
Social Security (Contributions) Regulations 1979, SI 1979/591	
reg 28B	5.37
Sch 1	5.37

Statutory Instruments

	PARA
Social Security (Contributions) Amendment (No 3) Regulations 1999, SI 1999/975	5.26
Social Security (Contributions) Regulations 2001, SI 2001/1004	
reg 3(2B)	5.54
26	9.63
31	5.54
50(2)	5.54
52(1)	5.54
(8)	5.54
54(3)	5.54
60	5.54
61(2)	5.54
65	5.54
67(1)	5.11
67A	5.22
71	5.36
76	5.36
77	
81	5.25
regs 90F–90H	5.21
reg 110(3)	5.54
Sch 4	5.04, 9.63
para 14	5.08
15	5.08, 5.10
17	5.35
19	5.41
20	5.41
Social Security Contributions (Decisions and Appeals) Regulations 1999, SI 1999/1027	5.48
reg 3(2)	5.58
4	5.61, 5.93
(1)	5.59
(2)	5.64
(3)	5.64
5(4)	5.66
6(1)	5.67
(2)	5.67
9	5.76
10	5.77
11	5.78
(4)	5.79
(5)	5.80
(6)	5.81

	PARA
Social Security (Crediting and Treatment of Contributions, and National Insurance Numbers) Regulations 2001, SI 2001/769	
reg 5	5.54
6	5.54
Special Commissioners (Jurisdiction and Procedure) Regulations 1994, SI 1994/1811	7.43, 10A.14
reg 15	11.81
21	11.90, 11.94
Statistics of Trade (Customs and Excise) Regulations 1992, SI 1992/2790	3.65
Transfer of Tribunal Functions and Revenue and Customs Appeals Order 2009, SI 2009/56	11.98
art 3	11.02
4	11.02
Tribunal Procedure (First-tier Tribunal) (Tax Chamber) Rules 2009, SI 2009/273	11.02
r 2	11.25
3	11.28
5	11.67, 11.89
10(1)(b)	11.94
15(2)	11.69
23	11.95
(4)	11.64
24	11.61
25(1)(b)	11.66
26(3)(c)	11.57
27	11.66
28	11.101
32	11.77
35	11.84
37	11.87
38	11.88, 11.89
39(2)	11.89
41(1)(b)	11.89
Tribunal Procedure (Upper Tribunal) Rules 2008, SI 2008/2698	11.02
r 2	11.25
(4)	11.27
3	11.28
5	11.113
7	11.113
11	11.116
21(3)(b)	11.106

Statutory Instruments

	PARA
Tribunal Procedure (Upper Tribunal) Rules 2008, SI 2008/2698 – *contd*	
r 22(2)(b)	11.108
24	11.108
34	11.116
40	11.117
42	11.119
43	11.119
44(1)	11.119

	PARA
Value Added Tax Tribunals Rules 1986, SI 1086/590	
r 24	11.82
29	11.98
Tribunal Procedure (Amendment) Rules 2009, SI 2009/274	
r 14	11.107

Table of Cases

	PARA

A

A v RCC [2007] SpC 650 .... 1.60
Accountant v Inspector of Taxes [2000] STC (SCD) 522 .... 1.60, 10A.20
Addison v London Philharmonic Orchestra Society Ltd [1981] ICR 261 .... 13.67
Al Fayed v Advocate General for Scotland [2004] STC 1703 .... 11.48
Alfred Crompton Amusement Machines Ltd v Customs and Excise Comrs
    (No 2) [1974]AC 405 .... 10.96
Anderson v Bank of British Columbia [1876] 2 ChD 644 .... 10.88
Application by Revenue and Customs Comrs to serve section 20 notice, Re
    [2006] STC (SCD) 71 .... 10.44
Application by Revenue and Customs Comrs to serve section 20 notice
    (No 2), Re [2006] STC (SCD) 360 .... 10.44
Application by Revenue and Customs Comrs to serve section 20 notice, Re
    [2007] STC (SCD) 202 .... 10.44
Application by Revenue and Customs Comrs to serve section 20 notice, Re
    [2007] STC (SCD) 208 .... 10.44
Application by Revenue and Customs Comrs to serve section 20 notice, Re
    [2007] STC (SCD) 216 .... 10.44
Application by Revenue and Customs Comrs to serve section 20 notice, Re
    [2007] STC (SCD) 222 .... 10.44
Application by Revenue and Customs Comrs to serve section 20 notice, Re
    [2009] STC (SCD) 493 .... 10.46
Asfar v RCC (2006 STC (SCD) 625 .... 1.60

B

B v B [1978] 3 WLR 624 .... 1.49
B v B [1978] Fam 181 .... 10.76
Barraclough v Brown [1897] AC 615 .... 11.125
Bayfine UK Products v Revenue and Customs Comrs [2009] STC (SCD)
    43 .... 11.42
Bennett v IRC [1995] STC 54 .... 11.128
Bensoor v Devine (2005 STC (SCD) 297 .... 1.65
Brady v Hart (t/a Jaclyn Model Agency) (1985) 58 TC 518 .... 13.81
Buxton v Public Trustee (1962) 41 TC 235 .... 11.126

Table of Cases

	PARA

C

CIR v Alexander von Glehn & Co Ltd, (1920) 12 TC 232 ...... 13.121
CIR v Nuttall [1990] STC 194 ...... 12.04
Capital Air Services Limited v HMRC ([2010] SFTD 671; [2010] STC 2726 ...... 11.64
Carter v Hunt [2000] STC (SCD) 17 ...... 11.90
Carvill v Frost (No 2) [2005] STC (SCD) 208 ...... 11.90
Chantry Martin v Martin [1953] 2 QB 286 ...... 10.93
Clark v Oceanic Contractors [1983] STC 35 ...... 10.86
Clinch case (1973) 49 TC 52 ...... 10A.30
Commane v HM Revenue & Customs [2006] STC (SCD) 81 ...... 10A.54
Commane v RCC (2006 STC (SCD) 81 ...... 1.60
Customs and Excise Commissioners v ApS Samex (Hanil Synthetic Fiber Industrial Co Ltd) [1983] 3 CMLR 194 ...... 11.133
Customs and Excise Commissioners v National Westminster Bank plc [2003] STC 1072 ...... 11.112
Customs and Excise Comrs v Young [1993] STC 394 ...... 11.75

D

DTE Financial Services Ltd v Wilson [1999] STC 1061 ...... 13.28
D'Arcy v HMRC [2006] UKSPC 549 ...... 11.39
Demibourne Ltd v Revenue & Customs Comrs SpC 486 ...... 13.70, 13.72
Derry v Peek 14 App Cas 337 ...... 2.18
Deutsche Morgan Grenfell Group plc v IRC [2007] 1AC 558 ...... 11.126
Direct Cosmetics v Customs and Excise Commissioners [1984] 1 CMLR 99 ...... 11.132
Duchy Maternity Limited v Hodgson [1985] STC 764 ...... 12.76

E

EMI Group Electronics Ltd v Coldicott [1999] STC 803 ...... 13.33
Eclipse Film Partners No 35 LLP v Revenue and Customs Commissioners [2009] STC (SCD) 293 ...... 11.39
Eder v RCC (2007 STC (SCD) 334 ...... 1.60
Edwards v Bairstow [1954]AC 14 ...... 11.105

F

FJ Chalke and AC Barnes v HMRC [2009] STC 2027 ...... 11.102
Fergusson v Noble (1919) 7 TC 176 ...... 13.21

G

Gamble v Rowe [1998] STC 1247 ...... 11.90
George v Ward [1995] STC (SCD) 230 ...... 13.40
Gilbert v Hemsley (1981) 55 TC 419 ...... 13.118
Government of India v Taylor [1955]AC 491 ...... 8.34
Grant v Downs [1976] 135 CLR 674 ...... 10.96
Grogan v HMRC, unreported, 20 November 2010 ...... 11.120
Guest House Proprietor v Kendall (2005 STC (SCD) 280 ...... 1.60
Guyer v Walton (2001 STC (SCD) 75 ...... 1.60

H

HMRC v Banerjee (No 2) [2009] STC 1930 ...... 11.83

Table of Cases

	PARA
Hall v Lorimer [1994] STC 23	13.67, 13.78
Hallamshire Estates Ltd v Walford (2004 STC (SCD) 330	1.64
Hanover Company Services Limited v The Commissioners for Her Majesty's Revenue and Customs [2010] SFTD 1047	11.112
Hartland v Diggines (1926) 10 TC 247	13.98
Health Response UK Ltd v The Commissioners for Her Majesty's Revenue and Customs [2010] UKFTT 123	11.112
Henn and Darby v DPP [1981] AC 850	11.131
Hochstrasser v Mayes (1959) 38 TC 673	13.146
Hochstrasser v Mayes (1959) 38 TC 673; Mairs v Haughey [1993] STC 569	13.107
Holly v Inspector of Taxes (2000 STC (SCD) 50	1.64
Horton v Young (1971) 47 TC 60	13.169
Howell v Trippier (Inspector of Taxes)[2004] STC 1245	11.82
Humbles v Brooks (1962) 40 TC 500	13.131

I

IRC v Rossminster Ltd [1980] STC 42	10A.44

J

Jacques v RCC (No 2) (2007 STC (SCD) 166	1.60
Jade Palace v Revenue and Customs Commissioners [2006] STC (SCD) 419	1.95, 11.38
John Wilkins (Motor Engineers) Ltd v HMRC [2009] STC 2485; [2009] UKUT 175 (TCC)	11.65, 11.102

K

Kilbride v R & C Commrs (2008) Sp C 660	1.96

L

L, Re [1997] AC 16	10.95
Langham v Veltema (2004) BTC 156	1.98
Lee Ting Sang v Chung Chi-Keung [1990] 2AC 374	13.75
Lee v R & C Commrs (2008) Sp C 715	1.96
Lonrho Ltd v Shell Petroleum [1980] 1WLR 627	10.79, 10.84
Lonrho Ltd v Shell Petroleum Co Ltd [1980] 1 WLR 627	1.49
Low v RCC (2006 STC (SCD) 21	1.60
Lucas v Cattell (1972) 48 TC 353	13.161

M

MacNiven v Westmoreland Investments Ltd [2003] 1AC 311	11.47
Market Investigations Ltd v Minister of Social Security [1969] 2 QB 173	13.65, 13.67
Marks and Spencer v Halsey [2003] STC (SCD)70	11.132
Marks and Spencer plc v Halsey (Case C-446/03)[2006] STC 237	11.135
Meditor Capital Management Ltd v Feighan (2004 STC (SCD) 273	1.49, 1.60, 10.83
Mobile Export 365 Ltd, Shelford IT Ltd v HM Revenue & Customs Comrs [2007] STC 1794	11.69
Moffat v CIR (2006 STC (SCD) 380	1.65
Monarch Assurance Co Ltd v Special Comrs and IRC [1986] STC 311	10.103
Morren v Swinton and Pendlebury Borough Council [1965]1 WLR 576	13.67

Table of Cases

	PARA
Mother v Inspector of Taxes (1999 STC (SCD) 279	1.60
Murat v HM Inspector of Taxes (aka Accountant v HM Inspector of Taxes) [2000] STC (SCD) 522	10A.51
Murat v Ornach (2004 STC (SCD) 115	1.65
Murphy v Gowers (2005 STC (SCD) 44	1.60

N

NMB Holdings v Secretary of State [2000] EWHC Admin 369	13.28
Nicoll v Austin (1935) 19 TC 531	13.98

O

O'Kelly v Trusthouse Forte plc [1984] QB 90	13.74, 13.78
O'Sullivan v Philip (2005 STC (SCD) 51	1.65
Owen v Burden (1971) 47 TC 476	13.131
Oxfam v Revenue & Customs Commissioners [2010] STC 686	11.112

P

Parikh v Back [1985] STC 232	11.46
Parikh v Sleeman (1990) 63 TC 75	13.131
Parto v Bratherton (2004 STC (SCD) 339	1.60
Pepper v Hart (1992) 65 TC 421	13.111, 13.112, 13.115, 13.127, 13.161
Pook v Owen (1969) 45 TC 571	13.169
Practice Direction (ECJ References: Procedure) [1999] 1 WLR 260	11.134
Price Waterhouse v BCCI Holdings [1992] BCLC 583	10.92
Purple Parking Services Ltd, Airparks Services Ltd [2009] [2009] SFTD 445	11.98

R

R v Allen [1999] STC 846	8.16
R v Charlton [1996] STC 1418	8.82
R v Da Silva [2008] EWCA Crim 1654	8.40
R v Gell [2003] EWCA Crim 123	10.04
R v Gill & Gill [2003] STC 1229	2.29, 2.30, 7.06
R v IK [2007] EWCA Crim 491	8.101
R v International Stock Exchange, ex p Else Ltd [1993] QB 534	11.133
R v IRC, ex p Mohammed [1999] STC 129	10A.07
R v IRC and Middlesex Guildhall Crown Court, ex p Tamosius and Partners [1999] STC 1077	10.126
R v IRC, ex p Lorimer [2000] STC 751	10A.22
R v IRC, ex p Taylor (No 2) [1990] STC 379	10A.22
R v IRC, ex p Ulster Bank Ltd [1997] STC 832	10A.33, 10A.35
R v IRC, ex parte Mead and Cook [1992] STC 482	7.12
R v Macdonald and CIR, ex p Hutchinson & Co Ltd [1998] STC 680	10A.14
R v NW, SW, RC and CC [2008] EWCA Crim 2	8.102
R v O'Kane, ex p Northern Bank Ltd [1996] STC 1249	10A.34, 10A.35
R v Special Comr, ex p Morgan Grenfell & Co Ltd [2003] 1AC 56	10A.17
R v W [1998] STC 550, CA	2.27, 8.94
R (on the application of H) v IRC [2002] STC 1354	10.122
R (on the application of Morgan Grenfell & Co Ltd) v Special Comr of Income Tax [2002] STC 786	10.89, 10A.21
R (on the application of Morgan Grenfell) v Special Comr of Income Tax) [2001] STC 497	10A.14

Table of Cases

	PARA
R (on the application of Prudential Plc) v Special Commissioner of Income Tax [2010] STC 2802	10.93
Ready Mixed Concrete (South East) Ltd v Minister of Pensions and National Insurance [1968] 2 QB 497	13.67
Red Discretionary Trustees v Inspector of Taxes [2004] STC (SCD) 132	11.82
Reed plc v Revenue and Customs Commissioners, unreported, 15 December 2010	11.112
Revenue and Customs Commissioners Application (Section 20 Notice: Tax Haven Co) [2006] STC (SCD) 376	10A.37
Revenue and Customs Comrs v Halcyon Films LLP [2009] STC 1741	11.42
Revenue and Customs Comrs v Micro Fusion 2004–1 LLP	11.42
Rheinmuhlen-Dusseldorf v Einfuhr-und Vorratsstelle fur Getreide und Futtermittel (Case 166/73) [1974] ECR 33	11.132
Rincham Limited v The Commissioners for HM Revenue & Customs [2010] UKFTT 502 (TC)	10.50

S

SCA Packaging Ltd v HMRC [2007] EWHC 270 (Ch)	13.31
Secretary of State v Baker (Re Barings) [1998] Ch 356	10.97
Self-Assessed v Inspector of Taxes (1999 STC (SCD) 253	1.64, 10A.50
Siwek v CIR (2002 STC (SCD) 247	1.65
Skoye v Bailey [1971]1WWR 144	10.78
Smart Voucher Ltd v HM Revenue and Customs Commissioners [2009] UKFTT 169 (TC)	11.98
Sokaya v RCC (2008 STC (SCD) 51	1.61
Space 2 Build Ltd v The Commissioners for Her Majesty's Revenue and Customs [2010] UKFTT 66 (TC)	11.112
Sparrow Ltd v Inspector of Taxes [2001] STC (SCD) 206	11.45
Spring Salmon & Seafood Ltd v RCC (2005 STC (SCD) 830	1.60

T

TC Coombs & Co [1991] STC 97	10A.35
Tanfern Ltd v Cameron-McDonald [2000] 1 WLR 1311	11.121
Taxpayer v Inspector of Taxes [1996] STC (SCD) 261	10A.34
Taylor v Bratherton [2005] STC (SCD) 230	10A.54
Three Rivers District Council v Governor and Company of the Bank of England [2005] 1 AC 610	10.97
Tod v South Essex Motors (Basildon) Ltd [1988] STC 392	11.47
Tower Cashback v HM Revenue & Customs Commissioners [2008] STC 3366; [2008] BTC 805	1.96, 11.40–11.42

V

Vandervell's Trusts, Re [1971] AC 912	11.125
Vodafone (No 2) (2006 STC 1530	1.95

W

Waugh v British Railways Board [1980] AC 521	10.96
Westek v HMRC Comrs (Sp C 629)	5.61
Wickens v Champion Employment [1984] ICR 365	13.67
Williams v Ingram (1900) 16 TLR 451	10.78
Wing Hung Lai v Bale (1999 STC (SCD) 238	1.64
Woolwich Equitable Building Society v IRC [1992] STC 657	11.126

Chapter 1

Enquiries under self-assessment

Martyn Bridges

Partner, Bridges & Partners

INTRODUCTION

1.01 An enquiry power is an essential element of a self-assessment system. Enquiries have two objectives. The first, and most obvious one, is to seek to detect fraud, errors and areas in which the applicable legal principles may be open to different interpretations so that HMRC may wish to challenge that adopted by the taxpayer. The second, less obvious, one is to test the system. If different taxpayers make the same error this may be due to poor design of the forms and guidance notes, or may suggest that an HMRC interpretation of the legislation is out of line with that adopted by others.

1.02 Direct tax enquiries are often categorised into full, aspect and random enquiries. These are not statutory divisions, but convenient descriptions. A full enquiry is one in which HMRC enquire into every aspect of the return – and in many cases seek to enquire into matters outside the return (albeit that it is questionable whether in most cases they have power to do so) to obtain an overall view of the taxpayer's financial affairs against which they can test what is shown in the return. An aspect enquiry is one that relates to only one, or selected, entries in the return. It is important to realise that an aspect enquiry can develop into a full enquiry, particularly if it is not handled well.

1.03 For example, in one case HMRC raised a number of questions in relation to estimates used in arriving at the figures of the taxpayer's Standard Accounts Information page. Conscious of costs, that estimates are to some extent a matter of opinion, and that the figures involved were all fairly trivial, the accountant made little effort to justify his figures but accepted without much protest the figures suggested by HMRC. The inspector, not surprisingly, finding that every figure he had challenged was conceded, concluded that the rest of the

1.03 *Enquiries under self-assessment*

figures shown in the return might well be unreliable and the enquiry, which had started in relation to fairly trivial issues, turned into a full enquiry.

1.04 The vast majority of enquiries begin because an inspector or other HMRC officer suspects that there is something wrong with the return. In other words there is either something on the face of the return that gives cause for concern or HMRC have information from other sources that conflict with what is shown on the return. A small number of returns are selected randomly for enquiry by the HMRC computer before the start of the tax year. These random enquiries are designed to test the tax system. They are not selected on the basis of risk (they are selected in advance of the return being submitted) and could well be cases where the HMRC risk assessment would not identify that anything might be wrong with the return. Random enquiries are full enquiries – although the inspector working the case may be able to verify some of the entries on the return from internal sources, so would not necessarily raise questions on every aspect.

1.05 Where an enquiry is opened into a return, some accountants seem to assume that the enquiry is a random enquiry because they have absolute faith in both their client's honesty and their own ability to avoid errors. This is a dangerous position to take. Roughly one in a thousand enquiries is a random enquiry. If there is no obvious reason why HMRC have opened an enquiry it is accordingly likely that it has been opened 'for cause' and that the factor or factors that caused the enquiry are simply not apparent to the accountant.

DISCLOSURE

1.06 Whilst it is not possible to avoid the risk of HMRC opening an enquiry into a tax return, the risk of an aspect enquiry at least can be reduced by anticipating which items in a return are likely to raise questions and forestalling such questions by providing the answer with the return. HMRC do not then need to open an enquiry in order to elicit that information. It needs to be realised that even if, when challenged, a convincing explanation can easily be given in relation to an item that looks odd, HMRC have only one bite of the cherry in relation to enquiries. Once they close an enquiry they cannot raise enquiries on any other issues in relation to the return (unless they can make a discovery). Accordingly if something in a return looks odd and HMRC have to open an enquiry to elicit why it does so, they are likely to review the remainder of the return much more thoroughly than they otherwise would have done, as once they close the enquiry they will reduce their ability to raise any other issues relating to that year. Accordingly, heading off an enquiry by forestalling questions about the oddity is also likely to head off the review of the return that would have been prompted by an enquiry into that item.

1.07 Accordingly, the pre-self-assessment strategy that many adopted of not volunteering information, but leaving it to the inspector to inspect the return, is dangerous in the era of self-assessment. Returns are selected for enquiry on the basis of an HMRC assessment of the risk that the return may not be wholly correct. Anything that can be done to reduce HMRC's perception of such risk therefore ought to be done. Explaining in advance items that are likely to call for an explanation might well eliminate the perception of risk in relation to such items, thus reducing the overall risk that HMRC place on the return.

1.08 Volunteering information can also have a second benefit of making it more difficult for HMRC to make a discovery in relation to the return at a later date. Unless they can establish negligence HMRC cannot make a discovery assessment unless at the time when the 'enquiry window' closed they could not have been reasonably expected, on the basis of the information made available to them before that time, to be aware of errors or omissions that they subsequently discover (Taxes Management Act 1970 (TMA), s 29(5)). Information which is contained in the tax return, or in any accounts, statements or documents accompanying the return (or in the return for either of the two previous years) is deemed to have been made available for this purpose, even if the officer who reviewed the return at that time chose not to look at it. Accordingly, it makes sense to volunteer accounts, dividend schedules, capital gains tax computations and other information created or used in arriving at the figures to be included in the return in order to enhance protection from discovery (TMA 1970, s 25(6)). HMRC sometimes seek to discourage the submission of such information, but they have no power to prohibit a taxpayer from providing it. In the early days of self-assessment they sometimes returned such information. If they do so it is sensible to send it back again and point out that they have no statutory power to refuse to accept it and that s 29(6) clearly envisages a taxpayer being entitled to submit accompanying documents. Indeed the legislation requires no more than that the document accompanies the return. What HMRC then do with it cannot thwart the statutory protection given to the taxpayer; that is already in place before HMRC send it back, although it is probably easier to convince the appeal tribunal of this if it can be shown that efforts were made to seek to persuade HMRC to accept the information. HMRC consider that 'reasonably expected' requires a taxpayer to point out that information sent to them is relevant to the return, but it is hard to imagine a tribunal holding that an inspector could not have expected something sent with the return to be relevant to it. Of course, an inspector might well not be expected to read through a long document only part of which is clearly relevant, so if the taxpayer wants protection for something else in it he may well be expected to point it out. For example, if shares in a private company are sold and the sale agreement is sent with the return it should be obvious that the name of the vendor, the date, and the existence or otherwise of warranties and indemnities that might give rise to contingent liabilities, is relevant to the return. However, if the inspector later discovers that the gain was declared in the wrong year because the contract was a conditional one, the tribunal could uphold his right to make a discovery on the basis that the taxpayer could be expected to have pointed out the relevant clause. Note in particular *Langham v Veltema* (2004) BTC 156 and HMRC SP 1/06.

HANDLING AN ENQUIRY

1.09 The enquiry process is laid down in the statute. However, HMRC have overlaid the statutory rules with their own, non-statutory, procedural rules. It is important to distinguish the two. A taxpayer is required to comply with a

1.09 *Enquiries under self-assessment*

statutory request; if he wishes to comply with a non-statutory request or procedure he is free to do so, but is equally free not to do so. That is not to say that he ought not to, but rather to make the point that a taxpayer should volunteer something in the full knowledge that he is volunteering and having made a positive decision to do so, rather than volunteer it under the mistaken impression that he is required to provide it.

1.10 It is accordingly unwise to seek to deal with an enquiry without first familiarising oneself with the statutory rules. For income tax these can be found in TMA 1970, ss 8–28B and for corporation tax in FA 1998, Sch 18, paras 3–35. These provisions do not relate solely to enquiries. They also cover the rules on tax returns. It is important to be aware of these as the requirements for what is to be included in a return set the parameters for what HMRC might need in order to check that return.

1.11 There are no similar statutory rules for VAT enquiries. These are dealt with elsewhere in this work and not considered further here.

1.12 It is also important to know who you are dealing with. Whilst the enquiry legislation applies to all tax enquiries, the Specialist Investigations Office (SI) adopts a different approach to inspectors in local tax districts and need to be approached in a different manner. SI (and its predecessors the Special Civil Investigations Office (SCI) and Special Compliance Office (SCO) which merged the old Special Offices and Enquiry Branch) have traditionally dealt with two distinct areas, tax avoidance and serious civil tax fraud. Whilst they still do both, they currently seem to be concentrating on the former and are taking on new fraud cases only if they believe that the tax underpaid is at least £500,000. Smaller cases of suspected serious fraud, which used to be dealt with by SCI are being dealt with by local CIF (Civil Investigations of Fraud) offices. These are headed by former SCI investigators. Their staff are trained by SCI, and their cases need to be handled in the same way as SCI cases. Whilst in the past it was easy to recognise if a case was being handled by SCI, it is often more difficult to identify where a CIF office is involved as this was not always apparent from the letterhead. CIF offices do not only deal with serious suspected fraud though. Where SI or a CIF office is dealing with such a case they will say that they are dealing with the case under COP (Code of Practice) 9. This is a procedure that replaces the old 'Hansard' procedure. Where COP 9 is issued, HMRC will not prosecute the taxpayer for the fraud; they are looking for a cash settlement. They may prosecute if false documents are given to them, or false statements made to them, in the course of the enquiry. CIF offices will usually work cases in the range of £100,000 to £500,000 however a case once opened will usually remain with the office responsible for taking it on.

1.13 Smaller cases of serious suspected fraud, normally where the tax at risk is initially thought to be under around £100,000 are dealt with in the local tax office network. Local tax offices are not empowered to issue COP 9. Only SI and CIF offices can do so. This is not necessarily a good thing as COP 9 affords protection against prosecution. In practice though, a network enquiry is unlikely to result in prosecution, if only because unless the case is identified as warranting prosecution at a very early stage, the network enquiries are likely seriously to prejudice the taxpayer's rights under the Police and Criminal Evidence Act (as network officers are not trained in PACE), which would make a prosecution very difficult.

1.14 There are also three HMRC publications that are very helpful in handling an enquiry. The first is the HMRC Enquiry Manual which is available on the HMRC website. This is HMRC's internal staff guidance. It not only gives an invaluable insight into how HMRC expect an enquiry to be conducted but also highlights areas where there may be doubt on the legal position and points out the limitations on an inspector's powers. The second is the Compliance Handbook which deals with penalties and compliance powers. The third is the relevant Code of Practice which is normally given to the taxpayer with the opening letter, at least where a full enquiry is involved. COP 11 deals with enquiries by local tax offices. SI and CIF offices use COP 9 (2005) in cases of serious suspected tax fraud and COP 8 for other cases.

THE START OF AN ENQUIRY

1.15 HMRC must start an enquiry by giving notice to the taxpayer of their intention to do so (TMA 1970, s 9A(1); FA 1998, Sch 18, para 24). The notice must normally be given by the first anniversary of the filing date, which is 31 January following the end of the tax year.

1.16 There is no right of appeal against such a notice. If there is something wrong with it, such as being given out of time, it is not a valid notice. The best option is to discuss matters with the officer responsible or his manager. Should this fail, the only practical way to establish whether or not it is valid is in the course of an appeal later in the enquiry process, such as an appeal against a s 19A notice, or an appeal against an HMRC amendment to the return – because if the original enquiry notice is not valid it will invalidate the entire enquiry process. A judicial review is unlikely to be a viable option.

1.17 The formal enquiry notice is normally accompanied by a letter asking for the information that the officer requires for the purpose of the enquiry. Officers are encouraged to ask up-front for everything they are likely to require, although they can, and often do, of course, ask for further information at any time during the course of the enquiry. The letter will normally give a time limit within which the officer expects the information to be supplied. This is normally a minimum of 30 days.

1.18 This opening letter is not part of the statutory enquiry process. Accordingly, the time limit is not a statutory one; it is a figure plucked out of the air by the officer. No penalty or other statutory sanctions arise if this time limit is not met. The officer's only recourse is either to chase for a reply or to issue a formal notice under Sch 36 FA 2008 for the information. It is obviously courteous to tell the officer as early as possible if his target date cannot be met and often this will achieve further time if reasons are properly advanced. However, there is no need to panic if the time limit is overlooked or, although the taxpayer or his agent aims to comply with it, he does not manage to do so.

1.19 *Enquiries under self-assessment*

1.19 Similarly, the officer is not entitled to compel the provision of information in response to the opening letter. Until 31 March 2009 he had two specific information powers. TMA 1970, s 19A (or FA 1998, Sch 18, para 27 in the case of a company) and TMA 1970, s 20. Section 20 was a general information power, but s 19A and para 27 were enquiry powers that are specific to self-assessment. However, each of these powers requires the use of a formal procedure (albeit a different one for each of the powers) that has built-in protections for taxpayers. From 1 April 2009 he will use the new powers contained in Sch 36 FA 2008. Accordingly, in reality in his opening letter the officer is requesting the taxpayer to volunteer information and indeed this will normally be the appropriate response.

1.20 That is not to say that the taxpayer should not volunteer to do so but instead insist on the use of the formal information powers. It is pointless to waste time on a statutory procedure when it is clear that at the end of that procedure the information is statutorily required to be provided. It will also clearly irritate the officer, which may well influence his approach to doubtful issues that arise during the enquiry.

1.21 However, it is sensible to consider each item of information requested by the officer in the context of the information powers. If it is clear that the item can be required under those provisions it should be provided. If it is not clear, the taxpayer or his agent ought to consider whether he believes it to be in his best interest to provide it. For example, an extended trial balance prepared by the taxpayer's agent is unlikely to be within Sch 36, as in most cases it is likely to belong to the agent and therefore will not be within the taxpayer's power to provide. Nevertheless, it is difficult to conceive of a reason not to volunteer it. Without it the officer will be forced to ask far more questions than he otherwise would have done and may make incorrect assumptions that needlessly prolong the enquiry and thus increase its cost. Where it is decided to volunteer information, it is sensible to make the point to HMRC that the taxpayer or agent does not believe that it falls within Sch 36, but that the taxpayer is happy nevertheless to provide it. This indicates co-operation and helpfulness.

1.22 If the taxpayer or agent does not believe that the information requested falls within Sch 36 and he chooses not to volunteer it there is nothing to prevent his declining to provide it. It is sensible to do so politely, such as telling the officer that its relevance to the tax return is not readily apparent and asking why he believes it to be relevant.

1.23 Each enquiry obviously depends on its individual facts. It is accordingly not possible to list what may or may not fall within FA 2008, Sch 36(1). Information that belongs to third parties, such as the taxpayer's spouse or children, or to his agent, clearly does not fall within these provisions (but might fall within FA 2008, Sch 36(2)). The author would normally challenge requests for the following:

- An analysis of drawings or of a proprietor's capital account or a director's loan account. There are things that do not impact on the quantification of profit. They relate to how the profit is spent and how funds to finance the business are raised. Normally, neither of these things has any relevance to the enquiry into the tax return, which is a return of income. HMRC argue that if drawings are minimal that may be an indication that income has been diverted from the business. However, that is far too wide a generalisation. The proprietor's or director's spouse may be generating the income to meet living expenses; parents may be helping to support an adult child whose business acumen is such that he cannot generate adequate income; a person may be living off borrowings such as a bank overdraft or may be realising past savings or using an inheritance to supplement his living expenses. It is hard to see a justification for HMRC to pry into a taxpayer's private life on the off chance that he may be diverting income from his business. Many taxpayers strongly resent such an intrusion and it does not seem right to ask them to submit to it merely to seek to prove the negative that income has not been diverted. Where a business does not handle cash at all but receives all of its income by cheque, diversion is clearly improbable as banks do not allow a cheque made out to one person to be banked in the account of another, but that fact does not seem to deter HMRC requests for analyses of drawings or loan account. Furthermore, the author's experience is that in many cases where such information is volunteered this does not satisfy HMRC, but they often go on to raise further questions on the information provided because the officer is searching for the possibility, no matter how remote, of some other theoretical source of undisclosed income.

- Personal bank statements of a sole trader or partnership where he keeps his personal finances separate from those of his business, or personal bank statements of a director of a company. Again these have nothing to do with the tax return under enquiry and have been requested on the off chance that something in them may suggest diverted takings. In this connection it needs to be appreciated that if such bank statements are volunteered the officer will often take the stance that, as it is for the taxpayer to disprove an assessment, he intends to assess every single receipt in the personal bank account as diverted business income and leave it to the taxpayer to prove that it is not. Very few people can identify – and evidence – the source of small payments into their bank accounts two years earlier. In most cases these are things like refunds from utilities or from mail order or online retailers for goods that are no longer available, receipts from friends for their share of a restaurant bill, premium bond or football pool winnings, insurance claims, and cheques as birthday presents and similar day-to-day personal receipts. It is of course highly improbable that if a person were to divert money from his business he would divert £8.46 or some other tiny sum, so the likelihood of such an item in a person's personal bank account representing diverted income is inherently improbable. However, such an improbability does not seem to deter most HMRC officers from making the allegation which, in appropriate cases, should be firmly resisted.

Sometimes an officer will put forward a non-business reason for needing to see personal bank statements. The author has seen for example claims that they are needed to check the receipt of dividends

1.23 *Enquiries under self-assessment*

from quoted companies, and to check the amount of bank interest earned. In such cases it is worth considering whether there is an alternative means to do what the officer says that he is trying to do. For example, in the dividends case he was sent the dividend counterfoils and pointed out that they provide far better evidence of the dividends than the bank statements do, particularly as the receipt of a dividend warrant is a receipt of income even if the warrant is not banked or is banked in a later year. In the case of interest most banks give a figure of interest for the year as a note on the first bank statement after 5 April or provide a certificate of interest paid and tax deducted. Accordingly, that one document or statement, rather than all of the statements for the tax year, will evidence that figure. A letter from the bank might be an alternative source of evidence. Providing such alternative evidence does not prevent HMRC from claiming that in the particular circumstances of the case the personal bank statements come within Sch 36, but it is likely to make it difficult for them to convince an appeal tribunal that the information is 'reasonably required' for that purpose when they already hold better evidence of the item that they have said that they wish to check.

- Appointment diaries. Most people do not keep their business and personal life separate. Accordingly appointment diaries invariably contain personal data for which the taxpayer is entitled to privacy. Furthermore, this author does not regard his diary as an historical record. It is merely a reminder of future engagements. If a client does not turn up for an appointment it does not get crossed out of the diary. If a client phones for an urgent appointment in a couple of hours' time it will probably not get put in the diary. Some of the appointments are of meetings that the author will attend if he has time, but not if he is too busy at the time, and those that are missed may well not be crossed out. Accordingly, the diary is a wholly inappropriate tool as a basis for HMRC to assume that every item in it should have generated a fee and, if it does not, to assume that income has been diverted. Electronic diaries tend to delete past entries on a monthly basis. Clearly, whether a diary is kept manually or electronically can have no bearing on the accuracy of a business's accounts. If accounts can be assumed to be reliable if the diary is electronic and does not retain past data, they ought to be assumed to be equally reliable if the diary is kept in a different manner.
- An accountant's working papers. These may be the property of the accountant and if so not in the power of the client to obtain.
- A statement of a director's or proprietor's personal assets and liabilities. Such a statement has no bearing to the tax return of a company or to the profits of an unincorporated business. Even where the individual has non-business income it is hard to see how a statement of assets can say anything about his income.
- Joint bank account: this is altogether much more difficult. Whereas the joint account holder is entitled to privacy and it may be unclear whether

- or not the bank statements of such an account are in the possession or power of the taxpayer, it is quite likely to be the case.
- Income of spouses or children. These are not normally in the possession or power of the taxpayer. They may be if the child is a minor and the taxpayer is the child's guardian, but this is unclear.
- Assets such as premium bonds or National Savings certificates which do not produce taxable income or capital gains.
- Assets held by the taxpayer as a trustee. It is not clear whether these are in his possession or power in relation to his personal affairs.
- Overseas assets and income of a non-UK domiciled taxpayer where there have been no remittances of income generated by such assets. It is hard to see how these can have any relevance to his UK tax return.

1.24 It does however need to be borne in mind that whether or not something is relevant depends on the circumstances. Although the above items are rarely relevant when an officer opens an enquiry, if during the course of the enquiry it were to become apparent that the business accounts are unreliable and the only satisfactory way to arrive at the taxable profits is to reconstruct what probably happened from some other source, then it clearly becomes relevant to look at whether one of the above sources provides an appropriate means to do this. However, this becomes the case only when the accounts are unreliable – what HMRC used to call 'breaking the accounts'. A handful of small errors or a few small unexplained items do not necessarily suggest that the accounts are unreliable as a basis for measuring the profits for the year.

MEETINGS

1.25 HMRC tell their staff that 'meetings play a vital part in full enquiries under SA and will often be appropriate in aspect enquiries of substance' (Enquiry Manual, para 1821). However, Parliament does not appear to have regarded meetings as vital when it introduced self-assessment. Had it done so it would surely have given HMRC power to require a taxpayer to attend meetings and answer questions, which it did not do. Furthermore, some agents refuse to countenance meetings, either at all or except where there is a good reason for a meeting, and such agents seem to settle enquiries as much as anyone else without recourse to the appeal Commissioners. Accordingly, 'vital' seems a wholly inappropriate adjective for HMRC to use.

1.26 HMRC tell their staff that meetings are vital because they enable you to:

- '– obtain facts from the taxpayer about the business, how it is run and the records that are kept;
- – obtain the facts in non-business enquiries;
- – explain the purpose of your enquiry. Taxpayers may not always be fully aware of the extent of Revenue enquiries;
- – establish whether the taxpayer wishes to disclose omissions;
- – agree what action is required and by whom to move the enquiry towards conclusion;
- – ensure that, where omissions have been found, the taxpayer is aware

1.26 *Enquiries under self-assessment*

what offence has been committed and the likelihood of penalties and of the benefits of co-operating in bringing about an appropriate settlement at the earliest possible date, but you should make it clear that it is entirely a matter for them to decide. You should also at this stage give them the public funding leaflet;
- quantify and agree omissions;
- settle the enquiry.'

(Enquiry Manual, para 1822).

1.27 Curiously, they also tell them that when they encounter resistance to a meeting from an agent they might reduce this by:

'– explaining that meetings can actually reduce the costs and length of an enquiry, because so much more can be covered at a meeting than in protracted correspondence.
- saying why you want to meet the taxpayer. You should make it clear that you are entitled to enquire into the taxpayer's return, the information you need can only be given by the taxpayer in person, and in the absence of co-operation, you will not give up.
- asking if the agent has passed on your views about the desirability of a meeting to the taxpayer.
- confirming to the agent that he or she will be provided with a copy of your notes following the meeting. The agent and taxpayer will be able to correct any misunderstanding of what was said and will be able to revise any explanations or information given at the time if, on reflection, these are felt to be inaccurate.'

(Enquiry Manual, para 1861).

1.28 It seems curious that the reasons that they are told to give agents for wanting a meeting seem to bear little relationship to their actual purpose in wanting it.

1.29 HMRC also tell their staff that, 'asking for meetings at business premises should be the norm rather than the exception' (Enquiry Manual, para 1830). Again, it is odd that when self-assessment was introduced, they did not seek to convince Parliament that they should be given power to hold meetings at business premises and this remains the case. From 1 April 2009 HMRC have the power to inspect business premises (Sch 36, Pt 2); nevertheless this does not compel 'a meeting', although one might expect the situation to develop particularly when the taxpayer is not represented. The Enquiry Manual, para 1861 states 'ultimately you do not have a power to compel a taxpayer or accountant to attend a meeting'.

1.30 In fact the tax legislation contains no references at all to meetings. These are purely voluntary. It follows that the terms on which they are held are equally voluntary. Sadly, most accountants can relate many horror stories of what has happened at meetings. The author's include the inspector who, when the Jewish refugee client started to give an explanation, jumped in and said 'Don't try to explain; just answer yes or no to my questions', the inspector who asked the Asian client how often his wife changed her underwear, and a number of inspectors who sought to put words into the client's mouth or harangued a client because the inspector seemed to think it incredible that a client could not remember details of a small transaction two or three years earlier. Clearly, an agent's reaction to a request for a meeting is likely to be coloured by his past experiences.

1.31 This author's own approach based on his personal experience is to welcome meetings between himself and HMRC, but to agree to meetings with the client present only where he can see a good reason for doing so and has agreed an agenda.

1.32 The Enquiry Manual tells HMRC staff, 'On some occasions an early meeting with the business's book-keeper or accountant will be valuable in understanding how the business records were built up and link together. Such meetings should lead to a better understanding of how the accounts have been prepared and may enable some issues to be resolved without troubling the taxpayer' (Enquiry Manual, para 1821). Such meetings seem sensible. Unfortunately, the author's experience is that they are rarely offered and where the agent himself suggests such a meeting that suggestion is invariably rebuffed. In many cases such a meeting could actually achieve virtually all of the purposes set out above for which HMRC believe meetings vital.

1.33 What about taking clients to meetings with HMRC? The circumstances in which this author will consider such meetings are where:

- HMRC have issued in advance a detailed agenda of what they wish to cover at the meeting. It is unrealistic to expect a list of questions as these ought, to a large extent, to be dependent on the answers to earlier questions. On the other hand, 'I wish to discuss how the business operates and the taxpayer's lifestyle' (or 'the gross profit percentage and living expenses') is not a detailed agenda. Indeed it is so vague that it probably does not justify a meeting at all. A detailed agenda is important because it indicates that the officer has identified what issues require help that only the taxpayer can give, and enables the accountant to satisfy himself that that is indeed the case and that some of the issues cannot be better resolved in advance of the meeting.
- All of the accounting issues and other issues that can be dealt with by the accountant have been resolved. HMRC tell their staff, 'You should bear in mind, however, that meetings can be expensive and inconvenient to taxpayers' (Enquiry Manual, para 1821). Sadly officers rarely seem to take much notice of this. The reality is that many clients have no knowledge of how the detailed figures in their accounts have been put together. Nor indeed is there any rational reason why they should. It is not information that they need to manage the business. It is information that has been generated partly by their book-keeper and partly by their accountant and it is reasonable for them to rely on the expertise of such people. It is unreasonable for an officer to expect a taxpayer to put aside running his business and attend a three-hour meeting, much of which is taken up by accounting issues that are outside the taxpayer's own knowledge and competence and which his accountant can deal with without the taxpayer's intervention.

1.33 *Enquiries under self-assessment*

- The taxpayer is the most appropriate person to deal with the remaining issues. Many HMRC officers seem to take the view that as the taxpayer has ultimate responsibility for his tax affairs they need to interview him because he ought to know precisely how the business operates. Such officers often become extremely suspicious when the client is unable to provide detailed explanations for things that his book-keeper or another staff member could well have been able to answer readily. If the taxpayer or company director is not the most appropriate person to provide the information that the officer says that he is seeking from the meeting consider offering a meeting with the appropriate staff member instead. If such an offer is rebuffed then the reasons the officer has given for wanting a meeting are probably not his real reasons. It is clearly inappropriate to subject a client to a meeting where the agent has any suspicion that the reasons the officer has given for wanting a meeting are either spurious or incomplete.
- If the agenda includes detailed questions on entries in the records that the accountant has been given an opportunity to deal with but has been unable to answer fully because the books and records were sent to HMRC at the start of the enquiry but have not been returned prior to the meeting. It is unreasonable to expect anyone to answer questions on individual transactions that occurred two or three years earlier without his having been able to review the records to refresh his memory in advance of the meeting.
- The issues that the officer wishes to discuss need to be of sufficient importance in the context of the accounts to justify taking the taxpayer or director away from his business. A meeting for the sake of having had a meeting is never justifiable.

1.34 If it has been decided that a meeting is appropriate, where should it be held? The answer is normally at either an HMRC office or the accountant's office depending on which is more convenient. HMRC increasingly deal with a taxpayer's affairs a long distance away. In such a case a meeting at the accountant's office is usually sensible, although the officer can usually arrange to hold a meeting at a local HMRC office if this is desired.

1.35 What about the HMRC desire to meet at the client's premises absent a notice under Sch 36, Pt 2? If the records are voluminous, or it is clear that a number of staff members are likely to be called on to deal with specific issues this may be sensible. In most cases though a taxpayer does not want someone arriving at his office and announcing to the receptionist that he is from HMRC. Even less do clients want to risk people wandering round the building, perhaps looking for the toilets, and telling other staff that they are from HMRC. Staff are likely to wonder why the tax authorities are visiting the business and could well draw incorrect conclusions from the presence of such people, which can be damaging to the operation of the business. There is also the risk an officer might add to his list of questions things that he notices while at the business premises but which actually have no bearing on the enquiry – other, of course, than to needlessly prolong the meeting. In reality these tactics used before the introduction of business inspections are likely to change as a result of the powers introduced on 1 April 2009. Thereafter the inspection powers are likely to be exercised first and the request for a meeting will follow.

1.36 HMRC usually make detailed notes of meetings. They are prepared to provide a taxpayer or his agent with a copy of such notes, but do not always volunteer to do so. If they do not send a copy of their notes after the meeting, it is sensible to request a copy. Where HMRC send notes they tend to sign them and ask the taxpayer and his agent to read them, sign them if they agree with them and send back a signed copy. It is unwise to sign such notes. Many firms of accountants, including my own, decline to do so as a matter of policy and explain to HMRC that it is their policy never to ask clients to sign such notes. Curiously, SI and its predecessors have always accepted this as reasonable, whereas some local offices get upset when notes are not signed. There are two good reasons not to do so. First, the notes tend to be slanted towards what the officer wanted to know. That is probably not deliberate. Meeting notes do not purport to be a transcript of what was said. They are a summary. Any summariser is likely to include in his summary the things that he regards as important and to omit things that he considers trivial. When people take notes of a meeting they do the same thing; their notes tend to cover only the points they consider significant. The result is that the notes often downplay or omit entirely things that may have been said, the relevance of which may not assume any importance until a later date. If the taxpayer has signed the notes as a complete and correct record of the meeting it becomes difficult, if not impossible, subsequently to convince a tribunal that he said something at the meeting that is not covered in the notes. The language adopted can itself slant the emphasis of what was said. The obvious example is that taxpayers seem never to 'say' anything at HMRC meetings; they 'allege' things. To many people 'allege' carries a connotation that what was said is not readily believable.

1.37 Secondly, the reason that HMRC want the notes signed is that in the event of a later dispute they can point to the signature as evidence that what the taxpayer is then claiming that he said at the meeting was not said. There is no advantage to the taxpayer in signing HMRC's notes. Accordingly, why risk them being regarded at a later date of evidence of precisely what was said at the meeting?

1.38 The HMRC notes should, of course, be read and any significant errors or omissions pointed out to the officer. Where the notes do not properly explain a point which the taxpayer was seeking to make it is sensible to re-explain that point. If the notes correctly reflect what was said but it has subsequently been found that the taxpayer's recollection was at fault, the information given at the meeting should of course be corrected. It is sensible to send HMRC any documentary evidence that shows that the corrected position reflects the facts. Often, if a taxpayer or his agent challenges what was said in an officer's notes the officer will seek to argue over what was said. Try not to get drawn into such a debate over the notes. At the end of the day, enquiries are resolved on the basis of the facts. If the tribunal is presented with a set of notes and a contemporary letter challenging aspects of those notes, they are likely to recognise that the issue is disputed and not regard the notes as evidence of what was said but look for alternative evidence to resolve the matter. If the purpose of a meeting is to

1.38 *Enquiries under self-assessment*

ascertain the facts, it is also curious that the officer should seem more concerned about what was and was not said than what the facts actually are.

BOOKS AND RECORDS

1.39 A person must keep all such records as may be requisite for the purpose of enabling him to make and deliver a correct and complete return (TMA 1970, s 12B(1); FA 1998, Sch 18, para 21(1)) as amended by Sch 37 FA 2008). In the case of a person carrying on a business such records must include records of:

- all amounts received and expended in the course of the trade, profession or business and the matters in respect of which the receipts and expenditure take place; and
- in the case of a trade involving dealing in goods all sales and purchases of goods made in the course of the trade

(TMA 1970, s 12B(3), FA 1998, Sch 18, para 21(5)) (as amended by FA 2008, Sch 37).

1.40 The records must be retained until the fifth anniversary of 31 January following the end of the tax year (the first anniversary for non-business records) or, if later, the completion of any HMRC enquiry. In the case of a company they must be kept for six years after the end of the accounting period (or if later the close of any HMRC enquiry). The duty to preserve the records listed at **1.39** above is specifically stated to include a duty to preserve 'all supporting documents relating to such items' (TMA 1970, s 12B(1)(b) and 3(b); FA 1998, Sch 18, para 21(2), (3) and (6)). Supporting documents is defined to include 'accounts, books, deeds, contracts, vouchers and receipts' (TMA 1970, s 12B(6), FA 1998, Sch 18, para 21(6)). It should be noted that there is no specific requirement to keep (in the sense of bring into existence) such records. It is only if the business in fact keeps them that it becomes under an obligation to retain them for the requisite period.

1.41 It is a question of fact what records 'may be requisite' for the purpose of delivering a correct and complete return. Unless and until it is demonstrated that the return is not correct and complete there is a strong inference that the records that were in fact kept satisfy the statutory obligation as they have enabled the statutory objective to be achieved.

1.42 Comments in the course of an enquiry that the officer considers the business records to be inadequate should be approached in the context of this statutory requirement. The records a taxpayer needs to keep are those that he considers appropriate, not those which the HMRC officer considers appropriate. The HMRC officer has no real knowledge of either the needs of the business or the abilities of its staff. Records that a person finds easy to keep are likely to be more accurate than more complex records that he finds it difficult to complete. This author's experience is that HMRC frequently expect records to be kept that are inappropriate to the circumstances of a business. For example, if cheques received are entered into a cash book and copied from there to a paying-in book, and the bankings agree with the cash book, it is hard to see any justification for keeping the paying-in book as that is not the prime record but is something prepared simply for the bank. Even if the paying-in book is completed first, it is difficult to see why it should form part of the records under s 12B once it is ascertained that the bankings agree with the cash book (although in that case it may be a supporting document). Similarly, cheque book stubs are unlikely to come within s 12B if they are not the prime document.

1.43 HMRC officers sometimes contend that the use of estimates breaches the requirement of s 12B. As the starting point for taxable profits is accounts prepared in accordance with UK GAAP (Generally Accepted Accounting Principles) and UK GAAP permits estimates, that cannot be right provided that the estimate can be justified under GAAP. Accounts that satisfy UK GAAP also satisfy the test of being correct and complete (subject to any adjustments required by law). Of course, if HMRC amend a taxpayer's return it is then up to him to justify any estimate used, but that is a different obligation from the record keeping requirement.

1.44 Schedule 37 of FA 2008 amends existing record-keeping legislation in respect of PAYE, VAT, income tax, capital gains tax and corporation tax and is aimed at alignment and clarification. This approach is designed to be flexible across a range of business and non-business taxpayers. For PAYE, employers are required to keep specified records. For VAT, income tax, capital gains tax and corporation tax the requirement is for taxable persons to keep adequate business and accounting records. Adequate does not mean excessive or prescriptive – it means keeping records to be sure that the right profit, loss, tax declaration or claim is made.

1.45 There are penalties for failure to keep appropriate records. One of the key elements in the new framework is the ability to inspect records before a return is submitted if such inspection is reasonably required to check a tax position. The basic requirements in relation to record keeping have not changed but rules have been aligned on how things are kept. The new measures will include: a generic requirement in primary legislation, an HMRC power to make regulations by secondary legislation, where necessary, to specify additional records (eg to comply with requirements of EU law), and published non-statutory HMRC guidance as to what is likely to meet the generic requirement, tailored to business, non-business and particular cases such as capital gains.

SECTION 19A AND PARA 27 NOTICES ISSUED PRIOR TO 1 APRIL 2009

1.46 The legislation relating to information powers was changed fundamentally by FA 2008, Sch 36 which entered into force on 1 April 2009. Whereas the legislation relating to self-assessment information powers was repealed the change is so recent that it was thought useful to continue covering the former legislation for the time being. This paragraph and those following under this heading relate to the former regime.

Section 19A is a limited information power. It seems likely that the limitations reflect the amount of work that Parliament envisaged HMRC doing in relation

1.46 *Enquiries under self-assessment*

to an enquiry. In particular, HMRC officers frequently say that they have a duty to satisfy themselves that the accounts are correct and complete. That is not the case. Section 9A (or para 24) gives him a right 'to enquire into a return', but does not specify the objective of such an enquiry. Section 19A (or para 27 enables him to obtain documents and information 'for the purpose of determining whether and, if so, the extent to which the return is incorrect or incomplete', but s 28A (and para 32) which deals with the completion of an enquiry merely requires the officer to 'state his conclusions and if necessary to amend the return to give effect to his conclusions'. It seems clear that if the officer believes that the return is not complete and correct all that statutorily he is seeking to do is to reach a conclusion and to form an opinion as to what the amendment to the return ought to be; not to satisfy himself about anything.

1.47 Section 19A imposes three limitations on the information that the officer can require (plus, of course, a valid enquiry notice must have been issued within the appropriate time limit).

1.48

- If he requires documents, these must be in the taxpayer's 'possession or power' (TMA 1970, s 19A(2)(a)).
- The documents or information sought must be required for the purpose of determining whether and to what extent the return is incorrect or incomplete.
- The documents or information must be 'reasonably required' for that purpose. (TMA 1970, s 19A(2); FA 1998, Sch 18, para 27).
- In the case of a company they can also require information (but not documents) to be produced in such form as they may reasonably require for the purpose of the enquiry (FA 1998, Sch 18, para 27(1)(b)).

1.49 As these provisions are central to the enquiry process, their limitations need to be looked at in more detail. Before doing so it may be worth noting that the draftsman has used the negative expression 'incorrect or incomplete' rather than the positive 'correct and complete'. This may well imply a lower test. In particular accounts require judgments to be applied in many areas. Using a judgment means that there cannot be one 'correct' figure of profit. There will be a range of figures permissible within the judgment and every one of those figures is potentially 'correct', or at least none of them are 'incorrect' (it is doubtful whether any of them can actually be described as correct when a different figure is equally correct). And what about estimates? By definition any estimate is unlikely to be correct because it is placing a value on something for which the actual value is unknown. Nevertheless, a reasonable estimate must surely make the return 'not incorrect' even though it may be uncertain whether it is 'correct'.

The expression 'possession or power' is a common legal expression. Nevertheless, its meaning is uncertain. In *Meditor Capital Management Ltd v Feighan* (2004 STC (SCD) 273) the Special Commissioner was asked to order disclosure of documents of another company with a common directorship. Reviewing the relevant law, he noted that:

'There is no case law on the phrase "possession or power" in the particular context of para 27, Sch 18 Finance Act 1998. Nor is there any case law on the same phrase in ss 20 and 20A of the 1970 Act. However, there is case law on the phrase in relation to the old disclosure rules, which confirms that the question is one of fact. RSC Ord 24, r 7(1) provided that the court had the power to order disclosure in certain circumstances if documents were in the "possession, power or custody" of a party. In *B v B* [1978] 3 WLR 624 a husband was ordered to disclose certain documents in divorce proceedings, although the documents belonged to a company which he controlled and of which he was a director. It was held by Dunn J that the documents were within his power. The question of whether this was the case was a question of fact, depending on the individual's shareholding, whether the minority shareholders were adverse to him, the constitution of the board of directors and whether they objected to disclosure of the documents. Documents would not be within his power merely because he had a right under s 12 of the Companies Act 1976 to inspect them; but where a company was a director's alter ego, so that he had unfettered control of its affairs, company documents would be within his power. In *B v B* the individual was the chairman and individual director of the company, which is not the case with Mr Shakerchi at present. He is no longer a director of the company, nor is he a shareholder. It is difficult to say that MCM(B) is the "alter ego" of Mr Shakerchi in the manner that the company was the alter ego of the director in *B v B* (at 807). The fact that Mr Shakerchi is not a director of the company means that this rule cannot be invoked ... In *Lonrho Ltd v Shell Petroleum Co Ltd* [1980] 1 WLR 627 it was said that "in the context of the phrase 'possession, custody or power' the expression 'power' must, in my view, mean a presently enforceable legal right to obtain from whoever actually holds the document inspection of it without the need to obtain the consent of anyone else" (per Lord Diplock, [1980] 1 WLR 627 at 635). In that case, the question arose of whether holding companies had the power over documents in indirectly controlled subsidiaries. The following observations were made: "The articles of association of all the subsidiaries vest the management of the company in its board of directors. It is the board that has control of the company's documents on its behalf; the shareholders as such have no right to inspect or to take copies of them. If requested to allow inspection of the company's documents, whether by a shareholder or by a third party, it is the duty of the board to consider whether to accede to this request would be in the best interests of the company" (at 634). The rule was limited however thus: "I say nothing about one-man companies in which a natural person and/or his nominees are the sole shareholders and directors. It may be that, depending upon their own particular facts, different considerations apply to these." '

1.50 The upshot of the above cases is that in cases in which a company is not simply a one-man company, the refusal of a company to allow inspection of its documents must be respected (Lonrho). In the case of one-man companies, if the company is the alter ego of the individual the company's refusal will have no effect on the individual's 'power' over a document (*B v B*).

1.51 *Enquiries under self-assessment*

1.51 Where it is unclear whether something is in the taxpayer's possession or power it is up to the appeal tribunal to decide the issue as a question of fact.

1.52 Whether or not something is required for the purpose of the enquiry requires an examination both of what the enquiry is and what its purpose is. The enquiry is 'into a return' (TMA 1970, s 9A(1); FA 1998, Sch 18, para 24(1)). This itself imposes a number of limitations. It is not a general enquiry in relation to the taxpayer's tax affairs. It relates only to one particular return; it does not extend to the return of any other year. It relates only to the return by the taxpayer; it does not extend to a return by the taxpayer's spouse or civil partner, to a return by a director of the taxpayer company or to a return by a subsidiary of the taxpayer company. It relates only to the income tax or company tax return under enquiry; it does not extend to a different return by the taxpayer such as a PAYE return or a return under one of the specific provisions requiring special returns (but a company return includes a return of tax due under ICTA 1988, s 419 (loans to directors)).

1.53 As indicated earlier, the purpose of the enquiry seems to be to enable the officer to state conclusions and to amend the return to give effect to such conclusions. As HMRC are adept at raising estimated assessments, the information that is reasonably required to enable the officers to amend a return to give effect to his conclusions may well not go beyond that which will enable him to make a rough-and-ready estimate of what amendment to make.

1.54 It needs to be realised though that this is a two-edged sword. If a taxpayer challenges a s 19A notice on the basis that the officer's wish to enquire into details is not necessary for him to be able to state his conclusions, he will put an onus on himself to displace the estimate which he forces the officer to make – and such an estimate is far more likely to be an overestimate than an underestimate.

1.55 Whether something is 'reasonably' required is a question of fact that must depend on the circumstances of an individual enquiry. It is not what a reasonable officer requires, ie it is not a test of whether or not the officer is being unreasonable. It is an objective test. What would 'the man on the Clapham omnibus' or the 'officious bystander with some knowledge of tax' think reasonable in the circumstances of the case?

1.56 This probably needs to be looked at in the context of what information the officer already has. If he already has the dividend vouchers can the bank statements be reasonably required to check the dividends? Probably not. It also needs to be looked at in the context that the officer is enquiring only into a single return, so what may be reasonably required to establish a course of conduct over several years may well not be reasonably required for the purpose only of enquiring into that single return.

1.57 An interesting issue arises in connection with electronic records. For income tax purposes the provision of a print-out seems to satisfy s 19A. In the case of a company the reason that the legislation enables HMRC to specify the form in which information is provided is to enable them to require the information on computer disk. The layout in the Queens Printer's version of the legislation and the version on the HMRC and Statute Law Database websites all tie 'in such form' only to information, not to documents. However, FA 1998, s 127(1) (which is headed 'Production of computer records') states that 'any provision made by or under the Taxes Acts which requires a person (a) to produce ... any documents ... shall have effect as if any reference in that provision to a document were a reference to anything in which information of any description is recorded'.

1.58 As para 27 deals separately with documents and information it may well be that the two are intended to be mutually exclusive and that something that constitutes a document cannot also constitute information. It is accordingly questionable whether HMRC are entitled to require the provision of a computer disk. The reason that they ask for such a disk is that they have an audit program that they wish to apply to it. The best advice is to provide a print-out of the information on the disk and to argue before the appeal tribunal that HMRC have already been provided with a document containing all of the accounts information held by the computer so it is not reasonable for them to require the same information again in a different form, particularly bearing in mind that Parliament has not given them the right to require the form which a document should take.

1.59 Because whether not an item falls within s 19A or para 27 is wholly a question of fact, the cases that have come before the Special Commissioners give little or no help in determining what does and does not fall within the section. The fact that in a particular case something was held to be reasonably required does not mean that it will also be reasonably required in another case where the circumstances may be different. Most people would prefer to take such a question before the appeal tribunal particularly where a point of principal is involved.

1.60 *Meditor Capital Management Ltd v Feighan* (2004 STC (SCD) 273) related to evidence to support a transfer pricing issue and one of the issues was what was in the company's possession or power. *Accountant v Inspector of Taxes* (2000 STC (SCD) 522) and *Parto v Bratherton* (2004 STC (SCD) 339) both raised the question, which the Commissioners answered in the affirmative, whether a person could be required under information to produce a document that did not exist. *Mother v Inspector of Taxes* (1999 STC (SCD) 279) was concerned with reasonableness, but as the challenge was more to whether HMRC was being reasonable rather than what was reasonably required it was not surprisingly dismissed. It was also held that records of the taxpayer's business which may reveal information concerning other taxpayers must nevertheless be supplied, but providing as little information concerning other taxpayers as is compatible with the requirement to produce documents relating to the taxpayer's business. *Guyer v Walton* (2001 STC (SCD) 75) involved a solicitor who unsuccessfully tried to claim legal professional privilege in relation to his own affairs. In *Guest House Proprietor v Kendall* (2005 STC (SCD) 280) some of the items requested did not exist and others formed part of the accountant's working papers, but the inspector told the Commissioners that he was not asking for documents to be produced that did not exist so it would be sufficient for the company to tell him that fact and which items were in the

1.60 *Enquiries under self-assessment*

accountant's working papers and thus not within the taxpayer's possession or power. In *Murphy v Gowers* (2005 STC (SCD) 44) it was held that it was irrelevant that the information requested had been supplied to another part of HMRC by Mr Murphy's employer, but as Mr Murphy did not appear and was not represented it was a very one-sided case. *Spring Salmon & Seafood Ltd v RCC* (2005 STC (SCD) 830) involved a tax scheme and the Commissioners felt that the information requested was reasonably required to enable HMRC to assess the motivation and commerciality of the transactions. The challenge in *Asfar v RCC* (2006 STC (SCD) 625) was that the information requested went too wide and that it infringed the taxpayer's human right to privacy, but the information was held to be reasonably required. *Commane v RCC* (2006 STC (SCD) 81) was an appeal by a taxpayer in person who did not appear before the Commissioners, but his main objection seems to have been that he thought the enquiry as such was unreasonable so the appeal was dismissed. *Low v RCC* (2006 STC (SCD) 21) was another case of a taxpayer in person who did not appear before the Commissioners. He complained that he had already provided the information in response to a tax credits enquiry, but the Commissioner held that as that was different legislation HMRC were entitled to ask for it again. It was held in *Eder v RCC* (2007 STC (SCD) 334) that information shown on a tax return that related to the tax liability of a different year (in that case an election to carry back a gift aid payment) was 'something contained in the return for the later year and accordingly within the scope of the enquiry for the later year'. In *Jacques v RCC (No 2)* (2007 STC (SCD) 166) the Special Commissioner expressed a view that 'produce' in the context of s 19A means 'allowing sufficient unrestricted use of all the documents in question to HMRC for HMRC to do such work, tests and other things (such as photocopying) in relation to the documents as is reasonable for HMRC to do in order to progress that stage of the enquiry. It includes allowing HMRC sufficient time to do what is necessary'. In *A v RCC* [2007] SpC 650 the question at issue was whether it was reasonable for HMRC to have issued a notice under s 19A. The Special Commissioner held that the jurisdiction of the Special and General Commissioners with regard to a challenge to the issue of a notice under TMA 1970, s 19A was limited to determining whether the production of the information was reasonably required for purposes of determining whether the taxpayer's return was correct and complete, and it was outside the Commissioners' jurisdiction to consider whether the issue of the notice was wholly unreasonable in view of the taxpayer's ill health.

1.61 In *Sokaya v RCC* (2008 STC (SCD) 51) the Special Commissioner commented, in relation to a demand for personal bank statements, 'Clearly the enquiry need not be limited to the entries in the return because the officer can require information to determine whether the return is incomplete ... The appellant says he has ordered his affairs so as not to pay any tax but has not said how. ... Since his income cannot support his expenditure it seems entirely reasonable to me that the Revenue should check his taxable income'. This ought to be a salutary lesson. If HMRC can point to a clear inconsistency it is likely that the tribunal will be sympathetic to allowing them access to whatever they claim that they need in order to resolve that inconsistency. It is accordingly advisable to identify in advance of the hearing that there is an obvious inconsistency and to seek to resolve it, if necessary by volunteering enough information that you believe falls outside s 19A for the tribunal to realise that the information sought by HMRC is not needed to explain the inconsistency because it can be explained by something else. For example, although an apparent deficiency of income may point to the possibility of other income, it could equally well be explained by an increase in bank overdraft facilities, a loan or gift from a third party or the taxpayer's spouse having sufficient income or assets to make good the shortfall. If no explanation is offered for the shortfall it is not surprising for the tribunal to feel it is reasonable for HMRC to assume that it suggests undisclosed income. If information to support the actual explanation has been proffered to HMRC the tribunal will have to consider the reasonableness of the information that HMRC are seeking in the context that an alternative explanation for the shortfall has already been evidenced.

1.62 Do not be disheartened by the fact that most of the published Commissioners' decisions have gone against the taxpayer. What is reasonably required is a pure question of fact. As such most taxpayers would take s 19A appeals (and requests for closure notices (see below) which are similarly pure questions of fact) to the General Commissioners as they feel that a layman with commercial experience is more likely to appreciate the practical questions involved in what might reasonable satisfy someone than do the Special Commissioners with their legal training. It is probable that the cases that came before the Special Commissioners (which were the only cases publicly reported) are those where the taxpayer or his adviser is either seeking to establish some legal principle or mistakenly believes either that listing the case before the Special Commissioners was some sort of deterrent to HMRC or that the Special Commissioners were more likely to be sympathetic to his arguments.

THE SECTION 19A PROCEDURE

1.63 A notice under s 19A (or para 27) must specify the time within which it must be complied with, which must not be less than 30 days (TMA 1970, s 19A(2), FA 1998, Sch 18, para 27(2)). The taxpayer has a right of appeal against such a notice. Such an appeal must be in writing and made within 30 days after the notice is given to the taxpayer (TMA 1970, s 19A(6) and (7); FA 1998, Sch 18, para 28(1) and (2)). A ground for appeal needs to be stated in the same way as for an appeal against an assessment (TMA 1970, s 19A(8)). This will normally be that some or all of the documents or information required by the notice does not fall within s 19A (or para 27). It could also be that the enquiry notice itself is invalid or that the s 19A (or para 27) notice is invalid. There have been several Special Commissioners' decisions dealing with the validity of both s 9A and s 19A notices.

1.64 The s 19A notice in *Wing Hung Lai v Bale* (1999 STC (SCD) 238) was held to be invalid as it was posted too late to have been received in the normal course of post by 31 January. HMRC sought, unsuccessfully, to overturn that principle in *Holly v Inspector of Taxes* (2000 STC (SCD) 50). In *Self-Assessed v Inspector of Taxes* (1999 STC (SCD) 253) a s 19A notice was held invalid as it

1.64 *Enquiries under self-assessment*

required the information to be produced 'within 30 days of this notice', whereas the taxpayer was entitled under the statute to a minimum of 30 days from receipt of the notice. In *Hallamshire Estates Ltd v Walford* (2004 STC (SCD) 330), the taxpayer unsuccessfully sought to contend as a matter of construction that the time limit for enquiring into an amended return ran from the date of the return, not that of the amendment.

1.65 In *Murat v Ornach* (2004 STC (SCD) 115), the taxpayer sought to challenge the validity of the s 9A notice in an appeal against a penalty for not complying with the resultant s 19A notice. It was held that as the decision on the s 19A appeal is final it was too late to seek to challenge the s 9A notice. Mr Murat appealed to the High Court (77 TC 122), but his appeal was dismissed as hopeless. *Siwek v CIR* (2002 STC (SCD) 247) was a taxpayer in person taking a forlorn point. In *Bensoor v Devine* (2005 STC (SCD) 297), the taxpayer challenged whether a s 9A notice could be issued by an officer who was not an inspector and also challenged HMRC's right to broaden an aspect enquiry. Unsurprisingly, he lost on both points. In *O'Sullivan v Philip* (2005 STC (SCD) 51) the taxpayer amended his return and after some correspondence HMRC accepted the amendment. In response to a subsequent enquiry notice the taxpayer contended, unsuccessfully, that such HMRC acceptance amounted to the completion of an enquiry into the return so they were debarred from opening a further enquiry. *Moffat v CIR* (2006 STC (SCD) 380) concerned a technical challenge based on the wording of the closure notice, but it failed.

1.66 The appeal freezes HMRC's ability to obtain the information sought until it has been determined either on appeal or by agreement. The tribunal can (and probably must) confirm the notice if it appears to them that the production of the documents or information is reasonably required for the purpose of the enquiry, and set it aside if it does not so appear to them (TMA 1970, s 19A(9): FA 1998, Sch 18, para 28(4)). There is no onus of proof on the taxpayer. Nor is there any right of appeal by either the taxpayer or HMRC against the decision of the tribunal. This is obviously because whether or not something is reasonably required for the purpose of the enquiry is a question of fact and the normal right of appeal against a tribunal decision applies only to questions of law (TMA 1970, s 19A(11), FA 1998, Sch 18, para 28(6)).

1.67 In practice it is generally accepted that the tribunal is entitled to look at each document or item of information individually as if it were contained in a separate notice and therefore uphold part of the notice and set aside part. The appeal on the other hand seems to be an appeal against the notice in its entirety. If the tribunal uphold the notice, the taxpayer has a period of 30 days from the determination of the appeal in which to provide the information (TMA 1970, s 19A(10), FA 1998, Sch 18, para 28(5)).

1.68 HMRC can issue as many s 19A (or para 27) notices as they wish during the course of an enquiry. Indeed there is nothing to stop them issuing a second notice for information that the tribunal hold not to be reasonably required under an earlier notice. This is not unreasonable as information may not be reasonably required at an early stage of an enquiry, but something might come to light later in the enquiry which affects its relevance. It might be worth drawing this to the attention of the tribunal. A decision that is adverse to the taxpayer is final whereas one that is adverse to HMRC is not necessarily so as they could issue a fresh notice for it at a later stage. Accordingly, if the decision is fairly evenly balanced justice might well require the notice to be set aside so that HMRC could revisit the need for the information at a later stage.

1.69 In practice HMRC rarely seem to list s 19A (and para 27) appeals for hearing. They generally make do without the disputed information provided that items that come clearly within the ambit of the provision are complied with.

1.70 Section 20 is considered elsewhere. There is nothing to prevent HMRC issuing a s 20 notice in relation to a self-assessment enquiry. However the following ministerial statement of 19 April 1999 should be quoted if HMRC threaten a s 20 notice to obtain information that has been held not to be reasonably required under s 19A.

> 'Dawn Primarolo: The powers in TMA 1970 ss 19A, 20 are not mutually exclusive. However, the Inland Revenue would not normally issue a notice under s 20 in order to obtain information that they had failed to obtain under s 19A. Very rarely, it might become clear, after the taxpayer had appealed against an s 19A notice, that s 20 was in fact the more appropriate section to use. A notice under s 20 cannot be issued by an inspector unless the taxpayer has failed to take an opportunity to provide the information voluntarily, and may be issued only with the consent of an independent Appeal Commissioner.'

(Hansard, HC Written Answer, Vol 329, cols 425, 426, 19 April 1999.) Section 20 was repealed with effect from 1 April 2009.

1.71 The main instances in which HMRC seemed to use s 20 notices in relation to self-assessment is to obtain information about the affairs of a company director when they are enquiring into the company's return. They cannot use s 19A in such circumstances, as the information is not in the possession or power of the company and the enquiry is not into the return of the director. Third-party notices under s 20(3) might also be used where the taxpayer is not prepared to co-operate with the enquiry. It might be easier for HMRC to obtain the information by another route than to have to enforce a succession of s 19A notices. However this is academic in relation to notices issued from 1 April 2009.

INFORMATION POWERS FROM 1 APRIL 2009: FA 2008 SCH 36

1.72 The self-assessment enquiry powers and the very different information powers under TMA 1970, s 20 were repealed with effect from 1 April 2009. In their place new information powers were introduced which are applicable to all enquiries and investigations in relation to income tax, capital gains tax, corporation tax, PAYE and VAT, Whilst the new powers are probably more straightforward than those under the previous regime they are wider in their application.

1.73 *Enquiries under self-assessment*

1.73 The provisions of FA 2008 Parts 1, 4–9 are considered elsewhere in this publication and are not replicated in detail in this chapter which deals solely with self-assessment enquiries.

1.74 The powers to obtain information and documents are contained within FA 2008 Sch 36, Part 1. Paragraph (1) provides that an HMRC officer may by notice in writing require a person ('the taxpayer') to provide information, or to produce a document, if the information is *reasonably required* by the officer for the purpose of *checking the taxpayer's tax position* (*'a taxpayer notice'*): note the difference in wording from the former self-assessment powers. Paragraph (2) applies similarly to third-party notices which may only be issued with the agreement of the taxpayer or the approval of the First-tier Tribunal (para (3)) which also imposes certain conditions. Paragraph (7) (2) specifies the place at which documents may be produced, clearly this could be specified as the business premises. Paragraph (8) relates to the production of copied and original documents. Note that 'checking' is defined as including carrying out an investigation or enquiry of any kind (para 58). 'Tax position' is defined in para 64.

1.75 Part 1 is subject to the restrictions in Parts 4 and 6. Paragraph 18 retains the important stipulation that a person can only be required to produce a document if it is his possession or power. Paragraphs 21(1) and (2) provide that where a person has made a return a taxpayer notice may not be given. Alas too good to be true as para 22(3) states that sub-paras (1) and (2) do not apply where, or to the extent that, any of the conditions in A to D is met!

1.76 Condition A is that a notice of enquiry has been given in respect of:

- the return, or
- a claim or election (or an amendment of a claim or election) made by the person in relation to the chargeable period in respect of the tax (or one of the taxes) to which the return relates ('relevant tax'), and the enquiry has not been completed: para 22(4).

1.77 In sub-para (4), 'notice of enquiry' means a notice under:

- s 9A or s 12AC of, or para 5 of Sch 1A to, TMA 1970, or
- para 24 of Sch 18 to FA 1998.

1.78 Condition B is that an officer of Revenue and Customs has reason to suspect that:

- an amount that ought to have been assessed to relevant tax for the chargeable period may not have been assessed;
- an assessment to relevant tax for the chargeable period may be or have become insufficient; or
- relief from relevant tax given for the chargeable period may be or have become excessive, para 22(6).

1.79 Condition C is that the notice is given for the purpose of obtaining any information or document that is also required for the purpose of checking that person's VAT position: para 22(7).

1.80 Condition D is that the notice is given for the purpose of obtaining any information or document that is required (or also required) for the purpose of checking the person's position as regards any deductions or repayments referred to in para 64(2) (PAYE etc): para 22(8).

1.81 There is a time limit in relation to deceased persons of four years after the person's death: para 22. Paragraphs 23–27 deal with the normal exclusions relating to privileged communications, auditors and tax advisers.

1.82 FA 2008 Sch 36 Part 5 deals with appeals against information notices. Note that there is no right of appeal against a taxpayer notice to provide any information or document that forms part of the taxpayer's statutory records: para 29(2). There are similar provisions for third-party notices: para 30. A decision by the First-tier Tribunal is final. 'Statutory records' are defined in para 62.

1.83 FA 2008 Sch 36 Part 6 relates to special cases including groups. Part 7 deals with penalties for non-compliance, Part 8 deals with offences, Part 9 deals with miscellaneous provisions and interpretation, Part 10 deals with consequential provisions.

1.84 Schedule 36 information powers combine, reinforce and widen those previous available to HMRC. Whereas the previous s 20 powers were used sparingly it is anticipated that Sch 36 will be used far more widely across the various taxes covered.

1.85 The meaning of such terms as 'reasonably required' and 'possession or power' which continue to be undefined will remain as interpreted by case law.

Business inspections: FA 2008 Sch 36, Part 2

1.86 These new powers will have a significant effect in relation to self-assessment enquiries and 'compliance checks'. HMRC's former powers to see records at business premises for VAT and PAYE were repealed with effect from 1 April 2009; FA 2008 Sch 36, Part 2 applies to income tax, capital gains tax, corporation tax, CIS, PAYE and VAT and allows an authorised officer of HMRC to enter business premises and inspect the premises, business assets and business documents that are on the premises. There is a provision that the inspection is reasonably required for the purpose of checking that person's tax position para 10(1). If an information notice has been issued, the documents required in the notice can be inspected at the same time. The powers do not extend to any part of the premises which is used solely as a dwelling. Inspections will normally be carried out at a time agreed with the taxpayer or at any reasonable time with a minimum of seven days' notice which may be given in writing or otherwise. There is also provision for an unannounced visit if a prearranged visit is considered to be inappropriate. There is no right of appeal against an inspection notice but the taxpayer can refuse entry and prevent the inspection being completed. The taxpayer can be penalised for such an obstruction but only if the inspection has been approved by the First-tier Tribunal under para 13. The inspection powers are in no way a substitute for a

1.86 *Enquiries under self-assessment*

PACE search warrant either as conferring the right of entry or conduct whilst on the premises.

1.87 Part 2 is subject to the restrictions in FA 2008, Sch 36, Parts 4 and 6. Significantly para 28 provides that:

> 'An officer of Revenue and Customs may not inspect a business document under Part 2 of this Schedule if or to the extent that, by virtue of this Part of this Schedule, an information notice given at the time of the inspection to the occupier of the premises could not require the occupier to produce the document.'

1.88 HMRC internal instructions relating to business inspections may be found in the Compliance Handbook at CH 25000–CH 25700.

1.89 Historically it was perhaps rare for professional advisers even to learn of a PAYE or VAT inspection visit at all or certainly until howls of anguish were to be heard from distraught clients when they received a tax bill in conclusion. The rules of the game have changed and professionals should now encourage clients to let them know when they receive a request for a visit from HMRC. Best practice suggests that it would normally be prudent for advisers to attend these events, at least in part so that they might ensure that the proper procedures are followed. In the rarer case where an unannounced visit is made the alarm bells should ring and HMRC should be refused entry until such time as proper professional advice has been taken. This process need not be rushed. In the even rarer case where a notice is issued with the approval of the First-tier Tribunal should entry be refused so that the taxpayer can take professional advice so potentially incurring a penalty? In the author's opinion a commercial view should be taken and this may well result in entry being refused so that advice may be taken. This may result not only in a penalty – there is no commentary in HMRC guidance as to whether this would constitute a 'reasonable excuse' – but in the most serious cases could lead to HMRC applying for a PACE search warrant where entry is not negotiable and the door can be forced!

Other ways to obtain information

1.90 Sometimes HMRC ask for a mandate from the taxpayer authorising his bank or another third party to provide direct to HMRC such information as they may request. This is not a statutory procedure. It is wholly voluntary. A taxpayer should think carefully before agreeing to provide such a mandate. It is normally better for the taxpayer to volunteer to obtain information from the bank himself. If HMRC obtain information direct from the bank the taxpayer may well not know what information they have been given, which places him at a disadvantage in negotiating with HMRC. Furthermore, in practice banks made available information to HMRC under the authority of a mandate which they would not make available to the taxpayer himself. The obvious example is the bank's own file notes of telephone conversations with the taxpayer. Note however that HMRC may decide to use their third-party notice powers under FA 2008 Sch 36 (2).

COMPLETION OF ENQUIRY

1.91 An enquiry is completed when the officer issues a closure notice to the taxpayer (TMA 1970, s 28A(1) and (3), FA 1998, Sch 18, para 32(1)). The closure notice takes effect when it is issued (TMA 1970, s 28(3), FA 1998, Sch 18, para 32(2)). An income tax closure notice must inform the taxpayer that the officer has completed his enquiries and state his conclusions. It must also state that in his opinion no amendment to the return is required, or must make the amendments to the return that are required to give effect to his conclusions (TMA 1970, s 28A(1) and (3)). This clearly implies that the conclusions must incorporate the amount of any adjustment that the officer concludes is required, as otherwise he would not be able to amend the return. A corporation tax closure notice merely has to inform the company that HMRC have completed their enquiry and state their conclusions (FA 1998, Sch 18, para 32(1)). The company then has 30 days in which to amend its return to accord with the conclusions stated in the closure notice (FA 1998, Sch 18, para 34(1)). This seems to imply an obligation on HMRC to state their conclusions in a manner which is capable of being put into effect, ie to either state what amendment is needed or how the amendment is to be arrived at. If the company does not amend its return within the 30-day period HMRC are entitled to do so, by notice to the company (FA 1998, Sch 18, para 34(2)).

1.92 At any time during the course of an enquiry the taxpayer can apply to the tribunal for a direction requiring HMRC to issue a closure notice within a specified period. Such an application is heard and determined in the same way as an appeal. The tribunal must give the direction applied for unless it is satisfied that there are reasonable grounds for not issuing a closure notice within a specified period (TMA 1970, s 28A(4)–(6); FA 1998, Sch 18, para 33). This places the onus on the officer to convince the tribunal that it ought not to direct a closure. The purpose of this provision is to prevent HMRC leaving an enquiry open indefinitely and thus defeating the taxpayer's right to finality in his tax affairs within a reasonable time. A taxpayer might make such an application where he considers that HMRC delays are unreasonable or where he feels that HMRC is raising new questions in relation to areas that have already been fully dealt with.

1.93 Such an application should not be made lightly, however. If successful, it does not force the officer to abandon his enquiry; it forces him to reach a conclusion on the basis of the information that is available to him by the specified date. If this is incomplete information he is likely to conclude that a greater adjustment to the self-assessment ought to be made than he would have concluded had he been able to obtain the missing information. Accordingly, a successful application is likely to force the taxpayer to appeal against the officer's amendment and on the appeal to disprove a larger assessment than he would have faced had he let the officer continue with his investigation. As usual timing is everything.

1.94 There is, of course, a right of appeal against the amendment to the self-assessment as a result of the closure notice or against HMRC's amendment of the assessment (TMA 1970, s 31, FA 1998, Sch 18, para 34(3)). Notice of

1.94 *Enquiries under self-assessment*

such an appeal must be made in writing within 30 days in the normal way. However, the issue of the closure notice brings to an end the self-assessment process and, in particular, may reduce the officer's ability to seek information under FA 2008, Sch 36, Pt 1 (para 21(4)). It does not, of course, prevent the taxpayer volunteering further information or the officer asking for further information informally.

1.95 Case law dealing with closure notices include *Jade Palace Ltd v RCC* (2006 STC (SCD) 419 which held that the legislation did not require the officer to be satisfied – she might never be so that would undermine the purpose of the provision – but merely to form a conclusion. It also held that the Commissioner does not have to require the closure by the date requested by the taxpayer, but can reach his own decision as to the appropriate date. In *Vodafone (No 2)* (2006 STC 1530), which is concerned with the validity of the UK's CFC rules, the company asked for a closure notice so that the case could be brought before the ECJ. The Commissioners decided that the substantive issue was one that ought to be referred and ordered the closure. HMRC appealed on the basis that the Commissioners had no power to decide the substantive point so ought not to have ordered the closure. The Court of Appeal held that para 33 gives the Commissioners power to do anything they consider reasonably necessary to decide whether or not to require a closure and that included deciding incidental points of law.

1.96 In *Kilbride v R & C Commrs* (2008) Sp C 660, HMRC had opened enquiries into two directors and their company, suspecting that the directors had not accounted for all their income as they had both declared considerably less income than was in their bank accounts. The taxpayers applied for closure notices arguing that HMRC had produced no evidence of any tax loss. The Special Commissioner dismissed the application. He held that there were reasonable grounds for not issuing closure notices with immediate effect, including the failure of the taxpayers to disclose the identity of directors of a related overseas company even though they were not under a legal obligation to do so. In *Lee v R & C Commrs* (2008) Sp C 715, the Special Commissioner decided that as there were unresolved questions about whether the taxpayer had made timely disclosure of savings income, it was not appropriate to direct closure at this stage of the enquiry. In *Tower Cashback LLP1 & Anor v R & C Commrs* [2008] BTC 805 the High Court held that the case raised a procedural question concerning the scope of appeals against closure notices: could an appeal be heard on grounds other than those set out in the closure notice? HMRC had issued a closure notice that stated that the LLPs were not entitled to the first-year allowances that had been claimed because the qualifying expenditure fell within one of the statutory exceptions. However, during the course of the Special Commissioners' hearing HMRC pursued other lines of attack. The court held that TMA 1970, s 31(1)(b) did not permit HMRC to challenge every aspect of a taxpayer's return but limited the scope of any appeal to the officer's conclusions and, or, the amendments (if any) to the return made by the closure notice.

DISCOVERY

1.97 Self-assessment is designed to give finality to the taxpayer. Once an enquiry has been closed or the enquiry window has passed without HMRC having opened an enquiry, they can no longer challenge the return.

1.98 The discovery power provides an exception to this general principle. It enables HMRC to assess tax in relation to closed years if they discover that tax has been under assessed and the under-assessment is attributable either to:

- fraudulent or negligent conduct of the taxpayer or a person acting on his behalf; or
- something of which the officer could not have been reasonably expected to be aware at the time the enquiry window closed on the basis of the information made available to him before that time.

In relation to the second of these points consider *Langham v Veltema* (2004) BTC 156 and HMRC SP 1/06.

1.99 Prior to FA 2008 a discovery assessment can be made at any time up to the fifth anniversary of 31 January following the tax year to which it relates (or up to six years after the end of the accounting period in relation to a company) (TMA 1970, s 34; FA 1998, Sch 18, para 46). In the case of fraud or negligence, a discovery assessment can be made up to 20 years after 31 January following the tax year to which it relates or, in the case of a company up to 21 years after the end of the accounting period (TMA 1970, s 36; FA 1998, Sch 18, para 46(2)).

New time limits for assessing and claims were introduces by FA 2008, Sch 39. The basic rules for PAYE, income tax, capital gains tax and corporation tax are:

- four years – normal time limit;
- six years – careless error (except for VAT which is four years);
- 20 years – deliberate error, failure to register for VAT, failure to notify chargeability to tax, failure to notify tax-avoidance schemes.

The new time limits apply from the end of the accounting period or tax year. The time limits for taxpayer claims are also aligned at four years.

1.100 As discovery is not part of self-assessment, the self-assessment enquiry procedures do not apply. Prior to 1 April HMRC had no power to issue a s 19A or para 27 information notice. Indeed, apart from TMA 1970, s 20, they had no power at all to require the taxpayer to supply information in relation to an investigation leading up to a discovery. They had to rely on the taxpayer volunteering information – but where a discovery involves negligence their power to determine the level of penalty can act as a powerful inducement to volunteer information. From 1 April 2009 HMRC can issue a notice under FA 2008, Sch 36 to compel the production of documents or information: para 21(6).

1.101 The reason for mentioning discovery in the context of enquiries is that HMRC take the view that in the absence of evidence to the contrary 'a presumption of continuity' can be made where an enquiry suggests that there is an understatement of income in the enquiry year and the reasons for that

1.101 *Enquiries under self-assessment*

understatement provide a pointer to under-declarations in earlier years (Enquiry Manual, para 3309).

1.102 In practice, HMRC invariably seek to adjust the previous six years in addition to the enquiry year where they believe that a presumption of continuity can reasonably be made. In general they do not seek to investigate the omissions for such earlier years, but quantify the supposed omissions by assuming that the figure quantified for the enquiry year is representative of the level of under declaration in earlier years and reducing it on some rough and ready basis to allow for inflation.

1.103 There are two points that need to be borne in mind. The first is that before agreeing to an adjustment on an enquiry for the sake of an easy life when the taxpayer does not believe any adjustment to be legally due, it needs to be appreciated that the adjustment may result in a tax bill seven times the size of that which was anticipated when agreeing it. The second is that if the taxpayer does not believe that adjusting the current year's amendment to reflect the effect of inflation is likely to give a reasonable approximation of any underpayment for earlier years, he ought to seek to establish the size of any appropriate adjustment on a more realistic basis using whatever information he has available in relation to the years in question and seek to persuade the officer to agree his calculation.

1.104 Where, in the course of a self-assessment enquiry, HMRC make a discovery in relation to earlier years they normally seek 'a contract settlement' rather than raise formal discovery and penalty assessments. A contract settlement is a contract between HMRC and the taxpayer under which the taxpayer offers to pay HMRC an agreed sum in respect of tax, interest and penalties in consideration of HMRC agreeing not to institute proceedings against him. The contract settlement will normally cover the enquiry year as well as the discovery years.

1.105 Where a contract settlement has been entered into, the amount due is not tax; it is a civil debt. HMRC will accordingly enforce it as such a debt. They cannot use their power of distraint or other statutory powers that they have to enable them to recover tax.

1.106 Where a contract settlement is entered into, HMRC do not in practice issue a closure notice. The reason is that their computer system would then seek to recover the tax due under the amendment to the self-assessment, as well as the collector collecting the debt under the contract settlement. In theory this leaves the enquiry window open indefinitely. The taxpayer could apply to the Commissioners for the issue of a closure notice, but as the issue of such a notice will trigger the computer problem and cause a lot of work and anguish for both the taxpayer and HMRC this is probably not a sensible thing to do. HMRC tell their staff, 'Once a contract offer has been accepted, it has the same effect as the issue of a closure notice. The year(s) included in the contract become final and you will not be able to make any further enquiries into those years, unless you consider that the conditions for making a discovery assessment are satisfied' (Enquiry Manual, para 6001). Whilst the legal basis for this statement may be dubious, the taxpayer can probably safely rely on it.

Chapter 2

Special Investigations

Gary Ashford

National Head of Tax Risk, RSM Bentley Jennison

THE ROLE OF SPECIAL INVESTIGATIONS OFFICE (SI)

2.01 SI is the recent successor office to SCI (Special Civil Investigations) and before that SCO (Special Compliance Office). It handles the larger cases as it was previously the case that all investigations of suspected serious fraud, in terms of direct taxes, were handled by Special Compliance Office (SCO). Cases of Suspected Serious Fraud were handled under Code of Practice 9.

2.02 SI also handles large and complex avoidance-type cases, regularly involving offshore structures where significant liabilities are at risk. SCO would also conduct large-scale projects looking at such groups as high-profile entertainers or sportsmen, sectors where significant amounts of PAYE and NIC or other taxes were at risk; for example in relation to city traders, the pharmaceutical industry etc. This sort of work was and is still undertaken under a separate Code of Practice, Code of Practice 8 (Cases other than Suspected Serious Fraud).

2.03 Historically SCO, staff were split into clearly defined roles within SCO dealing with the work arising under one or other of the Codes of Practice. SCO also was the home of the then Board's Investigation Office and Prosecution Groups. SCO also previously had responsibility for departments such as the Foreign Entertainers Unit (FEU); however, FEU became part of Centre for Non-Residents (previously FICO) and is now part of Charities Assets and Residence (CAR).

2.04 On 1 April 2005, the prosecution functions of the former Inland Revenue and former Customs and Excise were placed within a new independent prosecuting authority, the Revenue and Customs Prosecution Office (RCPO). This led the way for the criminal prosecution teams being removed to a new HMRC department, the Criminal Investigation Directorate. Whilst the Criminal Investigation Directorate remains, prosecutions are now

2.04 *Special Investigations*

conducted by the Criminal Prosecution Service (CPS). Special Civil Investigations (SCI) was created effectively to deal with the most serious civil cases of tax fraud and all other special civil investigation work. There were SCI offices strategically located throughout the UK; in London, Bristol, Manchester, Solihull, Edinburgh, Nottingham and Leeds. Various subsidiary SCI offices were created to handle the large increase in workload on tax-avoidance scheme arrangements, but the offices above remain the key SCI offices.

2.05 On 1 September 2005 the Civil Investigation of Fraud (CIF) procedures were introduced and specially trained CIF teams were set up within strategically located local Tax Districts throughout the UK to deal with those CIF cases that are not handled by SI and a majority of cases which were suitable to be worked under the these new procedures.

2.06 SI was created out of SCI in 2009 and currently remains responsible for the largest Code of Practice 9 investigations and investigations under Code of Practice 8. (See Section 8 below for the thresholds applicable to the SCI and CIF teams for COP 9 cases.). It also has other teams dealing with specific Customs and Excise matters including MTIC (Missing Trader Inter Company, Carousel fraud).

STRUCTURE OF SPECIAL INVESTIGATIONS OFFICE

2.07 SI is headed by a Director who is responsible directly to the Board of HMRC. Each individual SI office is headed by an Assistant Director. Various team leaders and investigators work directly to the Assistant Director.

Types of SI investigation

2.08 SI Investigations can arise in a range of ways and circumstances.

Suspected serious fraud (Civil Investigation of Fraud (CIF) Procedures (Code of Practice 9))

2.09 CIF investigations can arise in the following circumstances:

- from an investigation being conducted in the local area office where the local investigator identifies significant additions to profit as a result of an identified fraud, or activities which suggest that serious fraud may have taken place;
- from an investigation opened directly by SI or CIF team as a result of their own intelligence and research work;
- alternatively, where a taxpayer or their adviser identifies an issue or issues where additional liabilities are likely resulting from suspected fraudulent activity, subject to the limits (see SI thresholds), they might wish to approach the relevant CIF/SI team direct to seek the protection of CIF procedures for their client or clients.

Cases other than suspected serious fraud (Code of Practice 8)

2.10 SI also investigates non-fraud cases as follows:

- where significant tax is at risk, perhaps as a result of the use of offshore structures or trusts;
- where SI conduct projects for example to identify high-profile individuals, entertainers and sportsmen whose tax affairs may be complex or not up to date, or who have failed to register for tax altogether (an example of this is the well-publicised football and rugby project of the late 1980s and 1990s);
- where SI have been tasked to support local offices or for example the Anti Avoidance Group (AAG) by raising investigations into marketed avoidance schemes.

CRIMINAL INVESTIGATIONS

2.11 When considering cases of suspected serious fraud, with a view to CIF procedures, it is important to understand HMRC's approach to criminal investigation, as to some extent the two approaches overlap. There can be an overlap between a civil investigation and a criminal prosecution.

2.12 The overlap results from the fact that when HMRC consider whether a case is suitable for CIF procedures they will first look at the suspected offences committed and whether they are sufficiently heinous to warrant a criminal investigation.

2.13 HMRC's published criminal prosecution policy states the following:

'HMRC's aim is to secure the highest level of compliance with the law and regulations governing direct and indirect taxes and other regimes for which they are responsible. Criminal investigation, with a view to prosecution by the Revenue and Customs Prosecutions Office (RCPO) in England and Wales – or the appropriate prosecuting authority in Scotland and Northern Ireland – is an important part of HMRC's overall enforcement strategy.

It is HMRC's policy to deal with fraud by use of the cost-effective Civil Investigation of Fraud (CIF) procedures, wherever appropriate. Criminal Investigation will be reserved for cases where HMRC needs to send a strong deterrent message or where the conduct involved is such that only a criminal sanction is appropriate.

However, HMRC reserves complete discretion to conduct a criminal investigation in any case and to carry out these investigations across a range of offences and in all the areas for which the Commissioners of HMRC have responsibility.'

2.14 Examples of the kind of circumstances in which HMRC will generally consider commencing a criminal, rather than civil investigation are:

2.14 *Special Investigations*

- cases of organised criminal gangs attacking the tax system or systematic frauds where losses represent a serious threat to the tax base, including conspiracy;
- where an individual holds a position of trust or responsibility;
- where materially false statements are made or materially false documents are provided in the course of a civil investigation;
- where, pursuing an avoidance scheme, reliance is placed on a false or altered document or such reliance or material facts are misrepresented to enhance the credibility of a scheme;
- where deliberate concealment, deception, conspiracy or corruption is suspected;
- cases involving the use of false or forged documents;
- cases involving importation or exportation breaching prohibitions and restrictions;
- cases involving money laundering with particular focus on advisors, accountants, solicitors and others acting in a 'professional' capacity who provide the means to put tainted money out of reach of law enforcement;
- where the perpetrator has committed previous offences or there is a repeated course of unlawful conduct or previous civil action;
- cases involving theft, or the misuse or unlawful destruction of HMRC documents;
- where there is evidence of assault on, threats to, or the impersonation of HMRC officials;
- where there is a link to suspected wider criminality, whether domestic or international, involving offences not under the administration of HMRC.

2.15 When considering whether a case should be investigated under the Civil Investigation of Fraud procedures or is to be the subject of a criminal investigation, one important factor will be whether the taxpayer has made a complete and unprompted disclosure of the offences committed.

2.16 However, there are certain fiscal offences where HMRC will not usually adopt the Civil Investigation of Fraud approach. Examples of these are:

- VAT Missing Trader Intra-Community (MTIC) Fraud;
- VAT 'Bogus' registration repayment fraud;
- organised tax credit fraud.

DEFINITION OF FRAUD

2.17 As well as understanding the HMRC Board's policy to criminal prosecution when considering cases of suspected serious fraud some understanding of what constitutes fraud is also clearly helpful. There is an abundance of common law (both tax and non-tax related) on this subject.

2.18 The HMRC Enquiry Manual, reference EM5106, publishes the following extract from *Halsbury's Laws of England* (Butterworths), under the heading 'Misrepresentation and Fraud'.

'Section 757 What Constitutes Fraud?

Not only is a misrepresentation fraudulent if it was known or believed by the representor to be false when made, but mere non-belief in the truth is also indicative of fraud. Thus, whenever a person makes a false statement which he does not actually and honestly believe to be true, for purposes of civil liability, that statement is as fraudulent as if he had stated that which he did not know to be true, or knew or believed to be false*. Proof of absence of actual and honest belief is all that is necessary to satisfy the requirements of the law, whether the representation has been made recklessly or deliberately; indifference or recklessness on the part of the representor as to the truth or falsity of the representation affords merely an instance of absence of such a belief.

A representor will not, however, be fraudulent if he believed the statement to be true in the sense in which he understood it, provided that was a meaning which might reasonably be attached to it, even though the court later holds that the statement objectively bears another meaning, which the representor did not believe.

[* see *Derry v Peek* 14 App Cas 337, p374, per Lord Herschell: fraud is proved when it is shown that a false representation has been made (1) knowingly, or (2) without belief in its truth, or (3) recklessly, careless whether it be true or false; the third case being but an instance of the second.]

Section 759 Irrelevancy of Representor's Motive

It follows from the meaning of fraudulent misrepresentation that, given absence of actual and honest belief by the representor in the truth of the misrepresentation, his motive in making the misrepresentation is wholly irrelevant. It may be that he intended to injure the representee without benefiting himself, or to benefit himself without injuring the representee; it may be that he did not intend to do either, but solely to benefit a third person, or even the representee himself, or otherwise to do right. Lastly, he may have acted with no intelligible or rational notice whatsoever and told a lie from mere caprice, mischievousness or stupidity. In all these cases, provided that there was an absence of actual and honest belief in the truth of his assertion, the misrepresentation is accounted fraudulent and no proof of any wicked or other intention (other than an intention to induce) on the part of the representor is required by the law; or if it is necessary to establish an intention to deceive or injure, that intention is immediately and irrebuttably presumed in law from the mere act of making the misrepresentation without such belief.

Section 760 Representation Subsequently Discovered by Representor to be False

Where a representation is a continuing one and where, between the time when it was made and the time when the representee altered his position on the faith of it, either (1) the representor discovers that his original statement which, when he made it, he honestly believed to be true, was false, or (2) supervening events render, to the knowledge of the representor, his

2.18 Special Investigations

statement no longer true, a duty to disclose the changed situation to the representee may arise. In such cases the mere fact that the statement may have been innocently made, though false, or true when made, will not, it seems, prevent the representee from establishing fraud where he can show that the representor dishonestly failed to discharge the duty of disclosing the change in the situation.'

2.19 The above demonstrates that, particularly in terms of civil liability, the term fraud is widely drawn. For example it extends to the deliberate submission of understated accounts and incorrect tax returns.

2.20 Further guidance on fraud can also be drawn from the Fraud Act 2006.

THE FRAUD ACT 2006

2.21 In terms of the criminal law, the Fraud Act 2006 defines fraud in three categories:

- fraud by false representation;
- fraud by failing to disclose information;
- fraud by abuse of position.

2.22 The Act states that in all three categories the person committing the offence must have an intention to make a gain or loss, temporary or permanent, and defines loss or gain as extending only to money or other property (real or personal) but including things in action or other intangible property.

2.23 In terms of gain, this includes keeping what one has as well as what one does not have; and in terms of loss, this includes getting what one might get as well as parting with what one has.

CODE OF PRACTICE 9

2.24 In terms of direct taxes, Code of Practice 9 and its forerunner, the so-called 'Hansard procedure' has been around for a long time (its name derived from parliamentary statements made by the Chancellor of the Exchequer in relation to tax fraud) and dates from 1923.

2.25 Early versions of the Hansard procedures stated that where a person made a full disclosure of all tax irregularities as part of the formal Hansard process, the Board of the ex-Inland Revenue would take this into account when considering whether to accept a money settlement or institute criminal proceedings.

2.26 Whilst this provided no guarantee that criminal proceedings would not result from what amounted to full disclosure of tax fraud, in practice, the Inland Revenue approach was not to prosecute in such cases despite the legal facility to do so. (The approach of the ex-Customs and Excise was more clear cut, ie more like the current CIF procedures, in that once a case had been categorised as civil only in very defined circumstances could a criminal investigation occur.)

2.27 This position came to a head in the case of the case of *Regina v W* [1998] STC 550. In this case the Crown did institute criminal proceedings, despite the custom and practice of HMRC for many years of non-prosecution where full disclosure was made, and the case of *R v Allen* [2001] STC 1537 HL, where the courts referred to the inducement of the wording of the COP 9 leaflet effectively preventing prosecution where a full disclosure was made. (The matter of the inducement was incidental to the outcome of that case as the taxpayer was found not to have made a full disclosure under the terms offered.)

2.28 In order to clarify the position, a new statement was made by the Chancellor of Exchequer in November 2002 which resulted in the issue of a revised version of COP 9. This statement explicitly guaranteed for the first time for direct tax purposes that no prosecution would result where a full disclosure was made.

2.29 Further changes took place following the case of *R v Gill & Gill* [2003] STC 1229. In this case, the courts criticised the ex-Inland Revenue for not having formally cautioned the defendants before offering them an inducement to make a disclosure. (However, the courts did not free the defendants from their prison sentence, notwithstanding the criticism of the ex-Revenue procedures, as they found that the defendants had deceived despite the absence of the caution.)

2.30 As a result of this case, all the new Hansard investigations under the COP 9 procedures were suspended in the autumn of 2003, and new Hansard procedures were formulated to take account of the issues raised in the *Gill & Gill* case. It is worth recognising that in terms of investigating the extent of any irregularities and preparing disclosure reports, there was little difference in all of these variations of the Hansard and COP 9 procedures. The differences largely affected the procedures adopted in the formal opening of a case by SI, and, although the potential impact was significant, in practical terms the position only changed for those who did not make a full and complete disclosure when offered the protection of COP 9.

2.31 A new procedure was introduced by the ex-Inland Revenue to include a formal caution in line with that under The Police and Criminal Evidence Act 1984 (PACE) as well as the reading of the revised 2002 version of COP 9 which offered the inducement of non-prosecution in exchange for a full disclosure. The procedures for opening of Hansard cases under COP 9 was then amended to include a formal taped interview, at which the taxpayer would be formally advised of their rights under PACE. As a result of this, it became common for taxpayers and their advisers to attend the opening meetings with a criminal lawyer who could advise as to whether any self-incriminatory discussions could take place following the reading of the caution under PACE and the COP 9 questions. Consequently some opening meetings were very short, and were limited merely to the five formal questions (see **2.56**) with no other discussion of the issues in the case.

2.32 Following the merger of the Inland Revenue and HM Customs and Excise in April 2005, it was inevitable that further changes would be needed to the Code of Practice 9 procedures, given the different approaches to civil

2.32 *Special Investigations*

investigation of fraud by the two departments. The Customs and Excise approach (730 procedures) made very clear that once the decision had been made to go down either the civil or criminal route there was no ambiguity about the protection, or otherwise, available to the taxpayer when making a disclosure of irregularities. There was also the cumbersome approach of applying both COP 9 and the 730 procedures to the same case where both direct and indirect taxes arose from the same irregularity.

CIVIL INVESTIGATION OF FRAUD PROCEDURES

2.33 On 1 September 2005 a new Code of Practice 9 was published introducing the new Civil Investigation of Fraud (CIF) procedures to cover all taxes. The CIF procedures replaced all previous former Inland Revenue or former Customs and Excise procedures for the handling of serious fraud on a civil basis.

2.34 The most significant feature in the new CIF procedures from 1 September 2005 is an up-front guarantee, that HMRC will not conduct a criminal investigation in relation to the initial tax offence. The need for taped interviews under PACE has been disputed as there is no jeopardy of prosecution provided full disclosure is made. It is important to recognise that a criminal investigation might still be commenced if the taxpayer tries to deceive HMRC or provides false documents as part of the COP 9 investigation.

2.35 At **2.14** above reference is made to the various events that might result in a CIF investigation. Regardless of the origins of the investigation, the client will receive formal notification in writing from HMRC that their affairs are to be investigated in line with the CIF procedures under Code of Practice 9. A copy of the Code of Practice 9 booklet will be enclosed with that letter. The leaflet suggests that the taxpayer should consider seeking specialist advice. This is the recommended advice of the writer of this chapter.

2.36 The client who is the subject of the investigation under the CIF procedures will be invited to attend a meeting with specialist investigators from a CIF team or from SI. This is a formal meeting. The purpose of the meeting is for the HMRC investigator to set out in very prescribed terms the Board's approach to suspected serious fraud. Investigators are advised not to deviate from the Board's published statement.

2.37 The latest statement in relation to HMRC's approach to the civil investigation of fraud states the following:

> 'The Commissioners reserve complete discretion to pursue a criminal investigation with a view to prosecution where they consider it necessary and appropriate
>
> Where a criminal investigation is not considered necessary or appropriate, the Commissioners may decide to investigate using the CIF procedure
>
> Where the Commissioners decide to investigate using the CIF procedure they will not seek a prosecution for the tax fraud which is the subject of that investigation

The taxpayer will be given an opportunity to make a full and complete disclosure of all irregularities in their tax affairs

However, where materially false statements are made or materially false documents are provided with intent to deceive in the course of a civil investigation, the Commissioners may conduct a criminal investigation with a view to a prosecution of that conduct

If the Commissioners decide to investigate using the CIF procedure the taxpayer will be given a copy of this statement by an authorised officer.'

2.38 Having set out the formal policy, the investigator will hand out a printed copy of that policy to the client who is the subject of the CIF procedures.

2.39 The meeting then moves on to the point where the investigator asks a series of questions in relation to the taxpayer's affairs which are designed to result in either 'yes' or 'no' replies.

2.40 For investigations commenced before 1 September 2005 there were essentially five questions, which extended to all direct taxes and were without time limit (although HMRC was effectively time barred from action beyond HMRC's 20-year assessing time limit, clients could still be invited to pay out-of-date liabilities through voluntary restitution).

2.41 From 1 September 2005, the CIF procedures now include indirect taxes and there are also a series of four additional questions covering indirect taxes. (See **2.56** and **2.57** for the nine questions.)

2.42 Depending on whether the CIF investigation resulted from a voluntary disclosure or from HMRC's own investigation work, the meeting will then move to discussions of the irregularities, and the CIF or SI investigator will seek to understand more of the background to the disclosure. If the investigation has been opened by HMRC as a result of their own work they will ask the taxpayer whether they have anything to disclose or perhaps ask various questions around the issues already identified by the investigator or ask the taxpayer to respond to specific allegations.

2.43 Prior to any meeting where COP 9 is to be offered under the CIF procedures, it is clearly good practice to assist the taxpayer in preparing for the meeting. Such meetings can be very stressful for clients, and without any preparation they might inadvertently answer some or all of the questions incorrectly or provide misleading information to the investigator.

2.44 It is also good practice for the adviser to try and understand more about the client's affairs and identify any potential tax liabilities which might have arisen and which may have been overlooked by the taxpayer in compiling the disclosure. This should include a full review of areas where a liability might have resulted, including from technical points, as well as any liabilities that have arisen from any potential fraudulent activities.

2.45 The purpose of this is to assist the taxpayer in making an early disclosure of any such items, thus securing the maximum mitigation for penalties; but more importantly to demonstrate full cooperation and minimise

2.45 *Special Investigations*

any risk of losing the guarantee of no criminal proceedings and the withdrawal of Code of Practice 9, if the HMRC investigator believes the taxpayer is misleading them as part of the investigation.

2.46 A denial of any wrongdoing at the CIF meeting will result in the investigator conducting their own investigation, usually still within the protection of Code of Practice 9. If HMRC subsequently demonstrates that there are additional liabilities which were not disclosed, there is a risk of the withdrawal of COP 9 if they can demonstrate that they were misled or were provided with false documents. Also, mitigation for tax-geared penalties will be greatly reduced even if the case remains on a civil basis with COP 9.

2.47 The HMRC investigator will use the meeting to seek to understand the following information about the taxpayer's business. They will want to understand:

- detailed explanations around any disclosure being made;
- the taxpayer's response to any specific allegations being put before them;
- the nature and structure of the taxpayer's business (if appropriate);
- the business records maintained and controls applied;
- the accounting areas or practices where income/purchases may have been understated/overstated etc;
- any other areas where there might be a risk of a tax liability.

2.48 They will also use the meeting to understand fully the personal tax affairs of the taxpayer, including:

- personal history and background, including family relationships etc;
- details of sources of personal income and expenditure;
- details of personal assets and liabilities;
- any links to perceived tax-sheltering vehicles such as offshore trusts.

2.49 After the fact-finding part of the meeting, the investigator will ask whether the taxpayer formally wishes to instruct their adviser to prepare a disclosure report. If the taxpayer confirms that he or she does wish for this to happen, the investigator will make it very clear that HMRC will expect the disclosure report within six months of the date of the opening Code of Practice 9 Hansard meeting.

2.50 Following the formal meeting there will generally be a separate meeting with the adviser who has been commissioned to prepare the disclosure report in order for both parties to agree on what should be covered and what work should be undertaken. This is an opportunity for the adviser to set out to SI or the CIF team any practical difficulties that they may anticipate. This might include discussions on whether the six months' expectation for the report should be extended because of special circumstances, ie the case involves exceptional circumstances or is particularly large or complex.

2.51 Throughout the period of preparing the disclosure report there will be update meetings or telephone calls with the SI or CIF team investigator and again this is also an opportunity to set out any difficulties that the adviser is experiencing.

2.52 HMRC will generally expect the final disclosure report to include the following completed certificates:

- a certificate of bank and credit card accounts operated;
- a statement of personal assets and liabilities;
- a certificate of full disclosure.

2.53 The disclosure report will also be required to be adopted by the taxpayer as their own full and complete disclosure.

2.54 Where HMRC decides to investigate using the Civil Investigation of Fraud procedures, SI offices have remained responsible for the largest CIF cases and the remaining cases are dealt with by the CIF teams.

The nine questions of COP 9

2.55 There are five direct tax and four indirect tax questions:

The five direct tax questions

2.56

'1) Have any transactions been omitted from or incorrectly recorded in the books of any business with which you are or have been concerned whether as a director, partner or sole proprietor to the best of your knowledge or belief?

2) Are the accounts sent to the HMRC for each and every business with which you are or have been concerned whether as a director, partner or sole proprietor, correct and complete to the best of your knowledge and belief?

3) Are all the tax returns of each and every business with which you are or have been concerned whether as a director, partner or sole proprietor correct and complete to the best of your knowledge and belief?

4) Are all your personal tax returns correct and complete to the best of your knowledge and belief?

5) Will you allow an examination of all business books, and private statements and any other business and private records in order that HMRC may be satisfied that your answers to the first four questions are correct?'

The four indirect tax questions

2.57

'1) Have any transactions been omitted from, or incorrectly recorded, in the books and records of (name of legal entity) for which you are (responsible status)?

2) Are the books and records you are required to keep by HMRC for (name of legal entity) for which you are (responsible status), correct and complete to the best of your knowledge and belief?

2.57 *Special Investigations*

3) Are all the VAT returns of the (name of legal entity) for which you are (responsible status) correct and complete to the best of your knowledge and belief?
4) Were you aware that any of the VAT returns were incorrect or incomplete at the time they were submitted?'

In cases where the main offence is Failure to Notify Chargeability, HMRC may also include an extra direct tax question.

CIVIL INVESTIGATION OF FRAUD THRESHOLDS

2.58 HMRC apply their own internal financial limits to cases of suspected serious fraud. Historically the main threshold for Hansard (Code of Practice 9) investigations was whether the tax liability previously exceeded £100,000. With the setting up of the CIF teams, two thresholds effectively apply:

- £75,000–500,000, including interest and penalties, being dealt with by the CIF teams; and
- over £500,000 being dealt with by SI.

CODE OF PRACTICE 8 – CASES OTHER THAN SUSPECTED SERIOUS FRAUD

2.59 As well as cases of suspected serious fraud, SI also carry out other types of investigation.

2.60 Code of Practice 8 has historically been the Code used by SI to investigate complex tax-planning structures, and high-profile taxpayers with complex tax affairs, particularly involving offshore aspects, where HMRC believe there is a significant risk of substantial unpaid liabilities.

2.61 It is important to recognise that Code of Practice 8 does not bring with it any of the protections or guarantees of Code of Practice 9 (ie the guarantee of no prosecution where full compliance with the terms of the guidance on disclosure and cooperation are met). It must therefore be borne in mind that if SI identify fraud during any Code of Practice 8 investigation, it cannot be assumed that a civil settlement will result, and the enquiry could instead be handed over to the Criminal Investigation Directorate to commence a criminal investigation.

2.62 With HMRC's recent drive against marketed avoidance schemes, Code of Practice 8 has been used to conduct investigations in this field.

2.63 Code of Practice 8 investigators have historically demonstrated a strong leaning towards technical challenges on complex issues. However in recent times it is the case that SI investigators maintain a portfolio of both Code of Practice 9 and 8 work.

2.64 Code of Practice 8 investigations should be treated seriously and with care and the advice again would be that this should be handled by a specialist.

HANDLING SI/CIF INVESTIGATIONS

2.65 SI and CIF investigations involve highly specialised work and should only be handled in consultation with or by tax advisers with the appropriate specialist skills. Most professional indemnity insurers will state that they will not cover this work unless it is handled by specialists.

2.66 It is very important to recognise that all inspectors operating within SI or the CIF teams have been selected for their specific flair and interest in investigation work. These investigators are also recognised as possessing excellent negotiating skills.

2.67 New staff joining SI will shadow colleagues and work closely with experienced investigators and team leaders to ensure that they meet the standards required. One should therefore never view inspectors who have recently joined SI, or are of youthful appearance, as an easy touch or less experienced. There is a huge support network there to protect them.

2.68 SI investigators will not be easily deflected where they believe there is a need for an explanation. They are the recognised experts on the use of formal information powers in terms of information notices within the UK and overseas.

2.69 It is also important to recognise that any case which is taken on by SI will have been reviewed and identified as one where there is a clear risk of a significant loss of tax either as a result of fraud or otherwise.

2.70 SI does not take on cases lightly. Prior to April 2006 cases transferred to SI (and its predecessor named departments) resulted in an automatic credit in the yield records of the local tax office from where the case arose. From April 2006, the local area office will be given credit appropriate to the value of liabilities identified at the time of the transfer to SI or to the CIF teams. SI or CIF will only be able to claim the credit for the value they have added. It would therefore seem logical that they only take over cases where they are confident of additions substantially in excess of those already identified by the local area office.

2.71 Any case therefore registered by one of these specialist offices must be viewed as one that has passed all these tests and where the investigator believes that there are substantial further liabilities. It is good practice to ensure clients are aware of this and emphasise that SI and the CIF teams do not take on cases lightly. They believe there is a case to answer and will have strong evidence to support that view. Therefore as soon as an enquiry notice under either COP 8 or COP 9 is received, it is always worthwhile spending time with the client to explore if there is any reason they can think of why they are the subject of an SI or CIF investigation.

2.72 That said, SI or the CIF teams, like any other government agency, can occasionally get things wrong and so it is always worthwhile exploring with them their reasons for taking a case on. They may, of course, be reluctant to advise you of this, but a mature conversation can always help both parties explore the reasons for why the case has been selected.

2.73 *Special Investigations*

2.73 Good practice is to treat SI and CIF team staff professionally and courteously at all times whilst remaining firm and positive in your representation of your client. As experienced investigators they will not be put off track by an overly aggressive approach; SI inspectors are well-trained, well-supported and more than capable of holding their own in difficult and uncomfortable situations. Conversely, because of their clear professionalism and experience, SI personnel will generally respond very well where they are treated with respect, and will be more likely to share with you the reasons for the enquiry and the extent of the information which they already hold.

2.74 That said, there will be cases where it is necessary to stand your ground in representing your client and SI recognise this. But the skills lie in selecting the battles and most certainly not winning pyrrhic victories and ultimately losing the SI war. No client will thank you for starting (and generally) losing the long-term relationship with SI.

Specialists within SI

2.75 SI is staffed not only by direct and indirect tax investigators. In each office, there is also a team of qualified accountants whose role it is to assist the investigators in understanding accountancy issues.

2.76 SI is also the home of a number of the liaison points for HMRC with other UK Government agencies or overseas fiscal authorities. For example, SI London is the HMRC home for all UK exchange of information requests with other foreign fiscal authorities with whom the UK has reciprocal arrangements via such things as the OECD tax convention, double taxation treaties etc.

2.77 SI is the home of the teams that were responsible for the TMA 1970, s 20(8A) success against financial institutions which supported the 2007 Offshore Disclosure Facility (see **14.178**). They have also been responsible for the FA 2008, Sch 36, para 5 notices against financial institutions in support of the 2009 New Disclosure Opportunity (see **Chapter 14**). SI is also home to HMRC's liaison with the Serious Organised Crime Agency (SOCA), specifically in terms of money laundering.

2.78 Where SOCA receives a suspicious activity report (SAR) and tax offences are the predominant offence, the relevant SAR will be passed to SI for consideration of a tax investigation. Where SI decide they will not mount their own investigation, the SAR may then be handed over to the local office.

2.79 Whilst the criminal work of HMRC is no longer housed within SI, again SI is the liaison point for the Criminal Investigation Directorate.

HMRC COMPLIANCE PROJECTS

2.80 HMRC always conduct various investigations projects. This is also the case for SI, including projects on sportsmen (particularly rugby players and footballers). These projects could be into particular sectors such as the Special Investigations (previously SCI) project into sports clubs. Projects have also been run at local compliance level such as looking at particular trades, for example restaurants, public houses, taxi driving, and specific sectors for example professional practices, waste management businesses, cash and carries etc.

2.81 As well as all these various initiatives that will always run from time to time, HMRC have set out three areas that they will specifically consider: offshore, bank interest and property. These are large subjects and so we can expect to see various sub projects under those three headings, including activity at both local compliance and Special Investigations levels.

2.82 These projects will all feature in some capacity within HMRC's new approach of compliance checks. Compliance checks are covered in detail at **Chapter 14**. They have developed to reduce the resource burden on HMRC compliance staff and build on the work of the Tax Education, Enabling and Leverage teams (TEELs) working alongside the Risk Intelligence Service teams.

2.83 The concept is simple. HMRC undertake their various risk assessments, be it by trades, individuals or sectors. They can then decide, based on the scale and level of the risk, whether to open for example a full enquiry, or some lesser form of compliance check, be it telephone call or stencil letter.

2.84 We have seen the greatest development on this new project-based way of working in the work being done on disclosure campaigns, including the offshore disclosure campaigns and the campaign for medical professionals.

2.85 The Offshore Project group was set up, based in Liverpool SI, and they have spent much time successfully overseeing the numerous requests to issue TMA 1970, s 20(8A) and now FA 2008, Sch 36, para 5 information notices against UK financial institutions providing offshore banking and credit card facilities.

2.86 In order to manage the huge amounts of data from over 300 sources HMRC developed and introduced the Offshore Disclosure Facility (ODF) in 2007. This has been followed up in 2009 with the New Disclosure Opportunity (NDO) and the Disclosure Facility for holders of Liechtenstein accounts and assets (LDF). The LDF provides the same protection against prosecution as the COP 9 procedures.

OFFSHORE DISCLOSURE CAMPAIGNS

The Offshore Disclosure Facility (ODF)

2.87 On 1 April 2007 HMRC launched the Offshore Disclosure Facility (ODF) encouraging those holding untaxed offshore assets to make a disclosure to HMRC and pay the tax, interest and a small fixed penalty in return for HMRC operating a 'light touch' approach. Some called this the UK's first 'tax amnesty' but as penalties were still in point most commentators and certainly HMRC would disagree with this phrase. What is accepted is that it was the UK's first facility allowing people to regularise their tax affairs in a relatively simple way.

2.88 Special Investigations

2.88 The concept of such a disclosure facilities generally had already been examined and discussed by the Organisation for Economic Cooperation and Development (OECD) and had already been introduced in some shape or form in a number of OECD member countries.

2.89 All disclosure campaigns run by HMRC have a number of common features; pay the tax, late payment interest and a small fixed penalty. HMRC expect the disclosure to be full and complete and a Certificate of Full Disclosure must be signed to reflect this.

2.90 The disclosure campaigns also allow the person making the disclosure to summarise their tax liabilities in a series of forms and there is a requirement that a settlement is offered as part of the disclosure and where persons have difficulty in paying back the liabilities, it is sometimes possible to make an arrangement.

2.91 HMRC's approach to disclosure campaigns is to accept the majority of disclosures by way of risk assessing them and testing or enquiring into those it feels are higher risk.

Terms of the ODF

Notification period

2.92 There was a period from 1 April 2007 to 30 June 2007 whereby a person could register their intention to make a disclosure to HMRC.

Disclosure period

2.93 There was then a period from 1 July 2007 to 26 November 2007 when the person was required to make their disclosure.

The disclosure and the terms

2.94 As indicated earlier the disclosure was made via a series of forms providing HMRC with information such as the tax liabilities by year, the late payment interest and the penalty. The person was also required to provide a signed Certificate of Full Disclosure and Statement of Assets and Liabilities and formal offer to settle to HMRC.

2.95 The fixed penalty was 10 per cent.

2.96 The main benefits of the ODF were that HMRC provided very detailed guidance and stated in advance that while the ODF was not assurance against a criminal investigation a full and complete disclosure made voluntarily was the best protection against the risk of a criminal investigation. HMRC also stated the majority of disclosures would be accepted and they would apply a risk based approach in opening enquiries on some of these cases.

2.97 The ODF secured around £400 million for HMRC from around 45,000 disclosures. At the time of publication of this book, HMRC had secured around another £100 million from tens of thousands of tax enquiries arising from the ODF.

The New Disclosure Opportunity (NDO)

2.98 HMRC was pleased with the success of the ODF. HMRC recognised the scale of offshore data it had in its possession. It planned to obtain even more and so launched a follow up disclosure facility for those again holding untaxed offshore assets on 1 September 2009. This was the New Disclosure Opportunity (NDO).

2.99 The NDO largely followed the same approach of the ODF. At around the same time as launching the NDO, HMRC was issuing notices to over 300 financial institutions under para 5, Sch 36, FA 2008, the modern day s 20(8A), TMA 1970 which was repealed from 1 April 2009.

2.100 The NDO took notice of the ODF in that those persons who had already been written to by HMRC to alert that their details had been passed to HMRC would be offered only a 20 per cent penalty as opposed to the 10 per cent penalty being offered to everyone else.

2.101 Again the NDO was made up of several phases:

Notification

2.102 The notification period of the person's intention to disclose commenced on 1 September 2009 and ended on 4 January 2010.

Disclosure

2.103 The final disclosure date for paper disclosures was 31 January 2010 but if the disclosure was made electronically the deadline was 12 March 2010.

2.104 This facility secured around another £85 million for HMRC from 5,500 disclosures.

2.105 At the time of updating this book, HMRC had secured around another £6 million from enquiries which had been opened as a result of the banking data held. HMRC was still obtaining data from around 146 financial institutions remaining following the issue of the 300 notices mentioned above and after appeals etc.

2.106 As with the ODF, the NDO was managed by the Offshore Campaign team within RIS. However, this has now changed at the point of updating this book, so that the overall strategy and management of Offshore Banking investigation has transferred into Special Investigations. We have also already started to see a number of criminal investigations being opened by the Criminal Investigation Directorate using the data obtained from the banks.

2.107 *Special Investigations*

The Liechtenstein Disclosure Facility (LDF)

2.107 The Governments of the UK and Liechtenstein signed an agreement on a Tax Information Exchange (TIEA) on 11 August 2009. This was announced by way of a Joint Declaration between the Liechtenstein Government and HMRC relating to Cooperation in Tax Matters.

2.108 At the same time a Memorandum of Understanding (MOU) was signed by the Liechtenstein Government and HMRC introducing a five year taxpayer compliance assistance programme in Liechtenstein and a five year special disclosure facility for those with UK liabilities enabling them to regularise their tax affairs.

2.109 The LDF from the UK perspective became the third tax disclosure facility for those holding untaxed offshore assets and bank accounts. It was aimed at those with untaxed offshore assets, primarily in Liechtenstein. At the time of updating this book, the LDF remains open and will do so until 31 March 2015, unless the parties to the agreement terminate or amend it.

2.110 The facility commenced on 1 September 2009 for those who already held assets ('relevant property') in Liechtenstein at that date. The facility is also open to anyone who acquired a Liechtenstein asset after 1 September 2009 providing they held an offshore asset at 1 September 2009. This original offshore asset need not have been in Liechtenstein. There is therefore scope where a person has undeclared liabilities, and held an offshore asset to disclose them under this facility.

2.111 In September 2010 a Second Joint Declaration was issued which set out guidance on a number of areas, for example, that for any asset in Liechtenstein to qualify as relevant property for the purposes of the LDF it should be 'meaningful and of sufficient value and permanence to reflect the spirit of the MOU.' The Second Joint Declaration also sets out more information on the procedure for the retention of tax if the financial intermediary is unable to cease providing 'relevant services.' It states that such cases will be exceptional.

Demonstrating UK tax compliance

2.112 There are a number of ways that the person can satisfy their requirement to demonstrate their tax compliance with the UK authorities. The following are acceptable ways of doing this:

- Providing written confirmation by a legal, tax or accounting adviser duly qualified in the UK that the person is compliant with their tax obligations.
- The person providing evidence that they have submitted an application to disclose the relevant property under an HMRC tax disclosure facility.
- The person producing a form in a format approved by HMRC identifying the person and evidencing compliance in respect of their tax obligations.

- Providing a certified or notarised copy of their tax return showing that the relevant property at issue has been declared to HMRC.
- Providing a written waiver and identification form by the person, authorising the respective financial intermediary providing a waiver to HMRC a copy of tax information relevant to the person's tax obligations with respect to the relevant property.

The benefits of the LDF

2.113 The main benefits of the LDF are that HMRC will only assess years starting on or after 1 April 1999 where the full LDF beneficial terms apply. It will only assess four or six years, where the additional tax results from innocent error or where the tax arose from careless behaviour respectively.

Penalties

2.114 HMRC will apply a fixed 10 per cent penalty where the matters result from anything more serious than innocent error, for years up to and including 2008–09.

Assurance about criminal investigation

2.115 HMRC will not undertake a criminal investigation where the only offence is tax evasion and the money is not linked to more serious underlying criminal activity. The LDF is the only disclosure facility that has provided such assurance. In all previous tax disclosure facilities HMRC stated it would not give any guarantee regarding criminal investigations other than to state that a full and complete unprompted disclosure was unlikely to result in such an event.

Working out the tax

2.116 There are two ways that this can be done. The 'actual basis' can be applied which is to work out all tax liabilities in the normal way, for example taking into account relevant losses, reliefs and other deductions. There is also the facility to apply a composite rate option (CRO) of taxing the income and gains at a straight 40 per cent. However in this case there are no allowances, tax relief or deductions.

2.117 Where funds have been passed through family estates, the CRO is particularly attractive as providing the historical personal taxation liabilities are picked up under the CRO, any Inheritance Tax liabilities will potentially be foregone.

Who cannot participate

2.118 Anyone who is under investigation under Code of Practice 9, Civil Investigation of Fraud, will not be accepted into the LDF. Similarly anyone who has been arrested or cautioned as part of a criminal investigation also will not be accepted.

2.119 *Special Investigations*

2.119 Anyone who was previously under investigation and who did not disclose the offshore asset as part of that enquiry can participate in the LDF but will have a higher penalty (generally 30%). They can however benefit from the limited assessment position.

2.120 Anyone who was written to under the ODF or NDO can participate in the LDF but will have a 20 per cent penalty. Anyone holding an offshore asset outside Liechtenstein which was opened through a UK branch or agency can still use the LDF but will not benefit from the reduced assessment position, the reduced penalty or the composite rate option.

Time limits of the LDF

2.121 There are strict time limits in relation to the taxpayer assistance compliance programme and the LDF. In terms of Liechtenstein, financial intermediaries will be required to establish any clients who may have a UK tax liability who held a Liechtenstein asset at 11 August 2009 or afterwards.

2.122 The financial intermediary will have to notify the client within three months of identification and the person will then have 18 months to demonstrate they are UK tax compliant. If there are tax liabilities to disclose the person can also register for the LDF. If this is the case HMRC will issue a registration certificate within 60 days, provided the criteria are met.

2.123 The person must send the registration certificate to the financial intermediary within 30 days of receiving it. The person must then send their full disclosure to HMRC within seven months (if they are using the composite rate) or 10 months (if calculating the liability on an actual basis) of the registration certificate date.

2.124 HMRC will send a disclosure certificate within 30 days of receiving the disclosure providing it is complete. The person must then send the disclosure certificate to their Financial Intermediary within 30 days of receiving it.

Results of the LDF

2.125 At the time of updating this book, HMRC had published statistics showing that as at 31 March 2011, it had received 1351 registrations yielding £140 million.

PROFESSIONAL CAMPAIGNS

Tax Health Plan

2.126 In January 2010 HMRC launched yet another disclosure facility, this time directed at those in the medical and dentistry professions. This was launched as part of what was called 'the Professionals Campaign.'

As with all other campaigns, the RIS teams had secured data about those working in the medical professions, including data from the NHS and medical

Notification period

2.127 The end of the notification period was 31 March 2010.

Disclosure facility

2.128 The end of the disclosure period was 30 June 2010. Again the terms were such that a disclosure should be made and the tax, interest and a fixed penalty (10%) summarised via a series of forms, as well as the various certificates and an offer in settlement.

2.129 As part of this facility HMRC required those making a disclosure to provide their General Medical Association or British Dental Association registration numbers. HMRC also set out those who would not be able to benefit from this facility, including those with offshore bank accounts.

2.130 At the time of updating this book, the results from the THP were significantly lower than for the offshore campaigns at £10 million from 1,500 disclosures. This was considered to be disappointing.

TRADE CAMPAIGNS

Plumbers Tax Safe Plan (PTSP)

2.131 Another tax disclosure facility was launched on 1 March 2011 aimed at those in the plumbing and heating trade, HMRC's first disclosure campaign looking at trades. While this was aimed at a specific trade, HMRC confirmed that it would invite disclosures from anyone who wished to make a disclosure at the same time, and they could expect the same terms.

Notification

2.132 The end of the notification period was 31 May 2011.

Disclosure

2.133 The end of the disclosure period was 31 August 2011. Therefore at the time of updating this book the Plumbers Tax Safe Plan is still open.

2.134 The terms start to differ in the PTSP to reflect the way the new penalties work under Sch, 24 FA 2008. Where a person took 'reasonable care', there is no penalty. Where they were careless or did not notify the penalty is 10 per cent. There is no penalty for 2009 or 2010, although there might still be a small penalty for 2009 for failure to notify.

2.135 *Special Investigations*

2.135 Where deliberate behaviour is involved the penalty is 20 per cent. The PTSF is the first facility with multiple rates of penalty and offers the person the opportunity to self assess their behaviour and with that, the penalty that must be applied.

Who cannot participate

2.136 Those who are already under enquiry or are suspected of being involved in MTIC (carousel), repayment or tax credit fraud, or those suspected of involvement in wider (financial) criminality cannot participate.

2.137 As regards those who in HMRC's view should have disclosed under previous disclosure campaigns (ie those holding offshore assets at 4 January 2010), those written to under a previous campaign, or those in the medical profession, HMRC has stated it will expect any disclosure they make within the same time as the PTSP to file on the basis that their actions were deliberate.

VAT

2.138 The PTSP requires the person to consider whether there is also a VAT disclosure to be made and the PTSP will allow them to discuss this with HMRC. No special penalty arrangements exist for VAT, although a wholly voluntary unprompted disclosure should achieve a very low penalty.

Class 2 and 4 NIC

2.139 The PTSP requires the person to self assess the tax, and the penalty to Class 2 and 4 NIC as well as the income tax.

Chapter 3

VAT and Revenue & Customs visits

Kendra Hann

Partner, Deloitte LLP

OVERALL CONCEPT

3.01 In April 2005 HM Customs and Excise (HMCE) merged with the Inland Revenue (IR) to create a new department 'HM Revenue and Customs' (HMRC). Historically, HMCE had developed a personal and tangible contact with their 'customers'. HMCE's experience with, inter alia, importers, exporters, breweries, distilleries and the control of purchase tax necessarily led the department to propose a system for controlling the administration of VAT based on hands-on inspections. Although steps have been taken to harmonise the practices of both predecessor departments, the way VAT is currently controlled has not changed substantially. This is because, unlike corporation tax and other forms of direct taxation, VAT is an immediate tax. Every transaction made by a business impacts on the VAT affairs of that business, whether it be the liability of the supply made by the business or the amount of recoverable VAT that can be claimed by that particular business. The tax is, therefore, controlled at grass-roots level and will involve, to some degree, officers reviewing individual invoices on a sample basis.

3.02 Every business registering for VAT immediately enters the realm of the HMRC computer and the VAT Central Unit (VCU). This starts with VAT registration. Every business registered for VAT is allocated a VAT number. This is often initially notified to the business in a letter followed shortly after by a form VAT4 'Certificate of VAT Registration'. The VAT numbers are always in the same format: they consist of seven digits and two check numbers eg 123 4567 89. The validity of any VAT number can be checked at http://ec.europa.eu/taxation_customs/vies/vieshome.do?selectedLanguage=EN. If required, a certificate showing that the number has been checked can be obtained.

3.03 The time taken by HMRC's National VAT registration Unit for processing VAT registration applications has increased dramatically in recent

3.03 *VAT and Revenue & Customs visits*

years. This is due to additional checks undertaken as a result of the increase in Missing Trader Intra Community Fraud (MTIC). One of HMRC's strategies for countering this type of fraud is to restrict the ability of the fraudsters to obtain VAT registrations for entities that subsequently default on their VAT payments, through additional checks built into the registration process. This has an inevitable effect on all VAT registration applications. It has been known for VAT registration applications to take anything up to four months – and sometimes longer – for HMRC to process. This should be borne in mind if a business is considering registering for VAT.

Businesses typically fall within three main divisions: small and medium enterprises (SMEs), large and complex (L&C), and large business service (LBS). To be within the remit for L&C and LBS divisions, businesses will need to have at least 250 staff or a minimum turnover of £50 million.

3.04 For most businesses (with the exception of large and complex businesses), most initial contact with HMRC is now routed through the National Advice Service (NAS) (0845 010 9000). This centralised service takes all telephone enquiries and replaces the localised services which were provided by Business Advice Centres. The NAS also provides a centralised written enquiries service which can provide advice via email or letter. The address to contact is:

Written Enquiries Service,
Alexander House,
Victoria Avenue,
Southend,
Essex,
SS99 1BD
or email: enquires.estn@hmrc.gsi.gov.uk.

ASSURANCE VISITS

3.05 When VAT was introduced in 1973, the first visit to a business was a registration or educational visit. This enabled HMCE to ensure that a new business was aware of its obligations that the accounts maintained by the business were adequate for VAT purposes and the liability treatment of the supplies made by the business was correct. In the past, a newly registered business could expect to receive its first visit from the local VAT office (LVO) within about 18 months of being registered. These 'assurance visits', formed the basis of HMCE's control of the tax.

3.06 Now, the majority of assurance visits are assigned by a computer-based model based on a series of factors that assess the risk of errors, negligent or fraudulent returns. Occasional sector-based campaigns can also prompt a flurry of visits either nationwide or locally. For those businesses who remain under the compliance 'radar', more efficient ways of contact such as telephone advice to both correct and improve compliance are being trialled. As a result of this revised risk assurance methodology, some 'low-risk' businesses may not receive an assurance visit for ten years or more.

3.07 The VAT visit selection teams base their visits selections on risk assessments and have computer systems that draw data from a variety of sources such as the HMRC computer network known as 'VISION' (VAT Interrogation System Inter Office Network). This system allows the risk team to interrogate the trader database. Information contained on file includes core data such as name, address of the business, trade classification, date of last visit and VAT return data. The system will allocate points on the basis of, among other things, the amounts of VAT declared on a return and on the time elapsed since the last visit. After each VAT assurance visit, officers write a report allocating points based upon their findings and this is also fed into the visit selection process. The total level of points allocated to a business will dictate when the business is selected for subsequent visits and how much time is allowed for those visits.

3.08 HMRC may choose to carry out joint visits using officers checking more than one tax. For large and complex businesses that are allocated a customer co-ordinator (CC), or a client relationship manager (CRM) by HMRC, joint visits by usually two or more officers (looking at different taxes) are already undertaken. However different ways of working will no doubt be piloted to find the most cost-effective system. In normal circumstances however, HMRC should make it clear before the visit which taxes they will be inspecting and, usually, how many officers can be expected on the visit.

3.09 When a business is selected for an assurance visit, the officer will have at least the following information available:

- original VAT 1 application form (for the first VAT visit);
- copies of any correspondence between the business and HMRC including that with former HMCE;
- printouts containing, typically, up to the last 18 months of VAT return details and credibility analysis automatically performed by the VCU computer system (D1600 series);
- any earlier visit reports and internal departmental notes/memos;
- details of any written enquiries or telephone calls to the National Advice Service;
- if the business is a VAT group registration, details of group members; and
- information about the business from the internet.

3.10 Additionally, if the business sells goods to other EU states, the officer will be able to obtain information relating to the aggregate value of dispatches by that business for each quarterly period. Each VAT authority in every member state submits the data from the individual European Sales Listings (ESLs) into the VAT Information Exchange System (VIES). The data contained on ESLs enables VIES to identify, by VAT number, the value of sales from each supplier/member state. The officer can use this information to gain knowledge of where a business sells its goods and the level of such sales prior to his visit.

3.11 *VAT and Revenue & Customs visits*

3.11 The officer will also check acquisitions from other EU member states. Clearly, if the value ascribed to a particular UK business by VIES is greater than the acquisition value shown on the VAT returns, some difficult questions can be expected.

3.12 In addition to ESLs currently completed for goods supplied to other EU states, since 1 January 2010 businesses are also required to complete ESLs for the majority of services supplied to businesses in other EU member states. The officer will also verify these to ensure sales of services have been declared appropriately and, in addition, will be able to check (using data received from other EU states) that the taxpayer has declared the reverse charge VAT on services received from businesses established in other member states.

3.13 Often, the visit will be arranged by a centralised visit booking team, who usually telephone to make an appointment. This may then be followed up with a letter confirming the arrangements. When the VAT officer arrives for the visit he will have an identity card bearing his photograph. This should always be inspected before allowing the officer into the working area since bogus VAT visits have been known and are an effective way of finding out a lot about a business.

3.14 An assurance visit typically splits into three parts. First, general questions about the structure of the business, the way it operates and the build up to the VAT account; secondly a check of the VAT account and a detailed review of at least one VAT period; and, lastly, an overview of the business accounts including a number of credibility checks that will assist the officer in assessing the credibility of the figures on the returns.

General questions

3.15 For the first visit, the officer will be required to assemble/check basic information concerning that particular business including:

- name, status and contact details for the person responsible for VAT at the business;
- name, address and contact details for the auditors;
- financial year end;
- address of the principal place of business and registered office if different;
- confirmation that the details on the VAT4 (registration certificate) are still correct;
- a description of the main and, if applicable, subsidiary business activities;
- whether the business has contact with other parts of HMRC, eg whether the business has a bonded warehouse or operates under any HMRC duty regime;
- whether the business imports or exports goods;
- whether the business imports or exports services;
- principal sales (outputs) and purchases (inputs);
- which retail schemes are operated (if applicable);

- a list of the main, subsidiary and other non-accounting records maintained by the business;
- structure of the business;
- details of bank and building society accounts;
- tax point information (eg whether the business uses the 14-day rule for invoices);
- rulings given to the business;
- risk areas and special or unusual features; and
- any errors made by the business that the officer may need to be aware of prior to inspecting the records.

3.16 Since the introduction of a paperless electronic folder system this information will be held on the business's 'electronic folder', as will all other information regarding the business.

3.17 On subsequent visits to the business this information will be reviewed and amended as necessary to reflect changes in the business.

3.18 The above information is generally obtained whilst conducting a general discussion about the business. The information obtained allows the officer to establish an understanding of the business and how it is organised. Depending on the nature of the business, it is often followed by a request to see the premises. This general walk around adds to the officer's general understanding and allows him to see whether there is anything going on which was not disclosed in the general discussion. The officer will also be noting specific items of stock or machinery so that he can check these out later when inspecting the accounting system.

Review of VAT returns submitted

3.19 As mentioned earlier, the officer will invariably check at least one VAT return in detail. This involves checking from source documents, eg orders, purchase and sales invoices, etc, through the various accounting records to the VAT account and the completed VAT return.

3.20 The officer will also make other checks in order to verify the credibility of the VAT returns. For example, he will check that the sales figures indicated on VAT returns for a 12-month period correspond with the turnover figure disclosed in the annual accounts for the same period. Similarly, officers will check the annual accounts for any disposals of assets to ensure that output tax has been charged and declared and that the level of expenses declared in the accounts agrees with the input figures declared on the VAT returns. The credibility checks used will vary according to the specific activities of the business and the records available to the officer. Other credibility checks commonly used include cash reconciliations (more commonly used in smaller cash businesses such as restaurants and pubs), bank reconciliations and mark-up exercises.

3.21 Officers increasingly cross-refer invoices inspected at one business with the information disclosed at another business. For example, sales of confectionery items sold by a wholesaler will be checked against purchases

3.21 VAT and Revenue & Customs visits

declared by the wholesaler's customers. Although on the surface, the absence of purchases in the retailer's records might seem to suggest that eligible input VAT has not been claimed by the business, it is often a good indication, particularly in a cash business, that the business is not recovering input VAT in order to suppress sales. To continue to claim all input VAT whilst suppressing sales will eventually show that the business is being run on uneconomical margins. This will either mean that the business is in financial trouble or raise suspicions with HMRC that the business is failing to account for all of its sales.

3.22 The officer is required to prepare a report of his visit noting specifically:

- checks made and annual accounts examined;
- irregularities found, including particulars of misdeclarations and assessments made;
- rulings given during the visit and general comment;
- conclusions and comments on credibility; and
- matters for consideration on the next visit.

3.23 Depending on the size and complexity of the business and its accounting system, more than one officer may attend. It is unusual, however, for three or more officers to attend on the same day. This is regarded by HMRC as over-burdensome on the business.

3.24 If the business uses a sophisticated computerised accounting system, it is possible that the visit will be made by a computer accounts officer (CAO). This is an officer who has received additional training on procedures and methods of interrogating computerised accounting systems. The CAO may, for example, ask for special prints to be produced or interrogation software to be run against the business accounts, or for tapes/disks of data to be made for interrogation off site. If interrogation software is loaded on the business's computers it is imperative that HMRC are denied running the checks against the online data since this could corrupt current data. It is always advisable to run interrogation checks offline. If HMRC ask for data to be copied and downloaded for removal, it is important to take a copy of the data provided for checking by the business. It must be appreciated that when HMRC remove data they can then 'play with' that information to their hearts' content!

3.25 Again, depending on the sophistication of the system, the CAO may flowchart the procedures and processes conducted by the computer. These flowcharts will highlight, from a VAT perspective, the key controls and any weaknesses in the system. Subsequent assurance visits will check to see, in particular, whether the key controls are still in place. The removal of a key control could mean that the VAT accounting of that system is flawed or weakened in some manner.

3.26 Whether a business is visited by an officer, a higher officer, a CAO or a team of officers is generally dictated by its size and complexity. In addition to providing information about the checks conducted on a business, the visit report also requires the officer to provide information about the complexity of the business. This is done by requiring the officer to allocate points for certain aspects of the business following his review, including:

- Accounts – how complex is the accounting system, eg does the business have a simple cash book or does it use a multi-locational computerised system?
- Organisation – eg is the business a single shop or a multi-national company?
- Tax features – does the business sell goods or services attracting VAT at a single rate of VAT or does it supply goods and services at all rates including imports, exports, etc?
- Compliance – were any assessments issued and, if so, at what value?

3.27 The points allocated by an officer can be influenced by any suspicions he or she felt during the visit. The combination of the various points allocated by the officer is fed into the electronic folder system. These points are then used by the centralised risk team to determine when the next assurance visit should be conducted. The higher the points, the more frequent the visits are likely to be.

3.28 Businesses that are registered for VAT purposes as a VAT group will generally be controlled by the same team. However, where individual companies within the group registration are remote from the main site and are self-accounting these may, if their size and complexity merits it, be visited by a different team from their local VAT office. Likewise, a company may have self-accounting branches which could be controlled on a remote basis. Companies registered on a divisional basis will invariably be controlled by different teams from their regional office as opposed to being centrally controlled.

3.29 Typically, large and complex businesses and businesses allocated to the Large Business Service (LBS) are removed from the normal routine. Unlike businesses within the regular routine, these businesses are allocated to a particular officer or a customer co-ordinator (in the case of large and complex businesses) or a customer relationship manager (for LBS businesses). The rationale for this approach is that the bulk of business taxes and duties are collected from relatively few very large businesses. The payment of taxes from businesses handled by the large and complex teams and Large Business Service represents approximately 50% of total business taxes and duties. HMRC therefore, have determined that they should control these large traders with a systematic approach on a regular basis to ensure that the revenue take is maintained. Simple errors at large businesses can generate significant under-declarations of VAT. These businesses are often complex in organisation and frequently use several computer systems to produce data for the VAT return.

HMRC have introduced customer co-ordinators from June 2010 for the remainder of the large business segment that previously did not have a client relationship manager (CRM). Therefore, the majority of large and complex customers will now be assigned a customer co-ordinator.

Businesses with a customer co-ordinator will have a named point of contact who will have oversight of their issues, direct them towards appropriate specialists and published information, and follow up issues within HMRC to

3.29 *VAT and Revenue & Customs visits*

ensure they are concluded within an agreed time frame. The role of the customer co-ordinator is to also maintain a single, up-to-date overview of the customer, their issues and their risks.

3.30 Within HMRC's Large Business Service the CRMs responsible for each industry sector co-ordinate dealings with large traders with the aim of ensuring that businesses' governance and systems minimise tax risk and that compliance is achieved in that 'sector'. The LBS works with the UK's largest businesses.

3.31 LBS control will usually mean that all UK subsidiaries and branches of the business are controlled by the same team. This allows the LBS team to learn a tremendous amount about the business and how it operates. By allocating sector leaders, a common approach can be adopted by HMRC among similar large businesses. This also allows HMRC to learn a lot about the industry generally and to identify common problems and solutions.

3.32 Sometimes, officers carrying out routine visits may be accompanied by specialist anti-avoidance officers interested in any planning measures adopted by the business. Occasionally, independent visits may be undertaken by such officers outside the routine verification process. If a business becomes aware that it is being 'targeted' by HMRC's anti-avoidance teams, it would be well advised to obtain professional advice on how to deal with the situation.

CREDIBILITY VISITS

3.33 You may not just see the VAT officer on assurance visits. HMRC's computer system conducts routine checks on each VAT return submitted. The credibility routine, for example, not only checks that the figure shown in box 1 (VAT due in this period on sales and other outputs) is not significantly less than the VAT calculated on the box 6 figure (total value of sales and other outputs excluding any VAT), but it also conducts a series of comparison exercises.

3.34 When a business completes a VAT1 (Application for registration), it is required to describe its main business activity. This allows HMRC to assign a trade classification to the business. For example, all petrol filling stations will be allocated to the same trade classification. Thus, when each filling station puts in its VAT return, HMRC can compare any single VAT return for a petrol filling station with all other filling stations submitting VAT returns for that period. Trends can, therefore, be detected. If all petrol filling stations are showing an upturn in trade in any particular period and one filling station is claiming a repayment then, depending on the tax considered to be at risk, HMRC may send that VAT return to the nearest VAT office for verification prior to the repayment being made.

3.35 Often this type of verification will simply prompt a phone call to the business asking why an unusual VAT return was submitted. It may, for example, simply be that the business is stocking up or has incurred significant refurbishment costs for a building, etc. However, if the amount is large, the officer may decide to visit. The officer should agree the visit in advance, but it is usual to arrange the visit soon after the initial telephone call, particularly when it is a repayment return. This will usually simply be to verify the single queried VAT return and the checks will just be to satisfy the officer that the return is credible in the circumstances. It is worth noting that whilst the return is being queried, the clock for a repayment supplement is stopped. Thus, it is in the interests of the business to ensure that such credibility queries are dealt with and agreed with HMRC as soon as possible.

INTRASTAT VISITS

3.36 Businesses involved in the sale and movement of goods to other member states are required to prepare and submit European Sales Listings (ESL) and supplementary statistical declarations (supplementary declarations), subject to the value of these sales or movements being over a certain value. The ESL is used by all EU VAT administrations as a control document to monitor and check on the movement of goods (and, from 1 January 2010, many services) across EU borders. The information contained on the supplementary declaration is used by HMRC to build up the statistical data on what goods have been 'dispatched' from the UK and the 'arrivals' of goods in the UK from other member states. The Intrastat information, as it is called, is compiled from two sources: first, boxes 8 and 9 of the VAT return and secondly the supplementary declaration.

3.37 A package of changes has been introduced which took effect from 1 January 2010, to help modernise and simplify the current rules relating to cross-border supplies of services. One consequence is that businesses are now required to complete an ESL for services provided to businesses in other EU member states where the business in the destination country is required to account for 'reverse charge' VAT. Businesses report the supplies of services using the same format for reporting goods (form VAT101), submitted on a calendar quarterly basis. Businesses already reporting monthly (or which are obliged to do so in the future) also have the option to report cross-border services monthly as well.

3.38 Supplementary declarations must be submitted each calendar month when the level of dispatches (form C1501) and arrivals (form C1500) exceed a prescribed minimum threshold. Currently the annual threshold for arrivals is £600,000 and for dispatches is £250,000. These forms can now be submitted and amended online, via the HMRC website. Depending on the level of activity businesses may be required to submit returns only for dispatches or arrivals or both. The information required to be gathered and declared on the supplementary declaration by each member state can be different. However, the core information is always required. Failure to submit declarations or submitting persistently late, missing or inaccurate declarations could result in penalties.

3.39 Besides the header information (VAT registration number, number of items, period covered, etc) the statistical information required on a supplementary declaration in the UK is:

3.39 *VAT and Revenue & Customs visits*

- commodity code;
- goods value;
- delivery terms (unless the value of dispatches or arrivals is less than £16,000,000);
- nature of transaction;
- net mass;
- supplementary units;
- member state to which/from which consigned;
- trader's reference (optional).

3.40 The above information is not always contained on the main accounting system. This can, therefore, lead to delays in submitting the supplementary declarations and the date can slip through lack of time being spent on capturing accurate information. As a basic check, it is always worth comparing the values declared on the monthly supplementary declarations against the monthly/quarterly VAT returns for the same period. If the figures do not agree, a problem may have arisen in capturing the data.

3.41 VAT officers may inspect and check supplementary declarations as part of an ordinary assurance visit, although there are dedicated Intrastat officers who will arrange a visit specifically to verify the declarations. For large businesses a few days each year may be set aside to verify the data supplied on the supplementary declarations. This will usually be undertaken by a specialist Intrastat officer. HMRC will also visit when supplementary declarations have not been completed in order to ascertain why the returns have not been submitted.

MUTUAL ASSISTANCE THROUGH EXCHANGE OF INFORMATION

3.42 The continuing moves toward a single European market without border controls involving the liberalisation of capital movement and of payments is not only promoting intra-community trade, but undoubtedly encouraging tax dodgers. Missing Trader Intra Community (MTIC) fraud, a fraud which exploits the intra-community trade system by inserting in supply chains a trader that defaults on its VAT liabilities and then disappears, represents one of the most high-profile and serious attacks on the tax system and has prompted HMRC and the tax authorities in other member states to work closely together to combat this, and some other international frauds.

3.43 Member states are obliged to exchange information that might enable them to effect a correct assessment of taxes on income and capital under a Mutual Assistance Directive, which has been amended to include VAT. The European Commission operates the VAT Information Exchange System, which in 2005 received 26,000 information exchanges. The extent of this co-operation seems set to increase if the current climate persists regarding the need to combat not only MTIC, but other more sophisticated VAT avoidance schemes which may exist.

VAT and Revenue & Customs visits **3.49**

3.44 A number of multilateral VAT control visits have been carried out over the past few years as member states focus on the joint control of multi-national companies. The object of these visits has been to test the effectiveness of the tools provided by the EU legislative framework for administrative co-operation in controlling multi-nationals.

3.45 However, the national legislation of some member states has prohibited this type of exercise, even though EU legislation permits it. The EU Commission believes that these EU-wide controls should become a common part of each member state's national control strategies.

3.46 The tax authorities in the EU also co-operate over the recovery of VAT across borders, with the tax authority in one country (eg HMRC in the UK) taking action to collect VAT due in another member state. There is also an exchange programme to enable indirect tax officials to visit other member states, to learn from their experience of controlling VAT, and EU-wide controls may become commonplace over the next few years.

OTHER VISITS

3.47 Many businesses registered for VAT may also be involved with other aspects of the department's work on indirect taxes and duties. Usually, these other activities will involve visits from specialist officers trained in those HMRC matters. The information gleaned about the business from the department's involvement in these activities can also be expected to find its way onto the VAT officers' records. Recently there has been a move by HMRC to conduct joint VAT and excise visits at particular businesses, for example exporters. The degree of liaison by officers involved in the various aspects of the department's work has increased greatly over the last few years and allows HMRC better control over the various taxes and duties for which they are responsible.

PREPARING FOR VISITS

3.48 An assurance visit from HMRC must not be treated as a routine meeting. A degree of planning and preparation is required. Generally, prior to a VAT visit a letter should be issued from HMRC which should set out details the information and records the officer will require on the day. This provides an opportunity to review the material that the visiting officer will see and, perhaps, identify any issues that may exist.

3.49 Preparation for assurance visits must start well before the visit. Any business registering for VAT must accept that they will be visited by VAT officers. Generally, the larger and more complex the business is, the longer and more frequent the visits will be. When establishing accounting systems, the following points should, therefore, be borne in mind:
- establish documented procedures for all accounts staff;
- understand what system controls are in place and if staff can override these;

3.49 VAT and Revenue & Customs visits

- prepare guidance manuals for staff dealing with VAT;
- define default procedures should system failures occur; and
- ensure that staff dealing with VAT are trained.

3.50 Since 1 April 2009 there has been a single penalty regime dealing with inaccurate tax documents and returns across the main taxes (albeit that it differs in some details to cater for differences between the taxes). The concept of 'reasonable care' underpins the new penalty regime. If a business takes reasonable care to get its tax right, HMRC will not impose penalties, even if a mistake is made.

3.51 Patterns of behaviour that demonstrate reasonable care include keeping accurate records to make sure tax returns are correct, checking what the correct position is when you do not understand something, and telling HMRC promptly about any error you discover in a tax return or document after you have sent it. If a business does not take reasonable care HMRC will penalise inaccuracies. Documenting processes and demonstrating that staff are trained in their operation are important steps in showing that reasonable care has been taken.

3.52 Before the visit, try to arrange an office or meeting room for the VAT officer to use away from the normal office routine but in a position where he can be 'controlled'. This prevents the officer from overhearing conversations which may be misinterpreted. The office should be comfortable and tidy. Any confidential documents should be locked away securely. The following points should also be considered:

- upon arrival, check the officer's identity;
- give clear instructions to all staff that HMRC officers are on the premises and how to react if they are approached/asked questions by any of the visiting officers;
- make notes of the meeting with the HMRC officer, noting documents inspected and if possible checks performed;
- write to confirm rulings given verbally by HMRC;
- use HMRC's own controls – flowcharts/interrogation software;
- be polite but firm in your dealings with HMRC; and
- do not allow the officer free run of the premises.

3.53 Preparation for any visit from HMRC should also be part of the ongoing routine for any business. If any business ignores good accounting practice, a period of, say, two weeks' notice of a visit would not be enough to get accounts into good order. As indicated above, good accounting routines should always be established. It is also important that, wherever possible, the accounting procedures should be familiar to more than one person. There have been many appeals to the VAT tribunals against a default surcharge in which the business has argued that the director was 'on holiday' or the accounts manager was 'sick'. Some of these cases were successful, but only where it has been established that the missing person was away unexpectedly. Good accounting practices and procedures allow a business to be prepared for the unexpected!

3.54 It is worth taking time to establish a period end routine when completing VAT returns – a best practice approach to VAT. A key objective of HMRC is to 'direct resources away from the majority of compliant traders and to focus attention on the high-risk businesses'. In the 2009 Departmental Report, HMRC noted their commitment to ensuring the tax system operates fairly and effectively and in the current difficult economic climate recognised the importance of helping and supporting customers to fulfil their tax obligations while relentlessly pursuing those who bend or break the rules. An Anti-Avoidance Group was set up in 2005 to identify those taxpayers who are more likely to avoid paying tax. HMRC look set to continue in this vein, focusing resources on and identifying those who present the greatest threat of non-compliance. The more that a business can demonstrate, therefore, that it is managing its VAT affairs correctly, the less time HMRC are likely to spend inspecting that business – and that can only be good news.

3.55 A business should always seek to abide by two criteria: first, to minimise its VAT costs and secondly to maximise its cash flow. Effective planning for VAT can assist in achieving both of these criteria. Period-end routines can assist in recognising differences from the norm and serve to identify under- or over-declarations of VAT. Whilst HMRC officers are obliged to adjust for errors they discover that are in the taxpayer's favour, the checks undertaken during visits are generally aimed at identifying under-declarations. HMRC officers are unlikely to undertake detailed checks designed to ascertain whether a business has failed to take credit for input VAT or if it has been taken late. It is important, therefore, that each business has its own checks and procedures in place to ensure that it is not over-declaring its VAT liability, as well as check to identify any under declarations. When VAT is under-declared, HMRC can impose interest and penalties (in accordance with the new penalties regime, effective from 1 April 2009). Prior to 1 April 2009, disclosing any under-declarations prior to any prompt from HMRC (e g contact made with the business to arrange a VAT visit to look at the issue in question) would remove any liability to a penalty. Whilst it is still possible to adjust some errors on VAT returns, and to disclose errors to HMRC that cannot simply be corrected on a return, doing that now will not necessarily remove the exposure to a penalty.

3.56 For VAT periods ending on or after 1 April 2009, HMRC will impose a penalty if a business cannot show that it has taken 'reasonable care' to get things right. The penalty will depend on the type of inaccuracy involved, whether the error was careless, deliberate or deliberate and concealed, and whether any notification of the error to HMRC was prompted or unprompted. The penalty can range from 0% to 100% of the error. Taking reasonable steps to help avoid a penalty includes keeping accurate records, checking the position when a VAT liability is unclear, and telling HMRC promptly about any error discovered on a VAT return that has already been submitted. HMRC may suspend penalties for a careless inaccuracy for up to two years. HMRC will set out conditions for the business to improve its system to stop the inaccuracy occurring again. If at the end of the suspension period the business meets all the conditions, and has not made any further errors in the suspension period, the penalty will be cancelled. Note, though, that other errors made during the suspension period (not necessarily connected with the original misdeclarations) will normally trigger

3.56 VAT and Revenue & Customs visits

payment of the penalty. HMRC cannot suspend penalties charged for deliberate inaccuracies.

3.57 The concept of the credibility visit which, from HMRC's perspective, often identifies the one-off error made by a business has already been explained. Simply having a second person to check the figures for a VAT return and making sure that the figures shown in box 4 (VAT reclaimed in this period on purchases and other inputs including acquisitions from the EU) is not greater than 20% of box 7 (total value of purchases and all other inputs excluding any VAT) is a start. Businesses can also develop a bespoke package of internal documents or spreadsheets which serve to compile and check the VAT return data. Various checks can be built into these processes. It is also best practice to have a different person signing the VAT return from the person who prepares it and for the signatory to perform some independent credibility checks on the return to ensure that it does not contain obvious errors, is consistent with the activities of the business, etc.

3.58 A common criticism from HMRC is that the signatory to the VAT return is often at too low a level within a large business. A routine period-end procedure is an ideal way to get VAT taken more seriously within a business, especially if the finance director is required to check and sign the VAT return.

3.59 One reaction to concerns about how seriously VAT (and other taxes) is taken in some organisations is the new legislation that has been introduced (Finance Act 2009). This makes senior accounting officers (SAOs) of large UK companies (who are liable to taxes and duties in the UK) responsible for ensuring and certifying that appropriate tax accounting arrangements have been established and maintained. The new legislation will only apply to a UK-registered company with a turnover of more than £200 million or has gross assets of more than £2 billion, but it may be a hint of things to come for smaller businesses if it achieves the objective of persuading those large businesses to take tax (including VAT) compliance more seriously at a high level within the organisation.

3.60 The 'main duty' of the SAO is to take reasonable steps to monitor the accounting arrangements of the company and to identify any respects in which those arrangements are not appropriate tax arrangements. The SAO is a director or officer who in the company's opinion has overall responsibility for the company's' financial accounting arrangements. The SAO must provide HMRC a certificate for each financial year of the company stating whether the company had appropriate arrangements in place throughout the year. Breaches of the SAO regime may result in penalties for both the company and the SAO.

SEARCH AND ENTRY

3.61 Former officers of HMCE had some of the widest powers in UK law enforcement, with commentators often making the point that HMCE had, in certain respects, wider powers than the police. Many of these rights and powers have been bestowed on HMCE over their hundreds of years of history and have been rigorously defended. The fact that some of these old rights were retained is a testament to the generally judicious and appropriate use of the powers.

3.62 The Commissioners for Revenue and Customs Act 2005 (CRCA) which established HMRC transferred the powers of the former IR and HMCE to the new department. As a short-term measure, these powers were 'ring-fenced' so they could only be used for their original purpose. This means that powers bestowed on HMCE could only be used for administering VAT and the other HMCE responsibilities (customs and excise duties, insurance premium tax and so forth). It must be remembered, however, that information was shared between HMCE and the IR before the formation of HMRC and that the merging of the two departments has improved the internal communication network.

3.63 During the Parliamentary process for the CRCA, a major review of the powers, deterrents and safeguards for HMRC was announced. The purpose of the review was to address the issues of aligning and modernising the existing powers and safeguards of the newly formed department.

The review has since been completed and HMRC now have one set of powers covering VAT, PAYE, income tax, capital gains tax, corporation tax and the Construction Industry Scheme to:

- visit businesses to inspect premises, assets and records;
- ask taxpayers and third parties for more information and documents; and
- set record-keeping requirements.

3.64 The changes introduced by the new legislation are principally contained in Schs 36, 37 and 39 of the Finance Act 2008. Former HMCE powers (relating to VAT) were principally contained in the Customs and Excise Management Act 1979 (CEMA 1979) and the Value Added Tax Act 1994 (VATA 1994).

3.65 For Intrastat purposes, the powers of Customs are contained in the Statistics of Trade (Customs and Excise) Regulations 1992. All that will be dealt with here are the powers generally exercised during a routine VAT inspection.

3.66 VATA 1994, Sch 11 (amended in accordance with the FA 2008) deals with the administration, collection and enforcement of the tax. Paragraph 6 requires a business to keep records; para 7 requires a business to provide 'any documents relating to the goods or services or to the supply, acquisition or importation'. Paragraph 11 gives an officer the right to enter a person's business premises. This paragraph also permits an officer the right to inspect any business assets located on the business premises when he has reasonable cause to believe that those goods have been the subject of an acquisition or will be used to make a taxable supply. These paragraphs contain the basic powers that permit an officer to enter buildings, inspect goods and to inspect the books and records of a business. However an officer is not permitted to enter or inspect any part of the premises that is used solely as a dwelling or to conduct a search (generally, searches have to be authorised by a search warrant and would be undertaken only in the course of an investigation into suspected fraud).

3.67 *VAT and Revenue & Customs visits*

3.67 As mentioned earlier, VATA 1994, Sch 11, para 7 (as amended by s 36 of FA 2008) requires that all documents relating to a supply be produced to an officer. This will usually relate to, but is not restricted to, invoices (purchases and sales), delivery notes, ledgers, computer printouts of sales and purchases, control accounts, bank statements, etc. Paragraph 7 also requires the production of any profit and loss account and balance sheet relating to the business. It should be borne in mind that this only requires production of the statutory accounts. It is important to recognise, therefore, that this requirement does not immediately apply to the provision of management accounts produced by the business itself. Similarly, the statutory powers of HMRC concerning the provision of information do not mean that officers can immediately demand sight of confidential advice provided to a business by their tax advisers.

3.68 Following consultation with the ICAEW and the Institute of Taxation, HMCE issued VAT Leaflet 700/47 (February 1993) 'Confidentiality in VAT matters (Tax Advisers) – Statement of practice'. This leaflet acknowledges the confidential nature of such tax advice and recognises that tax advisers have a duty of confidentiality to their clients. The former HMCE policy in this area, therefore, is not normally to request the business to produce confidential opinion letters. This will typically include auditors' working papers and management letters, except to the extent that they contain information relating to a supply of goods or services. Where advice letters contain mixed information, ie general advice and guidance and advice relating to a supply of goods or services, HMRC will normally accept an extract from the document supported by a written statement from the tax adviser or business that in his opinion HMRC do not have the power to see the other part(s) of the document.

3.69 In practice, officers will ask for everything and anything on the basis that there is no harm in trying! If any business is in doubt as to whether to give any documents to HMRC they should consult their advisers. If documents of a confidential nature are given to HMRC – which should be resisted – ensure, as far as possible, that no copies are taken. It is worth remembering that, in dispute cases involving appeals, HMRC may seek and the tax tribunal may order disclosure of documents viewed as 'confidential'.

SURVEILLANCE OPERATIONS

3.70 In general terms, surveillance operations cover two types of activity: first, test purchases and second observation of premises and/or people. If VAT officers have reason to believe that a business is suppressing the value of its sales, for example, one device that can be used to good effect is to conduct a test purchase operation. This is a low-key investigation technique typically employed against suspicious retailers, particularly restaurants and hairdressers. A small team of VAT officers is sent to the target premises to, for example, purchase a meal and to observe the waiters and other staff to see what happens to the money, ie what procedures are operated.

3.71 The officers will complete a report (sometimes a witness statement) which typically details:

- what they purchased (a receipt is an essential feature);
- what the cash-taking routine is for the business, ie what does the waiter do with the cash or credit card slips, etc;
- the number of diners in the restaurant between certain times; and
- the general atmosphere in the restaurant.

3.72 This type of activity may go on for several days, or if the business and suspected misdeclarations is large enough, over a period of weeks. The output from this type of activity gives a rough idea of the level of takings for the restaurant for a given period. By extrapolation, an idea of the actual level of takings for a VAT period or year can be ascertained.

3.73 The 'test meal' will be followed fairly quickly by a routine assurance visit. The VAT officer, armed with the intelligence gained from the test meal operation, can compare known takings against the takings declared in the record of daily gross takings that must be maintained by every retailer. Clearly, if the test meal operation identifies a significant difference between declared and actual takings, the assurance visit is likely to turn very swiftly into an investigation.

3.74 If HMRC want to obtain information about premises and/or people they will, on occasion, mount an exercise to observe those premises or people (known colloquially as 'obs'). This procedure demands considerable skills which would not normally be expected of a VAT officer. Because of the level of expertise required and the manpower needed to conduct this type of operation, these techniques are usually employed only by trained investigators.

INVESTIGATIONS

3.75 Roughly coinciding with the formation of HMRC, two other agencies were formed to take over some of the responsibilities which were previously dealt with by HMCE. These are the Revenue and Customs Prosecutions Office (RCPO) and the Serious Organised Crime Agency (SOCA).

3.76 The RCPO now deals with prosecuting all tax fraud cases in England and Wales as an independent agency, while SOCA has now taken over responsibility for former HMCE investigation and intelligence work on serious drug trafficking and related criminal finances.

3.77 HMRC retained the responsibility for protecting the UK's borders up until April 2008, when the UK Border Agency was formed. The UK Border Agency brings together the work previously carried out by the Border and Immigration Agency, customs detection work at the border from HMRC, and UK Visa Services from the Foreign & Commonwealth Office (FCO).

3.78 Some areas involving investigations have been centralised. A centralised Intelligence Unit has been created, as has a Detection Unit dealing with anti-fraud and smuggling operations. The Special Civil Investigations Unit has also been created to deal with serious acts of evasion using civil powers. Due to its cost efficiency this remains the procedure of choice but HMRC

3.78 *VAT and Revenue & Customs visits*

reserve the right to pursue a criminal investigation where they deem appropriate.

ROLE OF THE PROFESSIONAL ADVISER

Business review

3.79 A professional adviser can, of course, take many roles and provide a variety of services. In an ideal world every accounting system should have rigorous procedures all of which are documented and involve staff having split responsibilities. However, in practice this utopian ideal may not always translate to the real world. It should also be remembered that professional advice is not cheap. A business invariably strikes a balance between the perceived risks and the cost of implementing a rock-solid accounting system.

3.80 Although the vast majority of businesses are subject to an annual audit, VAT errors or mistakes are rarely material to the accounts and VAT does not, therefore, form a large part of an audit. The role of the professional VAT adviser is something beyond the scope of an audit.

3.81 A typical role for a professional adviser can be to conduct an overview of the system operated by a business to determine key weaknesses and controls and to ensure that the systems suit that particular business. This type of VAT review is often likened to an assurance visit; the question then posed by the business is 'why do we pay an adviser to do that, when HMRC do it for free?' There are two fundamental reasons why a separate review should be considered by a business. First, HMRC's role, however they like to present it, is to maximise revenue. This means that HMRC will be looking mainly for errors where VAT has been under-declared or over-recovered. If such errors are found by HMRC, as stated earlier, this will result in an interest charge and, in some circumstances, a monetary penalty. Secondly, HMRC are not in the business of giving bespoke tax advice. Generally speaking, planning opportunities will not be pointed out by a visiting VAT officer!

Assessments

3.82 If a business has received an assessment following a VAT visit, it does not necessarily follow that the tax is due. The first thing a professional adviser will do on reviewing an assessment issued to a client is to ensure that it is not 'out of time'. It is also important to recognise that VAT officers are trained to use departmental instructions, public notices and leaflets – not all officers have the legislation, let alone read and understand it. This is not a criticism of VAT officers, but training a large number of staff and requiring them to treat transactions on the same basis does mean a standardised approach – hence a heavy reliance on public notices, etc. These occasionally do not reflect EU legislation or jurisprudence – on which of course a taxpayer may rely.

3.83 It must be remembered that most public notices and leaflets are simply HMRC's interpretation of the law. The number of successful appeals against

HMRC's view is a testament to the fact that HMRC's interpretation can and, where appropriate, should be challenged. It should also be appreciated that UK VAT legislation must reflect the provisions of EU VAT legislation. A business has the right, on appeal, to challenge HMRC's interpretation on both UK and EU law – HMRC can only defend the UK legislation, it cannot rely on EU law that has not been implemented properly into the domestic legislation. A professional adviser should be aware of the vast amount of UK and EU legislation and legal precedent and usually has far greater resources available than a normal business to ascertain the correct position.

Appeals

3.84 This can be a daunting thought for many businesses. The tribunal procedures can be obscure for the uninitiated as can the idea of building the legal arguments and giving evidence at the tribunal. A professional adviser can put the case together and remove a lot of the concerns usually experienced by a business going to a tribunal for the first time. Although businesses can take a cases on their own, with the complexity of today's legislation, particularly if a case involves VAT liability issue, they are well advised to seek professional guidance.

3.85 From 1 April 2009, a new two-tier tribunal system hearing all tax appeals replaced the old system. The First-tier Tribunal hears the majority of appeals, with larger and more complex cases being considered by the Upper Tribunal, which also hears appeals from decision of the First-tier Tribunal. Unlike the 'old' system, under the new regime costs will not generally be payable to the successful party in an appeal to the tax tribunal. In the more complex cases, however, the usual costs regime can apply and either party could find itself meeting its own and the opponent's costs. Experience has shown that even when a successful appellant is awarded costs, these will rarely cover the full economic cost of the appeal so it would be wrong to regard even a successful appeal as a 'no cost option'.

3.86 To coincide with tribunal reform, businesses are now entitled (but not obliged) to request an internal review of appealable tax decisions. This new legal right to a review will replace reconsiderations and mandatory reviews in indirect taxes. Reviews will be optional and will be undertaken by a trained review officer, who has not previously been involved with that decision and who will be able to offer a balanced and objective view. If the taxpayer does not agree with the result of the review, they can appeal to the tribunal for a decision.

The Revenue & Customs adjudicator

3.87 If a business has a grievance about the way it has been dealt with by HMRC, the business may be able to complain to the HMRC adjudicator. Appropriate complaints concern the way in which HMRC have conducted themselves in relation to a business's affairs and may include, for example:

- situations where HMRC have been excessively slow in dealing with a particular matter;

3.87 *VAT and Revenue & Customs visits*

- an officer being discourteous;
- a case where HMRC have made a mistake which they have failed to remedy; or
- situations where HMRC have used their discretion or powers inappropriately.

3.88 The adjudicator may award costs but can also require HMRC to make a consolatory payment, order things to be done to a particular timescale or recommend that the officer is changed.

3.89 The adjudicator does not examine cases which are appealable to a VAT tribunal.

Judicial review

3.90 In some cases where it is not possible to settle a dispute or to appeal it under the 'normal' appeal process to the tax tribunal, it may be possible to seek judicial review, either in the Administrative Court or the new Upper Tribunal (which has power to consider certain judicial review cases). Judicial review cases tend to be complex and involve tight time limits. Early professional advice would be essential in any situation where this process might be adopted.

Investigation

3.91 If an assurance visit becomes uncomfortable or an investigation team arrives at the business, the business' advisers should be contacted immediately. Trying to handle situations where interviews are being conducted under caution can be fraught and create a high degree of distress. The following are points to remember:

- phone the professional adviser immediately to seek specific advice;
- be polite and helpful at all times, as it is an offence to obstruct an officer in the course of his duties;
- politely but firmly refuse to give interviews under caution, whether taped or written;
- say something to the effect that 'we are happy to answer your questions, however, could you please outline your areas of concern so that due consideration can be given to providing the correct answer'; and
- always remember that when an investigation is instigated, it is an indication that the officer believes that offences may have been committed! If a comment is made under caution, it cannot be retracted. Trying to persuade HMRC that something said in a statement was wrong or inaccurate can be very difficult and expensive.

Chapter 4

National Insurance visits and investigations

Peter Arrowsmith FCA

National Insurance Consultant

4.01 With around £101 billion of National Insurance contributions due to be collected in a year (of which over £96 billion are Class 1 contributions), there is a clear duty on the National Insurance Contributions and Employer Office and HMRC generally to ensure that employers and the self-employed pay what is due and otherwise comply with the many NIC legislative requirements. The policing of the NIC systems largely, but not entirely, falls to HMRC employer compliance officers.

INSPECTORATE POWERS

4.02 Previous, and arguably heavier, powers available to employer compliance officers dealing with NIC matters were changed with effect from 6 April 2005 when SSCBA 1992, s 110ZA was rewritten by the National Insurance Contributions and Statutory Payments Act 2004. From that date, the tax and National Insurance powers of what are now HM Revenue and Customs officers to inspect records and obtain information have been aligned and Taxes Management Act 1970, ss 20B and 20BB – with appropriate modifications – applies to NIC (s 20 also applied prior to 1 April 2009). The rewritten s 110ZA does not deal with Class 3 contributions as they are entirely voluntary, and Class 4 contributions were already within the TMA regime in any event.

4.03 A revised compliance checking regime across most taxes applies from 1 April 2009: Finance Act 2008, Sch 36. This applies equally to National Insurance contributions, SSCBA 1992, s 110ZA having been further amended by Finance Act 2008, Sch 36, para 84 (see **10.13**).

4.04 *National Insurance visits and investigations*

4.04 All employer compliance officers carry a warrant card setting out their powers in addition to a standard identification card. Employers should ask to see such warrants if they are unsure of what rights the employer compliance officers have.

Reasons for visit

4.05 There are many reasons why an employer compliance officer would want to visit an employer. It could be because he is a new employer and the employer compliance officer wants to introduce himself and check that the employer is familiar with the basic rules for NIC, statutory sick pay (SSP), statutory maternity pay (SMP), statutory paternity pay (SPP) and statutory adoption pay (SAP) – the latter four collectively known as 'statutory payments'). There could be a small discrepancy in the year-end reporting forms and the employer compliance officer needs a quick look at the employer's records. It could be that there is a special check being made of specific industry type or an employer has been selected for a more in-depth examination. Given that most visits are fairly routine and will cause employers little or no trouble, the rest of this chapter will focus on how employer compliance officers carry out a full-scale investigation.

Which employers are chosen for investigation?

4.06 Although some random visits continue to be made, employer compliance officers are likely to have done a little bit of homework to identify employers worthy of a visit. They are under some pressure to collect additional NICs (and tax too) and so they will not want to waste time visiting employers who are unlikely to have underpaid or made other serious errors. Employer risk-profiling is used to identify suitable targets and factors taken into account include size, geographical location, industry type and make-up of workforce etc. Computer programs are regularly used to identify such targets.

Purpose of visit

4.07 Protecting the National Insurance Fund is the primary purpose of the NIC element of any visit but another very important purpose is ensuring that employee benefit rights are fully maintained by confirming that the correct amount of NIC has been paid. Other reasons for a visit are to identify instances where too little or too much NIC has been paid and to correct any errors, and to check that the statutory payments are being correctly and timeously paid out to employees when due.

Timing

4.08 Employer compliance officers will not want to visit too often and so they try to work on a five-year cycle, although where serious errors have been found or significant NICs collected check visits will be made in the interim period. Following the 1999 merger of the former Inland Revenue and the former

Contributions Agency all inspection visits now deal with both tax and NIC (including the related statutory payments issues) at the same time. This continues to be the case following the subsequent 2005 merger between HM Customs & Excise and the Inland Revenue. For larger employers, there will be a combined corporation tax and VAT visit, which will very probably encompass all PAYE/NIC matters too.

Notification of visit

4.09 It is extremely rare these days for employer compliance officers to make unannounced visits. Employers are more likely to receive a telephone call or letter at least two weeks in advance. Employers should not hesitate to seek to delay or defer a visit if there are work pressures caused by, for example, being at or near the end of the financial or trading year or because of staff shortages. However, the authorities are aware that sometimes requests for later dates are attempts to avoid a visit at all costs. Deliberately attempting to avoid being audited is severely frowned upon and appropriate measures will be taken if necessary.

4.10 Following wider tax changes effective from 1 April 2009, it is likely that visits with less than seven days' notice and unannounced visits will have been approved beforehand by a specially trained HMRC officer.

4.11 In larger employers, employer compliance officers may want to make a preliminary visit to explain how they see the inspection progressing whilst at the same time obtaining some background information such as who will be able to deal with the queries, the form in which the various records are kept and for how long the records are held and whether there is suitable accommodation for them to use. At that preliminary meeting the employer is likely to find out how many employer compliance officers and support staff will be involved in the inspection, how long it is likely to take and any specific areas in which the employer compliance officers are interested.

4.12 Equally, the visiting officer may well have used an internal computerised audit programme called 'IDEA' which – in advance of the visit – performs certain checks and procedures on the submitted P35 and P14 data and highlights key areas (down to individual employee level) for detailed examination and consideration at the visit.

Length of visit

4.13 It is virtually impossible to estimate in advance just how long an inspection will take and they will range from an hour to several weeks. It is safe to say that where there are, say, at least 1,000 employees the inspection will last for at least two weeks. It may well be that employer compliance officers are not on the premises for a continuous period but will simply check an aspect at a time, go away and put together their findings and then return and check something else.

4.14 National Insurance visits and investigations

Place of visit

4.14 Employer compliance officers will generally want to carry out their inspection at the employer's place of business and if the records are not readily available there they are likely to ask for the records to be brought to the place of business. Sometimes employer compliance officers can be persuaded to visit another location such as a payroll bureau or an accountant but that is the exception rather than the rule. Employer compliance officers will, however, want to visit other work locations to check paperwork held locally and maybe even to count the number of heads to make sure that they are all on the payroll.

Preparation for the visit

4.15 There is a lot an employer can do beforehand to make sure that the inspection runs smoothly. He should, for example, make sure that all the records requested by the employer compliance officer are readily available and that someone with knowledge of the employer's system and procedures is available to deal with any queries. That person should be senior enough to be able to answer queries without needing to refer matters elsewhere. An employer should also ensure that accommodation is made available for the employer compliance officers and it would be courteous to ensure that the room is lockable, that there is access to a telephone and that there are tea, coffee and toilet facilities.

Commencement of the visit

4.16 At the beginning of the visit the employer compliance officer(s) should make the necessary introductions and explain the process of conducting the examination of the records. This is the time for both the employer compliance officer and the employer to ask any questions and also to ensure that all the required records (listed below) are available. The employer compliance officer should also establish who should be contacted in the event of queries and questions. During the course of the audit the records of all employees and directors will be checked to ensure that contributions (including Class 1A, Class 1B and, in the case of unincorporated businesses, Class 2) are being correctly assessed and paid and also that SSP, SMP, SPP and SAP are being paid to employees who qualify and that only the correct recoveries are being made from the employer's monthly (or quarterly) remittances. While they will start with the current year they will usually check back into the preceding year and earlier years if they feel it is necessary.

Records to be made available

4.17 Employer compliance officers need to be able to examine any of the employer's records that could involve a liability for National Insurance contributions. The list of documents that may be required for examination for NIC purposes is extensive and, while not exhaustive, includes:

National Insurance visits and investigations 4.17

- *Accident book* – where there is a legal requirement to keep such a book, employer compliance officers will want to ensure that it is held and that it is being correctly completed.
- *Bank statements* – employer compliance officers will want to identify payments which do not go through the payroll and which could attract an NIC liability.
- *Cash book* – employer compliance officers will want to confirm that payments subject to NIC have been transferred to the payroll and have been correctly treated.
- *Certificates of deferment* – the visiting officers will want to ensure that these certificates are actually held.
- *Certificates of exemption* – employer compliance officers will want to ensure that these certificates are valid and have been correctly used.
- *Certificates of election for married women paying reduced rate National Insurance* – again employer compliance officers will want to ensure that these certificates continue to be valid.
- *Cheque stubs* – employer compliance officers will want to identify payments that should have gone through the payroll for NIC purposes.
- *Company accounts* – employer compliance officers will want to examine these as there are various clues to the NIC position. For example, does the employer NIC on the P35 broadly equal 11% or 12% (in 2010–11 and earlier years; otherwise 12% or 13%) of the total employee remuneration shown in the accounts and has all the remuneration paid to directors been considered for NIC purposes?
- *Contracting-out certificate* – is this valid and has the employer correctly identified those employees covered by the contracting-out arrangements?
- *Deduction working sheets (P11s)* – very few employers will use the standard P11s but they will have equivalent documentation (whether on paper or held electronically) and employer compliance officers will check a number of calculations to ensure that the correct NIC figures have been reached, often downloading electronic records onto their own computerised audit program 'IDEA' for further analysis work off the premises.
- *Sickness absence records* – employer compliance officers will look to see if employers have correctly dealt with sickness absences and in the main this will be to ensure that employees have received the equivalent of statutory sick pay.
- *Maternity absence records* – employer compliance officers will want to check a few SMP calculations and confirm that employers are holding the correct evidence of pregnancy.
- *Paternity and adoption pay records* – employer compliance officers will look to see if employers have correctly dealt with such absences and in the main this will be to ensure that employees have received the correct payments and the employer holds the appropriate certification from the employee(s) in question.
- *Minute book* – this is where employer compliance officers will identify additional payments to company directors and senior executives (this

4.17 National Insurance visits and investigations

- may include the awarding of shares, share options and other similar securities).
- *P30 BC paying-in book/P32 (or equivalent electronic records)* – employer compliance officers will want to ensure that monies have been paid over to HMRC when due.
- *Petty cash book* – again officers will be looking to identify payments that should have gone through payroll for NIC purposes.
- *Petty cash vouchers* – this is another area where the officers will be looking for payments liable for NIC which have not gone through the payroll arrangements.
- *Wage book/payroll* – this is where employer compliance officers will pay close attention and they will take a sample of entries to ensure that NIC liabilities have been fully met and that the correct reporting mechanisms are in place.
- *Dispensation* – officers will want to ensure that where NIC liabilities have not been met that this is because the terms of a dispensation granted by HMRC have been fully complied with. In appropriate cases HMRC can, and will, withdraw dispensations retrospectively if the terms on which they were issued have ceased to apply or if the circumstances were misrepresented in the original application.

4.18 When checking the above documentation employer compliance officers will pay close attention to the following aspects:

- *Basic pay* – they will want to ensure that NI has been paid on the full amount and that the correct contribution category letter and earnings period have been used.
- *Bonuses* – employer compliance officers will want to ensure that this has been added to the basic pay in the correct earnings period and that NIC has been assessed on the total. Employer compliance officers will pay very close attention to any bonus arrangements that have avoided NIC liabilities.
- *Company cars, fuel expenses and other benefits in kind* – officers are likely to carry out an in-depth examination of Class 1A contribution liabilities. They will also look to identify fuel used for private motoring and to ensure that all NIC liabilities are met. They will also look at mileage rates and allowances paid by employers to ensure that there is no profit element, as well as considering all other benefits in depth.
- *Other payments in kind* – the officers will want to satisfy themselves that payments in kind are genuine, that if they have not been subjected to NIC liabilities that such payments fall within the general Class 1 NIC exclusion provisions and, where appropriate, Class 1A accounted for nonetheless.
- *Casual and part-time workers* – they will want to ensure that they go through the payroll when earnings reach the NIC primary earnings threshold and that National Insurance numbers (NINOs) are held.
- *Directors* – employer compliance officers will want to identify all individuals who fall within the definition of a company director for NIC purposes and verify that an annual earnings period (or pro-rata in the

- *Employees with pension scheme contracted-out number (including directors)* – employer compliance officers will want to confirm that the correct category letter has been used and that the scheme numbers go on the end-of-year returns (P35 only for a salary-related scheme and both the P35 and all affected P14s in the case of a money purchase scheme).
- *Expenses payments* – this is an area where employer compliance officers will pay very close attention and they will be seeking to identify profit elements within payments as well as entirely non-business payments so that NIC liabilities can be assessed. They will look closely at what expenses employees are allowed to claim and the steps that employers have put in place for authorising such expenses.
- *Fees/commissions* – employer compliance officers will want to make sure that such payments are added to the basic salary in the correct earnings period and that full NIC liabilities are met.
- *Overtime* – employer compliance officers will again check that this has been added to basic pay.
- *Self-employed workers* – this is always an area which excites employer compliance officers simply because of the likely additional NIC yield if the individuals are in fact employees. They will look closely at the employment arrangements and in particular at any supervision, control or direction that is evident.
- *Workers exempt from payment of National Insurance/paying reduced rate National Insurance/not liable to pay National Insurance* – employer compliance officers will be looking for documentation to support the NIC position. This may involve employers in having to provide certificates of reduced rate authority, deferment certificates, age exemption certificates and certificates of coverage issued by foreign social security authorities.
- *Shares and other securities, including options* – employer compliance officers will examine all arrangements carefully including those in relation to approved schemes where transactions outside normal rules may give rise to liability.

More generally, the officers will also want to ensure that none of the business activities are such that either the personal service companies ('IR35') or management service companies provisions are applicable.

RECORD KEEPING

4.19 The legislation requires employers to keep records for the current tax year and the three previous years. It is likely that employer compliance officers will restrict their initial action to the current year and the last closed tax year. If errors are found they will go back further. If employers have records going back more than three years employer compliance officers are likely to look at the last six years. It is arguable, however, that if an employer only holds records for the three years the wording of the social security legislation precludes an employer compliance officer from going back any further simply because he would be

4.19 *National Insurance visits and investigations*

unable to identify a named employee who received a payment of earnings on a specific date. However, in practice, employer compliance officers will normally seek six years' arrears in all cases. It should be noted that whilst tax arrears are, at first instance, restricted to the collection of only four years' arrears with effect from April 2010, the old six-year limit under the Limitation Act 1980 is still applicable for NIC. It is understood that the previous government was to review the Limitation Act generally and no changes have been made pending this. It remains unclear whether the coalition government will, in fact, proceed with the review that was planned or in what timescale.

4.20 It is the employer's responsibility to make sure that the relevant records are made available to employer compliance officers. If the records are going to take a time to put together or to collect from different locations then employer compliance officers are usually agreeable to delay the inspection for a short time. Employers who do not make the relevant records available to the officers within a reasonable time may find that the employer compliance officer will take criminal proceedings.

4.21 It is always open to an employer compliance officer to take records away from the business premises but he will generally return them as quickly as possible. If an employer needs the records for his business purposes then the employer compliance officer will arrange for copies to be supplied to him.

ERRORS AND OMISSIONS

4.22 One of the main purposes of an inspection is to ensure that employers are not making errors. Yet with such a complicated scheme to operate it is inevitable that employers will make mistakes. The opportunities to get it wrong are wide and varied – some of the common areas include:

- accepting a person as being self-employed when the facts do not support the decision;
- using the wrong year's NI tables – whether hard-copy tables or through not having updated software either at all or on time;
- having incomplete identity details – usually the lack of NI numbers;
- deducting reduced rate contributions without holding the appropriate certificate;
- continuing to deduct reduced rate contributions when a woman has been divorced;
- paying employers contracted-out contributions as if the pension scheme were salary related when it is in fact money purchase and/or continuing to pay contracted-out rates (employer and employee) after the contracting-out certificate has been withdrawn;
- directors' annual earnings periods;
- errors with statutory payments;
- failing to account for employees' contributions without the required proof of age exemption or failing to account for any National Insurance contributions without the appropriate international coverage certification.

4.23 Using the wrong year's NI tables or having incomplete identity details – at least – will cause PAYE schemes filed electronically for 2005–06 onwards to be immediately rejected upon submission. Paper, etc returns containing such errors will also be returned in due course for correction by the employer. In either situation, the P35 is not then treated as having been submitted until the errors are successfully corrected.

4.24 Very few employers make mistakes deliberately. During visits employer compliance officers try to ensure that employers both understand and can operate the system. Where errors are found then the employer compliance officer will draw it to the employer's attention with guidance as to how the position should be rectified and how it should be avoided in future. Where the error results in an overpayment or underpayment of NIC then the employer compliance officer will again give guidance as to how this should be rectified. In simple terms if the error is in the current tax year then an adjustment can be made, but if it is in a closed tax year then either a refund application can be made, or the employer compliance officer will issue a demand for arrears.

INSPECTION REPORT

4.25 At the end of the inspection, the employer compliance officer will explain, in some detail, what has been discovered, answer questions, try to ensure that the employer (and staff) will be able to deal with problems in the future and know who to contact when faced with difficulties. Afterwards the employer will usually receive a written report of some kind, and will definitely do so, along with calculations, if arrears of NIC (and/or tax) are being demanded. It could merely be a letter or it could be a much more formal document. Whatever is issued will highlight the officer's findings and contain his recommendations to improve the record keeping. What employers will really be interested in is the usual demand for NIC arrears. Such demands will almost certainly accompany the inspection report with a request for payment. It is likely that some interest charge will also be levied, and in most cases penalties too. It is up to employers to pay over what is due or if they consider that there is no liability to set out in writing why they believe that is the case. This is often when advisers become involved and they will take the matter forward on behalf of the employer. The bigger the employer the more likely it is that employer compliance officers will want to have a formal meeting at the end of the inspection to discuss all the findings.

4.26 When assessing any arrears the employer compliance officers will also advise the employer of the implications of interest charges on contributions (and tax) that have not been paid by 19 April (22 April where the payment is made electronically) in the tax year following that in which they were due.

FUTURE VISITS

4.27 When the employer compliance officer decides to make a further visit will depend greatly on what he finds at the inspection. If there is little of concern

4.27 *National Insurance visits and investigations*

then it is likely to be five years or more before he returns. If, however, there are a large number of errors or significant NIC due then he may very well make a check visit within 12 months or so.

CONCLUSION

4.28 With employer compliance officers' growing ability to target firms for audit with greater effectiveness using risk-management tools, the potential for discovering financial irregularities is greater and the accent is now firmly on yield discovered rather than the number of visits carried out.

4.29 Targeting, by its very nature, involves the selection of businesses where experience indicates that there is more likelihood of employers making mistakes. Coming into this area are companies with a high turnover of staff, companies who employ large numbers of casual staff, those with numerous widespread sites with consequential long lines of communication, and companies who make large numbers of mistakes in their end-of-year returns. However, while being able progressively to identify such businesses employer compliance officers also have a duty to protect the NIC records of all types of employers. There must therefore be a balance between concentrating purely upon yield with the need to demonstrate that it is protecting employees in all types and sizes of employers.

4.30 From the above comments, it will be appreciated that there is not a lot that employers can do to avoid inspection visits. They will be selected as a target for any number of reasons and the employer compliance officer will follow that through. What employers can do, however, is check their procedures and ensure that they are following the legislative requirements. They could, in fact, mirror the type of checks that employer compliance officers carry out on a regular basis and ensure that all is in order. To this end, the HMRC Expenses and Benefits from Employment 'Toolkit' might be used (available at www.hmrc.gov.uk/agents/prereturn-support-agents.htm) as well as the National Insurance Contributions and Statutory Payments Toolkit that is also now available. However, users should appreciate that these documents are not comprehensive checklists but merely developed from the main errors that HMRC encounter in the respective fields covered.

Chapter 5

National Insurance: fines, penalties and appeals

Peter Arrowsmith, FCA

National Insurance Consultant

OFFENCES AND PENALTIES

General

5.01 New penalties came into effect in respect of underpayments associated with incorrect returns in the case of return periods commencing on and after 1 April 2008 where the return is lodged on and after 1 April 2009 – see **5.19** and **5.27**.

False information, delays and obstruction

5.02 The criminal penalties which once applied are dealt with as civil offences from 1 April 1999, following the transfer of responsibility from the former Contributions Agency to what was then the Inland Revenue and which merged with HM Customs & Excise in April 2005 to become HMRC.

Contravention of regulations

5.03 The previous criminal offences under SSAA 1992, s 113 are replaced with effect from 6 April 1999 by new s 113 inserted by Social Security Act 1998, s 60. This provides for regulations to be made setting out a scheme of civil penalties. It should be noted that, in the case of Class 1 NICs, it is the employer who is guilty of an offence, even if he delegated his duties of compliance to another (*Godman v Crofton* [1913] 110 LT 387). There is an extensive scheme of penalties applying to employers' failures in relation to statutory sick pay, statutory maternity pay, statutory paternity pay and statutory adoption pay (SSAA 1992, ss 113A, 113B, Employment Act 2002, ss 11, 12, Sch 1). These include:

- failure to produce documents or records or to provide information – up to £300, and for continuing failure a possible penalty of up to £60 per day;
- failing to maintain records – up to £3,000;
- repeated failure to make payments to employees – up to £3,000;
- incorrect payments due to fraud or neglect – up to £3,000;
- excessive advance funding by reason of fraud or neglect – up to £3,000.

These penalties will also be reformed in due course, but no changes have yet been made.

Offences relating to contributions

5.04 If an employer deducts or tries to deduct all or part of the employer's Class 1 secondary liability from the employee's pay he is guilty of an offence (SSCBA 1992, Sch 1, para 3A and SI 2001 No 1004, Sch 4, para 6(2), (3)).

5.05 The Social Security Act 1998 imposed a new *criminal* offence of fraudulent evasion and being knowingly involved in fraudulent evasion of contributions. The offence is brought to trial summarily or on indictment. When tried summarily the maximum fine is level 5 (£5,000) on the standard scale. When tried on indictment the maximum penalty is seven years' imprisonment and/or an unlimited fine (SSCBA 1992, s 114 inserted by Social Security Act 1998, s 61). It should be noted that this offence relates to 'any person' and so may extend to an accountant, tax advisor or junior payroll clerk.

Offences by bodies corporate

5.06 Where a company commits an offence by failing to pay a contribution, and it is proved that the offence was committed with the consent or connivance of, or to be attributable to any neglect on the part of a director, manager, secretary or other similar officer of the company, proceedings may also be taken against that individual (SSAA 1992, s 115 (1)). This applies equally to a company which is managed by its members (SSAA 1992, s 115 (2)).

5.07 The former Contributions Agency (CA) successfully prosecuted a director of two 'phoenix' companies under s 115 in 1995. Directors of such companies typically incur large debts through the non-payment of creditors and then liquidate the company, relying on its limited liability status to protect themselves. NICs are often deducted correctly from employees' wages, but are not passed on to what is now HMRC. This was the first criminal case of its kind (CA Press Release of 27 September 1995).

Employer failing to pay Class 1 and Class 1A contributions

Notice of amount due

5.08 If within 17 days of the end of any income tax period an employer has either failed to pay, or paid insufficient, Class 1 or Class 1A contributions and HMRC's Debt Management and Banking service believes that contributions are due, he may issue a notice to the employer instructing him to make a return within 14 days, showing the amount of contributions which he is liable to pay in respect of the period in question (SI 2001 No 1004, Sch 4, para 14(1), (3)).

5.09 The Debt Management and Banking service may alternatively, upon consideration of the employer's record of past payments, to the best of their judgment, specify the amount of contributions which they consider the employer is liable to pay and give notice of the amount (SI 2001 No 1004, Sch 4, para 15(1)).

Evidence of non-payment of contributions

5.10 If the employer has not paid either the estimated liability or the actual amount due within the seven days allowed in the notice, Debt Management and Banking's certificate of the amount due is, until the contrary is proved, sufficient evidence in any proceedings before the courts that the sum mentioned in the certificate is unpaid and due (SSAA 1992, s 118(1); SI 2001 No 1004, Sch 4, para 15(4)). A document purporting to be such a certificate is deemed to be such a certificate until the contrary is proved (SSAA 1992, s 118(3) and SI 2001 No 1004, Sch 4, para 15(4)). The Social Security Act 1998 broadens these arrangements to provide that a certificate of an authorised officer of HMRC confirming the non-payment of contributions, interest or penalty may be provided to court as evidence of non-payment of debt until the contrary is proved (SSAA 1992, s 118(1), substituted by Social Security Act 1998, s 62). The Social Security Act 1998 also provides for distraint action to be taken in England and Wales where a person served with a certificate confirming their debt, fails to make payment within seven days. A magistrate's warrant is required for forced entry to premises and, where necessary, the assistance of a constable may also be secured. Any goods distrained will be held for a five-day period and then sold by auction. In Scotland, poinding proceedings under Debtors (Scotland) Act 1987, Sch 5 can be instituted where a person has been served with a certificate confirming the debt (s 118(1) above) but fails to make payment within the longer period of 14 days. A sheriff's summary warrant is required for recovery and sale by way of poinding. Applications must be accompanied by the certificate of debt and a certificate stating that the certificate of debt was served on the person in question and the debt remains unpaid (SSAA 1992, s 121B inserted by Social Security Act 1998, s 63).

Recovery of Class 1 contributions

5.11 The provisions of ITEPA 2003 and PAYE Regulations relating to the recovery of tax apply also to Class 1 contributions which an employer is liable

5.11 *National Insurance: fines, penalties and appeals*

to pay to the Debt Management and Banking service, as if they had been tax charged by way of an assessment on the employer as 'general earnings' (ITEPA 2003, s 684 and SI 2001 No 1004, reg 67(1)).

5.12 Proceedings may be brought for recovery of Class 1 and Class 1A contributions in the same way as they are for income tax charged on 'general earnings' (TMA 1970, s 65(3)).

Class 1, Class 1A and PAYE penalties

5.13 FA 1989 introduced significant changes to the penalty regime for PAYE failures, including the penalty in respect of late and incorrect year end returns (forms P14 and P35) (TMA 1970, s 98A). With effect from 22 October 1990, these penalties also apply in relation to returns required under NI regulations of Class 1 and Class 1A contributions. For NIC purposes, the Social Security Contributions and Benefits Act 1992 (SSCBA 1992), Sch 1, para 7 mirrors the PAYE penalty provisions in TMA 1970, s 98A subject to the following modifications:

- Where a person has failed to render a tax return for a particular tax year within the time prescribed and is thus liable for (has been required to pay) a penalty for a default in the first 12 months, he is not liable for a similar penalty in respect of the associated contributions return (SSCBA 1992, Sch 1, para 7(3)).
- Where a person has failed to render a tax return and an associated contributions return for a particular tax year and the failure has continued beyond 12 months, a single penalty may apply of up to the sum of any tax and contributions remaining unpaid at the end of 19 April following the end of the tax year to which the return relates. An authorised officer must determine that a penalty is to be imposed in respect of both returns (SSCBA 1992, Sch 1, para 7(4)(5)).
- Where a person has fraudulently or negligently made an incorrect tax return and an associated contributions return for a particular tax year, a single penalty may apply of up to the sum of any tax and contributions remaining unpaid at the end of 19 April following the end of the tax year to which the return relates. Again, an authorised officer must determine that a penalty is to be imposed in respect of both returns (SSCBA 1992, Sch 1, para 7(4)(5)).

The provisions in Finance Act 2009, Sch 55 (see **14.126–14.166**) which relate only to various taxes, but including PAYE, are likely to extend to NIC also in due course.

5.14 Any penalties collected by HMRC in respect of NICs are, after the deduction of the collection costs, paid to the National Insurance Fund (SSCBA 1992, Sch 1, para 7(6)(8)).

Personal liability notices

5.15 With effect from 6 April 1999, officers of bodies corporate may be issued with a personal liability notice where the business has failed to pay the correct contributions at the correct time and the failure *appears* to be attributable to fraud or neglect on the part of one or more individuals (SSAA 1992, s 121C inserted by Social Security Act 1999, s 64).

5.16 The personal liability notice will transfer the whole or a specified part of the company's NIC debt to the director or company secretary as a personal debt of the individual, including the associated interest accrued to date. Further interest will accrue until payment is made. Appeals may be made against such notices.

Penalties for late returns

5.17 For 1994–95 and subsequent years, an employer who has not filed his end of year return of tax and NICs by the due date (19 May following the year of assessment) is liable to an automatic penalty of £100 for each month or part month it is delayed, in respect of every 50 employees (or part thereof) who should be on the return. For example, a return for 51 employees which is late by one day would attract an automatic penalty of £200 (TMA 1970, s 98A). Where the delay continues beyond 12 months, an additional penalty is due, equal to the amount of tax and NICs unpaid at 19 April following the end of the year to which the return relates.

The provisions in Finance Act 2009, Sch 55 (see **14.126–14.166**), which relate only to various taxes but including PAYE, are likely to extend to NIC also in due course.

5.18 Until the automatic penalties were imposed, an interim scheme, which was intended gradually to tighten up on PAYE compliance, applied in respect of late end of year returns for the years 1989–90 to 1993–94. Where an employer failed to make a return by the due date, the initial maximum penalty was £1,200 per 50 employees. Once the initial penalty had been imposed by formal proceedings before the Commissioners, there was a continuing penalty of £100 per 50 employees for each further month that the failure continued up to 12 months. The interim scheme was introduced gradually and penalty action was only taken against a proportion of defaulting employers.

Penalties for incorrect returns

5.19 In the case of return periods commencing on and after 1 April 2008 where the return is lodged on and after 1 April 2009 a new scheme of penalties applies under Finance Act 2007, Sch 24. The new regime applies to NIC because Finance Act 2007, Sch 24 applies the provisions of that schedule to SSCBA 1992, Sch 1, para 7. The new penalties are determined by reference to the amount of tax/NIC understated, the nature of the behaviour that gives rise to the understatement and the extent of disclosure made by the 'taxpayer'. No penalty will be charged where 'reasonable care' has been taken. The penalty will be 0–30% where there has been failure to take reasonable care (with a minimum of 15% where disclosure was prompted by HMRC), 20–70% where there has been deliberate understatement (with a minimum of 35% where disclosure was prompted by HMRC) and 30–100% where there has been

5.19 National Insurance: fines, penalties and appeals

deliberate understatement with concealment (with a minimum of 50% where disclosure was prompted by HMRC). In some circumstances, penalties may be suspended for up to two years, eg if the error is due to systems or record-keeping failure.

5.20 In the case of older returns, the penalty for an incorrect return, fraudulently or negligently made, is an amount up to the difference between the amount paid for the year of assessment to which the return relates and the amount which would have been payable if it had been correct (TMA 1970, s 98A (4) and SSCBA 1992, Sch 1, para 7(2)).

Penalties for incorrect manner of payment

5.21 In respect of Class 1 NIC and PAYE liabilities for 2004–05 et seq, large PAYE schemes (those with 250 or more employees) must make their monthly remittances by electronic means. Where the full amount due is not paid electronically then the employer is in default. The only ground for an appeal against a default notice is that there was no default. A surcharge is imposed for defaults on an increasing scale. This remains the case even where all payments were on time and complete but paid by cheque. There are three extra days to pay if doing so electronically, though cleared funds must be received within those extra three days (SI 2001 No 1004, regs 90F–90H).

Penalties for late payment

5.22 From April 2010 penalties will be applied for the first time to all sizes of employers who are late in making in-year (ie monthly/quarterly) PAYE/NIC remittances (SI 2001 No 1004, reg 67A).

5.23 The amount of the penalty will depend on the number of defaults in any 12-month period. There will be no penalty for the first default, but other defaults will attract a penalty starting at 1% and rising to 4% of the tax, etc unpaid. There will be further cumulative penalties of 5% of any amounts still unpaid at six months after the end of the year and again at 12 months after the end of the year. These penalties will not be charged during an agreed time to pay arrangement (unless the taxpayer defaults or 'misuses' the arrangement).

5.24 For an initial period, as HM Revenue and Customs systems are not yet in fact ready to impose these penalties on an automatic basis, they are being imposed on a risk-based assessment of HMRC internal records which means in practice that they will only be imposed on larger employers (or, perhaps more correctly stated – larger payers). In due course, but not for at least another year or two, they will be imposed automatically on all employers in default.

Class 1A contributions

5.25 For 2000–01 onwards there is a penalty of up to the amount of contributions underpaid where there is fraud or neglect (SI 2001 No 1004, reg 81(1)), otherwise £100 per 50 earners per part or full calendar month for the first 12 months, or the amount of contributions underpaid if the failure extends beyond 12 months (SI 2001 No 1004, reg 81(2), (3) and (4)).

The Finance Act 2007, Sch 24 regime mentioned in 5.19 also applies to Class 1A contributions but in a different way. In respect of the 2010–11 liability onwards there will be penalties of 5% on Class 1A contributions unpaid 30 days after the due date and a further 5% (each time) as at six months and 12 months after the due date (SI 2001 No 1004, reg 67B).

5.26 [*The practice outlined in the following paragraph has now been superseded, but has been retained in the text as it may still be of historic interest to practitioners*]

Where Class 1A contributions were paid through Forms P14 and P35 for years up to and including 1999–2000 the same penalties and interest consequences ensued as if the Class 1A NIC was Class 1 NIC for the year to which the P14/P35 relates, e g 1997–98 Class 1A NIC entered on Form P14 in July 1998 and 1998–99 P35 in April/May 1999, will be subject to interest from 19 April 1999 and to the 19 May 1999 P35 submission date. Previously, no interest charge or penalty could arise if the employer had applied to use the 'Alternative Payment Method'. This anomaly was rectified from 20 April 1999, i e in effect, for 1998–99 Class 1A onwards, by the Social Security (Contributions) Amendment (No 3) Regulations 1999 (SI 1999 No 975). However, interest and penalty charges arise from the due date for payment, e g 19 July 1999 for 1998–99 Class 1A NIC, whereas failure to pay will not, using the P14/P35 mechanism, attract interest until 19 April 2000 nor require the return to be rendered until 19 May 2000. This anomaly disappeared from 6 April 2000 as the former 'alternative payment method' formed the basis of the current Class 1A return structure – now using Forms P11D and P11D(b).

Class 4 contributions

5.27 In the case of return periods commencing on and after 1 April 2008 where the return is lodged on and after 1 April 2009 the new scheme of penalties applies under Finance Act 2007, Sch 24.

5.28 The new penalties will be determined by reference to the amount of tax/NIC understated, the nature of the behaviour that gives rise to the understatement and the extent of disclosure made by the 'taxpayer'.

5.29 The penalty will be zero for mistakes made despite 'reasonable care' having been taken, 0–30% where there has been failure to take reasonable care (with a minimum of 15% where disclosure was prompted by HMRC), 20–70% where there has been deliberate understatement (with a minimum of 35% where disclosure was prompted by HMRC) and 30–100% where there has been deliberate understatement with concealment (with a minimum of 50% where disclosure was prompted by HMRC).

5.30 In some cases penalties may be suspended for up to two years, e g if the error is due to systems or record-keeping failure.

5.31 *National Insurance: fines, penalties and appeals*

5.31 Where an inaccuracy does not result in tax/NIC being lost altogether but being declared in a later period than it should have been, the penalty is 5% for each year of delay.

5.32 There is a right of appeal against the imposition and amount of a penalty. The onus of proof is on HMRC.

5.33 In the case of older return periods, the penalty provisions of TMA 1970, Part X apply to Class 4 contributions which are payable by way of assessment made in accordance with income tax legislation (SSCBA 1992, s 16).

INTEREST

Overdue contributions

5.34 With effect from 1992–93, interest applies automatically to payments of PAYE and subcontractors' deductions outstanding at 19 April after the end of the tax year. Before this, and only from April 1988, interest arose in cases where tax, which the employer had failed to deduct under PAYE, was formally determined under what was then the Income Tax (Employments) Regulations 1993, reg 49. A similar charge did not apply for NIC purposes prior to 1992–93.

5.35 For 1992–93 and subsequent years, interest is automatically charged on primary and secondary Class 1 contributions paid more than 14 days after the end of the year in respect of which the contributions were due, eg 19 April 2011 for 2010–11 Class 1 contributions, or paid more than 17 days after the end of the year if payment is made electronically for 2004–05 onwards (SI 2001 No 1004, Sch 4, para 17). The same also applies to Class 1B contributions not paid by the due date.

5.36 Interest on late-paid Class 1A contributions is automatically charged for 1991–92 and subsequent years. In respect of 2000–01 onwards, interest on overdue Class 1A runs from the due date (normally 19 July) (SI 2001 No 1004, reg 76). The due day is extended by three days if payment in respect of 2004–05 onwards is made electronically (SI 2001 No 1004, reg 71).

5.37 Until 6 April 2000 interest on overdue Class 1A contributions accrued from the fourteenth day after the end of the year in which it was due to be paid, eg 19 April 1999 for 1997–98 Class 1A contributions (former SI 1979 No 591 Sch 1, reg 28B).

5.38 If, however, Class 1A contributions were paid by the 'Alternative Payment Method' (APM) up to 1999–2000 interest will run from the due date itself following a change in legislation effective from 20 April 1999, eg under the APM, interest for 1998–99 contributions will accrue from 20 July 1999. In earlier years, no interest could be charged under the APM.

5.39 In all cases, the rate of interest charged is the same as for late-paid income tax as set by FA 1989, s 178 (SSCBA 1992 Sch 1, para 6(3)).

Repaid contributions

5.40 With effect from 19 April 1993, Class 1, 1A and 1B contributions which are repaid after the 'relevant date' carry interest. The relevant date for 1999–2000 and subsequent years is:

- for Class 1 contributions, 14 days after the end of the tax year in respect of which the contribution is payable, for Class 1A contributions, 14 days after the end of the tax year in which the contribution is payable, for Class 1B contributions, 19 October after the end of the tax year to which the contribution relates; or
- if later, the date of payment,

and in the case of years up to and including 1998–99 the relevant date is:

- for contributions paid more than 12 months after the end of the year in respect of which the payment was made, the last day of the year in which it was paid; or
- in any other case, the last day of the year after the year in respect of which the contribution in question was paid

(SI 2001 No 1004, reg 77, Sch 4, para 18).

Repayment and remission of interest

5.41 Where an employer has paid interest on late-paid Class 1, Class 1A or Class 1B contributions which is subsequently found not to have been due, the interest will be repaid (SI 2001 No 1004, Sch 4, reg 19).

Interest will be remitted if the contribution in respect of which it was charged was paid late as a result of an official error on the part of HMRC or its predecessor bodies where the employer or his agent did not cause or materially contribute to the mistake or omission (SI 2001 No 1004, Sch 4, para 20).

Interest on Class 4 and 2 contributions

5.42 With effect from 19 April 1993, Class 4 contributions collected by assessment may attract an interest charge under TMA 1970, s 86. Prior to that date interest could only be charged in accordance with the former s 88, where an assessment was made for the purpose of making good to the Crown a loss of tax wholly or partly attributable to a failure or an error on the part of the taxpayer (SSCBA 1992, Sch 2, para 6).

5.43 The Social Security Act 1998 amends SSCBA 1992, Sch 2, para 6 so that references to TMA 1970, s 88 in that section are repealed (SSCBA 1992, Sch 2, para 6(1) as repealed by Social Security Act 1998, s 59).

5.44 Interest is not chargeable in respect of Class 2 contributions that are paid late, although a 'penalty rate' currently applies instead. This ensures that where payment is made later than one tax year after the end of the year to which the contributions relate they may be charged at the highest rate in force from the time payment was due to the time it was made (inclusive).

5.45 National Insurance: fines, penalties and appeals

APPEALS

5.45 Until April 1999 there was, in the Social Security Acts, no provision for appeals in connection with contribution matters and the appellate bodies which operate in connection with state benefits had no jurisdiction so far as the contribution side of the state scheme is concerned. Although, there was *effectively* an appeal procedure in connection with contributions it was not widely known or understood and entailed asking a 'question' of the Secretary of State for Social Security, who then determined the matter in a quasi-judicial capacity. A decision of the Secretary of State in favour of a contributor or employer could not be further appealed by the authorities, but an employer or contributor could appeal against a decision unsatisfactory to them although only to the High Court (and no further) and only on a point of law (see **5.93–5.98**).

5.46 However, with the transfer of the former Contributions Agency to the then Inland Revenue with effect from 1 April 1999 and the transfer of Contributions Policy functions from DSS to the Treasury from the same date, the opportunity was taken to modernise the appeals system, such as it was. It is now brought almost entirely into line with those procedures encountered in dealing with most other imposts for what HMRC are now responsible. This means that for exactly ten years National Insurance appeals were heard by the General and Special Commissioners but are now, from 1 April 2009, heard by the Tax Tribunal.

5.47 The fact that there remain some small differences, and the previous absence of a formal appeal system in relation to contributions, is explained by the fact that the Social Security Acts (unlike the Taxes Acts) make no provision for formal assessments of their levies – other than Class 4 contributions. The liability is either self-assessed at a fixed rate or employer-assessed by reference to earnings paid (e g Class 1 contributions) or to company cars, fuel and – from 6 April 2000 – other taxable benefits made available to employees (ie Class 1A contributions) or, from 6 April 1999, in respect of minor payments made to employees (ie Class 1B contributions).

5.48 Save for the Commissioners having been replaced by the Tax Tribunal, the current system has operated from 1 April 1999 and remains after the 2009 change still largely regulated by Social Security Contributions (Transfer of Functions, etc) Act 1999 (SSCTA 1999) and Social Security Contributions (Decisions and Appeals) Regulations 1999 (SI 1999 No 1027).

Decisions of officers of HMRC

5.49 Where a contributor or his employer is faced with a demand for payment that is considered to be wrong or excessive, the matter will first be considered informally. If the dispute cannot be resolved in this way, it will then be for an officer of HMRC to issue a formal 'decision' under SSCTA 1999, s 8.

5.50 The formal decision is then appealable in much the same way as an old-style tax assessment or an amendment to a self-assessment.

The subject matter of a decision

5.51 An officer may decide:

- whether a person is or was an earner and, if he is or was, in which category of earners he should be included;
- whether a person is or was employed in employed earner's employment for industrial injuries purposes (SSCBA 1992, Part V);
- whether a person is or was liable to pay any contributions of any class and the amount of the liability;
- whether a person is or was entitled to pay contributions, notwithstanding that there is no liability to pay, e g payment of voluntary contributions;
- whether contributions of a particular class have been paid for any period;
- on any issue in connection with statutory sick pay, statutory maternity pay, statutory paternity pay or statutory adoption pay;
- on matters concerning the issue or content of any notice under SSCBA 1992, s 121C (notices of company officer's personal liability for unpaid contributions);
- any issue arising under Jobseekers Act 1995, s 27 (back to work schemes for long-term unemployed);
- whether to give or withdraw approval for the transfer to the employee of the employer's Class 1 liability in respect of certain unapproved share options;
- whether a person is liable to a penalty and the amount;
- other issues as may be prescribed by regulations made by the Commissioners of HMRC.

(SSCTA 1999, s 8(1))

Decisions relating to the regional NIC Holiday that runs for new businesses set up from 22 June 2010 to 5 September 2013 inclusive are included within the above (National Insurance Contributions Act 2011, s 8(6)).

5.52 The third and fifth items above do not include decisions relating to Class 4 contributions which have, because they are invariably collected along with income tax, always been dealt with under tax appeal procedures (SSCTA 1999, s 8(2)).

5.53 The sixth item above does not extend to any decision as to the making of subordinate legislation since policy for statutory sick pay and statutory maternity pay remains with the Secretary of State for Work and Pensions (formerly the Secretary of State for Social Security), even though it is now administered by HMRC. Nor does it extend to any decision as to whether the liability to pay statutory sick pay, statutory maternity pay, statutory paternity pay or statutory adoption pay is that of HMRC or the employer. Likewise policy responsibility for statutory paternity pay and statutory adoption pay lies with the Secretary of State for Business, Enterprise and Regulatory Reform (SSCTA 1999, s 8(3)).

5.54 *National Insurance: fines, penalties and appeals*

5.54 With regard to the final item in the above list (**5.51**), further matters have been prescribed (with effect from 8 October 2002 except where stated) as follows:

- whether a notice should be given under SI 2001 No 1004, reg 3(2B) and if so the terms of such notice;
- whether a notice given under SI 2001 No 1004, reg 3(2B) should cease to have effect;
- whether a direction should be given under SI 2001 No 1004, reg 31 and if so the terms of the direction;
- whether the condition in SI 2001 No 1004, reg 50(2) is satisfied;
- whether late applications under SI 2001 No 1004, reg 52(8), reg 54(3) or reg 55(3) for the refund of (respectively) contributions generally, Class 1 contributions paid at the wrong rate, or Class 1A contributions should be admitted;
- whether, where a secondary contributor has failed to pay primary contributions that failure was with the consent or connivance of the primary contributor, as is mentioned in SI 2001 No 1004, reg 60;
- whether the condition in SI 2001 No 1004, reg 61(2) is satisfied;
- whether in the case of Class 2 contributions remaining unpaid at the due date, the reason for non-payment is the contributor's ignorance or error, and if so whether that is due to failure to exercise due care and diligence (SI 2001 No 1004, reg 65(2));
- whether the reason for non-payment of Class 3 within the prescribed period is the contributor's ignorance or error, and if so whether that is due to failure to exercise due care and diligence (SI 2001 No 1004, reg 65(3));
- whether the reason for non-payment of Class 3 within two years of the end of the year to which the contributions relate is the contributor's ignorance or error, and if so whether that is due to failure to exercise due care and diligence (SI 2001 No 1004, reg 65(4));
- whether a late application under SI 2001 No 1004, reg 110(3) for the return of a special Class 4 contribution should be admitted;
- whether a contribution (other than a Class 4 contribution) has been paid in error (SI 2001 No 1004, reg 52(1)(a));
- whether there has been a payment of contributions in excess of the amount specified in SI 2001 No 1004, reg 21 (SI 2001 No 1004, reg 52(1)(b));
- whether certain delays mentioned in the now superseded National Insurance (Contributions) Regulations 1969 are reasonable, etc;
- whether the delay in making payment of primary Class 1 contributions was neither with the consent nor connivance of the primary contributor (Social Security (Crediting and Treatment of Contributions, and National Insurance Numbers) Regulations 2001, reg 5);
- whether in the case of a contribution paid after the due date, the failure was due to ignorance or error and not failure to exercise due care and diligence (Social Security (Crediting and Treatment of Contributions, and National Insurance Numbers) Regulations 2001, reg 6);

- from 6 August 2007, whether the circumstances are such that the managed service company provisions apply.

5.55 The Board may make regulations with regard to the making of decisions and officers may direct that he shall have the assistance of an 'expert' where it appears that a question of fact requires special expertise (SSCTA 1999, s 9(1)(2)). 'Expert' means a person appearing to the officer of the Board to have knowledge or experience which would be relevant in determining the question of fact (SSCTA 1999, s 9(3)).

5.56 The Board may make regulations enabling decisions under s 8 to be varied or superseded (SSCTA 1999, s 10) and have done so.

5.57 A decision must be made to the best of the officer's information and belief and must state:

- the name of every person in respect of whom it is made, and
- the date from which it has effect, or
- the period for which it has effect

(Social Security Contributions (Decisions and Appeals) Regulations 1999, reg 3(1)).

5.58 An officer may entrust responsibility for completing procedures to some other officer, whether by means involving the use of a computer or not, including the responsibility for serving the notice on any person named in it (Social Security Contributions (Decisions and Appeals) Regulations 1999, reg 3(2)).

Giving notice of the decision

5.59 Notice of a decision must be given to every person named in it or, in the case of a decision relating to entitlement to statutory sick pay, statutory maternity pay, statutory paternity pay or statutory adoption pay to the employee and employer concerned (Social Security Contributions (Decisions and Appeals) Regulations 1999, reg 4(1)).

5.60 In the case of Class 1 contributions the notice will name the employer and each affected employee. Where the number of employees exceeds six, HMRC will normally seek to agree a representative sample of employees with the employer or the agent and will name only those selected employees (as well as the employer) in the notice. This is an extra-statutory arrangement, there being no legal basis for the selection of six employees as the number beyond which not to look at each case individually.

5.61 In *Westek v HMRC Comrs* (Sp C 629), a notice of decision sent to the employer had merely referred to 'earnings of employees' without naming the employees in question. W, inter alia, challenged the validity of the notices. The Special Commissioner upheld the view of HMRC that the decisions had been made under Social Security Contributions (Transfer of Functions, etc) Act 1999, s 8(1)(c) and it was only the employer that in the first instance was liable to pay both the primary and the secondary contributions. Accordingly, the notice needed only to name, as it did, the employer and it was therefore only the

5.61 *National Insurance: fines, penalties and appeals*

employer who had to be sent a copy of the decision notice (Social Security Contributions (Decisions and Appeals) Regs 1999, reg 4). In 1999 the then Inland Revenue had stated that the affected employees would always be named in notices of decision. Following Sp C 629 in 2007 it must therefore be expected that this policy will no longer be followed consistently.

5.62 Where the dispute relates to Class 1A contributions only the employer is affected as no employee's contribution arises. However, whilst there is therefore no obligation on the part of HMRC to name employees in the notice, they will usually do so where the decision concerns the provision of particular benefits. Similar procedures apply, as far as possible, in the case of disputed Class 1B liability.

5.63 In the case of Class 2, Class 3 or Class 4 decisions (the latter relating only to cases where Class 4 is not collected through the self-assessment tax return, eg deferment cases), there will invariably be only one person named in the notice.

5.64 The notice must state the date on which it is issued and may be served by post addressed to any person at his usual or last known place of residence or his place of business or employment. Notice to a company may be addressed to its registered office or its principal place of business (Social Security Contributions (Decisions and Appeals) Regulations 1999, reg 4(2)(3)).

5.65 A decision may be varied by an officer if he has reason to believe that it was incorrect at the time it was made. Notice of such variation must be given to the same persons and in the same manner as the original decision (Social Security Contributions (Decisions and Appeals) Regulations 1999, reg 5(1)(2)).

5.66 If a decision is under appeal, it may be varied at any time before the Tax Tribunal determines the appeal (Social Security Contributions (Decisions and Appeals) Regulations 1999, reg 5(4)).

5.67 A decision may be made superseding an earlier decision, including a varied decision, which has become inappropriate *for any reason*. A superseding decision will have effect from the date of the change in circumstances which rendered the previous decision (or varied decision) inappropriate. The previous decision ceases to have effect immediately the superseding decision comes into effect (Social Security Contributions (Decisions and Appeals) Regulations 1999, reg 6(1)(2)).

5.68 Decisions are issued on Form DAA1 (A) which tells the recipient to let their professional advisor or agent, if they have one, see it. Copies will be issued direct to agents, if acting. Where copies are sent to more than one person, the notes on the face of the notice will be varied on each copy to reflect the differing effects of the decision on different categories of people affected, eg where copies are sent to employers and one or more employees. The notice of decision also includes a payslip for making payment of the National Insurance contributions in question and will be sent with a letter of explanation which will, in practice, usually be a summary of what has been established in previous correspondence. A guide, DAA2 'A Guide to Your Notice of Decision' will also be sent to every recipient.

Appeals against officer's decisions

5.69 Any person named in a notice of decision has the right of appeal to the Tax Tribunal. The same right also extends to personal liability notices issued to company officers in respect of company contribution debts (SSCTA 1999, s 11(1), (2), (4); SSAA 1992, s 121D, as inserted by Social Security Act 1998, s 64).

Manner of making an appeal

5.70 Once a notice of decision has been issued any person named in it can appeal to HM Revenue and Customs with or without immediately also notifying the Tax Tribunal of the appeal. HMRC may offer a formal internal review but, the appellant may request a review even if not offered. If the review does not change the decision, then the appeal can still be notified to the Tribunal at that stage.

5.71 An appeal must be made in writing to HMRC within 30 days after the date on which the notice of decision was issued or the review decision notified. The Guide DAA2, sent with every notice of decision, contains a tear-off appeal form (DAA3) which may be used, but an appeal made in any format – provided it is in writing and made within the specified 30 days – is legally valid (SSCTA 1999, s 12(1), (2)).

5.72 Whilst National Insurance law specifies no particular form, the Tax Tribunal does provide one (TaxApp1) for notifications of appeals to it at www.tribunals.gov.uk/tax/FormsGuidance.htm which it says 'can' be used to make an appeal. It may be that the appeal will proceed more smoothly if the form provided is in fact used. The form can also be obtained by phone on 08452 238080. Once completed it should be sent to Tribunals Service, Tax, 2nd Floor, 54 Hagley Road, Birmingham B16 8PE.

5.73 The notice of appeal must specify the grounds of appeal, but on hearing by the Tribunal it may allow additional grounds, not stated in the notice of appeal, to be put forward if satisfied that the omission was neither wilful nor unreasonable (SSCTA 1999, s 12(3)).

5.74 The Board have the power to make regulations, with the concurrence of the Lord Chancellor and the Lord Advocate, in respect of contributions, statutory sick pay, statutory maternity pay, statutory paternity pay and statutory adoption pay appeals and may also make regulations regarding matters arising pending a decision of an officer under s 8, pending the determination by the tax tribunal, out of the variation of a decision or out of the superseding of a decision (SSCTA 1999, ss 13, 14).

Place of hearing of appeal

5.75 The Tribunals Service has a network of 130 hearing centres across the country and the facility for additional private hirings.

Late appeals

5.76   Late appeals may be admitted if the officer of the Board is satisfied that there was a reasonable excuse for not bringing the appeal within the normal time limit, provided that application is made without undue delay thereafter (Social Security Contributions (Decisions and Appeals) Regulations 1999, reg 9, applying the provisions of TMA 1970, s 49).

If HMRC declines a late appeal (which it may do if there is no 'reasonable excuse'), the potential appellant may apply to the Tribunal to make a late appeal and the Tribunal may consider factors beyond those that HMRC is required to consider.

Determination by Tax Tribunal

5.77   The Tribunal may decide at the hearing that the decision shall be varied in any manner or that it shall stand good. The Tribunal may examine the appellant on oath or affirmation or take other evidence (Social Security Contributions (Decisions and Appeals) Regulations 1999, reg 10).

Settling appeals by agreement

5.78   Appellants may, before an appeal is heard by the Tax Tribunal, come to an agreement with an officer that the decision under appeal should be treated as:

- upheld without variation, or
- varied in a particular manner, or
- superseded by a further decision,

and the same consequences will then ensue as would have ensued if the officer had made a decision in the same terms as that under appeal, had varied the decision or made a superseding decision, as the case may be. In any of these circumstances, all appeals against the original decision shall lapse and notice of the agreement must be given by the officer to all persons named in the decision who did not appeal against it (Social Security Contributions (Decisions and Appeals) Regulations 1999, reg 11(1), (2), (3)).

5.79   If such an agreement is not made in writing it is necessary for the officer to confirm by written notice to every appellant the fact that an agreement was come to and details of its terms (Social Security Contributions (Decisions and Appeals) Regulations 1999, reg 11(4)).

5.80   An appellant may, before an appeal is heard by the Tax Tribunal, notify the officer and every other person named in the decision, either orally or in writing, that he does not wish to proceed with the appeal. Unless, within 30 days, any person to whom that notice is given indicates that he is unwilling that the appeal should be treated as withdrawn then the appellant, the officer and every person named in the decision are treated as having reached an agreement that the decision should be upheld without variation (Social Security Contributions (Decisions and Appeals) Regulations 1999, reg 11(5)).

5.81 Where an appeal is to be settled by agreement in any manner mentioned above, the agreement may be made with any person acting on behalf of an appellant or any other person named in the decision and notices may be validly given to such persons (Social Security Contributions (Decisions and Appeals) Regulations 1999, reg 11(6)).

Dissatisfaction with Tribunal's determination

5.82 If HM Revenue and Customs, the appellant or another party to the proceedings think that the Tribunal's decision is wrong on a point of law, then an appeal may be made to the Upper Tribunal.

5.83 At this stage, the contributions in dispute must, if that is not already the case, be paid. If the appellant is successful, the amount will be repaid. If the hearing is with regard to statutory sick pay, statutory maternity pay, statutory paternity pay or statutory adoption pay, employers do not have to pay statutory sick pay, statutory maternity pay, statutory paternity pay or statutory adoption pay until the courts have finally settled the appeal.

5.84 The First-tier Tribunal may initially review its own decision on receipt of an application of appeal to the Upper Tribunal (TPC, r 41; Tribunals, Courts and Enforcement Act 2007, s 9). A refusal of appeal by the First-tier Tribunal must be accompanied by an explanation why and an option to have the rejection reviewed by the Upper Tribunal. Appeals against the Upper Tribunal decisions will be heard by the Court of Appeal in England and Wales or by the Court of Sessions in Scotland.

5.85 Upper Tribunal hearings will generally be held in London, Manchester, Birmingham, Belfast or Edinburgh.

Decisions under the Pension Schemes Act 1993 and in respect of the award of credits, etc

5.86 An officer is to make decisions in relation to questions referred to in Pension Schemes Act 1993, s 170(1) (SSCTA 1999, s 16(1)).

5.87 A dissatisfied party will not, however, appeal to the Tax Tribunal but has the right of appeal to the Social Entitlement Chamber of the Tribunals Service (which deals with State benefit disputes) (Social Security Act 1998, s 12, as amended by SSCTA 1999, s 16(6)).

5.88 The same procedure applies in the case of appeals against decisions of officers concerning the award of National Insurance credits, Carers' credits or (until replaced in 2010 by Carers' credits) Home Responsibilities Protection.

Class 4 appeals

5.89 Because Class 4 contributions are payable in accordance with assessments made under the Taxes Acts, the provisions of Taxes Management Act 1970, Pt V have always applied with necessary modifications in relation to such contributions as they apply in relation to income tax and this continues to be the case after 31 March 1999 (SSCBA 1992, s 15(1), (2), (5), Sch 8). The effect of this is that an appeal against any Class 4 assessment must be made in writing within 30 days of the issue of the notice of assessment or an unfavourable HMRC internal review decision and must state the grounds on which it is based. An appeal may be brought out of time if there is a reasonable excuse for the delay. An appeal against the decision of the Tax Tribunal may be made in the same manner as described in **5.82**.

5.90 Under 'self-assessment' from 6 April 1996, there will be few assessments issued now. However, in the case of a dispute, whether for income tax, Class 4 contributions or both, it will be necessary for HMRC, exceptionally, to issue an assessment in order to enable an appeal to be made by the taxpayer/contributor.

5.91 The only questions concerning Class 4 contributions which are excluded from this jurisdiction are:

- whether by regulations made under SSCBA 1992, s 17(1) a person is excepted from Class 4 liability or his liability is deferred; and/or
- whether he is liable for Class 4 contributions that may be collected directly by the NICO under SSCBA 1992, ss 17(3)–(6), 18.

5.92 These two matters previously fell within the Secretary of State's remit. However, from 1 April 1999, they become matters for a decision of an officer of the Board under SSCTA 1999, s 8 and then, only by those means, will the matter fall to be put before the Tax Tribunal.

Questions put to the Secretary of State before 1 April 1999

5.93 Where a person had made an application before 1 April 1999 for a question to be determined by what was then the Secretary of State for Social Security (renamed Secretary of State for Work and Pensions in summer 2001) but, as at that date, the question had not been determined, the matter is thereafter treated as being one for a decision of an officer of HMRC (Social Security Contributions (Decisions and Appeals) Regulations 1999, reg 4).

5.94 It will now therefore be necessary in such cases for a formal decision to be issued under SSCTA 1999, s 8 so that an appeal may then be made, within 30 days.

5.95 The then Inland Revenue issued, in May 1999, a temporary extra-statutory concession as regards interest on amounts of National Insurance contributions disputed by employers and others before 1 April 1999. Under the new arrangements, the disputed NIC and the interest on it need not currently be paid while an appeal is pending (although the Transfer Act does enable regulations to be introduced to require payment before an appeal may be heard). But, if the liability is confirmed, interest runs under the usual rules, e g for Class 1, from 14 days after the end of the tax year to which the contributions relate.

5.96 The Secretary of State's Question procedure provided that interest did not accrue from, broadly, the time the dispute arose and the time the question 'was disposed of'. Where an application had been submitted before 1 April 1999 for a determination by the Secretary of State but no determination had been made by that time, then interest will, under the extra-statutory concession, continue to be remitted until 1 August 1999 or the date the s 8 decision is made – whichever is the later. If, before 1 April 1999, a contributor had advised the Contributions Agency that they disputed liability, but it had been agreed that no formal application would be made pending the outcome of a lead case, then interest will also be remitted until the later of 1 August 1999 and a s 8 decision on the individual case (not the lead case). Where a determination was made before 1 April 1999, but a Statement of Grounds (needed before making an appeal to the High Court) was requested but not received until after that date, then interest will be remitted until the later of 1 August 1999 or 14 days after the issue of the Statement of Grounds.

5.97 The former regulation 28D, which provided for the 'freezing' of interest under the pre-1 April regime has now been largely repealed, but the amended provision continues to provide for the remission of interest in cases of official error (Inland Revenue Press Release 100/133, 9 July 1999) (SI 2001 No 1004, Sch 4, para 20).

Publication of decisions

5.98 SI 1986 No 2218, reg 16(1) gave the Secretary of State the authority to publish decisions 'in such manner as he thinks fit'. A decision is specific to an individual's contribution position and, while it was binding on the CA, Benefits Agency, Social Security Commissioners, social security appeals tribunals and the courts, in respect of the person (or persons) named in the decision, it had no wider application. Between 1950 and 1958 'Selected Decisions of the Minister on Questions of Classification and Insurability' were published but are now out of print. Subsequently, the Secretary of State, for reasons of cost and confidentiality, chose not to publish them.

5.99 As with other types of cases, National Insurance appeals heard by the Special Commissioners were published – anonymised where appropriate – and this continues to be the case under the new Tax Tribunal.

Chapter 6

NIC investigation trigger points

Peter Arrowsmith FCA

National Insurance Consultant

INTRODUCTION

6.01 Over a number of years employer compliance officers have adopted a much higher profile and there is clear evidence that considerably more thought is going into deciding which employers will be selected for a visit or investigation. In very simple terms HM Revenue and Customs (HMRC) is making the best use of the resources it has for visiting duties and it is clearly seeking value for money. To help it achieve this aim it has sought help from accountancy firms and management consultants and, from the way in which it now conducts investigations, that was clearly money well spent. In addition, computer-based risk assessment is undertaken.

6.02 Following the merger between the Inland Revenue and Contributions Agency on 1 April 1999 inspections are now, almost without exception, made into both tax and NIC – including statutory sick pay (SSP), statutory maternity pay (SMP), statutory paternity pay (SPP) and statutory adoption pay (SAP) – at the same time in a single visit. Another significant factor is the attitude of the current government where the perfectly valid use of legislation to avoid or reduce National Insurance contributions is regarded as akin to evasion. With such a prevailing attitude many employers are likely to suffer an investigation which is not really justified. Such activity is now also affected by the application of the disclosure of tax-avoidance schemes regime to any National Insurance contributions avoidance schemes that are not already reportable due to a tax saving too – the extension to National Insurance took effect from 1 May 2007.

6.03 There is no disputing that a certain amount of check visiting is necessary. The amount of public money involved makes this mandatory, although the number of employers visited (out of a total of around 1.2 million, with over 1.5 million PAYE schemes between them) was only around 18,000 in

6.03 *NIC investigation trigger points*

a recent year. However, with substantial staff reductions ordered by the previous government now largely implemented and yet more ordered by the coalition government, the likelihood of visits must inevitably reduce. It can be expected, however, that penalties will be applied with ever-decreasing laxity and the review of HMRC's powers that took place during 2006 and 2007 also provided from April 2009 a more rigid regime to encourage compliance without the need for too much human intervention (see **Chapter 5**).

6.04 Before looking at what can trigger a National Insurance investigation, it is worthwhile looking at the overall National Insurance funding position.

National Insurance funding

6.05 National Insurance contributions (NIC) are no longer cheap – the abolition of the employer's upper earnings limit in October 1985, the extension of employee liability from April 2003 and a separate upper accrual point and much increased upper earnings limit from 6 April 2009 have seen to that (although the latter is slightly reduced – temporarily – from April 2011). In the 2011–12 tax year HMRC expects to collect around £98 billion in NIC. This amount vies with VAT as the second largest source of government revenue after income tax. Of the money collected, virtually 96% comes in the shape of Class 1 contributions, ie from employees and employers. Estimated social security expenditure for 2011–12 is around £82 billion on the contributory benefits alone. There are in addition other benefits such as income support, tax credits and child benefit which are funded from general taxation. Even allowing for the fact that National Insurance contributions also make a contribution to the running of the National Health Service (around £20.6 billion in 2011–12) the National Insurance Fund is still expected to show a deficit in 2011–12 of only £4 billion having until 2009–10 accumulated surpluses for many years. Even despite temporary deficits, the position will be reversed by the April 2011 contribution rate increases and the gradual equalisation of the female state pension age, such that by 5 April 2016 it is estimated that there will be a surplus of nearly £53 billion. Since the Government Actuary recommends a working balance of only one-sixth of annual benefit expenditure, this suggests that there is an excess surplus in the medium term of virtually £40 billion – equivalent to a basic rate income tax reduction of nearly 5% a year for the lifetime of a parliament. It would seem that National Insurance rates are higher than they need to be!

6.06 The UK social security system is based on a pay-as-you-go principle – the contributions now being paid are used to fund the current payment of social security benefits. The money collected should be enough to cover HMRC's administrative costs and to pay all contributory benefits in the year. For a few years from 1985 the Government Actuary consistently underestimated the NIC yield mainly because earnings grew at a faster rate than expected. The result was an embarrassing surplus in the National Insurance Fund and one government minister actually described the Fund as being awash with money. In contrast, the twenty-first century surplus in the Fund appears to be a matter of pride for the government rather than embarrassment.

6.07 Furthermore and subject only to the temporary effect of the financial crisis and subsequent recession, the current surplus continues to increase year on year despite the fact that for a number of years early in the millennium the retirement pension increased at a rate higher than inflation (and in some years higher than earnings). In addition, National Insurance rates for employers were reduced for a time (thus reducing the income into the National Insurance Fund) to counterbalance the imposition of the climate change levy and aggregates tax – yet the proceeds from these duties go to the Treasury, not the National Insurance Fund. But for these factors, the National Insurance Fund surplus would be even greater. Despite the current surplus, rates have further increased by 1% in April 2011.

6.08 The most far-reaching measure, however, has been a change in the attitude of what is now HMRC. Employer compliance officers will no longer waste time visiting back-street garages or corner shops to confirm that the basic NIC rules are being complied with, but will visit large employers and investigate all aspects of social security going back as far as six years (as well as tax, of course). They will pay particular attention to those employers who have used structured NIC mitigation schemes and to those with an international exposure because that is where significant contributions are thought, often correctly, to be underpaid.

REASONS FOR INVESTIGATIONS

6.09 With virtually the whole social security system to police, employer compliance officers could realistically pop up anywhere and look at anything. In reality, however, there are a few specific instances where they are likely to show most interest.

6.10 As regards National Insurance contributions and related matters, they include:

- errors in an employee's end of year return;
- a large employer;
- an employer with an international exposure;
- a national drive against a specific industry;
- an employer failing to reply to correspondence;
- a routine audit visit;
- a complaint from an employee;
- a local HMRC initiative, though becoming less common since regionalisation.

End-of-year returns

6.11 Every employee who earns an amount equal to the National Insurance lower earnings limit in any week in a tax year must have submitted at the end of the year a P14 on his behalf. This is so even though no actual contributions may be payable – if earnings are below the earnings thresholds – because it is earnings at or above the lower earnings limit that gives rise to benefit

6.11 NIC investigation trigger points

entitlement. That P14 is the only real contact the National Insurance Contributions and Employer Office (NIC&EO) of HMRC has with most employees and it is not surprising that the form is subjected to a number of checks both immediately upon electronic submission and then at Newcastle using various computer routines which have been developed over the years. The very first check at Newcastle is to ensure that there is enough information to match the contributions paid against an individual's record on the NPS (the National Insurance and PAYE System) computer system (previously called NIRS2). Does the National Insurance number match with the identity details held for that number?

6.12 Where there is no match or a number is missing HMRC will attempt to trace the individual from the other information supplied. However, if it is a common name and no meaningful date of birth or address is supplied on the P14, then there is little chance of HMRC making a successful trace and they would have no option but to come back and ask further questions of the employer who submitted the P14. If there are too many enquiries for a single employer then that may be enough to trigger some form of investigation on the grounds that if an employer cannot be bothered getting numbers correct he is probably making other errors. Obtaining the correct National Insurance number is no longer an onerous task.

6.13 The former Contributions Agency identified that they were spending an inordinate amount of time sorting out missing numbers and so they introduced procedures to help employers. This includes extra information on form P46, the introduction of a separate enquiry form which can be sent to NIC&EO and the ability to contact NIC&EO by telephone. These various measures reduce the number of enquiries coming from Newcastle and employers should supply the additional information where it is easy to do so.

6.14 Once sufficient identity details have been established, then HMRC has two separate types of checks. The first concerns matching the contributions paid against those expected. For instance if contracted-out contributions have been paid and HMRC has no record of an individual joining a company pension scheme then questions will be asked. The same happens in reverse where they are expecting contracted-out, but they receive full-rate contributions. When did the individual leave the pension plan and how have his pension rights been secured are obvious questions that need to be answered.

6.15 It is this type of checking, called compatibility checking, which raises queries regarding individuals who have paid a lower rate of contribution and there is no evidence to support that level of contribution. Examples will include married women paying the reduced rate of contribution where no valid certificate is held, individuals paying the pensioners' rate when they have not yet reached state pension age and so on. Millions of enquiries are raised each year on this front and thousands of man hours are wasted by the authorities. They are showing less and less patience with employers who make regular errors and to bring these employers into line a check visit of some sort is likely to be made.

6.16 The second type of checking is called ratio checking and this is a consideration of the financial aspects of the payments. For example, has the employer paid roughly 12–12.5% of the taxable pay (if for 2010–11 or an earlier year) by way of employer NIC? Does the employer portion come out as more than the employee share? Do the total contributions exceed the employee contribution liability? If not there is likely to be something wrong. Has SSP been paid beyond a certain acceptable level? A similar sort of check is carried out for SMP although here it is much more difficult because there is no maximum rate payable for the first six weeks. Where the SMP paid looks excessive, however, or exceeds a certain amount, NIC&EO may very well ask an employer compliance officer to check the validity of the figures. Among other issues he will want to satisfy himself that any bonus payment used to calculate the entitlement has been treated properly.

6.17 Other checks carried out at Newcastle include an arithmetical check on the amounts on the individual P14 forms to ensure that the total agrees with that shown on the summary form P35. The checks will also confirm that the correct year's rates and limits have been used along with confirmation that the appropriate contributions have been paid on earnings that exceed the employee upper limit. A number of checks will be automatically included where electronic filing is undertaken. Where the data is not satisfactory the return(s) will be rejected. If correct and valid data is not resubmitted in time and/or electronically, then standard penalties will be imposed.

Category X notations

6.18 One important area where employer compliance officers show an interest is in the area of Category X – the contribution category letter which signifies that no contributions are payable. This creates some difficulty for HMRC simply because they have no earnings or contributions on which to base their validation checks. The Newcastle computer is simply programmed to accept the validity of such entries, but it would be a bit of a nonsense for NIC&EO to accept these returns without question. It would only be a matter of time before unscrupulous employers made fraudulent use of the X notation. In the past checking has been restricted to a sample of returns every few years, but the additional contribution yield from those checks has encouraged the authorities to instigate an annual check and so employers can now expect to see a considerable amount of activity on this front.

6.19 Because of this increased activity, employers should be aware of when it is in order to use Category X. The following uses will be accepted by employer compliance officers although they may well investigate the matter before giving approval:

- The employee is under age 16 at the time the payment of earnings is made. Employers should ensure that they have a record of when the employee reaches 16 so that liability begins with the correct payment.
- The earnings are below the relevant earnings limit. Care needs to be taken to ensure that the earnings fall below the lower earnings limit in each earnings period. Unless a company director (or other employee in

6.19 *NIC investigation trigger points*

respect of whom an annual earnings period has been imposed by a directive) is involved it is wrong to look at the total earnings at the end of the year and compare the amount paid with the annual limits. Another common mistake is the assumption that if an employee is given a weekly or monthly payment which is equal to the appropriate lower earnings limit then no NIC entries are required. This is incorrect because benefit entitlement starts at the lower earnings limit itself rather than at a penny over it. This mistake is common where a spouse helps out in the family business and the wage/salary payments are made to make use of tax allowances.

- The only payment being made is a pension. Employer compliance officers are a bit wary of payments made in the form of pensions and are likely to want to satisfy themselves that the pension is genuine and not some other payment wrongly described. Special attention will also be paid where there are contributions into or benefits from unapproved pension arrangements.
- The employee is working temporarily in the UK and is paying contributions to another country's social security scheme. All will be well if the employee has come from a treaty or EC/EEA country and holds the appropriate certificate of coverage. Employers should check every so often to ensure that certificates have not expired and that the employment details quoted on the certificate have not changed in any material way.
- The employee has been sent from a non-treaty country by his overseas employer to work temporarily in the UK. In such instances there is no contribution liability for the first 52 complete calendar weeks in the UK. To avoid difficulties employers should ensure that they have a workable system whereby they identify when the contribution liability begins.
- The employee has been sent to a treaty country and the appropriate certificate of coverage issued by the UK authorities has expired. If any earnings were still paid in the UK no contribution liability would arise.
- The employee is working abroad in a non-treaty country and has been out of the UK for more than 52 weeks.

6.20 Whilst the above circumstances are perfectly acceptable to HMRC, many employers continue to use Category X in other situations and so incur the wrath of an employer compliance officer when the matter finally comes up for investigation. The following are the more common examples of where employers incorrectly use Category X:

- no P14 entries are made where earnings are below the earnings threshold, even though they exceed the lower earnings limit;
- a non-working director, etc has some earnings in the form of fees or bonuses which reach or exceed the relevant limit;
- an employee from a non-treaty country has been in the UK for more than the exempt first 52 weeks;
- an employee from a treaty country holds a certificate of coverage which is either invalid or out of date;
- the earnings are thought to be exempt from NIC liability, eg paid via some avoidance scheme which is flawed. This is an area almost certain

to provoke an investigation because officials believe that few avoidance schemes now work on account of the many changes to the exemptions in the Contributions Regulations.

6.21 Employers should not be surprised to hear that when an employer compliance officer investigates matters and finds something amiss he will not restrict his actions to recovery of outstanding contributions to the year in question. In fact employer compliance officers are likely to try to collect arrears for as far back as the particular circumstances have existed. Since the merger in 1999, requests for more than six years' arrears are now almost unheard of, but should still be resisted where they occur. The time limit for NIC under the Limitation Act 1980 remains at six years and is not affected by the April 2010 changes to various tax time limits (including PAYE).

6.22 Although HMRC cannot be expected to issue any guidance on this matter, it would be reasonable for them to restrict the cases they select for investigation. There will always be times when the Category X notation is quite correct and allowance will have to be made for this. Employer compliance officers will not want to waste time investigating matters which are unlikely to throw up additional contributions. For instance, it is unlikely that employer compliance officers would want to look at cases where an employee is out of the UK or has been out of the country for part of the year. They are also unlikely to be very keen spending time looking at cases where the employee is dead or where it is likely that the payment could be some sort of occupational pension and the introduction of an internal age limit is probable with employer compliance officers not looking at cases where the employee is, say, 55 or over. A P14 with Category X contributions shown along with some other category of contributions would also be less likely to be examined on the reasoning that if an employer has shown at least one category letter in addition to Category X then he would seem to know what he is doing.

6.23 Investigation of Category X cases now features strongly in an employer compliance officer's regular routine work and any irregularities found in this area may well provoke a more detailed investigation.

Complaints from employees

6.24 From time to time complaints are received from employees alleging that:

- contributions are being deducted but not sent on to HMRC;
- too much is being deducted as employee contributions;
- the employee has to pay the employer's share;
- the individual is being made to work on a self-employed basis;
- the individual is not being paid the National Minimum Wage (NMW).

6.25 Whilst a single complaint will not be ignored it may not generate any activity other than a phone call or a letter to the employer, but it is reasonable to assume that a series of complaints will result in some sort of investigation. Such matters should never be taken lightly and steps should be taken to allay employee fears. Indeed, HMRC now actively solicits calls from 'people who

6.25 *NIC investigation trigger points*

have information relating to businesses or individuals that are not paying tax and/or National Insurance' on the Tax Evasion Hotline 0800 788 887 or online at www.hmrc.gov.uk/tax-evasion/

6.26 Separate staff in HMRC deal with all NMW matters. However, these employees are now allowed freely to exchange information with colleagues in other sections of the organisation.

Regional initiatives

6.27 It is entirely up to regional HMRC managers to decide whether they want to set up any local investigations. For example, a specific industry may be based in a particular area and bad habits creep in particularly where one employer obtains a commercial advantage and others follow. It is not uncommon for employer compliance officers to be sent in to tidy up matters. It is also quite common for personal prejudices to creep in and perhaps public houses, market traders and mini-cab drivers are singled out for investigation. More often than not the purpose behind a local initiative is to check that employees at a specific location are not working and claiming benefits at the same time. If employees at a particular location are prone to defraud the Department for Work and Pensions (DWP), then some thought will be given to whether the employer has been in collusion with the employee.

National programme

6.28 It has long been recognised that employers with operations at many locations create problems for employer compliance officers. At one time, employer compliance officers usually had to remain in their specific geographical area and so the larger employers often slipped through the net. Nowadays teams of employer compliance officers from the Large Business Service will assume responsibility for visiting all the branches irrespective of where they are located.

6.29 Specific industries or employment groups will sometimes be targeted for some form of investigation and, when that happens, control will be exercised from some central point to ensure continuity of action and equity of treatment.

Routine visits

6.30 Employer compliance officers have a theoretical and underlying objective to visit every employer via a five-year rolling programme but, given the more sophisticated targeting arrangements now in place along with the quest for additional contributions combined with significant staff reductions, this programme has inevitably fallen by the wayside and will no doubt continue to do so. Employer compliance officers, however, will still be responsible for policing their own geographical area and can decide to make a visit whenever they deem it to be necessary. A surprise visit especially where the findings are publicised will often have the result of making many others fall into line and so the value of such visits should never be underestimated and equally, small employers should never assume that they are exempt from investigation.

Failing to reply to correspondence

6.31 Most of the sections that make up HMRC will have to write to employers from time to time. The most common reason for them getting in touch is that their records are not complete enough to allow a benefit claim to be decided (HMRC at NIC&EO operates the NPS (National Insurance and PAYE System) computer – formerly known as NIRS2 – on behalf of both itself and DWP). Because a benefit claim is involved there is a fair degree of urgency, and if there is a delay in replying the papers are likely to be referred to an employer compliance officer to visit and collect what is needed. Such visits might then not be restricted to collecting purely what is needed, and a full check of the other National Insurance and perhaps tax issues may well be carried out. To avoid such an investigation is simple – reply quickly, but if that is not possible then tell the writer accordingly and indicate when a reply will be sent.

Large employers

6.32 As already mentioned above, large employers were historically left well alone simply because of the effort needed to carry out an investigation coupled with the fact that a number of different locations may be involved. The former Contributions Agency worked out that the bigger the employer the bigger the potential yield and so matters changed. Special teams of inspectors began to work together to investigate these larger employers. This approach has continued since the 1999 merger, these special teams being subsumed at first into what was the Large Business Office and, since the 2005 merger with the former HM Customs and Excise, has now become the Large Business Service dealing with all indirect taxes as well. The name of the game is additional contributions and as long as they are likely to be collected an investigation will continue. A large employer is generally one who has at least 1,000 employees either at a single location or spread all over the country. The employer compliance officers looking after the larger employers also have some responsibility for investigating the many structured National Insurance contribution avoidance schemes, irrespective of the size of the employer.

Employers with an international exposure

6.33 HMRC believes that employers who send employees abroad are significantly underpaying their National Insurance contributions and so in-depth investigations are likely to be carried out again by employer compliance officers from the Large Business Service. It is usually a simple task to identify the relevant employers because (in the case of many countries) the employer needs to hold a certificate confirming the contribution position and they are only issued by a central point at NIC&EO in Newcastle.

6.34 Employer compliance officers will want to satisfy themselves that where UK certificates are held contributions have been paid on the full

6.34 *NIC investigation trigger points*

remuneration package, with particular emphasis placed on the various allowances linked to employment abroad, payments made at the foreign location and the local income tax position.

6.35 In summer 2003, a revised approach to handling enquiries in relation to inbound expatriates was outlined. HMRC recognises that enquiries are often easier if it has established a working relationship with the relevant in-house tax department or professional advisers. Given the complex issues that are usually involved, there will be situations where the apparent Exchequer risk means that HMRC may need to pursue enquiries that will have substantial compliance costs for the employer. They recognise, however, that:

- such enquiries often relate to individuals not familiar with the UK tax and NIC system;
- directors and employees on tax-neutralised packages can sometimes fail to understand the need for the UK tax authorities to make detailed enquiries into their financial affairs;
- there can be considerable compliance costs in retrieving documentation, especially from overseas.

6.36 The former Inland Revenue stated that it 'will be aware of these factors when handling ... enquiries', and that these will increasingly be undertaken by specialist units. Such units will be able to develop greater expertise. However, some such enquiries will still be undertaken outside the specialist units. Where this is so, the section concerned may be Special Compliance Investigations (SCI). SCI will generally only undertake enquiries in relation to inward expatriates where there are additional features (such as suspected serious fraud, 'novel' avoidance or where SCI has a wider main interest). Both local area and also Large Business Service employer compliance teams will continue to carry out reviews of large employers and refer expatriate issues to the specialist units. The former may refer aspects relating to expatriates to specialist offices, such as the Centre for Non Residents (eg on residence and domicile issues).

Unlucky

6.37 Some employers may not have been selected for a visit but, nevertheless, an employer compliance officer appears. A good example of this happening is where it starts to rain and the employer compliance officer goes through the first doorway he sees. For this reason alone there is no room for complacency and all employers should keep in mind that a knock could come to their door at any time.

CONCLUSION

6.38 Despite the potential for up to 70,000 visits expected per year, in a recent year only 18,000 visits were conducted. Whether this number might yet revert to former levels remains to be seen but either way the arithmetic shows that there is less than a 1 in 20 chance of any employer suffering an investigation and considerably less than that if staff resources remain constrained. These numbers, however, are not the real story and given that the smaller employers will generally be ignored the odds move quickly against larger employers.

6.39 Little can be done to avoid an investigation if an employer is deemed to be large, although it will usually be possible to delay the event. What employers should aim to do is keep a low profile by ensuring that their end-of-year returns are as complete and accurate as possible and that any enquiries from the authorities are dealt with as quickly as possible.

Chapter 7

Criminal investigations in relation to direct tax

Andrew S Watt, MAE

BACKGROUND

7.01 Writing in his Association's journal in 1924 an Inspector of Taxes observed:

> 'The five or six years ending with 1920/21 will probably go down in our fiscal history as a period of maximum fraud and evasion. The weight of the tax burden in those years increased the temptation, the unavoidable relaxation of vigilance on the part of Inspectors and accountants under war conditions multiplied the opportunities, and as regards the methods of fraud the prevalence of abundant profits not needed as additional working capital, and therefore capable of being conveniently hidden away in secret hoards, greatly facilitated the practice of omitting transactions from trading books.'

It was in this climate that the Enquiry Branch – which became the Revenue's elite investigation unit – was set up to combat the evasion of excess profits duty which had been imposed to help fund the nation's efforts in the 1914–18 war.

7.02 Seventy years later, the realisation that tax evasion was still rife despite the fact that rates of direct taxation were, and still are, at almost unprecedentedly low rates, persuaded the then Board of Inland Revenue (the Board) to carry out a major reconstruction of its head office investigative effort, the main focus of which effort had previously been the Enquiry Branch, Special Office and the Board's Investigation Office [BIO]. This process of change has continued following the merger of the Inland Revenue with HM Customs & Excise in 2005 to create HM Revenue & Customs (HMRC).

INVESTIGATION STATISTICS

7.03 Published statistics suggest that the scale of tax evasion has continued apparently unabated. The following table shows the yield from the Revenue's

7.03 *Criminal investigations in relation to direct tax*

efforts to counter fraud and evasion as reported in the Board's annual reports. The yield from the Large Business Offices is surprising given that the offices deal with the tax affairs of some of the country's most prestigious businesses from which one might reasonably have expected a higher standard of compliance.

Results of work tackling non compliance (£m)

Summary of additional liability	2005–06	2006–07	2007–08	2008–09
Local Compliance	3,314	4,486	4,299	5,059
Large Business Service	3,581	3,917	4,964	4,904
Specialist Investigations			1,166	1,285
Business International	65	91	152	115
Stamps	6	11	5	25
Charity Assets and Residency	385	254	663	687
	7,351	**8,759**	**11,249**	**12,075**

7.04 It can, however, be seen from the criminal proceedings statistics that despite the widespread evidence of serious fraud, the rate at which HMRC have initiated prosecutions for false business accounts and tax returns, PAYE and subcontractor frauds has actually declined over recent years. With a view to speeding up the criminal investigation process, the Government gave the Revenue the power to require the production of documents under the authority of an order from a circuit judge (in England and Wales) (TMA 1970, s 20BA, see paragraph **7.25**). Furthermore, following the report by Lord Grabiner QC entitled *The Informal Economy* published in March 2000, the Government introduced a new statutory offence of evading income tax. This is contained in FA 2000, s 144 which came into force on 1 January 2001. The new offence may be tried either summarily in the magistrates' court or on indictment in the Crown Court (and in the appropriate courts in Scotland and Northern Ireland). The new power was intended to facilitate joint prosecutions of those who defraud the Benefits Agency and the Inland Revenue at the same time, say for example, where wages are paid to employees 'cash in hand' to avoid income tax deductions and then suppressed in claims to income-related benefits. There were 193 successful prosecutions in 2005 of individuals who had infringed the Working Family Tax Credit provisions.

Criminal investigations in relation to direct tax **7.04**

However, many will question whether this is the most appropriate use of HMRC investigative resources. The conclusions contained in the report of the House of Commons Committee of Public Accounts in December 2003 were particularly damning and are still relevant today:

> 'The Revenue should focus their work on making a reasonable estimate of the tax gap [i.e. the difference between full and actual compliance with the tax rules] so that they can judge the effort needed for a given reduction in losses.
>
> They should set a date for completing and publishing their revised compliance strategy including an explicit strategy for preventing, detecting, investigating and deterring fraud, and the performance measures by which they assess achievement.
>
> The low number of fraud investigations and prosecutions is not commensurate with the potential sums at stake in lost revenue ... Investigation work on tax fraud appears to have reduced as work on tax credit fraud has increased, despite additional resources being provided.
>
> To date the results of work aimed at using the new offence of evading income tax, which is particularly relevant in tackling fraud in the shadow economy, have been limited.
>
> More prosecutions should also bring opportunities to make greater use of the confiscation and restraint powers to deprive fraudsters of the wider proceeds of their crime.
>
> The Revenue should also publicise their awareness of new forms of fraud and evasion schemes, as a deterrent to further use, ... drawing on the experience of their overseas counterparts such as the US Internal Revenue Service.'

The Revenue and Customs Prosecutions Office (RCPO) was merged with the Crown Prosecution Service (CPS) on 1 January 2010. The Central Fraud Group within the CPS continues to prosecute cases in England and Wales investigated by Her Majesty's Revenue and Customs (HMRC) and provides a specialist tax and revenue prosecution service, together with expertise in the prosecution of arms dealing and sanctions violations.

Statistics relate to convictions for tax offences for the period April 2008 to the end of March 2010 and these are set out in the table below. They relate to prosecutions undertaken in England and Wales only since there are separate prosecuting authorities for Scotland and Northern Ireland from whom the same information has been requested but has not yet been received.

7.04 *Criminal investigations in relation to direct tax*

	2008–09			2009–10		
	Defendants	*Convictions*	*Conviction rate*	*Defendants*	*Convictions*	**Conviction Rate**
VAT (non-complex/ s 72(11) VATA)	90	77	85.6%	61	57	93.4%
VAT (complex/ MTIC)	22	20	90.9%	34	24	70.6%
Direct tax (non-complex/ Grabiner)	40	36	90.0%	16	14	87.5%
Direct tax (complex)	26	17	65.4%	14	11	78.6%
Tax Credits (non-complex)	71	68	95.8%	51	43	84.3%
Tax Credits (complex/ organised)	8	8	100.0%	16	13	81.3%

THE NEW REGIME

7.05 1 March 1995 became a landmark date in the history of the Revenue's efforts to counter serious tax fraud. On that date, the Enquiry Branch, Special Office and BIO ceased to exist as separate entities, thus completing the process of integration which had begun with the establishment of the Special Compliance Office (SCO) on 1 April 1992. The principal function of the BIO, until 1995, had been to police the proper operation of the subcontractor tax-deduction scheme in the construction industry and the PAYE system run by all employers. In the press release announcing the changes, the Revenue expressed the hope that they would 'improve operational efficiency and give greater opportunity for team working'.

7.06 At the same time as these structural changes were put into effect, the SCO published new codes of practice (COPs). The first (COP 8) set out the basis on which investigations other than those involving suspected serious fraud were to be dealt with. The other (COP 9) governed the conduct of investigations involving serious fraud where it was likely that a monetary settlement would be appropriate, ie the *Hansard* procedure. There was no Revenue code of practice governing the working of cases for prosecution. These were subject to the codes of practice promulgated in accordance with the Police and Criminal Evidence Act 1984, s 66.

Following the merger of the Inland Revenue (IR) and HM Customs and Excise (C&E) in April 2005 to form HM Revenue and Customs (HMRC), it became obvious the Departments had been investigating serious tax fraud in diametrically different ways. From April 2002, C&E had been conducting VAT civil investigations under their 'new approach' without invoking the Police and Criminal Evidence Act 1984 (PACE) procedures and with the threat of prosecution only where false declarations were made. Conversely, IR 'Hansard' Investigations had always carried the threat of prosecution for the original offence as well as for false disclosure. And, since December 2003, as a result of the decision in the Court of Appeal in *R v Gill and Gill* [2003] STC 1229, such investigations had been conducted in accordance with PACE procedures. Clearly, this difference in treatment was untenable given that VAT and direct tax investigators were working alongside each other. Accordingly, with effect from 1 September 2005, HMRC introduced a new Civil Investigation of Fraud (CIF) procedure. At the same time, SCO was re-branded as Special Civil Investigations (SCI) and a new chain of CIF offices was established in various locations around the UK, staffed in part by former SCI officers. It is important to note that once a CIF investigation has been launched the taxpayer receives a written guarantee that there can be no criminal prosecution in respect of the original offence(s). However, the threat of prosecution still remains for the making of false statements in the course of the investigation. SCI is now re-named Specialist Investigations (SI). Where the potential arrears exceed £10,000, cases are passed to the Evasion Referral Team which refers cases as appropriate to Criminal Division (see **7.12**), SI (tax at risk in excess of £500,000), CIF teams (tax at risk £75,000–£500,000), Cross Tax Evasion (tax at risk £75,000 or less).

7.07 Over the years, other Revenue head office investigative units have been set up to attack the hydra of serious tax fraud and avoidance. These include the Special Trades Investigation Unit and the Special Investigations Section. Both of these units still exist but are not part of the SCI structure, although they also apply the CIF procedure in some of their investigations.

Towards the middle of 2003, the Revenue launched the Offshore Arrangements Project. They acknowledged the legitimacy of many offshore arrangements, but claimed that there was evidence of their use as vehicles for avoidance and evasion. The launch document referred to the non-disclosure of beneficial shareholders and directors of offshore companies. It was said that companies in offshore centres controlled thousands of UK companies, whilst thousands more held minority shareholdings. In addition, a significant proportion of land and buildings in the UK was owned, or had been owned, by offshore companies.

As part of this initiative, the Revenue established a new Offshore Fraud Projects Group, as part of what was then SCO Liverpool. This team has begun to compile a database of UK residents with offshore bank accounts and British firms with offshore subsidiaries. Furthermore, enquiries were made of credit card companies using the power in TMA 1970, s 20(8A). This eventually culminated in HMRC serving notices on five major retail banks in the UK requiring them to provide details of customers – individual as well as corporate – with an address in the UK and a bank account offshore. In April 2007 HMRC launched the Offshore Disclosure Facility (ODF) which gave the opportunity for individuals and companies with undeclared offshore bank accounts to disclose the same and to pay the tax, interest and a 10% penalty. The time limit

7.07 *Criminal investigations in relation to direct tax*

for making such disclosures expired in November 2007 and HMRC had until 30 April 2008 either to accept or reject the disclosures as made. Approximately 400,000 pieces of information were received from the five banks and some 60,000 disclosures were made under the ODF of which about 40% were from customers of banks other than those which had received disclosure notices.

In 2009 HMRC moved against the customers of the next tier of 500 or so banks which have an offshore connection and which trade in the UK, by issuing information notices on the banks requiring details of UK customers with accounts in their offshore branches. In September 2009 HMRC launched the New Disclosure Opportunity (NDO) inviting those with undisclosed offshore assets to come forward. The NDO notification period ended on 12 March 2010 and without doubt the Criminal Investigation Directorate reviewed many of the cases reported by the banks in respect of which no disclosure was made either under the NDO or the ODF, but surprisingly there are no reports of prosecutions having ensued.

In August 2009 HMRC signed a Memorandum of Understanding with the Principality of Liechtenstein which established the Liechtenstein Disclosure Facility (LDF). This will ensure that by the time the amnesty ends on 31 March 2015 there should be no undeclared funds in Liechtenstein in the names of UK-resident individuals or entities. The most attractive feature of the LDF is that tax will have to be paid for only ten years rather than the statutory 20 years which HMRC is entitled to assess. And the LDF also allows UK residents with undeclared offshore accounts in another offshore jurisdiction, which were not opened via a UK bank branch or agency, to acquire an asset in Liechtenstein and take advantage of the LDF's favourable terms. Those participating in the LDF are guaranteed not to be investigated for tax fraud provided the undeclared funds arose solely from tax evasion and not from some other criminal activity.

In the summer of 2010 HMRC acquired, via their counterparts in France, data apparently stolen from the Geneva branch of an international bank. This led very quickly to a spate of CoP 9 investigations and two reported criminal investigations.

A disclosure initiative aimed at members of the medical profession – the Tax Health Plan (THP) – was announced in January 2010 and in March 2011 the Plumbers Tax Safe Plan (PTSP) was launched. In spite of its name the, PTSP is open to anyone who has underpaid tax and is a general amnesty in all but name.

PROSECUTION POLICY

7.08 The Board of Inland Revenue's approach to prosecution was clearly stated in a paper entitled 'Prosecution Policy' published in September 1980 in which it was said:

> 'In the main ... the Department deals with the tax evader not by prosecution but by money penalties graded according to the gravity of the offence ... criminal prosecution for tax offences is undertaken only in a small minority of ... the more serious cases of fraud.'

7.09 Underlying this policy of selectivity is a philosophy of deterrence. This was expressed in the same paper thus:

> '... to prosecute in some examples of all classes of tax fraud. This policy is essential because it is the possibility of prosecution which prevents the spread of tax fraud to unacceptable limits.'

This ethos is still reflected in HMRC's approach to criminal investigations.

7.10 The Board of Inland Revenue's report for the year to 31 March 1999 reaffirmed the intention to continue the policy of selective prosecution. To date, challenges to this approach under the *Human Rights Act,* which became law in 1998, have been largely unsuccessful.

It is important to note that the offences which constitute tax evasion also constitute money laundering offences and this issue is dealt with in **CHAPTER 8**. Increasingly, HMRC are using the powers contained in the Criminal Justice Act 1988 to confiscate assets which are deemed to be the proceeds of criminal conduct. In addition, the Proceeds of Crime Act 2002 introduced radical new powers to deprive criminals of their assets.

While HMRC is responsible for investigating suspected criminality in relation to tax, the decision as to whether or not to prosecute in England and Wales has since 1 January 2010 been made by the Crown Prosecution Service. In Northern Ireland this function is fulfilled by the Public Prosecution Service for Northern Ireland and in Scotland by the Crown Office and the Procurator Fiscal Service.

FACTORS SUGGESTING THE LIKELIHOOD OF CRIMINAL INVESTIGATION

7.11 Beginning with their evidence in 1983 to the Committee on enforcement powers of the Revenue Departments (the Keith committee), HMRC have set out the indices of serious fraud regarded as heinous, the presence of any one of which in a case would make the possibility of prosecution more likely. These have been altered and modified over the years as the threats to the tax-gathering system have changed. As an example, in recent years, significant losses were sustained as a result of massive frauds on the tax credit system perpetrated by organised criminal gangs.

HMRC reserve the right to conduct a criminal investigation in *any* case and to carry out these investigations across a range of offences and in all the areas for which they have responsibility. When considering whether a case should be investigated under the Civil Investigation of Fraud (CIF) procedure or should be the subject of a criminal investigation, one important factor to be considered will be whether the taxpayer has made a complete and unprompted disclosure of the offences committed. Professional advisors should have this in mind at all times. Apart from prosecution considerations, an unprompted, voluntary disclosure will attract significant mitigation of any civil penalties.

7.12 Clearly, HMRC simply do not have the resources to investigate with a view to prosecution more than a miniscule proportion of serious tax fraudsters,

7.12 *Criminal investigations in relation to direct tax*

and the following are examples of the sorts of circumstances which might lead HMRC to consider using the most potent weapon at their disposal:

- Cases of organised criminal gangs attacking the tax system or systematic frauds where losses represent a serious threat to the tax base, including conspiracy.
- Where an individual holds a position of trust or responsibility. Where the suspected offender is a professional tax adviser, eg an accountant or a solicitor HMRC take a particularly stringent view. A dishonest accountant is particularly reprehensible in the HMRC's eyes, being a source of 'infection' that is likely to have assisted a number of clients in the commission of serious fraud. However, the Board will not necessarily prosecute all the advisor's clients who may have been involved in fraudulent activities along with their advisor. This principle was tested in an application for judicial review *R v IRC, ex parte Mead and Cook* [1992] STC 482. In its judgment, the High Court upheld the Board's right to be selective in prosecuting persons alleged to have committed serious fraud.
- Another case (unreported) which highlights the dangers of prosecution for professional advisers is *R v Charlton* (see *Taxation* magazine, 4 January 1996). One of the defendants convicted on two counts of cheating the Revenue, for which he served a term in prison, was a barrister who had advised a corporate client on tax avoidance arrangements involving operations in a low-tax jurisdiction. In the case of *R v Chipping*, a UK solicitor and a Jersey-resident accountant were convicted of conspiracy to cheat the public revenue and received custodial sentences.
- Where materially false statements are made or materially false documents are provided in the course of a civil investigation. It is this determination which underpins the CIF procedure introduced in September 2005. In 1987, the case of *R v Piggott* culminated in a former British champion jockey receiving a three-year term of imprisonment after pleading guilty to serious tax fraud charges. One of the aggravating features of the case had been that the defendant had undergone two previous tax investigations, at the conclusion of which he had signed false statements of assets.
- Where, pursuing an avoidance scheme, reliance is placed on a false or altered document or such reliance or material facts are misrepresented to enhance the credibility of a scheme. This underlines the fact that although an avoidance scheme would normally be pursued under Code of Practice 8 – 'Cases where serious fraud is not suspected' – HMRC will not be inhibited from changing tack and initiating a prosecution in appropriate circumstances.
- Where deliberate concealment, deception, conspiracy or corruption is suspected. The siphoning off of profits into an offshore bank account in a false name would be one such example.
- In cases involving the use of false or forged documents. Modern-day technology has brought this particular fraud within easy reach of anyone with access to a computer and printer. The use of false invoices

or the keeping of a second set of books is likely to lead HMRC to at least consider applying the ultimate sanction.
- In cases involving importation or exportation breaching prohibitions and restrictions.
- In cases involving money laundering with particular focus on advisors, accountants, solicitors and others acting in a professional capacity that provide the means to put tainted money out of reach of law enforcement.
- Where the perpetrator has committed previous offences, or there is a repeated course of unlawful conduct or previous civil action.
- In cases involving theft, or the misuse or unlawful destruction of HMRC documents.
- Where there is evidence of assault on, or threats to, or the impersonation of HMRC officials.
- Where there is a link to suspected wider criminality, whether domestic or international, involving offences not under the administration of HMRC.

HMRC have made absolutely clear their unbending attitude to certain offences which they will almost always seek to prosecute rather than offer the CIF approach. These are:
- VAT missing trader intra-community (MTIC) fraud – generally involving the importation and onward sale of small high-value components such as mobile phones and computer chips;
- VAT bogus registration repayment fraud;
- organised tax credit fraud.

THE ORGANISATION OF CRIMINAL INVESTIGATION IN HMRC

7.13 HMRC Criminal Division is split into four directorates:
- Criminal Investigation – responsible for the bulk of the Department's criminal investigations. Following the creation of HMRC, responsibility for dealing with drug trafficking and associated criminal finance and organised immigration crime, was transferred along with a large number of C&E investigators, to the Serious Organised Crime Agency.
- Internal governance – handles civil and criminal internal investigations.
- Detection – looks for individuals and organisations bent on criminal activity whether at the border or inland. Where appropriate, responsibility for investigation is passed over to the criminal investigation directorate, the Serious Organised Crime Agency or the police.
- Risk and intelligence – uses criminal investigation powers to develop cases and highlight areas of potential criminal activity.

The maintenance of professional standards of criminal investigation within HMRC rests with a separate directorate in HMRC – Criminal Justice and Enforcement Standards – which was established no doubt at least partly in response to the criticisms made in the Gower Hammond and Butterfield reports.

7.14 *Criminal investigations in relation to direct tax*

HMRC'S CRIMINAL INVESTIGATION POWERS

7.14 The creation of the new department in 2005 brought into sharp focus the disparity between the respective powers of the former IR and C&E criminal investigators. The latter had historically always had significantly greater powers than their counterparts and it is understandable that this situation could not be allowed to continue. Following an extensive consultation process, Finance Act 2007 enacted a number of amendments to the Police and Criminal Evidence Act 1984 (PACE) aligning the powers of criminal investigators across the department. These mainly affect the powers of HMRC investigators to:

- Apply for production orders requiring information to be produced; Revenue investigators had previously relied solely on s 20BA of the Taxes Management Act 1970 (TMA) which remains on the statute book. However, HMRC are now required to use PACE 1984, Sch 1, para 4, if they require the production of 'special procedure material' (see later).
- Apply for search warrants. TMA, s 20C has been repealed and all HMRC investigators will now normally rely on s 8 of or Sch 1, para 12 to PACE, or in certain circumstances s 66, Serious Organised Crime and Police Act 2005 (SOCPA).
- Make arrests. Revenue investigators had previously relied on the presence of police officers to carry out this function on their behalf.
- Search suspects and premises following arrest.

In Northern Ireland these powers derive from the Police and Criminal Evidence (Northern Ireland) Order 1989 which has also been amended. PACE does not apply in Scotland, but similar powers have been introduced for HMRC investigators there.

7.15 Cross-border powers contained in FA 2007 enable HMRC's criminal investigation powers to be exercised in all parts of the UK. Thus, a search warrant issued by a court in Scotland can be exercised in England, if it is endorsed by an English court and vice versa. It may be possible to prosecute an offence in more than one part of the UK and guidance will be issued explaining how the prosecuting authorities determine in which UK country an offence is prosecuted.

Considerable concern was expressed during the consultation process especially about the extension of arrest powers to former Revenue investigators. In response, measures to control the use of the new powers have been introduced. They can only be used by officers who are authorised to use them (ie by HMRC officers who have been appropriately trained and are engaged on operational duties in the various Directorates mentioned above). PACE stipulates that certain powers can be exercised only by police officers of a particular rank. These ranks are converted to HMRC grades of an equivalent authority:

- Sergeant   Officer
- Inspector   Higher Officer
- Chief Inspector   Higher Officer
- Superintendent   Senior Officer

Criminal investigations in relation to direct tax **7.18**

HMRC has set internal authorisation levels requiring an authorised officer to obtain the approval of a higher graded officer before using certain powers. The police are the primary user of PACE powers and the authority levels within HMRC are no lower than those set in the police force. Indeed, for applications to a magistrate or a court for a production order or a search warrant, HMRC has set the main authority level at a minimum of Senior Officer Grade. By contrast, most authorities within the police force are held at the equivalent of a Higher Officer in HMRC.

7.16 Officers serving in the Criminal Investigation Directorate are trained in areas which include:

- custody time limits and procedures;
- powers to search persons;
- powers to search persons following arrest;
- transporting prisoners;
- safety training including personal safety and the use of handcuffs;
- responsibility for disclosure under the Criminal Procedures and Investigation Act 1996.

Over one and a half thousand officers in the Criminal Investigation Directorate have powers of arrest which can only be exercised for HMRC offences.

HMRC investigators also have assistance and advice available from HMRC criminal lawyers who may be assigned to work on the larger investigations and who will also consult the prosecuting authorities at an early stage on major prosecutions.

SEARCH WARRANTS AND PRODUCTION ORDERS

7.17 The clearest possible signal of the Revenue's intentions to investigate with a view to prosecution is a dawn raid carried out under PACE, s 8, or Sch 1 para 12, when HMRC invoke their powers to enter premises, by force if necessary, to search the premises and 'seize and retain anything for which a search has been authorised' (s 8(2), Sch1 para 13 and s 22), notwithstanding the fact that the thing found is not evidence of an offence which relates to a matter in relation to which HMRC have functions.

'Premises' includes any place and in particular:

- any vehicle, vessel, aircraft or hovercraft;
- any offshore installation;
- any renewable energy installation;
- any tent or moveable structure (s 23).

Where an HMRC officer is conducting a search under the authority of a PACE warrant, he may also carry out a same-sex search of any person found on the premises where he has reasonable cause to believe that person to be in possession of, material likely to be of substantial value (by itself or together with other material) to the investigation of the offence.

7.18 In the past it was almost certain that not only would the suspect taxpayer's home be raided, but also his business premises and quite probably

7.18 *Criminal investigations in relation to direct tax*

the offices of his professional advisers – both accountants and lawyers. This was so even if neither set of advisers was suspected of wrongdoing, since the Revenue wished to obtain documentary evidence at as early a stage as possible. This approach has changed significantly, now that HMRC have a production order power available to them.

In some respects the amendments to PACE introduced by FA 2007, ss 82–87 and as applied by SI 2007 No 3175 (the Police and Criminal Evidence Act 1984 (Application to Revenue and Customs) Order 2000) have made life more difficult for those HMRC criminal investigators accustomed to dealing with direct tax investigations.

TMA, s 20C has been repealed and in future it is likely that all HMRC search warrants will be authorised under either PACE, s 8, or para 12, Sch 1 to PACE (but see below regarding SOCPA).

To obtain a search warrant under the now defunct TMA, s 20C, HMRC had to persuade a circuit judge in England and Wales (a sheriff in Scotland or a county court judge in Northern Ireland) that there was 'reasonable ground for *suspecting* that an offence involving serious fraud in connection with … tax is being, has been or is about to be committed …'.

Now HMRC have to surmount a higher hurdle by convincing a Justice of the Peace (JP) that 'there are reasonable grounds for *believing* that an indictable offence has been committed …' (s 8(1)). On the other hand, whereas an application for a search warrant under s 20C had to be approved by the Board of Inland Revenue – in practice the head of SCI – an application under s 8 of or Sch 1 to PACE can, it appears, be approved at a much lower level. The application for a s 8 warrant is made *ex parte* and must be supported by information in writing. Various safeguards, mainly relating to the identification of the premises to be searched, are set out in s 15.

Note: actions preparatory to committing a tax offence are now no longer grounds applying for a warrant to raid premises.

7.19 Evidential material which is likely to be relevant, and of substantial value, to the investigation can be seized (s 8(i)(b)(c)). However, there is a protection for items subject to legal privilege, excluded material and special procedure material (s 8(i)(d)). And the search warrant application has to specify that there are no reasonable grounds for believing that the material on the premises to be searched consists of or includes items subject to legal privilege, excluded material or special procedure material. The JP also has to be satisfied that either it is not practicable to communicate with any person entitled to grant access to the evidence, or that entry to the premises will not be granted without a warrant, or that the purpose of the search is likely to be seriously prejudiced unless HMRC can gain instant access (s 8(3)). Computerised information must be provided in a form in which it can be taken away and in which it is visible and legible, or from which it can readily be produced in a visible and legible form.

7.20 The legal privilege protection applicable to both s 8 and Sch 1 search warrants is contained in s 10 and is worded in the same way as it was in s 20C.

'Excluded material' is defined in s 11(1) as personal records which a person has acquired or created in the course of trade business profession or other occupation or for the purpose of any paid or unpaid office and which he holds in confidence. Also included are human tissue and the like. Material of such a description would clearly include a patient's records held by a GP or psychiatrist. Excluded material also includes a journalist's notes or information obtained from a confidential source and held in confidence, or records other than documents.

7.21 'Special procedure material' is defined in s 14(2) as meaning material, other than material subject to legal privilege, acquired or created in the course of any trade, business, profession or other occupation and held subject to an express or implied undertaking that it is to be held in confidence or under a legal obligation of secrecy or restriction on disclosure. This would include business records held for example, by an accountant on a client's behalf and an accountant's working papers. Also included is journalistic material other than the type of journalistic material which is classed as 'excluded material'.

Where a search is likely to uncover special procedure material which may be required as evidence, HMRC will have to obtain a warrant signed by a circuit judge under Sch 1, para 12.

As with s 8, material subject to legal privilege cannot be seized under a Sch 1, para 12 warrant.

On the other hand, under the Criminal Justice and Police Act 2001, officers faced with large volumes of material during a search under a s 8 warrant, may take it from the premises to be sifted and examined elsewhere. Legally privileged, excluded or special procedure material seized under a s 8 warrant and which cannot be retained, must be returned as soon as practicable. Similarly, legally privileged and excluded material seized under a Sch 1 warrant must also be returned.

7.22 It should be noted that an officer of HMRC may, without a warrant, enter and search any premises occupied or controlled by a person who is under arrest for any relevant indictable offence if he has reasonable grounds for suspecting that there is on the premises evidence, other than items subject to legal privilege, that relates:

- to that offence; or
- to some other indictable offence which is connected with or similar to that offence (s 18).

Following a PACE raid, HMRC must supply a record of what was seized within a reasonable time of being so requested (s 21(1), (2)). And unless any investigation or criminal proceedings would be prejudiced, HMRC are also required to allow access under supervision to, and provide copies of, documents seized (s 21(3)–(8)).

The introduction in 2000 of a production order power in the form of TMA 1970, s 20BA was intended, at least in part, to obviate the need to execute a s 20C raid on a professional firm, such as a lawyer or an accountant, or on a bank that were not viewed as being implicated in criminal activity, but where speedy access to

7.22 *Criminal investigations in relation to direct tax*

information held by them was required. At the same time as s 20BA was enacted, s 20C was amended to say that the Board should not authorise an application for a search warrant unless they believed a request for a production order would seriously prejudice the investigation. HMRC are now bound by a similar provision in PACE. If, for instance, access to an accountant's working papers is required, and an application for a production order might seriously prejudice the investigation, HMRC may apply to circuit judge under PACE, Sch 1 para 12, for a search warrant. .The application must make it clear why HMRC believe a production order may seriously prejudice the investigation.

7.23 Where HMRC require access to 'special procedure material' such as an accountant's working papers or a solicitor's conveyancing files and they do not wish to invoke their search powers they can seek leave of a circuit judge to serve a production order under Sch 1, para 4.

The target of such an order is entitled to be present at the hearing before the judge. The material must be produced to HMRC within seven days from the date of the order or such longer period as is specified in the order and, if it is stored in any electronic form, must be produced in a form in which it is visible and legible.

A para 4 production order may be served on a person – whether an individual, company or any one of the partners in a partnership – either by delivering it to, or by leaving it at, the proper address or by sending it by registered post or recorded delivery. The proper address for a company is the registered or principal office; for a partnership it is the principal office of the firm; and in any other case it is the last known address of the person concerned.

Any person in receipt of a notice of an application for a para 4 production order must not conceal, destroy, alter or dispose of the material without the leave of a judge or written permission of HMRC until either the application is dismissed or an order made following the application has been complied with. Failure to comply with an order will be treated as contempt of the Crown Court.

Where HMRC require production of documents which are not special procedure material, they must continue to use TMA 1970, s 20BA. Such documents will be those which, although acquired or created in the course of business, are not held under a duty of confidentiality. Copy sales invoices would be such documents.

ORDER FOR THE DELIVERY OF DOCUMENTS UNDER TMA 1970, S 20BA

7.24 Following the changes introduced in FA 2007, HMRC may only use s 20BA if the officer thinks that an application under Sch 1, para 4 would not succeed because the material required does not consist of, or include, special procedure material.

Section 20BA and Sch 1AA give HMRC authority to order the production of documents:

'which may be required as evidence for the purpose of any proceedings in respect of an offence ... involving serious fraud in connection with, or in relation to, tax' (TMA, s 20BA(1)(a)(b)).

7.25 The Order for the Delivery of Documents (Procedure) Regulations SI 2000 No 2875 contains procedural rules governing the application for a production order and the resolution of disputes as to legal privilege. Finally, Code of Practice 22 (COP 22) explains how the power should be used.

An order to produce documents has to be made by 'the appropriate judicial authority' (a circuit judge in England and Wales). The person against whom the order is sought must be given not less than five working days' notice before the hearing of the application (SI 2000 No 2875, reg 4(2)).

Exceptionally, the right of the target of an order to appear and be heard at the hearing of the application can be waived if the appropriate judicial authority is satisfied that this would seriously prejudice the investigation of the offence (TMA 1970, Sch1AA, para 3(1)). It is difficult to imagine the circumstances in which a production order would be served on a professional firm in relation to a client of that firm without there being a simultaneous raid on the client. However, there are additional safeguards to protect the security of HMRC's investigation in the form of an anti-'tipping-off' provision on similar lines to that contained in the money laundering legislation.

Complying with a s 20BA production order

7.26 A person who has been given notice of the Revenue's intention to apply for an order must not – on pain of proceedings for contempt of Court:

'disclose to any other person information or any other matter likely to prejudice the investigation of the offence to which the application relates'(Sch 1AA, para 4(1) (b)).

7.27 It is not difficult to envisage the dangers for the Board's investigation when they are engaged in the delicate process of compiling a case against an unknowing suspect, say, by obtaining information from banks.

7.28 On the other hand, where the intended recipient of a notice is a 'professional legal adviser' there is no let or hindrance on him 'disclosing any information or other matter' to a client or his representative in connection with the giving of legal advice to the client or to any other person in contemplation of, or in connection with, legal proceedings and for the purpose of those proceedings (Sch 1AA, para 4(2), (3)). A lawyer's rights in this connection seem to be crystal clear, but where does the accountant stand? Is he a 'professional legal adviser'? The view of HMRC is that he is not, but if so, why does the legislation not refer to 'barrister, advocate or solicitor'? HMRC's view may be open to challenge.

7.29 It is strongly suggested that an accountant who finds himself in this dilemma should at least liaise closely with the investigator in charge of the investigation and possibly seek legal guidance on his own account. As has been indicated earlier, it is the writer's view that HMRC will in all probability solve

7.29 *Criminal investigations in relation to direct tax*

the problem by simultaneously raiding a client where his accountant is to be the recipient of a production order! Needless to say, any permission to disclose information does not apply to anything disclosed with a view to furthering a criminal purpose.

7.30 The legislation envisages that the person who has the documents required by HMRC in his power or possession will be given ten working days to comply with the order or 'such shorter or longer period as may be specified' (s 20BA(2)(b)). The time limits for giving notice of the intention to apply for an order and for the recipient to comply, run from the day of receipt at the 'proper address' (usually the last known place of residence, or business, or employment or a company's registered office) or, where that day is not a working day, from the next working day. There is also provision for such notices to be delivered 'by facsimile ... or other similar means' (but only by agreement of the intended recipient (COP 22), in which case the notice is deemed to have been given when 'the text is received in legible form' (SI 2000 No 2875, reg 5(1), (2), (3)). Readers will instantly recognise the scope for challenges against the validity of HMRC's operation of these procedures.

7.31 The order must specify or describe the documents which are the subject of the application, which will hopefully limit the scope for the over-zealous investigator to embark on an over-speculative enquiry. The order must also describe the suspected offence – 'serious fraud in connection with, or in relation to, tax' will no doubt suffice – and must also name the person suspected of having committed the suspected offence. It is an offence, punishable by up to two years' imprisonment and a fine, to falsify, conceal, destroy or otherwise dispose of (or permit the same to happen) any document required by a s 20BA order.

7.32 The statutory instrument, possibly anticipating the almost inevitable challenges, goes into fairly minute detail in setting down the procedures for complying with an order. For example, the order is complied with if the documents (originals – not photocopies) are delivered to the officer of the Board specified in the order, either by delivering them to him directly, or by leaving them marked for his attention at the address specified in the order. Should compliance within the time specified cause a problem, the target should not hesitate to agree an extension with HMRC. But, of course, do not wait until the time limit is about to expire or, even worse, has already expired, before asking for an extension. Where documents are sent by post, they will be treated, in the absence of evidence to the contrary, as having been produced on the second working day after first class posting and on the fourth working day if posted second class (reg 6(1), (2), (3)). One can imagine that a production order, particularly on a sole practitioner where the documents may already be in storage, could impose an almost intolerable strain on the business. Again, there must be a very real possibility of a challenge being mounted under human rights legislation.

7.33 There are a number of conditions which must be satisfied before a Sch 1 production order or search warrant can be applied for. These include:

- the application must be supported by a signed written authority from a Higher Officer of HMRC;
- HMRC must also have reasonable grounds for believing that:
  - an indictable offence has been committed;
  - there is material which consists of or includes special procedure material, and does not also include excluded material, on premises specified in the application or on premises controlled by a person specified in the application;
  - the material is likely to be of substantial value (on its own or together with other material) to the investigation; and
  - the material is likely to be relevant evidence.

In addition, other methods of obtaining the material have to have been tried without success, or have not been tried because it appeared that they were bound to fail.

It must also be in the public interest that the material should be produced or that access should be given to it, having regard both to the benefit which is likely to accrue to the investigation if the material is obtained and the circumstances under which the person in possession of the material holds it.

7.34 There are, in addition, further conditions which have to be satisfied before a Sch 1 search warrant can be issued:

Rather than specifying all the premises which they wish to search, HMRC may seek an 'all premises warrant', but the judge must not issue such a warrant unless he is satisfied:

- that there are reasonable grounds for believing that it is necessary to search premises occupied or controlled by the person in question which are not specified in the application, as well as those which are, in order to find the material in question; and
- that it is not reasonably practicable to specify all the premises which that person;
- occupies or controls which might need to be searched.

The judge must also be satisfied that:

- it is not practicable to communicate with any person entitled to grant entry to the premises;
- it is practicable to communicate with a person entitled to grant entry to the premises but not with any person entitled to grant access to the material;
- the material includes excluded material in the form of medical records held subject to a statutory obligation of secrecy which would be breached by disclosure other than as a result of a search under warrant;
- service of an application for a production order might seriously prejudice the investigation.

It is unlikely that the transition to PACE powers will lead to an increase in raids on professional firms. However, Sch 1 does not contain a prohibition on 'tipping off', as does s 20BA, so it is just possible that HMRC will be less

7.34 *Criminal investigations in relation to direct tax*

willing to rely on production orders if they have any fear that their investigation is in any danger of being prejudiced.

7.35 Code of Practice B of PACE gives extensive guidance to those using or intending to invoke the PACE search and production order powers and should also be consulted by those whose clients are subject to a raid or are, or are themselves, in receipt of a production order.

As was said earlier, most HMRC raids are likely to be conducted under PACE. However, SOCPA created a number of new powers of investigation including the power to force witnesses to answer questions or to provide documents or information. These powers are to be exercised by, among others, the Director of the RCPO, who may delegate these powers to a Revenue and Customs prosecutor who is any one of a number of senior officials and lawyers in HMRC.

Where someone has been served with a disclosure notice to produce documents under SOCPA, s 62 SOCPA and has not complied, or it is not practicable to give a disclosure notice, or the giving of a disclosure notice might seriously prejudice the investigation, a JP may issue a warrant to enter premises and seize documents (including computer discs) (SOCPA, s 66). Such a warrant may be applied for where the prosecutors 'suspect' (as for the repealed s 20C – not 'believe' as for s 8) that, for instance, the common law offence of cheating the public revenue has been committed. A very low threshold of loss of revenue of not less than £5,000 is stipulated – not quite the 'substantial financial gain' according to which 'serious fraud' was defined in s 20C.

7.36 However, it is understood that RCPO will in fact exercise its powers under SOCPA only in cases involving serious fraud – that is where the fraud has in fact resulted in substantial loss to the public revenue. The areas envisaged are tax credit and MTIC fraud. In other cases where HMRC have an existing power, PACE will almost certainly be applied.

As with other search powers, there is a protection for privileged material, but apparently none for excluded or special procedure material. Accordingly, a search warrant obtained under SOCPA, s 66, on application to a JP might cover, say, an accountant's working papers. To gain access to these by a search under Sch 1, PACE would require an application to a circuit judge.

DEALING WITH A DAWN RAID

7.37 The adviser's role on learning that his client is the object of a dawn raid is clear. First, he must immediately arrange for professionals with adequate knowledge of the search provisions to stand by his client both at his home and at the business premises. Without doubt the client, his family and, possibly to a lesser extent his staff, will be in a state of some fear and trepidation when faced with a determined search crew of HMRC investigators, possibly accompanied by a uniformed police constable whose presence is intended to deter any breach of the peace. (The adviser must also bear in mind that his own business premises may be being raided at the same time although there is now less likelihood of this happening (see **7.25**).)

Criminal investigations in relation to direct tax **7.38**

Arrests will frequently be carried out at a very early stage of the raid process. If that happens, arrangements must be put in hand immediately for clients to be represented by a suitably qualified solicitor since HMRC will be looking to conduct interviews under caution as soon as practicable. Certain officers of HMRC have been authorised to carry out arrests and to search and detain the persons arrested. Offices of HMRC may be designated as being suitable to be used for the purpose of detaining arrested persons. However, officers are not empowered to charge a person with an offence, to release a person on bail, or to detain or fingerprint a person after he has been charged with an offence. The Commissioners of HMRC are required to keep records relating to detentions and charges and to include the information in their annual reports.

7.38 Needless to say, nothing should or can be done physically to impede the search. However, that does not mean that the warrant itself must not be scrutinised in minute detail to ensure that the search is being conducted strictly in accordance with the terms on which it has been issued. Section 16 stipulates several requirements in relation to the execution of PACE search warrants:

- A warrant is valid for three months from the date of issue.
- A warrant may be executed by any officer of HMRC.
- Entry and search must be at a reasonable hour, unless the purpose of the search might be frustrated on entry at a reasonable hour. Criticism of the early morning raid was considered by the Keith Committee. One expert, in evidence to the Committee, maintained that the hours between 4am and 7am were the only hours when the hardened criminal could be guaranteed to be found at home. Thus the Revenue continues with their practice of commencing such raids in the early hours of the morning – usually 7am.
- The warrant may authorise persons to accompany the investigator. Such persons have the same power as the officer they are accompanying but they may exercise these powers only in the company, and under the supervision, of an officer. The presence during a raid of unauthorised persons has been successfully challenged in judicial review proceedings.
- If the warrant is an all premises warrant, premises which are not specified may not be entered or searched unless a senior officer has given written authority; nor may premises may be entered or searched for a second or subsequent time under a warrant which authorises multiple entries unless a senior officer has given written authority.
- The officer must identify himself to the occupier of the premises if he is present at the time the warrant is executed, and if not, to any other who is present, and provide him with a copy of the warrant.
- If no person is present a copy of the warrant must be left in a prominent place.
- A search may only be carried out to the extent required for the purpose for which the warrant was issued.
- The officer must endorse the warrant stating whether the articles sought were found and whether any articles were seized other than articles which were sought.
- On completion of the search, a s 8 warrant has to be returned to the

7.38 *Criminal investigations in relation to direct tax*

designated officer for the local justice area and a Sch 1, para 12 warrant to the appropriate officer of the court.
- A returned warrant must be kept for 12 months from its return, during which time it must be available for inspection by the occupier of the premises entered and searched.

The award of costs of any application under Sch 1 and of anything done in pursuance of an order are entirely at the discretion of the judge granting the order. By contrast there is no provision for the award of costs of complying with a s 20BA order.

INTRUSIVE SURVEILLANCE

7.39 HMRC are empowered to apply for authority to use surveillance powers in the Regulation of Investigatory Powers Act 2000 and the Police Act 1997. These are principally:

- the interception of post and telecommunications;
- intrusive surveillance;
- property interference;
- covert human intelligence.

These powers can only be used when investigating serious crime and even then only with the approval of certain members of senior management within the highest levels in the Criminal Investigation Directorate. The Home Secretary has personally to approve the interception of communications. And use of the power is overseen by the independent Interception of Communications Commissioner. The most intrusive surveillance has to be approved by the Office of Surveillance Commissioners which also reviews all other cases of intrusive surveillance.

LEGAL PRIVILEGE

7.40 Potentially one of the most difficult areas of the legislation relates to items which may be considered to be protected from disclosure by legal privilege and it is worth repeating the appropriate paragraph in its entirety.

Schedule 1AA, para 5 states:

'(1) Section 20BA does not apply to items subject to legal privilege.
(2) For this purpose "items subject to legal privilege" means –
    (a) communications between a professional legal adviser and his client or any person representing his client made in connection with the giving of legal advice to his client;
    (b) communications between a professional legal adviser and his client or any person representing his client or between such an adviser or his client or any such representative and any other person made in connection with or in contemplation of legal proceedings and for the purposes of such proceedings; and

(c) items enclosed with or referred to in such communications and made –
   (i) in connection with the giving of legal advice; or
   (ii) in connection with or in contemplation of legal proceedings and for the purposes of such proceedings, when they are in possession of a person who is entitled to possession of them.
(3) Items held with the intention of furthering a criminal purpose are not subject to legal privilege.'

The definition of legal privilege in PACE, s 10 is identical.

7.41 Readers will immediately note that, as far as production orders are concerned, the first arbiter as to whether or not a document is subject to legal privilege is the recipient of the notice himself. SI 2000 No 2875, reg 7(1)–(7) contains detailed provisions aimed at resolving disputes as to legal privilege which are far from being weighted in HMRC's favour (in contrast to the legislation in the Criminal Justice and Police Act 2001 which will allow investigators – including HMRC – to remove, in the course of a raid and in certain circumstances, privileged material from the premises for sifting). It is likely that these regulations will also apply to disputes over legal privilege arising out of orders under PACE. Where a dispute arises in a production order case, the person in receipt of the order can apply to the appropriate judicial authority to resolve the dispute. The disputed documents must be lodged with the court at the same time. Naturally, HMRC will have the right to be present and be heard at the hearing of the application and costs may be awarded against HMRC, except where the court holds that no document, or no part of a document, is subject to legal privilege.

7.42 There is an alternative and less formal means of resolving disputes as to privilege suggested in COP 22. This envisages an independent Counsel (or exceptionally an HMRC solicitor) considering the disputed documents in the light of the information previously seen by the judge who granted the order, to enable him to give a considered view on the claim to privilege and thus to enable HMRC to decide whether to challenge that claim.

INTERVIEWS

7.43 Not every prosecution, of course, is preceded by the drama of a dawn raid. Frequently, HMRC will feel that they already have sufficient evidence indicating the commission of serious fraud. The source of this material could be a spin-off from another investigation, information and possibly documents provided by an informer and by potential witnesses, or quite possibly documents supplied by the taxpayer during the course of an investigation whether voluntarily or in response to a notice under s 20(1) or in obedience to a precept issued under regulation 10 of SI 1994 No 1811 or 1812 by the Appeal Commissioners, or by a third party such as a bank under s 20(3).

7.44 In such circumstances as these HMRC's evidential jigsaw may be all but complete. All that is required to complete the final piece and guarantee the

7.44 *Criminal investigations in relation to direct tax*

required standard of proof to convince a jury beyond reasonable doubt may be the evidence obtainable under caution from the suspect's own mouth. The letter from HMRC inviting the taxpayer to an interview will make it clear that the taxpayer is to be cautioned and indeed will suggest that he or she may wish to be legally represented. Until 9 April 1995, the caution which investigators were required to administer in accordance with para 10 of the code of practice for the detention, treatment and questioning of persons issued under PACE read as follows:

> 'You are not obliged to say anything but anything you do say may be taken down in writing and given in evidence.'

Since that date as a result of a change brought in by the Criminal Justice and Public Order Act 1994, s 34, the caution now reads:

> 'You do not have to say anything. But it may harm your defence if you do not mention when questioned something which you later rely on in court. Anything you do say may be given in evidence.'

At the same time, if the person cautioned is not under arrest, he must be told that this is the case, that he is not obliged to remain with the investigator and that he may obtain legal advice (if he is not already legally represented).

7.45 This shift in the balance towards the investigative authorities requires careful consideration by the taxpayer and his advisers who must by this time include a specialist criminal solicitor and quite possibly a barrister. Whereas under the old caution, the taxpayer was well advised to exercise his right to remain silent, the same cannot be said of the new regime. However, before submitting to interview, HMRC, who have probably already had many months prior to the meeting to examine documents and speak to witnesses and generally to formulate the case, should be asked to provide details of the questions which they want to be answered and copies of the documents which they wish to put to the taxpayer for comment during the course of the interview under caution.

THE TRIAL

7.46 The preparation for any serious fraud trial can take many months and indeed can run into years. In such cases charges will generally be:

1. the common law charge of cheating HMRC;
2. offences under the Theft Acts;
3. forgery, perjury or conspiracy; or
4. fraudulent evasion of income tax.

7.47 Proceedings generally begin in the magistrates' court where, if it is demonstrated that the taxpayer has a case to answer, he will be committed for trial in the Crown Court in due course. HMRC will serve bundles on the defendant incorporating documentary evidence upon which the prosecution intend to rely including statements from witnesses. These can run to many thousands of pages and can be, and indeed frequently are, added to right up to the commencement of the trial in the Crown Court. Managing these bundles is of crucial importance, and the option of scanning them on to a computer should be considered since this process can greatly facilitate the constant referral to those documents which is usually necessary and the transfer of documents between the defence team.

7.48 Any opportunity to attack HMRC's case must not be overlooked and the services of a forensic accountant will frequently be invaluable. All this requires close co-operation between accountants and lawyers, and the concept of the team surrounding and supporting the taxpayer cannot be overemphasised.

7.49 The conclusion of the trial, whatever the outcome, is not the end of the matter. First, HMRC will seek to recover any tax lost as a result of the fraud (even if the taxpayer has been acquitted of any criminal offence). The Board's policy as regards penalties, is set out in SP2/88, and is:

1   to refrain from taking steps to recover civil money penalties on the basis of fraud in respect of an offence which has been before the criminal courts;
2   to seek appropriate civil money penalties in respect of any offence which has not been brought before the courts; and
3   to reserve the right to seek, where there are grounds to do so, a civil penalty in respect of negligence by a taxpayer who has been acquitted of criminal intent in respect of a prosecution for fraud.

Where a tax evader has been found guilty of fraud HMRC may seek, in accordance with the Proceeds of Crime Act 2002, to recover assets the value of which frequently exceeds the amount of tax lost. If that fails, civil recovery proceedings can be pursued under the same Act and, as a last resort, there is a form of taxation power available even if the source of the income is not known.

Chapter 8

The nexus between tax evasion and money laundering

Martyn Bridges

Partner, Bridges & Partners

INTRODUCTION

8.01 The purpose of this chapter is to give an appreciation of the relationship between tax evasion and money laundering. It is a widely held view that the money laundering legislation exists solely to deal with those involved in drug trafficking, terrorism or other 'serious crimes'. It is fair to say that this view is now more commonly held outside the UK than within. Whilst the original money laundering legislation applied only to offences related to drug trafficking and terrorism, since 1 April 1994 the net has been widened considerably to include all criminal conduct.

8.02 This chapter does not consider the history of anti-money laundering legislation and addresses only the regime imposed by the Proceeds of Crime Act 2002 (PoCA) (as amended) and the Money Laundering Regulations 2007.

8.03 The structure of the chapter is as follows:

- A brief history of tax evasion – considers tax evasion and the 'tax gap' or 'untaxed' economy.
- The money laundering legislation – details its applicability to the proceeds of domestic and foreign tax evasion.
- The view of government – briefly considers how the government's view of the tax evasion and money laundering issue has developed.
- Guidance for financial intermediaries and professional advisers – considers some of the existing guidance available.
- Role of the fiscal authorities – considers how the money laundering legislation is being and may be used by the fiscal authorities in

8.03 *The nexus between tax evasion and money laundering*

enhancing tax compliance and in prosecutions for tax-related money laundering offences.
- The risk to intermediaries and professionals – considers some of the risks posed to intermediaries by the tax evasion/money laundering issue.
- Conclusion.

A BRIEF HISTORY OF TAX EVASION

8.04 Taxation has been a curse of the human race since at least early Roman times. It would be fairly safe to assume that the concepts of tax avoidance and evasion were invented within hours of the first tax being introduced. Most people dislike paying tax and many, given the choice, would prefer to avoid (or evade) payment, in whole or in part. This chapter is concerned not with tax avoidance which, when properly implemented, is perfectly lawful and hence does not represent criminal conduct, but rather with tax evasion which is unlawful.

8.05 To some extent, the amount of taxes avoided or evaded will fluctuate in line with the level of applied taxation. However, while it is fair to say that tax avoidance and evasion will increase over whatever may be regarded as the norm when tax rates are high, it is unlikely that the level will decrease dramatically when tax rates are low. It is human nature to avoid or evade taxation whenever the opportunity arises, no matter what the level of taxation.

The most significant fraud

8.06 Tax evasion is the most significant fraud. Without doubt, losses to government from tax evasion far exceed the combined losses from all other forms of economic crime. This is inherent in the fact that few criminals believe in paying tax on the profits of their criminal enterprises. Indeed, it is almost impossible for them to do so without disclosing the nature and extent of their illegal activities which may lead to the fiscal authority disclosing such criminal activity to other law enforcement organisations. This is all the more true given the enhanced legal gateways now available which permit the fiscal authorities to exchange information with law enforcement and the introduction of the Assets Recovery Agency. The English civil courts have long held that the profits of most illegal trading activities are chargeable to tax and the fact that they are obtained illegally does not afford any relief. Any moral dilemma which may have existed has long been dismissed as irrelevant. In this context remember the demise of Al Capone!

The 'untaxed' economy

8.07 The 'untaxed' economy (also known, inter alia, as the tax gap, informal, hidden, parallel, shadow, black or underground economy) is usually a term which applies to the non-taxpaying formal economy rather than those involved in other forms of economic crime such as commercial fraud and drug trafficking.

8.08 While, obviously, no precise figures are available, it is thought that in the US the untaxed economy is equivalent to between 8% and 10% of the gross domestic product (GDP). In Germany that figure exceeds 10%, and Italy, Greece, Portugal and Spain are thought to have untaxed economies amounting to around 30% of GDP. In Russia and other former eastern bloc countries, it is thought that the untaxed economy may amount to as much as 50% of GDP.

8.09 In the UK the untaxed economy is equivalent to between 8% and 12% of GDP, somewhat over £100 billion. In the unlikely event that the untaxed economy in the UK amounted to as little as 5% of national income, it is estimated that the loss in tax revenue would exceed £10 billion per annum. Of this the fiscal authorities recover only a small fraction.

8.10 It is the author's view that the total amount of tax evaded or avoided in the UK is between £25 and 35 billion and, calculated at present-day values, the cumulative amount evaded or avoided over the last 20 years would exceed £500 billion. The distinction between tax evasion (which involves the proceeds of crime) and avoidance (which does not) is significant. Such niceties are outside the scope of this chapter. Clearly, even where the fiscal authorities have highly sophisticated investigative facilities, the amounts of money involved in tax evasion are astronomical; hence the earlier statement that tax evasion is the most significant fraud in fiscal terms.

Increased awareness

8.11 In the mid-1970s the UK government began to realise the magnitude of these losses and commenced an extensive programme to increase the investigative powers available to the fiscal authorities and to encourage them to become far more aggressive and proactive than had hitherto been the case. The result was a dramatic and progressive increase in the amounts of additional revenue raised.

8.12 Over the same period the judiciary noticeably changed their attitude to tax evaders coming before the criminal courts. In the mid-1970s a tax evader convicted in the criminal courts could expect a reasonably small fine or, if he was extremely unlucky, a short custodial sentence. Attitudes have hardened and today prison sentences are usually imposed, together with a confiscation order in respect of the 'benefit' derived from the crime.

8.13 Given the global financial recession of 2008, the budget deficits of most developed economies, including the UK, fears about the demographic time bomb, electronic commerce and globalisation, governments are looking to achieve greater fiscal efficiency. There are few votes in increased levels of direct taxation. Governments are seeking to extract the maximum amount possible from a diminishing tax base. Enhanced compliance methodologies and intelligence sources are actively sought out.

Why tax evasion is a crime

8.14 A widely held view is that tax evasion itself is not a 'real' crime, but represents no more than 'fair game' on the Exchequer. However, the UK

8.14 *The nexus between tax evasion and money laundering*

criminal law has difficulty in recognising this philosophy and there is a wide range of potential criminal offences available under both statute and common law.

8.15 In the UK anyone who wilfully misstates the truth of their financial position while rendering information to the fiscal authorities for the purposes of assessing their taxable status commits a common law criminal offence of cheating the Revenue. The actions of a person who creates false records to understate the amount of tax which they owe, or who provides misleading documentation, can constitute false accounting. These offences do not apply solely to income tax and VAT; for example failing to make proper returns for the purpose of evading National Insurance contributions is a similar criminal offence, while making false claims for state benefits or for the payment of government subsidies can be an offence of obtaining property by deception. All these offences can be prosecuted and punished under common or statute law such as the Theft Acts 1968 and 1978 and the Fraud Act 2006. All carry penalties of long prison terms and/or unlimited fines. In addition the courts can order the confiscation of the benefit obtained from the crime. The measure used to calculate the quantum of benefit is usually disproportionate and punitive.

8.16 In the Court of Appeal's judgment in *Regina v Allen* [1999] STC 846 (an appeal against a confiscation order relating to tax evasion), Laws LJ concluded:

> 'In short, the fact that the tax remains due does not mean that its evasion did not confer a pecuniary advantage ... by his crime the appellant evaded payment of £4 million tax. That sum constituted the proceeds of the offence. On the agreed figures, as we have indicated, he had realisable assets of £3.1 million. The fact that he remained in law liable to pay the tax, the fact even, were it so, that the Revenue might later recover it, does not, in our judgment, yield the proposition that the proceeds of his crime were one penny less than the whole of the tax evaded.'

THE MONEY LAUNDERING LEGISLATION

European Union Directives

8.17 The first Directive of the Council of the European Community dated 10 June 1991 on the prevention of the use of the financial system for the purpose of money laundering provides the foundation for the domestic money laundering legislation of the member states.

8.18 Nowhere in the Directive is the issue of tax evasion specifically exempted from the list of prohibited activities. Nowhere in the first Directive are the activities of those professionals who usually give advice on fiscal matters excluded from the list of persons subject thereto. On the contrary, the Second and Third Directives focused attention specifically on the professions.

8.19 UK domestic legislation on money laundering is based on the European Directives and, again, nowhere is the issue of tax evasion specifically exempted from those activities which are prohibited. The latest (2005 and Third Directive) entered into force in the UK on 15 December 2007 with the implementation of the Money Laundering Regulations 2007 (MLR).

8.20 As with the First and subsequent Directives, criminal activity means 'any kind of criminal involvement in the commission of a serious crime'. Certain serious offences are specified. Beyond this, member states may designate any other offence as a criminal activity for the purposes of the Directives (ie the Directives set a minimum standard). In the UK, legislation such as the Criminal Justice Act 1993 (CJA 1993) has long since been extended to cover the proceeds of all crime (including tax offences) and PoCA closes many legal loopholes which may have existed previously.

The Proceeds of Crime Act 2002

8.21 Part 7 of PoCA consolidates, replaces and expands the previous anti-money laundering legislation contained in the CJA 1993 and other legislation. There are three specific offences of money laundering.

Section 327 – concealing

8.22 A person commits an offence if he: conceals; disguises; converts; transfers or removes criminal property from England and Wales or from Scotland or from Northern Ireland.

Section 328 – arrangements

8.23 A person commits an offence if he enters into or becomes concerned in an arrangement which he knows or suspects facilitates (by whatever means) the acquisition, retention, use or control of criminal property by or on behalf of another person.

Section 329 – acquisition, use and possession

8.24 A person commits an offence if he: acquires uses or has possession of criminal property.

Section 340 – interpretation

8.25 Criminal conduct is conduct which: constitutes an offence in any part of the UK; or would constitute an offence in any part of the UK if it occurred there.

8.26 Money laundering is an act which:
(a) constitutes an offence under ss 327, 328 or 329;
(b) constitutes an attempt, conspiracy or inducement to commit an offence specified in paragraph (a);
(c) constitutes aiding, abetting, counselling or procuring the commission of an offence specified in paragraph (a); or

8.26 *The nexus between tax evasion and money laundering*

(d) would constitute an offence specified in paragraph (a), (b) or (c) if done in the UK.

8.27 SOCA (SOCA website 4 August 2009) defines money laundering as follows:

> 'Money laundering is any action taken to conceal, arrange, use or possess the proceeds of any criminal conduct. Criminals try to launder "dirty money" in an attempt to make it look "clean" in order to be able to use the proceeds without detection and to put them beyond the reach of law enforcement *and taxation agencies.*'

(emphasis added)

8.28 It should be noted that this primary legislation is drafted in extremely wide terms sufficient to embrace the conduct of the person involved in the criminal conduct himself; PoCA is not directed solely at intermediaries. Similarly, the primary legislation fails to provide any de minimis limit in relation to criminal property and applies to all criminal conduct no matter how petty.

8.29 In relation to the regulated sector as defined by the MLR, PoCA, s 330 creates a criminal offence for any person within the scope of the MLR if they do not report their knowledge, suspicion or information which gives reasonable grounds for knowing or suspecting that another person is laundering the proceeds of any criminal conduct, where the information comes to them in the course of a business in the regulated sector.

8.30 The legislation embraces all criminal conduct (including summary offences) which constitutes an offence in the UK or elsewhere if the offence would be recognised in the UK. In relation to criminal conduct there is no exception in relation to tax evasion, which is capable of being charged in a multitude of ways under common or statute law.

8.31 Similarly, the long and learned debate concerning the identity of funds representing the proceeds of crime under previous legislation (ie whether the proceeds represented the profits or gains not declared for tax purposes or a lesser amount, namely the tax due thereon) is now put to rest completely by the new statutory definition of criminal property referred to above. Any earlier doubt concerning the point at which funds became the proceeds of crime (ie before or after a tax return or other false account or document was submitted to the Revenue) are potentially overcome by the new definition of money laundering referred to in PoCA, s 340(11) and, in particular, paragraphs (b) and (c) thereof. It remains necessary for the Crown to demonstrate that an act of alleged money laundering involved both criminal conduct and the proceeds of crime.

Foreign tax evasion

8.32 PoCA, s 340(2)(b) extends the money laundering legislation to funds derived from criminal conduct in foreign jurisdictions to the extent that such conduct would constitute an offence in any part of the UK had it occurred there.

8.33 Historically, some have questioned whether the money laundering legislation applies to the proceeds of foreign tax evasion that pass through the UK.

8.34 There is case law to support the general principle that UK courts will not enforce foreign revenue law (*Government of India v Taylor* [1955] AC 491). It was therefore suggested that to bring the proceeds of foreign tax evasion within the ambit of the money laundering legislation would violate this principle. In many cases, evading foreign tax will involve conduct which breaches the general criminal law as well as specific revenue law. Obvious examples are false accounting, conspiracy to defraud and obtaining a pecuniary advantage by deception.

8.35 The offence of widest application is likely to be false accounting under Theft Act 1968, s 17. If an offence of false accounting is committed in a foreign jurisdiction (albeit as part of a wider scheme to defraud the foreign fiscal authority) PoCA, s 340(2)(b) treats this as having occurred in the UK. Hence it would seem difficult to argue that ss 327, 328 or 329 do not apply.

8.36 It is important to note that the test laid down by s 340(2)(b) is whether the criminal conduct would constitute an offence if it had taken place in any part of the UK. There is no need to enquire into the workings of foreign tax systems to determine whether a client's actions may amount to a criminal offence in the foreign jurisdiction. The only question which needs to be addressed when considering the applicability of s 340(2)(b) is 'If the conduct had taken place in the UK, would it constitute a criminal offence?'.

8.37 The Criminal Justice (International Cooperation) Act 1990, s 4 – which originally related to drug trafficking offences – gives the Serious Fraud Office the power to investigate UK aspects of foreign tax offences and to assist foreign fiscal/prosecuting authorities in this regard. These powers have been used with substantial effect.

What constitutes knowledge or suspicion?

8.38 Under PoCA, it is an offence for those in the regulated sector to fail to report where, inter alia, they have reasonable grounds to suspect someone has committed a money laundering offence.

8.39 What would constitute the requisite degree of 'knowledge or suspicion' for these purposes given the new objective test imposed on the regulated sector? For example, is anecdotal evidence that the vast majority of a country's inhabitants routinely evade tax sufficient to sustain the argument that the individual should have 'known or suspected' that the foreign national seeking help with a transaction or advice was guilty of an offence? If the individual is aware of such anecdotal evidence, does this equate with 'knowledge or suspicion' based on the objective standard now imposed on the regulated sector. Certainly not; however, this may indicate a need for enhanced due diligence following the MLR, regulation 14.

8.40 *The nexus between tax evasion and money laundering*

8.40 In *R v Da Silva* [2008] EWCA Crim 1654, the Court of Appeal held that 'suspicion' meant that 'there is a possibility, which is more than fanciful, that the relevant facts exist. A vague feeling of unease would not suffice'.

THE VIEW OF THE GOVERNMENT

8.41 This section considers how the UK government's view of the tax evasion and money laundering issue has developed over time.

Speech by Kenneth Clarke (Chancellor of the Exchequer), 5 October 1995

8.42 The link between money laundering and tax evasion was strengthened in a speech made by the Chancellor of Exchequer, Kenneth Clarke, at the Commonwealth Finance Ministers' meeting held in Jamaica on 5 October 1995. In discussing the definition of criminal conduct, he said:

> 'We must recognise that money laundering is associated with all types of crime – from fraud to extortion, arms smuggling to kidnapping. It is quite artificial to draw a distinction between drug related crimes and other crimes. In Britain we have responded to the shifting threat by passing legislation to cover the proceeds of all indictable offences. There is no moral difference between drug trafficking and other serious offences, and the risks from both are great, and this applies as much to fiscal offences as any other crime. All crimes should mean all crimes. Who is the victim is irrelevant. Tax crimes make the law abiding suffer. It is they who make up the shortfall caused by those who cheat.'

Speech by Helen Liddell (Economic Secretary to the Treasury), 6 November 1997

8.43 Speaking at a conference on financial crime, the minister said:

> 'There are international businessmen of intelligence and tact who require financial services. They trade in drugs, prostitutes and child pornography. They equip terrorists. They defraud the innocent or ill-informed. They bribe, forge and corrupt their way to greater market share.
>
> They have discovered that there are private bankers, brokers, accountants and other financial advisers who are comfortable providing services which help to obscure the relationship between the money and the man. But only if it is presented as "just a little problem with tax". They do not put their advisers in an awkward position by declaring the nature of their trade ... These people are money launderers and they sleep easy with the aid of their commissions and their self-deception; just helping out with a little tax problem.
>
> Their laundering supplies the financial lifeblood of international organised crime and in my book (and in the eyes of the law and for that matter the Criminal Justice Act 1988) people who assist criminals are criminals.'

8.44 This view is fully supported by the present government; indeed, since gaining power, they have both declared and demonstrated their intention to devote significant resources to tackling tax evasion. There is also evidence that this approach is gaining support in mainland Europe as governments seek to tackle their budget deficits.

G7 initiative on harmful tax competition, May 1998

8.45 Those who still doubt the government's resolve to utilise the money laundering legislation to tackle tax evasion should consider the May 1998 G7 initiative aimed at tackling the problem of harmful tax competition. As part of this UK-inspired initiative, the G7 members (US, Japan, Germany, Italy, France, Canada and the UK) agreed that financial institutions should be required to report suspicions about the movement of criminal assets irrespective of whether the suspected criminality is tax related.

8.46 The initiative also stated that the 'money laundering authorities' should be permitted to make information available to those investigating tax-related crimes domestically or overseas. In a speech given on 1 June 1998 to the Joint Meeting of Commonwealth Finance and Law Officials on Money Laundering, Helen Liddell stated:

> 'The [G7] Initiative is designed to ensure that financial institutions report suspicions of tax-related crime and that this information is shared both domestically and internationally. This work will begin to address the potential loophole which allows criminals to masquerade as tax-dodgers in order to avoid the reporting obligations of our money laundering systems.'

8.47 Whilst the G7 initiative has no legislative force, many of its policy recommendations are implemented, and not solely in the member countries. In this instance, given the fact that the initiative was inspired by the UK, the government will seek to implement them.

8.48 The UK's immediate response was to announce the attachment of an officer from the (then) Inland Revenue's Special Compliance Office to the Economic Crimes Unit of the National Criminal Intelligence Service (NCIS). NCIS (now SOCA) is the body responsible for analysing and allocating reports of suspected money laundering. HMRC will investigate the most serious cases of tax evasion and avoidance and in appropriate cases will institute criminal proceedings. Customs and Excise have been represented at NCIS since the service was formed.

8.49 HM Treasury acknowledged that the result of this will be that, for the first time, domestic and international intelligence on money laundering will flow to the Revenue. The assignment of a representative from a fiscal authority to the body which receives reports of suspected money laundering is likely to be mirrored in other countries.

8.50 Since UK banks are required to report suspicious transactions, and given that such reports are made to SOCA, a report is now also *effectively* made to HMRC (although HMRC do not see the reports themselves but rather a synopsis of material facts). Indeed, a report of a non-tax related suspicion which

8.50 *The nexus between tax evasion and money laundering*

is dismissed by SOCA as not indicating 'traditional' criminality may now be investigated by HMRC if there is a suspicion of tax evasion.

8.51 Given the extant statutory 'information gateways', the HMRC officers at SOCA will also serve as a formal conduit for the delivery to other authorities of intelligence regarding possible fiscal offences. Certainly there are significant flows of intelligence within the EU and to or from Australia, Canada, New Zealand and the USA.

8.52 This is an enormously valuable source of information for the fiscal authorities. The traditional focus and expertise of SOCA has been predicated upon identifying evidence of drug trafficking and terrorist-related offences since this was the basis for the original money laundering legislation. There was little or no expertise at SOCA when it came to the detection and investigation of fiscal offences. However, this is no longer the case since, following the initial trial of one person on secondment from HMRC; the presence has been expanded considerably.

Foreign tax evasion

8.53 The following is an extract from Hansard, 12 July 1999, Vol 335, No 121, col 82:

'Mr Flight: "To ask the Chancellor of the Exchequer if he has agreed, with the relevant professionals, guidance on the conduct by corporate clients which they should regard as evidence of overseas tax evasion in cases where they are obliged to report suspicion thereof to the NICS [sic]".

Reply given by Patricia Hewitt, Economic Secretary to the Treasury:

"Under the Criminal Justice Act 1993, financial institutions should report to the National Criminal Intelligence Service all transactions which they suspect involve the proceeds of criminal conduct. This obligation is a central element of our defence against money laundering, and provides valuable intelligence in the fight against crime.

The obligation applies equally to the proceeds of overseas offences (including overseas tax offences), where the conduct would have been criminal if it had occurred in the UK. 'Evidence' is not required; the obligation applies where there is knowledge or suspicion that the relevant conduct has occurred or is occurring." '

GUIDANCE FOR FINANCIAL INTERMEDIARIES AND PROFESSIONAL ADVISERS

Institute of Chartered Accountants in England and Wales

8.54 Section 7.3 of the ICAEW Members' Handbook relates to 'Professional Conduct in Relation to Taxation' and paragraphs 2.43–2.48 specifically deal with 'Fiscal Offences and Money Laundering' as follows:

'Fiscal offences and money laundering

2.43 Where members become aware of tax irregularities, they should also bear in mind that under the money laundering legislation, fiscal offences can amount to money laundering.

2.44 Tax-related offences involve evasion and not avoidance and are not in a special category. Tax evasion is a crime, the proceeds of which have to be treated in exactly the same way as those from drug trafficking, terrorist activity, theft, fraud, etc. Offences may relate to direct tax such as income tax or corporation tax, or they may relate to indirect tax such as VAT. Whilst not all tax-related offences are indictable, most are, including frauds against the Revenue or Customs. (*Note: there can be no money laundering until there are proceeds of crime, in other words, in respect of tax evasion, until the tax has become due and has not been paid.*)

2.45 A member who has knowledge of or reasonable grounds for suspecting money laundering should consider whether he has an obligation to make a report to the appropriate authorities (the Money Laundering Reporting Officer in his organisation or the Serious Organised Crime Agency). (*Note: formerly reports were made to the National Criminal Intelligence Service; NCIS has been absorbed into SOCA.*)

2.46 Where a report has been made to SOCA, the client should not be informed where this would be considered tipping off under the terms of the Money Laundering legislation. (*Note: advice on tax matters to a client to persuade him to stop breaking the law by evading tax is not tipping off.*) Members should also note that a report made to NCIS is not a substitute for a proper disclosure to the tax authorities.

2.47 This is an important subject and can involve the member in criminal penalties. There have been recent changes in EU and UK law. Members should familiarise themselves with the required rules and procedures in Part 7 of POCA 2002 and the Money Laundering Regulations 2003 (SI 2003/3075) (*Note: both as amended, for example, with effect from 21st February 2006, s. 330(6) POCA 2002 was amended by The Proceeds of Crime Act 2002 and Money Laundering Regulations 2003 (Amendment) Order 2006 (SI 2006/308) to extend exemption from reporting knowledge or suspicion of money laundering formed in privileged circumstances to a new but limited category of "other relevant professional advisers"* and should read carefully the current professional guidance on the avoidance, recognition and reporting of money laundering (see Section 9.5 of the Members' Handbook "Anti-money laundering guidance for the accountancy sector" at www.icaew.co.uk/membershandbook and CCAB and ICAEW Advisory Service and Tax Faculty guidance at www.icaew.co.uk/money-laundering). Members who are in any doubt about their responsibilities in this area should seek appropriate advice (for example from the Institute's money laundering helpline).

8.54 *The nexus between tax evasion and money laundering*

Members in employment

> 2.48 Whilst these guidelines are addressed primarily to members in practice, they apply equally to members employed in professional practice and in business. Additional assistance for such members will be found in Section 7.1 "Professional conduct and disclosure in relation to defaults and unlawful acts"; see www.icaew.co.uk/membershandbook/.'

Reference to these paragraphs is made in the section dealing with 'Acquiring Knowledge of Direct Tax Irregularities' at **4.7**, and **5.22** in the section dealing with 'Inland Revenue Errors' and at **8.6** in the section dealing with 'Acquiring Knowledge of VAT Errors and Irregularities'.

8.55 Members who are in any doubt about their responsibilities in this area should seek appropriate advice (eg from the Institute's money laundering helpline). Members seeking guidance from their professional body should note that the professional body as a supervisory authority under the MLR may be obliged to make a report to SOCA independently of the member himself. Professional advisers may be concerned that a report to SOCA may breach their duty of confidentiality and result in civil proceedings being instigated by their client – or former client! For example, it is possible to imagine a situation where a report to SOCA leads to bank accounts being frozen causing significant losses to the client. Should the original suspicions prove to be ill-founded; the client may feel understandably aggrieved and may seek legal redress, although there are a number of authorities which indicate a claim is unlikely to succeed.

8.56 PoCA, s 337 on protected disclosures exempts a person who receives information in the course of his trade, profession, business or employment from any legal or other obligations (ie professional) that would otherwise prevent him from making disclosures to the authorities. There are however three conditions:

1 that the information came to the attention of the discloser in the course of his trade, profession, business or employment;
2 that the information:
   (a) causes the discloser to know or suspect; or
   (b) gives him reasonable grounds for knowing or suspecting that another person is engaged in money laundering; and
3 the disclosure was made as soon as is practicable after the information comes to the discloser.

8.57 The disclosure must be made in good faith and as soon as practicable. It is possible that ill-considered disclosures would not be protected from suit. The potential for civil litigation must not be overlooked; for example, there may be exposure to claims predicated upon constructive trusteeship – knowing receipt or knowing assistance. However, a detailed consideration of the risk of civil liability is beyond the scope of this chapter. Professional advisers who are considering a report to SOCA and are concerned about the risk of litigation should seek specialist advice.

The Consultative Committee of Accountancy Bodies (CCAB)

8.58 In August 2008 the CCAB issued Anti-Money Laundering Guidance for the accountancy sector which has been approved by HM Treasury. Guidance on tax matters is included in Appendix A of the Guidance.

Chartered Institute of Taxation (CIOT)

8.59 The CIOT, in conjunction with the Association of Taxation Technicians (ATT), have issued 'Supplementary Anti-Money Laundering Guidance for the Tax Practitioner' as an Appendix to the CCAB main guidance. The guidance note dated 25 June 2009 has been approved by HM Treasury and is reproduced in Appendix 1 of this book.

Auditing Practices Board

8.60 The Auditing Practices Board (APB) issued Practice Note 12 (Revised) 'Money Laundering – Interim Guidance for Auditors on UK Legislation' on September 2010. The purpose of the Practice Note is to provide auditors with information on the money laundering legislation and guidance on its relationship with their responsibilities as auditors. The practice note offers some extremely useful guidance on money laundering legislation, but is now silent on the subject of tax offences. The guidance is generally intended to reflect that given by the CCAB referred to above.

Joint Money Laundering Steering Group

8.61 Joint Money Laundering Steering Group Guidance Notes (revised in December 2003) on the subject of money laundering recognise that there is a relationship between fiscal offences and money laundering. The guidance notes were revised in December 2007 and no longer deal with specific offences. It is perhaps relevant to refer to the earlier guidance on the subject of tax offences and this is reproduced below. The following is an extract from the notes as they related to this issue:

> '2.3 The term "criminal conduct" includes any conduct, wherever it takes place, that would constitute an criminal offence if committed in the UK, ie regardless of whether the conduct would also be an offence in the jurisdiction in which it was committed. This not only includes serious criminal conduct, e.g. drug trafficking offences, terrorist activity, corruption, tax evasion, burglary and theft, fraud, forgery and counterfeiting, product piracy, illegal deposit taking, blackmail and extortion. But also, any other offence which is committed and where benefit is gained of whatever size, for any person.
>
> 2.12 As with other criminal conduct, tax-related offences, where a benefit has been gained by any person, are reportable offences under the money laundering legislation. This includes tax offences committed outside the UK:

8.61 *The nexus between tax evasion and money laundering*

- that would amount to an offence if committed in the UK; and
- where the knowledge or suspicion came to a person in the course of his/her business within the UK regulated sector; and
- where there is a UK link, e.g. the "taxpayer" is resident in the UK, or where the proceeds of the foreign tax fraud have entered or passed through the UK institution (see paragraphs 5.76–5.77). The issues involved are set out in greater detail in Appendix C.

Appendix C

Reporting tax-related offences

Tax-related offences are not in a special category: the proceeds of a tax-related offence may, like the proceeds of a robbery or burglary, be the subject of money laundering offences, under the Proceeds of Crime Act 2002. Offences may relate to direct tax (such as income tax and corporation tax) or indirect tax (such as VAT or excise duty). As stated in Section 2 paragraph 2.12, most tax-related offences are triable on indictment and are therefore reportable offences under the money laundering legislation (*in fact 2.12 no longer states this*). This includes a tax offence committed abroad where the conduct would have been an offence if committed in the UK and where the proceeds have been received by, or passed through, a UK financial institution. Suspected tax evasion should be treated no differently to any other crime that is covered by the money laundering legislation.

However, as stated in Section 2 paragraph 2.4 there is no requirement for any financial institution to have knowledge of other countries' laws, including their tax laws. The issue under the money laundering legislation, for tax offences as for any other offences, is whether the conduct abroad would constitute an offence in this country. If, for example, it is known or suspected that an offence of fraud or false accounting has been committed by the customer against a foreign revenue authority, and the proceeds have entered or passed through the UK, then it should be reported to NCIS (*now SOCA*).

Financial institutions may reasonably assume that customers will meet their tax liabilities unless there is some reason to suspect otherwise, although they should not be taken in too easily by the tax avoidance excuse. Money launderers involved in other crimes may seek to explain transactions that might appear to be suspicious as being for the purposes of legal tax avoidance and financial institutions should remain on their guard. Such statements should not necessarily be taken at face value. If criminal conduct is suspected, then the normal reporting obligations apply.'

8.62 The former guidance notes were approved by HM Treasury for the purpose of PoCA on 17 July 2002.

HM Revenue & Customs

8.63 Following their appointment as a supervisory authority under the MLR 2007 HMRC issued guidance for those parts of the regulated sector in respect of which they were responsible. The guidance was contained in the HMRC Notice MLR 8 which was revised in August 2008 and withdrawn in July

2010. Paragraph 1.1 stated: 'All auditors, insolvency practitioners, external accountants and tax advisers, including those that are supervised by HMRC, should follow the guidance published by the Consultative Committee of Accountancy Bodies (CCAB)': see above. No specific guidance on tax matters was provided; however, HMRC has adopted the CCAB guidance referred to above. Notice MLR 8 was approved by HM Treasury.MLR8 was replaced by guidance notes specific to four specific sectors: money service businesses, high value dealers, and trust or company service providers. HMRC refer to the CCAB Guidance in relation to the accountancy sector, although they are considering issuing their own guidance.

Knowledge or suspicion of an offence

8.64 As with other offences, there is no requirement under the money laundering legislation for a UK financial institution, or a professional adviser, to investigate the affairs of its customers or clients to ascertain whether an offence has been committed. Financial institutions may not be in a position to judge whether a customer has paid tax due in the UK or in any other country. The money laundering legislation does not require a report to SOCA where there is a suspicion that a customer may be considering evading tax in the future. There has to be knowledge or suspicion that the conduct which has generated the proceeds of tax evasion has already occurred or is continuing. If knowledge or a suspicion does arise that the relevant conduct has taken place, then a report should be made to SOCA unless the client enjoys the benefit of legal professional privilege or the more limited benefits of the regulations relating to accountants. In these cases specialist advice should be obtained where necessary as these exceptions are limited in their application and certainly will not apply at all where conduct is capable of furthering a crime (the crime exception).

Procedures for processing the reports

8.65 It is possible that a special form will be prescribed for reporting suspicions of tax evasion. For the time being SOCA request that one of the two general forms in issue be used. SOCA will consider the disclosures received and will pass all or some of the intelligence contained in the suspicious transaction report to the enforcement agency with the power to investigate further. Disclosures which appear to provide evidence of a tax-related crime will be passed to HMRC. Each case will be judged on its merits and not necessarily on the amount of tax at risk.

8.66 Where the intelligence relates to offences committed overseas, SOCA will have the power to disclose the intelligence to Financial Intelligence Units overseas, subject to ensuring suitable safeguards. HMRC may also pass information to an overseas tax authority under various provisions, for example the double taxation agreements or the EU Mutual Assistance Directive.

8.67 *The nexus between tax evasion and money laundering*

THE ROLE OF THE FISCAL AUTHORITIES

8.67 Historically, whereas HM Customs & Excise charged money laundering offences in addition to predicate tax offences, the Revenue did not.

8.68 The quality of the intelligence flowing to the Revenue from 1998, and the results that quickly followed therefrom, led to a change of attitude which broadly coincided with the PoCA entering into force. The Revenue Publication 'Working Together' Issue 13 commented on the PoCA both generally and specifically where there was an impact from the tax perspective. The following extracts are of interest:

> '*Requirement for Professional Advisers to Report Knowledge or Suspicion of Tax Evasion*
>
> All SAR forms must be submitted direct to NCIS. This is the case whether the report concerns the proceeds of tax evasion or any other form of criminal activity. NCIS is the government body to receive these reports as only they have the information to check whether there are links to wider criminality.
>
> The Inland Revenue is not a receiving body for these reports. Where a voluntary disclosure about unpaid liabilities due to tax evasion is intended to be made to the Revenue the professional adviser is still required to make a SAR to NCIS at the earliest opportunity.
>
> *Reports that Concern Tax Evasion*
>
> Reports that relate to tax evasion will be referred within NCIS (now SOCA) to an Inland Revenue team who will analyse and evaluate them. Where the only criminality identified from this analysis is tax evasion, the reports will be forwarded by NCIS to the Inland Revenue or HM Customs & Excise as appropriate. For offences of evading direct taxes or NICs the Inland Revenue will be the investigating body and, in England and Wales, the prosecuting body for these offences. In Scotland the Procurator Fiscal and in Northern Ireland the Director of Public Prosecutions are the prosecuting bodies. Reports forwarded by NCIS to the Revenue will be received by Special Compliance Office (SCO) (now Specialist Investigations).
>
> *Effect on Inland Revenue Enquiries and Hansard (now Code of Practice 9)*
>
> Any Inland Revenue enquiries that result from or are informed by disclosures forwarded by NCIS will be carried out in the same manner as any other Inland Revenue enquiry.
>
> In particular reporting a case to NCIS ahead of notifying the Revenue will have no bearing on how the Revenue may treat a case, if the taxpayer is actively seeking to set their affairs straight. This also applies to cases dealt with under the Inland Revenue approach to civil settlements known as "Hansard".
>
> Confidentiality of information received by the Inland Revenue will of course remain of uppermost importance. In cases other than criminal investigations by SCO, procedures are in place such that investigators receive only the

factual information from a SAR with no knowledge of who made the original disclosure.

Tipping Off

Approaching the Inland Revenue to make a disclosure on behalf of a client about unpaid tax liabilities after the SAR has been sent to SOCA does not constitute tipping off.'

8.69 Commentary regarding the Hansard Practice may be found later in this chapter. In November 2003 the (then) Inland Revenue Special Compliance Office provided further insight to the matter.

Flow of intelligence

8.70 The number of reports disseminated by the Revenue team within NCIS were:

2000–01	2149
2001–02	287
2002–03	227
April 2003–20 October 2004	667

Commentary: Whereas the trend was down, following the initial bonanza, the more recent trend is upward and this is expected to continue, probably dramatically, following the first extension of the regulated sector on 1 March 2004 and the second extension on 15 December 2007. No further figures can be found in the public domain.

8.71 The number of consent applications in cases of suspected tax evasion was 594 (to October 2003). Consent will be given or refused by NCIS (now SOCA) after taking advice from HMRC. It is relevant to note that the actual STRs (now SARs) are not disclosed, but rather the intelligence derived from them using the 5x5 model. Thus the name of the reporter is not revealed although this may be capable or being inferred. HMRC also has access to overseas money laundering intelligence reports, including those received by SOCA from FIU's within the Crown Dependencies (eg Jersey, Guernsey and the Isle of Man).

HMRC's strategy

8.72 Clearly this fresh source of intelligence has served as a new source of investigation cases and will enhance existing investigations. The flow of intelligences will also inform the Revenue's risk-assessment processes, which are used as a basis for case selection. HMRC have stated in unequivocal terms that their first consideration in receiving intelligence will be to identity targets for criminal proceedings.

8.73 In their statement of Criminal Investigation Policy HMRC note that they will consider a criminal investigation 'In cases involving money laundering with particular focus on advisors, accountants, solicitors and others

8.73 *The nexus between tax evasion and money laundering*

acting in a professional capacity who provide the means to put tainted money out of reach of law enforcement.'

8.74 HMRC has responsibility for investigating money laundering cases where tax evasion is the predicate crime and will operate a selective prosecution policy. To this end a specialist unit has been established (the Criminal Taxes Unit). Officers within the unit will use powers under PoCA and will work closely with other law-enforcement agencies exchanging information under the legal gateways available. The prosecution of tax-related money laundering offences is now the responsibility of the Revenue and Customs Prosecutions Office.

8.75 In 2004 SOCA stated: 'the Inland Revenue indicates that around a fifth of disclosures received from SOCA identify a new target and a quarter lead to new enquiries'.

8.76 In November 2004 the Revenue published a press release concerning the Proceeds of Crime Act and money laundering. This document also contained a statement of the Revenue's anti money-laundering strategy (Appendix 2 of this book). In 2007 this was followed by the publication of the HMRC Criminal Finances Strategic Framework. The statements expand on the principles outlined above and are significant documents worthy of being read in full. Consequently the strategies are reproduced in full in Appendix 3 to this book.

8.77 Of the second document, paragraphs 71–73 are of particular note:

'HMRC operates a discerning approach to prosecution in respect of all offences within its remit. Where evidence of money laundering is uncovered during the course of the criminal investigation of a predicate offence, HMRC will ask the prosecutor to consider the addition of money laundering charges to the indictment in order to further dent an individual or gang's capacity to fund or commit future illegitimate activity. Equally, stand-alone money laundering prosecutions are valid where there is sufficient evidence to support charges under the Proceeds of Crime Act. There is no monetary threshold for prosecution.

Where the suspicion of money laundering mounts during a civil investigation, and there is evidence of other serious illegal activities which are not assigned matters, HMRC will consider disclosing this information to other agencies under statutory gateway provisions, either in the CRC Act or other legislation.

HMRC will normally investigate money laundering cases criminally where the money flows (benefit) are derived from fraud against HMRC regimes. HMRC will also investigate cases that will identify and investigate those persons benefiting from fraud by providing the means to launder the proceeds of crime, with particular focus on advisers, accountants, solicitors and others acting in a "professional" capacity who provide the means to put tainted money out of reach of law enforcement. The focus will be on cases where investigation and referral to RCPO will do most to promote compliance with the law and where HMRC can make a contribution to the over-arching HMG anti-money laundering strategy. HMRC will utilise all of the investigative powers in the Proceeds of Crime Act 2002 in the course of investigating money laundering. It will devote effort to counter the use of trusts, offshore mechanisms, internet banking and other devices in the cleansing of criminal monies and will refer appropriate cases to RCPO who will consider prosecution.'

THE RISK TO FINANCIAL INTERMEDIARIES AND PROFESSIONALS

8.78 Historically, UK professionals involved in giving tax advice should always have considered the subtle difference between (legal) tax avoidance and (illegal) tax evasion. Recently the concept has widened to include a further category, tax mitigation, which relates to very simple statutory relief which is available to reduce tax liabilities (personal allowances etc).

8.79 However, tax avoidance can involve an artificial series of apparently commercial transactions which may have little or no substance, and which are designed merely to avoid taxation. Conversely tax evasion is where someone deliberately sets out to defraud the fiscal authorities. This can represent an act of commission, or one of omission. An offence may be committed where information is deliberately withheld or misrepresented to the fiscal authorities (ie there is an inadequate disclosure of material facts that prevents a properly informed decision from being taken).

8.80 The dividing line between avoidance and evasion is becoming both thinner and more dangerous to cross. Professional advisers have taken the view that tax avoidance is capable of being recognised by the civil courts (or even in some circumstances, condoned by the Revenue) and is therefore legitimate, safe from the dangers of criminal litigation.

8.81 However, criminal law has difficulty in recognising the distinction, and when avoidance schemes are put before the criminal courts the court is likely to take a significant interest in the bona fides of the scheme and whether the transactions involved have any commercial substance or purpose. Should such transactions not pass the test of commerciality (reality), a criminal court, which will have little or no concept of the civil law distinction between avoidance and evasion, is unlikely to be sympathetic to the accused. Former Labour Chancellor, Denis Healey, is reported to have commented that 'the distinction between tax avoidance and tax evasion is the thickness of a prison cell wall'.

8.82 This lack of distinction became apparent in a case in the criminal courts, *R v Charlton* [1996] STC 1418, which challenged an offshore invoicing scheme which had always been regarded (by some) as tax avoidance rather than evasion. The jury disagreed and some of the professional advisers were duly convicted and imprisoned.

8.83 How then does the layman distinguish between lawful tax mitigation or tax avoidance and unlawful tax evasion which may involve the proceeds of

8.83 *The nexus between tax evasion and money laundering*

crime? Generally speaking, the more aggressive a 'tax planning' arrangement and particularly where it is accompanied by a reluctance to make a full and transparent disclosure of documents or facts to the fiscal authorities (either in filing a tax return, or on subsequent enquiry), the greater the risk of a criminal offence.

8.84 Consideration should be given to the activities with which professional advisers are often associated, namely:

- establishing and administering offshore corporate structures and trusts;
- handling cash for clients and/or the provision of client account facilities;
- the provision of investment advice.

Such activities are capable of being involved in laundering the proceeds of crime (including tax crime) and therefore potentially expose the professional adviser concerned to prosecution under the money laundering legislation.

8.85 In the UK the fiscal authorities have always regarded suspect tax practitioners as desirable targets for criminal proceedings because they occupy a position of trust in relation to the fiscal authorities (and also because they tend to produce high-profile criminal prosecutions). However, one problem for the fiscal authorities has always been proving (to criminal standards) that there has been a conspiracy between a taxpayer and his professional adviser. Informed application of the money laundering legislation to tax evasion may make it easier to bring criminal charges against financial intermediaries and professional advisers.

Developments in law and practice

8.86 There is little doubt that the European Directives on money laundering and the UK domestic legislation has imposed a huge burden on the financial community, both in terms of management time and the direct cost of compliance.

8.87 Ostensibly, these burdens and costs were introduced in order to make it impossible for those involved in organised crime to launder their profits and acquire a cloak of respectability. However, some cynics will assert that the underlying purpose of the money laundering legislation is to flush out the 'untaxed' rather than the criminal economy with a view to reducing losses to the Exchequer relating to tax evasion.

8.88 In the UK there is little evidence that the introduction of the legislation has had any material effect on organised crime. The fact is that since the 1930s organised crime has developed highly sophisticated money laundering techniques and, while the new legislation may make things slightly more difficult, it also creates a greater degree of awareness of risk, which will tend to drive the activities further underground.

8.89 It is also a fact that since the anti-money laundering legislation was introduced in the UK, there have been very few successful prosecutions (the exceptions have been mainly for drugs-related transactions), although this is by no means the only measure of success. It will be interesting to see whether this situation changes in the future following the current HMRC strategy. The jury is definitely out!

8.90 Certainly the authorities intend to target the professional services sector, from which there have been comparatively few disclosures of suspicious transactions. Until now it is doubtful whether life has been made much more difficult for the 'respectable' tax evader, particularly where he has been established in business for some time. Where such a person has established connections with financial institutions, it seems that he can continue to use them with little personal risk. Should he not wish to take that risk, he can either retain his 'profits' in cash or continue to exploit tax havens such as Switzerland (and certain EU member states) which still enjoy a strong degree of banking secrecy, certainly in relation to fiscal matters.

8.91 For the legislation to become an effective deterrent there must be successful and high-profile prosecutions. The legal framework and public interest policy is now in place to enable this. Certainly in this climate it would be foolhardy for a financial intermediary or professional adviser to claim a statutory defence based on the assertion that tax evasion does not constitute 'criminal conduct' for the purposes of money laundering legislation.

8.92 Consider a taxpayer under investigation by HMRC where the Code of Practice 9 procedure is used, this procedure is dealt with elsewhere in this publication.

8.93 The fact that the tax authorities decide to accept a monetary settlement rather than instituting criminal proceedings is purely a matter of administrative convenience. The monetary settlement does not in itself 'make good' the underlying criminal conduct.

8.94 One crumb of comfort which is capable of being drawn from the practice is that the Revenue cannot accept a monetary settlement *and* institute criminal proceedings. However, there was a potentially worrying development. The case of *R v W* [1998] STC 550 (Court of Appeal) established that a pecuniary settlement negotiated by the Revenue in relation to tax liability did not preclude the Crown Prosecution Service (CPS) from instituting proceedings for false accounting.

8.95 Essentially, one part of the Crown does not bind another. In this case the charge of false accounting was severed from an indictment alleging conspiracy to defraud and was ordered to be tried first. The author understands that the alleged false accounting arose solely in relation to a scheme designed to facilitate tax evasion and was not part of separate alleged criminal conduct by the defendants which was the subject of the conspiracy counts.

8.96 The decision has potentially serious ramifications. Say, for reasons of public interest, the CPS chose to institute proceedings against a taxpayer who had already reached a monetary settlement with the Revenue. If the CPS were able to gain access to statements and documents produced in connection with the tax investigation, they might have little difficulty in bringing a successful prosecution for non-tax-related predicate offences or money laundering.

8.97 *The nexus between tax evasion and money laundering*

8.97 In theory, this could lead to cases where, as a result of a monetary settlement reached with HMRC in respect of tax evasion, sufficient admissible evidence is generated to enable a money laundering charge to be brought by the CPS (or any other prosecuting authority such as the Serious Fraud Office, the Department of Trade and Industry) where the predicate crime upon which the money laundering charge is based was related to tax evasion.

8.98 Thus, a tax evader may find that having paid a sizeable amount of tax, interest and penalties to HMRC, he is charged with false accounting under Theft Act 1968, s 17 and a money laundering offence under PoCA. A money laundering charge would mean that the taxpayer is faced with the possibility of 14 years' imprisonment and/or an unlimited fine (interestingly, the charge of false accounting carries a maximum sentence of only seven years).

8.99 A trial in Scotland in July 1998 (not reported) should also serve to increase the likelihood of the tax evasion-money laundering link being utilised in what are ostensibly non-tax-related criminal prosecutions. A man accused of being one of the financiers of a huge drug trafficking operation had a majority verdict of 'not proven' returned by the jury. It was reported that defence counsel advanced the argument that he was an 'Arthur Daley' figure, 'ducking and diving' in the black economy, 'doing a bit of this and a bit of that' and not paying income tax or VAT. Coupled with his legitimate business activities, his objection to paying tax was advanced in order to explain why he was in possession of huge sums of money.

8.100 Should the report be correct, no doubt HMRC would have viewed the proceedings with interest and acted accordingly. However, consider the position if the defendant had also been charged with offences relating to the evasion of direct and/or indirect taxation, coupled with money laundering charges. A failure to convict on the drug-related charges would have been a pyrrhic victory had there been a conviction on charges relating to tax evasion; this would almost certainly have resulted in conviction on the money laundering charges.

8.101 In the case of *R v IK* [2007] EWCA Crim 491 the Court of Appeal held that profits from a legitimate trade upon which tax had been evaded could, in part, represent the proceeds of crime. In this case the criminal property was represented by the tax evaded. Dyson LJ said that cheating the public revenue had to have already taken place for the funds to represent the proceeds of crime (ie the date for payment of tax due must have passed).

8.102 In the case of *R v NW, SW, RC and CC* [2008] EWCA Crim 2 the Court of Appeal confirmed that the Crown could not simply point to unexplained wealth and assert that there was no legitimate explanation and therefore it must be from the proceeds of crime. The Crown had to identify the criminal conduct or at least the category of criminal conduct alleged to have generated the money.

8.103 Life for the alleged tax evader who enjoys a criminal lifestyle will be made more difficult by other provisions of PoCA 2002 (ie the civil recovery process or revenue functions of SOCA).

8.104 It is now clear that HMRC will make use of the money laundering legislation. HMRC will be tempted to utilise the money laundering legislation in the most serious cases where financial institutions and/or professional advisers have assisted in or have otherwise facilitated tax evasion.

8.105 In the US the Internal Revenue Service will bring money laundering charges in relation to tax offences only where under-declared income emanates from a criminal source. Where profits arise from a legitimate business, tax evasion, though remaining a criminal offence, is not a predicate crime for money laundering purposes; a stark contrast with the position of the UK.

CONCLUSION

8.106 It is to be hoped that this chapter assists in dispelling the myth that tax evasion, or offences related to it, are not predicate crimes for money laundering purposes. Financial intermediaries and professional advisers must acquaint themselves with the relevant legislation and establish procedures to deal with situations where they suspect their clients are involved in tax evasion (and hence, potentially, money laundering). It is also vital that professional advisers ensure that their action or inaction, once they know or suspect money laundering is taking place, does not risk implicating them in any criminality.

8.107 Professional advisers should note that the money laundering legislation does not prevent them from acting on behalf of a client seeking to make a full disclosure of irregularities to one or more of the fiscal authorities. However, advisers acting for such clients should ensure that they do not give any 'transactional advice' which may implicate them in an 'arrangement' for the purposes of PoCA, s 328. In this context, consider a professional adviser representing a client seeking to make a disclosure to HMRC whilst at the same time offering the client some hypothetical advice on how to 'ring fence' certain assets from the fiscal authorities. In the author's opinion, this is unlawful.

8.108 A former version of ICAEW's 'Professional Conduct in Relation to Taxation' points out at para 2.32:

> 'The money-laundering legislation does not prevent a member from advising clients on negotiations with the tax authorities in respect of evaded tax liabilities, *on a bona fide basis of full disclosure* in accordance with the guidelines' (emphasis added).

8.109 As the line between tax avoidance and tax evasion becomes increasingly important, the money laundering legislation adds a 'double jeopardy' for those who either cross the line or assist another to do so. Professional advisers involved in devising and/or implementing aggressive tax avoidance schemes would be well advised to ensure that they genuinely deserve the 'avoidance' label – although this label is becoming far less comforting than it once was. Perhaps the test for any scheme should be whether a credible explanation could be provided to a Crown Court judge and a jury of 12 lay people. If in doubt, it may be prudent to seek counsel from a member of the criminal bar.

Chapter 9

Meetings with HMRC

Chris Chadburn BSc (Econ)

Founder member of Venntax – an association of independent specialist tax consultants

INTRODUCTION

9.01 Meetings with HMRC arise in many circumstances. This chapter focuses on meetings between advisers, their clients and HMRC officers relating to day-to-day direct tax business return enquiries, interventions and compliance checks by the Local Compliance Small & Medium Enterprises business unit. Many of the points made are of general application and **9.63** et seq cover meetings in the employer inspection context. Ensuring you have a 'good' meeting will often be crucial to getting the results both you and your client are looking for at the end of the enquiry process.

9.02 These notes refer to the current position on meetings. HMRC's approach at the top end of tackling non-compliance is now to work very closely with the taxpayer in an open and collaborative way. In their Large Business Service's brochure 'Working with Large Business', HMRC have published 'the types of generic risk factors we use to develop our risk assessments' which they say will be discussed with customers as part of the risk-review process: 'we will publish risk assessment guidance that will help you understand our thinking on what we consider to be key risks'.

9.03 They state that their resources will focus on customers who do not comply. Low-risk taxpayers will receive light touch checking and those seen as high risk will receive significantly more attention. Taxpayers will however be clear from the outset where HMRC intend addressing the issues.

9.04 This approach is now applied to larger and higher risk businesses dealt with by Local Compliance and the new High Net Worth Individual teams. Other substantial companies will see their risk assessments and may take part in the preparation and review of these.

9.05 *Meetings with HMRC*

9.05 Clearly this approach of matching HMRC resource with the tax at risk is not appropriate for the vast majority of SMEs given the staffing implications for the department. A different approach to enquiries was trialled between November 2007 and April 2008. HMRC have advised that openness and early dialogue will be adopted in most cases, leading to more transparency and improved rapport in compliance checks. This will involve an explicit, realistic but flexible timescale for:

- an initial discussion;
- the production of any information and documents;
- a records examination; and
- a discussion of the findings.

9.06 It was envisaged that the initial discussion would help HMRC understand:

- the nature of the business;
- the circumstances of the individual;
- the records kept and the work done by the accountant;
- the key risk points on which the enquiry is focused.

PURPOSE OF THE MEETING

9.07 Detailed notes on meetings relating to enquiries are at HMRC's Enquiry Manual (EM) 1820 et seq. Meetings are described as a vital part in full enquiries and appropriate in aspect enquiries of substance. Explanations will invariably be needed from the taxpayer and it is suggested that these are best obtained directly at an early stage rather than by correspondence (EM 1821).

9.08 HMRC's compliance officers are told that they should know exactly why they are holding the meeting, what they want to achieve and what information they want to obtain. Meetings are considered the best way to:

- explain the purpose of the enquiry;
- obtain facts about how the business is run and the records kept;
- establish whether the taxpayer wishes to make a disclosure;
- explain the position on interest and penalties where omissions are established;
- agree the action needed to move the enquiry forward;
- quantify the omissions;
- settle the enquiry.

This list is from EM 1822 which for some reason fails to mention a key point, obtaining the facts about the taxpayer's private finances.

9.09 Although some full enquiries are randomly selected, the vast majority are taken up because it is considered by HMRC that tax is at risk. When tackling non-compliance, officers are under constant pressure to deliver results in terms of yield and turnaround. This results in a detailed consideration of the risk of something being wrong with the return and the likely scale of the problem.

9.10 The typical opening letter will involve a request for books and records and some additional information. This will normally relate solely to the

Meetings with HMRC **9.14**

business rather than the finances of the proprietors. There is no compulsion on the officer to say why the enquiry has been started, but bear in mind HMRC's commitment to transparency. In larger cases there may be a request for a 'pre-meeting meeting' before any records are examined, but this will typically be with the firm's accountant and the adviser to discuss how the business records are kept and link together and how the accounts have been prepared. It should then be possible to agree on how the records can most effectively be examined by HMRC.

9.11 In examining the books etc the officer is seeking to establish whether there is evidence to indicate that the initial doubts on the accuracy of the return have been validated. Unless the review shows there to be no problem or is inconclusive, the officer will usually proceed by requesting a meeting with the client.

9.12 HMRC envisage that there may be a reluctance to attend and in advising on how to overcome objections to a meeting. EM 1861 confirms that the officer should say why a meeting with the taxpayer is desirable. You should note that EM 1827 says that 'an agenda covering the main areas for discussion should always be provided. This should enable the agent to carry out any necessary preparation or research in advance'. In practice at the outset there is usually little by way of explanation of the need for a meeting beyond the assertion that experience shows this is the most cost-effective way of dealing with the HMRC's concerns. Comment on what the officer wants to talk about is often restricted to generalities or the need to know more about the business or the client's personal finances or whatever. However, a detailed agenda can be requested if it is not offered, to assist the adviser in preparing the client for the meeting (**9.21**).

9.13 EM 1861 concludes by saying that 'ultimately you do not have a power to compel a taxpayer or accountant to attend a meeting'. The relevant Codes of Practice (COP 11 and 14) also make that clear although the equivalent Compliance Check factsheets do not. You will need to deal with the enquiry in a cost-effective manner and this will be very difficult if you have little or no idea where the officer's attack is coming from. Clearly you need to discuss the meeting request with the client but invariably every effort should be made to establish with HMRC why a meeting is considered necessary and the aspects to be covered. If the officer considers the quality of the records to be at best indifferent, this will be a principal reason to say they need to look at the business and private finances in more detail to validate the figures returned. Officers may well talk in generalities at this point and keep specifics to themselves until after the taxpayer has provided explanations, without prior notice of the questions.

9.14 If you are not convinced that a meeting at this stage is the best way forward for your client you can suggest to the officer that you are sure that many of the questions can be dealt with perfectly adequately by correspondence. Usually at this stage HMRC will not have a convincing case and will probably take you up on your offer. It is a fact that you can provide considerable detail in this way that will take the enquiry forward. Your client has the benefit of giving

9.14 *Meetings with HMRC*

answers after deliberation and research and you should be in a position to take a much firmer view on where HMRC's interest really lies and whether a meeting is appropriate at that stage.

9.15 The officer may point out that not agreeing to a meeting may be regarded as a lack of cooperation if penalties arise and this will affect the abatement. This is referred to in leaflet IR 160 'Enquiries under Self Assessment' when explaining what happens at the end of an enquiry.

> **'*Co-operation* – A reduction of up to 40%**
>
> If you supply information quickly, attend interviews, answer questions honestly and accurately, give all the relevant facts and pay tax on account when it becomes possible to estimate the amount due, you will then get the maximum reduction for co-operation.'

The abatement for co-operation now only applies where penalties can be charged under the old penalty system, which is currently running alongside the new.

9.16 The Compliance Handbook (CH) includes guidance on the new penalty regime that generally relates to returns due to be filed on or after 1 April 2009. CH 82450 covers penalty reductions for actively helping quantify inaccuracies, providing positive assistance and volunteering information. This says that there are many different ways of achieving all this and included in several examples is 'attending meetings where that is the best way to quantify the inaccuracy and test the disclosure'. CC/FS7 sets out how the taxpayer can reduce any penalty but there is nothing prescriptive about attending meetings.

9.17 Given the fact that your client has a right not to attend a meeting it is difficult to see how the penalty reductions would be affected if your client did everything that could reasonably have needed to be done except attend a meeting. It seems difficult to argue that proactively establishing the extent of any tax loss must involve a meeting with HMRC after the records review. To help in any future negotiation on penalties you should make it clear to the officer why you do not agree that a meeting at that particular time is the 'best way' forward. See more detail on penalties in **Chapter 14**.

9.18 An officer may take the line that if the taxpayer continues to refuse to attend a meeting then it may well be the case that they will have to be questioned under oath before the Tax Tribunal if the case progresses that far. It will be rare for a case to progress in that way. After the initial records examination the officer will invariably still be looking for a lot of information to determine whether suspicions are well founded and the likely extent of the problem. You and your client may be more than happy to provide information but not at a meeting, because the officer has not provided any detail on what the key issues are.

9.19 There will certainly come a time in many cases where the officer says that progress will now be made using formal means if there is to be no meeting. Experience shows that this approach will only usually arise several months from the start of the enquiry. By then you should be clear on the merits of the

HMRC case and any meeting is likely to be on relatively narrow ground because plenty of information has been provided in the meantime.

9.20 It is of course generally accepted that a co-operative and constructive approach to HMRC enquiries is adopted, but it must also be recognised that the objectives of the officer and those of the adviser and the client may not always coincide.

PREPARING FOR THE MEETING

9.21 Compliance officers will prepare extensively for any meeting with a taxpayer and adviser. HMRC do not have your cost constraints and invariably officers will be able to devote significantly more time to preparation than you. This is a primary reason for ensuring that before agreeing to a meeting you are as clear as possible on where your preparation time should be spent. The following notes are really a counsel of perfection but as a minimum:

- the client needs to be aware of:
  - the background to the enquiry and the meeting;
  - the advantages of being cooperative and making early and complete disclosures;
- there needs to be consideration of the general areas to be covered at the meeting and the likely areas of particular interest to HMRC;
- the client needs to be briefed on:
  - what is likely to happen at the meeting;
  - how direct and open questions should be approached;
  - potentially difficult areas and how to deal with these;
  - the adviser's role.

Review your knowledge of the client

9.22 The adviser should generally review the case and identify strengths and weaknesses. Particular attention should be paid to those areas to which the officer's attention might usefully be directed if a speedy and beneficial resolution for the client is to be reached. There should be a focus on:

- the quality of the client's records;
- issues arising during the preparation of the accounts and/or tax returns and how these were dealt with;
- previous tax issues;
- the position on any previous enquiries;
- general knowledge of the adviser (and adviser's staff) of the business and private finances.

Identify any problem areas

9.23 If omissions or understatements are identified prior to a meeting with HMRC it is critical that these are considered in some detail and disclosed to HMRC at an early stage. This will signify a constructive and cooperative

9.23 *Meetings with HMRC*

approach and will assist in optimising the penalty position. If disclosures are not made at an early stage of a meeting but are revealed in a piecemeal fashion this will have a damaging effect not only on the penalty loading but also on the client's (and possibly your own) credibility.

9.24 On making a disclosure it may be agreed that an early meeting with the client is dispensed with and the adviser agrees to provide an investigation report. There will be a meeting with the officer to agree the scope of such a report and a provisional timescale.

9.25 If the review process identifies no particular issues it will be useful at some stage to detail the research which has been done and the conclusions. Care needs to be taken on the timing of this and usually it will be appropriate once you have established that the officer has 'fired all the bullets' or that there are none. There may be advantages to starting the process by saying you have looked at the papers and discussed the position in some detail with your client and you believe the return is correct. If, however, the officer has strong evidence to the contrary then you and your client may finish up looking less than competent and possibly dishonest.

Pre-meeting client issues

9.26 At the time of receiving the opening letter the client should have been briefed on the background to HMRC enquiries and the likely course that will be taken. In particular you should outline:

- the obligations to keep proper records;
- the absolute right to enquire into tax returns;
- the power to call for relevant documents and particulars;
- the rights of appeal and review.

9.27 The advantages of admitting problems at an early stage should have been spelt out. There will have been a subsequent dialogue on the upsides and downsides of having a meeting at this stage and the client should be reminded of all this.

9.28 The adviser may be thoroughly familiar with HMRC meetings but most clients will experience a fair degree of stress when face to face with one of HMRC's officers. The client should be briefed as far as possible on what to expect on the day. Much of the meeting, certainly the opening explanations, issue of HMRC leaflets etc, will follow a fairly predictable course. Your approach and behaviour in dealing with HMRC in a mature and professional manner will settle the client. The officer will expect your role to be as a facilitator. The client will be expected to answer the questions and should appreciate this.

9.29 As a general rule clients should be encouraged to keep answers to questions factual and concise and to avoid overly lengthy replies. In particular they should be made aware that if they do not know the answer to a specific question then they should not guess and should only provide estimates when they are comfortable doing so. Any false impressions given at the initial meeting may be difficult to correct at a later stage. This is another excellent reason for only agreeing to a meeting when you and the client are confident that

Meetings with HMRC **9.33**

you are aware of the key issues for the officer and it is unlikely that there will be any surprises for anyone. The client should be made aware that the officer's usual objective in the early stages of the meeting is to put the taxpayer at ease and get them talking. The client should be encouraged to:

- remain calm and avoid aggravating the officer;
- participate actively and constructively;
- answer specific questions directly;
- answer more general questions with circumspection.

You should be prepared to suggest a 'review and report back procedure' which should be quite acceptable and may even be expected by HMRC.

9.30 The client cannot be expected to remember details from many years ago. Ideally the request for a detailed agenda will have resulted in identifying such questions before the meeting and appropriate answers given. Areas of weakness should be considered in detail. It is not possible to be prescriptive on what these will be but **9.08** sets out the areas of interest for the officer and your judgment should throw up some likely issues. If the officer is looking at private finances in any detail at all then questions will invariably arise in relation to non-taxable sources. See EM 2051.

> 'Taxpayers may claim that deficiencies ... or money introduced were funded from ... non-taxable receipts. You should at an early stage in an enquiry try to pre-empt such claims by asking the taxpayer about matters such as cash accumulation, loans and gifts received and so on. If the claim is first made at a meeting you should question the taxpayer closely about it, before he or she has had time to invent plausible circumstances to surround a false story.'

9.31 Further general guidance is then given at EM 2053 and then more specific details are given from EM 2056 through to EM 2097 although most of the text is withheld. Common explanations are:

- cash hoards;
- betting wins;
- legacies and sales of personal effects;
- illegal or immoral activities.

9.32 In these circumstances you should ask the client about such issues before the meeting – although it will not usually be wise to raise a specific query on illegal or immoral income! If there are matters of substance in the relevant period then these should be discussed in considerable detail. Are you satisfied with the explanations given and is the compliance officer likely to be? In any event the client needs to understand that HMRC will require evidence to substantiate the claims and you need to agree how best this can be obtained. See **9.23** regarding early disclosure of any irregularities.

9.33 One reason for the officer preferring to see the client is that it helps in forming a view on the latter's overall credibility. The adviser should do all that is possible to ensure that the client comes across as honest, open, knowledgeable, and helpful. You want to come out of the meeting feeling that the client would make a very credible witness if appeals were taken to the Tax

9.33 *Meetings with HMRC*

Tribunal. There is no substitute for sound preparation but over-coaching can easily give the wrong impression.

WHAT THE COMPLIANCE OFFICER WANTS

9.34 The officer will have a combination of the following objectives which should be clearer to you when considering the reasons for the meeting and the agenda:

- to obtain detailed information about the individual's personal and financial background, the nature of the business being carried on and the economics on which it operates;
- to obtain detailed information about the business records with a view to testing their reliability;
- to obtain detailed and specific information about the individual's personal finances to establish whether these stack up with the returns and accounts;
- to check facts and explanations against third-party information held.

9.35 The officer has to be able to cast significant doubt on the accuracy of the return in order to justify continuing with the enquiry. The Taxes Management Act (TMA) 1970, s 9A obliges the inspector to establish whether the return 'is incorrect or incomplete'.

9.36 It is important to HMRC officers to find problems with the records. They can then justify preparing a recalculation of the client's sales figure based on a business economics exercise which suggests that the figure in the accounts may have been understated. The preparation of a business economics exercise which casts doubt on the accuracy of the sales figure is not enough to justify displacing the accounts, if there is no reason to cast doubt on the accuracy of the records from which those accounts were prepared.

9.37 The officer may be able to show that the evidence about the client's lifestyle and the day-to-day expenditure of him and his family exceeds significantly the cash available from drawings from the business and other sources for the client to live on. Similarly the funding of private assets may be unclear from the known borrowings and other established funds. If the officer can show that any of these 'doubtful' features are present there may well be a strong case for establishing omissions. Invariably, though, HMRC will be in a much stronger position if it can be shown that there is evidence of material inaccuracies in the records supporting the return.

CHECKLIST FOR PREPARING FOR A MEETING

9.38 The adviser should:
- review the case history;
- review all knowledge of the client and business;
- prepare and review schedules from the accounts and tax returns;

- discuss case with accounts and tax staff;
- identify areas of weakness;
- discuss briefly areas of interest with the compliance officer (consider a pre-meeting meeting);
- clear up any accountancy queries and brush up on relevant technical knowledge;
- agree with HMRC that accounts queries are to be handled before the meeting;
- agree an agenda for the meeting;
- agree who is to be present and a suitable place, date and time;
- agree what information should be brought to the meeting.

9.39 The advisor should cover the following points with the client:

- explain the reason for the meeting;
- outline the history of the case to-date;
- explain what HMRC already know;
- explain the officer's likely objectives;
- summarise the expected control and format of the meeting;
- advise on approach and demeanour;
- identify areas of weakness and strengths;
- identify and go through key questions and answers;
- provide briefing note.

THE MEETING ITSELF

Format of the meeting

9.40 Most full HMRC enquiries will follow a fairly predictable format, at least in outline and will cover some combination of the following:

- Reasons for the interview, provisions of TMA 1970, ss 8 and 9A (TMA 1970, s 12AC for partnerships, FA 1998, Sch18 for companies) the rights of HMRC to make enquiries into a return and the rights of the taxpayer to ask for an internal review and for the Tax Tribunal to determine when an enquiry should be terminated.
- Background to the business, business history, particular expertise, types of products, types of goods sold, business performance over the years, problems encountered in running the business, wastage, expertise and experience of the proprietor, specific nature of the trade, prices, pricing policies, stock-holding policies, cash-control policies, economics of the business, general trends.
- Business records: who keeps them, where, how often, what are they, what do they cover, nature of 'prime' records; details of any 'non-financial' records kept; points from the officer's initial review demonstrating a clear problem and profit adjustment.
- Business economics in detail: how the business is organised.
- Level and frequency of drawings from the business; personal and

9.40 *Meetings with HMRC*

       private expenditure, personal assets and liabilities, funding of major assets etc, other sources of income, cash windfalls and legacies, etc.
- Technical adjustments: own use and own goods, private car adjustments, private telephone, etc, other private benefits/expenses.
- Any omissions or additions disclosed during meeting, proposals for further investigation.
- Agreements for subsequent action: information to be provided, records to be reviewed, investigations to be undertaken by the accountant, etc, scope of future enquiries and an agreed timetable for action.

Who will be present?

9.41 Always ascertain before the meeting who is to attend on behalf of HMRC. There will usually be at least two officers, one essentially conducting the meeting and the other taking notes. You need to establish whether there will be anyone there outside the norm, for example a very senior officer or a qualified accountant. Why are they attending and does this affect your approach to the meeting?

9.42 The adviser should always consider who should attend on the client's behalf and ensure HMRC are aware of the position. If the meeting is likely to be protracted, complex and generally difficult, then assistance from the adviser's office may be necessary to take notes and provide general support.

9.43 It may be appropriate from time to time to get a specialist's technical input at the opening meeting if the agenda warrants it. If personal finances are to be discussed it may be appropriate for the client's spouse or partner to attend even though they have no business responsibilities.

9.44 If a meeting is likely to cover detailed reviews of business records or particular areas of commercial expertise it may be advisable to have an appropriate member of the client's staff at the meeting. Questions to be directed to the employee may have to be dealt with at a separate meeting or at the beginning of the discussion after which the employee can leave. They should be given clear guidelines and support in preparation for the meeting and their terms of reference, areas of expertise and knowledge about the business and the proprietor's affairs must be made clear to the officer.

9.45 Where the business is conducted by a husband and wife, civil partners or cohabiting couples in a business partnership or as directors in a limited company it is important to verify before the meeting the exact degree of involvement of both parties in the business. Should any query about the level of involvement of one of the couple in the business be raised by the officer, it can then be addressed properly. Where omissions are to be disclosed it will be of considerable importance to ascertain the extent of the involvement and knowledge of both parties in the relevant events. HMRC's instructions tell the officer to offer separate interviews to both initially (EM 1852 et seq). It may be necessary to insist on separate meetings where it is clear that one party has had no involvement in or no knowledge of what has gone on. In such cases it may be necessary for one or both of the couple to seek independent advice.

9.46 For businesses run by partners or directors of a limited company the officer will indicate who it is believed should attend the meeting or meetings. There will usually be a clear line drawn between meetings where personal finances and business matters are to be discussed. At the former, only the relevant partner or director will be present with the adviser and at the latter either all partners and directors or those with specific responsibilities for example the finance partner/director. Clearly the larger the organisation the more likely it is that not all partners/directors will attend the business side of the meeting.

9.47 The officer's views on which taxpayers should attend should be fully considered with the clients. Having a number of partners/directors tied up for several hours in a meeting with HMRC, together with essential preparatory time, may be a very significant commitment. The officer should be prepared fully to justify the assertion that the suggested attendees are necessary to progress the enquiry.

Where and when should the meeting be held?

9.48 HMRC's view is that 'asking for meetings at the business premises should be the norm' (EM 1830). Their rationale for this is said to be that in many cases it will be easier to examine the business records there.

9.49 Given that there is no obligation to have a meeting with HMRC, the adviser and the client need to take a view on the advantages and disadvantages of holding a meeting at the business premises, in the tax office or at the adviser's office. It will rarely be suggested that the meeting take place at the client's home and unless there are issues such as age and infirmity any such suggestion should normally be rejected. The logistics and potential disruption to the business as well as lack of privacy from employees will be principal factors to consider, but deciding where the client is likely to feel most comfortable should usually be the key point. This is unlikely to be at the tax office. The adviser's office might sensibly be regarded as the venue of choice, where the taxpayer and adviser will be most at ease.

9.50 Although it will be sensible to have a degree of flexibility, the time and day best suiting the client should be 'the norm'.

9.51 Wherever and whenever the meeting is held it should be arranged that the room and set up provide for a reasonable degree of comfort and minimal opportunity for disruption. It will usually be sensible to establish approximately how long the meeting is expected to last and manage expectations if necessary.

9.52 As a separate matter, you should note that under the compliance checks regime which came into effect from 1 April 2009, HMRC have the power to enter a person's business premises and inspect business documents. Further information is given at **9.65** et seq.

9.53 *Meetings with HMRC*

Conduct of the meeting

9.53 HMRC's Personal Contact Manual, now withdrawn, set out how HMRC officers should:

- be helpful, courteous and considerate;
- have a polite and professional manner;
- be fair and impartial;
- give clear, honest and accurate explanations when needed;
- have regard to confidentiality;
- handle matters promptly.

EM 1850 gives general points to compliance officers on meetings gives some insight into expected conduct. It is interesting to note that the officer will be striving to gain and maintain control of the meeting.

9.54 All enquiries and all meetings are different and however well you and the client have prepared, unexpected and potentially difficult issues may be raised. The adviser should be alert to this and recognise potential stress points quickly. You should always be prepared to ask for a brief adjournment of the meeting to reassure the client, to provide professional guidance and to review the progress of the meeting to establish whether or not the client wishes to proceed. There may be occasions on which the adviser deems it necessary to bring the meeting to a close either because new and unwelcome information has come to light, or because HMRC adopt specific procedures about which the adviser is unsure or unprepared.

9.55 A good example of the latter situation would be where it appears from the client's comments during the meeting that HMRC may regard this as a case of serious fraud. See www.hmrc.gov.uk/prosecutions/crim-inv-policy.htm and **Chapter 7** of this book for details of HMRC policy on prosecutions. HMRC prosecute few cases for false accounts/returns but the case may be taken over by a Civil Investigation of Fraud team if the yield is likely to be £75,000 or more. If the yield is likely to be over £500,000 the Specialist Investigations team may be involved.

9.56 Prolonged pauses or silence during a meeting are sometimes used by HMRC's officers and can appear oppressive and quite stressful for the client. The client should avoid unnecessary or irrelevant statements simply to keep the meeting moving and the adviser should normally fill such silences if the client is uneasy.

9.57 The adviser should be prepared to participate actively or intervene in the meeting even if at times this is clearly not to the satisfaction of the officer.

9.58 Officers should not tape or video record a meeting. If the client or agent wants to tape record the meeting this should normally be allowed if it is agreed that a copy of the unedited tape be provided to HMRC or a full typed transcript. Requests for video recordings will normally be refused on the basis that there is no obvious business advantage over an audio recording. See EM 1835.

How should the meeting conclude?

9.59 The officer is told to ensure the taxpayer knows exactly where they stand at the end of the meeting. If there is likely to be additional liability then the taxpayer needs to be informed and reminded of the benefits of co-operation and what needs to be done next. The officer will most likely raise the possibility of a penalty being charged at this stage and is then obliged to issue factsheet CC/FS9 the Human Rights Factsheet. Factsheets CC/FS7 may also be issued. If further information is needed then the officer should make it clear what is needed; a realistic timescale should be agreed. The position should be summarised by letter shortly after the meeting. See EM 1855.

Notes of meetings

9.60 The officer or his assistant will prepare a detailed note of the meeting usually shortly after it has been held. A copy should be sent to the adviser either:

- asking for the client to signify agreement to its accuracy by signing a copy and returning it; or
- at least commenting on any amendments that are considered necessary.

9.61 There will usually be no advantage to the client in signing the notes and there is no statutory obligation to do so. If however there are points of dispute or a particular spin on what was said then these should be pointed out reasonably quickly. Similarly if what was said is properly recorded but the client or the adviser on reflection wants to give better particulars then this may be an appropriate time to do so. Clearly if points on the notes are not raised until many months after the notes were sent out then their evidential value is likely to be substantially weakened.

Ten key areas

9.62

1. Lack of preparation and attention to detail will result in an inability to answer questions properly. Clients may be faced with questions for which they are not ready leaving them feeling exposed and vulnerable. This in turn will jeopardise the client/agent relationship.
2. Most enquiries are settled without recourse to formal appeal proceedings and the adviser should be aware throughout any meeting that he may have to reach a compromise settlement at some stage. Identifying strengths and weaknesses and continually reinforcing the best arguments with references to points and facts in the client's favour is a key area of negotiating.
3. A list of priorities and certain key points to make helps the adviser redirect the route a meeting is taking in some cases. The adviser must be prepared to insist that the discussion is moved on if it is felt that the meeting is bogged down.
4. An ability to see the other side's viewpoint, to accept HMRC's statutory authority and to take a constructive approach towards resolving areas of

9.62 *Meetings with HMRC*

        doubt and difficulty is generally to be recommended. It is likely to prove more cost-effective in the long run. Advisers must however be prepared to exercise their judgement on where co-operation ends and obsequious collaboration begins. The client is entitled to representation and to feel that he has been afforded the correct level of support.

5   Many enquiries will at some stage cover or at least touch on areas where HMRC's right to information or to take certain action is not clear cut. Advisors who are known to avoid disputes on such areas may be viewed as a 'soft touch' and will do clients an injustice.

6   A thorough awareness of the provisions of TMA 1970, FA1998, Sch 18 (companies) and FA 2008, Sch 36 (compliance checks) and the rights and obligations under the statute is needed. Cases may involve specific areas of the Taxes Acts and careful research should always be undertaken if such technical issues are to be the subject of discussion during any meeting.

7   The adviser who lets the compliance officer know that he would not take a case to appeal is sacrificing a solid negotiating tactic and, more fundamentally, is depriving his client of one of the latter's basic rights under the enquiry process.

8   The adviser should always be prepared to call a halt during a meeting to be satisfied that the client fully understands the statutory position and what the various options are, even if this is just done to give the client breathing space or a comfort break.

9   The adviser should adopt a questioning and challenging approach to the officer's statements where appropriate.

10   Where detailed calculations are presented during an interview it will rarely be possible to test them properly. An interview is inevitably a pressurised situation and even simple points or errors can easily be overlooked. Generally no comment should be made on detailed calculations presented under these circumstances and they should be reviewed later. Similarly, any request for the client to sign any document at the meeting should be resisted; the document should be taken away for later review.

Employer compliance checks

9.63   All references to employers include contractors. A broad summary of the regulations under which PAYE and NICs are deducted is given at HMRC's Compliance Operational Guidance manual (COG) 903520 and 903540. PAYE records must be retained for at least three years after the end of the tax year to which they relate (Income Tax (PAYE) Regulations 2003, reg 97 and Social Security (Contributions) Regulations 2001, reg 26 Sch 4).

9.64   In general the points made in relation to the opening meetings in self-assessment enquiries will apply to inspection visits for employers. The essential objectives of these inspections are to ensure that employers:

- pay what is due;
- keep accurate records;
- submit accurate returns;

- submit returns within the statutory time limits.

9.65 A new framework for inspections generally was introduced from 1 April 2009 and detailed guidance is provided in the Compliance Handbook (CH) 21660 et seq. See also **9.69** below.

9.66 If an inspection is reasonably required to check the tax position of any person an HMRC officer has the power to enter a person's business premises and inspect:

- the premises, see CH 25180;
- the business assets on those premises, see CH 25260;
- the business documents on those premises, see CH 25280.

The employer may agree a time and date for an inspection but otherwise HMRC must give at least seven calendar days' notice unless the inspection is carried out by or with the agreement of a senior HMRC officer. Such unannounced visits will only take place where it has not been possible to make an appointment or there are identified concerns, such as a reason to believe tax is being deliberately evaded. See CH 25520.

9.67 Entry into the premises may be refused and the officer may not force entry (CH 25120). In these circumstances HMRC are likely to get approval for the inspection from the First-tier Tribunal. This allows HMRC to impose penalties for deliberately obstructing an officer in the course of an approved inspection. The initial penalty is £300 and up to £60 a day for continuing failure.

9.68 As in other areas of tackling non-compliance it is clear that the selection of employers for inspection is based on risk assessment and that yield is the name of the game. An employer inspection may be undertaken if a full enquiry into a business and its principals is being considered. Full enquiries into larger businesses will often have a review of PAYE and benefits as part of the overall compliance check. In short these are not routine matters.

9.69 Although detailed guidance on employer compliance checks can be found in COG (previously the Employer Compliance Handbook). It should be noted that the factsheets: EC/FS1, FS2, FS3 and FS5 have been withdrawn. This is because HMRC now carry out employer compliance checks under their new powers at FA 2008, Sch 36. Further information can be found at www.hmrc.gov.uk/about/new-compliance-checks.htm. The notification letter SC105 and factsheet EC/FS4 (penalties) are still available and there is a suite of new factsheets covering compliance checks: CC/FS1 to FS13. Factsheets CC/FS3, CC/FS4 and CC/FS5 cover visits.

9.70 If there is to be a pre-arranged visit, clearly it makes sense to establish in advance exactly which records are needed and for which period. COG 905015 says that an explanation of the types of records required should be given when making the appointment. Before inspecting the records the officer will want to talk about the business, the workforce and the systems.

9.71 HMRC should notify the adviser of the commencement of the compliance check (COG 905020). It is common for advisers not to attend such

9.71 *Meetings with HMRC*

visits and this may be appropriate. However, given the risk-based decision to undertake the check, the benefits and costs of the adviser attending the visit should be carefully discussed. At the very least clients need to know:

- how the review is likely to unfold;
- the risk areas;
- how to handle the visit.

9.72 COG 905045 sets out details of the 'intervention plan' which provides a framework for the check and is produced before the visit. It is used to record:

- specific risks to be addressed;
- key steps planned to address those risks;
- results of the work/tests undertaken;
- outcomes, conclusions and yield.

9.73 COG 905075 sets out details of HMRC's risk-based systems audit which gives a good idea of the questions likely to be asked and the approach to testing the systems allegedly operating in practice. COG 905085 says that it is important that the 'talk through' of the systems is conducted:

- with the owner, partner, director or company secretary as they will have knowledge of the business, and, if applicable;
- the person with the knowledge of the systems in operation.

9.74 Where there is a request for copies of the intervention plan, etc the officer is told to consider whether 'any other information should [also] be released' although it is expected that the usual answer will be that a note of the meeting will be provided and other details are withheld under an exemption in the Freedom of Information Act.

9.75 COG 905165 says that where the employer or agent refuses to attend a meeting or cancels two pre-arranged meetings the officer should explain why a meeting is preferred and how it will assist the compliance check and encourage them to reconsider. A further letter may be issued, reminding the employer of his obligations. If there is still a refusal to co-operate then the officer and senior manager should consider forcing action in terms of:

- a formal notice of the visit with possible approval by the tribunal;
- an unannounced visit;
- a formal information notice;
- formal determinations or decisions of tax and NI.

9.76 CC/FS3 says that '[the taxpayer does] not have to be present at the visit' but it will be helpful if [they] are available particularly at the beginning and at the end. The officer may ask to speak to the people who keep the records. COG 905030 says that when making an appointment '[the officer] should ask that the proprietor or director and the person responsible for maintaining the records is present'. Clearly the officer has a right to inspect relevant records and it is sensible and practical to have someone senior at the meeting who can help the officer understand the systems and how they work in practice.

9.77 HMRC officers will not usually highlight particular areas of interest before the meeting and in these circumstances it can be difficult to establish who should be around to answer detailed questions. For example, in terms of expenses policy that may be a director with responsibilities for human resources or for the arrangements with sub-contractors a director responsible for production. Whatever the situation, there should be a conscious decision as to who will be at or available for the meeting and they should all be fully briefed.

9.78 If there is any doubt it will usually be sensible to keep the meeting at a relatively low level to allow the officer to flag up areas of interest, but not to allow the employer to go into any great detail on these without proper consideration. Because it is relatively unusual in smaller cases for advisers to be present during the visit, their presence may put the officer on notice that the employer has particular concerns.

9.79 The officer, either at the visit or in terms of follow up, may be very keen to meet a particular director or principal of the business. HMRC may overlook the fact that their rights relate purely to inspecting records. They have no rights to meet a particular client and every request needs to be considered on its merits. In short they should meet the client when it suits you and the client, not when it suits HMRC. When referring to 'meetings' COG 905165 seems to be referring to the visit rather than to the presence of any particular person at any part of the visit. There is no indication of forcing action to be taken (including a penalty for obstruction) unless there is a problem with the officer gaining access to the premises and records.

9.80 The visit will usually begin with general fact finding in terms of the nature of the business; number of directors and employees; responsibilities of key people; the payroll system used and who does what in relation to wages, PAYE returns etc. This is basic information and may be more cost effectively covered by way of a detailed note provided by the employer and adviser before or at the meeting. With the notes in front of them the compliance officer can then focus on any particular points of detail or areas of concern.

9.81 HMRC may ask for sight of records kept electronically. CH 23360 says that electronic documents and records can include the actual computer or server, including an internal hard drive system and an external storage device holding backed up information or scans of previously printed documents. If it is not possible to produce a copy electronically, then HMRC are instructed to accept a printed copy instead.

9.82 Status issues will often be a significant risk area and will be covered in detail. Note that compliance officers may approach workers or ex-workers to validate the client's version of the facts relating to the engagement. It is possible that such approaches may have been made before the compliance visit.

9.83 On the conclusion of the visit the compliance officer should ensure that all questions have been answered and relevant facts obtained. HMRC are empowered to copy, make extracts from or remove for a reasonable period documents relating to the inspection. If removing documents, the officer is advised to provide a written receipt.

9.84 Meetings with HMRC

9.84 At the end of a compliance check, if nothing is wrong then the employer will get a letter of confirmation. Otherwise the results of the check will be set out in a letter and the employer will be encouraged to co-operate in establishing the correct amount of tax and NIC payable. Bear in mind that HMRC may collect the amount owing from when the mistakes first started, although frequently they will only go back up to six years, provided they can establish that mistakes are due to at least careless inaccuracies. CC/FS7 sets out the position on penalties applicable for returns due to be filed after 31 March 2009. The factsheet makes no direct reference to attendance at the visit in relation to the penalty reduction.

9.85 COG 906170 says the officer should consider further meetings as necessary to:

- see additional records;
- ask further questions;
- challenge explanations;
- avoid lengthy correspondence;
- maintaining the initiative and continuity.

9.86 In practice the areas highlighted by the review will need to be looked at in detail to establish whether tax is likely to have been lost and arrive at a reasonable quantum. Sometimes the conclusions of the officer are sound and often they are not. The earlier the adviser provides input the easier and less costly the visit is likely to be.

PRE-PLANNING CHECKLIST

9.87

- What records do they want to see?
- What state are those records in?
- Is all relevant information easily accessible?
- Extract all irrelevant items.
- Is the suggested date too early? Consider postponement?
- Where is the meeting to be held?
- Arrange suitable accommodation?
- Who is to attend the meeting?
- Appoint someone to accompany the visitors?
- Find out exactly who is coming.
- Get a list of what/who they will want to see.
- Ask if there is a specific reason for the visit.
- Check up on statutory powers.
- Ascertain statutory obligations and rights.
- Identify any areas of risk or vulnerability.
- Quantify any problems, potential errors or omissions.
- Prepare statements for early disclosure if relevant.
- Prepare explanations in mitigation if necessary.
- Identify likely exposure to interest and penalties and quantify.

DURING THE VISIT ITSELF

9.88 General:

- Be concise and factual.
- Do not guess – if unsure adopt a 'report back' approach.
- Ensure that the officers have adequate accommodation.
- Give access only to:
  - the relevant records;
  - parts of the premises;
  - relevant (and fully briefed) staff.

9.89 Review of records:

- Agree a timetable.
- Delegate secretarial assistance/copying facilities if needed.
- List all records seen and examined.
- Resist removal of records and offer copies.

9.90 Conclusion of visit:

- Establish when the results of the review will be explained – agree a timescale.
- Agree a timescale within which the officers will report their conclusions.
- Agree a schedule of any matters outstanding.
- Identify the specific areas for further research.
- Establish who is to do what, and when.
- Ask for a copy of HMRC's meeting note.

CHECKLIST FOR AREAS THE COMPLIANCE OFFICERS ARE LIKELY TO REVIEW

9.91 Formal returns:

- P11Ds;
- VAT returns and the VAT account;
- wages books and records;
- cash records, nominal ledgers, private ledgers;
- subcontractor records.

9.92 General records:

- clock cards, timesheets, worksheets, job cards;
- sickness records, absence records;
- holiday pay records;
- cash books, bank books, expense invoices, etc.

9.93 The danger areas:

- directors' benefits and expenses payments;
- accommodation and related benefits;
- casual labour records, overtime records;

9.93 *Meetings with HMRC*

- bonuses paid and weekend working records;
- the subcontractors' scheme;
- students and part-time workers;
- status of subcontractors and consultants;
- travel and subsistence payments;
- overnight allowances and clothing allowances;
- Class 1A insurance records and mileage records;
- telephone logs;
- tips and gratuities systems;
- tronc systems in operation;
- seasonal workers;
- payments to wives;
- cars provided for family members, entertaining and gifts, staff canteens and vending machines.

CONCLUSIONS

9.94 A meeting with HMRC is a potentially difficult experience for a client. The adviser's role is to participate actively and constructively during these meetings, to represent the client, to ensure that their rights are observed and upheld and to provide professional and positive guidance before and throughout the course of a meeting on the legal, technical and practical aspects of any case.

9.95 The adviser needs to be familiar with:

- relevant legislation;
- HMRC's statutory rights and duties;
- the client's rights and obligations;
- codes of practice on investigations and relevant parts of HMRC manuals.

9.96 This chapter is not an exhaustive review of all the aspects of HMRC meetings. It aims to provide some guidelines on how such meetings are best conducted. There can be little substitute for experience in this area of tax practice. Most practitioners can, however, perform more than adequately, even very effectively in interview situations, with the right preparation – and perhaps a little luck!

9.97 The opening meeting is frequently the key stage of an enquiry. This is so for both the client and the HMRC officer. The latter's training includes help and guidance on interviews. The rapid realisation that the ability to conduct a well-structured and successful meeting is a major factor in conducting successful enquiries should be appreciated by advisers. The accountant or tax practitioner who performs well during interviews is likely to achieve the best settlement for the client.

Chapter 10

The information powers of HMRC

Hartley Foster

Partner, Olswang LLP

INTRODUCTION

10.01 HM Revenue & Customs' new system of information powers has been introduced in stages. Finance Act 2007 included enabling legislation under which the criminal investigatory powers of HMRC in England, Wales and Northern Ireland became based on the powers contained in the Police and Criminal Evidence Act 1984 (PACE); and Finance Act 2008 introduced a new regime of civil information powers that enables HMRC officers to obtain information and documents for the purpose of 'checking a taxpayer's tax position'. Finance Act 2009 amended and extended the new regime that had been introduced by Finance Act 2008; and Finance (No 3) Act 2010 aligned the record-keeping rules and time limits for excise duties in accordance with the changes that had been made to other taxes and duties. It is intended that legislation that 'modernises' and brings the bulk information powers in line with the other powers that HMRC currently possess in relation to third parties will be introduced in Finance Act 2011.

10.02 In general terms, the powers that the new legislation replaced are repealed at the same time and consequentially. There are, however, transitional provisions that keep in force the pre-1 April 2009 rules relating to appeals and penalties for information notices issued before 1 April 2009. For that reason, a summary of the pre-1 April 2009 rules is set out as an appendix to this chapter.

10.03 After this introductory section, this chapter comprises two sections. The first section contains an analysis of HMRC's civil investigatory powers (under Finance Act 2008, Sch 36); and the second contains an analysis of the powers that are available to HMRC in relation to criminal investigations (under PACE, SOCPA and TMA, s 20BA).

10.04 *The information powers of HMRC*

The rationale for change

10.04 The Commissioners for Revenue and Customs Act 2005 (CRCA) received Royal Assent on 7 April 2005. It provides the legal basis for the integrated department of HM Customs & Excise and the Inland Revenue – HMRC, and for the independent prosecutions office – the Revenue and Customs Prosecutions Office (RCPO). HMRC are responsible for all the functions that were previously the responsibility of the Commissioners of Inland Revenue and the Commissioners of Customs & Excise. The exception to this is prosecutions, for which, as a result of CRCA, s 35, RCPO has responsibility. (This removal of the prosecution function from HMRC was, in part, following the recommendations of His Honour Judge Butterfield. In his 'Review of Criminal Investigations and Prosecutions conducted by HM Customs and Excise' (15 July 2003), which examined the reasons for the collapse of the prosecution of 15 defendants for conspiracy to cheat the revenue in *R v Gell* [2003] EWCA Crim 123 (such reasons including: (1) that it was apparent that a prosecution witness had lied in the course of a *voir dire*; and (2) that HM Customs and Excise Officers had withheld relevant evidence from the defence), HHJ Butterfield recommended that all prosecution (as opposed to investigation) functions should be removed from HM Customs and Excise's power and instead should be conducted by an entirely separate authority.)

10.05 Both HM Customs & Excise and the Inland Revenue had powers that were set out in legislation that applied only to each department (e g the ability to apply for a search warrant under s 20C of the Taxes Management Act 1970 (TMA) applied only to the Inland Revenue). The legislation that was available to the two departments was inconsistent. In particular, in relation to criminal investigations it did not provide any powers of arrest to HMRC officers in respect of offences related to ex-Inland Revenue matters. In such cases, it was necessary for HMRC to seek the assistance of the police. Although HM Customs & Excise had different functions, responsibilities and powers from those of the Inland Revenue, when HMRC was established, the powers of each body were transferred unchanged to HMRC. The powers were 'ring fenced' so that they could be used only for their original purpose. Thus, the basis on which it was determined which powers were available to HMRC was by reference to the specific tax that was being investigated. The powers of the former Inland Revenue were applicable to direct taxes; the powers of the former HM Customs & Excise were applicable to indirect taxes, and to customs and excise duties.

10.06 However, the government had recognised, prior to the merger of the departments, that it was important to consider whether the heterogeneous powers of HMRC could be rationalised. This would make it easier for taxpayers to understand and comply with their tax obligations, and potentially could reduce the administrative burden of the tax system that fell on them. A major review of HMRC's powers, deterrents and safeguards was undertaken. (During the second reading of CRCA, the Paymaster General announced that a consultation process entitled 'Modernising Powers, Deterrents and Safeguards: A Consultation on the Developing Programme of Work' would be commenced in 2006. This consultation process included a review of the information powers available to HMRC in relation to civil tax matters, as well as where criminal activity was suspected. HMRC indicated that, in their view, PACE should become the statutory framework for the investigation of all tax-related criminal activity.) Following that review and a subsequent consultation, including consultation on draft clauses, the government, in Finance Act 2007, introduced enabling legislation under which HMRC's investigatory powers in England, Wales and Northern Ireland became based on the powers contained in PACE. (A statutory code was introduced for Scotland, where PACE does not apply.) By Treasury Order that was introduced with effect from 1 December 2007 (see further below), these powers now apply across all taxes and mean that HMRC criminal investigations are subject to the statutory codes of practice and safeguards that attach to criminal investigations generally. A notable change is therefore that HMRC officers now have the PACE powers of search, seizure and arrest in connection with ex-Inland Revenue matters.

10.07 The amendments in Finance Act 2007 increase the powers available to ex-Inland Revenue investigators; and mean that HMRC no longer need to follow different procedures in the same investigation where both direct and indirect tax fraud are suspected. Finance Act 2007 repealed s 20C of the TMA and para 10(3), Sch 11 to the Value Added Taxes Act 1994 (VATA) and ss 82(2) and 83(2) of that Act enabled the Treasury to make an order applying the provisions of PACE to investigations conducted by Officers of HMRC: The Police and Criminal Evidence Act 1984 (Application to Revenue and Customs) Order 2007, SI 2007 No 3175. SI 2007 No 3175 was laid before Parliament on 9 November 2007; it applies the relevant provisions of PACE to all functions of HMRC (except where the department acts as an agent for other government departments) with effect from 1 December 2007. Thus, since 1 December 2007, HMRC officers have had access to the appropriate powers in PACE to investigate all tax matters where criminal activity is suspected. In particular, since that date, search warrants have been obtained under PACE, s 8 and Sch 1, rather than TMA, s 20C, (for offences concerning direct tax) or VATA, Sch 11, para 10(3) (for offences concerning indirect tax).

10.08 The changes introduced by Finance Act 2007 resolve a number of the problems that arose when HMRC officers sought to investigate combined instances of direct and indirect tax fraud. For example, prior to the introduction of these changes, if a taxpayer was suspected of both VAT and corporation tax fraud, separate warrants for each of these offences were required to search and seize evidence from the same premises and, arguably, the taxpayer had to be arrested twice (once by the police for the suspected direct tax offence and once by HMRC officers for the suspected indirect tax offence). There remain a number of police powers (such as the power to charge and bail suspects and the power to take fingerprints) that HMRC are unable to exercise; and it is anticipated that further rationalisation of the powers available to HMRC officers, in accordance with the fundamental underlying principle of the proposed changes, namely that the nature of the activity, rather than the tax, should determine the ambit of the statutory power, will be introduced in due course.

10.09 Finance Act 2007 also introduced a new regime for penalties for incorrect declarations and returns. Finance Act 2007, Sch 24 (Commencement

10.09 *The information powers of HMRC*

and Transitional Provisions) Order 2008 (SI 2008 No 568) brought into force the provisions of Finance Act 2007, Sch 24 in relation to return periods beginning from 1 April 2008, but provides that Sch 24 shall not apply to any tax period for which a return is required to be made before 1 April 2009. This new regime is examined in more detail in Chapter 14. However, in short, under Sch 24, a single penalty regime applies to returns (and similar documents) for income tax (including PAYE), capital gains tax, the construction industry scheme, corporation tax, National Insurance Contributions and VAT. In the 2009 Budget, it was announced that the Finance Bill 2010 will include legislation to align the remaining VAT (and other indirect tax) penalties; also new penalty rules for unauthorised issue of VAT invoices and for breach of the obligation to notify chargeability to tax come into effect on 1 April 2010). Under the new regime, an error in a 'taxpayer's document' (which is broadly a tax return or the accounts that accompany the return) gives rise to a penalty if that inaccuracy amounts to or leads to an understatement of the taxpayer's liability to tax and that inaccuracy was 'careless or deliberate'. The new approach relates the determination of penalties to the underlying behaviour that gave rise to the inaccurate return or assessment. If it was caused by a mistake or misinterpretation of fact or law and reasonable care was taken, then there is no penalty. Otherwise, to reflect the increasing seriousness of the behaviour, penalties at three different levels may be imposed:

1   failure to take reasonable care;
2   deliberate understatement; and
3   deliberate understatement with concealment.

There are reductions for disclosure. In general terms, early and truthful explanation of why the arrears arose and their true extent, supplying information promptly, including full written disclosure, will result in mitigation of the penalty.

10.10   Finance Act 2008 homogenised HMRC's powers in relation to civil tax matters. Schedule 36 applies to enquiries into income tax, corporation tax, capital gains tax, VAT, PAYE, NICs and construction industry scheme (CIS) liabilities (and relevant foreign taxes) with effect from 1 April 2009 (Finance Act 2008, Schedule 36 (Appointed Day and Savings) Order 2009 (SI 2009 No 404)). It contains a new regime of information powers that enable HMRC officers to obtain information and documents for the purpose of 'checking a taxpayer's tax position'.

10.11   SI 2009 No 404 also repealed, with effect from 1 April 2009, a number of the old HMRC information powers (including TMA, s 20) and self-assessment information powers (including TMA, s 19A), subject to transitional provisions. The transitional provisions keep in force the pre-1 April 2009 rules relating to appeals and penalties for information notices issued before 1 April 2009. Documents in respect of which a penalty is exigible under TMA 1970, s 98 are expressly excluded from the Finance Act 2007, Sch 24 penalty regime. Thus, the 'old' regime remains in force in relation to penalties for failure to comply with a s 20 notice.

10.12 Finance Act 2009, ss 95 and 96 and Schs 47 and 48 contain amendments to the information and inspection powers contained in Finance Act 2008, Sch 36 and extend the Sch 36 regime to:

(1) insurance premium tax;
(2) inheritance tax;
(3) stamp duty land tax;
(4) stamp duty reserve tax;
(5) petroleum revenue tax;
(6) aggregates levy;
(7) climate change levy;
(8) landfill tax; and
(9) relevant foreign taxes.

They also provide for the repeal (by statutory instrument in due course) of other information and inspection powers that are no longer required. Schedule 48 also introduces the concept of an 'involved third party' – namely a person who is 'closely involved' in a potentially taxable event or transaction and who has obligations to provide information in relation to certain taxes that are similar to the obligations of a taxpayer. Involved third parties are specifically defined; they include, for example, a manager of an individual investment plan, a body approved for the purposes of payroll giving to charity and an account provider in relation to a child trust fund. Involved third parties are brought within the scope of the powers of inspection that apply to taxpayers, and some of the restrictions that apply to HMRC's information powers as regards 'uninvolved' third parties are removed. The legislation is not yet in force, but is expected to apply from 1 April 2010.

FINANCE ACT 2008, SCH 36

Summary

10.13 Schedule 36 introduced a common compliance checking structure. It is intended to provide a more flexible approach than was possible with the heterogeneous information powers that HMRC possessed previously; it is now different taxpayer behaviours, rather than different taxes, that determine the approach to be taken by HMRC. Schedule 36 provides a new framework for:

- the records to be kept and the requirement to make them available to HMRC;
- the powers to obtain information from taxpayers and third parties;
- inspection powers; and
- time limits for assessment.

10.14 Schedule 36 introduced two classes of information powers with effect from 1 April 2009:

- the power to obtain information and documents; and
- the power to inspect premises.

10.15 *The information powers of HMRC*

The power to obtain information and documents

10.15 Under Schedule 36, an HMRC officer may, by notice in writing ('an information notice'), require the taxpayer or a third party to provide information or documents if the 'information or document is reasonably required for the purpose of checking the taxpayer's tax position'.

10.16 'Tax position' is defined in Sch 36, para 64 as a person's position as regards any tax, including: (1) past, present and future liabilities to pay tax; (2) penalties and other amounts payable in connection with any tax; and (3) claims, elections, applications and notices in relation to that person's liability to pay tax (between 1 April and 21 July 2009, it extended to claims, elections, applications and notices in connection with any tax (see Finance Act 2009, Sch 47, para 22)).

10.17 A person served with an information notice must provide the information or documents within such period as is 'reasonably specified or described' in the notice (para 7). Thus, in contrast to, for example, s 20 notices, there is no minimum 30-day limit for compliance. Whether the time limit for compliance is 'reasonable' will depend on the circumstances of the notice and the information sought under it. The legislation also gives HMRC the right to 'reasonably specify' the place where the information should be produced for inspection (para 7(2)).

10.18 A person who receives an information notice is only required to produce a document if it is in that person's possession or power (under Sch 36, para 18). This reflects the pre-1 April 2009 position regarding documents. However, 'information' can require the creation of new documents on service of an information notice. The information requested in an information notice may be specified or 'described' by HMRC (para 6(2)). This means that HMRC are not restricted to asking for documents that they can identify specifically. In the Explanatory Notes to the Finance Bill 2008, it is indicated that 'information' includes both explanations and the creation of schedules or documents that do not already exist. Provision is also made that the information should be supplied in such form (if any) as is specified by HMRC. This would appear to imply that HMRC may request information and/or documents in electronic form. Finance Act 2008, s 114 gives HMRC, at any reasonable time, access to computers used in connection with relevant documents and a power to insist (with threat of a penalty for obstruction) on 'reasonable assistance' in relation to the same. Although, prior to 1 April 2009, Finance Act 1985, s 10 and Finance Act 1988, s 127 gave HMRC access to computers for VAT and direct taxes purposes respectively, in practice, these powers were rarely exercised. It is anticipated that HMRC will increasingly specify that business records be supplied in electronic form and demand that computer records be produced.

10.19 There are three main information notices that HMRC may issue under Sch 36:

- a taxpayer notice;
- a third party notice; and
- an identity unknown notice.

The information powers of HMRC **10.24**

10.20 Schedule 48, Finance Act 2009 introduced a power that enables HMRC to issue 'involved third party notices'. The power was introduced with effect from 1 April 2010.

Taxpayer notice (Sch 36, para 1)

10.21 The power to issue a taxpayer notice, in effect, replaces the powers under: (1) TMA, ss 20(1) and 20(2), relating to HMRC information notices; (2) TMA, s 19A relating to personal tax self-assessment; (3) Finance Act 1998, Sch 18, para 27 relating to corporation tax self-assessment; and (4) VATA, Sch 11, para 7 relating to VAT enquiries.

Taxpayer notice: key points

10.22 Paragraph 1 bestows on HMRC a free-standing power to obtain information and documents. The issue of a notice requiring production of information is no longer related, as it was in respect of the self-assessment information powers (TMA, s 19A and Finance Act 1998, Sch 18, para 27), to the issue of a notice of enquiry (under TMA, ss 9A or 12AC, or Finance Act 1998, Sch 18, para 24). Nor is it issued for the purpose of 'determining whether a return is incomplete', but, instead, for the purpose of checking the taxpayer's 'tax position' (which includes future liabilities to pay tax). Thus, the power allows HMRC to inspect records before a return is filed.

10.23 A restriction on the use of notices under paragraph 1 is, however, provided by paragraph 21. Paragraph 21 provides that if the taxpayer has already filed a corporation tax or personal self-assessment return, then an HMRC officer cannot issue a taxpayer notice in relation to the period covered by the return in order to check that person's corporation tax position or income or chargeable gains tax position unless one of the following conditions is satisfied:

1   there is an open enquiry in relation to that period; or
2   the officer has reason to suspect one of the following:
      (a) an amount that ought to have been assessed to tax for the chargeable period may not have been assessed;
      (b) an assessment to tax for the chargeable period may be or have become insufficient; or
      (c) relief from tax given for the chargeable period may be or have become excessive;
3   the notice is given for the purpose of obtaining any information or document that is required for the purpose of checking that person's position as regards any tax other than income tax, capital gains tax or corporation tax;
4   the notice is given for the purpose of obtaining any information or document that is required for the purpose of checking the person's position as regards any deductions or repayments of tax or withholding income (eg under PAYE or CIS).

10.24 HMRC are not restricted to the seeking of existing identifiable documents. The information that can be requested by a taxpayer notice may be specified or 'described' by HMRC. As is indicated in the *Explanatory Notes to*

10.24 *The information powers of HMRC*

the Finance Bill 2008, 'information' includes both explanations in respect of existing documents and the creation of schedules or documents that do not already exist.

10.25 There is no statutory pre-condition that HMRC ask the taxpayer to provide the information or documents voluntarily before service of a taxpayer notice. In contrast, TMA, s.20 contained a statutory requirement that the taxpayer be given a reasonable opportunity to provide the documents voluntarily (s 20B(1)); and, whilst there was no such legal requirement before issuing a notice under TMA 1970 s 19A, in practice, it was rare for HMRC to serve a s 19A notice without having first made an informal request for the information or documents.

10.26 There is no obligation on HMRC to obtain prior judicial approval of the taxpayer notice (as had been the case in relation to notices under s 20(1) (under s 20(7))). Under Sch 36, the HMRC officer can choose whether or not to seek approval from the First-tier Tribunal in advance. Whether or not the officer has sought approval has consequences for the ability of the taxpayer to appeal the notice to the Tribunal (see further below). Finance Act 2009 ensures that the taxpayer has no right to appeal against a decision of the First-tier Tribunal to approve the issue of a notice (new Sch 36 para 6(4), inserted by Finance Act 2009, Sch 47, para 4). From 21 July 2009, HMRC have been permitted to make an application to the First-tier Tribunal for approval without notice to the taxpayer (Sch 36 para 3(3A), inserted by Finance Act 2009, Sch 47, para 3(2)).

10.27 A taxpayer notice can require the taxpayer to produce documents more than six years old, provided that the request has been made by an 'authorised officer' of HMRC (defined in para 58 as an HMRC officer who has been authorised by HMRC for the purposes of Sch 36). By contrast, judicial approval was required for an extension of the six-year time limit in relation to notices under s 20; it was given only if the Commissioner was satisfied that there were reasonable grounds for believing that there was a tax loss by reason of the fraud of the taxpayer (s 20B(6)).

10.28 A taxpayer who is required to provide information or documents must do so within the period, at the time, and by the means and form reasonably specified in the notice (Finance Act 2008, Sch 36, para 7).

Third party notice (Sch 36, para 2)

10.29 An HMRC officer may by written notice to any person require that person to provide information or to produce a document if either is reasonably required for checking the tax position of a known person (a 'third party notice'). The power under Sch 36, para 2 has, in effect, replaced TMA, s 20(3) and VATA, Sch 11, para 7(2).

Third party notice: key points

10.30 As with taxpayer notices, third parties can now be required to provide 'information' (as well as existing documents), potentially by creating new documents. The predecessor third-party power (TMA, s 20(3)) was frequently used by HMRC to obtain documents from banks that concerned the tax affairs of their customers. Paragraph 2 extends the scope of the power to included requesting 'information'. Thus, for example, HMRC may seek explanations for transactions from bank employees in the context of seeking evidence for or understanding the 'motive' of taxpayers when entering into transactions.

10.31 A copy of the third party notice must be given to the taxpayer to which it relates, unless the First-tier Tribunal disapplies this requirement. It may not disapply the requirement unless the application for consent has been made by (or with the agreement of) an authorised officer of HMRC and it is satisfied that the officer has reasonable grounds for believing that giving a copy of the notice to the taxpayer might prejudice the assessment or collection of tax. Under the pre-1 April 2009 rules, the taxpayer had to have been named in the notice and be given a copy, unless the Commissioners were satisfied that there were reasonable grounds for suspecting fraud (s 20B(1B)).

10.32 The issue of a third party notice requires judicial approval, unless the taxpayer consents to the issue of the notice. Under Sch 36, para 3(3)(b) the First-tier Tribunal must be satisfied that, in the circumstances, the HMRC officer is justified in issuing a third party notice. HMRC can make an application to the First-tier Tribunal for approval without notice.

Judicial approval of taxpayer and third party notices

10.33 As indicated above, HMRC may request approval from the First-tier Tribunal for the giving of a taxpayer notice, but they are not obliged to do so. However, they may not issue a notice to a third party without the approval of the First-tier Tribunal, unless the taxpayer has agreed. The First-tier Tribunal will not approve the giving of a taxpayer or third party notice unless the conditions in Sch 36, para 3(3) are satisfied:

1 The application is made by an authorised HMRC officer.
2 The First-tier Tribunal is satisfied that, in the circumstances, the HMRC officer is justified in issuing an information notice.
3 The person to whom the notice is addressed is given a summary of the reasons why HMRC require the information or documents and has had an opportunity to make representations to HMRC concerning the information request.
  However, there is no express provision, as existed under s 20B(1), for the taxpayer or third party to have been given a reasonable opportunity to supply the information before any application is made for a formal notice.
4 A summary of the representations made by the person to whom it is addressed (ie either the taxpayer or the third party) has been given to the First-tier Tribunal.
  The legislation does not specify whether the summarising is to be undertaken by HMRC or the person to whom the notice is to be addressed. It is recommended that taxpayers or third parties that wish to make representations should send these directly to the First-tier Tribunal, with a copy to the relevant HMRC Inspector.
5 In the case of a third party notice, the taxpayer has received a summary

10.33 *The information powers of HMRC*

of the reasons why the officer requires the information and/or documents from the third party.

10.34 The First-tier Tribunal may disapply requirements (3) to (5) if satisfied that taking the specified action might prejudice the assessment or collection of tax. Accordingly, HMRC can obtain a third party notice without notice to either the third party or the taxpayer. There is no right of appeal against a tribunal's decision to disapply any of these conditions (Sch 36, para 6(4) (inserted by Finance Act 2009, Sch 47, para 4)).

10.35 An information notice that is given with the approval of the First-tier Tribunal must so state (para 6(3)). If the First-tier Tribunal has approved the issue of an information notice, then there is no route of appeal available to the taxpayer or to the third party (see para 29(3) and para 30(3) respectively, and Sch 36, para 6(4) (inserted by Finance Act 2009, Sch 47, para 4)). The only routes available to the taxpayer or the third party are judicial review of the First-tier Tribunal's decision to approve the notice or challenging the imposition of a penalty on the basis that the notice was not lawfully issued.

10.36 If HMRC serve the taxpayer with an information notice that has not been approved by the First-tier Tribunal, then the taxpayer has a right of appeal to the First-tier Tribunal against the notice itself, or any requirement in it. However, this right of appeal does not apply to a requirement in a notice to produce any document that forms part of the taxpayer's statutory records. If approval from the First-tier Tribunal was not obtained in relation to the service of a third party notice (which would only be in the case where the taxpayer agreed to the issuing of notice on the third party), then the third party may appeal to the First-tier Tribunal against the notice; the only basis on which the third party may appeal against the notice is on the ground that it would be 'unduly onerous' to comply with (Sch 36, para 30(1)).

10.37 'Statutory records' are defined by Sch 36, para 62(1) as 'information or a document which a person is required to keep and preserve ... under the Taxes Acts or any other enactment relating to a tax'. To the extent that any information or document that is required to be kept and preserved does not relate to the carrying on of a business and is not also required to be kept or preserved under any other enactment relating to tax, it only forms part of a person's statutory records to the extent that the chargeable period or periods to which it relates has or have ended (Sch 36, para 62(2)). Information and documents cease to form part of a person's statutory records when the period for which they are required to be preserved by the enactments above referred to has expired (Sch 36, para 62(3)). HMRC have said that, although there is provision for them to specify further the records to be kept, they have no plans to do this at present.

There is no right of appeal under the Tribunals, Courts and Enforcement Act 2007 against a decision of the Tribunal to approve an information notice (Sch 36, para 6(4)).

Involved third party notices (Sch 36, para 34A)

10.38 The Finance Act 2009 introduced a hybrid regime between taxpayer notices and third party notices, namely 'involved third party' notices. The power came into force on 1 April 2010. If an 'involved third party' is given a third party notice for the purposes of checking the position of a person in relation to the 'relevant tax' and referring only to 'relevant information or relevant documents', then the involved third party is treated as if he had received a taxpayer notice, rather than a third party notice (Finance Act 2008, Sch 36, para 34A introduced by Finance Act 2009, Sch 48, para 11).

10.39 Involved third parties are, in essence, third parties who are involved in transactions that may give rise to a taxable transaction. In broad terms, involved third parties are intermediaries of taxpayers. FA 2008, Sch 36, para 61 specifies 12 categories of 'involved third parties', and what constitutes a 'relevant tax' and 'relevant information or relevant documents' for each category. Paragraph 61 also provides a list of the relevant information and relevant documents which can be requested in relation to that involved third party, in relation to a specified tax. For example, an account provider in relation to a child trust fund is an involved third party; if the information and documents sought from that person by a third party notice are 'information and documents relating to the fund, including investments which are or have been held under the fund' and are sought in respect of checking the fund's position in relation to the fund as regards income tax, then the account provider is treated as if he had received a taxpayer, rather than a third party, notice.

10.40 HMRC can serve an involved third party notice without the taxpayer's consent or approval from the First-tier Tribunal. An involved third party can appeal against a notice on any grounds (if the notice was not approved by the First-tier Tribunal), as can the recipient of a taxpayer notice, rather than solely on the grounds that compliance would be 'unduly onerous' (the only grounds of appeal for third party notices).

Identity unknown notice (Sch 36, para 5)

10.41 The power under para 5 enables HMRC to obtain, from a third party, information about a taxpayer whose identity is not known (an 'identity unknown notice'). This replaces TMA, s 20(8A). Under para 5, an HMRC officer may by written notice to any person require that person to provide information or to produce a document if that is reasonably required for checking the tax position of either of the following:

1 a person whose identity is not known to the HMRC officer; or
2 a class of persons whose individual identities are not known to the officer.

10.42 HMRC may not issue an identity unknown notice to a third party without the approval of the First-tier Tribunal. The First-tier Tribunal must be satisfied that:

- the information or documents are reasonably required by the officer;
- there are reasonable grounds for believing that the person or any of the class of persons to whom the notice relates may have failed or may fail to comply with any provision of the Taxes Acts or VATA;
- any such failure is likely to have led or lead to serious prejudice to the assessment or collection of UK tax; and

10.42 *The information powers of HMRC*

- the information or documents are not readily available from any other source.

The like preconditions applied to notices under TMA, s 20(8A) (absent the references to 'information' and to VAT).

10.43 By TMA, s 20(7), a Special Commissioner was to give his consent to, inter alia, a s 20(8A) notice 'only on being satisfied that in all the circumstances the Inspector was *justified* in proceeding under that section'. There was thus a balancing act between the reasonable requirements of HMRC to obtain information, in order to carry out the effective investigation of tax affairs, and the protection of the personal property rights of taxpayers against invasion to be carried out by the Special Commissioner. The obligation on the Special Commissioner to carry out this balancing act was most stringent in the case of s 20(8A) notices. Here, not only did the burden fall on a third party (as was the case with all s 20(3) notices), but also there was the likelihood that the burden would be a significant one. That this is so was recognised by the courts. It was also recognised by Parliament. (In the Standing Committee debates on Finance (No 2) Bill 1988 with regard to the clause that was to introduce what became s 20(8A) and (8B), an amendment was tabled that a person complying with a s 20(8A) notice be entitled to claim from the Revenue his reasonable expenses for so complying (ie as per Lord Keith's recommendation). Mr Howarth MP, for example, referred, in particular, to the 'enormous obligation' that would be imposed, on, for example, banks who might be required to provide details of a class of taxpayers who might have drawn cheques over a number of years.) Further, contrary to the express recommendation of the Keith Report, there is no possibility of reimbursement from HMRC of any reasonable costs incurred by a third party in complying with the significant burden.

10.44 However, the approach taken by the Special Commissioner in relation to 16 applications by HMRC where the power under s 20(8A) was sought to be used to obtain, from banks, information in relation to individuals with a UK address and a non-UK bank account or a credit card that was associated with a non-UK bank account suggests that, even in relation to s 20(8A) notices, the scales were strongly weighted in HMRC's favour. The first six cases are: *Re an Application by Revenue and Customs Comrs to serve section 20 notice* [2006] STC (SCD) 71; *Re an Application by Revenue and Customs Comrs to serve section 20 notice (No 2)* [2006] STC (SCD) 360; *Re an Application by Revenue and Customs Comrs to serve section 20 notice* [2007] STC (SCD) 202; *Re an Application by Revenue and Customs Comrs to serve section 20 notice* [2007] STC (SCD) 208; *Re an Application by Revenue and Customs Comrs to serve section 20 notice* [2007] STC (SCD) 216; and *Re an Application by Revenue and Customs Comrs to serve section 20 notice* [2007] STC (SCD) 222.

10.45 In these cases, the Special Commissioner considered that the statistical evidence presented by HMRC in relation to the additional tax yield that would be generated consequent on the disclosure of the information sought was sufficient to enable him to conclude that the 'class' of taxpayers was in default and that this non-compliance by the class had led to serious prejudice to the proper assessment or collection of tax. In the first two cases to be decided

The information powers of HMRC **10.48**

(which concerned the same bank), HMRC's estimate was that 20% of the cases investigated following disclosure would result in additional tax yield. The total additional tax yield from customers of that bank who fell within the 'class' was estimated at £1,855 million. The figure given in relation to the following four banks was £40 million, £55 million, £36 million, and £150 million respectively. Given that the estimated anticipated total additional tax yield in the four subsequent cases was based on a similar percentage of cases leading to additional tax yield, but the average anticipated total additional tax yield consequent on the notices served on each bank was only approximately 4% of the tax yield that was estimated would be generated from customers of the first bank (and all five banks were (broadly) comparable in size), it would have been incumbent on the inspector to provide a reasonable explanation for that extremely significant difference. For the judicial control introduced by s 20(8A) to have been effective, the Special Commissioner should have evaluated that explanation and accepted it as legitimate before giving his consent. There is nothing in the decisions to suggest that any explanation at all was given or requested by the Special Commissioner.

10.46 In *Re an Application by Revenue and Customs Comrs to serve section 20 notice; Note* [2009] STC (SCD) 493, which concerned a similar application by HMRC for a s 20(8A) notice, the Special Commissioner noted that the estimate of £1.5 billion additional tax yield given in [2006] STC (SCD) 360 was an overestimate by HMRC, stated that 'this error had been made known to me earlier' and concluded that this had no effect on his conclusion that the condition that there must be serious prejudice to the proper collection of tax is satisfied. This was notwithstanding that the estimate of serious tax prejudice was approximately six times its true quantum. A similar approach to the legislation was adopted by the Special Commissioner in relation to all 16 s 20(8A) applications that were made against banks between 2006 and 2009.

10.47 There is no 'balancing act' to be carried out by the First-tier Tribunal in relation to paragraph 5 notices. This and the decision of the First-tier Tribunal in *Application by the Commissioners for Her Majesty's Revenue and Customs to serve 308 notices under paragraph 5 of Schedule 36 to the Finance Act 2008 on Financial Institutions in respect of customers with UK addresses holding non-UK accounts* [2009] SFTD 780 gives rise to a concern as to whether tribunal approval, under paragraph 4, provides any form of check against HMRC's use of the power under paragraph 5. In *308 notices*, the First-tier Tribunal approved the issue of 308 paragraph 5 notices (seeking details of non-UK bank accounts held by persons with a UK addresses) to be served by HMRC on financial institutions.

10.48 In determining whether failure to have complied with the tax legislation 'is likely to have led or to lead to serious prejudice to the assessment or collection of tax', the Tribunal considered that generic evidence (rather than evidence specific to each financial institution) was sufficient. The approach that the Tribunal seems to have adopted was to hold that, as the disclosures made under the Offshore Disclosure Facility proved that the tests had been satisfied in relation to the previous 16 applications made by HMRC for s 20(8A) notices, therefore the tests also must be satisfied in relation to these (similar)

10.48 *The information powers of HMRC*

applications. Yet, paragraph 5 bestows on HMRC a power to require 'a' person to provide information and documents if the relevant conditions are met. Thus, even though the Tribunal was right in its decision that 'there is nothing in the statute preventing the issue of many notices in the same form', the relevant conditions should have been met in relation to each recipient individually. That clearly did not occur; and, in any event, many of the recipient banks were operating in a way that meant that their accounts were dissimilar to accounts (held with other banks) in respect of which ODF disclosures were made. Moreover, it seems that HMRC were not put to proof as to whether the information could have been obtained 'from another source'; particularly given that it seems that the purpose of obtaining the information and documents was to enable HMRC to carry out a 'cross-check' against disclosures made under the New Disclosure Opportunity or under the Liechtenstein Disclosure Facility, It is at best moot as to whether this test would have been satisfied had it received any detailed judicial consideration.

10.49 If the approach taken by the tax tribunal in the banking sector cases is to be followed by the First-tier Tribunal in relation to applications made by HMRC in relation to other sectors of industry, then there will be no bar on HMRC undertaking Micawberish 'fishing expeditions', based on a generalised suspicion, by serving generic notices that impose a massive compliance burden on third parties. In the consultation paper on bulk and specialist information powers, HMRC noted that 'a relatively common form of income tax non-compliance is for taxpayers not to pay tax on income from letting a property'. Accordingly, generic paragraph 5 notices that require details of every bank transaction undertaken over say a six-year period being served on every letting agent in the UK could be permissible.

Identity unknown notices: key differences between the old rules and the new rules

10.50 The main differences between the power under paragraph 5 and the power in TMA, s 20(8A) are as follows:

- Approval from the Board of HMRC is no longer required for issue of a notice.
- There is no statutory pre-condition that HMRC ask a person to produce the information or documents voluntarily before service of an identity unknown notice.
- Paragraph 5 applies to VAT.
- As with third party notices, information (as well as documents) can be sought under identity unknown notices.
- An identity unknown notice can be appealed, but the basis of appeal is that it would be 'unduly onerous' to comply with the notice (Sch 36, para 30). The test under TMA, s 20(8B) was that the s.20(8A) notice would be 'onerous' to comply with. In the recent cases concerning financial institutions with offshore bank accounts, the Special Commissioner gave (at most) limited consideration of the estimated cost of compliance with the notices, on the basis that the financial institutions had a separate right of appeal against the notice on the basis

that compliance with the notice would be onerous. There is only one case on s.20(8B): *Rincham Limited v The Commissioners for HM Revenue & Customs* [2010] UKFTT 502 (TC). In *Rincham*, the First-tier Tribunal rejected the company's arguments that it would be onerous for it to provide details of some 40 capital redemption policies, particularly as it had no direct employees. The Tribunal stated that it considered that it should be a relatively inexpensive matter for them to employ, if necessary, a temporary or part-time person to obtain the details and provide them to HMRC.
- Section 20(8A) was a subset of s 20(3) so that the restrictions on the use of the s 20(3) powers applied also to the powers under s 20(8A) (although the question of whether the six-year time restriction that applied to s 20(3) notices applied also to s 20(8A) was not fully decided). Paragraph 5 creates a free-standing identity unknown notice regime.

The power to inspect premises

10.51 Finance Act 2008, Sch 36, Pt 2 introduces the new inspection power. VAT and PAYE inspections habitually involved visits to premises to check records; now inspections can take place in relation to all taxes covered by Sch 36. 'Inspect' means to examine; this power does not give HMRC the right to force entry, or to search. The power to inspect is restricted to the business premises of the person whose tax liability is being checked, other than in relation to VAT or the premises of involved third parties in certain circumstances. Absent involved third parties, the ambit of the power does not extend to third parties.

Power to inspect taxpayer's business premises: Sch 36, para 10

10.52 An HMRC officer may enter a person's business premises and inspect the premises and business assets and business documents on the premises, if the inspection is reasonably required for the purpose of checking that person's tax position. HMRC have indicated that this power will not be used routinely, and that they will carry out an inspection only where they consider it to be the best and most effective way to tackle tax risk.

What can be inspected?

10.53 The premises that HMRC can inspect are those used by the person whose liability is being checked. The inspection may extend to the premises and to business assets and business documents on the premises, if their inspection is reasonably required for the purposes of checking the person's tax liability. The power does not extend to inspection of any part of the premises used solely as a dwelling.

10.54 'Business premises' are any premises (or a part thereof) that an HMRC officer has reason to believe are used in connection with the carrying on of a

10.54 *The information powers of HMRC*

business by or on behalf of the taxpayer. They include land, buildings, and 'means of transport'. Schedule 36, para 10 does not give HMRC a power of entry to premises that are used wholly as a dwelling. HMRC consider that there are circumstances where it may be reasonable to conduct an inspection at a person's home. These include the following:

> 'In the case of an outworker – the stock or assets kept at their home may be inspected. The person should be given an opportunity to make the items available for inspection elsewhere if this is practical.
>
> At a farm – the office, fields, barns and areas involved in business activity can be visited. The private areas of the farm house and private garden cannot be visited without invitation.
>
> In a pub – the cellar, bar, commercial kitchen, store rooms and any vacant rooms which are let can be visited. The private living accommodation cannot be visited without invitation.'

10.55 'Business assets' are assets that an HMRC officer has reason to believe are owned, leased or used in connection with the carrying on of a business by any person. The definition of business assets excludes documents other than documents which are trading stock or plant (Sch 36, para 10(4) (inserted by Finance Act 2009, Sch 47, para 5)). 'Business documents' means documents that relate to the carrying on of a business by any person and that form part of any person's 'statutory records' (statutory records are defined in Sch 36, para 62 as information or documents required to be kept and preserved under the Taxes Acts and enactments relating to VAT). Thus, any person's business records can be reviewed if they are found on the inspected premises, but only if that inspection is reasonably required for checking the tax position of the person in connection with whose business the premises are used.

10.56 HMRC cannot review documents that could not have been required to be produced had the occupier been given an information notice at the time of inspection (Sch 36, para 28). In particular, this means that HMRC cannot view documents that are protected by legal professional privilege.

10.57 As with information notices, HMRC are not required to obtain judicial approval before conducting an inspection; under Sch 36, para 13(1), an officer may ask the First-tier Tribunal to approve an inspection. There is no appeal to the First-tier Tribunal against an inspection.

10.58 A person who deliberately obstructs an HMRC officer in the course of an inspection that has been approved by the First-tier Tribunal is liable to a penalty of £300 and daily default penalty of £60. There is no penalty if there is a reasonable excuse for the obstruction (Sch 36, paras 39 and 45). In the event that the First-tier Tribunal has not approved the notice, then the penalty regime in Sch 36, para 39 (and in para 40), does not apply.

Timing of inspections

10.59 Inspections should normally take place at a time agreed with the occupier of the premises.

10.60 Absent agreement, HMRC may carry out an inspection 'at any reasonable time' in two circumstances:

- where the occupier has been given at least seven days' notice; or
- where an authorised HMRC officer has agreed that the inspection can be carried out (Sch 36, para 12).

10.61 HMRC have said that, in practice, the notice period is likely to be longer than seven days and the time and date of the inspection will be both by negotiation and at the taxpayer's convenience.

10.62 However, inspections can be made without advance warning (Sch 36, para 12(2)(b)). In 'A New Approach to Compliance Checks: Responses to Consultation and Proposals' (issued on 10 January 2008), HMRC indicated that unannounced visits would be 'the exception, and need higher levels of safeguards to reassure the majority of the population'. As indicated above, no external judicial authorisation is required for unannounced visits; such visits need only the agreement of an 'authorised' HMRC officer. An 'authorised officer' is defined in the legislation simply as an HMRC officer authorised by HMRC for the purposes of Sch 36. It is understood that HMRC do not consider that officer grade is the appropriate criterion, but rather someone with the appropriate training. Information on the training that is required for an officer to become authorised is awaited.

10.63 There is also no provision for a right of appeal to the Tribunal. HMRC have said that a code of practice will be published to cover such visits and has indicated that, in their view, the requirement for powers to be used reasonably and in accordance with the Code of Practice (to be published) will provide an adequate safeguard.

Inspection of premises used in connection with taxable supplies: Sch 36, para 11

10.64 As originally enacted, para 11 provided for the inspection of premises used in connection with VAT taxable supplies where an HMRC officer had reason to believe any of the following:

- The premises were being used in connection with the taxable supply of goods and such goods were on those premises.
- The premises were being used in connection with the taxable acquisition of goods from other member states and such goods were on those premises.
- The premises were being used as a fiscal warehouse.

10.65 This reproduced the power in VATA, Sch 11, para 10(2). The power was widened slightly by Finance Act 2009 (with effect from 21 July 2009): an HMRC officer is now able to inspect premises if he has reason to believe that documents relating to a taxable supply or taxable acquisition of goods are on the premises or if the premises are used in connection with a fiscal warehouse (Finance Act 2009, Sch 47, para 6).

10.66 *The information powers of HMRC*

10.66 Under para 11, the HMRC officer may inspect the premises, any goods that are on the premises and any documents on the premises that appear to relate to the goods. This power to inspect is not restricted to the premises of the person whose tax liability is under enquiry (unlike the general inspection power: see above), but it only applies to VAT. In the *Explanatory Notes to the Finance Bill 2008*, it was stated that it is important that HMRC retain the power to inspect third-party premises, goods on the premises and documents relating to those goods, in order to combat certain VAT frauds (such as missing trader intra-community fraud).

Power to inspect premises of involved third parties (Sch 36, para 10A)

10.67 Finance Act 2009 introduced a power for an HMRC officer to inspect:

- an 'involved third party's' business premises; and
- business assets and 'relevant documents' on those premises;

for the purpose of checking the position of any person in relation to any 'relevant tax' (Finance Act 2008, Sch 36, para 10A inserted by Finance Act 2009, Sch 48, para 3). The power came into on 1 April 2010.

10.68 Finance Act 2008, Sch 36, para 61A (inserted by Finance Act 2009, Sch 48, para 14) includes a table which comprises a list of 'involved third parties' and the 'relevant tax' and 'relevant documents' to which the inspection of that third party's premises must relate. Involved third parties are closely related to a potentially taxable event or transaction. The ambit of this power is fairly narrow; it is restricted to those involved in payroll giving, individual investment plans and child trust funds for income tax purposes, managing agents of Lloyd's syndicates, those involved in insurance business or contracts of insurance for the purposes of insurance premium tax, accountable persons for the purposes of stamp duty reserve tax and certain persons in relation to petroleum revenue tax and environmental taxes.

Power to inspect premises for valuation (Sch 36, para 12A)

10.69 Finance Act 2009 introduced a power for HMRC to inspect any premises (business or private) for the purpose of valuing, measuring or determining the character of the premises, provided that the valuation is reasonably required for the purpose of checking any person's position as regards income tax, corporation tax, capital gains tax, inheritance tax, stamp duty land tax or stamp duty reserve tax (Finance Act 2008, Sch 36, para 12A introduced by Finance Act 2009, Sch 48, para 5). The HMRC officer can be accompanied by any person whom the officer considers is needed to assist with the valuation, such as a surveyor. The power came into force on 1 April 2010.

10.70 An inspection can be carried out only if one of the following two conditions is met:

- the occupier (or person who controls the premises, if the occupier cannot be identified or the premises are vacant) has agreed the time of the inspection and has been given a written notice; or
- the inspection has been approved by the First-tier Tribunal and the occupier (or person who controls the premises) has been given at least seven days' notice in writing of the inspection.

10.71 The First-tier Tribunal may not approve the inspection unless the person whose tax position is being checked and the occupier have been given a reasonable opportunity to make representations to HMRC about the inspection and the Tribunal has been given a summary of those representations (Finance Act 2008, Sch 36, paras 12B and 13 as amended by Finance Act 2009, Sch 48, para 6).

Restrictions on the use of the powers by HMRC

10.72 A number (but, by no means all) of the restrictions that applied in relation to the old HMRC information powers (including under TMA, s 20) and self-assessment information powers (including under TMA, s 19A) have been carried over to Finance Act 2008, Sch 36. These include:

- An information notice only requires a person to produce a document if it is in that person's 'possession or power'.
- Privileged communications are excluded from disclosure.
- Auditors and tax advisers' documents are protected from disclosure.

These concepts are analysed further below.

Possession or power

10.73 Schedule 36, para 18 provides that an information notice only requires a person to produce a document if it is in that person's 'possession or power'. This restriction does not apply:

1   to the provision of 'information' on service of an information notice; or
2   in respect of HMRC's power to enter business premises and inspect.

10.74 The terms 'power' and 'possession' are not defined in any of the taxing statutes; and there is little case law on the meaning of the phrase 'power or possession' in the context of requests for information from HMRC.

Possession

10.75 The term 'possession' applies in a variety of contexts and has a number of meanings (Palmer *Bailment* (2nd edn, 1991) notes, at p 103 that 'Possession is a ductile and intuitive concept'; and Stroud's *Legal Dictionary* (5th edn, 1986) lists 49 different meanings). The meanings of the term 'possession' include:

1   de facto control or 'custody', that is, actual physical possession;
2   the right to possession where actual physical possession is not present;

10.75 *The information powers of HMRC*

3   ownership; and
4   'legal' possession in the sense of physical possession combined with a right to possession.

10.76   The most relevant to the meaning of the term in the context of s 20 is the phrase that formerly appeared in the Rules of the Supreme Court in relation to the inspection and discovery of documents for the purposes of civil litigation in the High Court. (The duty of disclosure under the Civil Procedure Rules is limited to documents which are or have been in a party's control; and so does not assist interpretatively here.) Under these Rules a party was required to list, for the purposes of disclosure, the documents that were in his 'possession, custody or power' (with the term 'custody' being added in 1964). The meaning of the threefold test was considered in a matrimonial case, *B v B* [1978] Fam 181, where Dunn J said that:

> '... for this purpose "possession" means the right to the possession of a document. 'Custody' means the actual, physical or corporeal holding of a document regardless of the right to its possession, for example, a holding of a document by a party as servant or agent of the true owner. "Power" means an enforceable right to inspect the document or to obtain possession or control of the document from the person who ordinarily has it in fact. The requirements of the rules are disjunctive in their operation, so far as possession, custody and power are concerned.'

10.77   Thus, it is clear that Dunn J was of the view that 'possession' is limited to lawful possession. De facto control, or physical possession without a right to possession is not sufficient. If a document has been entrusted to an individual who is acting as the owner's agent or bailee, and is physically held by that individual subject to an obligation of confidentiality to the owner, then that document is not in the legal possession of the agent or bailee, because although he has custody (or physical possession) of the document, he does not have an unfettered right to possession of the document. Although this definition was in the context of a threefold test of 'possession, custody or power', there seems to be no reason why that definition should not apply equally in s 20, which refers to 'possession or power'.

10.78   Documents that are in the custody or physical possession of an officer or employee of a company, if held as servant or agent of the company, or by such individual in his capacity as an officer or an employee of the company, will be treated as being in the possession of the company (see *Skoye v Bailey* [1971] 1 WWR 144 and *Williams v Ingram* (1900) 16 TLR 451).

Power

10.79   Although 'power' has a number of meanings, its meaning in the context of access to information is clear. The term has been defined by the House of Lords in *Lonrho Ltd v Shell Petroleum* [1980] 1 WLR 627. In *Lonrho*, the claimants sought disclosure of documents held by foreign subsidiaries of Shell. The claimants argued that, even though the subsidiary companies had refused to supply the documents further to a request from Shell, the documents were in the 'power' of Shell and were thus disclosable under Ord 24, r 2 of the

Rules of the Supreme Court (which provided that 'all documents must be disclosed which the party giving discovery has or has had in his possession, custody or power'). Shell owned 100% of the shares of the subsidiary companies; and so it could remove the directors or change the articles so as to require disclosure of the documents. This argument was rejected by the Court of Appeal ([1980] QB 358). Shaw LJ noted that, in a general philosophical sense, there was a latent power that could be used to achieve possession of the relevant documents. However, no note of futurity could be read into Ord 24. As it specified documents that 'were or had been' within a party's power, that constituted the limits on what could be obtained. It could only be in the situation where company A was so subservient to the wishes of company B that compliance was guaranteed that it could be said that company B had the documents in its power.

10.80 The House of Lords upheld the decision of the Court of Appeal, Lord Diplock saying (at 635) that the term 'power' means:

> 'a presently enforceable legal right to obtain from whoever actually holds the document inspection of it without the need to obtain the consent of anyone else'.

10.81 The following observation (at 634) was made:

> 'The articles of association of all the subsidiaries vest the management of the company in its board of directors. It is the board that has control of the company's documents on its behalf; the shareholders as such have no right to inspect or to take copies of them. If requested to allow inspection of the company's documents, whether by a shareholder or by a third party, it is the duty of the board to consider whether to accede to this request would be in the best interests of the company.'

10.82 The rule was caveated, however: 'I say nothing about one-man companies in which a natural person and/or his nominees are the sole shareholders and directors. It may be that, depending upon their own particular facts, different considerations apply to these' (at 636–7).

10.83 The decision of the House of Lords was considered in the context of the information powers of HMRC in *Meditor Capital Management v Feighan* [2004] STC (SCD) 273. *Meditor* concerned, inter alia, documents that were held by Meditor Capital Management (Bermuda) Limited ('MCM(B)') in Bermuda and sought by HMRC by service of a notice under the Finance Act 1998, Sch 18, para 27 on Meditor Capital Management Ltd ('Meditor'), a UK resident 100% subsidiary of MCM(B). Meditor adduced evidence of correspondence between itself and MCM(B), which showed that it had asked MCM(B) twice to supply to it the documents requested by the Revenue and that MCM(B) had twice refused to do so. The Special Commissioner held that these letters were not sufficient proof that the particular documents were not in the power or possession of Meditor. He hinted that the *Lonrho* test may not be the correct test to apply for these purposes, and that simply a de facto ability to obtain the documents or particulars might suffice. However, this decision was in the context of Meditor having previously agreed to provide the particular

10.83 *The information powers of HMRC*

documents (under the terms of agreed directions) and having provided other information that had been, both legally and factually, held on an identical basis to the particular information that it claimed was not in its power or possession.

10.84 In the context of the s 20(8A) and paragraph 5 notices served against financial institutions, HMRC have indicated that they consider that *Lonrho* was incorrectly decided by the House of Lords and/or does not apply in a tax context. It is understood that they will bring test cases in order to determine whether a UK head office has power over documents and information held by an offshore branch and whether a UK parent company has power over documents and information held by a non-UK subsidiary.

10.85 Notwithstanding this indication by HMRC, it is considered that the current state of the law in respect of documents held offshore by non-UK resident companies in a group of companies with a UK-resident parent company is, provided the relevant company is a separate legal entity and it cannot be said that it is so subservient to the wishes of the parent company that, with regard to requests from that company, compliance will always be guaranteed, then it cannot be said that all documents in the possession of a subsidiary company are in the power of the parent company. If the parent company is unable to recover the documents without taking further steps, such as amending the articles to allow the shareholders to have a right of inspection of the documents, then the parent company does not have power over the documents. This is on the assumption that the autonomy which the overseas subsidiaries enjoy is conferred on them bona fide, and that the local directors 'run their own show' with comparatively little interference from the parent company.

10.86 It is possible (but unlikely) that HMRC could try to obtain disclosure of documents in the power or possession of a non-UK resident company by service of a separate information notice directly on that company. There is no express statutory or judicial limitation on the territorial scope of Sch 36; and, indeed, HMRC have expressed the view that, for example, the reporting obligations imposed on professionals under Inheritance Taxes Act 1984, s 218 have extra-territorial effect. However, it is unlikely that HMRC would try to obtain disclosure of 'offshore information' from an offshore entity (unless that entity has a 'sufficient presence' in the United Kingdom (as that term was defined by the House of Lords in *Clark v Oceanic Contractors* [1983] STC 35)), particularly if such disclosure could expose the offshore entity to penalties or legal challenge in its own jurisdiction, as HMRC are unlikely to wish to be drawn into a test case as to the scope of their statutory powers in this context.

Legal professional privilege

10.87 Paragraph 23, Sch 36 provides that an information notice does not require a person to provide information or produce any part of a document which is protected by legal professional privilege. Similarly, the business premises inspection power does not permit HMRC to inspect a business document that is protected by legal professional privilege (Sch 36, para 28).

10.88 Legal professional privilege is a fundamental aspect of the legal system in this country. It allows a person to consult a lawyer without fear that the information that he reveals will be disclosed in court contrary to his wishes. It thus enables the client to have confidence in the confidentiality of his legal adviser and so encourages him to 'make a clean breast of it to the gentleman whom he consults' (per Sir George Jessell MR, *Anderson v Bank of British Columbia* [1876] 2 ChD 644 at 649). Further, legal professional privilege has been recognised as an aspect of the right to privacy under Art 8 of the European Convention on Human Rights by the European Court of Human Rights and by the European Court of Justice to be part of European Community Law.

10.89 That privilege is a fundamental human right has been recognised in the UK by the House of Lords in a series of cases. (See *R (on the application of Morgan Grenfell & Co Ltd) v Special Comr of Income Tax* [2002] STC 786, *per* Lord Hobhouse of Woodborough at 798f and Lord Hoffmann at 796g–j and 790d, where he said that: '[privilege] has been held by the European Court of Human Rights to be part of the right of privacy guaranteed by art 8 of the Convention for the Protection of Human Rights and Fundamental Freedoms'.) There are two heads of privilege: legal advice privilege and litigation privilege.

Legal advice privilege

10.90 There is no requirement that such documents be produced for the 'dominant purpose' of legal advice. Provided that there is a 'relevant legal context', a lawyer/client communication will be privileged. This will cover most lawyer/client communications.

10.91 Internal communications between employees of a company, even if for the purpose of seeking legal advice or preparing 'raw material' in respect of which advice may be given are not privileged, unless those employees are the 'client'. Only those employees in an organisation who are given the role of obtaining or receiving legal advice can be classified as 'the client' for the purposes of privilege.

10.92 Communications between third parties and lawyers or clients are not privileged under this head, even if they are made in connection with the seeking or giving of legal advice. The only exception to this rule is if that third party is an agent of either the lawyer or the client and is simply a medium of communication. This is strictly construed. (See *Price Waterhouse v BCCI Holdings* [1992] BCLC 583 where Millett J (as he then was) held that reports produced by accountants and sent to lawyers were not privileged, as the accountants acted as more than mere agents of communication.)

10.93 Communications with other professionals, such as accountants or chartered tax advisers, will not attract legal professional privilege under this head, even if they are giving advice on strictly legal matters, such as tax law. (See *Chantry Martin v Martin* [1953] 2 QB 286 and *R (on the application of Prudential Plc) v Special Commissioner of Income Tax* [2010] STC 2802.)

Litigation privilege

10.94 Litigation privilege covers communications that came into existence for the dominant purpose of being used in connection with or in contemplation of litigation. There is an overlap between advice and litigation privilege in that, once litigation is in prospect, then lawyer/client documents produced for that litigation will be protected under both heads.

10.95 There are two important limits on litigation privilege. First, it does not arise in respect of non-adversarial proceedings. In *Re L* [1997] AC 16, the House of Lords held (by a majority) that litigation privilege could not apply to proceedings under Part IV of the Children Act 1989 in respect of child care orders, because the proceedings were not adversarial in nature; privilege was excluded by necessary implication from the terms and overall purpose of the Act.

10.96 Secondly, the documents must be produced for the 'dominant purpose' of litigation. In *Waugh v British Railways Board* [1980] AC 521, the House of Lords adopted and applied the 'dominant purpose' test that had been put forward by Barwick CJ in his minority judgment in the High Court of Australia in *Grant v Downs* [1976] 135 CLR 674, at 677 to determine whether a report that had been prepared both for safety purposes and for the purpose of obtaining legal advice in anticipation of litigation was privileged. (Lord Edmund-Davies described the 'dominant purpose' test as the 'touchstone' of the privilege.) The dominant purpose test (which must be applied at the time of creation) acts as a filter mechanism and prevents privilege attaching to documents brought into existence for purposes other than that of legal advice. If a document has been produced partly for the purpose of litigation and partly for another purpose, that document will not be privileged if the relevant litigation purpose is a secondary or even an equal purpose. Thus, for example, communications by a tax authority with third parties in order to ascertain the value of goods for the purpose of tax legislation, even though such communications would also enable the authority to meet an inevitable challenge by taxpayers, were not protected by litigation privilege. (*Alfred Crompton Amusement Machines Ltd v Customs and Excise Comrs (No 2)* [1974] AC 405.)

10.97 There is a further important difference between the two privileges in that communications between the client or lawyer with third parties can be protected by litigation (but not advice) privilege. Although no lawyer need, in fact, have been engaged at the time of the communication, as the dominant purpose for which the communication is made must be either: (1) obtaining legal advice from the client's lawyer; or (2) use by the lawyer in aid of litigation that has commenced or is contemplated, whether litigation privilege applies to third party/client communications when no lawyer is contemplated is doubtful. This is particularly the case in the light of the recent judicial trend to seek to limit the ambit of litigation privilege. Lord Scott, for example, in *Three Rivers District Council v Governor and Company of the Bank of England* [2005] 1 AC 610 suggested that there should be a limit on third-party communications being protected under the head of litigation privilege. In Lord Scott's view, even if such documents were produced for the dominant purpose of litigation, they should not be privileged unless they constitute or disclose the seeking or giving of legal advice. (See also Scott V-C in *Secretary of State v Baker* (*Re Barings*) [1998] Ch 356.)

10.98 The consequence of this is that if an accountant or tax adviser is instructed in relation to a tax dispute and instructing a legal adviser is not anticipated, then it is likely that communications between the adviser and the client will not be protected by litigation privilege. Such documents may, however, be protected by the statutorily created quasi-privileges under Sch 36, paras 19, 24 and 25.

Resolving privilege disputes

10.99 Regulations have been issued covering disputes about privileged information for the purposes of Finance Act 2008, Sch 36: the Information Notice: Resolution of Disputes as to Privileged Communications Regulations 2009, SI 2009 No 1916, which came into force on 7 August 2009, provide a procedure for the First-tier Tribunal to resolve disputes about whether a document or information is protected from disclosure by reason of legal professional privilege.

10.100 Where a dispute arises in correspondence, the recipient of an information notice must serve on HMRC a list of the documents that the recipient believes are privileged. The list must describe the nature and contents of each piece of material, unless that description would itself give rise to a dispute about privilege. The recipient must serve the list within the time for complying with the information notice. HMRC then have 20 working days in which to tell the recipient which material on the list they require and which they consider is not privileged. Assuming that the matter is not resolved between the parties, the recipient must then make an application (which notice must be accompanied by the disputed material) to the First-tier Tribunal for it to resolve the dispute, The application must be made within a reasonable time, to be agreed between HMRC and the recipient, but no later than 20 working days after HMRC have indicated which material they require and which they consider is not privileged.

10.101 Where the dispute arises during an inspection of premises, the recipient of the information notice must tell the HMRC officer carrying out the inspection which material it considers is privileged and any disputed material must be placed in a sealed opaque container. The HMRC officer must then deliver the container to the First-tier Tribunal within 42 working days, with an application that it resolve the dispute about privilege.

The process under the Regulations is potentially of particular use in relation to premises inspections, first, because there is no appeal against an inspection and, secondly because a reasonably held belief that a document is or may be privileged amounts, in the author's view, to a reasonable excuse for obstructing the HMRC officer by not providing that particular document. (A person who deliberately obstructs an HMRC officer in the course of an inspection that has

10.101 *The information powers of HMRC*

been approved by the First-tier Tribunal is liable to a penalty, unless there is a reasonable excuse for that obstruction (FA 2008, Sch 36, paras 39 and 45).)

10.102 HMRC and the recipient of the information notice can also resolve a dispute about privilege by agreement at any time. A recipient who complies with these regulations is treated as having complied with the information notice in relation to the disputed material until the Tribunal decides whether privilege applies or the dispute is settled by agreement.

Schedule 36, para 19(1)(a)

10.103 Paragraph 19(1)(a) is in similar terms to the old TMA, s 20B(2). It is not coterminous with litigation privilege. It protects documents 'relating to the conduct of any pending appeal relating to tax' from disclosure under service of an information notice. The reference to 'conduct' of appeals indicates that only documents that are brought into existence for the purposes of the preparation and presentation of the appeal are protected (see *Monarch Assurance Co Ltd v Special Comrs and IRC* [1986] STC 311). It applies only in respect of 'pending' appeals; thus, until an appeal has been made by the taxpayer, para 19(1)(a) does not apply to protect documents, even if they came into existence for the purpose of contemplated litigation.

Auditors and tax advisers' documents (Sch 36, para 24)

10.104 Paragraph 24 provides that, subject to certain qualifications, which are described below, an auditor cannot be required either to provide information held in connection with the performance of carrying out a statutory audit or to produce documents that are his property and that were created in the course of carrying out a statutory audit. In practice, HMRC allowed equivalent protection in relation to s 20 notices where an accountant was appointed to carry out a non-statutory independent audit to standards similar to those required for a Companies Act audit, provided that the work on the audit was kept separate from any work on the preparation of the accounts. It is reasonable to assume that a like approach will be adopted by HMRC in relation to para 24.

10.105 Paragraph 25 provides that, subject likewise to the qualifications described below, anyone appointed to give advice about the tax affairs of another person cannot be required to produce documents that are his property and which consist of 'relevant communications' with his taxpayer client or another tax adviser of the client for the purpose of giving or obtaining advice on that client's tax affairs. HMRC consider that the term 'relevant communications' can include notes of meetings and telephone calls, and internal memoranda, as well as client correspondence.

10.106 The protection for documents of tax advisers and auditors is subject to two qualifications:

- Under para 26(1), no protection is provided in relation to information or documents that contains workings or analytical information showing how a particular entry on the return, accounts etc was arrived at.

The information powers of HMRC **10.112**

- Under para 26(2), where the notice requiring production of documents or information relates to an unidentified taxpayer (ie it is a notice under para 5), no protection is provided for such part of a document which contains information as to the identity or address of a taxpayer to whom the notice relates or in respect of any person who has acted on behalf of such a taxpayer.

10.107 Paragraphs 26(1) and (2) are subject to para 26(3), which provides that the protection for a document or information in the possession of an auditor or tax adviser is not lost, as a result of these qualifications, if the explanatory information or the information identifying the taxpayer or adviser respectively is also contained in another document that has already been produced to HMRC.

10.108 In relation to s 20 notices, HMRC stated that the formal power to require access to an accountant's working papers was to be used only where the information needed could not be obtained on a voluntary basis and HMRC had no other means of satisfying themselves that a taxpayer's accounts or returns are accurate. A like assurance has yet to be given expressly in relation to the new regime.

Penalties

10.109 Transitional provisions keep in force the pre-1 April 2009 rules relating to appeals and penalties for information notices issued before 1 April 2009. Documents in respect of which a penalty is exigible under s 98 are expressly excluded from the Finance Act 2007, Sch 24 penalty regime. Thus, the 'old' regime remains in force in relation to penalties for failure to comply with a s 20 notice. This regime is described in the appendix to this chapter.

10.110 Failure to comply with an information notice issued under Sch 36 renders the taxpayer liable to a penalty of £300 and an additional £60 for each day on which the failure continues after the day on which such penalty was imposed (Sch 36, paras 39 and 40). A further tax-geared penalty may be imposed for continued failure to comply (Sch 36, para 50).

10.111 However, failure to comply within the time limit will not necessarily attract a penalty, provided that there is compliance within such further time as HMRC may allow (Sch 36, para 44). A penalty does not arise if the person satisfies HMRC (or the First-tier Tribunal on appeal) that there is reasonable excuse and, if relevant, the failure is remedied without unreasonable delay after the excuse ceases (Sch 36, para 45).

10.112 There is also a penalty for providing inaccurate information or a document containing an inaccuracy in complying with an information notice where both of the following conditions are satisfied that:

- the inaccuracy is careless or deliberate;
- the person who provided the inaccurate information or document discovers the inaccuracy some time later and fails to take reasonable steps to inform HMRC.

10.113 The maximum penalty in relation to inaccurate information is £3,000 (FA 2008, Sch 36, para 40A introduced by Finance Act 2009, Sch 47, para 15 from 21 July 2009).

THE CRIMINAL INVESTIGATORY POWERS OF HMRC

TMA, s 20A

10.114 Section 20A applies to any tax accountant, who has been convicted by a UK court of any tax offence, or has had a penalty imposed on him for assisting in the preparation of a tax return or accounts or any information or document to be used for tax purposes that he knows to be incorrect. (For the purposes of s 20A, 'tax accountant' includes any person who assists in the preparation of a return. It may therefore include a lawyer.) Pages 743–46 of *Inland Revenue Bulletin* April 2000 set out HMRC's interpretation of the scope of this power.

10.115 An inspector can seek consent for the issue of a s 20A notice from the appropriate judicial authority, who is to give consent only if he is satisfied in all the circumstances that the inspector is justified in so proceeding. The appropriate judicial authority in England and Wales is a circuit judge. A notice under these provisions against a barrister, advocate or solicitor can be issued only by the Board, with the consent of the appropriate judicial authority. It cannot require the production of any document for which a claim for professional privilege can be maintained.

10.116 Under a s 20A notice, HMRC may seek delivery of documents that are in the possession or power of the tax accountant, and which, in the inspector's reasonable opinion, contain information relevant to the tax liability of any of his clients.

PACE powers

10.117 Not all the powers that are available to the police under PACE are available to HMRC officers. In particular, the power to take fingerprints, and the power to charge and bail suspects have not been made available to HMRC officers. Article 4 of the Police and Criminal Evidence Act 1984 (Application to Revenue and Customs) Order 2007, SI 2007 No 3175, ensures that HMRC officers do not have powers to charge a person, release a person on bail or to detain a person after charge. PACE has been amended so as to apply four categories of PACE powers to all taxes. These categories are:

- search warrants;
- production orders;
- arrest powers; and
- search and entry powers in order to arrest.

10.118 In 'Criminal Investigation Powers: Publication of Draft Clauses and Explanatory Notes' (which was published on 17 January 2007), it was proposed that the use of the PACE powers would be restricted to suitably trained officers authorised by the Commissioners of HMRC; and at para 7.7 of 'The

Explanatory Memorandum to The Police and Criminal Evidence Act 1984 (Application to Revenue and Customs) Order 2007 SI No 2007 3175', it was indicated that, before 1 December 2007, HMRC would publish material on its internet site in respect of 'how criminal investigation work is organised in HMRC, which officers are entitled to use the powers and how use of the powers is authorised'. This proposal has, to an extent, superseded by the introduction of the enabling Treasury Order. Nonetheless, on 6 December 2007, HMRC issued a release in which it was stated, inter alia:

> **'Authorisation to use powers**
>
> The criminal investigation powers can be used only by officers who are authorised to use them. An authorised officer is an officer of HM Revenue and Customs, appropriately trained and engaged on operational duties in Criminal Investigation, Detection, Risk and Intelligence and Internal Governance Directorates. PACE provides that some powers can be exercised only by police constables of a particular rank. When those powers are applied to HMRC the police ranks are converted to HMRC grades of an equivalent authority –
>
> - Sergeant   Officer
> - Inspector   Higher Officer
> - Chief Inspector   Higher Officer
> - Superintendent   Senior Officer

10.119 HMRC have set internal authorisation levels requiring an authorised officer to get the approval of a higher graded officer before using certain powers. The authority levels for HMRC are set no lower than the authority levels in the police, the primary user of PACE powers. However in most cases HMRC have set the main authority level required at a minimum of senior officer grade, for example applications to a magistrate or court for a production order or search warrant. The majority of authorities in the police service are held at inspector level, equivalent to HMRC's higher officer grade.

The PACE power to search

10.120 All applications for HMRC search warrants since 1 December 2007 have been made under PACE, s 8 or Sch 1. On an application by an HMRC officer, a magistrate may issue a warrant for the HMRC officer to enter and search premises if he has reasonable grounds for believing that an indictable tax offence has been committed and that there is material on the specified premises that is likely to be of substantial value (whether by itself or together with other material) to the investigation of the offence and is likely to be admissible at the trial for the offence.

10.121 The powers of seizure under PACE have been considerably extended under CJPA 2001. Its provisions aim to overcome the problems that arose either where it could not be conveniently determined in situ whether a particular item

10.121 *The information powers of HMRC*

(such as a computer) was subject to seizure or where there were issues relating to whether or not material was protected by reason of legal professional privileges.

10.122 Under CJPA 2001, Sch 1, Pt 1, the s 50 powers of seizure under that Act are extended to PACE, s 8. This power applies where it is not reasonably practicable to determine on the premises whether the material is, or contains, something HMRC are entitled to seize. It entitles HMRC officers to remove material (eg computer hard drives) if they have reasonable grounds to believe that the material may contain items they are authorised to seize. In *R (on the application of H) v IRC* [2002] STC 1354, which concerned a s 20C warrant, the High Court held that a hard disk could not be regarded as simply a container of the files visible to the computer's operating system. It was a single object: a single thing. There was no basis, therefore, for a computer not being considered a 'thing' within the meaning of s 20C(3)(b). The fact that there was also on the hard disk irrelevant material did not make the computer any less of a thing that might be required as evidence for the purposes of criminal proceedings. Accordingly, if a Revenue Officer who entered into premises under the authority of a warrant under s 20C found a computer, and he had reasonable cause to believe that the data on the computer's hard disk might be required as evidence for the purpose of relevant proceedings, then he was entitled to seize and remove that computer, even though it contained irrelevant material also. It is considered that the ratio of this case applies equally to PACE warrants.

10.123 Once the material is removed from the premises, HMRC are empowered to sift the material to determine whether it contains any relevant items that they wish to seize. When powers of seizure under s 50 are exercised by an HMRC officer, the taxpayer or third party must be provided with a written notice of this in accordance with CJPA 2001, s 52. The warrant must be endorsed to provide a record of those documents or items that have been removed.

10.124 Access to all the documents or items may be permitted, on request and under supervision. Copies may be taken at the time of access, or requested. If requested, the copies must be provided within a reasonable time. There is no right to allow a copy to be taken at the time of search.

10.125 An HMRC officer exercising powers under PACE, s 8 is bound by the PACE Codes of Practice. Code B provides, inter alia, that a person from whom any items are seized must, on request, be provided with a list or description of the property within a reasonable time. If an original document has been removed and is of such a nature that a copy would be sufficient (1) for use as evidence at a trial for an offence, or (2) for forensic examination or for investigation in connection with an offence, it may not be retained longer than is necessary to establish that fact and to obtain the copy.

10.126 Items held with the intention of furthering a criminal purpose are not subject to legal privilege. In *R v IRC and Middlesex Guildhall Crown Court, ex p Tamosius and Partners* [1999] STC 1077, the High Court held that s 20C(4) prevented only the removal of documents with respect to which a claim to professional privilege could be 'maintained' – the seizure did not become unlawful merely because the firm of American lawyers that had been raided claimed that the documents were privileged. HMRC will often adopt the practice of applying in advance to the Attorney General to nominate a counsel and then using that counsel to review material to determine whether or not legal privilege applies. However, this process is undertaken only to protect HMRC; it does not preclude a taxpayer or third party challenging a decision by counsel that material is not privileged. If there is a dispute as to whether legal privilege applies, attempts should be made, at the time of the search, to persuade HMRC to put the material in opaque, sealed envelopes and the issue of privilege resolved subsequently.

Key points in respect of the PACE search powers
10.127

- There must be reasonable grounds for 'believing' that an offence has been committed (suspicion is not sufficient). The judge is only able to issue an order where he is satisfied that there are reasonable grounds for believing that an offence 'has been' committed (that it is 'being, or is about to be' committed will not suffice). In contrast, the grounds for issuing an s 20C warrant were that: 'there is reasonable ground for *suspecting* that an offence involving serious fraud in connection with, or in relation to, tax *is being, has been or is about to be committed* and that evidence of it is to be found on premises specified in the information' (emphasis added).
- An application for a warrant under PACE, s 8 is made to a magistrate. If special procedure material is involved, a search warrant cannot be issued under s 8, and a warrant can be issued only by a circuit judge (see further below). (Applications for s 20C warrants were made to a circuit judge.)
- Applications for search warrants under PACE do not require the approval of the Board of HMRC as a matter of statute (although, as a matter of practice, do need internal authorisation at a senior level). (Under TMA, s 20C(1), the judge had to be satisfied that the officer was acting with the approval of the Board of HMRC given in relation to the particular case before consenting to issuance of a warrant.)

Production orders

10.128 'Special procedure material', items subject to legal professional privilege, and 'excluded material' are excluded from the scope of a s 8 warrant. Special procedure material consists broadly of business records that are held by a person under an obligation of confidence to a third party (see PACE, s 14).

10.129 If it is suspected that special procedure material needs to be obtained, HMRC can apply to a circuit judge (*ex parte*) for a warrant under PACE, Sch 1, para 12. If granted, this enables an Officer to enter premises and search for excluded material or other special procedure material. (There are a number of conditions as to access and other criteria that must be satisfied (see Code B of the PACE Codes of Practice).)

10.130 *The information powers of HMRC*

10.130 An alternative to an order authorising such material to be seized under a search and seizure exercise is a production order (under PACE, Sch 1, paras 7–11). If a circuit judge is satisfied that there are reasonable grounds for believing that an indictable tax offence has been committed, he may consent to the issue of a PACE production order. The hearing before the judge is *inter partes* (in contrast to applications under s 20BA).

10.131 Currently, the production order powers under s 20BA (direct tax) and VATA, Sch 11, para 11 (VAT) are preserved. However, if the documents sought are believed to include special procedure material, then those documents may not be obtained under the s 20BA or para 11 production order process: a production order under PACE, Sch 1 must be used instead. (Article 7 of the Police and Criminal Evidence Act 1984 (Application to Revenue and Customs) Order 2007, SI 2007 No 3175 provides that PACE is to be interpreted as if s 14B was inserted after s 14A, with s 14B providing that an HMRC officer may only make an application under TMA, s 20BA or VATA, Sch 11, para 11 if the officer considers that an application under PACE, Sch 1 would not succeed because the material required does not consist of or include special procedure material).

Safeguards

10.132 The PACE Codes of Practice apply when PACE powers are exercised by HMRC officers and when HMRC officers are investigating tax offences (see PACE, s 67). They contain detailed regulations on the exercise of PACE powers and notes for guidance. They are admissible in evidence and any relevant provision must be taken into account by a court (under PACE, s 67(11)). PACE Code B deals with the powers to search premises and to seize and retain property found on premises and persons.

The SOCPA powers

10.133 SOCPA, ss 60–70, Sch 1, Part 2, introduced, inter alia, new investigatory powers in relation to tax crimes. Under SCOPA, s 60 use of these powers can be delegated by the director of RCPO to any HMRC prosecutor. The offences to which the powers relate include common law cheat of the public revenue and false accounting (Theft Act 1968, s 17), provided that, in the opinion of the investigating officer, the potential loss to the public revenue is of an amount not less than £5,000. The powers came into effect on 1 April 2006.

10.134 An HMRC prosecutor can give, or can authorise an officer of HMRC to give, a disclosure notice to any person who has information which relates to a matter relevant to the investigation of the offence, provided that there are reasonable grounds for belief that the information in question, whether or not by itself, is likely to be of 'substantial value' to the investigation. A recipient of the notice not only has to produce documents relevant to the investigation, but also has to 'answer questions with respect to any matter relevant to the investigation' and to 'provide information with respect to any such matter as is specified in the notice' (under SOCPA, s 62(3)). There is a similar protection for privileged information or documents as was contained in TMA, 20C(4); a person may not be required to answer any privileged question, or provide any privileged information, or produce any privileged document (except that a lawyer may be required to provide the name and address of his client).

10.135 Two offences are created with regard to SOCPA disclosure notices. The first is failure to comply with the requirements set out in a disclosure notice (punishable by a maximum sentence of 51 weeks' imprisonment, with a 'reasonable excuse' for failure to comply being a defence); and, second is making a false or misleading statement in response to the requirements imposed by a disclosure notice (punishable by a maximum of two years' imprisonment).

10.136 If the recipient of a disclosure notice fails to comply with its terms, then the HMRC prosecutor can obtain a search and seize warrant from a justice of the peace. Such a warrant will enable an HMRC prosecutor to enter and search premises, using force where necessary, and to take possession of any documents that appear to be of a description specified in the disclosure notice, or to take any other steps that appear to be necessary for preserving, or preventing interference with, any such documents. A warrant can also be issued if it is not practicable to issue a disclosure notice, or where the service of a disclosure notice might seriously prejudice the investigation (under SOCPA, s 66(2)).

10.137 It was intended that these powers would be used primarily against third parties, including professional advisers. (See the comments of the Parliamentary Under-Secretary of State for the Home Department at the Committee stage of the Serious Organised Crime and Police Bill.) However, to date, HMRC have not made any particular use of these powers.

Section 20BA – the production power

10.138 HMRC's ability to obtain possession of documents in the case of suspected serious fraud was enhanced by the introduction of s 20BA (and Sch 1AA), which was inserted by Finance Act 2000, s 149(1). Section 20BA does not require HMRC to apply for a search and seizure warrant to obtain documents from a third party, who may have evidence relating to suspected fraud; a judge may issue an order requiring the person to deliver the documents to HMRC. The appropriate judicial authority (a circuit judge in England and Wales (see s 20D(1)) may, if satisfied on information on oath given by an authorised officer of the Board of the grounds set out below, make an order under s 20BA requiring a person who appears to have in his possession or power the documents specified in the order to deliver them to a specified HMRC officer within 10 working days (working days exclude Saturdays, Sundays and public holidays), or such other period as may be specified. Section 20BA was intended to limit the occasions on which it is necessary for HMRC to enter the premises of persons not themselves suspected of fraud; a warrant could be issued under s 20C if the production order procedure under s 20BA is more appropriate. Section 20C(1AA) provided that the Board of HMRC shall not approve an application for an s 20C warrant unless 'they have reasonable grounds for believing that use of the procedure under s 20BA ... might

10.138 *The information powers of HMRC*

seriously prejudice the investigation'. There is no such equivalent requirement to consider s 20BA before applying for a warrant under PACE, s 8.

Section 20BA has been amended in one regard following the changes introduced by Finance Act 2007: the procedure under s 20BA cannot be used to obtain 'special procedure material' (see Art 7 of the Police and Criminal Evidence Act 1984 (Application to Revenue and Customs) Order 2007, SI 2007 No 3175, and further below); instead an application under PACE, Sch 1 must be made.

10.139 The grounds for issuing the order are that:

- there is reasonable ground for suspecting that an offence involving serious fraud in connection with, or in relation to, tax is being, has been or is about to be committed; and
- documents which may be required as evidence for the purposes of any proceedings in respect of such an offence are or may be in the power or possession of any person (under s 20BA(2)).

10.140 A person is entitled to notice of the intention to apply for an order against him under s 20BA and to appear and be heard at the hearing of the application, unless the appropriate judicial authority is satisfied that this would seriously prejudice the investigation of the offence (under Sch 1AA, para 3).

10.141 A recipient of the notice of intention to apply for an order must not do any of the following:

- conceal, destroy, alter or dispose of any document to which the application relates; or
- disclose to any other person information or any other matter likely to prejudice the investigation of the offence to which the application relates (under Sch 1AA, para 4) unless permission is obtained from the appropriate court, or in writing from an HMRC officer, or after the application has been dismissed or abandoned, or after any order has been complied with.

10.142 This is an exception to the anti-tipping of provision in the case of professional legal advisers. A professional legal adviser may disclose information to his client in connection with the giving by the adviser of legal advice, or to any other person in contemplation of, or in connection with, legal proceedings and for the purposes of those proceedings. However, this exception does not apply in circumstances where disclosures are made with a view to furthering a criminal purpose.

10.143 Schedule 1AA, para 5 provides the same protection to privileged materials with regard to the exercise of a power under s 20BA as s 20C(4) did in the context of s 20C notices. In addition, Orders for the Delivery of Documents (Procedure) Regulations 2000, SI 2000 No 2875, reg 7 sets out a procedure for the resolution of disputes as to legal privilege. If there is a dispute as to whether any document or parts of documents are protected by legal privilege, the person concerned may apply to the appropriate judicial authority (in England and Wales, a circuit judge) to resolve the dispute. If the application is made within the time allowed for the delivery of the documents, then they are deemed to have been delivered in accordance with the notice until the dispute is resolved. In the meantime, all the documents concerned are to be lodged with and held by the court. The Board of HMRC is entitled to at least five working days' notice of the hearing of the application, and to attend and be heard at the hearing. If the authority upholds the claim for legal privilege in whole or in part, the costs of the application are to be met by the Board of HMRC. Before the hearing of the dispute, it may be resolved by agreement between the Board and the applicant.

10.144 HMRC do not have a statutory duty to provide copies or an inventory, although there are rights to access/request copies: if an original document has been delivered and is of such a nature that a copy would be sufficient (1) for use as evidence at a trial for an offence, or (2) for forensic examination or for investigation in connection with an offence, the original shall not be retained longer than is necessary to establish that fact and to obtain the copy (s 20CC, Sch 1AA, para 8).

Section 20BA offences

10.145 Failure to comply with an order made under s 20BA is punishable as a contempt of court. Failure to comply with the obligations under Sch 1AA, para 4 is also punishable as a contempt of court.

Appendix

The pre-1 April 2009 direct tax powers

INTRODUCTION

10A.01 Before the changes introduced by Finance Act 2008, HMRC had an extremely wide range of powers that it could call on to ascertain the quantum of tax due from a particular taxpayer, to confirm and collect the tax due and then to enforce payment of the tax. The tax information-gathering powers could be divided into:

- the issue of returns of various types or 'bulk information powers'; and
- the issue of notices requiring the production of documents or information.

10A.02 The first of these categories include the provisions of TMA 1970, ss 13–19, 21 and 23–28, under which notices can be served on certain persons requiring them to make returns containing information relevant to the taxable income of other persons. These include:

- the names of employees, and details of payments to them, from an employer under s 15;
- details of payments, such as commissions, made for services to persons other than their employees from traders (and certain others), under s 16; and
- interest payments made by banks, under ss 17 and 18.

These provisions remain in force. However, they are likely to be amended or replaced following the consultation in respect of 'bulk and specialist information powers', and possibly in Finance Act 2010.

10A.03 With regard to the second of these categories, the two main sets of provisions were:

- the powers given to HMRC under TMA, ss 20–20D ('the s 20 powers'); and

10A.03 *The pre-1 April 2009 direct tax powers*

- the powers that were introduced under the personal and corporate self-assessment regimes (under TMA, s 19A and the Finance Act 1998, Sch 18, para 27 respectively) ('the self-assessment powers').

10A.04 Wide and general information powers were bestowed on HMRC under s 20. These powers were among the most important in HMRC's arsenal of weapons to detect, quantify and prevent any loss of tax that may have arisen through either a failure to make returns or the submission of incomplete or incorrect returns (whether innocently incorrect or not). The s 20 powers were distinct from (and additional to) the self-assessment powers, which enabled an inspector to issue a notice to the taxpayer requiring 'such documents as are in the taxpayer's possession or power' and 'such accounts or particulars' as he may reasonably require in order to determine the accuracy of the return, in two important ways. First, the s 20 powers were 'free-standing' in that they could be used even if there was no open enquiry; and, secondly, third parties could be required to produce documents in their power or possession that contained information relevant to another person's tax liability. The powers that HMRC possessed in relation to direct taxes that were most relevant (and which have been repealed) are s 20(1), (3), and (8A) (which gave information powers), and s 20C (which gave a search and seizure power). Section 20BA (which gives a production power) remains in force. In this appendix, the s 20 powers are analysed first before the self-assessment powers are outlined.

OVERVIEW OF TMA 1970, S 20

10A.05 There were four main s 20 powers:

- s 20(1);
- s 20(3) (which includes s 20(8A));
- s 20BA; and
- s 20C.

10A.06 The first two were information powers, and the third is a production power. Section 20C was a search and seizure power. With regard to the information powers, notices under s 20(1) (and under s 20(2)) were served on a person in relation to his own tax liability and were known as 'first-party notices'; and notices under s 20(1) and (3) as extended by s 20(8A) were served on third parties in relation to another person's tax liabilities and thus are known as 'third party notices'. A further distinction could be drawn between notices that could be issued by an inspector and those that could be issued only by the Board of HMRC. Although it was rarely used in practice, s 20(2) was similar in ambit to s 20(1), but it could be used only by the Board of HMRC.

The information powers – s 20(1) and (3)

10A.07 A s 20(1) or (3) notice required the taxpayer or third party respectively to produce documents in their 'possession or power' which, in the inspector of taxes' reasonable opinion, contained or may contain information relevant to the tax liability of any person named in the notice. The subjective nature of the words 'reasonable opinion' gave a significant discretion to inspectors to determine what information they considered was necessary to determine the amount of any tax liability to which a person may have been subject (and there was a presumption that the inspector was acting reasonably in this regard – see *R v IRC, ex p Mohammed* [1999] STC 129).

10A.08 There were a number of statutory restrictions on the exercise of the s 20 information powers by HMRC. The restrictions are outlined in more detail below, but they included the following:

- The taxpayer or third party must have been given a reasonable opportunity to produce the requisite information or documents voluntarily; this was usually done by the service of a 'precursor notice' requesting the provision of the documents within a certain time limit (often 30 days) (s 20B(1)).
- Notices under s 20(1) and (3) could be issued by an officer only after permission had been granted by a General or Special Commissioner (or in the case of a s 20(8A) by a Special Commissioner only), who must have been satisfied in all the circumstances that the officer was justified in proceeding under this section (s 20(7)).
- An officer of HMRC could not give a s 20(1) or (3) notice to a barrister, advocate or solicitor; the decision to give such a notice had to have been taken by the Board (s 20B(3)).
- Notices had to specify a date for compliance, which had to be not less than 30 days after the date of the notice (s 20(8D)(a)).
- Privileged materials in the possession of either the taxpayer or a legal adviser were protected from disclosure.
- Neither the taxpayer nor a third party was obliged to produce documents relating to a 'pending appeal' by the taxpayer. This was a limited, but additional, form of 'litigation privilege' (s 20B(2)).
- Tax accountants were protected from disclosing audit papers or working papers that contained tax advice (s 20B(9)).
- Personal records which were excluded from police search powers and journalistic material were protected from disclosure (s 20(8C)).

Issue of a precursor notice

10A.09 Before a s 20(1) or (3) notice could be issued, the inspector had to have provided the taxpayer or third party with a reasonable opportunity to deliver voluntarily (or, in the case of s 20(3) only, make them available for inspection) the documents that would be specified in the notice (under s 20B(1)). This was normally done by the issue of a 'precursor' notice, requesting the voluntary provision of the specified documents within a certain time limit, often 30 days.

10A.10 The issue of a precursor notice 'froze' the documents concerned. A taxpayer or third party was guilty of an offence (under s 20BB(1)) if he intentionally falsified, concealed, destroyed, or otherwise disposed of, a document whose production was requested by the precursor notice, or if he caused or permitted any of the aforementioned to occur. If found guilty, a

10A.10 *The pre-1 April 2009 direct tax powers*

taxpayer or third party could be liable, on summary conviction, to a fine not exceeding £3,000 or, on conviction on indictment, to a maximum of two years' imprisonment, a fine or both.

10A.11 In contrast with the situation under s 20BA, where a third party cannot advise the taxpayer of receipt of such a notice (under TMA, Sch 1AA, para 4(1)(b), there is an obligation not to 'disclose to any other person information or any other matter likely to prejudice the investigation of the offence to which the application relates') a third party could inform the relevant taxpayer that he had received a s 20(3) precursor notice. Often informing a taxpayer would give that taxpayer the opportunity to contact HMRC directly before any s 20(3) notice was served on the third party, and, therefore, could negate the need for issuance of the s 20(3) notice. Under s 20B(1A) (introduced by Finance Act 1989, s 144), a copy of the third party notice had to have been sent to the taxpayer whose affairs were being investigated, unless a Commissioner had directed to the contrary in the case of suspected fraud.

Consent from a Commissioner of Tax

10A.12 After the period specified in the precursor notice for voluntary production of the specified documents had expired (without production of the documents), the inspector was able to apply for consent to the issuing of the s 20(1) or s 20(3) notice. Consent to a s 20(1) or a s 20(3) notice could be granted by either a General or Special Commissioner; consent to an s 20(8A) notice could be granted only by a Special Commissioner.

10A.13 The Commissioner had to have been satisfied that, in all the circumstances, the inspector was justified in proceeding under s 20. The reasonableness of the inspector's opinion as to the potential relevance of the information contained in the documents was a necessary, but not a sufficient, condition for the Special Commissioner to give his consent. The wording of s 20(7) clearly encompassed the possibility that, notwithstanding the fact that the inspector had reasonable grounds for believing that the use of the power under s 20 was justified, the Special Commissioner was not satisfied that this course was justified and so should exercise his discretion not to give consent. The further step that the Special Commissioner had to carry out was a balancing act between the reasonable requirements of HMRC to obtain information, in order to carry out the effective investigation of tax affairs, and the protection of the personal property rights of taxpayers against invasion. As this duty to give effect to this balancing act rested on the Special Commissioner alone, it was the Special Commissioner who had the role of acting as an important safeguard of the rights of citizens. Before consent was given, the Special Commissioner had to have been satisfied in all the circumstances that the inspector was justified in invoking his compulsory powers. The Special Commissioner was 'the independent person entrusted by Parliament with the duty of supervising the exercise of the intrusive power conferred by section 20 …' (per Lord Lowry in *R v IRC, ex p TC Coombs* [1991] STC 97 at 108*f*).

10A.14 The hearing before the Commissioner was without notice. The Court of Appeal held in *R* (*on the application of Morgan Grenfell*) *v Special Comr of*

Income Tax) [2001] STC 497 that Morgan Grenfell had no right to attend the hearing and that the Special Commissioner had no discretion to permit its attendance. That issue was not taken to the House of Lords (who reversed the Court of Appeal's decision on the issue of legal professional privilege). There was thus a potential argument that the basis on which the House of Lords overturned the Court of Appeal's decision on privilege rendered that court's decision on attendance *per incuriam*, but this issue was never taken to the courts (Finance Act 2009, Sch 47 amends Finance Act 2008, Sch 36 so as to provide that an application for approval of an information notice may be made without notice). However, the inspector was under a duty to ensure that all relevant facts, including those unfavourable to HMRC, were put before the Commissioner and that a full record of the proceedings was kept (*R v Macdonald and CIR, ex p Hutchinson & Co Ltd* [1998] STC 680). The Commissioner had a general power to receive evidence that would be inadmissible in a court of law (see the Special Commissioners (Jurisdiction and Procedure) Regulations 1994, SI 1994 No 1811).

10A.15 Section 20D(3) defined 'documents' as 'anything in which information of any description is recorded'. Thus, included within the definition of document was:

- correspondence, whether by letter, email or fax;
- any disk, tape or other device from which data can be reproduced;
- any film, negative, tape or other device from which a visual image can be reproduced; and
- maps, plans, graphs, drawings and photographs.

10A.16 Excluded from this definition (under s 20(8C)) were personal records (eg medical records) or journalistic material, as defined by PACE, ss 12 and 13 respectively.

10A.17 Following the decision of the House of Lords in *R v Special Comr, ex p Morgan Grenfell & Co Ltd* [2003] 1 AC 56, documents in respect of which a claim to legal professional privilege could be asserted were excluded from the scope of s 20 notices.

10A.18 It was permissible to provide copies of documents instead of the originals, but these had to have been photocopies or facsimile copies (under s 20B(4)(a)). Originals had to have been made available for inspection by a named officer of the Board if required (under s 20B(4)(b)). Failure to comply with this requirement was regarded as a failure to comply with the notice.

10A.19 A taxpayer or third party could also be required to provide a person authorised by the Board of HMRC with access to any computer or any associated apparatus or material that was or had been in use in connection with any document within the ambit of the notice (under Finance Act 1988, s 172(2)). Access had to have been granted at any reasonable time and suitable assistance from a computer operator or other appropriate person had to be provided, if requested, to assist in accessing, inspecting or checking the computer and associated equipment. The maximum penalty for failing to allow access to a computer or provide reasonable assistance was £500.

10A.20 *The pre-1 April 2009 direct tax powers*

10A.20 Under s 20(1)(b), a taxpayer could be required to produce, on service of a notice under s 20, 'such particulars as the Inspector may reasonably require as being relevant to, or to the amount of, any' tax liability to which the person is or may be subject. It is considered that, by reason of this subsection, taxpayers could be required to create new documents under s 20(1) (and under s 20(2)). In *Accountant v Inspector of Taxes* [2000] STC (SCD) 522, the Special Commissioner noted that whilst s 19A(2)(a) refers to the production of documents as are in the taxpayer's 'power or possession', s 19A(2)(b), which requires that the taxpayer 'furnish such accounts or particulars as the officer may reasonably require' was not so limited expressly and thus concluded that, under this subsection, a taxpayer could be asked to create new documents. It is considered that this reasoning applied equally to s 20, and therefore applied to s 20(1) and (2). Section 20(3) (and (8A)) did not contain the equivalent of s 20(1)(b), and so could not be used to require the third party to create a document (or documents).

Protection of privileged material

10A.21 Material over which a claim to legal professional privilege could be sustained was protected from disclosure whether it was in the possession of the taxpayer, or his legal adviser, following the decision of the House of Lords in *R on the application of Morgan Grenfell & Co Ltd v Special Comrs* [2002] STC 786. It is considered that the decision of the House of Lords applied also so as to protect privileged material that was in the possession of a third party from disclosure consequent on a s 20(3) notice.

10A.22 Although a barrister, advocate or solicitor could not be obliged to produce privileged documents in his possession without the consent of his client in response to a s 20(3) notice (under s 20B(8)), the claim of privilege was not available in relation to notices issued to a legal adviser *qua* taxpayer (see *R v IRC, ex p Taylor (No 2)* [1990] STC 379, and *R v IRC, ex p Lorimer* [2000] STC 751).

10A.23 In addition to legal professional privilege, two statutorily created quasi-privileges restricted the documents that could be sought by services of notices under s 20(1) and (3):

- Under s 20B(2), documents 'relating to the conduct of any pending appeal' did not need to be provided.
- Section 20B(9) created a privilege in relation to documents that are the property of 'tax advisers' or accountants.

Auditors and tax advisers' documents

10A.24 Section 20B(9)(a) provided that, subject to certain qualifications, which are described below, an auditor could not be required to produce documents that were his property and that were created in the course of carrying out a statutory audit. In practice, HMRC allowed equivalent protection where an accountant was appointed to carry out a non-statutory independent audit to standards similar to those required for a Companies Act audit, provided that the work on the audit was kept separate from any work on the preparation of the accounts.

10A.25 Section 20B(9)(b) provided that, subject likewise to the qualifications described below, anyone appointed to give advice about the tax affairs of another person could not be required to produce documents that were his property and which consisted of 'relevant communications' with his taxpayer client or another tax adviser of the client for the purpose of giving or obtaining advice on that client's tax affairs. HMRC considered that the term 'relevant communications' could include notes of meetings and telephone calls, and internal memoranda, as well as client correspondence.

10A.26 The protection for documents of tax advisers and auditors was subject to two qualifications:

1. Under s 20B(11), if the auditor or tax adviser had assisted a client in completing a return, accounts or other document or information for production to HMRC, then no protection was provided for such part of any document which contained workings or analytical information showing how a particular entry on the return, accounts etc was arrived at.
2. Under s 20B(12), where the notice requiring production of documents related to an unidentified taxpayer (ie it was a notice under s 20(8A)), no protection was provided for such part of a document which contained information as to the identity or address of a taxpayer to whom the notice related or in respect of any person who had acted on behalf of such a taxpayer.

10A.27 Section 20B(11) and (12) were subject to s 20B(13), which provided that the s 20B(9) protection for a document in the possession of an auditor or tax adviser was not lost as a result of these qualifications if the explanatory information or the information identifying the taxpayer or adviser respectively was also contained in another document that had already been produced to HMRC.

10A.28 HMRC stated that the formal power to require access to an accountant's working papers would be used only where the information needed could not be obtained on a voluntary basis and HMRC had no other means of satisfying themselves that a taxpayer's accounts or returns were accurate.

TMA, s 20(8A)

10A.29 Section 20(8A) was introduced by the Finance Act 1988, s 126. The *fons et origo* of s 126 was the Report of the Committee on Enforcement Powers of the Revenue Departments (Cmnd 8822) produced by Lord Keith of Kinkel ('the Keith Report'). The Keith Committee had carried out a wide-ranging review of the enforcement powers of both the Inland Revenue and HM Customs and Excise; and it recommended changes to the existing information powers of the Inland Revenue (principally s 20 as it was then enacted). At that time, the power to issue 'third party notices' under s 20(3) was limited. There were

10A.29 *The pre-1 April 2009 direct tax powers*

various restrictions placed upon the availability of that power in relation to the class of persons on whom it could be served; and a third party notice could be served in relation to an identified taxpayer only. The Keith Committee concluded, at 15.4.1, that:

> '... in particular it seemed to us that limitation of the third party information power in s 20(4)(b) to a person carrying on a business was unnecessary and undesirable in principle. In our view the Inspector ought to be free to serve a production notice upon any person he reasonably believes to be in possession of relevant information.'

10A.30 The Keith Committee then considered the issue of identification of the taxpayer. At para 15.5 it was stated:

> '15.5.1 We consider that as a matter of principle the Inspector should wherever possible be required to identify the taxpayer under investigation when making a formal information production demand on a third party and we so recommend. We received a considerable body of representation against the principle of "fishing" being associated with a general information power. Those witnesses who admitted a possible need for a fishing power, for example in relation to a specific anti-avoidance provision (Chapter 7), considered that it should be particularly enacted in each situation when it is required.
>
> 15.5.2 This seemed to us to be appropriate in relation to the kind of "fishing" notice used in the *Clinch* case ((1973) 49 TC 52)), where a professional agent is asked for particulars of any transactions of a specified kind in which he has acted for a client. We consider, however, that it is not reasonable to attempt to exclude every information enquiry that does not relate to an identified taxpayer from those proper to the general information power. Between the ground covered by an information power associated with a specific anti-avoidance provision and the ground within a general information power where it is possible to identify the taxpayer in question, lies a middle ground which the Department represented to us is quite extensive. We consider that this middle ground lies legitimately within the scope of the general information power, because it is important that the Inspector should be able to obtain information connecting a specific transaction or situation with an, as yet, unidentified taxpayer.'

10A.31 Thus, the purpose of what was to become s 20(8A) was to deal with the 'middle ground', that is the intersection between specific anti-avoidance measures and general information powers. That the context for the introduction of this power was tax-avoidance schemes was recognised by the Inland Revenue and by the Government. During the debates on the Finance Bill 1988, the Economic Secretary to the Treasury (Peter Lilley) explained that 'the clause ... is intended to cover circumstances in which an Inspector may suspect abuse by a group of people and wants information' (Hansard, Standing Committee A, 28 June 1988, col 676). On 15 March 1988, when cl 118 of the Finance Bill 1988 (which was enacted as s 126 Finance Act 1988) was laid before Parliament in draft, the Inland Revenue published a press release, which commented on the draft provision. In this press release, which was entitled 'measures to improve tax compliance', it was stated, at paras 10–12:

'Information about serious tax defaulters

10. It is proposed to allow the Revenue to call for information about taxpayers whose identity is not known to the Revenue, but who are suspected of serious tax default.

11. The Revenue can already ask for information about a particular, named taxpayer. But this authority does not cover documents giving the names of people the Revenue cannot identify, even where it is known that something is seriously amiss. This might happen, for example, where a tax avoidance scheme is marketed, which the Revenue investigate and establish to be not legally effective. The sponsor of the scheme may have told his clients that there is no tax liability on the profits covered by the scheme and no need to include them in their tax returns. There may therefore be reason to believe that there are large amounts of income which are liable to tax, but which have not been reported to the Revenue.

12. The proposal will enable the Inspector, but only after obtaining the approval of a Special Commissioner, to require the sponsor to reveal information about those using the failed scheme. The new power will be restricted to cases of serious tax loss, and an order from the Board of Inland Revenue will be needed before the Inspector may apply to the Commissioners.'

10A.32 That the power under s 20(8A) was introduced primarily for the purpose of enabling the then Inland Revenue to obtain information from sponsors of tax avoidance schemes with regard to their clients is reflected in the Enquiry Manual of HMRC, where it is stated, at EM 2406, that:

'The Revenue may be aware of the existence of serious tax irregularities but not of the identity of the person(s) involved. A tax adviser may, for example, have sold an avoidance scheme to a number of clients which is proved ineffectual in the case of one of them. This power enables the Revenue to serve a notice requiring the adviser to provide information about the others.'

10A.33 Section 20(8A) enabled HMRC to serve a s 20(3) notice that did not name the taxpayer to whom the notice related (a 's 20(8A) notice'), provided that the additional tests under s 20(8A) were met. Section 20(8A) notices were a subset of s 20(3) notices (as the Court of Appeal in *R v IRC, ex p Ulster Bank Ltd* [1997] STC 832 indicated ('… notices given under sub-s (8A) are but a subset of notices which may be given under sub-s (3). Thus a notice under sub-s (8A) must comply with all the same conditions as apply to a notice under sub-s (3) except with regard to the naming of the taxpayer' (*per* Morritt LJ said at 838))). Thus, the restrictions on the powers under s 20(3) applied, *mutatis mutandis*, with the following differences:

1   Consent of the Board of HMRC was required.
2   Only a Special Commissioner could consent to issuance of an s 20(8A) notice.
3   The Special Commissioner could exercise his discretionary power to

give consent to issuance of a s 20(8A) notice only if he was satisfied that each of the additional tests in s 20(8A) had been met:
(a) the notice related to a taxpayer whose identity was not known to the inspector or to a class of taxpayers whose individual identities were not so known (s 20(8A)(a));
(b) that there were reasonable grounds for believing that the taxpayer or any of the class of taxpayers to whom the notice related may have failed or may fail to comply with any provision of the Taxes Acts (s 20(8A)(b));
(c) that any such failure was likely to have led or to lead to serious prejudice to the proper assessment or collection of tax (s 20(8A)(c)); and
(d) that the information which was likely to be contained in the documents to which the notice related was not readily available from another source (s 20(8A)(d)).

Section 20(8A) had its own appeal route: under s 20(8B).

Appeal of s 20 notices

10A.34 There was no straightforward right of appeal against the issue of a s 20(1) or (3) notice. Once the notice had been issued, there were two means by which it could be contested. The first was to raise the legitimacy of the notice at penalty proceedings for non-compliance with the notice (see *R v O'Kane, ex p Northern Bank Ltd* [1996] STC 1249 and *Taxpayer v Inspector of Taxes* [1996] STC (SCD) 261). The second was by means of judicial review of the decision of the General or Special Commissioner.

10A.35 Those cases where taxpayers or third parties, such as banks, sought to prevent HMRC's use of its formal information powers against them by means of judicial review did not give much encouragement to potential litigants who wished to halt HMRC in this regard. Absent *R v O'Kane and Clarke ex p Northern Bank* [1996] STC 1249, when the courts carried out the balancing act between the effective investigation of evasion and avoidance and the protection of the rights of companies and individuals, investigation was favoured strongly over protection of rights. For example, the Court of Appeal in *R v IRC, ex p Ulster Bank* [1997] STC 636 did not comment adversely on the possibility of Ulster Bank having to incur (without possibility of recovery) costs in the region of £350,000 in order to comply with the s 20 notices that it had been served with. (For the low points in the protection of the rights of third parties, see the decision of the House of Lords in *TC Coombs & Co* [1991] STC 97 and also the recent decisions of the Special Commissioner/First-tier Tribunal in respect of applications for s 20(8A) notices and paragraph 5 notices respectively against financial institutions.)

The s 20(8A) appeal route – s 20(8B)

10A.36 Section 20(8A) had its own appeal route – s 20(8B). Section 20(8B) gave a third party 30 days in which to appeal in writing to the inspector against the issue of the s 20(8A) notice on the grounds that it would be 'onerous' for him to comply with it. If the matter could be settled by agreement between the third party and the inspector, it was referred to the Special Commissioners who could confirm, vary or cancel the notice. The term 'onerous' was not defined in s 20, nor, as far as the author is aware, in any statute. The dictionary definition of the term is 'burdensome; oppressive'. There are no reported cases on the meaning of 'onerous' in this context. However, it is thought that, had the matter been considered then the Special Commissioners should have weighed the burden that compliance would impose on the third party versus the likely benefit to HMRC in terms of collection of revenue. If such an approach had been adopted, then, in order to succeed, it would have to have been necessary to have shown that the burden imposed on the third party in terms of, for example, staff costs, IT time and physical constraints outweighed the potential benefit to the Exchequer that would result from compliance with the notice.

Time limits

10A.37 Under s 20B(5), a s 20(3) notice did not oblige a third party to provide any document, the whole of which originated more than six years before the date of the notice, unless the inspector had obtained approval from a Commissioner to extend the time limit on the basis that he was satisfied that there were reasonable grounds for believing that tax had, or may have been, lost as a result of fraud by the taxpayer. Also a s 20(3) notice could not be issued in respect of a deceased taxpayer if more than six years had elapsed since his death. In *Revenue and Customs Commissioners Application (Section 20 Notice: Tax Haven Co)* [2006] STC (SCD) 376, the Special Commissioner indicated that he preferred HMRC's argument that the six-year provision in s 20B(5) did not apply to s 20(8A), but that as there were reasonable grounds to suspect fraud, he was satisfied that the inspector was justified in proceeding under s 20.

Section 20 offences

10A.38 There are transitional provisions that keep in force the pre-1 April 2009 rules relating to appeals and penalties for information notices issued before 1 April 2009. These penalty provisions remain in force in relation to s 20 notices that were issued before 1 April 2009.

Destruction of documents

10A.39 A taxpayer or third party is guilty of an offence if he intentionally falsifies, conceals, destroys, or otherwise disposes of, a document whose production is requested by a precursor notice, or if he causes or permits any of the aforementioned to occur. If found guilty, a taxpayer or third party can be liable, on summary conviction, to a fine not exceeding £3,000 or, on conviction on indictment, to a maximum of two years' imprisonment, a fine or both.

10A.40 No offence is committed if documentation is disposed of or destroyed:
- where written permission had been obtained from a (Special or General) Commissioner, inspector or an officer of the Board;

10A.40 *The pre-1 April 2009 direct tax powers*

- after a document had been delivered or inspected, or a copy had been delivered and the original has been inspected;
- where no s 20 notice has been issued and six months have elapsed since the issue of the precursor notice; or
- after a Commissioner has refused the application for consent to issue an s 20 notice requiring the production of the documents. **[QUERY: Should this paragraph be in the present or the past tense?]**

10A.41 Unless an inspector or an officer of the Board notifies a taxpayer or third party in writing that the notice has not been complied with to HMRC's satisfaction, then the taxpayer or third party can dispose of documents after two years from the date of issue of the s 20 notice (subject to other document preservation requirements).

Failure to comply

10A.42 An initial penalty of £300 can be levied for failure to comply with a s 20 notice, followed by a penalty of £60 per day for continuing failure. If a taxpayer or third party fails to comply with a s 20 notice, then it shall be liable to a penalty not exceeding £300 under s 98(1)(i). However, as the level of any penalty to be imposed under s 98(1)(i) cannot be determined by an authorised HMRC officer, if an HMRC officer wishes to impose such a penalty on a taxpayer, then he must commence proceedings by information in writing to the First-tier Tribunal. Following the commencement of proceedings, the First-tier Tribunal issues a summons to the taxpayer to appear before them, under s 100C(2), and hear and decide the case in a summary way. Any penalty so determined by the First-tier Tribunal to be exigible is treated as due and payable as if it was tax charged in an assessment (under TMA, s 100C(3)) and can be appealed by the taxpayer to the Upper Tribunal, under TMA, s 100C(4).

10A.43 After the level of the initial penalty has been determined by the First-tier Tribunal, HMRC may impose a daily penalty for non-compliance (of up to £60) from the date of issue of the initial penalty up to the date of compliance with the notice (under s 98(1)(ii)). The daily penalty imposed by an HMRC officer may be appealed by the taxpayer or third party to the First-tier Tribunal (under s 100B). Under s 100B(2)(a), the First-tier Tribunal may:

- set aside the penalty determination (if they consider that no penalty is exigible);
- confirm the penalty determination (if they consider that the amount of the penalty is correct); or
- increase or reduce the penalty to the correct amount (if it appears to them that the amount is incorrect).

The search and seizure power under TMA, s 20C

10A.44 Section 20C was repealed, and replaced with a power under PACE, s 8 with effect from 1 December 2007. For comparative purposes, a brief analysis of the power under s 20C is set out below.

Section 20C enabled an inspector (after obtaining a warrant from a circuit judge) to enter private premises (if necessary by force) to search for and remove documents that he reasonably believed to be evidence of tax fraud. No particular offence needed to be specified in the warrant other than 'serious fraud' (see *IRC v Rossminster Ltd* [1980] STC 42). The occupier of the premises had no right to be informed of the precise grounds on which the warrant was issued.

The grounds for issuing the warrant were that:

- there is reasonable ground for suspecting that an offence involving serious fraud in connection with or in relation to tax is being, has been, or is about to be committed and that evidence of it is to be found on premises specified in the information; and
- in applying under this section, the officer acts with the approval of the Board given in relation to the particular case (under s 20C(1)).

The judicial authority also had to be satisfied that the officer concerned was acting with the specific approval of the Board (not merely with the approval of an officer acting under the Board's authority) given in relation to the particular case (see s 20C(1)(b), and (2)). Under s 20C(3)(a) the officer could take with him such other persons as appeared to him to be necessary (this was not limited to people with a purely ancillary role eg locksmiths). In practice, as Inland Revenue officers had no powers of arrest, normally they would be accompanied by police officers. With effect from 1 December 2007, the relevant officers of HMRC have the power of arrest for all indictable tax offences under PACE.

Under s 20C(1B), the powers conferred by a warrant under this section could not be exercisable:

- by more than such number of officers of the Board as may be specified in the warrant (there was no requirement to specify the names);
- outside such times of day as may be so specified (there was no limit as to when these might be);
- if the warrant so provided, otherwise than in the presence of a constable in uniform.

Under s 20C(3)(b), an officer of the Board who entered the premises under the authority of a s 20C warrant could seize and remove any 'things' whatsoever found there which he had reasonable cause to believe may be required as evidence for the purposes of proceedings in respect of a serious tax fraud offence (not necessarily the one that the warrant was obtained in respect of). Under s 20C(3)(c), the officer could search or cause to be searched any person found on the premises whom he had reasonable cause to believe to be in possession of any such things, but no person could be searched except by a person of the same sex.

10A.45 A single 'thing' could include irrelevant as well as relevant material. The power of seizure under s 20C(3) included a power to require information stored in electronic form accessible from the premises, and which the officer had reasonable cause to believe may be required as evidence, to be produced in

10A.45 *The pre-1 April 2009 direct tax powers*

legible, visible form (or from which it could readily be so produced). (See s 20C(3A).)

Under Criminal Justice and Police Act 2001 (CJPA 2001), Sch 1, Pt 1 the s 50 powers of seizure under that Act were extended to s 20C. This power applied where it was not reasonably practicable to determine on the premises whether the material was, or contained, something HMRC was entitled to seize. This power is analysed further under the PACE powers section of this chapter.

Access to all the documents or items was permitted, on request and under supervision (under s 20CC(4)). Copies could be taken at the time of access or requested. If requested, the copies had to have been provided within a reasonable time (s 20CC(6) and (7)), unless the officer had reasonable grounds for believing that to do so would prejudice the investigation (s 20CC(8)). There was no right to allow a copy to be taken at the time of search.

10A.46 HMRC officers exercising powers under s 20C followed the codes of practice of PACE. They are now bound by them statutorily when exercising PACE powers; see further under the PACE powers section of this chapter.

The power under s 20C was rarely used by the HMRC where the relevant documents were believed to be in the possession of non-suspect third parties. HMRC recognised that a search warrant is a very draconian tool to be used against third parties; and, in 2000, s 20BA was introduced in order to allow the Inland Revenue to gain access to original documents from unsuspected third parties without the need to have recourse to the intrusive power under s 20C. Before a warrant under s 20C could be obtained, the Board must have had reasonable grounds for believing that the use of the s 20BA procedure might seriously prejudice the investigation.

Section 20C(4) provided that HMRC are not authorised to seize items that are subject to legal privilege. Section 20C(4A) provided a definition of legally privileged documents for the purpose of s 20C. It extended the protection given to such documents to whenever they are held by 'a person who is entitled to possession of them'.

Section 19A – power to call for documents for purposes of certain enquiries

Introduction

10A.47 The 1990s saw a significant reform of the machinery of administration, particularly in the system for assessing personal tax. The essence of the reform was that those taxpayers who used to be required to make an annual tax return (mainly those self-employed persons who were assessable to tax under Cases I and II of Schedule D) are now allowed to work out their own tax bill. Assessment on a 'preceding year' basis for the self-employed has been abolished, so that all taxpayers pay tax on a current-year basis. This enables taxpayers to receive one statement dealing with all their income from whatever source and one tax bill (albeit that there are separate rules for computing the amounts from each source).

10A.48 The key feature of the self-assessment system is that the primary responsibility for making an assessment of the tax payable each year falls on the individual taxpayer, not on HMRC. With the introduction of self-assessment came the introduction of powers that enabled HMRC to obtain information that it may 'reasonably require' for the purpose of enquiring into the accuracy of self-assessment returns. These powers are the self-assessment powers (contained in TMA 1970, s 19A and Finance Act 1998, Sch 18, para 27 (personal and corporate self-assessment respectively). Although the self-assessment powers, in many aspects, resemble the powers that HMRC already possessed under s 20 (which powers were first introduced in 1970 and significantly extended in 1976), there were important differences between the two sets of powers: the self-assessment powers co-existed with, rather than replaced, the s 20 powers. The powers under s 19A in respect of personal self-assessment and under Finance Act 1998, Sch 18, para 27 in respect of corporate self-assessment were to a significant extent identical in scope. For ease, references in this section are to s 19A, with differences set out only.

10A.49 Once an enquiry is in progress, generally HMRC first will seek to obtain information by means of an informal request to the taxpayer. If that did not succeed, then, before 1 April 2009, recourse would generally be had to s 19A. In contrast to s 20, there was no statutory requirement to give the taxpayer a reasonable opportunity to produce documents voluntarily before a s 19A notice could be issued. In practice, it was rare for HMRC to serve a s 19A notice without having first made an informal request for the information or documents. HMRC acknowledged that their aim should be to ask for all the information that they considered was necessary at the outset of the enquiry; there was, however, no statutory restriction on the number of information notices that could be issued in relation to an enquiry.

10A.50 Section 19A did not give HMRC a free-standing power to obtain information. A s 19A notice could be issued only 'for the purpose of an enquiry'; it was a precondition for issue that HMRC must have commenced an enquiry (under either TMA, s 9A(1) (individuals), TMA, s 12AC(1) (partnerships) or Finance Act 1998, Sch 18, para 24 (companies)). If there was no open enquiry, HMRC instead had to rely on their s 20 powers to obtain information that it could not obtain voluntarily.

A notice issued under s 19A had to have been given in writing. A time limit (of not less than 30 days) had to be imposed for production of the information. In *Self-assessed v Inspector of Taxes* [1999] STC (SCD) 253, a notice was quashed because it required production of documents within 30 days of the date of the notice.

What could be sought under service of an s 19A notice?

10A.51 Under s 19A, an officer of HMRC could issue a notice to the taxpayer requiring 'such documents as are in the taxpayer's possession or power' and 'such accounts or particulars' as he may reasonably require.

'Documents' were widely defined by Finance Act 1988, s 127(1) as anything in which information of any description is recorded. This included, for example,

10A.51 *The pre-1 April 2009 direct tax powers*

information held on computer disk. The word 'particulars' is synonymous with information. HMRC indicated that the word 'particulars' in s 19A is used in the ordinary sense of 'detailed account' and may include answers to specific questions or require the creation of documents that do not already exist, such as, for example, a set of accounts. In *Murat v HM Inspector of Taxes* (*aka Accountant v HM Inspector of Taxes*) [2000] STC (SCD) 522, the Special Commissioner observed that it was reasonable for an inspector's enquiries not to be limited to existing documents and held that it was reasonable for HMRC to require the preparation of a balance sheet.

10A.52 The equivalent CTSA power adopted the same wording in relation to requests for documents, but para 27(1)(b) required the production of such information (as opposed to particulars), 'in such form' as HMRC may reasonably require for the purpose of the enquiry. The use of the wording 'in such form' was thought likely to enable HMRC to request that information be provided electronically.

The taxpayer was not obliged to produce documents, accounts or particulars relating to the conduct of any appeal (s 19A(5)).

Appeals

10A.53 The taxpayer could appeal against an information notice within 30 days. HMRC's view was that the taxpayer could appeal on three grounds:

- that the information was not reasonably required for the purpose of the officer's enquiry;
- that the information was not within the taxpayer's possession or power; and/or
- that insufficient time had been allowed for production of the information.

10A.54 Despite the onus being on the taxpayer to show why the information was irrelevant to the question of whether or not a return is correct or complete, the inspector was obliged to provide his reasons for why he considered that the information was reasonably required. A frequent area of disagreement was where the inspector requested information contained in 'non-business' records, such as private bank accounts. Requests for details of personal expenditure may be intrusive and the Special Commissioners held that they should not be sought if that could be avoided (*Taylor v Bratherton* [2005] STC (SCD) 230). However, requests for documents and information concerning the taxpayer's income were held to be reasonable for the purposes of the enquiry into the taxpayer's affairs (*Commane v HM Revenue & Customs* [2006] STC (SCD) 81).

10A.55 If the documents that had been requested did not exist, then they could not, of course, be provided. In such circumstances, HMRC should have been advised of this fact and the notice should, as a consequence, have been set aside by the inspector. Depending on the documents sought, this could lead the inspector to consider whether a penalty should be sought for failing to comply with the self-assessment record-keeping provisions. If HMRC did not accept the validity of the taxpayer's claim that he no longer had possession of the documents in question, then, ultimately it was for the Commissioners to determine as a fact whether this was so, either on hearing an appeal against the notice or the determination of a penalty.

10A.56 Although HMRC considered that the time allowed to comply with a notice was ground for an appeal, the self-assessment legislation did not bestow on the Commissioners a power to extend the time allowed for production. The Commissioners could, however, direct that the hearing be adjourned.

Penalties for non-compliance

10A.57 The penalty provisions for failure to comply were contained in TMA, s 97AA and Finance Act 1998, Sch 18, para 29. An initial fixed penalty of £50 could be determined by an authorised HMRC officer. If the failure continued after the determination of the fixed penalty, it was then open to the officer to determine a further penalty of up to £30 for each day from the date of the initial determination up to the date when the notice was complied with. Alternatively, the officer could commence penalty proceedings before the General or Special Commissioners under s 100C, in which case the Commissioners could impose a penalty of up to £150 per day.

10A.58 The taxpayer had a right of appeal against the imposition of penalties under s 97AA or para 29, Sch 18, to the Commissioners under s 100B. In the case of a determination by the Commissioners, the appeal lay to the High Court in England and Wales and to the Court of Session in Scotland (s 100B(3)).

THE INDIRECT TAX POWERS

10A.59 The most relevant powers in relation to VAT were in VATA, Sch 11. There were two distinct powers under Sch 11: para 7 gave a power to obtain information and documents; paragraphs 10(1) and (2) bestowed on authorised representatives of HMRC a right to enter premises at any reasonable time. VATA, Sch 11, para 10(3) gave HMRC a right to search and seize under the authority of a warrant.

10A.60 HMRC now has powers to obtain information and documents and to inspect under Finance Act 2008, Sch 36 and powers to search and seize under PACE, s 8 and Sch 1. Before the reform of the information powers, the legislation provided also for a system of sanctions that aimed to render a trader's lack of cooperation a self-defeating exercise. These sanctions remain in force. They are as follows:

- HMRC may, as a condition of repaying any input tax to any person, require the production of such evidence relating to VAT as may have been supplied to him (Sch 11, para 4). Thus, the obvious sanction to be imposed if the person declines to produce the required evidence is to withhold repayment of VAT.

10A.60 *The pre-1 April 2009 direct tax powers*

- HMRC may issue an assessment where a person has failed to keep any documents and afford the facilities necessary to verify his return (VATA, s 73(1)).

Paragraph 7 – powers to obtain information and documents

10A.61 HMRC has a number of statutory sources of information, including suppliers and their customers. Under Sch 11, para 7, HMRC had power to demand information and documents from:

1. every person concerned (in whatever capacity) in the supply of goods or services in the course or furtherance of a business;
2. every person to whom such a supply was made;
3. every person concerned (in whatever capacity) in the acquisition of goods from another member state;
4. every person concerned (in whatever capacity) in the importation of goods in the course or furtherance of a business; and
5. in relation to documents only, any other person who appeared to be in possession of documents which HMRC could demand from a person in categories 1–4 above.

10A.62 A person 'concerned in' a supply included a person who had been assigned a right to receive the whole, or part, of the consideration for a supply of goods or services. Such a person was required to furnish such information relating to the goods, services, supply, acquisition or importation as the Commissioners might reasonably specify. The specified information had to have been furnished to the Commissioners within such time and in such form as they might reasonably have required.

10A.63 Legal professional privilege could protect documents from being provided. HMRC's view was that an officer could demand to see copies of the tax invoice, and the corresponding bill, produced by a legal adviser, but not a copy of the advice to which the charge related. The documents that could be sought under para 7 were limited to those relating to the goods, services, supply, acquisition or importation concerned. A further limitation was that the documents had to be produced 'for inspection' by an authorised person. This prevented HMRC officers using this power after an investigation had commenced, as the documents would not be used for the purpose of inspection.

10A.64 For the purposes of this provision a 'document' meant anything in which information of any description was recorded; and a copy of a document was defined as anything onto which information recorded in the document had been copied, by whatever means and whether directly or indirectly (under VATA, s 96(1)). This included information held or copied on paper or an electronic medium, as well as in the form of photocopies, faxes, photographs or photographic film.

10A.65 An HMRC officer could take copies of any documents produced and could make extracts from them. He could also remove any such document at a reasonable time and for a reasonable period where he considered this necessary. A person producing documents under these provisions had the following rights:

- to be provided with a receipt on request;
- to be provided with a copy, free of charge, of any document reasonably required for proper conduct of his business; and
- to compensation for expenses reasonably incurred in replacing documents which had been lost or repairing documents which had been damaged.

10A.66 Where an HMRC officer had a right of access to any document, he was also entitled, at any reasonable time, to have access to any computer, associated apparatus or material (ie including software) used in connection with such a document. This power extended to inspecting a computer, apparatus or material and checking its operation. A person was required to afford such reasonable assistance as may be required for these purposes if the computer was used by him or on his behalf, or if he controlled or operated the computer, apparatus or material.

10A.67 Failure to comply with a demand for information could give rise to a liability to civil or criminal penalties. The prescribed civil penalty was the greater of: (1) an amount equal to the prescribed rate multiplied by the number of days on which the failure continued (up to a maximum of 100); or (2) £50. The prescribed rate was determined by the number of previous failures (if any) taking place in the period of two years preceding the beginning of the failure in question. If there were no previous failures, the prescribed rate was £5, one £10 and two or more £15. **[QUERY: Is this correct as shown?]** In practice, the action taken by HMRC was often in the first instance to issue a formal warning letter and not approve any relevant VAT repayment claims.

Paragraph 10(1) and (2) – the power to enter

10A.68 VATA, Sch 11, para 10(1) enabled any person acting under the authority of the Board of HMRC (an 'authorised person') to enter premises used in connection with the carrying on of a business at any reasonable time for the purpose of exercising any powers under the VAT legislation. Business premises did not have to be occupied by a taxable person; the right of entry therefore extended to business premises occupied by a trader who was not registered for the purposes of VAT, regardless of whether or not he should have been so registered.

10A.69 Under para 10(2), an authorised person could enter and inspect any premises, and could inspect any goods found thereon, at any reasonable time if he had reasonable cause to believe that they were used in connection with the taxable supply of goods or the taxable acquisition of goods and that goods to be so supplied or acquired were to be found there, or that the premises were used as a fiscal warehouse. The clear wording of para 10(2) excluded inspection of premises concerned solely with the provision of services. The right was to 'inspect'. The distinction between 'inspection' and 'search' is not absolute. However, the general maxim is that 'inspection is by eye, search by hand'. The power to inspect encompasses walking around premises and examining goods

10A.69 *The pre-1 April 2009 direct tax powers*

in packing cases; it does not cover searching for hidden things or rummaging through the contents of a waste-paper basket.

The power to search under VATA, Sch 11, para 10(3)

10A.70 VATA, Sch 11, para 10(3), has been repealed and replaced by PACE, s 8 (and related powers under PACE) by Finance Act 2007 and the Police and Criminal Evidence Act 1984 (Application to Revenue and Customs) Order 2007, SI 2007 No 3175, with effect from 1 December 2007. For comparative purposes, a brief analysis of the power under para 10(3) is set out below.

VATA 1994, Sch 11, para 10(3) enabled any person acting under the authority of the Board of HMRC (an 'authorised person') to enter premises, if necessary by force, at any time within one month from the time of the issue of the warrant and search them. Any person who entered the premises under the authority of the warrant could:

- take with him such other persons as appeared to him to be necessary;
- seize and remove any documents or other things whatsoever found on the premises which he had reasonable cause to believe may be required as evidence for the purposes of proceedings in respect of a fraud offence which appeared to him to be of a serious nature; and
- search or cause to be searched any person found on the premises whom he had reasonable cause to believe to be in possession of any such documents or other things (no woman or girl could be searched except by a woman).

The warrant was given in writing. It had to specify:

- the name of the person who applied for it;
- the date on which it was issued;
- the enactment under which it was issued; and
- the premises to be searched.

A warrant had to identify the articles or persons to be sought in so far as it was practicable to do so. It could:

- authorise persons to accompany any officer executing it;
- specify the maximum number of authorised persons who may execute it;
- specify the times of day when it may be executed; and
- provide that it may be executed only in the presence of a uniformed constable.

In addition, the authorised person could take with him such other persons as appeared to him to be necessary. This authorised the presence of, for example, police officers, locksmiths and translators, but it did not authorise them to take part in the search. The warrant had to have been executed within one month from its date of issue. A copy of the warrant had to have been given to the occupier of the premises (if he was present when the search began) or, in his absence, the person who appeared to be in charge of the premises. In any other case (ie if the premises were empty), the copy had to have been left in a prominent place. The copy of the warrant had to have been endorsed with the name of the person searching the premises (if he was alone) or the person in charge of the search.

10A.71 The person executing a warrant had to endorse it and return it to the clerk to the justices for the relevant petty sessions area. The clerk had to retain the endorsed warrant for one year and he had to allow the occupier of the premises to inspect it on request during this period.

The power to search premises was used only in serious cases of suspected evasion (ie where the actual or potential amount of VAT involved exceeded £10,000), and where other methods of investigation were either unlikely to succeed or, when tried, had failed. A justice of the peace could issue a warrant only where he was satisfied judicially by information given on oath that there were reasonable grounds for suspecting that an offence under VATA 1994, s 72(1)–(8) which appears to be of a serious nature, was being, had been, or was about to be committed on the premises, or that evidence of the commission of such an offence was to be found there.

Chapter 11

Tax appeals

Hartley Foster, Partner, and Louisa Warburton, Solicitor

Olswang LLP

INTRODUCTION

The tax appeals system

11.01 The tax appeals system in the UK changed fundamentally on 1 April 2009. Before that date, rather than having one specialist tax tribunal that could hear all tax-related appeals, different taxes carried with them different methods and routes of litigation. Litigation that concerned income tax, corporation tax, capital gains tax and the stamp taxes fell within the purview of the General Commissioners and the Special Commissioners (the Commissioners) (with the division of jurisdiction being complicated; some was reserved to the General Commissioners, some to the Special Commissioners, and some could be heard by either body); the jurisdiction of the s 706 Tribunal was limited to determining whether a person being in a position to obtain, or having obtained, a 'tax advantage' in consequence of a transaction in securities or of the combined effect of two or more transactions in securities could suffer the nullification of that tax advantage; and the jurisdiction of the VAT and Duties Tribunals encompassed VAT, customs duties, excise duties, insurance premium tax, landfill tax, aggregates levy, climate change levy, and airport passenger duty.

11.02 The new rules governing the reform and operation of the Tax Tribunals are set out in the Tribunals, Courts and Enforcement Act 2007 (TCE). TCE received Royal Assent on 19 July 2007. It is an enabling Act, under which, and the secondary legislation issued thereunder (arts 3 and 4, Transfer of Tribunal Functions and Revenue and Customs Appeals Order 2009, SI 2009 No 56), the General Commissioners, Special Commissioners, s 706 Tribunal, and VAT and Duties tribunals were abolished and their functions and jurisdiction transferred,

11.02 *Tax appeals*

with effect from 1 April 2009, to a unified tribunal that comprises a first tier and an upper tier (the First-tier Tribunal and Upper Tribunal, respectively). The procedural rules for the First-tier Tribunal and the Upper Tribunal are set out in the Tribunal Procedure (First-tier Tribunal) (Tax Chamber) Rules 2009, SI 2009 No 273 (the First-tier Rules) and the Tribunal Procedure (Upper Tribunal) Rules 2008, SI 2008 No 2698 (the Upper Tribunal Rules) respectively.

11.03 References to HM Revenue & Customs (HMRC) include references to its statutory predecessors.

11.04 This chapter is divided into five sections, after this introductory section. The first section, by way of summary and introduction, describes briefly the new tribunal system, and contains a short history of why the system was introduced. Section two explains the procedures that apply in tax matters before cases are notified to the First-tier Tribunal. The third section sets out in detail the jurisdiction and powers of the First-tier Tribunal. The fourth section comprises an analysis of the Upper Tribunal, and an outline of the procedure on appeal from the First-tier Tribunal to the Upper Tribunal. The fifth section comprises an analysis of the various matters that may be heard by judicial bodies that adjudicate on tax-related matters outside the new tribunal system.

Use of litigation as a tactic

11.05 Many tax practitioners have little or no experience of taking an appeal to the Tax Tribunal. Indeed, there is a school of thought that regards the reaching of some form of compromise settlement with HMRC as a panacea. Although, as a general rule, reaching a negotiated settlement is preferable to resolution via litigation, that is only a general rule and the approach that should be adopted in any particular case can be arrived at only after considering fully what is best for the taxpayer, and should not be influenced by any predisposition against litigation. Being mindful of the adage 'if you want peace, prepare for war' and thus dealing with enquiries from the perspective that, ultimately, the underlying issues may be heard by a tribunal or court can achieve considerable improvements, both in terms of the cost of compliance and the ultimate outcome of the case.

11.06 This is particularly since, under its litigation and settlement strategy (LSS), HMRC also are adopting a litigation-focused approach to disagreements with taxpayers. LSS was published in June 2007; it is the strategy that inspectors are required to adopt to all contentious matters. In an article in the *Tax Journal* (11 June 2007), Dave Hartnett (who was, at the time, HMRC Director General, Business) set out the aims of HMRC's LSS strategy:

> 'The LSS sets consistent standards for the way we settle disputes with our customers, whether by agreement or litigation. It ensures that where we are confident about the strength of our case and the disputed point is a significant one, we will insist on 100% of the tax or other liabilities that HMRC believes to be due. Where we accept that we do not have strong grounds for our position or the issue is less important to us, we will aim to avoid disputes altogether.'

11.07 LSS is part of HMRC's wider aim of promoting positive customer behaviours and deterring non-compliance with the tax laws. LSS covers all types of dispute about liability to pay taxes or duties, or entitlement to tax credits, absent litigation to recover debts or concerning employment matters. The term 'dispute' means any situation where HMRC are in disagreement with a taxpayer and 'the disagreement is not readily resolved'. Once this stage has been reached, LSS must be applied by the inspector to the matter and a litigation-focused approach adopted.

11.08 The two fundamental aspects of LSS are as follows:

1 Each dispute is to be settled on its own merits. There are no 'package deals' that settle a range of issues for a single undifferentiated sum of money.
2 Disputes that have an 'all-or-nothing' character involving a single point of law that would be decided one way or the other by the courts must be settled on an 'all-or-nothing' basis. Thus, for example, no discount will be provided for an agreement not to litigate.

11.09 The dominant factor in determining whether or not to litigate is the chance of success. If HMRC consider that the chance of success is less than 50%, then they will not pursue the case unless it can be justified by the particular circumstances, such as a very large amount of tax in question (in the case itself or from immediate precedent value), or a fundamental point of principle at stake. In all cases, the legal advice from HMRC Solicitor's Office will be a critical factor in decision making.

An analogous approach by the taxpayer not only brings greater rigour and enables greater focus when responding to HMRC, but also allows litigious tactics to be used.

11.10 However, currently, there is an element of flux as regards HMRC's overall approach to tax disputes. It is understood that it is HMRC's intention to focus more on the 'settlement' element of LSS; and Dave Hartnett, Permanent Secretary for Tax, announced a change to LSS in an interview that he gave to the *Financial Times* on 19 August 2010. He indicated that 'increasingly, inspectors will be encouraged to reach agreement' in relation to disputes with businesses, and that inspectors may conclude a settlement, provided that the amount of tax payable is based on a 'plausible' technical conclusion on the point at stake.

SECTION ONE – INTRODUCTION OF THE NEW TRIBUNAL SYSTEM

The origin for change

11.11 The pre-April 2009 tax appeals system was a complex one. As indicated above, rather than (as is the case in many other European countries) having one specialist tax tribunal that could hear all tax-related appeals, in the UK different taxes carried with them different methods and routes of litigation.

11.11 *Tax appeals*

Moreover, not all tax-related matters could be litigated before the specialist tax tribunals (eg only the High Court could judicially review the actions of HMRC).

11.12 Reform of this labyrinthine system had been mooted for many years. It was over 14 years ago that the Institute of Fiscal Studies' Tax Law Review Committee started its work on the subject. In 2001, a consultation document (the LCD paper) that was based, to a large extent, on recommendations in the Institute of Fiscal Studies' Tax Law Review Committee's Report of October 1999 was issued by the Lord Chancellor's Department. It was released as part of the consultation exercise that was undertaken to ensure that all government departments operated in a way that was compatible with individuals' rights under the European Convention of Human Rights. In essence, the Lord Chancellor's Department proposed refinements to the existing system. The LCD paper proposed (in accordance with a recommendation of the Tax Law Review Committee) a move to a unified tax tribunal that would hear all tax appeals. Under the proposal, the unified tax tribunal would be centrally administered, but would comprise special and general lists, which would be heard centrally and locally respectively. The other significant issue that was addressed in the LCD paper was that of costs, and, in particular, the divergence of regimes between the Special Commissioners, the General Commissioners and the VAT and Duties tribunals. The Tax Law Review Committee recommended that the Special Tax Tribunal should adopt the rule that applied in indirect tax appeals (ie a costs jurisdiction, but with HMRC having agreed that it would seek costs only in certain circumstances); and, in its reply to the LCD Paper, the Special Commissioners endorsed this recommendation.

The Leggatt Inquiry

11.13 Many tax practitioners were of the view that the timing of the release of the LCD paper by the government was an indication that the Leggatt Inquiry, which was, almost simultaneously, considering the tribunal system in general, would not lead to fundamental changes to the operation of the tax appeals system being proposed. In contrast to the reforms suggested in the LCD paper, which were, in essence, refinements, rather than changes, to the existing system, in his Report, Sir Andrew Leggatt proposed a revolutionary change: a single homogeneous system for all tribunals. Sir Andrew Leggatt was concerned that the tribunals, as they had developed in piecemeal fashion, were not cost-effective, and often appeared to lack independence: 'Because they are many and disparate, there is considerable waste of resources in managing them, and they achieve no economies of scale. Most importantly, they are not independent of the departments that sponsor them.' It was stated in relation to the General Commissioners that 'although now sponsored by the Lord Chancellor's Department, [they] are still wholly dependent on the Inland Revenue for case listing and for the flow of information to enable them to take decisions'.

11.14 It was proposed by Sir Andrew Leggatt that the existing 'system' of tribunals, where each tribunal had evolved its own rules and procedure as a solution to the particular requirements in its particular area of law, be replaced

Tax appeals **11.17**

by a single consistent procedure and structure for all tribunals. Thus, regardless of the area of law within which the particular tribunal operated, the same procedure would apply. The tax tribunals were expressly included within the proposed new system. As it pertained to tax, the proposed outline structure was as follows:

- a general tax tribunal (the general tax tribunal), with jurisdiction to hear the cases heard by the General Commissioners and straightforward VAT cases, such as those dealing with 'reasonable excuse';
- the second-tier tribunal (which would largely be a successor to the Special Commissioners and the VAT and Duties Tribunal) would hear appeals from the general tax tribunal and would be able to set precedent binding on the general tax tribunal;
- the second-tier tribunal would also hear, at first instance, the most complex appeals arising from decisions made by HMRC;
- appeals from the second-tier tribunals would go direct to the Court of Appeal;
- permission would be needed for an appeal from the general tax tribunal to the second-tier tribunal; and
- permission would be needed for an appeal from the second-tier tribunal to the Court of Appeal.

11.15 In July 2004, the government published its response to the Leggatt Report in a White Paper entitled 'Transforming Public Service: Complaints, Redress and Tribunals'. The key proposal that was set out in the White Paper was a unified tribunal service organisation. Most of the proposals of Sir Andrew Leggatt were accepted. Under the White Paper, it was proposed that the current jurisdictions of the VAT and Duties tribunals, the Special Commissioners and the General Commissioners would be combined. The High Court's role in tax appeals would be eliminated; and, instead, there would be a two-tier tax tribunal system, with a right of appeal from the second-tier tribunal to the Court of Appeal. The first-tier would be responsible for hearing most direct and indirect tax appeals at first instance; the second-tier tax tribunal (the upper tribunal) would be an appellate tier to which an appeal would lie with permission from the first tier on a point of law (it would also have a first-instance jurisdiction for cases of sufficient size and complexity to justify being started at that level). Decisions of the second-tier tribunal would be binding on the first-tier tribunal.

11.16 A further impetus to reform the system was the merger in April 2005 of the Inland Revenue and HM Customs & Excise and the creation of HMRC. Although each of HM Customs & Excise and the Inland Revenue had different functions, responsibilities and powers, these were transferred unchanged to the new body, and 'ring-fenced', so that they could be used only for their original purpose. The consequence was that different rules and procedures applied across different taxes that were now administered by a single department.

The Tribunals, Courts and Enforcement Act 2007

11.17 The majority of the proposals of Sir Andrew Leggatt were accepted by the government and TCE reflects the approach set out in the Leggatt Report.

11.17 *Tax appeals*

TCE is divided into eight parts. The principal reforms relating to tax appeals are contained in two parts:

- Part 1: Tribunals and Inquiries (ss 1–49).
  This creates a new statutory framework for the tribunals, and brings the tribunal judiciary together under a senior president.
- Part 2: Judicial Appointments (ss 50–61).
  This revises the minimum eligibility requirements for appointment to judicial office, and enables eligibility to be extended by order.

Summary of the new system

11.18 A single UK-wide first-instance tribunal with the competence to hear every form of tax appeal and every tax-related application by either the taxpayer or HMRC with one set of procedural rules (including a notice of appeal that is common to all tax appeals) has been introduced. The Special Commissioners and chairmen of the VAT and Duties Tribunals have transferred into the new tribunal, with the majority transferring to the First-tier (where they are known as 'judges of the First-tier Tribunal'). The membership of both the First-tier Tribunal and the Upper Tribunal consists of legally qualified judges (tribunal judges) and of members with specialist expertise in tax matters (tribunal members) (see TCE, Schs 2 and 3).

11.19 The First-tier Tribunal is the first instance tribunal for most jurisdictions; the majority of appeals commence in this tier. The First-tier Tribunal is organised into specialist divisions or 'chambers'. Each chamber is headed by a chamber president and the Tribunals' judiciary is headed by the Senior President of Tribunals, Carnwath LJ. The chambers are intended to be flexible groupings, able to maintain and expand expertise and to incorporate new jurisdictions where most suitable. There are five chambers in the First-tier: (1) social entitlement; (2) general regulatory; (3) health, education and social care; (4) taxation; and (5) land, property and housing.

11.20 The Upper Tribunal is divided into three chambers: (1) administrative appeals; (2) tax and chancery; and (3) land. A system of 'ticketing' has been introduced within each chamber. The president can issue tickets to judges and members that identify their suitability to sit in a particular jurisdiction. Thus, for example, a Special Commissioner, who was also a VAT and Duties Tribunal chairman, may be issued with an indirect and direct tax ticket that enables him (or her) to hear both such appeals. A procedure known as 'assignment' has also been introduced; this enables cross-chamber transfer (with the consent of the relevant president). Judges of the Upper Tribunal may sit in the First-tier Tribunal where the weight of the case justifies it.

11.21 In essence, the First-tier Tribunal replaces the General and Special Commissioners, the VAT and Duties Tribunal, and the s 706 Tribunal, and the Upper Tribunal replaces the High Court as an appellate jurisdiction. Appeals from the First-tier Tribunal to the Upper Tribunal are possible only on points of law and with permission from the Upper Tribunal itself. Whilst the role of the Upper Tribunal is primarily to hear appeals from the decisions of the First-tier Tribunal, it also hears some first-instance appeals in more complex tax cases and it may take over the judicial review function of the High Court in certain cases (see **11.110**). For a case to be heard by the Upper Tribunal at first instance, the parties must consent to the transfer. The First-tier Tribunal refers the matter to the President of the Tax Chamber with a request that the case be considered by the Upper Tribunal. The agreement of the President of the Tax and Finance Chamber of the Upper Tribunal is also required.

11.22 HMRC do not perform any listing or case management procedures under the new system (in contrast to their role in relation to hearings before the General Commissioners). That function is performed by the Tribunal's administration.

11.23 There are two concepts that are likely to seem novel to many tax practitioners, but which are likely to be familiar to those who have experience of litigation before the civil courts, that have been introduced to the Tax Tribunal system. These are the 'overriding objective' and alternative dispute resolution.

THE OVERRIDING OBJECTIVE

11.24 Lord Woolf introduced the overriding objective that courts deal with cases 'justly' as a fundamental part of his reforms to civil court procedure. Rule 1 of the Civil Procedure Rules 1999 (CPR) provides that 'these Rules are a new procedural code with the overriding objective of enabling the court to deal with cases justly'. Dealing with a case justly includes, so far as is practicable:

1 ensuring that the parties are on an equal footing;
2 saving expense;
3 dealing with the case in ways which are proportionate:
 (a) to the amount of money involved;
 (b) to the importance of the case;
 (c) to the complexity of the issues; and
 (d) to the financial position of each party;
4 ensuring that it is dealt with expeditiously and fairly; and
5 allotting to it an appropriate share of the court's resources, while taking into account the need to allot resources to other cases.

11.25 Rule 2 of the First-tier Rules and r 2 of the Upper Tribunal Rules introduce a similar concept to the Tax Tribunal system; they provide that the overriding objective of the Rules is to enable the Tribunal to 'deal with cases fairly and justly'. Rule 2(2) states that:

'Dealing with a case fairly and justly includes –
 (a) dealing with the case in ways which are proportionate to the importance of the case, the complexity of the issues, the anticipated costs and the resources of the parties;
 (b) avoiding unnecessary formality and seeking flexibility in the proceedings;
 (c) ensuring, so far as practicable, that the parties are able to participate fully in the proceedings;
 (d) using any special expertise of the Tribunal effectively; and

11.25 *Tax appeals*

(e) avoiding delay, so far as compatible with proper consideration of the issues.'

11.26 The obligation in the CPR that the courts seek to ensure that the parties are 'on an equal footing' is not included in the Tribunal version of the overriding objective. This obligation has been interpreted in the civil courts as referring to equal financial footing and has been used by the courts to allow parties that are in a weaker financial position than their opponents to be given, for example, additional time to comply with deadlines. Given that, in tax matters, the taxpayer's 'opponent' will invariably be the state, and so the parties to a tax case will never be on an equal footing, this obligation would have been difficult to impose in a reasonable or meaningful sense.

11.27 Rule 2(4) imposes on the parties an obligation to help the Tribunal to further the overriding objective and an obligation to co-operate with the Tribunal generally.

ALTERNATIVE DISPUTE RESOLUTION

11.28 Rule 3, First-tier Rules and rule 3, Upper Tribunal Rules impose an obligation on the respective tribunals to bring the availability of any appropriate alternative procedure for the resolution of the dispute to the attention of the parties. HMRC are currently conducting a small pilot programme with regard to the use of alternative dispute resolution (ADR). In addition, HMRC have also indicated a willingness to consider 'collaborative dispute resolution' or 'facilitated dispute resolution' (where an 'independent' third party assists the negotiations between HMRC and the taxpayer) in relation to the large corporate sector. A number of 'disputes' have been resolved in this way. However, this approach has only been applied at the stage before the enquiry has been closed (ie before the matter falls within the jurisdiction of the Tribunal).

Given that HMRC have, in recent times, adopted a far more aggressive stance towards tax disputes, and, in particular, has a compliance goal of changing what they consider is unacceptable behaviour in relation to taxation, the extent to which ADR will be used to resolve tax disputes is likely to be limited. ADR is likely to be of most use in cases where, as described in LSS, there is 'a range of plausible figures for tax due', ie where there is a dispute over facts or valuation. The obligation on HMRC to consider the impact of an issue on other taxpayers and the constraints of LSS mean that HMRC will not often be in a sufficiently flexible position to resolve a dispute via ADR.

SECTION 2

Introduction

11.29 The procedures before appeals are made against HMRC decisions remain the same as they were before 1 April 2009. Whilst the Tribunal procedure is now, broadly, the same across all the taxes, there remain different 'pre-appeal' procedures for direct and indirect tax matters. In this section, the provisions relating to indirect tax matters are considered first.

INDIRECT TAXES

The right to appeal

11.30 HMRC conduct various checks to ensure that the correct amount of tax has been reported and paid. If HMRC consider that insufficient tax has been paid, then they have the power to issue a decision on a number of aspects of a taxpayer's affairs, including for example: (i) whether a taxpayer should be registered for VAT purposes; or (ii), the amount of input tax credited to a person. A taxpayer can appeal against decisions made by HMRC to the extent that the decision comes within the statutory jurisdiction of the Tribunal. For example, in relation to VAT, an appeal will lie to the Tribunal for any matters listed in Value Added Tax Act 1994 (VATA), s 83 and for matters relating to landfill tax, Finance Act 1996, s 54 lists those that are appealable.

The internal review process

11.31 Prior to 1 April 2009, there was a semi-formal procedure under which HMRC encouraged taxpayers, who disagreed with a decision of HMRC, to seek a reconsideration of that decision by their local VAT office, before commencing an appeal. This local reconsideration procedure did not form part of the appeals procedure. Whilst there was, initially, some doubt as to whether or not this procedure had been replaced by the new statutory review process, in *Revenue and Customs Brief* 10/09, it was stated: 'This new legal right to a review will replace reconsiderations … in indirect taxes.' Taxpayers may still, however, make informal representations to HMRC.

11.32 At the time of notifying an appealable decision to a taxpayer, HMRC must also offer the taxpayer a review of that decision. The aim of the review process is to provide an inexpensive means of resolving disputes without the need for a hearing. Use of the review process is voluntary.

A taxpayer has 30 days to accept the offer for a review, unless HMRC extend the time period. (HMRC must review a decision out of time where they are satisfied the taxpayer had a reasonable excuse for not accepting the offer for a review in time and the request was made thereafter without unreasonable delay.) A taxpayer need not accept the offer of a review, and may not accept the offer if an appeal against the decision has already been lodged at the Tribunal.

11.33 HMRC determine the nature and extent of the review as appears appropriate to them having regard to the steps taken by HMRC to reach the decision and they should take account of representations made by the taxpayer. Unless agreed otherwise, HMRC must provide a notice of the conclusions of the review and their reasoning within 45 days from the date that HMRC received notification from the taxpayer accepting the offer of a review. Where HMRC are required to undertake a review, but they do not give notice of their

11.33 *Tax appeals*

conclusion within the relevant period, then the review is to be treated as having concluded that the decision is upheld. Although HMRC are required to notify the taxpayer of this conclusion which the review is treated as having reached, there is no applicable time limit for provision of this notification of the deemed conclusion.

The outcome of a review will be that the decision is upheld, varied or cancelled. Of the 6,863 non-penalty cases which were reviewed in the period 1 April 2009 to 31 March 2010 (both direct and indirect taxes), 60% were upheld, 7% varied and 32% were cancelled.

11.34 A taxpayer appeals a decision by HMRC by lodging a notice of appeal at the First-tier Tribunal. The time limits for appealing are as follows:

- if the taxpayer chooses not to accept the offer of a review, within 30 days of the date of the document notifying the decision to which the appeal relates;
- if a review has been requested and the taxpayer has received notice of the review conclusion, within 30 days of receiving the conclusion of the review;
- if a review has been requested, but HMRC have not notified the taxpayer of their conclusions within the 45-day time limit, then the 30-day time period within which to appeal commences at the end of the 45-day period.

Where any amount of tax is payable consequent on the appealable decision of HMRC, that amount of tax, interest or penalty must be paid. If the tax, interest or penalty assessed is not paid, the appeal cannot proceed before the Tribunal unless either HMRC are satisfied, or the Tribunal decides that the requirement to pay the unpaid amount would cause the taxpayer to suffer hardship.

DIRECT TAXES

The right to appeal

11.35 Following the introduction of self-assessment for both individuals and corporations, most assessments are made either by the taxpayer or by an HMRC officer on his behalf, based on the information in the taxpayer's tax return. There is no right of appeal against such assessments.

Instead, under s 31(1), Taxes Management Act (TMA) there is a right of appeal against:

- an amendment to a self-assessment by an HMRC officer during an enquiry in order to prevent loss;
- any conclusion stated or amendment made by a closure notice under s 28A or s 28B following completion of an formal enquiry;
- any amendment of a partnership return under s 30B(1); or
- any assessment to tax which is not a self-assessment.

Similar provisions exist in relation to other direct tax matters (Finance Act 1998 para 48, Sch 18 for appeals relating to company tax matters and Finance

Act 2003 para 35, Sch 10 for appeals relating to stamp duty land tax assessments). Appeals must be made within 30 days of the relevant date under the statute (broadly the date that the decision (be it an assessment or closure notice was issued).

The appeal must be made in writing to HMRC.

Self-assessment closure procedure

11.36 The procedure on completion of an enquiry for corporation tax self-assessment is set out in Finance Act 1998, Sch 18. It can involve up to four stages:

- issue of a closure notice, stating HMRC's conclusions;
- a 30-day opportunity for the taxpayer to amend the self-assessment return;
- a 30-day opportunity for HMRC to amend the self-assessment return; and
- the taxpayer's right of appeal against HMRC's amendment to the self-assessment return.

11.37 This procedure has been recognised by HMRC as being unnecessarily cumbersome; and, following a joint report by the Chartered Institute of Taxation and the Inland Revenue into income tax enquiries under self-assessment, a new 'two-stage' procedure for personal (and trustee) self-assessment was inserted into the TMA by FA 2001. Under s 28A, an enquiry into a personal self-assessment is completed when, by closure notice, the HMRC officer informs the taxpayer that he has completed his enquiries and states his conclusions. The closure notice must either state that no amendment of the return is required, or make the amendments of the return that the officer considers are necessary to give effect to his conclusions. The taxpayer may then appeal against any conclusion stated or any amendments of the return.

Closure notice applications

11.38 HMRC not only have very wide powers during the enquiry stage, but also considerable scope for prolonging this stage. This is significant for taxpayers, as, in general, they can appeal only after the enquiry has been completed. However, valuable protection is provided to the taxpayer against HMRC by TMA, ss 28A(4) and 28B(5) and Finance Act 1998 para 33, Sch 18 (in relation to personal partnership and company returns respectively) which enable the taxpayer to apply to the Tax Tribunal, during the enquiry, for a direction that the enquiry should be closed. The burden of proof is then on HMRC to show that there are 'reasonable grounds' for not closing the enquiry. As the Special Commissioner noted in *Jade Palace v Revenue and Customs Commissioners* [2006] STC (SCD) 419:

> '… the issue on [a closure notice] application is not simply whether a closure notice should be directed, but whether it should be directed within a specified period. The reasonable grounds must cover the setting of a period.'

11.39 *Tax appeals*

11.39 This procedural rule is intended to protect taxpayers against protracted and unfocused enquiries and to enable taxpayers to take control of a dispute with HMRC. In *Eclipse Film Partners No 35 LLP v Revenue and Customs Commissioners* [2009] STC (SCD) 293, the Special Commissioner noted that s 28B (and the corresponding provisions relating to companies discussed in *HMRC v Vodafone 2* [2006] STC 483) are 'constructed so as to produce a reasonable balance' between the taxpayer's 'legitimate concern that the enquiry is concluded as soon as it is reasonable so to expect, so that he has the certainty of knowing either that his return is accepted unamended, or that he may appeal so as to determine any matter of dispute identified in the closure notice' and HMRC's caution as to 'when their enquiries may be regarded as sufficiently complete to enable them to issue a closure notice'. The Special Commissioner concluded that:

> 'it is implicit in the powers given to the General or Special Commissioners to give a direction requiring the issue of a closure notice, and is part of that "reasonable balance", that a closure notice can be required notwithstanding that the officer has not pursued to the end every line of enquiry or investigation – what is required is that he should have conducted his enquiry to a point where it is reasonable for him to make an informed judgment as to the matter in question, so that, exercising such judgment, he can state his conclusions and make any related amendments to the taxpayer's return. The exercise of that judgment may require the officer to express his conclusions in broad terms, or even express alternative conclusions (see the observations made in the case of *D'Arcy v HMRC* [2006] UKSPC 549 at [12]) – which should at the practical level allow an officer of the Commissioners to avoid the pitfalls identified in the *Tower MCashback* case of a closure notice too restrictively drafted in its conclusions.'

The form of a closure notice

11.40 In the closure notice, the inspector's conclusions can be stated in the alternative (see *D'Arcy v HM Revenue & Customs Commissioners* [2006] at paragraph 12) and there is no obligation on the inspector to give reasons for them (see *Tower MCashback v HM Revenue & Customs Commissioners* [2011] STC 1143). What matters for the purpose of TMA is the conclusions, not the process of reasoning by which the conclusions are reached. Section 31(1)(b) provides that an appeal may be brought against 'any conclusion stated or amendment made by a closure notice'. The legislation thus distinguishes between 'a conclusion stated' and 'an amendment required to give effect to the conclusion'. The ambit of any appeal is delimited by reference to the conclusion stated and/or amendment made to the return.

11.41 In *Tower MCashback*, the taxpayer claimed first-year allowances (under CAA 2001, s 45) in respect of certain expenditure. HMRC considered that the expenditure was precluded from being first-year allowance expenditure under s 45(4). The Inspector expressly stated in correspondence that the 'scheme' failed on that point alone; and, in the closure notice he stated that the reason for disallowing the claim for relief was 'as previously indicated'. During the hearing before the Special Commissioner, HMRC abandoned the s 45(4) argument and sought to introduce new legal arguments. On appeal to the High Court, Henderson J held that HMRC were precluded from raising legal grounds other than in respect of s 45(4). The referential statement ('as previously indicated') brought the conclusion expressed in correspondence into the closure notice; and so it was as if the inspector had stated in the closure notice: the claim for relief under s 45 is denied for the sole reason that s 45(4) applies. Henderson J said at paragraph 128:

> 'the limitation on the scope of the appeal is part of the protection given by Parliament to taxpayers under the self-assessment system. There is always a balance to be struck between the interests of individual taxpayers on the one hand, and the interests of the state and the general body of taxpayers on the other hand. Parliament has decreed how the balance is to be struck, and in the present case the result is in my judgment that the scope of the appeals was limited to matters arising under s 45(4). If there is a moral to be drawn, it is that HMRC should ensure that they have considered all the points on which they may wish to rely before a closure notice is issued. Issue of the notice is an irrevocable step, and once it has been taken the battle ground on any future appeal will be defined by reference to it.'

The Court of Appeal (Arden LJ dissenting on this issue only) held that the Special Commissioners had jurisdiction to hear any legal argument relevant to the subject matter of the conclusions stated in a closure notice. To a large extent, there is little difference between the majority of the Court of Appeal and Henderson J as to the principles to be applied. The difference, and the reason for allowing HMRC's appeal, was by the application of those principles. The Court of Appeal (Moses and Scott Baker LJJ) held that: (i) the question as to the subject matter of the appeal was one of fact for the Special Commissioner, and he had correctly identified the conclusions; and (ii) the conclusion stated in the closure notices was, in plain terms, a refusal of relief under s 45. They went on to say that s 45(4) was the reason for the officer issuing the closure notice, but it was not the conclusion stated in the notice (which was that the s 45 claim was excessive). The Court of Appeal also emphasised that the tribunal may entertain any evidence or legal argument relevant to the subject matter of the enquiry, subject to its obligation to ensure a fair hearing.

The Supreme Court dismissed the LLPs' appeal on the procedural issue. Both the High Court and Court of Appeal had undertaken a detailed analysis of the self-assessment provisions in order to answer this question. In contrast, the Supreme Court adopted a 'broad-brush' approach (by way of contrast, the Court of Appeal's decision comprises 103 paras, 68 of which pertain to the closure notice issue; only 17 paras of the Supreme Court's 94-para decision concern the issue). The Supreme Court held that it preferred the approach of Moses LJ to that of Henderson J as regards the application of the principles (on which principles there was broad agreement). Lord Hope added the comment that, although the scope and subject matter of the appeal was defined by the conclusions in the closure notice, TMA 1970, s 50 meant that the tribunal was not tied to the precise wording of the closure notice when hearing the appeal.

11.42 As the Supreme Court has confirmed that the tribunals are not limited by the precise wording of a closure notice when hearing an appeal, it will be harder for HMRC to contend that there are reasonable grounds for keeping the enquiry open, because the officer has not pursued to the end every line of enquiry or investigation. Accordingly, it should now be easier to obtain closure notices. However, while the time that should be saved by the shortening of the length of enquiries is welcomed, this approach brings with it a residual uncertainty as to the issues that may be articulated before the tribunal. As the Supreme Court hinted at, this is a matter that will need to be controlled by the tribunals.

Referral of questions during enquiry

11.43 FA 2001 inserted a new Part IIIA 'referral of questions during enquiry' into the TMA. Sections 28ZA–28ZE set out a procedure for personal self-assessment that enables questions relating to the subject matter of an enquiry to be referred to the Special Commissioners whilst the enquiry is still in progress. A similar procedure of referral has been introduced with regard to corporation tax self-assessment also (see Finance Act 1998, Sch 18, paras 31A–31D).

11.44 Referral can be made only jointly by the taxpayer and HMRC. Whilst proceedings on a referral are in progress in relation to an enquiry and until the matter referred is finally determined, no closure notice will be issued, nor can an application for a direction to give such a notice be made. A question is not finally determined whilst there remains a possibility of a determination by the Tribunal being set aside (e g by appeal on a point of law).

The determination is binding on both parties, subject to any further appeal rights, in the same way as a decision on a preliminary issue in an appeal. HMRC must take the determination into account in reaching their conclusions on the enquiry and in formulating amendments to the return. The referred point cannot be reopened on an appeal against HMRC's conclusions at the end of the enquiry.

Application for postponement of tax

11.45 Where the taxpayer has lodged an appeal and he considers that the tax charged is excessive, he can apply to HMRC, under TMA, s 55, for postponement of payment of part or all of the tax charged, pending the determination of the appeal. HMRC may agree with the taxpayer the amount of tax in respect of which payment may be postponed; and most cases are determined in this way. However, if agreement cannot be reached, then the taxpayer may refer the application for postponement to the First-tier Tribunal. The taxpayer is not required to prove all the facts or succeed in the legal arguments that will have to be proved or established at the substantive appeal; instead, the taxpayer just must show 'reasonable grounds' for believing that he has been overcharged to tax. 'Reasonable' means that the grounds must be based on reason and must not be irrational, absurd or ridiculous (see *Sparrow Ltd v Inspector of Taxes* [2001] STC (SCD) 206).

11.46 Only the amount of tax that depends on the outcome of the appeal is postponed until the appeal is heard. In the meantime, HMRC are entitled to seek payment of the balance (which is payable within 30 days of the agreement or the Tribunal's decision under TMA, s 55(5) – see *Parikh v Back* [1985] STC 232). In the event that the taxpayer does not apply for postponement, then the whole of the tax charged is payable as if there had been no appeal (but without prejudice to the appeal).

Agreements settling appeals

11.47 Litigation which has been commenced by notice of appeal can be validly settled by agreement only if the agreement complies with the relevant statutory provision, namely TMA, s 54. In short, a s 54 agreement has the same consequences as a determination to the same effect by the Tax Tribunal; and the agreement binds the parties to it in the same way as a determination binds the parties to an appeal (see *Tod v South Essex Motors (Basildon) Ltd* [1988] STC 392). It cannot be determinative of tax liabilities for years after that to which the assessment in question relates (see *MacNiven v Westmoreland Investments Ltd* [2003] 1 AC 311 in which, although the inspector's reasoning in the agreement referred to the amount of excess management expenses that were intended to be carried forward, the House of Lords held that this did not bind HMRC to take those into account in future years). Save as otherwise provided in the Taxes Acts, the determination of the Tax Tribunal is final and conclusive (under s 46(2)). Thus, a s 54 agreement is similarly final and conclusive and the issues that are resolved by it cannot be re-litigated by the parties.

11.48 An agreement between HMRC and a taxpayer made outside s 54 will be binding only in limited circumstances. Whilst HMRC, under its care and management powers, may enter into 'back duty' agreements (whereby it agrees to settle for less than the tax that may be due), HMRC do not have power to enter into 'forward tax agreements' (where it is agreed, in advance, that specified amounts will be paid annually in lieu of tax that otherwise would be due, because HMRC do not have power to agree not to perform their duty to collect tax in accordance with the statutory procedure (see *Al Fayed v Advocate General for Scotland* [2004] STC 1703). If a taxpayer enters into such an agreement, it will be enforceable only by way of judicial review proceedings, and HMRC will be bound only if their failure or refusal to abide by the agreement amounts to an abuse of power.

The internal review procedure

11.49 The review procedure is a new procedure that applies before any notification of an appeal to the First-tier Tribunal. There are certain differences between the review procedure for direct and indirect tax matters.

11.50 The review is carried out by an HMRC case officer who has no connection to the decision under review.

11.51 After a taxpayer has notified HMRC of his decision to appeal, he has three options:
- to request that HMRC review their decision;

11.51 *Tax appeals*

- to respond to any offer from HMRC to review their decision; or
- to bypass the review procedure by notifying the First-tier Tribunal of the appeal.

11.52 If a review is requested or offered, then the decision must first be considered by the officer who made it. That officer has 30 days in which to give the taxpayer his view of the matter (which may remain the same as when the appeal was made). The matter is then referred to a specialist review team. The review is carried out by specially trained staff, who are not only independent of the officer responsible for the case, but also outside his management chain. HMRC have confirmed that the review will be a genuine 'second look' at the case. HMRC must notify the taxpayer of the conclusions of the review within 45 days of, where the taxpayer requested the review, the initial officer notifying the taxpayer of his view of the matter or, where HMRC offered the review, when HMRC received notification from the taxpayer that the offer of a review was accepted.

11.53 If the taxpayer decides that a review would not be worthwhile, then he notifies the First-tier Tribunal of the appeal. This starts the appeal process. However, if the taxpayer proceeds to a review, then it will not be possible to notify the First-tier Tribunal of the appeal until after the review has been concluded. If the taxpayer disagrees with HMRC's post-review decision, then it is the taxpayer's responsibility to notify the First-tier Tribunal of the appeal within 30 days. Failure to do so means that HMRC's original decision stands. TMA, ss 49A–49I specify the rules as to when the taxpayer may notify the Tribunal of its appeal, namely:

- at any time after an appeal has been notified to HMRC, provided that:
  - a review has neither been requested nor an offer of a review accepted; or
  - the appeal is one to which the review process does not apply (s 49A);
- within 30 days of the conclusion of a review (s 49G(5)(a));
- within 30 days of the end of the period when HMRC should have given notice of their review conclusion but have failed to do so (s 49G(5)(b)); or
- if HMRC offer to conduct a review, but the taxpayer has not accepted, within 30 days from the date that HMRC notified the taxpayer of the offer to review the matter (s 49H).

SECTION THREE – THE FIRST-TIER TRIBUNAL

Introduction

11.54 The First-tier Tribunal is the court of first instance for nearly all tax appeals. The judges, for every appeal, are selected on a case-by-case basis from a pool that comprises both legally qualified and non-legally qualified members. The composition of the panel of judges that hears the case depends on the nature of the case. All members of the Upper Tribunal are able to sit as members of the

First-tier Tribunal. A substantial number of the current Special Commissioners have transferred to the First-tier Tribunal (but most General Commissioners have not). The First-tier Tribunal sits in local centres, with larger centres in London, Manchester and Edinburgh having been established to deal with matters of greater complexity.

11.55 A new central processing centre (based in Birmingham) has been established to handle the administration of all appeals. To commence an appeal, the taxpayer submits a Notice of Appeal to the First-tier Tribunal and, on receipt by the First-tier Tribunal of the Notice of Appeal, the central processing centre will allocate the case to one of four categories: (1) default paper; (2) basic; (3) standard; or (4) complex.

Once a case has been allocated to a category, either party may apply (or the Tribunal may decide on its own initiative) for the case to be re-allocated to a different category.

The categories

(1) Default paper cases

11.56 The simplest appeals (such as late filing penalties) are dealt with under this track. They are dealt with by means of written submissions only, unless either party requests a hearing. An appeal against, for example, (1) penalties for late income tax and corporation tax self-assessment returns (including penalties under TMA, ss 93(2) and 93(4), and Finance Act 1998, Sch 18, para 17(2) and (3)); and (2) fixed percentage surcharges for late payment of income tax under TMA, s 59C, must be allocated to the paper track, unless the Tribunal considers that there is a reason why it is appropriate to allocate the case to a different category. Once a case has been categorised as a default paper case, a copy of the notice of appeal is sent to HMRC by the Tribunal. HMRC then have 42 days within which to file their statement of case (which must set out the legislative provision under which the decision under appeal was made and their position in relation to the appeal) with the Tribunal and serve it on the appellant. HMRC may ask for the appeal to be dealt with at a hearing (First-tier Rules, r 25(3)). It is anticipated that HMRC are unlikely to do this unless they consider that there is an important issue that arises.

11.57 The appellant may (but is not obliged to) respond to HMRC's statement of case by sending a reply to the Tribunal. If the appellant wishes to reply, then he must do so within 30 days of receiving HMRC's statement of case. In the reply, the appellant may address the arguments raised by HMRC in their statement of case and may also bring any information that he considers is relevant to the appeal to the attention of the Tribunal. The appellant may request an oral hearing (First-tier Rules, r 26(3)(c)).

11.58 If neither party has made a written request for a hearing, then the Tribunal will determine the case on the papers. However, if either party has requested a hearing, the Tribunal must hold a hearing before determining the case; such a hearing will be heard by a single tribunal judge or tribunal member

11.58 *Tax appeals*

(see *Tribunal Composition Practice Statement*, 10 March 2009, para 3). It is anticipated that only a small number of default paper track cases will proceed to a hearing.

(2) Basic cases

11.59 Appeals where it is considered that little or no case management is required (and which do not fall within the default paper category) will be categorised as basic appeals. All standard tax penalties and surcharges that are not suitable for the default paper category will be allocated to the basic track, as will appeals against information notices. In addition, applications for:

- permission to make a late appeal;
- postponement of the payment of tax pending an appeal (under TMA 1970, s 55); and
- a direction that HMRC close an enquiry

will generally be classed as basic.

11.60 Basic cases, generally, proceed directly to a hearing without the need for further documents to be exchanged.

11.61 The procedural rules in relation to the preparation and service of a statement of case do not apply to basic cases. However, if HMRC wish to raise at the hearing any grounds for contesting the proceedings that they have not raised previously, then they must inform the appellant of these before the hearing (under First-tier Rules, r 24(3)) and as soon as reasonably practicable (under First-tier Rules, r 24(4)). No particular time is specified in relation to this; it is considered that the length of this time will vary according to the nature of the appeal and the issues raised.

11.62 Basic cases are heard by a panel of one, two or, where the Chamber President considers it appropriate, three, consisting of judges or members as determined by the Chamber President (see *Tribunal Composition Practice Statement*, 10 March 2009, para 4).

(3) Standard cases

11.63 Any case that does not fall within the basic or default paper categories will, as a rule, be allocated as a standard case. The cases that will be allocated as standard (or complex) cases are those that require substantial case management, exchanges of documentary evidence and witness statements. The rules governing the composition of the panel are similar for both standard and complex cases. If preliminary issues are to be determined or the panel is disposing of the case, the panel must consist of at least one tribunal judge, who may sit with two others, who may be either tribunal judges or tribunal members, as determined by the Chamber President. Any other decision, including giving directions (whether or not at a hearing) must be presided over by a single tribunal judge.

(4) Complex cases

11.64 For a case to be allocated to the complex track, the Tribunal must consider that one or more of the following criteria are satisfied: (a) the case will require lengthy or complex evidence or a lengthy hearing; (b) it involves a complex or important principle or issue; or (c) it involves a large financial sum (First-tier Rules, r 23(4)).

The circumstances when it is appropriate to categorise a case as complex were considered by the First-tier and the Upper Tribunal in *Capital Air Services Limited v HMRC* ([2010] SFTD 671 and [2010] STC 2726 respectively). The First-tier Tribunal declined to categorise the case as complex, holding that, in order to be complex, it must be the type of case that ought to be treated exceptionally and start in the Upper Tribunal. The Upper Tribunal disagreed. It allocated the case as a complex case. The Upper Tribunal also made a number of observations regarding the general approach that should be taken to allocation.

1 A case has to satisfy one or more of the three criteria. Accordingly, a case which is, overall, complex within the ordinary meaning of the word but does not quite meet any of the criteria separately cannot be allocated as a complex case.

2 Alternatively, a case that is not complex as a matter of ordinary meaning, but which nonetheless satisfies one or more of the criteria could be allocated as complex. However, if for example, a case would involve no lengthy or complex evidence and no complex or important principle or issue, then it may be appropriate not to allocate the matter as complex simply because it involves a large amount of tax. This could be either because a case must be complex, as that term is ordinarily understood, in order to be allocated to the complex category or because the First-tier Tribunal has a discretion not to allocate such a case to the complex category. (It is considered by the authors that the latter is the better justification.)

3 There is an element of objectivity to be applied. Thus, for example, a hearing of half a day can never be 'lengthy', whereas a three-month hearing always would be. Likewise, a case involving tax of £1,000 could never be said to involve a large financial sum and a case involving tax of £100 million always would. Absent broad indicative limits such as these, there is not a single 'right' answer that could be ascertained objectively as a matter of law.

11.65 Once an appeal has been allocated as a complex case, the First-tier Tribunal may, with the agreement of the parties, refer the case to the Chamber President with a request that the case be transferred directly to the Upper Tribunal. The agreement of the President of the Tax and Finance Chamber of the Upper Tribunal is also required (First-tier Rules, r 28). The first appeal to be heard in the Upper Tribunal, *John Wilkins (Motor Engineers) Ltd v Revenue and Customs Comrs* [2009] UKUT 175 (TCC) was so transferred. It is considered that only small numbers of cases will be transferred to the Upper Tribunal. Where a complex case is transferred to the Upper Tribunal, the rules relating to

11.65 *Tax appeals*

the composition of the panel are the same as those governing complex cases in the First-tier Tribunal.

Statement of case/exchange of documents

11.66 For all categories, except the basic category, HMRC must file a statement of case that sets out HMRC's position in relation to the case. The statement of case must include the legislative provision under which the decision under appeal was made also. In standard and complex cases, HMRC have 60 days from the date that the Tribunal sent the notice of appeal to provide their statement of case (First-tier Rules, r 25(1)(b)); and in default paper cases they have 42 days. In standard and complex cases, unless any other directions are given, each party must send to the Tribunal and to each other, within 42 days after the date that the statement of case is sent by HMRC, a list of the documents that it has in its possession or power and which it intends to rely on in the proceedings (First-tier Rules, r 27).

Case management powers

11.67 Rule 5 of the First-tier Rules provides that, subject to TCE, the First-tier Tribunal may regulate its own procedure. The First-tier Tribunal has wide-ranging powers to manage the proceedings before it, such as the ability to require expert evidence, to compel the production of documentary evidence or the attendance of witnesses, and to select preliminary issues, consolidate cases and appoint lead cases.

11.68 The aim of directions is to prepare the appeal for hearing. The practice in all courts is now to require that all evidence and argument be committed to writing in advance of the hearing. This means that all witnesses (including the appellant) are required to prepare written statements of the evidence that they will give and both parties are required to set out their legal arguments in outline. These documents, together with any other document which is to be produced in the appeal, must be lodged with the Tribunal, and served on the other side, in advance of the hearing.

11.69 There are many advantages to this approach. It shortens the length of the hearing, because all the evidence and argument can be read by both sides and the Tribunal before the hearing begins. It means that each witness can prepare his evidence in advance and it means that each party is fully aware of the other's case. It is no longer regarded as reasonable, or in the interests of justice, for late evidence (oral or written) or argument to be sprung on the opposing party at or during the hearing of the appeal. In *Mobile Export 365 Ltd, Shelford IT Ltd v HM Revenue & Customs Comrs* [2007] STC 1794, the Administrative Court criticised the approach that counsel had adopted before the VAT Tribunal. In relation to counsel having produced 'from his papers (as a conjurer produces a rabbit out of his hat) a skeleton argument and a bundle of authorities', Lightman J said:

> 'I should conclude by saying a word about springing surprises on opponents, as were sprung on the Commissioners and the Tribunal in this case. Such

tactics are not acceptable conduct today in any civil proceedings. They are clearly repugnant to the Overriding Objective laid down in CPR 1.1 (where applicable) and the duty of the parties and their legal representatives to help the court to further that objective. The objection to them is not limited to proceedings to which the CPR are applicable.'

Under Rule 15(2) of the First-tier Rules, the Tribunal has the power to admit evidence and the power to exclude evidence that is admissible but would otherwise be unfair to admit. In considering what is 'unfair to admit', the Tribunal will start from the presumption that all relevant evidence should be admitted, unless there is some other compelling reason not to admit it. In identifying whether there is a compelling reason not to admit evidence, the Tribunal will weigh up the fairness to the parties in admitting it or not admitting it. So, for example, the Tribunal may conclude that a party would be unfairly prejudiced if the other party were able to adduce evidence shortly before or at the hearing, such that there is a compelling reason that the evidence should not be admitted.

11.70 The Tribunal may issue a specific direction itself on its own initiative or, alternatively, the parties may apply for directions. If a direction is requested, it must be made in writing (unless it is requested at a hearing) and reasons must be given for the request. Once promulgated by the Tribunal, the directions must be sent to the parties and to any person affected by the direction (unless the Tribunal considers that there is good reason not to do so).

11.71 The only procedural directions that are prescribed by the First-tier Rules are in respect of service of a statement of case by HMRC and exchange of lists of documents by the parties. In nearly all complex cases (and in many standard cases), further directions will be required. In general, the parties will agree directions for the management of the case between themselves, but if they are unable to do so, the Tribunal will list the matter for a preliminary hearing at which a Tribunal judge will issue relevant case management directions.

Case management directions will typically include some or all of the following steps:

1   exchange of witness evidence of fact;
2   exchange of expert evidence;
3   agreement of a statement of agreed facts;
4   agreement of a statement of issues;
5   exchange of skeleton arguments;
6   preparation of a paginated bundle of documents.

11.72 The time estimate of the length of the hearing is left to the parties. If there is any doubt as to the length of hearing, time should be over-estimated rather than under-estimated. If a hearing has to be adjourned part-heard and further dates fixed, the gap between hearings could be weeks or even months, depending on how much further time is required and the availability of the particular First-tier Tribunal judge or judges who heard the first part of the appeal.

Strike out

11.73 The case management powers under the First-tier Rules are backed up by sanctions. If a taxpayer fails to comply with a direction that states that failure to comply would lead to the striking out of the proceedings or that part of them, then the proceedings, or an appropriate part of them, will be struck out automatically. The Tribunal may strike out the whole or part of the proceedings if:

- the taxpayer has failed to comply with a direction that states that failure to comply could lead to the striking out of the proceedings; or
- the taxpayer failed to co-operate with the Tribunal to such an extent that the Tribunal cannot deal with the proceedings fairly and justly; or
- the Tribunal considers that there is no reasonable prospect of the taxpayer's case (or part of it) succeeding.

11.74 The Tribunal may not strike out under the second or third heads above without first giving the taxpayer an opportunity to make representations in relation to the proposed striking out. In relation to the third head, whilst the power to strike out hopeless cases without need for a full hearing is a sensible provision, it is to be hoped that there will be guidance provided to and by the First-tier Tribunal to ensure that it is not used inconsistently by different judges in relation to analogous cases.

11.75 If the proceedings have been struck out by reason of the taxpayer's failure to comply with a direction, then the taxpayer may apply in writing within 28 days after the notice of the striking out was sent to have the proceedings reinstated. If the approach that the First-tier Tribunal takes is in line with its predecessor tribunals, then it is likely that the cogency of the reasons given by the taxpayer for failure to comply with a direction will be determinative as to whether or not the appeal will be struck out. If so, a failure to give any reasons (or any proper reasons) for the breach could result in the case being struck out (see *Customs and Excise Comrs v Young* [1993] STC 394). The First-tier Tribunal does not have an inherent jurisdiction to review an assessment outside a taxpayer's appeal. Thus, if the appeal is struck out (for whatever reason), the assessment of tax payable by the taxpayer stands and the tax thereunder is due, even if it is incorrect or unlawfully demanded.

11.76 The above rules apply to HMRC, save that the references to 'striking out' must be read as references to 'the barring of HMRC from taking any further part in the proceedings'. If HMRC are barred from taking part in the proceedings, then the Tribunal is not obliged to consider any submissions made by them. The Tribunal *may* summarily determine any or all the issues against HMRC, but it is not obliged to do so. It is considered that the bestowing of this discretionary power on the Tribunal is to enable the Tribunal to prevent taxpayers from receiving 'windfalls' in cases where it considers that the tax has been correctly demanded, but HMRC are barred from taking part in the proceedings due to procedural delays. Whether the bias in the rules in this way in favour of HMRC is appropriate is moot; it is to be hoped that a similar approach is adopted to HMRC and taxpayers in relation to failure to comply with directions.

Hearings

11.77 Hearings in basic cases are informal; in many cases, the taxpayer represents himself. Hearings in standard and complex cases are more formal, and representation is more common. Either party can appoint someone to represent him at the hearing (First-tier Rules, r 11), but that person need not be a legal representative (regardless of which category the case has been allocated to).

If a party does not attend the hearing, then the Tribunal has a discretionary power to continue to hear the appeal if it is satisfied that: (1) the party has either been informed of the hearing or reasonable steps have been taken to notify him of it; and (2) it considers that it is in the interests of justice to continue (First-tier Rules, r 33).

11.78 All hearings are held in public, unless the Tribunal directs that all or part of the proceedings are to be held in private (First-tier Rules, r 32). The Tribunal will give a direction to this effect only if it considers that restricting access to the proceedings can be justified:

- in the interests of public order or national security;
- to protect a person's right to privacy;
- to maintain the confidentiality of sensitive information;
- to avoid serious harm to the public interest; or
- because it is in the interests of justice.

11.79 It is anticipated that the number of cases that are held in private will be very small. Although the tests are not identical, it is considered that the approach that was taken by the Special Commissioners and the VAT and Duties Tribunals to the issue of publicity provides some guidance to the likely approach that will be taken by the First-tier Tribunal.

THE POSITION BEFORE THE PREDECESSOR TRIBUNALS

11.80 Prior to September 1994, proceedings before the Commissioners were held in private. After 1994, the general rule was that proceedings of the Special Commissioners were held in public; and, in December 2002, legislation was introduced to make General Commissioners' hearings open to the public. In contrast, proceedings before the VAT and Duties Tribunals were held in public.

11.81 Until 31 December 2002, an appellant before the Commissioners had the right to have his appeal heard in private. However, since that date there was no longer an unqualified right. A hearing before the Commissioners could be held in private only if the particular tribunal was satisfied that this was necessary in the interests of morals, public order, national security, juveniles or for the protection of the private life of the parties, or if they considered that publicity would prejudice the interests of justice (see the Special Regulations, reg 15 and the General Regulations, reg 13). Agreement by the parties that the appeal should be heard in private was not sufficient. The Practice Statement that accompanied the Standard Directions in respect of proceedings before the Special Commissioners stated that: 'The Special Commissioners will rule on

11.81 *Tax appeals*

applications for hearings in private even where these are agreed.' If such a Direction was applied for, it was considered by the Special Commissioners on its merits having regard to the facts of the case. However, if the only argument that was put forward is that the appellant did not want his tax affairs discussed in public, then that was unlikely to satisfy the conditions for a Direction.

11.82 In *Red Discretionary Trustees v Inspector of Taxes* [2004] STC (SCD) 132, a company related to the appeal owned a high-profile asset that had attracted a considerable amount of press attention; the settlor's family wealth had made the family a target for theft and violence. They had suffered a serious personal attack in which members of the family were handcuffed by robbers at the home and a substantial amount of property was stolen. Press reports of the event were provided. HMRC indicated that they had no objection to the hearing in private. The Special Commissioners allowed the application for the hearing to be heard in private. They said:

> 'As we believe this is only the second such application under the amended rule we are setting out the chairman's reasons for granting the application in this decision for the benefit of those reading this decision when it is published in an anonymised form. The rules clearly state that consent of both parties is in itself not enough; the tribunal must be satisfied about the matters set out in (i) or (ii) of reg 15(2). There is a public interest in open hearings and a presumption that sittings will be in public unless sufficient reasons are shown that one of those matters is satisfied. In this case given the circumstances of the robbery and its press publicity the chairman considered that sitting in private is necessary for the protection of the private life of the appellant to a greater extent than would ordinarily be the case. Protecting the taxpayer's private life could not be achieved if part of the hearing were in private. Accordingly the chairman agreed that the hearing would be in private. If it had not been for the press publicity about the robbery the tribunal would probably have decided to sit in public and for figures to be omitted where these were not necessary to an understanding of the decision.'

(The decision of the Special Commissioners was appealed directly to the Court of Appeal, where it was heard in public: *Howell v Trippier (Inspector of Taxes)* [2004] STC 1245.The anonymity protection afforded by the tribunal did not automatically extend to the higher courts.)

A party in proceedings before the VAT and Duties Tribunals could apply for the hearing or any part of the hearing to take place in private (under Rule 24, VAT Tribunals Rules). A direction that a hearing be held in private would only be made in exceptional circumstances. An example of where such circumstances were found to arise was where the disclosure of information could have caused harm to an appellant's business (see *Consortium International Ltd* (VTD 824)).

APPROACH OF THE HIGH COURT

11.83 In *HMRC v Banerjee (No 2)* [2009] STC 1930, the High Court refused an application from a taxpayer that its judgment be anonymised in order to protect her private life. The application was made after the proceedings had taken place in open court; and Dr Banerjee's previous appeal to the General Commissioners had been heard in public. The application was opposed by HMRC. Henderson J said

> 'It is relevant to bear in mind, I think, that taxation always has been, and probably always will be, a subject of particular sensitivity both for the citizen and for the executive arm of government. It is an area where public and private interests intersect, if not collide; and for that reason there is nearly always a wider public interest potentially involved in even the most mundane seeming tax dispute. ... in tax cases the public interest generally requires the precise facts relevant to the decision to be a matter of public record, and not to be more or less heavily veiled by a process of redaction or anonymisation. The inevitable degree of intrusion into the taxpayer's privacy which this involves is, in all normal circumstances, the price which has to be paid for the resolution of tax disputes through a system of open justice rather than by administrative fiat.'

Henderson J also went on to note that there was nothing 'inherently sensitive or embarrassing about the information disclosed'. The judge concluded that 'it will only be in truly exceptional circumstances that a taxpayer's rights to privacy and confidentiality could properly prevail in the balancing exercise that the court has to perform'.

Decisions

11.84 First-tier Rules, r 35 provides that the Tribunal may give an oral (extempore) decision at the hearing. The decision also must be communicated in writing to the parties within 28 days after making a decision by a decision notice that states the Tribunal's decision and informs the party of its appeal rights. Unless both parties agree that it is unnecessary, the decision notice must either include a summary of the findings of fact and the reasons for the decision or be accompanied by full written findings of fact and reasons for the decision. If the decision notice includes summary findings and reasons only or does not include any reasons or findings then either party may apply in writing (to be received within 28 days of the date that the decision notice was sent) for full written findings and reasons to be provided. On receiving such an application, the Tribunal is obliged to send the full statement of findings and reasons within 28 days 'or as soon as practicable thereafter' (First-tier Rules, r 35(6)). A party who wishes to apply for permission to appeal the Tribunal's decision must apply for full written findings and reasons before making such an application.

11.85 It is anticipated that the general practice will be that, in basic appeals, decisions will be given orally at the hearing, but in standard and complex appeals, judgment will be reserved and full written decisions will be provided subsequently.

11.86 Decisions where full reasons have been provided are published on the Tribunal's website and are reported in: *Simon's First tier Tax Decisions*.

11.87 *Tax appeals*

Review of decisions

11.87 The First-tier Tribunal has power to correct administrative or clerical errors (such as spelling mistakes) in decisions, either of its own motion or consequent on an application by either party. If a decision or direction is amended, a copy will be sent to all parties and the Tribunal will amend the published version (First-tier Rules, r 37).

11.88 A decision may be set aside if there has been a procedural irregularity and the Tribunal considers that it is in the interests of justice to do so (First-tier Rules, r 38). Procedural irregularities include documents either not being sent or being sent late or one party's representative not being present at the hearing.

11.89 An application to set aside a decision must be made to the Tribunal in writing within 28 days of the decision being sent by the Tribunal (First-tier Rules, r 38(3)). A party wishing to challenge a decision of the First-tier Tribunal must apply in writing to the First-tier Tribunal within 56 days of the latest date of receipt of: (1) the fully reasoned decision; (2) notification of amended reasons for, or correction of, the decision following a review; or (3) notification that an application for the decision to be set aside has been unsuccessful (First-tier Rules, r 39(2)). The Tribunal has the power to extend time under First-tier Rules, r 5(3)(a). An application for permission to appeal outside this period must include a request for an extension of time and state the reason why the application is being made late. On receiving an application for permission to appeal, the First-tier Tribunal must first consider, in accordance with the overriding objective, whether to review the decision (First-tier Rules, r 40). The First-tier Tribunal may only undertake a review if it is satisfied that there was an error of law in the decision (First-tier Rules, r 41(1)(b)) and it may not take any action without first having given all parties the opportunity to make representations. If the Tribunal decides not to review the decision or, having reviewed it, decides to take no action then it must consider whether to give permission to appeal. There is no prescribed test; and, as a general rule, the First-tier Tribunal judges tend to allow permission unless there is no reasonable prospect of success.

If the First-tier Tribunal refuses permission to appeal, then it must send to the parties a statement of its reasons for such refusal and notification that the party wishing to appeal may make an application direct to the Upper Tribunal for permission to appeal (see **11.106**).

Costs

11.90 Each of the General Commissioners, Special Commissioners, and the VAT and duties tribunal had different costs rules. The VAT and Duties Tribunal had power to direct any party to an appeal or an application to pay the other party's costs which were 'incidental to and consequential upon' the appeal or application. Costs could not be awarded in the General Commissioners and in the Special Commissioners, costs could only be awarded if a party had 'acted wholly unreasonably in connection with the hearing' (under Special Regulations, reg 21).

Regulation 21 was extremely restrictive as to the circumstances in which a cost order could be made by the Special Commissioners (see the comments by Park J in *Gamble v Rowe* [1998] STC 1247); and it was rare for such awards to be made, particularly against HMRC. Regulation 21 imposed a three-fold test that had to be satisfied before costs could be awarded:

- 'wholly unreasonable';
- 'action'; and
- 'in connection with the hearing'.

Each of these was construed narrowly.

The system of having three different costs regimes was criticised widely, not merely by tax practitioners, but also by the Special Commissioners. For example, in *Carter v Hunt* [2000] STC (SCD) 17 the Presiding Special Commissioner said at 24:

> 'In the present situation the protection given to the Revenue by Regulation 21 of the 1994 Regulations, in an appeal like this where large costs are involved and the amount of tax at stake is relatively small, has imposed a real injustice on the taxpayer. The costs rules are in urgent need of overhaul and I hope this case will be seen as a starting point.'

In *Carvill v Frost (No 2)* [2005] STC (SCD) 208, the Special Commissioners again indicated that, in their view, they should have a proper costs jurisdiction.

11.91 In the Leggatt Report, it was recommended expressly that no change to the existing costs system should be made. Sir Andrew Leggatt's recommendation was that there be no changes to the current costs system in *any* tribunals (the consequence of this in relation to the Tax Tribunals would have been that the old tripartite system was maintained). In the Consultation Paper 'Transforming Tribunals' (which was published on 28 November 2007), it was proposed that 'no costs' will be the default position. That approach remains the default position, but the ability of the Tribunal to award costs has been expanded. TCE, s 29 provides that costs shall be in the discretion of the tribunal in which the proceedings take place, subject to Tribunal Procedure Rules. In the explanatory notes to the Tribunals, Courts and Enforcement Bill it is stated in relation to the clause that became s 29:

> 'Many tribunals' powers to award costs are currently limited, either because they have no powers to award costs, or because the scope of any power they have is limited. This clause grants the tribunals the discretion to order costs and expenses in the same way as courts. It is not intended that these provisions will apply in all jurisdictions, rather that there will be flexibility as part of the creation of the new system to determine where a costs regime would be appropriate and whether there should be any limits to such a regime (for example, that costs should be awarded only against a party who has acted vexatiously or unreasonably). This is why subsection (1) is subject to provision made under the Tribunal Procedure Rules.'

11.92 There are four circumstances when the First-tier Tribunal may award costs. These are described below. The quantum of costs may be ascertained by the Tribunal by summary assessment, by agreement between the parties or by assessment upon application to the High Court or county court (First-tier Rules, r 10).

(1) Wasted costs

11.93 TCE, s 29(4), enables the Tribunal to make a wasted costs order. Wasted costs are costs that have been incurred by a party either (1) as a result of improper, unreasonable or negligent conduct by any legal or other representative; or (2) which the Tribunal considers that it would be unreasonable to expect that party to pay. The costs of a hearing to deal with a failure to comply with directions, for example, could give rise to a wasted costs order being made against a party's representative.

(2) Unreasonable conduct

11.94 Under First-tier Rules, r 10(1)(b), the Tribunal may award costs if it considers that a party (or their representative) has acted unreasonably in bringing, defending or conducting the proceedings. The adverb 'wholly' that was in reg 21 of the Special Commissioner Regulations is not included and there is no requirement that the unreasonable conduct be 'in connection with the hearing' as was the case before the Special Commissioners. Although this test is less stringent than the reg 21 test, it is not anticipated that costs will be awarded against a party under this head unless that party has acted in a capricious or vexatious fashion. It is considered that it is prima facie reasonable for a taxpayer to assert that a taxing statute does not apply to his particular factual circumstances, if there is a tenable argument to support that.

(3) Complex cases

11.95 If the proceedings have been allocated as a complex case under First-tier Rules, r 23 then the Tribunal has a costs jurisdiction. The default costs approach will be as in the High Court: the losing party pays the costs of the successful party. However, a taxpayer can elect to opt out of the default approach and submit to a 'no costs' environment, as for default paper, basic and standard cases, by making a written request to the Tribunal within 28 days of receiving notice that the case has been allocated as a complex case.

11.96 A written ministerial statement that sets out HMRC's policy in relation to costs was made by the Financial Secretary to the Treasury (Mr Stephen Timms) and the Financial Services Secretary to the Treasury (Lord Myners) on 30 March 2009 (*Hansard* HC Vol 490, col 29WS and *Hansard* HL Vol 709, col WS60). This replaces the statement that was made on 12 March 1980 by Mr Peter Rees, then Minister of State at the Treasury. In the 2009 ministerial statement, it is indicated that HMRC may waive their right to seek costs in certain circumstances:

> 'The general rule in the appeal courts is that the losing party risks having to pay the other side's costs, and I do not think it would be right to treat tax cases differently as a matter of course.

Tax appeals **11.98**

However, HM Revenue and Customs (HMRC) exercise their discretion and are willing in appropriate circumstances, and in particular where it is they who are appealing against an adverse decision, to consider waiving any claim to costs in cases before the Upper Tribunal or the appeal courts, or to consider making other arrangements – this may also extend to cases before the First-tier Tribunal.

In the minority of cases categorised as complex, where costs can be awarded in the Tax Chamber of the First-tier Tribunal other than for unreasonable behaviour, the appellant can ensure that there is no risk of them bearing HMRC's costs by opting for the costs rules not to apply.

In considering the exercise of HMRC's discretion, influential factors include the risk of financial hardship to the other party, the involvement of a point of law the clarification of which would be of significant benefit to taxpayers as a whole and the efficient collection and management of revenue for which HMRC have responsibility.

If HMRC are to come to an arrangement of this nature, they would expect to do so in advance of the hearing and following an approach by the taxpayer involved.'

11.97 It is considered that if the outcome of a particular appeal may affect a significant number of taxpayers (but particularly where the tax in issue for the particular taxpayer is not significant), then the taxpayer should, at an early stage, approach HMRC to discuss whether an agreement under which he has no liability to HMRC's costs can be reached in advance of an appeal.

(4) Pre-1 April 2009 appeals

11.98 Where a taxpayer has appealed against a decision before 1 April 2009, but the hearing has not taken place before that date, the First-tier Tribunal may make directions to apply the old procedural rules (Transfer of Tribunal Functions and Revenue and Customs Appeals Order 2009, para 7(3), Sch 3) in order to deal with cases fairly and justly. Under the transitional rules, an order for costs may be made only if, and to the extent that, an order for costs could have been made before 1 April 2009, regardless of when the costs have been incurred (Transfer of Tribunal Functions and Revenue and Customs Appeals Order 2009, para 7(7), Sch 3). Thus, it is considered that there are two particular circumstances when the old costs rules are likely to be applied by the First-tier Tribunal. The first is pre-1 April 2009 cases that would have been heard by the VAT and Duties Tribunals and which, probably, would not be allocated as complex cases had they been appealed post-1 April 2009. In this regard, it is noted that in *Smart Voucher Ltd v HM Revenue and Customs Commissioners* [2009] UKFTT 169 (TC), for example, the Tribunal directed that 'having regard to the fact that the appeals against the assessments were made in August and September 2008, to ensure that the proceedings are dealt with fairly and justly, pursuant to para 7(3), Sch 3, Transfer of Tribunal Functions and Revenue and Customs Appeals Order 2009, rule 29 of the Value Added Tax Tribunals Rules 1986 shall apply to this appeal, and rule 10 of The Tribunal Procedure (First-tier Tribunal) (Tax Chamber) Rules 2009 shall be disapplied'. The

11.98 *Tax appeals*

second circumstance is a case that would have been heard before the VAT Tribunal and where the taxpayer's appeal is dismissed. In *Purple Parking Services Ltd, Airparks Services Ltd* [2009] [2009] SFTD 445 the old conditions of 'importance, complexity and difficulty set out in the Parliamentary statement [of 12 March 1980]' were considered by the Tribunal before it decided that costs should be awarded to HMRC.

SECTION FOUR – THE UPPER TRIBUNAL

The function of the Upper Tribunal

11.99 The Upper Tribunal's main role is to act as a court of appeal from the First-tier Tribunal. It replaces the High Court as an appellate tax court in this regard. The Upper Tribunal also has jurisdiction to hear references against decisions of the Financial Services Authority (FSA) and the Pensions Regulator. In some cases, such as tax and FSA cases, the Upper Tribunal's jurisdiction is UK-wide; in other cases the geographical jurisdiction is slightly more limited. The Upper Tribunal also has jurisdiction in relation to judicial review cases in certain instances. This is analysed in more detail at **11.100** below.

11.100 In addition to tax appeals from the First-tier Tribunal, some cases go directly to the Upper Tribunal:

- direct referrals;
- appeals in which there are conflicting First-tier Tribunal decisions;
- some tax-related judicial review cases; and
- applications by HMRC for the imposition of additional penalties where they consider that significant tax is at risk (under Finance Act 2008 para 50, Sch 36).

Direct referrals to the Upper Tribunal

11.101 Complex cases may, with the consent of the parties, be referred directly to the Upper Tribunal by the First-tier Tribunal. In order to transfer a complex case directly to the Upper Tribunal, the First-tier Tribunal may, with the consent of the parties, refer a case to the President of the Tax Chamber, who may, with the agreement of the President of the Tax and Finance Chamber of the Upper Tribunal, direct that the case be transferred to the Upper Tribunal (First-tier Rules, r 28). Once a complex case has been transferred to the Upper Tribunal, the rules relating to the composition of the panel are the same as those that govern complex cases in the First-tier Tribunal.

11.102 For a case to qualify for such a referral, it will have to (1) raise a point of law of wide importance or particular complexity; and (2) not involve a complex factual dispute. The policy intention is that the number of cases that will be heard by the Upper Tribunal acting as a first instance tribunal will be very small. The first case to be heard by the Upper Tribunal in such capacity was that of *John Wilkins* (*Motor Engineers*) *Ltd v HMRC* [2009] STC 2485. This was an unusual case procedurally; it was the Tribunal limb of claims by taxpayers for compound interest on overpaid VAT, where the same substantive legal issue had already been heard by the High Court (*FJ Chalke and AC Barnes v HMRC* [2009] STC 2027).

Appeals from the First-tier Tribunal

11.103 There is no automatic right of appeal from a decision of the First-tier Tribunal to the Upper Tribunal. This is in contrast to the pre-1 April 2009 position, where taxpayers could appeal to the High Court as of right in most cases.

11.104 The following decisions are not appealable:

- a decision by the First-tier Tribunal not to review its own decision;
- a decision by the First-tier Tribunal to take no action following a review;
- a decision to set aside an earlier Tribunal decision;
- a decision that has already been set aside; and
- any other decisions of the character specified in the Appeals (Excluded Decisions) Order 2009, SI 2009 No 275.

11.105 Appeals from the First-tier Tribunal are on points of law only (TCE, s 11(1)), as was the case with appeals from the Special or General Commissioners or the VAT and Duties Tribunals to the High Court. Although TCE, s 12 which prescribes the powers of the Upper Tribunal to make determinations on an appeal involving an error on a point of law, expressly bestows on the Upper Tribunal a power to make 'findings of fact', an appeal to the Upper Tribunal does not give the appellant the opportunity to re-litigate factual issues in respect of which the First-tier Tribunal has made findings (see para 7.19, 2004 White Paper *Transforming Public Services: Complaints, Redress and the Tribunals*), and the hearing will not be a rehearing. Thus, it is considered that the ability of the Upper Tribunal to make findings of fact is limited and is analogous to the ability that the High Court possessed under TMA, s 56A, applying *Edwards v Bairstow* [1954] AC 14. In essence, findings of facts may be challenged only if they are outside the ambit of 'reasonable judgment'.

11.106 As set out above, an application for permission to appeal a decision of the First-tier Tribunal must first be made to the First-tier Tribunal. If the First-tier Tribunal refuses permission to appeal, an application may be made to the Upper Tribunal (TCE, s 11(4)(b)). Applications for permission to appeal must be made in writing to be received within one month of the date on which the First-tier Tribunal previously refused the application (Upper Tribunal Rules, r 21(3)(b)). Application for permission to appeal will be considered by the Upper Tribunal on the papers filed in the first instance.

11.107 If permission is refused on the papers, the party seeking to appeal the decision may apply in writing (to be received within 14 days of the Upper Tribunal sending notice of its refusal to give permission to appeal) for an oral hearing before the Upper Tribunal of the application (Upper Tribunal Rules,

11.107 *Tax appeals*

r 22(3)–(5), as substituted by the Tribunal Procedure (Amendment) Rules 2009, SI 2009 No 274, r 14).

11.108 If permission is granted, the appellant must provide a notice of appeal to the Upper Tribunal within one month after permission to appeal has been sent to the appellant. If it is the Upper Tribunal (rather than the First-tier Tribunal) that has given permission to appeal, generally the application for permission will be treated as the notice of appeal and a copy of it will be sent to the respondents by the Upper Tribunal (Upper Tribunal Rules, r 22(2)(b)). The Upper Tribunal may, with the agreement of all parties, determine the appeal without the need for any further papers (although, in practice, it is considered that this power will be exercised rarely).

In cases where the First-tier Tribunal gave permission to appeal, the Upper Tribunal, having received notice of the appeal will send a copy of the notice of appeal to the respondents to the appeal. The respondents will then have one month within which they may file a written response. The response must state whether the respondent opposes the appeal and give the grounds on which they intend to rely. It must also state whether or not the respondent wants the case to be dealt with at a hearing (Upper Tribunal Rules, r 24). The appellant then has one month within which they may reply to the response (Upper Tribunal Rules, r 25). Having received the papers, the Upper Tribunal will either decide the appeal without a hearing, if the parties have agreed, or will arrange for the case to be listed and heard.

11.109 The Upper Tribunal must decide if the First-tier Tribunal made an error of law. If it does so decide, then it may set aside the original decision (although it is not obliged to do so). If the decision is set aside, the Upper Tribunal must either remit the matter back to the First-tier Tribunal for it to reconsider or give a new decision itself. If the Upper Tribunal does not remit the case to the First-tier Tribunal, it may make any decision on the case that the First-tier Tribunal could have made (under TCE, s 12(4)(a). In the event that the Upper Tribunal remits the case to the First-tier Tribunal, it may give directions as to how the case should be managed by the First-tier Tribunal. This can include directing that the case be heard by a differently constituted panel (under TCE, s 14(3)(a)).

Judicial review

Jurisdiction of the Upper Tribunal

11.110 TCE creates a statutory regime that enables the Upper Tribunal to exercise judicial review powers in appropriate cases. Where it has jurisdiction, the Upper Tribunal has power to grant the following kinds of relief: (1) a mandatory order; (2) a prohibiting order; (3) a quashing order; (4) a declaration; or (5) an injunction ('the judicial review reliefs'). These powers may be used either where:

- a direction has been made by the Lord Chief Justice, with the agreement of the Lord Chancellor, specifying a class of case that is to be heard in the Upper Tribunal, rather than the High Court (under TCE, s 18); or

- the High Court has ordered the transfer of an individual case, because it considers that it is just and convenient to do so (under TCE, s 19(3)).

11.111 Whilst the legislation allows for an application for permission to judicially review a matter to be made in the first instance to the Upper Tribunal, the Upper Tribunal must transfer such an application to the High Court unless it meets the four conditions set out within TCE, s18, so that the Upper Tribunal has the function of deciding the application. The first condition is that the application does not seek anything other than the judicial review reliefs. The second condition is that the application does not call into question anything done by the Crown Court. Condition 3 is that the application falls within a class specified for the purposes of s 18 in a direction given in accordance with Part 1 of Sch 2 to the Constitutional Reform Act 2005. A Practice Direction was made for this purpose by the Lord Chief Justice on 28 October 2009. It specifies the class of cases that fall within condition 3 as decisions of the First-tier Tribunal where there is no right of appeal to the Upper Tribunal only. The fourth condition is that the judge who will hear the application is either a judge of the High Court or the Court of Appeal or 'such other persons as may be agreed from time to time between the Lord Chief Justice ... and the Senior President of Tribunals'. Conditions 1, 2 and 4 are likely to be met in the majority of tax judicial review cases; however, condition 3 will be met (at present) in very few cases. Consequently, the present situation (ie unless and until a further Practice Direction is released in this regard) is that almost all judicial review cases will need to be commenced in the High Court.

Where a claim for judicial review is commenced in the High Court, then a different condition 4 applies. It is highly unlikely to be relevant to a tax case, and, accordingly, condition 4 is likely to be satisfied in the vast majority of tax cases. If all four conditions are met, then the High Court must transfer the application to the Upper Tribunal. Where only conditions 1, 2 and 4 are met, the High Court may transfer the application if it appears to be just and convenient to do so. Accordingly, although the majority of tax judicial review cases must be started in the High Court, the majority of these applications will be suitable to be considered for transfer from the High Court to the Upper Tribunal. After transfer, the case will then be decided by a High Court judge sitting in the Upper Tribunal, applying the rules of the Upper Tribunal.

JURISDICTION OF THE FIRST-TIER TRIBUNAL IN RESPECT OF PUBLIC LAW MATTERS

11.112 There are competing decisions of the High Court in relation to whether or not the First-tier Tribunal (or its statutory predecessors) has jurisdiction to decide issues of a public law nature. There is a long line of authority that includes the decision of Jacob J in *Customs and Excise Commissioners v National Westminster Bank plc* [2003] STC 1072 to the effect that: 'the proper remedy for unfair treatment is judicial review, not an appeal to the tribunal'. More recently, however, Sales J in *Oxfam v Revenue & Customs Commissioners* [2010] STC 686, said that, on the basis that VATA, s 83(1)(c), brought within the First-tier Tribunal's jurisdiction the amount of input tax

11.112 *Tax appeals*

which may be credited to a person, the First-tier Tribunal jurisdiction extended to the public law issue which arose between Oxfam and HMRC (being legitimate expectation) as far as that issue related to the amount of input tax to be credited. This decision has been followed by the First-tier Tribunal in some cases (*Hanover Company Services Limited v The Commissioners for Her Majesty's Revenue and Customs* [2010] SFTD 1047), but distinguished in others (*Space 2 Build Ltd v The Commissioners for Her Majesty's Revenue and Customs* [2010] UKFTT 66 (TC) and *Health Response UK Ltd v The Commissioners for Her Majesty's Revenue and Customs* [2010] UKFTT 123 (TC), where the First-tier Tribunal held that it did not have jurisdiction).

Reed plc v Revenue and Customs Commissioners (unreported, 15 December 2010) is a case where the tax appeal and the legitimate expectation issues are highly interconnected, both factually and in law. Warren J and Judge Avery Jones (sitting as judges of both the Upper and First-tier Tribunal) considered the appropriate procedure to be adopted. Warren J exercised his casting vote and directed that the tax appeal be heard in the First-tier Tribunal (by Judge Avery Jones) and the judicial review proceedings be stayed until after release of the tax appeal decision. However, it was indicated by the judges that they did want this case to be seen as a pointer towards any practice. Accordingly, it is considered that the appropriate procedure to be adopted in similar cases will have to be decided on a case-by-case basis.

It is considered that the First-tier Tribunal does not have jurisdiction to grant judicial review remedies. Even if the consequence of Oxfam is that under VATA, s 83(1), the determination of the relevant amount of VAT which may be creditable remains within the jurisdiction of the Tribunal when the doctrine of legitimate expectation can affect the amount of it, it remains the case that the ability of HMRC to enforce their collection of VAT is not within the Tribunal's jurisdiction. In order to avoid falling within a potential jurisdictional lacuna, taxpayers who have a 'legitimate expectation' ground of challenge are recommended to both seek permission for judicial review from the Administrative Court (on a protective basis) and to raise the 'legitimate expectation' issue as a ground of appeal before the First-tier Tribunal.

Case management powers

11.113 The Upper Tribunal may regulate its own procedures and it has the same case management powers as the First-tier Tribunal. In addition, under Upper Tribunal Rules, r 5 it may also, inter alia:

- suspend the effect of a decision where a party has made an application for permission to appeal or whilst an appeal is ongoing; and
- ask the First-tier Tribunal to provide information or documents in relation to any decision and the reasons for that decision.

11.114 Under Upper Tribunal Rules, r 7 the Upper Tribunal may take any action that it considers 'just' to deal with a failure to comply with directions. There is no definition as to what would be considered just in the legislation; each case is likely to be considered by the Upper Tribunal by reference to the circumstances of the failure, and in accordance with the overriding objective. The actions that can be taken include:

- waiving the requirement;
- requiring the failure to be remedied;
- striking the case out; or
- restricting a party's participation in the proceedings.

11.115 Also, as a superior court of record, the Upper Tribunal has the power to treat failure to comply with an order of the Upper Tribunal as contempt; a custodial sentence could be imposed.

Hearings

11.116 Whilst the Upper Tribunal may make any decision without an oral hearing, it must have regard to the views of the parties when deciding whether to hold a hearing (Upper Tribunal Rules, r 34). This is in contrast to the First-tier Tribunal, which can decide cases without a hearing only if both parties consent. Absent this difference, the rules applying to hearings before the two tribunals are broadly the same. Legal representation before the Upper Tribunal is not mandatory; and a party's representative need not be legally qualified (see Upper Tribunal Rules, r 11).

Generally, it is expected that most cases will be heard by one Upper Tribunal judge, but the Chamber President may require a hearing before up to three Upper Tribunal judges.

Decisions

11.117 The Upper Tribunal may give a decision orally at the hearing (Upper Tribunal Rules, r 40). A written decision, with reasons, together with information on appeal rights, must be sent to all parties as soon as is 'reasonably practicable' after making the decision (the term 'reasonably practicable' is not defined) under Upper Tribunal Rules, r 40(2). The Upper Tribunal is a superior court of record and so its decisions are published (in *Simon's Tax Cases*).

Costs in the Upper Tribunal

11.118 The Upper Tribunal has full costs jurisdiction. However, the Upper Tribunal may not make an order for costs against a person without first (i) giving that person an opportunity to make representations; and (ii) if the person is an individual and either the proceedings were a judicial review or if the Upper Tribunal considers the person (or his representatives) has acted unreasonably, considering the person's financial means.

Appeals from the Upper Tribunal

11.119 As in the First-tier Tribunal, the Upper Tribunal has power to correct clerical errors (such as spelling mistakes) in decisions by sending notification of

11.119 *Tax appeals*

the amended decision to all parties and making any necessary amendments to any information published in relation to the decision (under Upper Tribunal Rules, r 42).

Also as at the First-tier Tribunal, the Upper Tribunal may set aside a decision if there has been a procedural irregularity and the Upper Tribunal considers that it is in the interests of justice to do so (Upper Tribunal Rules, r 43). A written application to set aside a decision must be made to the Upper Tribunal so that it is received within one month of the decision being sent by the Upper Tribunal.

An appeal from the Upper Tribunal lies to the Court of Appeal. In the first instance, permission to appeal must be sought from the Upper Tribunal (Upper Tribunal Rules, r 44(1)). Following the Upper Tribunal's decision, the unsuccessful party has one month in which to seek permission to appeal. If the Upper Tribunal refuses to give permission, it must inform the parties in writing of the reasons for refusal. If permission is refused, the party may then apply to the Court of Appeal.

11.120 The available grounds for appeal are the same as those for an appeal from the High Court to the Court of Appeal (as set out in Access to Justice Act 1999), first it must be an appeal on a point of law; and, secondly, the proposed appeal raises an important point of principle or practice; or there is some other compelling reason for the Court of Appeal to hear the appeal (para 2 of the Appeals from the Upper Tribunal to the Court of Appeal Order 2008).

In *Grogan v HMRC* (unreported, 20 November 2010), the Upper Tribunal indicated that it viewed this power with circumspection. It considered that permission should not be granted by the Upper Tribunal unless the appeal has a real prospect of success and that, in case of doubt, it would leave the matter to the Court of Appeal

11.121 Under Access to Justice Act 1999, s 55(1) 'second appeals' are to be granted only in exceptional circumstances. The above test applied for appeals from the High Court even if the taxpayer succeeded at first instance, but lost on appeal. Although the change was introduced to ensure that 'second appeals would ... become a rarity' (per Brooke LJ in *Tanfern Ltd v Cameron-McDonald* [2000] 1 WLR 1311 at 1320C), it was often not too difficult to demonstrate an 'important point of principle' in tax matters when applying for permission for a second appeal to the Court of Appeal.

The Court of Appeal grants permission for appeals from specialist tribunals more sparingly. Whether the fact that the Upper Tribunal (Tax and Chancery Chamber) is a specialist tribunal (whereas the High Court was not, even when it heard tax cases) will have any impact on the number of tax appeals that are granted permission to be heard by the Court of Appeal is not yet known.

11.122 Access to Justice Act 1999, s 54(4) provides that there is no appeal from a decision of the Court of Appeal refusing permission to appeal to that court.

Consequently, if the Court of Appeal refuses to grant permission, the appeal process will end.

SECTION FIVE – THE TAX COURTS

The High Court

11.123 As set out above, prior to 1 April 2009, the High Court sat as an appellate court from the Commissioners, the s 706 Tribunal, and the VAT and Duties Tribunals. The Upper Tribunal has effectively assumed the jurisdiction of the High Court as regards this appellate function.

11.124 In very general terms, before 1 April 2009, the High Court also existed as a potential jurisdiction of first instance where, in a tax-related matter, there was no statutory route of appeal to the Tax Tribunals. The High Court's jurisdiction has not been expressly transferred to the Upper Tribunal and so the extent to which this jurisdiction has been assumed also by the Upper Tribunal is, to a degree, unclear.

11.125 The principle of 'exclusive jurisdiction' applies to delimit the jurisdiction of the High Court. In very broad terms, the principle of 'exclusive jurisdiction' has the consequence that the jurisdiction of the High Court is ousted at first instance if there is a statutory scheme containing its own system of remedies in place to deal with claims and Parliament has assigned resolution of such disputes to that scheme. Whether the correct analysis of the principle is that, where the proceedings come within the area that has been assigned to a statutory tribunal and thus concern matters over which the specialist tribunal should have exclusive jurisdiction, but jurisdiction has not been explicitly confined by statute to that tribunal (as, for example, Taxes Management Act 1964, s 5(6) and (as originally enacted) s 29(6) confined the right to challenge assessments to the tax tribunals), then the jurisdiction of the High Court is excluded (cf the House of Lords' decision in *Barraclough v Brown* [1897] AC 615) or, alternatively, retained, but subject to the rule that the High Court should exercise its discretion to refuse jurisdiction (cf the House of Lords' decision in *Re Vandervell's Trusts* [1971] AC 912) remains an open question. It is the authors' view that it is only where a taxpayer's High Court claim is an indirect way of seeking to achieve exactly the same result as it would be open to the taxpayer to achieve directly by appealing to the Tax Tribunals, that the High Court's jurisdiction is excluded absolutely (as this is, or is tantamount to, abuse of process). However, if there are elements of the claim that differ, including, for example, the seeking of a remedy that the tribunal has no power to grant, the High Court jurisdiction is not ousted and it is an issue of discretion.

11.126 Matters that could be taken to the High Court before 1 April 2009 included:

- claims to recover overpayments of tax (although, if s 33 applied, this potentially provided an exclusive procedure. See *Woolwich Equitable Building Society v IRC* [1992] STC 657, and *Deutsche Morgan Grenfell Group plc v IRC* [2007] 1 AC 558);
- claims for declaratory relief (see, for example, *Buxton v Public Trustee* (1962) 41 TC 235, where a declaration was sought that trusts were charitable);

11.126 *Tax appeals*

- claims for damages in tort (such as proceedings for negligence or misfeasance in a public office against HMRC); and
- judicial review of decisions of HMRC or the tax tribunals.

11.127 It is considered that the matters listed at **11.126** above may still be taken to the High Court, save that the position regarding: (i) judicial review; and (ii) claims to recover overpayments of tax with effect in relation to claims made on after 1 April 2010 is now more complicated. The issue of judicial review is addressed further above at **11.110–11.112**. TMA, Sch 1AB (which was inserted by Finance Act 2009) is intended to provide a complete code with regard to claims to recover overpayments of tax; consideration as to whether it achieves that purpose is outside the scope of this chapter.

11.128 Under Inheritance Tax Act 1984, s 222(3) the High Court is also an alternative first-instance venue for certain inheritance tax appeals. An appeal against a determination by HMRC may be notified to the High Court where either the appellant and the Board agree that the matters for decision on appeal 'are likely to be substantially confined to questions of law' or, in the absence of such agreement, if the appellant applies for and obtains leave from the High Court, having satisfied the court that the subject matter falls within that category. In *Bennett v IRC* [1995] STC 54, where Lightman J gave leave for an inheritance tax appeal to be heard at first instance at the High Court, he held that, whilst it was a precondition for leave that the appeal be substantially confined to questions of law, it was also necessary to determine whether the issue, by reason of its novelty, importance or otherwise, was one which could and should proceed by way of appeal directly to the High Court. Leave was granted on the basis that a short but important issue of law was raised and it was likely that any decision of the Special Commissioners would be appealed.

The European Court of Justice

11.129 The jurisdiction of the European Court of Justice (ECJ) is defined in the EU treaties. It has jurisdiction over the following matters:

- failure by a Member State to fulfil an obligation under the Treaty on the Functioning of the European Union (previously known as the EC Treaty);
- legality of acts of the institutions of the European Union; and
- interpreting EU law at the request of national courts and tribunals (preliminary rulings).

11.130 The ECJ comprises one judge from each of the 27 member states. The court may sit as a full court, but rarely does so. It usually sits in chambers of three or five judges, depending on the importance or complexity of the issues, and occasionally as a Grand Chamber of 13 judges. Cases are dealt with via a two-stage procedure. The first stage requires the parties and any interested member states (and the European Commission) to submit written statements to the ECJ (known as 'written observations'). An appointed judge then summarises the statements into a report. The second stage of a case is the oral hearing, at which the parties and the interested member states (and the European Commission) have the opportunity to give short, oral submissions to the court.

Tax appeals **11.134**

The court is assisted by eight Advocates General. At the end of a hearing, the Advocate General appointed to the case may prepare a detailed written opinion which is publicly released. Since 2003, Advocates General are only required to give an opinion where the court decides that the case deals with a new point of law. If the Advocate-General does provide an opinion, it is authoritative, but not binding on the ECJ. However, the ECJ does often (albeit not always) follow the Advocate-General's opinion.

11.131 The general rule is that, where a question concerning EU law arises before a national court or tribunal, the matter may be referred to the ECJ if a decision on the question is necessary to enable the national court to give judgment. However, under Article 267 of the Treaty on the Functioning of the European Union (previously Article 234 of the EC Treaty), the matter must be referred to the ECJ if there is no right of appeal from a decision of the court or tribunal. Thus, courts of last resort (typically the Supreme Court in the UK) do not have a discretion as to whether to make a reference on an EU law issue which it is necessary to resolve before judgment can be given (although the court in question retains its discretion to decide whether a decision on a question of EU Law is necessary to enable it to give judgment (see *Henn and Darby v DPP* [1981] AC 850). If the answer to the EU law point is 'acte clair' (in essence so obvious that there is no scope for any reasonable doubt), then there is no obligation to refer the question to the ECJ.

11.132 The decision to make a reference is a matter for the national court or tribunal, not for the parties to the case. The court is not even bound to accept a joint submission by the parties that an issue of EC law that is not acte clair arises (see *Rheinmuhlen-Dusseldorf v Einfuhr-und Vorratsstelle fur Getreide und Futtermittel* (Case 166/73) [1974] ECR 33). Similarly, a reference may be made by a court against the wishes of all the parties (see, for example, *Direct Cosmetics v Customs and Excise Commissioners* [1984] 1 CMLR 99). Thus, if one of the parties disagrees with the decision regarding the making of a reference to the ECJ, he must appeal under national law to challenge that decision – there is no direct right of access to the ECJ (see for example, *Marks and Spencer v Halsey* [2003] STC (SCD) 70: the Special Commissioners declined to refer questions to the ECJ; that decision was appealed to the High Court, where Park J referred questions to the ECJ).

11.133 In *R v International Stock Exchange, ex p Else Ltd* [1993] QB 534, Sir Thomas Bingham set out guidelines that courts should be mindful of when deciding whether or not to refer issues of EU law to the ECJ. If the issues are almost certain to be conclusive of the outcome of these appeals, and it cannot be said that the court can resolve the issue itself 'with complete confidence', the issues should be referred. If the delay and costs of an appeal can be avoided by the making of a reference at an early stage, then that is a relevant consideration for a court to consider (see Bingham J in *Customs and Excise Commissioners v ApS Samex* (*Hanil Synthetic Fiber Industrial Co Ltd*) [1983] 3 CMLR 194).

11.134 It is the responsibility of the UK court, rather than the parties, to settle the terms of the reference, although, in practice, the parties are normally involved in the drafting process. *Practice Direction* (*ECJ References: Procedure*) [1999] 1 WLR 260 states that the reference should 'identify as

11.134 *Tax appeals*

clearly, succinctly and simply as the nature of the case permits the question to which the British court seeks an answer. It is very desirable that language should be used which lends itself readily to translation.' If a reference is made, the ECJ will not concern itself with the question of whether or not a reference was necessary; it will simply give a decision.

11.135 When questions are referred to the ECJ by national courts or tribunals, the ECJ's sole function is to decide what the EU law is and to assist the referring court on the point of law in abstract. It does not have jurisdiction to interpret national law; and it is for the referring court or tribunal to apply the relevant rule of EU law, after it has been interpreted by the ECJ, in the specific case pending before it (see, for example, *Marks and Spencer plc v Halsey* (Case C-446/03) [2006] STC 237, where the decision of the ECJ has been applied by the referring High Court ([2006] STC 1235), and further by the Court of Appeal ([2008] STC 526)).

Chapter 12

Settlement negotiations

Phil Berwick, CTA, ATT

Director, Tax Disputes and Investigations, McGrigors LLP

INTRODUCTION

12.01 Dictionary definitions of 'negotiate' include 'to reach an agreement or compromise by discussion' and 'to get over an obstacle'. In the context of HM Revenue and Customs (HMRC) investigations, both meanings are equally valid: there are a multitude of potential obstacles to be overcome. These include an intransigent HMRC officer, the client, and the practitioner himself. This chapter will explore ways of navigating the various obstacles that the practitioner may face.

12.02 The practitioner will often be instructed by his client to get the best settlement possible. What is the officer's authority to negotiate? This can be found in Taxes Management Act (TMA) 1970 and common law. TMA 1970, s 1(1) as amended by the Commissioners for Revenue and Customs Act 2005, states the Commissioners for HMRC shall be responsible for the 'collection and management' of income tax, corporation tax and capital gains tax. The 'care and management' authority is an important part of HMRC's powers. Without it, HMRC would not be able to issue extra-statutory concessions (departures from the strict interpretation of the law where such an interpretation could give an unfair result).

12.03 In the context of an investigation settlement, the authority enables an officer to reach an informal agreement with a taxpayer where complex matters of statutory interpretation are concerned, where precedents derived from case law appear to be in conflict with the particular matter in hand, or even where the facts themselves are open to dispute and different interpretations.

12.04 The 'care and management' power permits negotiations so that an agreement can be reached which is acceptable to both parties, i e HMRC and the client. The authority permits the agreement to be reached without recourse to the legal process, which would be time-consuming, expensive and may result in

12.04 *Settlement negotiations*

a decision that was unacceptable to both parties. The Court of Appeal held, in *CIR v Nuttall* [1990] STC 194, that the power to enter into settlement negotiations and make agreements was not overridden by the specific provisions of TMA 1970, s 54.

START THE NEGOTIATING GROUNDWORK EARLY

12.05 For the purpose of this chapter, it is assumed that there have been omitted profits from the client's tax return. Where, in practice, this is established, the practitioner should direct his attention to minimising the level of the additions sought by the officer.

12.06 It is important for the practitioner to appreciate that the groundwork for settlement negotiations should start at the beginning of an investigation. Co-operation of the advisor, as well as the client, is taken into account by the officer when considering the level of penalty at the end of an investigation. The practitioner should ensure that, from the time of the officer's opening letter, he is not responsible for any unnecessary delays in providing information reasonably requested by the officer, or in respect of the general progress of the enquiry.

12.07 Where there are going to be delays in, for example, the provision of information, the officer should be kept informed. The practitioner should instil a sense of urgency into his client so that he appreciates the seriousness of the situation, and will qualify for the maximum penalty abatement for co-operation.

ARE INTEREST AND PENALTIES DUE?

12.08 Historically, HMRC did not pursue a penalty unless omitted profits exceeded £2,000. Following the introduction of the new penalty regime (see **12.10** below), HMRC's published instructions do not give details of a de minimis limit that will apply in relation to the imposition of a penalty. Unless the practitioner can demonstrate that his client has taken reasonable care, the officer is likely to seek the imposition of a penalty.

CALCULATION OF INTEREST

12.09 When the additional liabilities have been agreed, the resulting tax will be calculated together with any interest. This is automatic and there may not be scope for reducing the interest charged. Interest is charged under the provisions of TMA 1970, s 86.

PENALTY NEGOTIATION

12.10 Where HMRC has suffered a loss of tax, the officer will seek, in addition to the tax due, interest and a penalty, except in the smallest of cases. A new penalty regime was introduced by FA 2007, Sch 24, para 1 for inaccuracies in returns or other documents. The new regime applies to an inaccuracy contained in a return or other document which was due to be filed on or after 1 April 2009 and the return or other document relates to a tax period beginning on or after 1 April 2008. The new regime consists of a series of 'stepped' penalties based on taxpayer behaviour. The penalty is calculated by reference to the 'potential lost revenue' rather than tax lost.

12.11 The previous penalty regime, where tax was mitigated by reference to disclosure, co-operation and seriousness (which incorporates size and gravity), will continue to apply in relation to inaccuracies in returns for earlier tax periods. Practitioners will need to ensure that they are applying the appropriate penalty regime when negotiating with the officer. Where an investigation straddles 6 April 2008, both regimes will need to be considered.

12.12 The maximum penalty under the new regime is 100% of the 'potential lost revenue'; under the old regime it is 100% of the tax lost. The likelihood is that, under the new regime, HMRC will recover a higher level of penalty than they would have done for the same offence under the old regime. This increases the importance of negotiation when considering penalties – for example, in determining the appropriate taxpayer behaviour and the corresponding band of penalty that applies. Further details of the new penalty regime, including the bands of taxpayer behaviour, are considered in **Chapter 14**.

12.13 The officer will consider whether there has been a disclosure, and, if so, whether it was prompted or not. He will also take into account what he thinks is the appropriate behaviour and level of mitigation, and, consequently, penalty. It should be noted that the officer's figure is not cast in stone. It is important to remember that it is the client who is making the offer to HMRC: the officer should only be giving an indication of the level of penalty that is likely to be accepted by the Board.

12.14 Practitioners should bear in mind that some officers do not give detailed consideration to each of the relevant steps when calculating the penalty considered due. Practitioners are advised to contact the officer to discuss penalty mitigation. When they do so, they should request a breakdown of the penalty loading, as set out in **Chapter 14**. If the officer has not fully thought out the penalty mitigation in this way, he may have no choice but to agree to a lower figure.

12.15 The penalty mitigation does not depend solely on the actions of the client. An inaccuracy by the agent, or delay by him, will count against the client as if it was him that was directly responsible for the inaccuracy or delay. However, where the taxpayer can establish that the inaccuracy relates to information supplied (or not supplied) by another person, and the taxpayer has taken reasonable care to check the information supplied (or not supplied) by the other person the taxpayer will not be liable to a penalty. Practitioners should note that the other person may be charged a penalty where they give the taxpayer false information, or withhold information from the taxpayer, with the intention of the taxpayer submitting a false document. Where the taxpayer

12.15 Settlement negotiations

suffers an adverse penalty loading because of an inaccuracy or delay by his advisor he may decide to seek compensation from the agent.

12.16 When considering the relevant penalty mitigation, the officer will consider any delays, etc from the time that the investigation started. That is why it is important for practitioners to prepare for their settlement negotiations at the start of an enquiry, by ensuring that the officer's reasonable requests are complied with without unnecessary delay. That does not mean that you agree to unreasonable demands, either in timescale or nature of information requested, by the investigator. Your client should not be penalised because you challenge an overzealous officer.

12.17 The practitioner needs to be particularly careful where he has taken over a case from another advisor. This situation can be fraught with difficulties for the new advisor, who should ensure that the client is fully aware of the seriousness of the position.

PAYMENTS ON ACCOUNT

12.18 Officers are instructed to ask for a payment on account in investigation cases. Making such a payment has two advantages for the client. It shows the officer that the client is treating the investigation seriously, and should assist when negotiating the penalty mitigation at the end of the enquiry. Secondly, it helps to mitigate the interest, accruing on a daily basis, where there has been an underpayment of tax. When a practitioner is aware that there are additional liabilities, he should recommend to his client that a payment on account is made.

12.19 During the course of an investigation further liabilities may become apparent, and the practitioner should recommend the making of such additional payments on account as are deemed necessary. If the client is not able to make a lump-sum payment, he should be advised to make monthly payments of such amount as he can afford. It should be noted that the client will not always make payments on account when recommended to do so by the practitioner. Some may prefer to wait until the settlement figure is known, and then arrange finance to meet the liability in full. It is imperative that the practitioner makes the recommendations regarding payments on account, and, preferably, puts them in writing, even where the client has stated that he will settle in full, so that he is protected against any claims from his client regarding the imposition of interest or an adverse penalty loading.

12.20 The officer's interest computation should be checked carefully. This is particularly important where payments on account have been made, or there are tax repayments due to the client, to ensure that the correct interest credit has been included.

12.21 For a sole trader or partnership, it is important to remember that an increase in the tax payable for years under enquiry will automatically increase the payments on account which should have been made for the following year(s) under TMA 1970, s 59A. Surcharges on late-paid tax for self-assessment years under TMA 1970, s 59C may also be included within contract settlements, but not where a tax-geared penalty has been charged on the same tax (TMA 1970, s 59C(4)).

VAT DISCLOSURE

12.22 Where there has been a disclosure made to the officer, it is extremely likely that there are VAT implications. The practitioner should consider the possibility of VAT irregularities, and make sure that appropriate action is taken. Although the Inland Revenue and HM Customs and Excise merged in April 2005, there are very few HMRC officers who are trained in both disciplines.

12.23 Until that time, it is advisable to put the VAT office on notice at an early stage in the investigation that there is a disclosure to be made. This should assist in minimising the penalty position in relation to the VAT offences. Final details of the irregularities can be provided when the settlement has been agreed with the officer. The VAT officer will usually accept adjustments based on the settlement figures with the officer. It should be borne in mind, that, where there are VAT implications, the figures agreed with the officer take this into account.

PROFESSIONAL COSTS

12.24 HMRC has set out its position regarding accountancy expenses arising out of self-assessment enquiries (EM 3981). Where the enquiry does not result in an addition to profits, or there is an adjustment to the profits for the year of enquiry only and that alteration does not arise as a result of a failure to take reasonable care or a deliberate understatement (negligent or fraudulent conduct in relation to periods covered by the old penalty regime) the additional accountancy expenses will be allowable.

12.25 In all other cases, ie where there has been a failure to take reasonable care or a deliberate understatement (fraudulent or negligent conduct in relation to periods covered by the old penalty regime), or there are adjustments for more than one year, the professional costs of dealing with an HMRC investigation are not allowable deductions for income tax or corporation tax purposes. Where the fees include work done in connection with ongoing compliance obligations, eg the preparation of accounts, or P35 completion, that element will be allowable in the normal way.

12.26 Where such costs may be allowable, they should be agreed with the officer during the settlement negotiations, rather than waiting until the next tax computation is submitted, when the practitioner's position is weaker.

12.27 When the client is VAT-registered, the VAT element can be reclaimed to the extent that it relates to the business. If the client is not billed separately for the work done on the business affairs and the personal tax affairs of its proprietor or directors, the VAT reclaimed must be restricted. Also, the appropriate entry must be made in the owner's drawings account. When dealing with a company, the relevant amount should be debited to the director's current account, or a benefit returned on form P11D, as appropriate.

WHY NEGOTIATE?

12.28 Some practitioners may query why they should negotiate with the officer. They should remember that the officer's role is to establish the amount of tax etc, to be paid by the client. The officer has various statutory powers to enable him to do his job. The practitioner's role is to obtain the best settlement for his client. This can usually be best achieved by negotiating the level of additional liabilities etc with the officer, rather than proceeding down a formal route. There are several practical reasons why it is advantageous for the advisor to reach a negotiated settlement, and these are considered below.

Reduce the length of the investigation period

12.29 If additional profits can be agreed between the officer and the practitioner, this should be quicker than the officer going down the formal route. Under this process, the officer issues a closure notice for self-assessment years (where there is an open enquiry), discovery assessments for other self-assessment years, and estimated assessments for pre-self-assessment years. The closure notice and, if issued, discovery and estimated assessments must be appealed against, with a subsequent hearing of the appeals before the First-tier Tribunal. This process takes time, and can add several months, if not longer, to the investigation period.

Finality for the client

12.30 A negotiated settlement gives the client finality, without the uncertainty of taking the case before the Tribunal.

Financial (professional fees)

12.31 Although there may be meetings or telephone conversations with the officer to reach a negotiated settlement, the time costs for the client should be cheaper than becoming embroiled in the time-consuming, and costly, process of assessments, appeals and Tribunal hearings.

Financial (tax, etc savings for the client)

12.32 The outcome of a negotiated settlement should be that both sides benefit. When reaching an agreement with the officer, without recourse to the formal route, the additions should be lower. This has the consequential effect that the tax, interest and penalty will be reduced, resulting in a lower overall settlement. The negotiated settlement will also be reflected in the penalty loading, the client enjoying higher mitigation because the officer has not had to use his formal powers to bring the investigation to a conclusion.

Finality for the practitioner

12.33 It should be remembered that handling an HMRC investigation is time-consuming for the accountant. This is particularly an issue for smaller firms of advisors. The practitioner has a duty to all his clients, not just those under enquiry, and the strain of dealing with only a handful of HMRC investigations, or one large one, can severely stretch the resources of the smaller practice. A practitioner in such a position should consider engaging the services of an investigation specialist.

What is negotiable?

12.34 As in any negotiating situation, when settling an investigation case, anything is potentially negotiable. The officer may say that he cannot give ground on a particular area because of, for example, case law, but the practitioner may be able to obtain a concession in another area.

12.35 The interest and penalty figures follow from the amount of tax due. It makes sense to start by considering how the level of tax can be mitigated. Where the additional tax arises from income, the practitioner should concentrate on minimising the figure for the year under enquiry, as this will determine whether the officer also seeks additions for earlier years, and, if so, for how many.

12.36 It may be possible to restrict the number of earlier years that the officer seeks additions for. Was there, for example, a change in the nature of the business that gave rise to the omissions starting? By reducing the level of additional income etc, the practitioner keeps the tax down, which will lead to lower interest and penalty. Where the enquiry has been ongoing for a number of years, the officer may also seek additions for later years. The comments above also apply to restricting any such additions sought by the officer.

12.37 The practitioner should explore all options when negotiating, including alternative treatments of particular items. Conceding that an item should be taxed under a different provision may result in more tax payable in relation to that aspect, but should not be dismissed if it leads to a lower settlement because of, for example, favourable penalty mitigation.

CONSIDERATION OF GREY AREAS

12.38 In most investigation cases, there will be three broad areas into which potentially taxable items fall. There will be those items that are agreed by both parties as being taxable; there will be certain items that are accepted as being non-taxable; and there will be those items that fall in between the first two categories.

12.39 Before accepting that an item is taxable, the practitioner should consider all available options. Although the client's case may not be absolute, the officer may be prepared to offer concessions. The practitioner should also be prepared to do the same, although he will be seeking to ensure that he gains more than he concedes!

12.40 There are various examples of grey areas: the distinction between income (liable to income tax) and capital (liable to CGT, or possibly not taxable

12.40 *Settlement negotiations*

at all) is a common area of difficulty. Protracted negotiations may be required to agree on the treatment of such items. The practitioner should be aware that different allowances, exemptions and reliefs may apply which reduce or eliminate the tax bill, or transfer liability from the client to someone else. A compromise solution can often be the best conclusion for both parties.

12.41 Tax avoidance schemes can be another area of complexity. The client may have implemented a strategy that is at the very edge of current tax understanding. Where HMRC has a contrary view it will challenge any such arrangements. HMRC is taking an increasingly aggressive view of avoidance, and has established specialist units within Specialist Investigations to deal with the more serious or complex cases.

12.42 It is often in the interest of both parties to reach a compromise settlement where there are complex technical issues. This avoids the need for lengthy, and costly, recourse to the legal process to obtain a definitive answer. Once the courts have given their decision, it is too late to negotiate a better settlement if that decision did not go in the client's favour.

LITIGATION AND SETTLEMENTS STRATEGY

12.43 HMRC introduced its litigation and settlements strategy (LSS) on 11 June 2007. Guidance sets out HMRC's principles for bringing tax disputes to a conclusion. A central theme of the LSS is seeking non-confrontational solutions 'where possible'. The LSS sets out the principles determining whether HMRC will litigate to resolve a case. HMRC anticipates that most of its discussions with taxpayers will not fall within the term 'dispute'. HMRC has recently updated its guidance notes on the LSS, which should make it easier for a negotiated settlement to be reached. Where there is a substantial and material difference of opinion about tax liabilities in a case, particularly where that difference will not be easily resolved, a practitioner should refer to the detail of the LSS (available on HMRC's website) for consideration as to how HMRC may proceed.

THE ART OF NEGOTIATION

12.44 An investigation settlement is no different in many respects to negotiating in other areas of life. Each side wants to win more than they lose. There are numerous publications available which detail negotiating skills, and here it is intended to give a few pointers relevant to tax investigations.

Negotiate

12.45 The first point to remember is that it is perfectly acceptable to negotiate. Tax investigations are contentious and adversarial arenas into which the practitioner is entering on behalf of his client. Some practitioners are wary of negotiating, especially where the officer's case seems cut and dried. It is the practitioner's duty to do whatever he legitimately can, within the law and the ethics of his profession, to seek to minimise the amount of tax, etc that his client has to pay.

12.46 If the practitioner is not comfortable with negotiating, he should seek specialist help for this part of the enquiry process – even if only for a second opinion as to the reasonableness of the officer's proposals, and the merit of the client's position.

Pitch at the right level

12.47 When starting discussions, the practitioner must ensure that his figures are not too high (from the client's point of view). It is inevitable that the opening figures will not be the final ones, so the practitioner should allow room for movement, and be prepared to make concessions from his starting position. The officer will always be looking for an increase on the opening figures, as he will be looking to maximise the position for HMRC.

12.48 With this in mind, the practitioner should work backwards from what he thinks will be the finishing position. It is important not to concede too much before negotiations begin as this will inevitably result in an unsatisfactory settlement figure. As well as dealing with the demands of the client, and managing his expectations, the practitioner must also take into account the officer's position in the negotiations.

How strong is the client's case?

12.49 When deciding where to pitch an offer, the practitioner must take into account the relative strengths and weaknesses of the client's case. Serious irregularities cannot be brushed aside, and must be taken into account in the negotiations. Where the issues concern highly technical matters, ambiguity over the taxability of transactions, etc, this should be brought to the officer's attention.

12.50 It should be remembered that the officer does not have the final say on the level of a settlement. The client can appear before the First-tier Tribunal to present his case, although the risks in taking the dispute there should be stressed. As the practitioner reviews the case, he should consider what view the Tribunal would make of the evidence available. This can help the practitioner to plan his dealings with the officer.

Consider the outcome

12.51 When negotiating with the officer, it is important that the practitioner has a clear idea of the best possible outcome, what he thinks will be the result, and the worst position that will be acceptable to the client. These positions may change during the course of the meeting, or several meetings, if the situation cannot be finalised in one session.

12.52 Discussions with the officer to finalise the additional liabilities may take place over the telephone or at a meeting. It is preferable for the client not to be present, so that you can concentrate on the issues. Thorough preparation is important, so that you know the strengths and weaknesses of your client's case.

12.53 *Settlement negotiations*

The officer is not the enemy

12.53 You should regard the officer as a partner, rather than as an enemy to be defeated. You may have to deal with the same officer in the future, and you do not want him to be seeking revenge for a previous 'defeat'. For the same reason, it makes sense not to say or do anything rash.

12.54 There are some practitioners who take great delight in 'bashing' HMRC. Others relish lengthy delays in dealing with correspondence from the officer and attach little priority to progressing enquiries. These types of attitude are not conducive to effective negotiation.

Agree on minor issues

12.55 If agreement cannot be reached on the level of additional profits, try to see if there are any areas that can be agreed, e g treatment of a particular receipt, or even the level of a private usage adjustment, and then return to the main area.

12.56 The best result is one when both sides are satisfied that the outcome is in their best interests and the best they could have achieved.

No two cases are the same

12.57 The practitioner should approach each settlement for what it is – a unique situation. You cannot treat each case the same because the facts will be different and you are dealing with an individual, the officer. There is no tried and tested formula that can be used in every case. Officers will react differently, depending on the approach taken.

Avoid premature concessions

12.58 After thorough preparation, and having assessed the relative strength of the client's case, the practitioner should not give concessions too soon, or too many. He should be prepared to stick by his arguments. Investigations are adversarial by nature, and the practitioner must be prepared to argue his side with the officer.

12.59 The practitioner should not be rushed into making concessions by the officer. The investigator is also under pressure to settle for the reasons mentioned earlier. If the practitioner gives in too easily, the officer may regard him as an 'easy touch' and may seek more concessions than he would otherwise do so. The practitioner should ensure that concessions are not given away; they should, if possible, be given in exchange for a concession by the officer.

Previous experience

12.60 Your settlement discussions should be planned, taking into account what you have learnt about the officer in your previous meetings and conversations with him. If you have been brought in at a late stage, and are meeting the officer for the first time, you will need to assess the officer at the meeting, and from whatever discussions you have had with him.

CLAIMS, ALLOWANCES AND RELIEFS

12.61 The re-opening of accounts and tax returns for earlier years provides an opportunity to make any claims that have been overlooked, or make claims to relief earlier than has been the case. Before starting negotiations with the officer, the practitioner should conduct a thorough review of the case to establish whether there are any potential claims, allowances or reliefs that should be made. This includes the ability to make claims that would otherwise be out of time.

12.62 The officer can be expected to challenge claims for expenses that are not supported by vouchers. Often, the officer can be persuaded to concede an allowance for some additional expenditure, depending on the circumstances of the case. The officer cannot resist a claim for additional expenditure where he is seeking additional profits that required, for example, additional materials, labour or fuel.

REMITTANCES BY NON-DOMICILED INDIVIDUALS

12.63 Wealthy non-domiciled individuals have long been a favourite target for officers. Often, there is considerable difficulty in identifying the source of funds remitted by non-domiciled individuals resident in the UK. The amounts involved can be substantial, and officers are aware of this. The practitioner is advised to undertake a thorough review of funds remitted, and the bank accounts from which the amounts were made, if appropriate, and establish the arguments that can be made. The officer will expect to see an audit trail, demonstrating the origin of the funds. Time spent by the practitioner will usually be worthwhile, because of the substantial sums often involved. Legislation, which came into effect from 6 April 2008, has reduced the risk represented by non-domiciled individuals to HMRC.

INNOCENT ERROR AND REASONABLE EXCUSE

12.64 Penalties will be due under FA 2007, Sch 24, para 1 where HMRC can establish that there is an inaccuracy in a tax return and the taxpayer failed to take reasonable care when completing that return or there was a deliberate inaccuracy in the return (The position was broadly the same under the old penalty regime, although the requirement was whether HMRC could establish fraudulent or negligent conduct – TMA 1970, s 95.) Failure to take reasonable care can be likened to the long-standing concept in general law of negligence – the failure to do what a reasonable person should recognise as his duty. A deliberate inaccuracy occurs when a person knowingly and intentionally gives HMRC an inaccurate document. HMRC will usually resist claims for penalty

12.64 *Settlement negotiations*

mitigation on the grounds of an innocent error or reasonable excuse; although it does recognise that there are situations when mitigation is appropriate. Practitioners should note that the HMRC officer does not have the final say as to what constitutes 'reasonable excuse', and there is always recourse to the Tribunal. Practitioners should consider carefully before proceeding to the Tribunal where there has been an accepted understatement of profits, and should consider seeking a second opinion on the strength of their client's position.

12.65 Where a person has a serious illness this would qualify as a reasonable excuse, and the officer will often be sympathetic. What the taxpayer would have to ensure is that he gets his tax affairs in order following recuperation. Few illnesses are so serious that a person is unable to instruct someone else to deal with matters on his behalf, or advise HMRC of the reason for the delay. The wording of TMA 1970, s 118(2) indicates that a 'reasonable excuse' defence will not protect a taxpayer who fails to take the necessary action once the 'excuse' has ceased to apply.

12.66 Ignorance of the law is not a defence, and would not qualify as a reasonable excuse. HMRC will not automatically accept that a person did not know that a receipt or transaction gave rise to a tax charge. The credibility of the excuse will depend on the complexity of the transaction, and the client's background and technical knowledge.

12.67 Where the amounts involved are anything other than minimal, it will be difficult to claim innocent error. If, however, the client was not aware of, for example, accumulated income from a trust where he was unaware that he was a beneficiary, he cannot be expected to include the details on his tax return.

12.68 Where the officer cannot establish that an inaccuracy by a person in a document was neither careless nor deliberate at the time the document was sent to HMRC, it will be treated as careless if the person discovers the inaccuracy at some later time and does not take reasonable steps to inform HMRC. There was a similar provision at TMA 1970, s 97 in relation to the old penalty regime.

ADVANTAGES FOR THE OFFICER

12.69 As with any negotiation situation, it is worthwhile considering the position from the other side – what's in it for the officer?

Time

12.70 The officer does not have the cost issues that the practitioner and his client need to consider. He can spend weeks, or even months, pursuing minor issues. What the investigator does have to consider is his portfolio of investigation cases. The process of issuing assessments or closure notices is a relatively straightforward task for the officer, with instructions usually passed to a clerical officer, although this can be onerous, particularly where numerous years are involved.

12.71 Although some officers relish the prospect of taking a case to the Tribunal, many more seek to avoid this route, unless absolutely necessary.

Preparing a case for the Tribunal is a labour-intensive and time-consuming process for the officer, even where responsibility for conducting the hearing is passed to one of HMRC's specialist Appeals Units. Most officers do not like the thought of, perhaps, weeks of intensive preparation, and will prefer to reach agreement by negotiation.

12.72 Remember that any 'without prejudice' offers will be withdrawn once formal proceedings have been commenced. Often, though, officers will be prepared to reach a negotiated settlement up to, and on, the date of the Tribunal hearing.

WORKLOAD

12.73 Although the practitioner may handle only a few investigations at any one time, the officer will often have a large portfolio of such cases. He is under pressure to settle cases, and register new ones. When your client's case is finished, he can move on to another taxpayer. A negotiated settlement gives him that opportunity far sooner than finalisation via the formal route.

WHEN AGREEMENT CANNOT BE REACHED

12.74 It is recognised that not every case can be settled by negotiation. There may be particular issues on which agreement cannot be reached, or there may be an intransigent officer who will not move from his unreasonable opening proposals. In these cases, there may be no alternative other than to go to the Tribunal, particularly if the officer in charge does not encourage his officer to adopt a conciliatory position.

12.75 The practitioner faced with this situation should still seek to agree as much as possible with the officer, so that it is only the contentious issues that have to be considered by the Tribunal. Details on presenting a case at the Tribunal are contained in **Chapter 11**.

12.76 Where there is an assessment under appeal, it should be noted that the officer can issue a further assessment even though the main assessment could be increased under the provisions of TMA 1970, s 50(7). The officer is likely to take this course of action where there is a substantially inadequate assessment under appeal and the client has not made a suitable payment on account. Case law has confirmed that the officer can raise a further assessment under TMA 1970, s 29(3) in these circumstances, see *Duchy Maternity Limited v Hodgson* [1985] STC 764.

THE SETTLEMENT PACKAGE

12.77 When considering what the best possible settlement for the client is, the answer will not usually rest only on the amount of tax to pay. The practitioner needs to consider the overall position and aim to get the most

12.77 *Settlement negotiations*

advantageous result for the client in the circumstances of the case. This will include a review of the following:

- the level of tax, interest and penalty;
- what amounts are included in the settlement (eg the officer may be persuaded to include non-investigation liabilities, effectively giving your client more time to pay);
- the funding of the settlement;
- the period of time to repay the liabilities;
- the level of forward interest charged by the officer in an instalment arrangement; and
- agreement from the officer on the future treatment of a contentious issue.

12.78 Often, the client is looking at the overall settlement package – what is it going to cost, and over what period does he have to repay HMRC – rather than a detailed consideration of the individual component parts (tax, interest, penalty, etc). Before embarking on negotiations with the officer, it is important that the practitioner discusses the situation with the client. The practitioner can ensure that he is aware of his client's expectations, and that they are reasonable.

12.79 The client must be made aware of the possible outcomes to the negotiations. It will usually be helpful to give the client the 'best-case' and 'worst-case' scenarios. This can help to stabilise the client's level of expectation about the settlement. The client should have been kept informed throughout the investigation process, and this practice should continue until the formalities have been finalised. The client needs to be able to make an informed decision about the level of offer to be made to HMRC.

12.80 During the negotiating process, there will be various proposals and counter-proposals. The practitioner should recognise when he has gained as many concessions as possible from the officer, taking into account materiality. There is no point continuing to negotiate where the saving to the client may only be a few hundred pounds in tax, etc when it costs him more than that in the advisor's time.

FUNDING THE SETTLEMENT AND TIME TO PAY

12.81 The advisor should discuss the client's means, and how he intends to repay HMRC. A person who has deliberately understated income for tax purposes does not usually make provision for the eventual settlement with HMRC. Banks and building societies are not always agreeable to lending funds to meet an investigation settlement. HMRC prefers to reach agreement about the level of settlement, rather than make a person bankrupt. Taking that course of action would result in them only obtaining a proportion of the money due, and they will, usually, reluctantly provide time to pay.

12.82 Practitioners should be aware that HMRC are taking a more robust stance with regard to settlement of liabilities. Bankruptcy is being pursued by HMRC more vigorously than two or three years ago. This course of action is a possible outcome if the client is unable to pay a significant proportion of the agreed liabilities. In the current financial climate, HMRC are adopting a realistic approach to the settlement of liabilities. The officer may be prepared to accept a lower figure than might normally be expected, although it will depend on the financial circumstances, and attitude, of the client.

12.83 If the client is not in a position to make a standard offer, the officer will seek a certified written statement of means. This will include details of all assets and liabilities (including those of his spouse and children or anyone to whom he has transferred assets), full details of current income and outgoings, and details of any likely changes in the following three to five years, for example, the maturing of an endowment policy, or impending retirement.

12.84 The officer will always want any liabilities settled as soon as possible, usually within 30 days of the acceptance letter (see below). During the course of an enquiry, the investigator will regularly request further payments on account, and ask the practitioner to ensure that any payments made reflect the additional liabilities established. At the end of the investigation, the officer will want HMRC to be repaid in full in the shortest possible time.

12.85 If the client is unable to make immediate payment, details of his current and future income will need to be established. The client's assets, and liabilities, will already have been identified, from the statement that the officer will have requested as part of the settlement process. The officer will not agree to a lengthy instalment arrangement if the client has substantial funds in a bank account, or, for example, several properties unencumbered by loans.

12.86 In cases where the client does not have sufficient funds to make immediate repayment of the settlement in full, an instalment arrangement must be considered. Repayments can be made over several months, or even years.

12.87 Officers are reluctant to accept instalment offers, particularly those extending beyond two years. An offer where there is a repayment period not exceeding three years can be agreed locally. A longer instalment period requires approval from HMRC's compliance division. Where an instalment arrangement is accepted, the officer will seek to apply forward interest for the duration of the repayment period. This should be included in the negotiations with the officer. He may agree not to charge forward interest for a period of time, perhaps three or six months.

12.88 The 'time to pay' aspect should not be overlooked when negotiating with the officer. The officer may agree to a period longer than 30 days for repayment to be made, and for this to be interest-free. That will depend on the amounts involved, and the negotiating skills of the practitioner. Readers should be aware that officers are, generally, taking a tougher stance in all matters relating to settlement, and that includes their position on any interest-free period.

12.89 HMRC's Enquiry Manual does not comment on the length of interest-free period that is acceptable. Practitioners should seek as long a period as possible, although the extent of any interest-free period granted will depend on the circumstances. A period of 60 to 90 days would not be unreasonable, or longer where the amount involved is substantial. The officer will need to be

12.89 *Settlement negotiations*

satisfied that the client needs further time to obtain funding for the settlement, and the client will be making a cash offer, rather than paying by instalments.

THE LETTER OF OFFER

12.90 Where settlement of an HMRC investigation is by negotiation, the agreement is set out in a written contract, called a 'letter of offer', submitted by the client, detailing the amount to be paid. Where the offer is agreed, HMRC sends the Board's formal acceptance letter, which creates a legally-binding contract with the client. In practice it would be unusual for an offer not to be accepted where agreement had been reached with the officer about the level of offer to be made. An acceptance letter may not be sent when the client has made a sub-standard offer (see below).

12.91 The payment terms are contained in the offer letter. The usual terms are that payment will be made within 30 days from the date of the acceptance letter. Where payment is to be made over a period of time, the offer letter sets out the date of the first and subsequent instalments. As mentioned above, the time granted will depend on several factors, including the practitioner's negotiating skills.

12.92 As with any contract, action can be taken if the terms are broken. The client must be made aware of the implications of, for example, failing to make an instalment payment, before he signs the offer letter. The officer will be reluctant to renegotiate the terms of a contract at a later date if, for example, future income does not meet the projected figure and the client is unable to meet both his obligations under the contract and his ongoing self-assessment liabilities. The practitioner should ensure that the settlement terms are reasonable, and that the client will be able to adhere to them.

12.93 Contract settlements will continue to be the normal way in which investigations are concluded. The process does not sit comfortably with the provisions of TMA 1970, s 28A(5) which requires the issue of a formal notice at the completion of an enquiry into a self-assessment return. The officer will not normally issue a completion notice where there is a contract settlement including 1996–97 and later years. The contract settlement provides finality in the investigation proceedings. The practitioner can seek a completion notice, if desired, although this may not give the client any additional protection.

MAKING SUB-STANDARD OFFERS

12.94 There may be a temptation to submit a sub-standard offer. This should be resisted. Once the level of a settlement has been agreed with the officer it would be unwise to submit an offer in a lower figure. If there are genuine reasons why the client cannot make a 'full' offer, this should be taken into account when negotiating with the officer, before submitting a formal offer. If a sub-standard offer is submitted it may be accepted, providing it is reasonably close to the expected offer, but the officer is likely to exercise extreme caution when negotiating with the practitioner on subsequent cases.

12.95 There may be exceptional circumstances where the submission of a sub-standard offer may be justified, for example, where the officer is intransigent, but it is not recommended that this is done as a matter of course.

SETTLEMENT MEETINGS

12.96 Most officers requested settlement meetings in the past. The purpose of the meeting was for the client to sign the letter of offer, and, usually, for the officer to deliver a moral lecture on tax evasion. Now, most settlements, particularly in smaller cases, are dealt with by correspondence. The officer accepts an assurance that the significance of the various documents signed by the client (offer letter, statement of assets, certificate of bank accounts operated and certificate of full disclosure) has been explained by the practitioner. It is important that the advisor does this in unequivocal terms to the client, in writing, to ensure that he fully appreciates the seriousness of the situation.

12.97 The dangers of signing an incomplete statement of assets or certificate of full disclosure, ie the possibility of criminal proceedings by HMRC, should be stressed to the client. Often, at this late stage in the investigation, the client may disclose additional assets. Although the officer will not be impressed by late disclosure of further assets or sources of income, and this can impact on the penalty mitigation, it is preferable to the client signing an incomplete statement or certificate and being prosecuted.

12.98 Although a settlement interview may be requested, particularly in larger cases, there is no statutory obligation on your client to attend such a meeting. If a formal meeting is held, it is important that the client is fully briefed beforehand. The client should be advised merely to listen to the officer, and sign the documentation when requested.

12.99 The practitioner should be aware that the meeting is not for the benefit of the client, but provides the officer with an opportunity to give the client a rap on the knuckles and warn him about his future conduct. The practitioner should ensure that any debate about, for example, the level of penalty, is agreed before the settlement meeting. At the meeting the client only has to listen, and sign the relevant documentation (which should have been checked in advance by the practitioner).

RELATIONSHIP WITH THE OFFICER

12.100 It is important for the practitioner to establish a good rapport with the officer conducting the investigation. A frosty relationship with the officer will not be helpful when it comes to negotiating a settlement. It is equally important that the relationship does not become 'cosy'. What is desired is a healthy professional respect between the officer and the practitioner.

12.101 If the advisor does not know the officer from previous dealings with HMRC, he should endeavour to establish a rapport at an early stage of the investigation. The following steps can help to achieve this:

12.101 *Settlement negotiations*

- agree the work to be done by the practitioner at the beginning of the investigation;
- carry out the work agreed, within an approved realistic timescale, or keep the officer informed of any unforeseen delays;
- use the telephone, email (where the officer has the facility) or meetings to make progress, rather than lengthy letters, particularly those of a legalistic nature, which tend to prompt replies of similar length and style;
- comply with reasonable requests for information or documentation by the officer, or be prepared to say why certain items are not considered reasonable or relevant to the investigation; and
- adopt an appropriate tone in correspondence – some practitioners adopt an unnecessarily aggressive stance, which is not conducive to establishing a good rapport with the officer.

RELATIONSHIP WITH THE CLIENT

12.102 The relationship with the client can be fraught with difficulty during a HMRC investigation. If the practitioner has acted for the client for many years, there can be a sense of betrayal when it emerges that the client has been guilty of irregularities. The advisor can also feel disappointed that he did not identify the misdemeanours when preparing the accounts. These thoughts must be banished from the practitioner's mind if he is to best represent his client at this difficult time. Often, particularly in large or complex cases, investigation specialists are engaged to deal with HMRC; the client is then handed back to the practitioner 'clean'.

12.103 Clients will want different things from their advisors during the investigation. They will all want, initially, to be spared from criminal proceedings. Their priority then shifts to a desire for the settlement cost to be as low as possible. Some clients will let the practitioner get on with his job without much contact other than to supply information or records. Others want to know all the detail of the discussions with the officer. Whatever level of detail the client wants, it is imperative that the practitioner makes the client aware of the seriousness of the situation, and the implications where irregularities have been discovered.

12.104 Some clients may try to bury their head in the sand and ignore the consequences of their actions. The practitioner should ensure that his client is not in the dark about the final outcome. The advisor is not doing the client, or himself, any favours in withholding details of the case until presenting the officer's settlement proposal – particularly where the amounts sought are substantial. This can only create difficulties for the practitioner, both in settling the case with the officer and tarnishing the relationship with the client.

12.105 The client should be kept fully informed during the progress of the investigation, and made aware of his options, if any, at a particular stage of the case. Some clients will want to fight all the way, and may seek their 'day in court'; others will take a commercial view and want the investigation concluded as soon as possible, almost regardless of cost. The practitioner needs to deal with both extremes, and every position in between, but must act in accordance with his client's instructions.

12.106 Much of the advice on handling clients is common sense, and good case management. Dealing with the client should extend to billing arrangements. Although the client may normally receive one bill a year, following preparation of the accounts, it is recommended that practitioners bill monthly during an investigation. Time spent in dealing with the officer's enquiries can be substantial. There is a better prospect of recovery where monthly bills are issued, rather than one large bill issued at the end of a lengthy investigation.

12.107 The effect of an investigation on a client should not be underestimated. Even with the practitioner acting as a buffer between the client and the officer, the strain can be immense. There will be a tremendous pressure on the client's business and personal affairs. The practitioner should watch for signs that the stress is taking its toll on the client.

12.108 The penalty mitigation process should be explained to the client. The practitioner should highlight the arguments that can be used to mitigate the penalty. He should also mention any areas of weakness that the officer will use to argue for a higher penalty. The client may come up with further arguments, and should be encouraged to do so.

12.109 Handling the client during an investigation can be as demanding as the negotiations with the officer. With thorough preparation, a good understanding of the relative strengths and weaknesses of the client's case, and an appreciation of the officer's position, the practitioner will be best placed to negotiate the obstacles in his way during the investigation and achieve a successful conclusion.

Chapter 13

Employees and directors

Alastair Kendrick

Tax Director, Mazars LLP

SCOPE OF CHAPTER

13.01 The review of employees and directors used to be carried out by a number of different Revenue agencies. These have now been refocused to form Employer Compliance Units, who can be expected to cover both the tax and the NIC implications of both salary and benefits paid to employees and directors. At the present time we are seeing HMRC deciding how employer compliance reviews will be conducted, with this aspect now involving a relationship manager within HMRC for the employer. With the introduction of the new penalty rules there is greater reliance on voluntary disclosure by employers who find that they have not complied fully with the rules. The main exception to this single focus is Special Civil Investigation Office, which may become involved in serious cases.

13.02 HMRC have been considering for some time how they manage employer compliance activity in the future. We are seeing HMRC employing far less traditional auditors and their approach to be risk based and centred on the new world of self compliance. Whilst the picture for the larger corporates seem to be totally centred on this aspect which is managed by the inspector responsible for that company within the Large Business Service (LBS) we still await clarification as to whether a similar approach is to be adopted to those employers who do not fall within the LBS.

13.03 The purpose of this chapter is to look specifically at the points which an audit or investigation team may raise in respect of employee/director tax issues. It aims to identify those points which are most vulnerable to challenge and, where possible, it suggests how such challenges can be best dealt with. It cannot cover all areas and in particular does not attempt to deal with the tax rules applicable only to certain occupations, such as those of footballers, divers and farm-workers. In general, directors are swept up in the category of 'higher paid employees' although when a particular point is relevant to directors only, this is identified.

13.04 *Employees and directors*

13.04 Another chapter of this work covers the penalties and interest which HMRC may charge following a review of employee tax issues. The way negotiations should in general be conducted is also separately dealt with, and this chapter will thus only identify those negotiation points which are specific to employees and directors. Self-assessment is also dealt with elsewhere although where this has a significant impact on PAYE/ Schedule E tax compliance, it is referred to briefly in this chapter. The review requirements relating to certain National Insurance contributions, (NICs) are covered elsewhere in this book, but the NIC treatment of payments and benefits is also mentioned here, where appropriate.

INTRODUCTION

13.05 As is well known, an employee is taxable on all 'emoluments' from his or her employment (ITEPA 2003, s 6 and 7). Emoluments are defined to include 'all salaries, fees, wages, perquisites and profits whatsoever' (ITEPA 2003, ss 10(2), 62(2)). Emoluments may include payments from third parties.

13.06 National Insurance contributions (NICs) are payable on 'earnings'. This is similar to the HMRC definition of emoluments, and now includes most benefits in kind.

13.07 In order to review compliance with the tax legislation, HMRC have broad authority to examine records held by the employer. These include:

- copies of P9Ds and P11Ds;
- P46s;
- petty cash records;
- expense claims;
- cash book/purchase ledger/cheque requisition records;
- timesheets and clock cards;
- tachographs;
- cheque book stubs; and
- bank statements.

It should be noted that at the time of updating the chapter HMRC are consulting over the introduction of a new PAYE/National Insurance procedure which requires the reporting of earnings with tax and National Insurance deducted to be accounted for on a 'real time' reporting basis. This if introduced will enable HMRC to ensure that the correct tax and National Insurance is being accounted for. In addition, it will ensure that the correct levels of tax credits are being paid. The proposed changes will mean that many of the existing procedures will be obsolete and replaced with the sole requirement to provide regular payroll information. If these changes happen they will seriously change the reviews which will be conducted by HMRC.

13.08 In addition such powers extend to enable HMRC to ensure the following aspects have been correctly dealt with:

- minimum wage;
- student loan repayment;
- tax credits.

13.09 They will in addition wish to carry out what is called a 'payroll cleanse' which is to ensure that the employer is using the correct National Insurance number for the employee. Whilst this review is voluntary it is sensible to permit it to be undertaken, given there is the threat in that the rules may at some point be changed which would enable penalties to be imposed for the use of an incorrect NI number.

13.10 It is the inspection of these records which allows HMRC to check both compliance with the PAYE regulations and the more general rules for the taxation of benefits. The appropriate application of National Insurance (NI) is likely also to be reviewed. The way HMRC carries out compliance checks changed at April 2009. This change is said by HMRC to make the arrangement simpler and more consistent. The legislation is set out at Sch 36 of the Finance Act 2008.

13.11 This chapter analyses the review/investigation approach into four main areas:

- compliance with the PAYE regulations;
- directors;
- Schedule E benefits; and
- liability for tax arising.

PAYE COMPLIANCE ISSUES

13.12 The overall reason for reviewing PAYE records is to ensure that the correct amount of PAYE and NICs has been deducted from the earnings of the employees and directors of the business. This requires that the company has:

- deducted PAYE and NICs from all relevant payments;
- calculated the correct amount of PAYE and NICs;
- included all employees and directors on the payroll.

13.13 It is in the employer's interest that these areas are regularly reviewed, either by in-house specialists or an external adviser, so as to ensure that an HMRC visit will not produce unwelcome and expensive surprises. It is recommended that the employer apply for appropriate dispensations and make himself aware of any working rule agreements (WRAs) applicable to his industry.

13.14 If the company is conducting any pre-review or check, it is worth noting that HMRC standard procedures require them to question those responsible for completing wages and similar records. Similar discussions should be conducted by the internal review team. It is common to find, in the course of such a review, that the procedures actually being carried out in practice are not exactly as management imagine.

13.15 The employer should also not forget that HMRC officials carrying out a PAYE or Schedule E review are under instructions to keep their eyes open for any indications that the employer has been deliberately evading tax. This includes VAT for example; the HMRC team will then introduce colleagues responsible for those areas.

13.16 *Employees and directors*

13.16 The following are some review points relevant to employee/director issues:

- Does the workforce on the books look like the workforce on the premises?
- Are there indications of shiftwork (and possibly an additional workforce paid through a second set of books)?
- Does the business look prosperous?
- Have there been any recent improvements or alterations to the premises?
- Is the apparent lifestyle of directors in keeping with the level of remuneration?
- Are any directors paid less than employees?
- Do the directors control the wages records and payments?
- Is the wages clerk related to the directors?
- Are cash wages paid?
- Are significant round sum payments made? (Even if it seems reasonable that these represent genuine business expenditure, large amounts paid without supporting documentation point to a lack of control.)
- Is there a large casual wages charge (ie large relative to the size of the business)?
- Are wages paid to domestic staff or gardeners?
- Do spouses or other relatives receive excessive wages?
- Is there the opportunity to earn extra income?
- If the main income is by cheque, is there a subsidiary business generating cash?
- Are the directors personally in control of cash/petty cash/chequebooks?
- Is there a poor system of cash control?
- Are there cash takings where you would not expect them?
- If there is a high level of cash takings, is it all banked?
- Is cash in hand kept at a steady level or does it fluctuate?
- What was the cash in hand figure at the beginning and end of the year?
- Are the records inaccurate, not up to date, written up after a period from memory and not from vouchers and receipts?
- How often is the cash book balanced?
- Is personal expenditure paid by the business?
- Is the expenditure not supported by receipts or vouchers?
- Is there evidence of altered or false invoices, that is where Special Civil Investigation Office (previously Special Compliance Office (SCO)) have not taken up the case?
- Are unusual benefits provided (eg yachts, caravans, holiday homes, trips abroad, fines paid, school fees, upkeep of animals, prizes awarded by third parties)?
- Are round sum entertaining expenses paid?
- Are any company vehicles rarely used for business (including those used by relatives)?

13.17 If the employer is using a computerised payroll system (or if this is outsourced to a third-party payroll provider) the Revenue team will be interested to know the particular system and what security is in place over the overrides to the system. One area looked at would be payroll parameter reports which show that payments made through the system are dealt with for income tax and National Insurance. They will also be interested to ascertain who is authorised to override electronic systems and what exception reports are then generated. Is the system kited? This means have HMRC carried out the appropriate checks of the payroll software and satisfied themselves that the calculations it performs are correct?

13.18 As well as a review of employment taxes being the trigger for an investigation of other areas, the reverse can also be true. When HMRC review business accounts they are instructed to consider whether costs in the profit and loss account may point to PAYE irregularities. Such costs may include:

- payments to casuals;
- commissions, fees, or consultancy payments;
- wages payments where there is no evidence of a PAYE scheme; and
- suspiciously large items which may conceal additional payments to employees or uncertified subcontractors.

13.19 In particular, whenever a close company is investigated for whatever reason, the official is required to review the company's compliance with its PAYE obligations.

Subjecting earnings to PAYE/NICs

13.20 As has been stated above, not all emoluments are within the scope of PAYE and/or NICs. Even a cursory overview shows up significant differences in tax and NIC treatment, despite recent attempts at greater alignment of the two systems. Some particular points to note are set out below.

Round sum allowances

13.21 These are allowances paid to an employee whether or not he spends them in a particular way. As such they are taxable and subject to NICs (*Fergusson v Noble* (1919) 7 TC 176). However, where an allowance is set at a level which is simply intended to reimburse the employee's actual expenditure for 'a specific and distinct business expense', it will not be regarded as a 'round sum allowance'. Ideally such flat rate payments, eg for travel or subsistence, should be discussed with the local inspector in advance and a dispensation agreed. HMRC published set rates which they consider to be reasonable. Whilst it is not necessary to comply with these rates if the payment exceeds the amount set, HMRC would want to be satisfied that the amounts paid do not give rise to a profit in the hands of the employee. HMRC are expected to announce international rates in April 2011.

13.22 Where there is no dispensation, and *an audit review* identifies the payments, the employer should see how far he can establish that his allowances were a reasonable estimate of actual necessary expenditure incurred by employees in performing their duties and seek to exclude this from the settlement. It will be the practice of HMRC to ensure that the specific

13.22 *Employees and directors*

arrangements in place for payment of round sums, which had been disclosed when the dispensation was agreed, is being followed.

Sick pay

13.23 Sick pay paid to employees is generally within the scope of PAYE. Exceptions do occur, eg where sick pay is provided by a third party after an employment has ceased, or when an employee has contributed to a sickness insurance scheme. In the latter case only the part of the sick pay attributable to the employer's contribution, if any, attracts PAYE and NICs (SE 1340).

Tips and service charges

13.24 This is an area in which we have seen significant interest over recent years and the approach of HMRC change. The position is now set out in booklet E24 which clarifies that there is little change from the historical position save that where the employer is using tips to form part of the minimum wage of the employee then National Insurance arises on these irrespective of how the tips are paid.

13.25 Tips paid in cash to the employee or into a communal pool are taxable as earnings from the employment, and may be subject to PAYE and NICs, depending on the role of the employer. The table below summarises the position (ECM 13203; CWG2 (1998) 29).

Employer decides basis of distribution	*Employer distributes tips*	*Employer to deduct/ account for:*
Yes	Yes	PAYE/NICs
Yes	No	NICs
No	Yes	PAYE

13.26 Service charges are more complex. Where employees receive a share of the service charge made by the employer to customers, the employer must *always* account for NICs (CWG2 (1998) 28).

13.27 However, PAYE has to be deducted by the person responsible for distributing the service charge to employees. This may not be the employer, but may, for example, be the bar steward or head waiter (Income Tax (Employments) Regulations 1993, reg 5). Such an arrangement is generally known as a tronc. Where the troncmaster has been found not to operate PAYE satisfactorily, the principal employer can be made responsible, but only for future amounts (reg 3). The troncmaster is still responsible for amounts underpaid in the past. However, it is true to say that in such cases an auditor will look very carefully at the arrangements to see if the troncmaster was genuinely independent of the employer. It is in my experience rare for anyone to be willing to take on the responsibility of running the tronc and when they fully understand the implications of this role they resign.

In a recently introduced note HMRC have made the point that it is essential that the employee is earning in excess of the minimum wage without account taken of any tips.

Remuneration in non-cash form

13.28 Over recent years a number of schemes have sought to avoid NICs and PAYE by paying remuneration other than in cash, e g by using gold bullion, coffee beans or fine wines. However, successive anti-avoidance legislation has sought to prevent the use of such devices. HMRC have also had some success when challenging schemes before the courts, see *DTE Financial Services Ltd v Wilson* [1999] STC 1061 and *NMB Holdings v Secretary of State* which was heard on 14 July 2000. Whether a particular method or asset is caught may thus depend on the years for which it was in force and the case law position. See Revenue Press Release 18 May 1999 for treatment of interest on NICs found to be overdue as a result. The remaining areas will be covered within the disclosure rules.

13.29 There have been a number of methods used to provide bonuses to employees without the requirement to apply PAYE or National Insurance at the time of the award. These have largely been the subject of HMRC scrutiny and in many cases it is not possible for the payer of the bonus to receive any tax relief for the payments made until the PAYE and National Insurance is settled. The most popular route adopted in this area was the payment of the bonus via an employee benefit trust (EBT). It is generally the case that HMRC in discovering such an arrangement in place will refer the matter to a specialised team to consider. It is essential that payments passed into an EBT were not contractually entitled to be paid to the employee and that they sacrificed their rights to the remuneration to be paid into the EBT. This is an aspect which HMRC will wish to consider.

At the time of updating this chapter HMRC have issued new rules which aim at catching 'disguised remuneration'. These rules are expected to be introduced in April 2011. There are however anti-forestalling provisions which apply in the period 5 December 2010 to 5 April 2011. These rules are very widely drafted and will catch a significant number of employer-related arrangements. Whilst there is still discussion over the exact extent of the restrictions which this proposed legislation will impact upon, it is clear that it will attract EBT arrangements, some share scheme arrangements and some other forms of remuneration arrangement when payments or benefits are provided by one group company to another. Clearly it will be important to see after the current round of consultation what changes are introduced by this legislation when it beomes law.

Terminations

13.30 A pre-audit review should also check that any termination payments have been correctly included for PAYE purposes. While it is widely known that there is an exemption for the first £30,000 of a termination payment (ITEPA

13.30 *Employees and directors*

2003, s 403) this does not apply to every payment made on cessation of an employment, and a single lump sum may be composed of a number of different amounts. Points to note are set out below.

Contractual payments

13.31 HMRC will seek to tax any termination payment, which is contractual. They have sought to tax termination payments both where the contract provided explicitly for such a payment, and where there was an expectation that such a payment would be made. In the latter situation HMRC argue that the payment is an implied contract term. This situation was the subject of the case of *SCA Packaging Ltd v HMRC* and also the subject of a *Tax Bulletin* 63. We are still seeing HMRC paying significant interest in the arrangements of the employer and whether there is clear evidence of a pattern over how such payments are dealt with. If it is, for instance, customary for the employer to not permit employees into work following their termination to serve out any notice period, then it is possible HMRC will argue that the case of *SCA Packaging Ltd v HMRC* is in point and their pay for this period is taxable. It is therefore very important for an employer to ensure that PILON'S cannot be considered contractual on grounds of custom.

13.32 NICs are also sought on contractual amounts, and the same comments apply. However, with NICs there is an extra point: the employer should also resist any attempt to charge NICs on any redundancy payment, as such payments are specifically excluded from NIC liability.

Payments in lieu of notice (PILONs)

13.33 The HMRC view of contractual payments extends to PILONs (*Tax Bulletin* 24 August 1996). If a PILON is contractual, HMRC will seek to exclude it from ITEPA 2003, s 403. HMRC's view was supported in *EMI Group Electronics Ltd v Coldicott* [1999] STC 803. However, in this case, the Revenue accepted that payments in lieu of notice to junior employees were not taxable emoluments, since the employees had no contractual right to them.

Restrictive covenants

13.34 HMRC have also sometimes sought to argue that part or all of the termination payment is in respect of a restrictive covenant and therefore taxable (ITEPA 2003, s 225). However, HMRC significantly reduced the scope and believe these only to be of relevance if the payment being made is a restriction on the employee, which is not specified in their employment contract. Where a restrictive covenant would apply, the employer should seek to apportion the payment being made to apportion the covenant and the balance.

Dismissals

13.35 There have also been attempts to argue that s 403 is only applicable to redundancies, and not, for example, where someone is dismissed. There are no grounds for this restrictive interpretation within the very broad wording of the section:

> 'This section applies to any payment (not otherwise chargeable to tax) which is made, whether in pursuance of any legal obligation or not, either directly or indirectly in consideration or in consequence of, or otherwise in connection with, the termination of the holding of the office or employment or any change in its functions or emoluments.'

Retirement

13.36 A further line of HMRC attack has been on payments made to individuals nearing retirement. They have sought to argue that the termination payment is in effect a non-approved retirement benefits scheme, which would make it taxable (ITEPA 2003, s 394). This should be resisted as it is difficult to believe that a court would agree with the Revenue, and it is doubtful whether HMRC would be prepared to take such a case to court.

13.37 If this point is raised by HMRC it should be noted that in particular the termination of employment because of redundancy or inefficiency is frequently referred to as 'early retirement' even though the employee has been deprived of his employment prematurely, often against his wishes. In both these situations, any ex-gratia lump sum paid by the employer should not be regarded as chargeable. This is so even if the employee also becomes entitled, at the time of termination, to immediate pension benefits from the employer's approved superannuation scheme.

Continuing benefits

13.38 On termination some employees are provided with continuing benefits, such as the use of a company car or a beneficial loan. New rules were introduced by FA 1998, s 58 which rewrote TA 1988, s 148 (ITEPA 2003, s 403) and they were further explained in a *Tax Bulletin* article (September 1998). These rules apply to payments received after 5 April 1998, unless the sums were already taxed in earlier years. It is necessary to monitor the benefits provided to former employees and to report these at the end of the tax year. Since the changes to the pension rules there is a significant change in approach to benefits provided to retired employees

Employment termination settlements

13.39 The HMRC view of continuing benefits pre-FA 1998 is explained in the HMRC press release dated 17 March 1997: 'Taxation of Benefits received after the Year of Termination'. This press release also describes special arrangements available for employment termination agreements entered into from 6 April 1996. These special arrangements offer taxpayers a simpler

13.39 *Employees and directors*

approach to taxing such continuing benefits. A *Tax Bulletin* article (June 1997) further expands on the issues involved.

13.40 Employers who are attacked under the continuing benefits rules for these years are advised to read the Press Release and *Tax Bulletin*. However, despite the detailed arguments set out therein by the Revenue, it is arguable that continuing benefits which cannot be transferred have no market value and thus were not assessable. The only reported case on the point is *George v Ward* [1995] STC (SCD) 230 (Sp C 30), when the taxpayer lost the argument that there was no tax to pay on a continuing benefit. It was, however, held that tax should be charged by reference to the period for which the benefit was actually made available rather than for the longer period set out in the termination agreement. If *George v Ward* is raised by HMRC in support of their taxation of continuing benefits, they should be reminded that it is merely a Special Commissioner's case, and thus does not create a binding precedent. It is also the view of many tax advisers that it was wrongly decided.

13.41 Since ITEPA 2003, s 403 only applies where an item is 'not otherwise chargeable to tax', but the Revenue official may argue that certain continuing benefits cannot form part of the £30,000. Targets include gifts of assets, taxable under ITEPA 2003, s 203, and loan write-offs, taxable under ITEPA 2003, s 188. Such problems could be avoided if the employee was given the cash which was then used to buy the asset at its market value, or to repay the loan. If this route was not taken, and the official seeks to argue that the amounts are taxable, reference should be made in the HMRC press release of 17 March 1997 which clearly suggests that both cars and loans can fall within the £30,000.

13.42 Where the 'continuing benefit' is a small regular gift, such as a Christmas box to pensioners, the employer could argue that, if it is taxable at all, it should be exempted.

Other issues

13.43 Terminations are complex and are occurring with increasing frequency. Their cumulative cost and the value of the tax-free amounts are significant, and thus can be expected to draw an inspector's attention. In addition to the points raised above, other relevant issues arise where:

- The employee has been made redundant and then subsequently re-employed. The inspector will review such cases to ensure that the redundancy was genuine at the time it was made.
- The employee has 'retired', received a lump sum from his pension tax free, and then been re-employed. In these cases the Pension Schemes Office may challenge the tax-free status of the lump sum and may even threaten the qualifying status of the pension scheme itself. For a discussion of this issue, see Adrian Waddingham's article in *Taxation*, 18 May 2000. Therefore, it is important to demonstrate that there has been a genuine cessation of employment, with a re-employment on wholly different terms. It may be worth consulting an employment lawyer.

- The employee is given 'garden leave', ie continues to receive his salary but is not required to report to the office. This is taxable under Schedule E in the normal way.
- The employee has spent some time abroad. In this case a higher amount can be paid tax free; if he or she is retiring through ill health, there is no £30,000 limit (ITEPA 2003, s 413).

Salary sacrifice arrangements

13.44 A salary sacrifice is an arrangement under which the employee agrees to take a cut in future remuneration in exchange for some other benefit, such as an increased employer contribution to the employee's pension fund. It is becoming very common to use salary sacrifice to avoid the employer National Insurance and to pass on some savings in employee National Insurance to the employee. It is the case that HMRC are keen to ensure that the rules around salary sacrifice are observed and difficulties with compliance can prove expensive.

13.45 An HMRC official may check a sample of such salary sacrifices to ensure that they:

- are in writing, signed and dated;
- stating clearly that the employee is varying his or her right to remuneration; and
- are not retrospective.

13.46 Failure in any respect will mean that HMRC will view the sacrifice as ineffective, so that the employee remains entitled under his contract to the originally sacrificed amount and should thus have been taxed on it. The NIC implications will follow, plus a possible over-funding of the pension scheme if the re-categorised amount takes the employee above his contribution limit.

13.47 There are special rules relating to life changing circumstances. HMRC have given guidance of what significant lifestyle changes warrant an early exit from a salary sacrifice arrangement. HMRC at the time of any review will want to be satisfied that those who have exited early from a salary sacrifice had circumstances, which they would consider to fall within their guidance.

HMRC have issued significant guidance on what they consider is essential to meet the qualifying conditions for a salary sacrifice arrangement. The HMRC guidance makes clear that the arrangement, which must be available to 'all employees', must not discriminate against employees who for instance cannot obtain credit, ie employees below the age of 18. In addition, in respect of the 'bike to work' scheme, the price at which the bike is transferred to the employee at the end of the hire period must represent market value. HMRC have issued guidance over what they consider that value to be. From April 2011 the provision of canteen meals using salary sacrifice is stopped.

13.48 *Employees and directors*

Calculation of the correct amounts of PAYE/NICs

13.48 In these days of computerised PAYE, it is often thought that calculation errors are unlikely to occur. This is not the case, although some of the errors occur not because of the system itself but through faulty inputs – the 'garbage in, garbage out' principle. Particularly vulnerable are PAYE systems which are supplied with information from more than one source, such as two or more departments or subsidiaries. As part of any *pre-audit* review some mechanical checks on the operation of the system are therefore useful. HMRC's review will make similar checks. Some areas where the wrong amounts may be erroneously brought into the calculation are set out below.

Timing of taxing the earnings

13.49 Specific rules exist to establish when earnings are taxable, and these are different for employees and directors. Employees are taxable on the earlier of receipt and entitlement (ITEPA 2003, s 10). Particular care needs to be taken with bonus payments and commission.

13.50 The special rules for the taxing of directors' remuneration are likely to be checked by HMRC. The remuneration is taxable on the earliest of:

- receipt of the emoluments;
- entitlement to the emoluments;
- determination of the emoluments; or
- crediting the emoluments to an account with the company.

13.51 It is the fourth of these which most commonly gives problems, because companies do not always realise that the account in question does not have to be the director's own account. A credit in the company's salaries account is enough, or a written note in a minute book. Neither does a restriction (a 'fetter') on drawing out the money prevent the credit from being regarded as remuneration (TA 1988, s 203A(1)(c)), although in such cases there are no NICs until payment is made. Companies should also be aware that 'director' includes a shadow director (TA 1988, s 202B(6)). However, the company should note that to be taxable:

- the entry must identify the director, and
- it must be for an emolument. In particular, an accounts provision which has not been agreed, or remuneration which is contingent on the happening of some future event, is not an emolument.

(SE 5351)

13.52 Inspectors will review this area by:

- asking if any directors' remuneration has been deferred;
- paying particular attention, when examining records, to any annual fees, bonuses, etc and establishing the date on which they should have been subject to PAYE.

13.53 There are also special NIC rules for directors, under which the earnings period is a year rather than a month or a week (their regular earnings period). This has the effect of accelerating the payment of NICs. These rules were softened by s 49 of the Social Security Act 1998. Directors may now pay primary contributions for 11 months as if they were employees, with a recalculation and 'catch-up' payment in month 12 if necessary. Failures in earlier periods are often treated leniently by auditors as long as the correct amount of NICs has been paid in the tax year. However, problems can arise with directors who leave in the year.

13.54 This is an area often overlooked by payroll departments especially when using electronic payrolls. This special rule does, however, only apply to statutory directors and not those who simply carry the title of 'director'.

13.55 With effect from April 2010 it is proposed that interest and penalties can be sought from an employer if income tax or National Insurance is not paid on time. At this point in time we wait to see how these proposed changes will apply. **[QUERY: Does this text need to be updated?]**

New employees

13.56 Sometimes the first month's salary is paid by cheque whilst the administrative arrangements to include the employee on the payroll are in process. Ensure that any such payments are included in PAYE pay.

NICs, SSP, SMP issues

13.57 The cost of errors in these areas, and particularly in employer's NICs, can be substantial. HMRC will check that these amounts have been correctly calculated for a sample of employees. The accuracy of the following may be reviewed:

- any non-standard calculations, such as reduced rate NICs and small employer's relief for SSP;
- contracted-out amounts;
- National Insurance contributions;
- SMP amounts paid and the amounts offset against NICs due – the SMP rules are complex and in general less well supported by either computer systems or trained staff than PAYE. For employers with relatively low numbers of women on maternity leave, the cost of errors in this area may be small, but for organisations with large female workforces it may be worth checking that the rules are understood and being operated correctly;
- correct application of the NIC aggregation rules.

13.58 One important point for employers is the limited scope they have to collect under-deductions of NICs from employees. Such sums can only be recovered if they occur in the current tax year; if later, the cost is purely one for the employer.

13.59 *Employees and directors*

Payroll giving schemes

13.59 If the company is operating a payroll giving scheme, the inspector will ask to see:

- the employer's contract with the approved agency;
- form CHY 140(1) if for a period prior to 2000 (form abolished by FA 2000, s 38);
- the employer's written authority to make deductions from the employees' pay.

13.60 He will also check that:

- PAYE is being operated on a 'net pay' basis but that NICs are calculated on the true gross pay;
- for years before 2000–01, that the deductions are within the maximum annual limit (the annual limit was abolished by FA 2000, s 38); and
- the company has paid the donations to the agency within 14 days of the end of the income tax month in which they were deducted.

Third parties

13.61 Where a cash payment, such as a round sum allowance, is paid as a reward in connection with an individual's employment, the paying company has to deduct PAYE. This is because of ITEPA 2003, s 684.

13.62 An 'employer' is defined as 'any person paying emoluments'. This means that PAYE obligations may stretch more widely than is sometimes presumed. It should, however, be noted that the client is not liable for the NICs on these payments. For the position of benefits paid to third parties see **13.162–13.164** below.

Including all employees and directors on the payroll

13.63 Ensuring that all employees are correctly included on the payroll is a key audit task. HMRC will look particularly closely at any individuals paid by the company who have not been included in PAYE, such as casuals, agency workers, students, those regarded as self-employed, and one-man companies. Recently they have paid particular attention to subcontractors.

13.64 There will also be particular attention paid to directors. HMRC review instructions say that all directors should be identified at the time of interview, and that the records should be checked to see if there is any director whose remuneration has been concealed.

Self-employment v employment: basic principles

13.65 There is no definition of either 'employment' or 'self-employment' in the legislation, and the HMRC/CA will thus rely on the principles established in a series of tax cases. These have sought to distinguish between the individual who works under a contract of service (and is thus employed) and one who works under a contract for services. The distinction was summarised in the case of *Market Investigations Ltd v Minister of Social Security* [1969] 2 QB 173:

> 'Is the person who has engaged himself to perform these services performing them as a person in business on his own account? If the answer to that question is "yes" then the contract is a contract for services. If the answer is "no" then the contract is a contract of service.'

13.66 This is a developing area and regard should always be had to recent case law in establishing the latest position. There is increasing interest in this area caused by the introduction of the personal services legislation.

13.67 Currently the basic principles which a court would adopt in deciding whether an individual is an employee or not are:

- Is the person in business on his own account? This was discussed in the case of *Hall v Lorimer* [1994] STC 23, in which the judge said: 'In order to decide whether a person carries on business on his own account it is necessary to consider many different aspects of that person's work activity. This is not a mechanical exercise of running through items on a check list to see whether they are present in, or absent from, a given situation. The object of the exercise is to paint a picture from the accumulation of detail. The overall effect can only be appreciated by standing back from the detailed picture which has been painted, by viewing it from a distance and by making an informed, considered, qualitative appreciation of the whole.'

    Some of the details that will be considered (*Market Investigations Ltd v Minister of Social Security* [1969] 2 QB 173) include:
    (1) How much control is exercised over the individual? Control includes control over *where* the individual does his work, *when* he does it, *what* he does and *how* he does it. The relative importance of each will vary, e g a surgeon is not told how to perform an operation (*Morren v Swinton and Pendlebury Borough Council* [1965] 1 WLR 576).
    (2) Does he provide his own equipment? There is a presumption that employers will generally provide major items of equipment which are necessary for employees to do their job. Similarly many self-employed people own their own equipment. However, there are many exceptions to this. 'Little significance can be attached to the provision of small tools (or even major items) where it is customary for them to be provided' (SE 604). Cases on this point include *Ready Mixed Concrete (South East) Ltd v Minister of Pensions and National Insurance* [1968] 2 QB 497.
    (3) Can he hire his own helpers? If he can, he is more likely to be self-employed.
    (4) Does he take financial risk, so that he can make a loss as well as a profit? If he can, he is likely to be self-employed. If there is no financial risk, it is still possible, albeit unusual, that the individual will be self-employed. (*Addison v London Philharmonic Orchestra Society Ltd* [1981] ICR 261).

13.67   *Employees and directors*

    (5) Can he 'profit from sound management'? A self-employed person is often in this position: the efficiency with which he carries out his job will affect his income. The same may, however, apply to some employees, such as those paid on piece work.

- Can the individual send a substitute to do the job? If he can, this is almost conclusive evidence in favour of self-employment, as the requirement for personal service is a normal ingredient of most service contracts.
- What were the intentions of the parties? Although not conclusive, what the parties intended should be taken into account.
- How is the individual paid? Again, this is not conclusive, but generally only employees have paid holidays, sick pay, maternity pay and pensions.
- Is the individual effectively selling his skills to a succession of different companies? This is a very difficult test to apply, and the tax case of *Hall v Lorimer* [1994] STC 23 is the best illustration of its application. Mr Lorimer was a vision mixer who customarily worked for 20 or more production companies. Most of his engagements lasted for only a single day. HMRC have said that they believe that *Lorimer* will have particular relevance to engagements where:
   (1) the worker provides similar services to many engagers; and
   (2) there is a mutual intention not to create employment; and
   (3) the worker has a businesslike approach to obtaining and organising his engagements and incurs expenditure in this area of a type not normally associated with employment.

  In addition the following pointers may be present although their absence would not inevitably mean employment:
   (4) the worker has many short-term engagements;
   (5) the worker is providing professional services or services requiring the exercise of rare skill and judgment;
   (6) the worker is engaged for a specific task;
   (7) as a result of the number of different engagers the worker incurs expenditure travelling to various workplaces similar in nature to 'home to work' travel but considerable in amount when compared to the level of expenditure that is likely to be incurred by an employee who resides close to his/her workplace;
   (8) the worker bears a greater financial risk than an employee because payment is made after the payer has been invoiced, exposing the worker to the risk of delayed payment and bad debt; and
   (9) the extent to which the worker is able to influence the rate of pay is greater than is normally the case in employment situations, for example evidence of tendering.

- It is, however, possible for a person to be neither an employee, nor in business on their own account, see the comments of Nolan J in *Wickens v Champion Employment* [1984] ICR 365.

Self-employment v employment: the audit approach

13.68 As stated above, in seeking to establish whether individuals are employees, HMRC will apply the above case law principles to the facts of each case. To establish these they will:

- interview some or all of the individuals. This may well occur without the engager being aware;
- ask to see any documentation concerning the terms under which the individual was engaged. This may include the original job advertisement, any oral instructions given when he started work, the written contract (if any) and written company procedures;
- seek to confirm actual practice which may be other than described in the written agreements. Remember that this works both ways: the written documentation may not be helpful, but if the company can establish that the actual procedures are otherwise, this should also be taken into account;
- seek to discover whether there are other workers doing similar duties and if so, whether they are employed or self-employed;
- ask whether the worker was previously an employee of the 'employer' – if so they will ask when the change occurred and what differences exist in the terms of engagement.

13.69 HMRC have developed an employment status tool indicator on their website in to which the detailed terms of a contract can be populated and from which it will give an indication of whether that person engaged should be treated on a self-employed or employed basis. Clearly in any Revenue review in this area they will want to see if the status tool was used and also whether the information fed into this was correct and therefore its conclusion can be relied upon. This may result in a formal ruling that the individuals the company has been treating as self-employed are in fact employees. If the company disagrees with the ruling it may be necessary to take a test case to the courts. Whether the ruling is to be applied for past years or only for the future is a matter for negotiation, often as part of an overall audit settlement.

13.70 Where an individual is retrospectively recategorised as an employee, there will be a recalculation of the outstanding tax and NICs. In such cases the Schedule D tax and Class 4 NICs should be allocated against the Schedule E tax, and the Class 2 against the Class 1 NICs (*Hansard (1984) vol, 55 No 108 cols 62–3*). The shortfall (plus possibly interest and penalties) is to be paid by the employer, with the limited recovery rights. The position is now changed following the principles outlined in the case of *Demibourne*. HMRC will not only accept an offset which is equivalent to the Schedule D tax paid by the contractor. This could leave an employer facing a significant liability in respect of the past.

13.71 Even before their merger, HMRC and the CA used the same case law in arriving at their status decisions, and agreed that they would accept each other's rulings. However, the CA, and now HMRC, had the power to *determine* that particular groups of workers should be treated as Class I (employed) or

13.71 *Employees and directors*

Class II (self-employed). They made use of these powers for the following groups of workers:

- electoral workers (generally exempt from NICs);
- examiners, moderators, etc of certain examining bodies (generally treated as self-employed);
- domestic employment by close relatives (generally exempt from NICs);
- ministers of religion (generally treated as employees);
- office and telephone cleaners (generally treated as employees);
- part-time or visiting lecturers, teachers or instructors (generally treated as employees);
- engaging of a person by his or her spouse (generally treated as an employee).

13.72 The practice of HMRC in this area is currently changing following the case of *Demibourne Ltd v Revenue & Customs Comrs* SpC 486. This case outlined the position of how income tax paid under Schedule D by the worker could be used against the tax liability of the engager. Whilst the future approach is still not final HMRC are now only prepared to offset tax paid by the worker if that person consents and this will be given in the form of a credit against the engager which is still likely to leave a balance of liability payable.

Casual workers

13.73 A 'casual' in common parlance is someone who is not permanently employed by an organisation. There is no special legislation covering such people, and the normal rules for employment status, described in the preceding section, therefore apply.

13.74 However, it is in the case of casuals that the concept of mutuality of obligation comes into its own. For an individual to be an employee there must be an ongoing obligation on the part of the person who employs him to supply him with work and an ongoing obligation on the part of the worker to take work which is offered. There is a long line of cases on this point, of which *O'Kelly v Trusthouse Forte plc* [1984] QB 90 is perhaps the most significant.

13.75 From the employer's point of view, casuals represent a review vulnerability. The company may genuinely believe the casual worker to be self-employed, e g because the worker has no sick pay or holiday pay and is known to undertake a succession of similar contracts. However, the individual may nevertheless be a employee, see the comments of Lord Griffiths in *Lee Ting Sang v Chung Chi-Keung* [1990] 2 AC 374:

> '... the picture emerges of a skilled artisan earning his living by working for more than one employer as an employee and not as a small businessman venturing into business on his own account as an independent contractor with all its attendant risks. The applicant ran no risk whatever save that of being unable to find employment which is, of course, a risk faced by casual employees who move from one job to another ...'

13.76 Organisations with a large number of branches are particularly vulnerable if the branch manager has authority to cover short-term staff shortages. The amounts paid to each casual may be small, but if multiplied across a branch network and carried back for six years, the total cost can be substantial.

13.77 Another risk area is casual payments made to existing employees for extra duties such as unscheduled overtime. This may also not have been correctly dealt with under the NIC aggregation rules. A classic case is the teacher who does occasional evening classes for the same local authority which employs him during the day.

13.78 In dealing with an audit attack on casuals, the company should:

- check whether there is any scope for arguing that some of the individuals are genuinely self-employed, applying the principles set out above, and in particular *O'Kelly v Trusthouse Forte* and the *Hall v Lorimer* case;
- review whether any of the workers were supplied by bona fide employment agencies, in which case the agency rules may apply;
- perform a detailed sample check to establish whether and how many workers are below the threshold for taxation and NICs – this may be possible where the casuals are known to other workers in the organisation, eg family members or friends;
- consider writing to the individuals asking them to complete forms P46 on a retrospective basis;
- if the payment should have been taxable, seek to have it reduced by the personal allowance which would have been available, on the basis that such individuals are unlikely to have used it elsewhere. Likewise full use should be made of the lower rate band in assessing tax underpaid (this argument may be resisted by HMRC but may be useful when negotiating an overall settlement).

Agency workers

13.79 People supplied by a third-party agency who are not employed either by the agency or the company can be *deemed* employees (ITEPA 2003, s 44). In this case PAYE is operated by whoever pays them. The deeming provision operates where: 'an individual ("the worker") renders or is under an obligation to render personal services to another person ("the client") and is subject to, or to the right of, supervision, direction or control as to the manner in which he renders those services' (ITEPA 2003, s 44). Exceptions to this deeming provision include musicians, entertainers, models and (until 6 April 1998) subcontractors (ITEPA 2003, s 44).

13.80 Where an organisation engages a worker through a foreign agency without a branch or agent in the UK, the UK organisation is deemed to be the employer for PAYE and NIC purposes.

13.81 The inspector will seek to establish whether the deeming provisions should be applied, and in so doing will:

- review the contractual relationships. If the agency has only introduced the worker to the company then the deeming provisions will not apply

13.81 *Employees and directors*

(*Brady v Hart (t/a Jaclyn Model Agency)* (1985) 58 TC 518). However where this is the case the auditor will then review whether the worker is an employee of the organisation for which he is working;
- check whether any travelling expenses or associated subsistence have been paid to cover the worker's travel costs in getting to the job. Such expenses are regarded as home to work travel and as such are taxable. PAYE is deductible by the person making the payments, which may be the company for whom the individual is working. Before settling on this point with the auditors, the company should check whether in fact some of the expenses cover detached duty away from the normal place of work, in which case they will be allowable. There is also a concessional relief available for travel between clients.

One-man companies

13.82 One-man companies are common in some industries, such as computer consultancy. There should be no problem with using the services of such companies. An attempt to make the client liable for the PAYE and NICs on payments to such personal service companies was defeated (IR Press Release 23 September 1999). The company is registered and will receive its own tax return; the salary paid to the director will be subject to PAYE by the one-man company. There will only be a liability on the payer if the amount represents non-business costs, such as a round sum allowance (see Frequently Asked Question on IR35 Number 17). The personal service company's client may also have a reporting obligation if benefits are provided and should also:

- ensure that the individual *has* such a company and not be misled by business names on headed paper, such as 'Jim Brown Computing' which may simply be a trading name with no corporate identity;
- be sure that a formal contract has been entered into with the company to make it clear that the individual is not being employed directly.

13.83 HMRC is likely to ask to see copies of the contracts between the service companies and the organisation using the company's services.

13.84 If however, the one-man limited company is not UK resident for tax purposes it is likely that HMRC will expect the engager of the services to withhold tax on payments it makes. It is sensible though that the engager should take the precaution of deducting tax on the payments made.

Students

13.85 Students are likely to be outside PAYE, but to establish this they need to have completed a form P38(S). Where this has not been completed HMRC will seek back tax. The employer should try to obtain the forms retrospectively, as with casuals or put forward the arguments at **13.78** bullet points 3, 5. Other points to watch are that:
- there is no exemption from NICs, so that the normal rules apply – thus NICs should be operated where the student's earnings exceed the lower earnings limit;

- where a student's period of vacation work is at Easter, two tax years may be straddled. In such cases a form P38(S) is required for each year.

Special arrangements may apply to foreign or agricultural students.

Cleaners

13.86 Certain cleaners are deemed to be employees for NIC purposes. These deeming provisions apply to cleaners who work in an office or other non-domestic premises and are accepted as self-employed for tax purposes. However, the deeming rules will not be applied if the cleaners are operating in partnership, or have their own employees. The rules also do not apply to window cleaners, but do apply to cleaners of telephone kiosks.

13.87 The employer in the office which they clean must operate Class 1 NICs on what he pays them. An official will seek back payment of Class 1 NICs on payments to a 'self-employed' cleaner if non-deduction is discovered during a review.

DIRECTORS

13.88 In many respects the investigation of directors is the same as that for higher paid employees, but there are a number of special points:

- The Revenue take a special interest in anyone who may be able to override an organisation's normal accounting controls. Apart from deliberate fraud, the HMRC official will also look for expense claim forms from directors where the expenses are not fully vouched, or are self-certificated. It will be for the company to prove that the payments were for genuine business expenses, rather than a benefit to the director.
- For the same reason the interface between the individual's own returns and the company's may also be checked. In the case of a more complex investigation each director may be asked whether his own returns are correct and complete to the best of his knowledge and belief. The personal files of the directors may also be called for.
- Directors of close companies are subject to particularly close examination, eg to ensure that personal expenditure has not been put through as a business expense.

SCHEDULE E BENEFITS AND REIMBURSED EXPENSES

Dispensations

13.89 A dispensation releases an employer from the obligation to include expenses payments and benefits on employees' P11Ds. It also releases the employee from including the items on his tax return. Without a dispensation HMRC may argue that *all* reimbursed expenses and all benefits must be reported on the P11D and the individual's tax return, even where the reimbursed expenses were incurred solely for business purposes.

13.90 *Employees and directors*

13.90 However the legal position is that only 'benefits provided for the employee such as give rise to any charge to tax' need to be reported. Thus if the business reason is quite clear, the employer should resist any penalty for not having included an amount on the P11D. It is of course simpler if employers pre-empt such problems by applying for dispensations where appropriate (IR Leaflet IR 69 explains how to do this).

13.91 To obtain a dispensation the employer will need to show that:

- the expenses are necessarily incurred in the performance of the employees' duties;
- claims to expenses are independently checked and authorised;
- where possible expense claims are accompanied by receipts or other evidence;
- the employer has procedures to ensure that advances of expenses are fully accounted for, and any excess advance has been repaid by the employee.

13.92 HMRC will check current dispensations at the beginning of their review. Problems can arise where:

- an examination of the company's records shows that the terms of the dispensation have not been complied with, eg if amounts in excess of agreed subsistence allowances have been paid;
- the dispensation was for a limited period and has not been renewed;
- the dispensation only covered some companies or individuals in the group but has been applied to others.

If either the second or third point are found to apply, the employer should seek to prove that, had a dispensation been applied for, the company would have satisfied the requirements. We have recently seen HMRC move to bring all dispensation applications to be reviewed in one office so that they can ensure consistency of treatment.

Working rule agreements

13.93 Working rule agreements (WRAs) are collective agreements drawn up between representatives of employers and trade unions to govern rates of pay and conditions of work in a number of industries. HMRC is not a party to these agreements but have agreed that certain WRA allowances paid for daily travel and lodging should not be taxed or liable for NICs.

13.94 This is broadly on the basis that the employees would otherwise be able to claim a deduction for the expenses under ITEPA 2003, s 336, although HMRC have indicated that 'it now seems likely that many such expenses payments might not be deductible under the general expenses rule, with the result that the tax treatment of WRAs is, at least in part, concessionary'.

13.95 The WRA allowances generally cover travel, accommodation and subsistence and are normally payable only to specific groups of employees within the construction and allied industries. The modified tax procedures are negotiated nationally and apply only where the employer adopts the terms and conditions of the relevant WRA. However, the employer does not have to be a member of the relevant employers' federation, nor do employees have to belong to the union negotiating the allowances, for these procedures to operate (IR Press Release of 13 February 1981).

13.96 It is possible that some payments made by an employer could fall within a WRA, but the employer is ignorant of its existence. HMRC may point out the WRA and apply its provisions to past payments; if the employer wishes to check for himself, a complete listing of current WRAs and their tax consequences are given in and this should be available at every tax office and on the Revenue website.

13.97 If the employer is aware of the WRA but has not been operating it correctly, he will be invited to make a settlement to cover the difference between the WRA amounts and the amounts actually paid. Should such a settlement be resisted, HMRC can make a determination under the legislation, which would of course be on the stricter provisions of ITEPA 2003, s 336 without the concessional WRA elements.

Scope of benefits

Benefits assessable on all employees

13.98 Although the benefits legislation is commonly thought of as applying to 'higher paid' employees, some benefits are assessable on *all* employees. These are:

- all vouchers other than those for meals worth less than 15p per day). Note that:
  (1) vouchers exchangeable for cash are taxable as earnings ITEPA 2003, s 7; and
  (2) a travel voucher includes a season ticket;
- gifts of assets. The second-hand value is assessable. It may be possible to argue that the gift was not 'by reason of the employment' but was made to the employee in a personal capacity, see *Reed v Seymour* (1927) 11 TC 625, HL, although HMRC can be expected to challenge this;
- living accommodation, where the rules in ITEPA 2003, s 7 apply to determine the value;
- payments made by the employer to meet the employee's pecuniary liability, such as telephone bills or school fees (*Hartland v Diggines* (1926) 10 TC 247; *Nicoll v Austin* (1935) 19 TC 531).

National Insurance

13.99 From 6 April 2000, Class 1A NICs are due on all benefits unless *either* Class 1 already applies, *or* the benefit is:

- covered by a dispensation;
- included in a PAYE settlement agreement;
- provided to employees (other than directors) earning less than £8,500;

13.99 *Employees and directors*

- a reimbursed expense which is wholly for business; or
- shares or options. In some cases these will already be subject to a Class 1 NIC charge.

13.100 In years before 2000–01, benefits in kind were not generally subject to NICs. However, Class 1A NICs have been due on cars and fuel since 1991, and NICs were also payable where the company settled the employee's liability rather than providing the asset or benefit directly. Thus if a company provided clothing for its employees, there were no NICs; if it reimbursed the employees for the cost of the clothing, NICs were payable. It was generally possible to replace contracts between the employee and a supplier with a contract between the company and the supplier, and thus avoid the NICs. However, the inspector may resist this where the benefit being provided is clearly an individual's personal liability, such as a child's school fees, although a properly structured contractual agreement may withstand attack.

13.101 The reimbursement of expenses is strictly subject to NICs ie there is no deduction equivalent to the tax rules. However, reimbursements could be excluded if 'they are specific and distinct payments of, or a contribution towards, expenses actually incurred by the employee in carrying out his work'.

13.102 It is important to bear in mind that Class 1A National Insurance only arises on benefits provided to employees who are themselves liable to Class 1 National Insurance on their earnings. If therefore benefits are provided to 'inpat' employees who are continuing to have social security deductions collected in some overseas territory then Class 1A National Insurance will not arise on any benefits they may receive.

Benefits assessable on higher paid employees and all directors

13.103 A 'higher paid' employee is one who is remunerated at the rate of £8,500 per year (ITEPA 2003, s 66(4)). There are two potential traps for the unwary:

- benefits and reimbursed expenses must be included in calculating the £8,500, even if these are covered by a dispensation or would be allowable under the normal expenses rules;
- the £8,500 is a *rate* of pay. Thus an employee paid £2,000 a month for three months of the year is 'higher paid' within the definition.

13.104 However, employee pension contributions on a 'net pay' basis and payroll giving amounts are both deductible in this calculation.

13.105 At the time of writing this update there are proposals to overhaul these rules and to take out the current concessions to 'lower paid' workers.

13.106 A director is within the scope of the benefits legislation irrespective of his earnings level unless he has no material interest in the company and either is a full-time working director or the company is a charity or non-profit-making concern (TA 1988, ss 167–168).

13.107 Benefits and reimbursed expenses are taxable if they are made or provided 'by reason of the employment'. Although the HMRC Manual says that 'the legislation deems this to be the case if it is the employer who is making or providing them' (ITEPA 2003, s 71), there remain cases where something can be provided by the employer to the employee which is not a benefit, if it is not given in return for 'acting as or being an employee' (*Hochstrasser v Mayes* (1959) 38 TC 673; *Mairs v Haughey* [1993] STC 569). Nevertheless it must be accepted that the deeming provision is wide ranging in scope.

13.108 Points which may be picked up on a Revenue review include the following:

- Any amounts paid to the employee's family or household must also be included on the P11D (or P9D, where applicable). Note, however, that 'family or household' does not include an unmarried partner who is not a dependant or a member of the employee's household (ITEPA 2003, s 721(5)).
- The amount included on the P11D or P9D must be the full VAT-inclusive cost. The fact that some or all of the VAT may be recovered by the employer from Customs and Excise is irrelevant.

Self-assessment

13.109 Under self-assessment the employer is required to show the cash-equivalent value of the items included on P11Ds and P9Ds. Suffice it to say that under self-assessment the need to understand the benefits legislation and the penalties for non-compliance are both greater than before 1996–97 (when self-assessment came in to force).

Value of benefits

13.110 The general rule on valuing a benefit is that the employee is taxable on the money's worth of the benefit, ie its cash equivalent. ITEPA 2003, s 203(2) and ITEPA 2003, s 204 state that the cash equivalent of the benefit is its cost, less any part made good by the employee to those providing the benefit. VAT is included whether or not it is recoverable by the employer.

13.111 The case of *Pepper v Hart* (1992) 65 TC 421 established that by 'cost' the statute did not mean full cost but marginal cost. Thus an airline employee who has the use of a spare seat on the airline which would otherwise be unused is only taxed on the extra cost to the airline of carrying one more passenger, not on the total cost of the flight divided by the number of passengers.

13.112 HMRC have agreed that the marginal cost principle should apply to in-house benefits and to the use of assets employed in the business. Thus where a telephone is provided for business use it is accepted that the employee does not have to pay a proportion of the line rental or any other standing charges. However, there are cases other than in-house benefits and assets used in the business where marginal cost can be applied. Where appropriate the Revenue can be successfully challenged on this restrictive interpretation of *Pepper v Hart*.

13.113 *Employees and directors*

13.113 A further point to note is that where an employee is charged for part of the cost of the benefit, there may be VAT on the amount so charged, depending on the normal VAT rules. The area in practice most affected by this used to be payments for the private use of company cars but this has now changed. However, the same point continues to apply to other supplies, such as the use of holiday accommodation.

Areas likely to be investigated

13.114 In investigating the taxation of benefits, the Revenue official will concentrate on areas where the employer is most likely to have made mistakes. Some of the main ones are covered below. It should, however, be emphasised that this is a review of vulnerabilities and not a complete summary of the benefits legislation. In particular, for years 2000–01 and subsequently, the National Insurance costs should be taken into account.

Accommodation (ITEPA 2003, ss 97–113)

13.115 Where living accommodation is provided by the employer for employees, HMRC may check that:

- Any job-related accommodation (ITEPA 2003, s 99(1)) is so in fact. Accommodation is job-related and thus exempt from tax if it is:
  (1) *necessary* for the proper performance of the duties, or
  (2) provided for the *better* performance of the duties in an employment where the provision of accommodation is *customary*, or
  (3) required to protect the employee's *security*.

  The difficult area here is (2), which is subject to erosion by HMRC. For example, they are currently challenging the customary right of cemetery attendants to live on site, although most people would not consider this to be a perk. In job-related accommodation cases it may be worth considering an appeal to the Commissioners if the facts are strong and HMRC continue to challenge the position.

  The job-related exemption does not, however, apply to the payment by the employer for household furniture, which is subject to the 20% rule for assets. Nor does it apply to the payment by the employer of household bills or ancillary costs such as cleaning. However, it should be noted that:
  (1) P9D employees escape tax if the liability is met directly by the employer, but not if the employer reimburses the employee's costs.
  (2) Structural alterations, or alterations which would be the landlord's responsibility under the Landlord and Tenant Act 1985, s 11 are also not taxable.
  (3) Where the accommodation is provided in an institution, such as a hospital or school, the benefit of such ancillary costs as cleaning can be reduced using *Pepper v Hart* principles.
  (4) Where there is a liability, it is capped at 10% of the employee's net emoluments, ie his emoluments after deducting pension

contributions, capital allowances and allowable expenses and before including the benefit of the household costs (ITEPA 2003, s 315).
- The calculation has been carried out correctly. This is based on the rateable value; for new properties with no rateable value an estimate is used (IR Press Release of 19 April 1990).
- 'Expensive' accommodation (broadly that which cost more than £75,000 (ITEPA 2003, s 105)) has been correctly identified and that the benefit has been accurately calculated. Note here that properties which originally cost less than £75,000 do not fall within the 'expensive' category even if the current market value is more than that, unless improvements subsequent to the purchase and before the year of assessment, together with the purchase price, have taken the cost above £75,000.
- Any 'perk' accommodation, such as London flats or holiday homes, have been correctly assessed.
- Any accommodation provided to a shadow director has been taxed.

13.116 Many employers who provide expensive accommodation set up lease premium arrangements to minimise the benefit-in-kind charge. These arrangements work with the employer paying a premium to the landlord which then means that the monthly rent is reduced. On this basis given that the rent is reduced, then the benefit in kind is reduced. The premium lease arrangements are the subject of HMRC attack and from 22 April 2009 are no longer available to be used for leasing entered into after the 2009 Budget. For employers who have existing arrangements in place, it is important that these arrangements are not varied following the 2009 Budget, otherwise they will cease to benefit from the previous tax position.

13.117 If such arrangements have been organised, HMRC at the time of any review would want to be satisfied that there is a valid arrangement in place and it is worth checking whether the arrangements were cleared with HMRC at the outset. It is the opinion of HMRC that these arrangements are only applicable when the lease premium covers an extensive period. At present HMRC are challenging employers who have set schemes up for a period below what they would consider acceptable. It is likely that HMRC will seek to take cases on this matter to tribunal. For those employers who previously used the lease premium arrangement, we are finding that despite the change of tax rules going forward, HMRC are looking to seek a settlement of the liability in regard to the past.

Assets used by employees (ITEPA 2003, s 203(3))

13.118 Where an asset remains the property of the employer but the employee can use it privately, the taxable benefit is on the 'annual value' of the use of the asset, unless specific provisions exist to tax it separately, such as company cars. The 'annual value' is 20% of the market value of the asset when first used privately. Points to note in an audit context are that:
- The 20% charge is replaced by the actual cost of hiring the asset if this is greater.

13.118 *Employees and directors*

- If the original cost is enhanced by further expenditure, this must be added when calculating the annual value.
- If ownership of an asset is transferred to an employee, the normal rule is that there is only a benefit if the asset is transferred at less than market value at the date of transfer. However, these rules are amended where there has been private use, see ITEPA 2003, s 203(3).
- The cost of the asset includes VAT, whether or not this can be recovered by the employer.
- If the asset is provided part way through the fiscal year, there is no pro-rating of the benefit charge.
- If the private use of an asset has been prohibited, the company can argue that there was no benefit (*Gilbert v Hemsley* (1981) 55 TC 419).
- From 2000–01 there is a specific exemption for any assets where the private use is 'not significant'. This covers the use of telephones, photocopiers and fax machines, as well as computers provided for work which do not fall within the ITEPA 2003, s 320 exemption. Unsurprisingly, this relief does not extend to the private use of aeroplanes, boats or cars, even if private use is not significant.

Cars

13.119 The provision of cars for employees is a fruitful area for a compliance review. Under self-assessment employers are required to calculate the cash equivalent of the benefits. This will increase the employer's exposure to interest and penalties.

13.120 The cost of incorrect handling of company cars is compounded when one looks at Class 1A contributions. If an error is made in calculating the value of the car, or the business miles, this will affect the value of the car and the fuel for both tax and Class 1A purposes. Thus an error in this area can prove extremely expensive.

13.121 Particular points to note are that:

- All cars with private use have been included on the P11Ds. A fleet listing may be used for this purpose. Check especially:
  (1) new cars;
  (2) second hand cars;
  (3) cars provided other than by the company's fleet department, e g by a branch for use by a salesman;
  (4) hire cars provided before the employee's company car could be made available.
- Since 1994–95 cars have been included on the P11D at original market value, not cost:
  (1) The original market value is broadly the manufacturer's list price, and is defined as the price which was 'published by the car's manufacturer, importer or distributor (as the case may be) as the inclusive price appropriate for a car of that kind if sold in the United Kingdom singly in a retail sale in the open market on the relevant

Employees and directors 13.121

day' (ITEPA 2003, s 216(3)). The inclusive price means the price including delivery, VAT, customs duty and car tax.

(2) Particular care is needed when the car is acquired second-hand, as the original market value must still be used, not the second-hand cost.

(3) As the definition in s 216(3) quoted at (1) above makes clear, cars obtained by the employer at a volume discount must be included at the price that would have been charged if only a single car had been bought by a retail customer.

- Any accessories also need to be treated correctly (ITEPA 2003, s 125). Standard accessories will be included in the car's list price. If optional accessories are provided with the car, then their price must be added to the list price when calculating the total price of the car. Note that:

(1) car phones provided by the employer are exempt;

(2) only those optional accessories attached to the car are added to the price (this includes accessories such as a roof-rack which is attached although it can be removed, but does not include emergency triangles, first aid kits, car rugs, etc – in practice the value of such excluded items can be regarded as de minimis, although strictly there is an annual value charge of 20% on their cost);

(3) optional accessories paid for by the employee such as car stereo equipment are not added to the car price;

(4) optional accessories necessarily required for the employee's job, such as a towbar, are also not added to the price;

(5) the removal of an item from the car which would have been provided as standard does not reduce the list price;

(6) the price to be used for accessories, as for the car, is the open market list price and not the actual cost (ITEPA 2003, s 126). Personalised number plates on a company car are not generally assessable (SE 3439);

(7) complex rules apply to replacement accessories.

- Where the individual 'in the year concerned ... is required, as a condition of the car being available for his private use, to pay any amount of money for that use' the scale charge can be reduced. The strict wording here means that if the payment is not *required*, or the requirement was not *in the year concerned*, the inspector may argue that the payment was ineffective. He may also question whether the payment was for private use, or merely, for example, to obtain a better model than that otherwise available at his grade. The company should have made clear the purpose of the contribution in its documentation (IR *Tax Bulletin* November 1991).

From 1 August 1995 there is no need to charge VAT on the private use payment, provided the input tax is also excluded (VAT Information Sheet 12/95 of 1 June 1995). Different rules applied before 1 August, see Customs and Excise News Release 9/92 of 19 June 1992.

- Capital contributions to the cost of the car by the employee reduce the price of the car for assessment purposes, as long as the contribution does

13.121 *Employees and directors*

not exceed £5,000 (ITEPA 2003, s 132). Note that this only applies to reduce the value of the car when used by that employee and not when it is transferred to another employee.

- Where a car is classified as a pool car, the inspector will check that the strict conditions in ITEPA 2003, s 167(1) are being complied with. These are that:
  (1) the car is available to, and actually used by, more than one employee and is not ordinarily used by any one of them to the exclusion of the others;
  (2) any private use of the car by any of the employees is merely incidental to its business use;
  (3) it is not normally kept overnight at or in the vicinity of the residence of any of the employees except while it is being kept on premises occupied by the person providing the car.

  Note that *all* the conditions must be met. Pool cars are a frequent target of inspectors and can cost employers significant sums in settlement where cars do not in practice meet the requirements.

  Particularly difficult is the second requirement and the interpretation of 'merely incidental', which is a qualitative test. If the private use follows from the business use then the incidental test is passed, but not if the private use of the car is independent of its business use (HMRC have a rule of thumb that a car is not regarded as 'normally kept overnight' at employees' homes if the total number of nights on which it is taken home by employees, for whatever reason, is less than 60% of the total number of nights in the period under review (IR Booklet 480)). However they also warn, at SE 3492, that: 'If a car is taken home often enough to approach the 60 per cent limit – though without breaking it – it is unlikely that all the home to work journeys will satisfy the "merely incidental" test.'

  Note that where a chauffeur employed to drive pool cars is obliged to take the car home overnight this will not disqualify the car from being a pool car.

- The inspector will also check that there has been correct calculation of the total taxable car benefit. In addition to items 1 to 6 above this will include adjustments to the list price for:
  (1) business mileage;
  (2) periods when the car was unavailable – the period of unavailability must be for at least 30 consecutive days and it is not enough that the driver cannot drive for the period, eg because of illness or a driving ban (TA 1988, Sch 6, paras 6 and 9).
- Where a company car is sold to an employee at less than the open market value the difference will be assessable as a benefit on the employee. If the price at which the car was transferred is significantly different from that given for a car of that age and type in, say, *Glass's Guide*, then the employer may need to prove that the market value of this particular car was less than would be expected, eg because the car was in poor condition.

- Although car parking is exempt from tax under ITEPA 2003, s 237(2) there is an NIC cost if the car parking charge at an employee's permanent place of work is reimbursed to the employee (CWG2 (2000) page 75).
- Where a chauffeur is used by an employee for private journeys, his costs are taxable on the employee. SP 2/96 discusses HMRC's view on the use of a chauffeur to collect senior personnel from home so they can work in the car. While discouraging, the statement of practice does not preclude a claim that such a car is a pool car and that the private use is incidental, but it does increase the difficulty of having such a claim accepted. If it is not, then the inspector will seek the cost of both car and fuel benefit, as well as the chauffeur costs.

  The latter is based on the relevant proportion of his wages, including waiting time, overtime, pension contributions, and NIC costs. The amount of exposure can be reduced if the chauffeur does other jobs.
- Parking fines are taxable on an employee if the penalty notice was actually handed to him at the time of the offence, or if the employee owns the car. But if the notice was fixed to a car owned by the employer, and the employer pays the fine as the registered owner, there is no Schedule E liability on the employee. The Revenue Manual (IM 699) says that: 'If the employee voluntarily pays a fine in these circumstances, and the employer reimburses it, the employee will be chargeable on the emolument arising. A deduction for the expense may then be allowed to the employer.'

  Where the fine is not taxed on the individual, HMRC will, however, seek to disallow it in the company's tax computations. This is on the basis that it was not 'wholly and exclusively' in the course of the company's trade (*CIR v Alexander von Glehn & Co Ltd*, (1920) 12 TC 232).

13.122 A number of employers have offered employee car ownership schemes which use their purchasing power to obtain discounts for employees to permit the employee to purchase a car from a third-party provider. This provider offers an arrangement to manage the vehicle to ensure that the vehicle is maintained and with a guaranteed buy-back price on the vehicle at the end of the loan period. In addition employers involved in this area will often provide insurance on the vehicle to ensure this is adequately insured for any business travel.

13.123 It is the case that the employer will often support the employee car ownership scheme with some financial support which is either paid directly to the employee or to a third party e g the provider. It is the case at the time of any employer compliance review that HMRC will wish to ensure that any financial support met by the employer is identified and tax/NIC on this correctly dealt with.

13.124 To make employer car ownership schemes financially viable many employers will use the approved mileage allowance payments (AMAP) to cushion the tax impact on any payment made to the employee. This is an area

13.124 *Employees and directors*

which will be of particular interest to HMRC who will want to be certain the payment fits in to the category of approved mileage allowances and, in regard to National Insurance, falls within the appropriate earnings period. The rules at reg 22A are complex but need to be followed to ensure that the NIC relief can be obtained. This is a very topical issue for HMRC.

13.125 The rules on vans changed over recent years and the level of the benefit is now significantly increased to £3,000. However, the benefit only arises if the van is made available for private use. The change in the rules however takes account of private use as well as normal commuting journeys. Therefore if the van's use is available to the employee for business travel but is taken home each day then no benefit will arise subject to the employee not being permitted to use the van for additional private use. At the time of any HMRC compliance visit they will want to ensure that the policy and practice of employers do not permit unlimited private use.

Credit cards

13.126 These are taxed under the vouchers legislation, ITEPA 2003, s 7. Employers should ensure that any corporate credit cards are properly controlled, so that expenditure is analysed between private and business. There is no tax liability if all private expenditure is reimbursed to the employer, and there is also no tax on credit card interest or annual/joining fees for the card (SE 2011).

Commissions and discounts

13.127 Until the publication of HMRC Statement of Practice SP4/97, the taxation of commissions, rebates and discounts was in disarray. SP4/97 states that where an employee receives commission by reason of his employment, this is taxable. If in cash, the amounts should be subjected to PAYE. If invested, for instance in a financial product, then the value of the uplift should be reported on the employee's P11D. Particular areas of interest or difficulty include:

- If the employee receives a discount rather than a commission, there will be no tax if either the discount is also available to the public or the amount paid by the employee is above cost to the employer (*Pepper v Hart* (1992), 65 TC 421).
- The taxable commission can be reduced by any rebate which passes the 'wholly exclusively and necessarily' test. This is likely to be the case where the product is sold to a third party at arm's length, but employers should beware of rebates passed on to friends and relatives.
- The previous Statement, SP 5/95 contained many errors, and its predecessor, SP 3/79 was much narrower in scope. The confusion over taxability could be used as a defence against too robust an attack by the Revenue's officials on past years.

Conferences

13.128 The official is likely to ask if the employees attend conferences, and be particularly interested in any which are overseas and/or where a partner is invited. He will ask to see itineraries and programmes for the conference, as well as other relevant documentation, such as invitations. Because of the cost of such meetings, especially those overseas, and the number of attendees, the expense of a settlement in this area can be substantial. The official is likely to ask a number of questions.

13.129 *What is the business content?* The Revenue official may argue that any business purpose was de minimis, indeed a mere front for the overseas trip. The Schedule E Manual (SE 4261) instructs him as follows:

> 'Overseas trips variously described as conferences, conventions or seminars are often no more than incentives intended either to reward past performance or to motivate employees for the future. Although a minimal "business" element such as an address by a company executive may have been included in the programme do not give a deduction if it otherwise consists of social occasions, excursions and leisure activities.'

13.130 Where the conference does have some business content, the best the company can achieve is a reasonable apportionment of costs between business and private, but the Revenue now discourage this. Their Manual (SE 4260) says:

> 'Avoid accepting an apportionment of travel expenditure on a percentage basis calculated by looking at the relative time spent on business and non-business activities. Such an apportionment cannot be readily justified in law. In any potentially contentious case an "all or nothing" approach should be taken with regard to travel costs.'

13.131 *Was the trip necessarily incurred?* Here HMRC may not accept that a conference was necessary if the employee himself decided to go (*Owen v Burden* (1971) 47 TC 476). Senior employees should therefore ensure that they are 'instructed' to attend, and do not simply authorise their own attendance. Similarly HMRC may argue that a seminar to improve an employee's qualifications to do his job or to keep his knowledge up to date is not allowable (*Humbles v Brooks* (1962) 40 TC 500; *Parikh v Sleeman* (1990) 63 TC 75), unless the education forms an integral part of the performance of the duties of the employment.

13.132 *Did partners attend?* Attendance of partners at a conference is likely to increase the Revenue's doubts about the business purpose of the conference. In addition they will check whether the cost of the partner's attendance has been included on the P11D for the employee. Note that there is no benefit where the person attending is not a member of the employee's family or household (ITEPA 2003, s 721(5)). The employee must show that the expense of taking his spouse with him is necessarily incurred in the performance of his duties. In assessing whether the 'necessarily' test is satisfied, the Revenue will ask whether his duties would have required someone else to go with him, such as a secretary or interpreter. The company will need to prove that:

13.132 *Employees and directors*

- the partner has some special skill or qualification associated with his or her partner's job which is needed on the trip (although not necessarily full-time). An example might be where the wife is a competent linguist and acts as an interpreter at business meetings; or
- the partner's presence is essential to host a series of business entertaining occasions which the employee is required to organise as part of his or her duties. It is insufficient that the employee and partner merely attend functions where other guests are accompanied by their spouses; or
- the employee's health is so poor that it would be unreasonable for him or her to travel alone.

Entertaining clients

13.133 This has long been a favourite of HMRC, who have a dual weapon:

- CAA 2001, Sch 2 para 51(1)(a) prohibits a deduction for entertaining costs from *trading profits*.
- ITEPA 2003, s 356(1) states that no deduction for such expenses shall be made from emoluments chargeable to tax under Schedule E.
- However, ITEPA 2003, s 357 prohibits a double disallowance where the employer pays for, or reimburses, the cost of the entertaining, and the cost is disallowed in the trading computation. Where this is the case, the employee still has to satisfy the test in ITEPA 2003, s 328(1).

13.134 HMRC may thus wish to check that there was a genuine business reason for the entertainment, and that the company is not simply being used as a tax-efficient vehicle for private entertaining by senior management or directors.

13.135 It is true that genuine entertainment of third-party business contacts, such as customers or suppliers, would qualify. However, in such cases HMRC may check that the amounts have been correctly identified as disallowable in the company's corporation tax return (TA 1988, s 577(3)). Indeed, under self-assessment the P11D requires the employer to state whether any entertaining expenses included on the P11D (ie those not covered by a dispensation) have been or will be disallowed.

13.136 The position is different where the employer is a non-trading entity, such as a local council or charity (SE 4151).These organisations, and their employees, are not affected by s 577 because any entertainment which they may provide is not 'in connection with a trade' and therefore is not 'business entertainment' as defined in s 577(5). The employees of such organisations are therefore entitled to a deduction for any entertainment expenses they may incur which satisfy the conditions of ITEPA 2003, s 328(1) provided only that the expense is incurred out of their taxable emoluments.

13.137 The position is different again where the employer is a representative office of an overseas company. In that case the company's profits, whilst chargeable to tax overseas, are not subject to UK tax. As a result there can be no disallowance on the company under s 577(1)(a), and s 577(3) thus cannot operate to protect the employee, while s 577(1)(b) denies the employee a deduction for business entertainment expenses irrespective of whether the expenses are, or are not, reimbursed by the employer. This often results in the employees being taxed under Schedule E in respect of their reimbursed entertainment expenses with no possibility of an off-setting deduction under s 198. This harsh position is set out in *Tax Bulletin* 42, August 1999. However, it may be possible to change the Revenue's mind if the overseas company is in a treaty country, on the grounds that the tax exemption derives from the treaty. There is always the possibility of arguing that the position is unfair and not within the Revenue's commitment to human rights which requires that all taxpayers should be treated equally.

Entertaining – staff

13.138 For many years, HMRC adopted a tolerant attitude where staff entertaining was concerned. As long as the cost was either included as a benefit on their P11D (the technically correct position) or disallowed in the company's tax computation, they accepted the position. However, a stricter approach was set out in *Tax Bulletin* 42, August 1999, which said that the disallowing of staff entertaining 'is inconsistent with the concept of self-assessment, and should no longer be adopted'. The old approach will continue to apply for accounting periods ending not later than 30 April 2000 (*Tax Bulletin* 45, February 2000); thus for these earlier periods it should be possible to agree a disallowance in the company computations in preference to the more onerous (and usually more expensive) adjustment to an individual's emoluments.

13.139 There remain many areas of difficulty, eg where the employer entertains an employee or two employees have lunch 'on the firm' this is taxable on the employees as a benefit. This includes a meal out as a reward for doing a good job, or having lunch in a restaurant to provide a relaxed ambience for a team meeting. In general the Revenue take the view that 'meetings over a meal with other members of the same organisation are normally social, with work matters being insufficient to make the meeting a necessary business occasion' (ECM 13029). You can therefore expect that such costs will be challenged.

13.140 However, the Revenue are prepared to accept that there is no benefit where the nature of some meetings would qualify for ITEPA 2003, s 328(1) relief, eg:

- meetings for the negotiation of the renewal or alteration of a service contract; or
- a briefing visit where local staff are detained beyond normal hours to fit in with a visit from head office.

13.141 However, the employer is on weaker ground when the person being entertained is from a branch rather than a connected company, as a branch has no separate existence. Here some use may be made of HMRC's agreement that 'where the colleague being entertained would be entitled to tax free subsistence, (his) costs can be discounted' (NAG 5.130).

13.142 *Employees and directors*

13.142 The company has no grounds for a defence where the individuals are from the same site, unless the costs involved are no more than they would have been had they eaten in the company's subsidised or free restaurant.

13.143 A problem may arise where one employee has paid for the mutual staff entertaining, in that the full bill should have been entered on his P11D. However, HMRC will normally agree that the bill should be shared among all attendees. Where a higher rate taxpayer paid the bill, this apportionment will have the effect of reducing the overall tax charge. In practice, the company may wish to include such items in a PAYE settlement agreement.

Gifts

13.144 Gifts provided by the employer are generally taxable under the deeming provisions of ITEPA 2003, s 71. However, HMRC will accept that there is no benefit if the gift is either provided on personal grounds (eg a wedding present), or as a mark of personal esteem (SE 1182). See also long-service awards and third-party benefits.

Loans

13.145 Cheap or interest-free loans supplied by, or by arrangement with, the employer are taxable if they fall within the detailed rules of ITEPA 2003, s 7(5). Particular points to note are as follows:

- Certain loans are classed as 'qualifying' and are exempt from these provisions (ITEPA 2003, s 180). These include loans to buy into a partnership, to buy shares in, or lend money to, a close company, and to buy machinery or plant for use by the partnership or employment. From 6 April 2000, loans to acquire a main residence are no longer qualifying, and from the same date qualifying loans do not have to be included on a P11D (ITEPA 2003, s 180(5)). For earlier years the loan should have been reported by the employer, leaving it for the individual to claim ITEPA 2003, s 328(1) relief. However, it would be unusual for HMRC to take this point.
- Allowable relocation loans are also not a benefit, but see **13.153** for details of the rules which must be satisfied here.
- Loans on the same terms as those provided to members of the public are excluded (ITEPA 2003, s 180(5))), if the lending of money is part of the business of the employer. A deregulatory amendment introduced by FA 2000, Sch 10(5)(1) improved the position for such loans, and the rules were backdated to cover the previous six years. Previously the 'same terms' requirement was strictly interpreted, so that a relaxation of lending criteria or a waiver of fees for staff loans, as compared to those for the public, caused the loan to fall outside this exemption (IR Interpretation, August 1994).
- There is a de minimis exemption for cheap or interest-free loans below £5,000. Where the total amount loaned has exceeded £5,000, the full amount, and not just the excess, will come within the rules. The total

value of loans to each individual must therefore be checked. In practice, loans can be granted from different sources within the company, e g one department may provide season ticket loans, and another loans for car purchase. Because all season ticket loans are below the de minimis amount, they may have been ignored when looking at whether there is a benefit.
- The de minimis exemption is only valid if the loan does not exceed the £5,000 limit at *any time* in the tax year.
- The loan interest must not simply be *payable* in a tax year, it must actually be paid (ITEPA 2003, s 7(5)). Where the loan is interest bearing but the interest has not been paid, the loan must be reported on the P11D. The employee can recover the tax charged once he has paid the interest (s 174(1)). In an audit situation the employer should check whether the employee has now paid the interest, and if so should seek to limit the cost of settlement to sufficient interest to cover the period during which HMRC would have had the tax if the P11D had been correct originally.
- Loan guarantees are also included within the loan benefits legislation.
- In some cases the company may argue that the loan has not been granted 'by reason of' the employment, but because of the private circumstances of the employees. They may find support for this in *Hochstrasser v Mayes* (1959) 38 TC 673.
- Loans written off are taxable, even when the write-off happens after the individual has left (ITEPA 2003, s 188(2)).
- For years before 2000/01 a benefit could arise if the loan interest rate fell below the Revenue approved rate for any part of the tax year. This could happen where the company follows a market rate and HMRC rate falls more slowly. For 2000–01 and subsequent years, the official rate is set at the beginning of the tax year, making it easier to monitor whether a benefit has arisen (IR Press Release, 25 January 2000).
- Under self-assessment the actual benefit of the loan must be calculated. HMRC will check a sample of such calculations to ensure that they have been carried out correctly.

Long-service awards

13.146 The tax rules exempt certain long-service awards from tax. However, the requirements of the concession have to be met; it is not enough that, for example, the total sum spent is less than that allowed by the Concession but the gifts are made more frequently. A small gift made every five years can cause expensive gifts made after 20 years to be taxed.

Mobile phones

13.147 Finance Act 1999 changed the rules for mobile phones, to the enormous relief of all those involved in PAYE reviews with the possible exception of the HMRC official (ITEPA 2003, s 316(1)). For years from 1999–2000 onwards, the following points are relevant:

13.147 *Employees and directors*

- Mobile phones provided by the employer are exempted from tax from 6 April 1999 (however, limited to one phone per employee).
- However this does not cover the reimbursement of private calls made on the employee's own phone, which remain taxable.
- Neither does it cover the cost of vouchers used by employees to make calls, unless covered by ITEPA 2003, s 328(1).

13.148 For years before 1999–2000, mobile phones were a notoriously difficult area for employers to police, as many departments of an organisation may have had authority to buy such phones, and their existence may not have been notified to the tax department. Apart from this general control issue, the following points should also be considered:

- There was no tax charge on a mobile phone used privately if the employee was both *required* to pay, and did pay, the cost of any private use. If the employee was not required to pay, e g by written instructions before the beginning of a tax year, even if the costs were reimbursed, HMRC had argued that this would not allow the employee to escape a tax charge. However, the wording of the section was that the payment must be made *for* a tax year and thus retrospection should be permitted.
- The reimbursement must have been of the full cost, not just the call charges. Full cost required that the employee paid a proper proportion of the equipment rental or, if the employer owned the equipment, the 20% annual value charge. In practice this was generally covered by requiring the employee to reimburse private calls, plus a certain mark-up.
- The tax was chargeable in full even if only one private call had been made and not reimbursed. There were no de minimis rules. However, if the telephone was first made available part way through the year, or ceased being available at a date during the year, or was unavailable for at least 30 days at some point, the charge could be reduced.

Personal incidental expenses (ITEPA 2003, s 240)

13.149 Employees often incur incidental expenses when staying away from home, such as laundry, personal phone calls and newspapers. Until FA 1995 these items tended to be covered by dispensations, although under strict law they do not meet the requirements of ITEPA 2003, s 328.

13.150 From 6 April 1995 a specific relief was introduced. Now, an employee is not taxable on personal incidental expenses up to £5 per night (£10 outside the UK) if he is away on business for at least one night. The new relief was heralded as deregulatory, in practice it is more likely to cause problems for employers when audited.

13.151 Particular note should be taken of the following:

- If the payment is more than £5, the whole amount is taxable and subject to NICs.
- If an employee stays away for several nights consecutively, the total allowance is the £5 times the number of nights away. For example, where an employee stays away for four nights and claimed £5 on the

first night, £5 on the second, £6 on the third and £4 on the fourth he would be within the exemption because the total does not exceed £5 × 4. Where the number of nights is not consecutive, no averaging is allowed.
- Where the limit is exceeded the employer should check that the employee was not bearing some costs of other employees. If he was, HMRC will accept an apportionment (HMRC Booklet 480 App 8).

Prizes

13.152 A prize won in a competition only open to employees is within the scope of Schedule E. See also gifts (**13.144**), suggestion schemes (**13.160**), and third-party benefits (**13.162**).

Relocations

13.153 The rules for relocations were made infinitely more complex by the introduction in 1993 of TA 1988, Sch 11A. This lays down detailed rules as to which relocation costs are allowable, or, as the legislation puts it, eligible. Eligible expenses of up to £8,000 per relocation will not be taxed.

13.154 Note that there is no requirement for overpayments of such eligible expenses to go through PAYE, even where the excess is a cash sum. However, payments of ineligible amounts must be taxed under the normal rules, which include the application of PAYE where appropriate.

13.155 In particular a reviewer will check that:
- The employer has clearly separated eligible and ineligible relocation costs, and that the latter have been either taxed under PAYE or included on the employee's P11D as appropriate. Ineligible costs include:
    (1) abortive relocation costs (ie where the employee does not actually relocate after all);
    (2) council tax;
    (3) duplicate costs of any items which are not 'domestic', such as school fees or season ticket costs;
    (4) higher cost housing payments for moving to a more expensive area – these were allowed, within limits, until the new legislation was introduced;
    (5) transport and installation costs of non-domestic items, such as boats or horses;
    (6) travel allowances paid to employees who choose not to relocate.
- The £8,000 limit on eligible expenses has not been exceeded in the tax year, and if it has, whether the excess has been included on the employee's P11D.
- Where a relocation crosses a tax year, the amount spent in the previous tax year has been carried forward in calculating whether the £8,000 limit has been exceeded.
- The time limits on paying or providing eligible relocation expenses/ benefits have been adhered to. If expenses have been paid after the time limit, has permission been sought from the local inspector to extend the

13.155 *Employees and directors*

limit? In practice, where permission has not been sought but it is reasonable to believe that an extension would have been granted had a request been made, the inspector will generally accept this.
- The payment of any flat rate allowances as part of the £8,000 limit has been agreed in advance with the local Inspector of Taxes (IR Press Release 14 April 1993). If not, the employer can argue that the allowance should be accepted if it is:
    (1) required to be spent on eligible costs; and
    (2) broadly within the limits allowed to the civil service. Unfortunately these are no longer published, as each government department has been given authority to set its own limits. The most recent allowances were set in 1993 as follows:

Married householder	£2,705
Single householder	£1,645
Single non-householder	£635

Reasonable increases on these amounts to allow for inflation should be accepted by HMRC.
- The complex rules for beneficial bridging loans have been complied with. Interest on bridging loans can be included as an eligible cost but only insofar as the £8,000 limit has not been used to cover other eligible relocation expenses. Interest therefore forms the top slice of eligible costs. This unused slice of relocation relief is then used to determine how long the beneficial loan can be outstanding before it becomes taxable. The formula for calculating this is given in ITEPA 2003, s 288(4).
- Any guaranteed price scheme is being correctly operated. Again, this is complex, and failure may mean that significant sums fall into tax. HMRC explained the legal position in the *Tax Bulletin* of April 1995.

13.156 Note that until 6 April 1998 the Contributions Agency rules on relocation were not affected by the Schedule 11A rules and thus some elements of a relocation package were taxable but not subject to NICs (CWG2 (1998) 78). However for relocations after 6 April 1998 the NI rules broadly follow the tax legislation, although a number of important differences remain. In particular, there is no £8,000 cap for NI purposes, so if an expense qualifies as allowable, no NI was charged, irrespective of the amount. A further year of grace was allowed for relocation payments made via a PSA agreement, with no contributions being due until 1999. Employers should thus analyse the position of their relocated employees with care before agreeing to any audit settlement.

Staff social functions

13.157 The inspector will check whether staff social functions fall within ITEPA 2003, s 264. It is important to ensure that:
- the allowable limit (currently £150 per attendee) has not been exceeded;
- in calculating the £150 the employer has:
    (1) included VAT, and

Employees and directors **13.161**

- (2) where relevant, travel to the function and accommodation, and
- (3) that the cost is on a per head basis of those who actually attended, not those who could have attended;
- the function was open to employees generally. In practice a number of departmental functions which are of a similar nature will be accepted as falling within this condition;
- if the allowable limit for a single function has been exceeded, the full amount is taxable and not just the excess;
- if there have been a number of functions and the total cost is more than £150, HMRC will disregard those functions which total £150 or less but will tax the others in full.

Note that the concession currently in place is more generous than the previous version, and that more restricted rules apply to tax years before 1995–96.

Subsistence

13.158 Along with travel, this is perhaps the most fruitful area of review for an HMRC official. Particular points which will be checked are whether:

- The payments of subsistence allowances or the reimbursement of actual costs are reasonable in amount. HMRC have now published rates that they consider can be paid free of income tax. These limits do not apply if an employer simply met the costs incurred by the employee.
- Allowances are paid or amounts reimbursed only when the employee is away from his normal place of work or holding a travelling appointment.
- Meals for late working have been taxed. However, the Revenue concession can be argued to apply if the meals are available to all who work late.
- Where a working rule agreement applies, the terms have been followed.

13.159 Complex new rules on travel and subsistence were introduced with effect from 6 April 1998 (ITEPA 2003, s 328). However, it should be noted that subsistence is treated as part of travel, and thus any food or accommodation provided in conjunction with travel which does not fall within the new rules, will itself be taxed and subject to NIC.

Suggestion schemes

13.160 These are exempt from tax if they fall within ITEPA 2003, s 321. Note that the NIC rules are more generous (CWG2 (2000) 70). See also Incentive Valuation Unit.

Telephones

13.161 The official will check whether the employer has reimbursed any part of home telephone costs. See also mobile phones at **13.147**.

13.161 *Employees and directors*

- All home telephone calls paid should have been included on the P11D (other than necessary business calls). Evidence will be required to support the business calls unless they are covered by a dispensation.
- Line rental is regarded as taxable (*Lucas v Cattell* (1972) 48 TC 353) unless:
  (1) employees can show that it is genuinely part of their duties to deal with emergencies; or
  (2) the employee's home is the place of employment; or
  (3) the contract for the telephone is in the employer's name; or
  (4) the telephone is used exclusively for business.

In (1) and (2) a proportion of the rental charge is allowable. HMRC generally seek to allow only the same proportion as the business use of the telephone is of the overall use. In (3) there is no charge to either tax or NICs (*Pepper v Hart*; CWG 2: 79 and (d)).

Third-party benefits

13.162 To date this has not been a significant review area but the position is changing with self-assessment. Many gifts are covered by the concession, which exempts from tax gifts received by employees from a third party by reason of their employment and totalling £150 or less from the same source in a single tax year. Until 1995–96 the limit was £100. This concession does not cover gifts provided by, or by arrangement with, the employer. The only review risk here is that if the limit is exceeded the full amount, not just the excess, is taxable.

13.163 The reporting rules for third parties under self-assessment have increased the risks to employers. These cover expenses payments or benefits provided to employees by a third party other than those covered by the concession. They took effect for 1996–97 onwards and require that where a third-party benefit is provided, the third party must provide the employee with details of the cash equivalent of the benefit in writing by 6 July after the end of the tax year. The employer of the employee who has received these third-party benefits is also required to tell HMRC the name and address of the provider (FA 1995, s 106(9)(c); SAT2 and SAT3). Where the benefit has been provided by arrangement with the employer, the latter must provide details of both the amounts and the name and business address of the other person (FA 1995, s 106(9)(b)).

13.164 These are extensive requirements and, combined with the self-assessment enquiry powers will have a significant effect on companies' audit settlements.

Travel

13.165 Reimbursing employees' travel expenses, or paying an allowance to cover travel costs, is invariably the subject of Revenue review. New legislation on travel and subsistence was finally introduced with effect from 6 April 1998 (ITEPA 2003, s 337). This was supplemented by the publication, in January

Employees and directors **13.168**

1998, of the Revenue's 'Employee Travel: a Tax and NIC Guide for Employers'. This booklet is destined to become the reviewers' bible, and any employer who wishes to ensure compliance with the new rules would be advised to study its numerous examples. The Guide has been further extended by *Tax Bulletin* articles (*Revenue Tax Bulletin* December 1997; February 1998 and April 1998).

13.166 Problems are likely to arise when considering the operation of:

- the two-year rule for site-based employees;
- the interpretation of 'substantially ordinary commuting';
- whether an employee has more than one permanent workplace;
- the difference between employees with an 'area' and those with 'travelling appointments'.

13.167 It should be remembered that the Guide is only a guide, not dogma. In cases of dispute, reference should be made both to the legislation and to its purpose: see IRPR 24 September 1997 and 9 January 1998.

13.168 For earlier years, the Revenue will look in particular for:

- Payment of travel costs other than those necessarily for business. Note that the 'wholly and exclusively' test does not apply to travel, see ITEPA 2003, s 337. This will include any reimbursement of home to work travel other than those included in a WRA, eligible relocation costs, emergency call outs (see point (4) below) and amounts payable on a secondment which is expected to last less than a year (see point (5) below). Note that where an employer reimburses home to work costs HMRC may seek to recover the fuel scale charge which applies when petrol costs for private use are paid by the employer.
- Cases where employers reimburse business miles. Here HMRC applied the 'triangular travel' principle. This only allowed the employer to reimburse on a tax-free basis the lower of the actual miles travelled on business and the miles which would have been travelled to reach that location if the employee had set off from his normal place of work rather than from home. Failure to tax any payments in excess of this can be very expensive for the company. However, it should be noted that this principle is a deviation by HMRC from the law, and has never been established as such in either statute or case law. It is unclear whether HMRC would be prepared to take a contested case to court, and an employer faced with a large retrospective liability may want to obtain a counsel's opinion on the law as it stands.
- Proper controls over mileage reimbursements to ensure that only allowable business miles, according to HMRC's definition, are being reimbursed. The rates of reimbursement will also be reviewed: are they in line with the fixed-profit car scheme rules? Have they been agreed with the local inspector? Excess payments for mileage can be an expensive part of a review settlement, as what appear to be relatively small amounts are spread over a large number of miles and employees. Note that under self-assessment the employer must report details of the

13.168 *Employees and directors*

mileage paid, including any profit, on P11Ds, unless this has been covered by a dispensation.
- Transport vouchers (including season tickets and travel passes) provided for any employees by reason of their employment, including those in the form P9D category. These are taxable unless the travel is genuine business and does not include home to work. Employees who worked at a succession of different places (site-based employees) were regarded as having a 'normal place of work' at each site, and thus any reimbursement of travel costs or a travel allowance was taxable as was subsistence. Since the employee was likely to have counted this travelling as business rather than private, the reclassification was also likely to affect his car benefit calculation and the employer's NICs. This has in practice resulted in some very large settlements following HMRC reviews. Contrast this with secondments at point (5) below. Both areas are significantly affected by the new rules.

13.169 In addition, the following general points on the review of travel should be noted:

(1) Cases where an employer pays for or reimburses the cost of late-night travel home. This is taxable unless it falls within the concession, which requires that:
  (a) public transport has ceased or could not reasonably be used; and
  (b) the employee travels from home to work by public transport; and
  (c) normally works fairly regular hours; but
  (d) is occasionally required to work late (HMRC in practice accept that 60 occasions a year or fewer is occasional);
  (e) the pattern of late working must not be regular, e g every Friday.

  The same rules apply to NICs.

(2) Where an employee holds a travelling appointment, the reimbursements or allowances are more flexible and are likely to include travel from home. It may be necessary for the employer to establish that an employee or a group of employees hold a travelling appointment, for which there is no definition in law. HMRC's view is that 'for an employee to hold a travelling appointment ... travel must be a fundamental part of the job and not just to put the employee in a position to do the job' (ECM 13099).

(3) Employees who are based at home and travel from there. These are regarded by HMRC as working from home, usually as a matter of personal choice. To have the costs of home to office travel allowed, the employer must demonstrate that it is an objective requirement of the employment that the employee must work at home. Often the inspector will ask whether the employee has a desk and other facilities on the employer's premises, and if they do will reject the premise that the employee is home-based. Such a finding is expensive for the employer with a number of employees who work in this fashion. It is advisable to obtain clearance in advance of any review that the employees are 'home-based'. The current HMRC position is described at para 2.13.1 of the Consultative Document on Employee Travel of 13 May 1996. For

a defence, see *Horton v Young* (1971) 47 TC 60 and HMRC's view of this in SE 4402.
(4) Where an employer pays emergency call-out expenses, these will be taxable unless the employee has given instructions before leaving home and had continuing responsibility for the emergency whilst travelling to the normal place of employment (*Pook v Owen* (1969) 45 TC 571). Health service employees have for some time generally been required to certificate any such travel expenses to say that they met these criteria. If this is not done, the inspector is likely to attack any such reimbursement.
(5) Under the pre-FA 1998 rules, home to work travel (and subsistence) was not taxable if the employee had a normal place of work and was temporarily seconded to another. For periods before 6 April 1998 the payment was tax free if:
  (a) the absence did not exceed 12 months; and
  (b) the employee returned to his normal place of work at the end of the secondment.

13.170 If it became obvious at some point in the period that the employee would not return within 12 months, payments were taxable from that date (P7 (1996) T5). The same rules applied to NIC (NI 269 164:83).

LIABILITY FOR TAX ARISING

13.171 Where an employer does not tax an item which should have been included in PAYE, the primary liability for any back tax, interest and penalties is with the employer). The employee cannot currently be made to pay the tax unless it was reasonable to assume that he knew the item should have been taxed and that it had not been onwards.

13.172 There is a statutory exception for directors, on the basis that 'in practice the failure to deduct tax from remuneration nearly always occurs in respect of certain directors'. So special legislation was introduced to treat the amount of any tax paid by someone other than the director as a benefit chargeable on the director (ITEPA 2003, s 223(7)). Note that this only applies to directors as defined at **13.106**.

13.173 The position is different for benefits. Here the primary liability for paying the tax rests with the employee, and the employer can therefore refuse to settle the unpaid tax on benefits which is uncovered during a review, and require that HMRC assess the individuals. However, HMRC can penalise the company for filing an incorrect P11D, and this can result in fines of up to £3,000 for each incorrect form.

13.174 The refusal to settle the tax under-deducted on P11Ds can be used judiciously to reduce the costs of a settlement, as HMRC will often be reluctant to go to the trouble and expense of assessing hundreds of employees on what is, individually, often a fairly small amount.

Chapter 14

The new penalty regime

Graham Funnell

Independent Tax Journalist

(From original material by John Newth FTII)

14.01 Tax advisers and accountants became familiar with the former tax penalty regime under TMA 1970, s 95 and the corresponding legislation for corporation tax defaults, PAYE defaults and VAT offences, as well as the penalties for failure to notify chargeability to tax, late filing of returns and late payment of tax. However HMRC and the government obviously took the view that the charging of tax penalties was being imposed unevenly, and in the view of HMRC, some penalties were far too lenient for the type of tax offence committed. Another issue was the desire for the standardisation of penalties following the merger of the Inland Revenue and Customs & Excise.

14.02 It was also clear that HMRC had the capacity to extract a substantial amount of revenue through the imposition of penalties on individual taxpayers, companies and partnerships. This is illustrated by the amount of revenue received from the late filing penalties imposed on self-assessment taxpayers. In the current economic climate this has no doubt proved to be a miniature 'goldmine' for the department.

CONSULTATION DOCUMENTS

14.03 The views of HMRC resulted in the publication of a number of consultation documents between 2005 and 2009. The overall theme of these consultation documents was 'HM Revenue & Customs and the Taxpayer: Modernising powers, deterrents and safeguards'. Other consultation documents were entitled 'A new approach to penalties for incorrect returns' and 'Penalties reform: The next stage'. Results of consultations were published in a Document entitled 'A new Approach to Compliance Checks: Responses to Consultation and Proposals'.

14.04 *The new penalty regime*

14.04 The result of these consultations has been a fundamental change in tax law regarding the powers of HMRC and the imposition of penalties. It is the latter issue that forms the main focus of this chapter.

14.05 Such has been the volume of new legislation regarding this subject in the past three years, as well as the publication of comment by HMRC, that it is impossible to cover every detail of tax penalties legislation and practice in one chapter of a book. The HMRC Compliance Handbook alone includes enough material for a complete book in its own right.

14.06 The writer will therefore attempt to point readers to detailed sources of information about tax penalties, and also highlight the main principles of the new regime.

NEW LEGISLATION

14.07 The legislation regarding HMRC information powers and the new penalty regime is as follows:

- s 97 of and Sch 24 to the Finance Act 2007 – penalties for errors;
- s 113 of and Sch 36 to the Finance Act 2008 – information and inspection powers;
- s 114, Finance Act 2008 – computer records;
- s 115 of and Sch 37 to the Finance Act 2008 – record keeping;
- s 116 of and Sch 38 to the Finance Act 2008 – disclosure of tax avoidance schemes;
- s 118 of and Sch 39 to the Finance Act 2008 – time limits for assessments, claims etc;
- s 119, Finance Act 2008 – correction and amendment of tax returns;
- s 122 of and Sch 40 to the Finance Act 2008 – penalties for errors;
- s 123 of and Sch 41 to the Finance Act 2008 – penalties for failure to notify etc;
- s 93 of and Sch 46 to the Finance Act 2009 – responsibilities of senior accounting officers of large companies;
- s 94, Finance Act 2009 – naming and shaming tax defaulters;
- s 95 of and Sch 47 to the Finance Act 2009 – amendment of some existing information powers;
- s 96 of and Sch 48 to the Finance Act 2009 – amendment of information powers included in Sch 36 to the Finance Act 2008;
- s 97 of and Sch 49 to the Finance Act 2009 – provision that HMRC may issue notices requiring third parties to provide contact details for those in debt to HMRC;
- s 98 of and Sch 50 to the Finance Act 2009 –extension of record-keeping rules to other taxes;
- s 99 of and Sch 51 to the Finance Act 2009 – amendment of time-limits applying to certain taxes;
- s 100 of and Sch 52 to the Finance Act 2009 – explanation of changed rules regarding overpaid income tax, corporation tax and capital gains tax;

- ss 101–105 of, and Schs 53 and 54 to the Finance Act 2009 – provisions regarding interest on tax paid to and by HMRC;
- s 106 of and Sch 55 to the Finance Act 2009 – creation of new penalty regime for late filing of tax returns;
- s 107 of and Sch 56 to the Finance Act 2009 – creation of new penalty regime for late payment of taxes;
- s 108 of the Finance Act 2009 – cancellation of penalties where taxpayers have entered into an agreement with HMRC to defer payment of taxes;
- s 109 of and Sch 57 to the Finance Bill 2009 – amendments to Sch 24 to the Finance Act 2007 (penalties for errors) and Sch 41 to the Finance Act 2008 (penalties for failure to notify and certain other wrongdoing).

HMRC MATERIAL

14.08 The legislation up to Finance Act 2008 is reflected comprehensively in the HMRC Compliance Handbook. Paragraphs CH 81001 to CH 84974 and CH 401100 to CH 451540 deal with every aspect of the new penalty regime at great length, and are invaluable resources for the busy tax practitioner.

14.09 There are two provisos regarding this HMRC Manual. First, it will need to be updated to reflect the new legislation included in the Finance Act 2009. Second, it must always be remembered that the contents of HMRC manuals are not law but the department's view of any particular situation. Practitioners should always go back to the law itself for confirmation of any particular issue. Having said that, the Compliance Handbook is an excellent resource.

14.10 HMRC also issued Notice 160, dated 25 June 2009, entitled 'Enquiries into indirect tax matters', which explains the procedure for checks into indirect tax matters if HMRC suspects conduct involving dishonesty.

DEFAULTS AND ERRORS

14.11 The legislation introduced by Sch 24 to the Finance Act 2007 concerns defaults and errors and applies to income tax, corporation tax, capital gains tax and VAT. As previously mentioned, its application and that relating to the Finance Act 2008 is dealt with exhaustively in the HMRC Compliance Handbook at CH 81001–CH 84950.

14.12 The FA 2007 legislation commenced for income tax periods which commenced after 31 March 2008, where the return is filed after 31 March 2009. Correspondingly the legislation commenced for corporation tax periods for the year ended 31 March 2009 and later where the company has a 12-month accounting period.

14.13 FA 2008 extended the penalties for tax errors to insurance premium tax, inheritance tax, the two stamp duty taxes, petroleum revenue tax, excise duties and a whole list of other taxes and duties. The provisions in respect of

14.13 *The new penalty regime*

these particular taxes become effective for return periods commencing on or after 1 April 2009, where the return for that period is filed on or after 1 April 2010.

14.14 FA 2008 also introduced new legislation in respect of HMRC information and inspection powers, computer records, record keeping, disclosure of tax-avoidance schemes, time limits for assessments, claims etc, correcting and amending tax returns and penalties for failure to notify.

14.15 Exceptions to the normal rule for commencement dates are set out in the HMRC Compliance Handbook at CH 81012 and CH 81013.

POTENTIAL LOST REVENUE

14.16 Tax penalties are applied to 'potential lost revenue' of HMRC. The new regime is intended to focus on taxpayer behaviour. As will be seen in the following paragraphs, penalties are 'stepped' so that they will increase depending on the seriousness of the taxpayer's failure, although 'size and gravity' is not mentioned in the legislation or associated literature. Accordingly the idea is to move from a 'nil' penalty for an innocent mistake to much higher penalties for deliberate understatements of tax, particularly when compounded by concealment. Guidance as to how HMRC will interpret taxpayer behaviour has been published.

14.17 Penalties are applied to 'potential lost revenue', which Sch 24, para 5(1) describes as the additional amount due or payable in tax and national insurance as a result of correcting the inaccuracy or assessment.

14.18 Potential lost revenue includes over-repayments made by HMRC. Calculations of group relief and close company relief for loans under TA 1988, s 419(4A) are ignored for the purposes of assessing potential lost revenue, but this does not prevent a penalty being imposed for an inaccurate claim for relief (see CH 82282–CH 82284).

14.19 The HMRC Compliance Handbook at CH 82301–CH 82370 makes it clear that losses over-claimed will contribute to potential lost revenue.

14.20 Examples of the calculation of the penalty based on potential lost revenue are illustrated in CH 82161 and at CH 82260 and CH 82272 for overstatements.

DOCUMENTS SUBJECT TO THE NEW REGIME

14.21 These are listed in FA 2007, Sch 24, para 1 and apply to documents which contain an inaccuracy which amounts to or leads to:

- an understatement of an individual's liability to tax,
- a false or inflated statement of a loss by an individual, or
- a false or inflated claim to repayment of tax.

14.22 It should be noted that giving a document to HMRC includes a reference to communicating information to HMRC in any form and by any method. This includes by post, fax, e-mail and verbally.

Income tax or capital gains tax

14.23 Documents relating to income tax and capital gains tax subject to the penalty regime within FA 2007 are:

- personal tax returns under TMA 1970, s 8;
- trustee returns under TMA 1970, s 8A;
- a return, statement or declaration in connection with a claim for an allowance, deduction or relief;
- partnership returns under TMA 1970, s 12AA;
- statements or declarations in connection with a partnership return under TMA 1970, s 12AB;
- accounts in connection with a partnership return;
- a return for the purposes of PAYE regulations;
- returns under the CIS Scheme.

Corporation tax

14.24 Corporation tax documents coming within the provisions are:

- company returns under the FA 1998, Sch 18, para 3;
- return, statement or declaration in connection with a claim for an allowance, deduction or relief;
- accounts in connection with ascertaining liability to tax.

VAT

14.25 For VAT, documents described in the legislation are:

- VAT returns;
- returns, statements or declarations in connection with a claim.

Income tax, capital gains tax, corporation tax and VAT

14.26 Also included within the new penalty regime is any document which is likely to be relied upon by HMRC to determine without further enquiry a question about:

- the taxpayer's liability to tax;
- payments made by the taxpayer by way of or in connection with tax;
- any other payment by the taxpayer including penalties;
- repayments or any other kind of payment or credit to the taxpayer.

DEGREES OF CULPABILITY

14.27 FA 2007, Sch 24, para 3 states that inaccuracy in a document provided to HMRC is:

14.27 *The new penalty regime*

- 'careless' if the inaccuracy is due to failure by the taxpayer to take reasonable care;
- 'deliberate but not concealed' if the inaccuracy is deliberate but the taxpayer does not make arrangements to conceal it; and
- 'deliberate and concealed' if the inaccuracy is deliberate and the taxpayer also makes arrangements to conceal it, for example by submitting false evidence in support of an inaccurate figure.

14.28 An inaccuracy in a document given by a taxpayer to HMRC, which was neither careless nor deliberate when the document was given, is to be treated as careless if the taxpayer:

- discovered the inaccuracy at some later date, and
- did not take reasonable steps to inform HMRC.

CH 81168 illustrates that a penalty may be imposed for an inaccuracy due to the actions of another person.

Innocent error or mistake

14.29 The position has not really changed in this respect, although the new legislation confirms what will be accepted and gives taxpayers a modicum of protection. No penalty is imposed when the taxpayer has taken reasonable care to prepare and submit his or her self-assessment tax return. This default is only treated as 'careless' (see definition above and explanation below) where the taxpayer discovers the default and does not inform HMRC within a reasonable time.

Reasonable excuse

14.30 The term 'reasonable' was considered in the draft consultation documents. It is interpreted according to the situation of the individual taxpayer. It reflects materiality in the sense of the size of the default compared with the size of the taxpayer's business. In effect the previous 'size and gravity' or 'seriousness' concepts are retained, but in another form.

14.31 CH 81120 states that HMRC do not expect the same level of knowledge or expertise from a self-employed unrepresented individual as they do from a large multi-national company. It would therefore seem that HMRC have higher expectations from professionals than tradespersons and will penalise accordingly.

14.32 Comments in the Consultation Document of December 2006 suggest that HMRC might regard the following as innocent errors:

- an innocent error after taking reasonable care;
- a reasonable view of the law that proves to be wrong or is not pursued;
- an act or omission that does not form part of a pattern of behaviour and is untypical of the taxpayer concerned;
- the adoption of a treatment for tax purposes that is clearly disclosed to HMRC in a return or accounts, even if it is subsequently changed by agreement or Tribunal decision.

14.33 Examples given include:
- an arithmetical error but not as big so as to produce an error which should have been noticed;
- misclassifying an unusual item which is not big enough to prompt the need for professional advice;
- a mistake made by an assistant or employee;
- omitting a small (relative to overall liability) item from the return;
- a reasonable judgment is made eg on a valuation;
- a reasonable view of the law is adopted even if this differs from HMRC guidance.

14.34 Other actions that would be regarded as taking reasonable care are set out in CH 81130, with examples in CH 81131. In CH 81141, HMRC state:

> 'People do make mistakes. We do not expect perfection. We are simply seeking to establish whether the person has taken the care and attention that could be expected from a reasonable person in similar circumstances.'

14.35 CH 431010 sets out factors that may demonstrate that the taxpayer was not taking reasonable care with their affairs, and CH 431020–CH 431040 give illustrations of such behaviour. CH 84540 illustrates the issues that HMRC will consider when deciding whether the taxpayer has taken reasonable care.

Carelessness

14.36 The penalty for 'carelessness' is 30% of the potential tax lost. This is subject to mitigation down to nil where there is an 'unprompted disclosure' and to 15% where there is a 'prompted disclosure'.

14.37 An additional ingredient of this penalty is that it may be imposed in respect of a document submitted to HMRC on the taxpayer's behalf. This clearly applies, inter alia, to the accountant or tax adviser.

14.38 This level of penalty also applies when HMRC discover an inaccuracy later, but no reasonable steps had been taken to inform the department.

14.39 It can be seen that mitigation of the penalty is only granted for 'disclosure' although, as will be seen later in this chapter, account is also taken in effect for cooperation by the taxpayer and the seriousness of the case. The December 2006 Consultation Document gives examples of behaviour that would be construed as not taking reasonable care, including:
- a breach of duty existing at a time when the duty should have been performed;
- not doing something that the person knew or should have known ought to have been done and which the person concerned had the power to do;
- the absence of such skill, care and diligence as it was the duty and capacity of the person to bring to the work;
- omitting to do something that a reasonable person would do and the person concerned could do, or doing something that a reasonable person would not do;

14.39 *The new penalty regime*

- negligence. Importing some duty of neglect of duty in relation to facts or the interpretation of the law, provided the capacity to perform the duty is present.

14.40 Specific examples of carelessness are:

- making large arithmetical mistakes;
- mis-classifying items of income and expenditure without giving the matter adequate consideration or taking professional advice;
- keeping incomplete books and records;
- omitting occasional items of income and gains;
- having insufficient quality control over the work of others;
- applying PAYE wrongly, occasionally or to an unusual item without checking on the correct treatment.

14.41 CH 81145 gives specific examples of careless inaccuracies.

QUALITY OF DISCLOSURE

14.42 It should be noted that mitigation of penalties is now only given for disclosure. Disclosure is defined in FA 2007, Sch 24, para 9(1) as:

- informing HMRC about the return inaccuracy or under-assessment of tax;
- providing reasonable help to HMRC in quantifying the potential tax loss; and
- allowing HMRC access to books, records and information for the purpose of ensuring that the inaccuracy or understatement has been completely corrected.

14.43 CH 82410 outlines the penalty reductions for disclosure, and CH 82430 and CH 82432 explain the weighting that may be given to elements of disclosure. CH 82440–CH 82460 explain the penalty reductions for 'telling', 'helping' and 'giving access'.

Prompted and unprompted disclosure

14.44 A disclosure is 'unprompted' if it is made at a time when the taxpayer has no reason to expect that HMRC has discovered the default or is about to discover it or an under-assessment. In any other circumstances the disclosure is 'prompted'.

14.45 CH 82420 and CH 82421 elaborate on these definitions, and CH 82422 illustrates penalty reductions.

Aspects of disclosure

14.46 The quality of a disclosure is judged principally in terms of timing, nature and extent, although other factors may be considered.

14.47 In comparing this aspect of the new regime to the previous penalty regime, it is noticeable that no mitigation is given specifically for co-operation by the taxpayer (and his or her agent). However, co-operation is taken into account in effect because disclosure includes providing help to HMRC and allowing access to books, records and information.

14.48 Similarly, seriousness will be reflected in the category of the penalty imposition in respect of the tax deemed to be potentially lost by the taxpayer's default.

14.49 The HMRC Compliance Handbook at CH 82430 sets out three elements of disclosure. These are telling HMRC about the facts, giving HMRC reasonable help and allowing HMRC access to records. The elements of disclosure may be weighted as follows:

- telling – 30%;
- helping – 40%;
- giving access – 30%.

14.50 CH 82440–CH 82460 elaborate on the three elements of disclosure.

Failure to notify HMRC of under-assessment

14.51 A completely new penalty is announced for failure to notify HMRC of an under-assessment of income tax, corporation tax, capital gains tax or VAT. This penalty is imposed when the taxpayer fails to take 'reasonable steps' to notify the under-assessment of tax to HMRC within 30 days. This penalty is also a mitigable amount up to 30% of the potential tax lost, but can be reduced to 0% for an unprompted disclosure or 15% in the case of a prompted disclosure.

14.52 As in the case of taxpayer carelessness, this penalty is extended to acts by a third party acting for the taxpayer, notably the accountant or other tax adviser.

14.53 In assessing whether the penalty should be imposed, account is taken of the competence of the taxpayer to recognise that tax has been under-assessed, and what steps should have been taken by him or her if the under-assessment was recognised. This initial review is quite apart from the consideration of mitigation for disclosure.

14.54 Examples of penalties for under-assessment based on potential lost revenue are illustrated in CH 82162.

Deliberate understatement of tax

14.55 Where the taxpayer deliberately understates the tax liability, but such understatement is not concealed, the maximum mitigable penalty is 70%. This is mitigable by 50% in the case of an 'unprompted disclosure' and 35% in the case of a 'prompted disclosure', so that the penalty under these circumstances may be mitigated to either 20% or 35%.

14.56 Deliberate understatement of tax without concealment is defined as:

14.56 *The new penalty regime*

- deliberately not doing something which ought to be done; or
- deliberately getting something wrong.

14.57 Examples of this behaviour include:

- not recording all sales, especially where a pattern of under-recording appears to rule out a genuine misunderstanding.
- including personal expenditure in business expenditure in circumstances that rule out a genuine misunderstanding.
- making inadequate private use adjustments where the amounts are significant.
- omitting significant amounts of income.
- adopting inappropriate accounting treatment.
- describing transactions in a misleading way.
- deliberately misinterpreting the law with a view to understatement.

14.58 CH 81150 gives other examples of deliberate inaccuracies, with illustrations at CH 81151 and CH 432030 gives examples of indirect evidence of such behaviour.

14.59 It should be noted that within the examples is deliberately withdrawing money from an incorporated business and not making any attempt to make sure that it is treated correctly for tax purposes.

Deliberate understatement with concealment

14.60 Where the taxpayer understates tax deliberately, and this default is also concealed, the maximum penalty is 100% of the potential loss of tax, but once again can be mitigated. This level of penalty also applies to an inaccuracy due to the deliberate behaviour of another person.

14.61 Mitigation of up to 70% can be gained in the case of an 'unprompted disclosure', making the penalty 30%. In the case of an 'unprompted disclosure' mitigation of up to 50% is available, which would produce a penalty of 50%. The 'quality of the disclosure' is all important.

14.62 There is no statutory definition of concealment. However an example is the making of a deliberate error for tax purposes, covering it up, perhaps by producing a false document, and then destroying incriminating documentary evidence. Basically, it is submitting false evidence in support of figures known to be incorrect. This type of default is one step down from a situation where HMRC and the Revenue and Customs Prosecution Office (RCPO) would consider a criminal prosecution.

14.63 Examples of deliberate understatement with concealment are:

- creating false invoices or altering invoices;
- backdating or post-dating contracts or invoices;
- creating false minutes of meetings or minutes of fictitious meetings;
- destroying books and records;
- deliberately misleading accountants or HMRC;
- systematic diversion of income into undisclosed bank accounts and covering up the traces of this action;

- invoice routing, for example the purported sale or purchase of goods through a tax haven company (with no activity undertaken by that company even though contracts exist showing the contrary) leaving profits untaxed in that company;
- creating sales records that deliberately understate the value of the goods sold, the balance of the full price being paid separately to the person;
- describing expenditure in the business records in such a way as to make it appear to be business related when it is in fact private (possibly with the supplier agreeing to change the description on the relevant invoices);
- alteration of genuine purchase invoices to inflate their value.

14.64 CH 81160 also includes compiling false business accounts to support the availability of agricultural or business relief for IHT and misdeclaring the strength of alcoholic products. Specific examples are given at CH 81161.

Special reduction

14.65 Another new concept is the 'special reduction' that HMRC may apply in special cases. This penalty reduction will be applied rarely, and the taxpayer and his or her advisers will have to make a strong case for special circumstances to apply. It is not yet clear in what circumstances this reduction will apply, but inability to pay the tax or penalty will not be valid, and neither will the proposition that tax underpaid has been covered by an overpayment by another taxpayer. CH 82490 outlines HMRC thinking on the subject.

Timing differences

14.66 In cases that do not involve unrelieved losses, where timing differences are involved, a non-mitigable penalty of 5% may be imposed. The penalty is 5% for each year of the delay or part thereof.

Suspended penalty

14.67 Another new concept is the suspended penalty. At the lower end of the penalty scale, where HMRC allege carelessness, involving a penalty of between 0% and 30% of the potential tax loss, HMRC may agree to suspend the penalty for up to two years. In order for this to happen the taxpayer must agree steps to remedy the situation. HMRC will impose conditions during the suspension period. If the taxpayer complies with the conditions and satisfies HMRC, then the suspended penalty will be cancelled. HMRC must state:
- what part of the penalty is being suspended;
- the period of the suspension, which must not exceed two years; and
- the conditions which must be complied with by the taxpayer. These can include specific actions and time limits.

14.68 CH 83130–CH 83160 explain in what circumstances a penalty might be suspended. CH 83190 details the remedial action taken by the taxpayer that will affect penalty suspension, and CH 450660 and CH 450670 outline the

14.68 *The new penalty regime*

issues that HMRC will consider before granting a suspension. CH 450680–CH 450730 deal with conditions for granting a suspension and CH 450740 with the period of suspension.

14.69 HMRC have used the acronym SMART in the Compliance Handbook at CH 83250 to illustrate the conditions that must be fulfilled, as follows:

- Specific – directly related to the business or individual being penalised;
- Measurable – in order to have a penalty cancelled the person needs to be able to demonstrate that conditions have been met;
- Achievable – the person must be able to meet the conditions;
- Realistic – unrealistic conditions cannot be imposed (for instance a condition that a business employ a full-time resource may be unreasonable for a small business with few business transactions);
- Time bound – the conditions must be met by a certain date.

Third-party errors

14.70 Paragraph 3 of Sch 40 to the FA 2008 provides that where an error in a taxpayer's document is attributable to another person, penalties of up to 100% of potential lost revenue may be imposed, but subject to reductions and the special reduction based on taxpayer behaviour.

NEW PENALTY CONCEPTS

14.71 The new legislation has spawned a number of new concepts applicable to the imposition of penalties for the type of income tax, corporation tax and VAT defaults already described. These are as follows:

- As already discussed there is a potential penalty for failing to notify HMRC of an under-assessment of tax.
- The penalties are applied to the 'potential lost tax revenue'. Broadly speaking, this is the additional tax found to be due as a result of the inaccuracy, default or failure to report under-assessment. Note that it is equally applicable to VAT.
- Group relief is ignored in estimating the potential tax lost relating to a given accounting period.
- The 5% penalty for timing differences, as described above.
- Extension of the penalties for carelessness and failure to report under-assessment of tax to actions or failures by a third party acting for the taxpayer. This is aimed principally at the accountant or other tax adviser. This is in sharp contrast to the current regime, where the HMRC Enquiry Manual at EM 5140 exempts the taxpayer generally for the defaults of the agent.
- Where there has been a deliberate understatement of tax, HMRC will have the power to attribute CTSA penalties to directors. This applies to cases where the potential maximum penalty is 100% or 70%. Where the taxpayer is a company and the default is due to the actions of an officer of the company, the penalty may be imposed on both the company and

the officer. However, to avoid double counting, HMRC is not permitted to recover a penalty of more than 100% in total.
- The scope of corporation tax extends to other bodies such as unincorporated associations (but excluding limited liability partnerships) and in these situations the definition of an officer means:
  - a director;
  - a manager;
  - a secretary;
  - any other person managing or purporting to manage any of the company's affairs.

14.72 However, FA 2008 provides that there can be no 'doubling up' of penalties, so that the total penalty cannot exceed 100%. This is of particular significance where both a company and one or more of its officers both attract a penalty.

14.73 The overstatement of losses may attract a tax penalty.

AMOUNT OF THE PENALTY

14.74 In assessing the penalty HMRC will proceed by:
- fixing a penalty for the nature of the action;
- basing the penalty on the 'potential lost revenue';
- taking into account whether any disclosure was prompted or unprompted;
- considering the 'quality' of the disclosure.

14.75 CH 82510–CH 82512 describe the penalty calculation process.

TIME LIMIT

14.76 The time limit for making a penalty assessment has been reduced. The current provision for direct tax allows a penalty determination to be made up to three years after the final determination of the tax lost. This is reduced to 12 months from either:
- the end of the appeal period for the decision correcting the inaccuracy; or
- if there is no assessment, the date on which the inaccuracy is corrected; or
- where the taxpayer has failed to tell HMRC of an under-assessment, the end of the appeal period in respect of the assessment relating to the tax understated.

APPEALS

14.77 Taxpayers will be able to appeal to the Tax Tribunal against the imposition or amount of any penalty or a decision not to suspend a penalty.

14.77 *The new penalty regime*

Where the appeal relates to whether a penalty should be suspended or whether HMRC should reduce the penalty due to special circumstances, the appeal body may consider whether HMRC's decision is reasonable. Paragraph 6 of Sch 57 to the Finance Act 2009 makes it clear that the taxpayer is not required to pay a penalty until the appeal against the penalty has been determined.

THE PREVIOUS PENALTY REGIME

14.78 Those practitioners who undertake investigation and enquiry work on behalf of clients will be familiar with the current penalty regime under TMA 1970, s 95 in connection with errors and defaults in connection with accounts and returns.

14.79 HMRC could impose a mitigable penalty of up to 100% of the tax deemed to have been lost due to fraudulent or negligent conduct of an individual, partnership or company.

14.80 No penalty was imposed where the taxpayer (or his or her adviser) made an error innocently and the error was remedied without delay. Where a penalty was imposed, the 100% maximum was mitigated on the following bases:

- up to 20% for disclosure or up to 30% for unprompted disclosure;
- up to 40% for co-operation;
- up to 40% based on the seriousness of the case (this used to be termed size and gravity).

The total mitigation could not exceed 100%.

14.81 Generally speaking, HMRC have not previously penalised taxpayers for the defaults of agents, as set out in the HMRC Enquiry Manual at EM 5140.

14.82 It appears that tax penalties of over 25% were rarely imposed except in serious cases, and this is one of the reasons that led to the consultations and new legislation. The views of HMRC also stated that:

- the average rates of penalties actually charged fell within a narrow band which provided insufficient room to differentiate between different types of behaviour;
- some of the terminology, such as 'negligence' is opaque to most taxpayers;
- there is not one regime but three, which adds to the lack of clarity for taxpayers about the rules and the potential outcomes; and
- the VAT misdeclaration penalty is not explicitly behaviour-rated and the high objective tests means that for many there is no sanction where a return is incorrect due to a failure to take reasonable care.

14.83 Whether one agrees with HMRC views or not, it is clear, as will be illustrated later, that the new regime is likely to yield higher penalties in the future in enquiry and investigation cases.

14.84 For failure to notify chargeability under TMA 1970, s 7 within six months of the end of a tax year a mitigable penalty of up to 100% of the tax unpaid at 31 January after the year of assessment could be imposed. The penalty for late submission of a self-assessment return was £100, a further £100 if the return was six months late and a continuing penalty of up to £60 a day in serious cases and where the Commissioners imposed the penalty.

14.85 For failure by an employer to submit returns such as Forms P11D timeously, the penalty was up to £300 plus £60 a day for the continued failure to file after the initial penalty had been imposed.

14.86 For an individual who failed to inform HMRC of the commencement of self-employment within three months of starting, a penalty of £100 could be imposed by the NI contributions section of HMRC.

14.87 For companies a flat rate penalty of £100 was imposed if the CT return was submitted late within three months of filing date, or £200 in other cases. The amounts were increased to £500 and £1,000 respectively for a third successive failure. For serious delays in filing where the return was not filed within 18 months, an additional tax-related penalty could be imposed of up to 10% of the unpaid tax where the return was filed within two years of the due date or 20% of the unpaid tax in other cases.

TRANSITIONAL RULES

14.88 The new legislation is not retrospective. This means that the two penalty regimes will run side by side for the next 20 years or so. The new regime will apply to defaults occurring after 31 March 2008 for defaults in connection with the main taxes and to defaults occurring after 31 March 2009 for other taxes, failure to notify chargeability and obstruction of HMRC information powers. The previous legislation under what were TMA 1970, ss 7, 93 and 95, the Finance Act 1998, Sch 18, paras 17–18 and other existing legislation will apply to tax defaults occurring before either 1 April 2008 or 1 April 2009.

COMPUTER RECORDS

14.89 Finance Act 2008, s 114 provides that a penalty of £300 may be imposed for obstruction in or failure to provide computer records required by HMRC.

INFORMATION AND INSPECTION POWERS

14.90 Section 113 of and Sch 36 to the Finance Act 2008 deal with HMRC information and inspection powers. Paragraph 39(2) of Sch 36 to the Act imposes a penalty of £3,000 for obstruction and failure to comply with HMRC requirements. This includes concealment, destruction or disposal of documents and is subject to the reasonable excuse provisions.

14.91 Paragraph 15 of Sch 47 to the Finance Bill 2009 extends the legislation to provide for the penalty to apply where a person carelessly or deliberately

14.91 *The new penalty regime*

provides inaccurate information and produces inaccurate documents in response to an information notice.

14.92 A daily penalty of up to £60 may be imposed where the offence continues. Both the initial and daily penalty must be imposed within 12 months of the 'relevant date'. An appeal procedure is available.

14.93 Where the offence continues HMRC may apply to the Upper Tribunal for a tax-related penalty, which is additional to the initial and daily penalties. All penalties must be paid within 30 days.

14.94 FA 2009 provides that existing rules are now applied to standard and daily default penalties only, and to ensure that the time limit works properly in relation to daily penalties a third 'latest date' is added.

14.95 Concealment, destruction and disposal of relevant documents are treated very seriously. The penalty is a fine or imprisonment for up to two years in addition to the fine.

14.96 These provisions will apply to obligations entered into after 31 March 2009.

FAILURE TO NOTIFY

14.97 Section 123 of and Sch 41 to the Finance Act 2008 deal with penalties for failure to notify etc. This legislation applies to obligations entered into on or after 1 April 2009 and will have effect on or after 1 April 2010.

Legislation affected

14.98 The legislation affects or replaces:

- TMA 1970, s 7 for income tax and capital gains tax;
- FA 1988, Sch 18, para 2 for corporation tax;
- various VAT obligations including obligation to notify and liability to register;
- various obligations for IPT, aggregates levy, climate change levy, landfill tax, excise duty and numerous other taxes and levies.

Penalty imposition

14.99 Penalties will be imposed, inter alia, on the basis of acts that are 'deliberate and concealed' or 'deliberate but not concealed'. The maximum rate of penalty is:

- 100% for acts that are deliberate and concealed;
- 70% where the default was deliberate but not concealed;
- 30% in other cases.

14.100 The penalty is applied to potential lost revenue, and for income tax and capital gains tax relates to tax unpaid on 31 January after the end of the tax year.

For corporation tax purposes the date is 12 months after the end of the accounting period.

14.101 Schedule 41, para 2 imposes a penalty on the unauthorised issue of a VAT invoice.

Reductions for disclosure

14.102 Schedule 41, paras 12 and 13 deal with reductions for disclosure by the taxpayer. The actions that will trigger this are:

- letting HMRC know about the default;
- giving HMRC reasonable help in quantifying the tax unpaid by reason of the default;
- allowing HMRC access to the business or other records for the purpose of checking how much tax is unpaid.

Quantification of disclosures

14.103 Disclosure is quantified by HMRC on the basis of the following:

- whether the act of failure by the taxpayer is unprompted and the taxpayer has no reason to think that HMRC has discovered or is about to discover the relevant act or failure;
- whether the act is prompted.

14.104 HMRC consider the quality and completeness of the disclosure and its timing (how promptly). The nature of the disclosure is also considered, in the sense of the level of evidence provided and degree and extent of access provided to test the disclosure.

Penalty reductions

14.105 The potential reductions in penalties are:

- the unprompted disclosure penalty of 100% can be reduced to not less than 30%;
- the prompted disclosure penalty of 100% can be reduced to not less than 50%;
- the unprompted disclosure penalty of 70% can be reduced to not less than 20%;
- the prompted disclosure penalty of 70% can be reduced to not less than 35%;
- in the case of an unprompted disclosure where the 30% penalty could be imposed, HMRC may reduce the penalty to nil or 10% where HMRC become aware less than 12 months after tax becomes unpaid by reason of failure to notify the relevant items. This reduction will depend on the quality of the disclosure;
- in the case of a prompted disclosure where a 30% penalty could be imposed, this may be reduced to not less than 10%, or in any other case

14.105 *The new penalty regime*

20%, depending on the quality of the disclosure, where HMRC become aware of the failure within 12 months.

14.106 Paragraph 14 of Sch 41 provides that in some instances HMRC will consider a special reduction.

Companies officers' liability

14.107 Paragraph 22 of Sch 41 provides that where a penalty is chargeable on a company for a 'deliberate action' offence, but the action is attributable to an officer of that company, HMRC may pursue all or part of the penalty from that officer. The position of 'officer of the company' means:

- a director;
- a manager;
- a secretary; and
- any other person managing or purporting to manage any of the company's affairs.

14.108 In these circumstances, the company officer is liable to pay such proportion of the penalty (which may be up to 100%) as is specified by HMRC within 30 days of the issue of the relevant notice.

Other issues

14.109 There is an appeals procedure, and the concept of reasonable excuse applies. Paragraph 21 of Sch 41 describes the provisions in respect of agents. When the taxpayer can satisfy HMRC that he has taken reasonable steps to avoid the failure, no penalty will be due despite a careless action taken by someone on his behalf.

14.110 It should be noted that the concept of suspended penalties does not extend to failures to notify chargeability to HMRC.

Previous penalty regime

14.111 Previously there was a diverse penalty regime for failure to notify, which included the following provisions:

- For income tax the penalty was a mitigable amount of up to 100% of the tax due but unpaid 10 months after the tax period in the case of income tax and 12 months for corporation tax. The £300 penalty for failure by a company to notify when it comes into charge was rarely imposed.
- For Class 2 NICs the penalty was £100 for failure to notify chargeability within three months of commencing business. Two-thirds of such penalties were cancelled for a variety of reasons.
- VAT penalties were complex. Failure to notify where the intention is to evade tax and the actions involve dishonesty could produce a penalty of up to 100% of the tax evaded (mitigable).

14.112 In other VAT cases involving late notification the penalty depended on the degree of lateness, as follows:

- 5% of the tax due for a failure of up to nine months;
- 10% where the late notification is between nine and 18 months; and
- 15% for over 18 months.

14.113 There was a minimum penalty of £50 where no VAT is due, but all the former VAT penalties were mitigable on the grounds of reasonable excuse. For excise duties there was a fixed penalty of £250 for failure to notify and in some instances criminal sanctions could be imposed. HMRC could also seize goods and equipment. Environmental taxes and insurance premium tax had penalties for failing to notify of 5% of the tax due.

SENIOR ACCOUNTING OFFICERS

14.114 Section 93 of and Sch 46 to the Finance Act 2009 introduced a provision whereby senior accounting officers of qualifying companies and the company itself could suffer a tax penalty in certain circumstances.

14.115 The company and its senior accounting officer must take reasonable steps to:

- establish and maintain appropriate tax accounting arrangements;
- monitor the accounting arrangements; and
- identify any respects in which the arrangements are not 'appropriate' for the accurate calculation of taxes and duties.

14.116 In addition the company must certify annually on or before the statutory accounts filing deadline:

- that appropriate arrangements were in place throughout the year; or
- an explanation of why arrangements were not appropriate.

14.117 Penalties of up to £5,000 may be imposed on the company for failing to notify the identity of the senior accounting officer during the financial year; and up to £5,000 on each count on the senior accounting officer personally for failure to:

- take reasonable steps to establish, maintain and monitor arrangements; or
- provide a certificate, or providing one with a careless or deliberate inaccuracy.

14.118 A later amendment to the draft legislation was passed at committee stage of the 2009 Finance Bill, defining a 'qualifying' company and limiting the new legislation to a company or group which has, at the end of its financial year:

- turnover of more than £200 million, and/or
- a balance sheet total of more than £2 billion.

NAMING AND SHAMING

14.119 Section 94 of the Finance Act 2009 provides for HMRC to publish information (including names) of persons who have been penalised for

14.119 *The new penalty regime*

deliberate defaults: inaccuracies, failing to notify, and certain VAT and excise duty wrongdoings, in each case where the tax lost exceeds £25,000.

14.120 No details will be published if the person has made a full disclosure, either prompted or unprompted, within a time considered appropriate by HMRC. Any details must be published within 12 months from the relevant penalties becoming final and may not continue to be published beyond 12 months from when first published.

14.121 This scheme mirrors the one that has been in existence in the Republic of Ireland for some years.

POWERS TO OBTAIN CONTACT DETAILS FOR DEBTORS

14.122 Section 97 of and Sch 49 to the Finance Act 2009 provides that HMRC may issue notices requiring third parties to provide contact details for those in debt to HMRC.

14.123 A person who fails to comply with a notice is liable to a penalty of £300. The procedures for penalties are similar to those for information powers under Sch 36 to the Finance Act 2008.

TIME LIMITS FOR ASSESSMENTS

14.124 Paragraph 16 of Sch 51 to the Finance Act 2009 reduces the period during which HMRC may make a determination of penalties or bring proceedings for penalties from six to four years from the date the penalty was incurred or, in the case of daily penalties, first incurred.

14.125 However the time limits remain at six years when the penalty relates to a loss of tax brought about carelessly and is increased to 20 years where it relates to a loss of tax brought about deliberately or when certain obligations have not been met.

These provisions take effect from 1 April 2010, with transitional arrangements.

PENALTIES FOR FAILURE TO MAKE RETURNS

14.126 Section 106 of and Sch 55 to the Finance Act 2009 creates a new penalty regime for late filing of tax returns for income tax, corporation tax, PAYE, national insurance contributions, the Construction Industry Scheme, stamp duty land tax, stamp duty reserve tax, inheritance tax, pension schemes and petroleum revenue tax.

14.127 Taxpayers have a right of appeal against all penalties and no penalty can be charged if the taxpayer has a reasonable excuse for his or her failure.

14.128 Implementation of the provisions will be staged over the next few years, and the provisions will be/have been brought into effect by Treasury Order.

MULTIPLE PENALTIES

14.129 More than one penalty may be charged in respect of the same failure. Each penalty can be applied and pursued in isolation and a person has a right of appeal against each of them. This is subject to the proviso that tax-geared penalties may not exceed 100% of the relevant liability to tax.

AMOUNT OF PENALTY

Occasional returns and annual returns

14.130 The initial penalty is fixed at £100, provided that the taxpayer's failure continues after the end of the period of three months beginning with the penalty date.

14.131 A daily penalty of £10 is imposed for each day that the failure continues during the period of 90 days beginning with the date specified in the penalty notice.

14.132 A penalty of the greater of £300 or 5% of the liability to tax shown in the return is imposed where the return is still outstanding six months after the filing date and there would have been a liability to tax shown in the return.

14.133 Where the failure continues after the end of a period of 12 months, and the taxpayer withholds information that would enable HMRC to assess the liability to tax:

- if the withholding of the information is deliberate and concealed the penalty is the greater of :
  - 100% of the liability to tax; and
  - £300.
- if the withholding of the information is deliberate but not concealed the penalty is the greater of:
  - 70% of the liability to tax; and
  - £300.
- in any other case the penalty is the greater of:
  - 5% of the liability to tax; and
  - £300.

CIS returns

14.134 A penalty of £100 is imposed if the taxpayer fails to submit a CIS return on time.

14.135 A penalty of £200 is imposed if the failure continues after the end of the period of two months beginning with the penalty date.

14.136 Where the failure to file a CIS return continues after the end of a period of six months beginning with the penalty date, the penalty is the greater of 5% of the liability to make payments under the CIS return and £300.

14.137 If the failure to file continues after the end of the period of 12 months beginning with the penalty date the penalty is the greater of 5% of any liability

14.137 *The new penalty regime*

to make payments and £300. However, where by failing to make a return, the taxpayer withholds information which would enable or assist HMRC to assess the tax due:

- if the withholding of the information is deliberate and concealed the penalty is the greater of 100% of the payments which should have been made and £3,000.
- if the withholding of information is deliberate but not concealed the penalty is the greater of 70% of payments which should have been made and £1,500.

14.138 Where the failure continues after the end of a period of 12 months beginning with the penalty date, and the information required in the return related only to persons registered for gross payment, and by failing to make the return information is withheld:

- a penalty of £3,000 is imposed if the withholding of information is deliberate and concealed;
- if the withholding of information is deliberate but not concealed, a penalty of £1,500 is imposed.

14.139 Fixed sum penalties are capped at £3,000 where the person has just entered the CIS scheme.

REDUCTIONS FOR DISCLOSURE

14.140 Reductions in penalties are given where a taxpayer discloses information which has been withheld by a failure to make a return. This involves:

- telling HMRC about it;
- giving HMRC reasonable help in quantifying any tax unpaid; and
- allowing HMRC access to records for the purpose of checking how much tax is unpaid.

14.141 Disclosure may be prompted or unprompted and the 'quality' of it includes timing, nature and extent.

14.142 Reductions of penalties will be made:

- Where the person who is otherwise liable to a 100% penalty makes an unprompted disclosure, HMRC must reduce the 100% penalty to not less than 30%.
- Where an individual liable to a 100% penalty makes a prompted disclosure, HMRC must reduce the 100% penalty to a percentage of not less than 50%.
- Where a person who is liable to a 70% penalty makes an unprompted disclosure, HMRC must reduce the penalty to not less than 20%.
- Where a person who would otherwise be liable to a 70% penalty makes a prompted disclosure, HMRC must reduce the penalty to not less than 35%.

14.143 HMRC must not reduce the penalty for occasional returns and annual returns below £300, and the CIS penalty to less than £3,000 where the failure to submit information was deliberate and concealed or £1,500 where the failure was deliberate but not concealed.

Special reduction

14.144 HMRC have a power to reduce any penalty, including the minimum amount penalty, where they consider it right because of special circumstances.

Interaction with other penalties

14.145 Where the taxpayer is liable to more than one penalty in connection with the same tax liability, then the appropriate reduction is made. Tax-geared penalties cannot exceed more than 100% of the relevant liability to tax.

Assessment and appeals

14.146 Provisions are made for the assessment, notification and enforcement of penalties, which are to follow the same procedures as for assessments to tax. Penalties must be paid within 30 days of notification.

14.147 The assessment of penalties must be made on or before the later of two dates. The first date is the last day of the two-year period beginning with the filing date. The second date is the last day of the period of 12 months beginning with the end of the appeal period for the assessment of the tax or the date when the tax was ascertained.

14.148 A taxpayer is not required to pay a penalty before any appeal against the assessment is determined. When a Tax Tribunal substitutes its decision for that of HMRC it may vary the special reduction if the original decision by HMRC was flawed.

Reasonable excuse

14.149 No penalty arises when the taxpayer satisfies HMRC or a Tax Tribunal that there was a reasonable excuse for the failure.

Determination of penalty geared to tax liability when no return made

14.150 It is provided that a liability to tax that would have been shown in a return means an amount that, if a complete and accurate return had been delivered on the filing date, would have been shown as due and payable by the taxpayer.

FAILURE TO PAY TAX

14.151 Section 107 of and Sch 56 to the Finance Act 2009 create a new penalty regime for late payment of income tax, corporation tax, PAYE, national

14.151 *The new penalty regime*

insurance contributions, The Construction Industry Scheme, stamp duty land tax, stamp duty reserve tax, inheritance tax, pension schemes and petroleum revenue tax.

14.152 The provisions of the Schedule are being brought into force over the next few years by Treasury Order.

Penalty imposed

14.153 The legislation introduces a table setting out the amounts of tax to which the new penalty provisions apply and the date after which the penalty will be incurred. The table defines the penalty date both for principal amounts of tax and amounts that might become due as the result of an assessment or determination of an amount of tax by HMRC, and a correction to a return by HMRC or a taxpayer. It states that if a taxpayer fails to pay an amount of tax in column 3 of the table by the date specified in column 4 of the table, the taxpayer will be liable to a penalty. A taxpayer may be liable to more than one penalty in the Schedule.

Amount of penalty: occasional amounts and amounts in respect of periods of six months or more

14.154 The Schedule defines the taxes to which this penalty model applies by reference to the table. The penalty is 5% of the unpaid tax. The penalty is incurred if the taxpayer fails to pay the tax in full by the date provided for in column 4 of the table. This date is normally 30 days after the due date for the tax.

14.155 It is provided that a taxpayer who has tax unpaid five months after the penalty date is liable to an additional penalty of 5% of the remaining unpaid tax. Where the tax is unpaid 11 months after the penalty date an additional penalty of 5% of the remaining unpaid tax is imposed.

Corporation tax

14.156 The first penalty date for corporation tax is the day after the filing date for the CT return rather than the day after the due date for the tax, which is usually three months earlier.

14.157 A penalty of 5% of the amount unpaid is imposed where the tax is unpaid the day after the CT filing date. Additional penalties of 5% of the remaining unpaid tax are imposed when the tax is unpaid three months after the penalty date, and a further 5% where failure to pay extends to nine months after the penalty date.

PAYE and CIS amounts

14.158 Penalties for PAYE and CIS defaults are imposed by reference to the number of defaults of payments made of the same tax during the tax year.

The new penalty regime **14.166**

14.159 The first failure does not count as a default. Where a taxpayer makes more than one, two or three defaults in a tax year, the taxpayer is liable to a penalty of 1% of the *total* amount of those defaults.

14.160 Where four, five or six defaults occur in a tax year, a penalty is imposed of 2% of the total of the defaults. For seven, eight or nine defaults the penalty is 3% of the total amount of the defaults, and for 10 or more defaults the penalty is 4%.

14.161 Additional penalties of 5% of the unpaid tax are imposed, initially, where the tax remains unpaid six months after the penalty date, and a further 5% penalty is imposed where the tax is unpaid 12 months after the penalty date.

Special reduction

14.162 A special reduction of the penalty may be granted by HMRC if special circumstances apply.

Suspension of penalty

14.163 Where a taxpayer makes a request to HMRC that the amount of tax already due be deferred, commonly referred to as a time-to-pay arrangement, and agreement is reached to defer the payment, then no penalty is imposed. This also applies when the agreement is extended. If the taxpayer breaks the agreement any penalty that would have been imposed before the deferral request is reinstated.

Assessments and appeals

14.164 A penalty must be paid before the end of 30 days from the issue of a notice of assessment. Assessments must be made on or before the later of two dates. The first date is the last day of the period of two years beginning with the date specified in column 4 of the table. The second date is the last date of the period of 12 months beginning with the end of the appeal period for the assessment of the amount of tax in respect of which the penalty is assessed, or if there is no such assessment the date on which the amount of tax is ascertained.

14.165 Where an appeal has been made, the taxpayer is not required to pay a penalty until the penalty has been determined. Where the Tax Tribunal substitutes its decision for that of HMRC, then it may apply its own special reduction if it considers that the original decision of HMRC in this respect was flawed.

Reasonable excuse

14.166 No penalty arises where the taxpayer satisfies HMRC or the Tax Tribunal that there is reasonable excuse for the failure.

14.167 *The new penalty regime*

SUSPENSION OF PENALTIES: DEFERRED PAYMENT

14.167 Section 108 of the Finance Bill 2009 provides that taxpayers who enter into agreements with HMRC to defer payment of taxes are not liable to certain surcharges or penalties that would otherwise become due because of late payment. The change becomes effective for deferral agreements reached on or after 24 November 2008.

14.168 If the taxpayer breaks the agreement, or fails to pay the tax when the deferral period ends, then the taxpayer becomes liable to the relevant penalty.

14.169 The taxes to which this provision applies are income tax and capital gains tax, VAT, aggregates levy, climate change levy, landfill tax, insurance premium tax and excise duties.

OFFSHORE DISCLOSURES

14.170 UK taxpayers with undisclosed income from offshore accounts were invited to reveal their earnings and suffer a limited penalty under HMRC's New Disclosure Opportunity (NDO), which ran from 1 September 2009 until 12 March 2010.

14.171 HMRC has begun to brief professional bodies regarding this new initiative. HMRC will impose a fine equal to 10% of the total unpaid tax, in line with the previous offshore disclosure facility. However, customers of high street banks who received letters under the 2007 offshore disclosure facility, but chose not to contact HMRC, will face a 20% penalty if they now use the NDO to make a disclosure. It is understood that where the tax due is less than £1,000, HMRC do not intend to charge a penalty.

14.172 All undeclared UK tax liabilities for the past 20 years, (whether or not connected with an offshore account), must be covered by the disclosure. Full payment of tax, interest and penalty must accompany the disclosure, although time to pay arrangements may be considered exceptionally provided proposals are made before the end of the NDO period. Interest is imposed as well as the penalty. Duties must be calculated using correct rates. This will, in some cases, lead to duties being chargeable in excess of 40%, for example where PAYE and NIC are in point.

14.173 The penalty percentages compare with a penalty percentage of 35–100% likely to be imposed by HMRC in cases where the department has discovered an offshore account without prior disclosure. Taxpayers who do not come forward could also face criminal prosecution. Criminal prosecution is unlikely if a disclosure is made under the NDO.

14.174 Tax advisers had to notify HMRC in paper form from 1 September 2009 and online from 1 October 2009 on behalf of clients, and advisers and taxpayers had until 30 November 2009 to register and notify their intention to disclose.

14.175 Taxpayers choosing to submit details of their disclosure in paper form had until 31 January 2010 to do so, while those preferring to disclose online had

The new penalty regime **14.181**

a deadline of 12 March 2010. Full payment of taxes and duties, interest and penalties must be made with any disclosure, although HMRC may consider time to pay if such a request is made during the disclosure 'window'. Disclosures must include undisclosed onshore income as well as offshore income.

14.176 HMRC originally stated that this is the last occasion on which taxpayers will be given the opportunity to 'clean up their act' on such favourable terms. After the end of the NDO date, taxpayers who failed to take advantage of the NDO are likely to face a full investigation and a tax penalty of at least 35%, or more. However, the more recent Disclosure Opportunities, for the medical profession, and plumbers etc, indicate that such specific campaigns by HMRC are going to continue.

14.177 HMRC will issue acceptance letters within four months of 12 March 2010 in most 'low risk' cases. Those deemed 'high risk' may have to wait for a longer period before finding out whether their disclosure has been accepted.

The Liechtenstein Disclosure Facility

14.178 The Liechtenstein Disclosure Facility is a bespoke service to support the reviews to be carried out by the financial intermediaries in Liechtenstein to identify those who may have a liability to UK tax. The LDF allows people with unpaid tax linked to investments or assets in Liechtenstein to settle their tax liability under this special arrangement.

14.179 The LDF runs from 1 September 2009 until 31 March 2015. Basic information will be posted on the HM Revenue & Customs website for taxpayers who consider they may qualify to register and for tax advisers with clients who may qualify to register. Only undeclared UK tax liabilities for the past ten years need to be disclosed under the LDF.

14.180 The LDF will cap penalties on unpaid tax at 10% of the tax evaded over the past ten years, provided the taxpayer provides full disclosure of his or her financial dealings. The penalty will be 20% where the taxpayer was notified of the Offshore Disclosure Facility (ODF) in 2007. However, where a person has been investigated by HMRC in the past and knowingly did not disclose his or her interest in the relevant property, then a 'significantly higher penalty' than the special rate of 10% will be applied. There is an assurance of immunity from prosecution for tax-related offences unless the source of the funds constitutes 'criminal property'. Individuals whose offence amounts to no more than innocent error will have to pay no more than six years of back tax, and no penalty will apply.

14.181 Tax can either be calculated using correct rates or a composite rate of 40% can be applied, without deductions or reliefs. Liability under the LDF, including penalty and interest, is payable when the disclosure is made, but HMRC will consider offers of instalment payments (with forward interest) subject to evidence as to means and the timing of the sale of assets.

14.182 *The new penalty regime*

14.182 Those taxpayers who are identified by banks and financial intermediaries in Liechtenstein as UK resident, and who fail to reveal all to HMRC by the end of the programme, will find their accounts in Liechtenstein closed down.

14.183 It is believed that up to 5,000 taxpayers may be affected by this new agreement between the UK and Liechtenstein governments.

BREACH OF MINIMUM WAGE LEGISLATION

14.184 From 6 April 2009, new laws mean that employers who fail to pay the minimum wage will face an automatic penalty of between £100 and £5,000 based on the amount they owe to their workers. This penalty will apply even if the underpayment was a mistake. In the most serious cases employers could also face an unlimited fine.

CONSEQUENCES AND ACTION

14.185 Taxpayers and their advisers will have to decide on their reaction to the new legislation. Accountants and tax advisers may well consider that this subject should be highlighted in a client newsletter, or as part of a client seminar. Whether they will wish to advertise the fact that penalties are extended to errors by the adviser of which the client was unaware is something that each firm will need to consider.

14.186 The new regime certainly underlines the need for good professional indemnity insurance, as clients are unlikely to be too pleased to have to pay a tax penalty for the default of their agent.

14.187 Other actions that could be considered are:

- a review of the risk-management programme relating to the tax affairs of the particular client. This may bring the opportunity for some added value services by the accountant;
- the marketing of professional expenses insurance by the professional practice. This will not cover any additional tax, interest or penalties imposed on the client, but would help towards the professional fees incurred, which are likely to be substantial in the case of any investigation or enquiry;
- revision of self-assessment procedures for clients, as Sch 36 of FA 2008 has dramatically altered previous safeguards regarding the HMRC powers of information seeking and inspection.

14.188 It should also be remembered that the new penalty regime still leaves room for negotiation of penalties by the professional adviser, and this aspect of investigation work remains extremely important. Current investigation practitioners will have to review their tactics in the light of the new legislation.

Chapter 15

Tax avoidance investigations

Andrew Hinsley

Ernst & Young

INTRODUCTION

15.01 Tax avoidance is a broad and emotive subject: one man's avoidance is another's legitimate planning. The term 'avoidance' has been used throughout this chapter as opposed to expressions such as tax planning but should be taken to mean any form of legal planning, whether acceptable or unacceptable from the perspective of Her Majesty's Revenue and Customs (HMRC).

15.02 A detailed review and analysis of avoidance, both in terms of statute and case law, is beyond the scope and purpose of this chapter (although a number of key cases will be considered). Rather, the aim is to provide an insight into the current avoidance environment in terms of HMRC's objectives and approach, the attitude of the tribunals and courts and the implications of this environment for practitioners.

15.03 Whilst this is essentially a practical book, it is essential to be mindful of the ever-evolving views of the courts to the interpretation of statute. Similarly, the fact that tax avoidance has recently become an issue of such strategic significance to HMRC, means it is essential for practitioners to have regard to the bigger picture, as well as to the detailed technical analysis.

15.04 This chapter therefore attempts to cover a mixture of strategic, technical and practical issues under the following headings:

- An introduction to tax avoidance
- HMRC's approach to combating avoidance covering the following areas:
  - strategic
  - operational
  - legislative
- The evolution of avoidance case law

15.04 *Tax avoidance investigations*

- HMRC's approach to working avoidance enquiries
- Key implications and considerations for the practitioner.

WHAT IS TAX AVOIDANCE?

15.05 Tax avoidance is not defined in statute and the judiciary has tended to shy away from attempts at a universally applicable definition. Lord Nolan in *CIR v Willoughby* [1997] STC 995 defined tax avoidance as 'a course of action designed to conflict with the evident intention of Parliament'. At first sight this appears to be a seemingly sensible working definition until one considers the difficulty divining the intention of Parliament has presented over the years and still does.

15.06 Michael J Graetz, a Yale law professor, defines a US tax shelter (the US equivalent of an avoidance arrangement) as 'a deal done by very smart people that, absent of tax considerations, would be very stupid'. Lord Templeman sought to differentiate between 'acceptable' and 'unacceptable' avoidance but this proposition has since been rejected, although arguably it persists but without formal judicial approval.

15.07 Whilst Templeman's approach has officially fallen out of favour with the courts, unofficially it is a commonly held view of practitioners operating in this area that judge's personal preferences or instincts can play a significant part in their interpretations. As such, whilst rejected as a judicial principle, Templeman's acceptable and unacceptable distinction perhaps plays a greater part in the rationale for judgments than most judges would care to admit.

15.08 The Economic Secretary to the Treasury, in providing assurances that straightforward tax planning would not be caught by the anti-avoidance provision at para 13 Sch 9 Finance Act 1996, quoted the following comment by a top adviser:

> 'companies will know when they are into serious tax avoidance; apart from anything else they are likely to be paying fat fees for clever tax advice and there will commonly be wads of documentation'.

15.09 In 2007, HMRC's Anti-Avoidance Group published guidance (available on its website (which can be accessed by the search facility on the HMRC site)) to enable taxpayers to better understand how it addresses the risks it perceives arise from tax planning. The guidance originally took the form of 'signposts' or features of transactions that HMRC is likely to challenge. More recently, HMRC has taken this concept a stage further by highlighting in its 'Spotlight' section the types of arrangement it believes are ineffective.

THE CURRENT AVOIDANCE ENVIRONMENT

Background

15.10 During the early part of 2000 the government was increasingly forming the view that the avoidance industry was getting out of control and action was required to curb its perceived excesses.

15.11 The merger of Customs and Excise and the Inland Revenue in 2004 undoubtedly gave a significant boost to the process of clamping down on avoidance. Customs had considerable success in curbing VAT avoidance and following the merger Chris Tailby (originally with Customs and Excise) headed up the Anti-Avoidance Group (AAG), the specialist HMRC department dealing with both direct and indirect tax avoidance.

15.12 HMRC's response can be split into three broad categories strategic, operational and legislative.

15.13 The strategic has involved:

- a fight to win 'hearts and minds' over the notion that tax avoidance is morally unacceptable and taxpayers should follow the spirit as well as the letter of the law in their approach to their tax affairs;
- the litigation and settlements strategy (LSS).
- Focusing resources on those companies which are perceived to represent the greatest risk via the 'High Risk Corporate Programme' (HRCP) for companies within Large Business Service and 'Managing Complex Risk' (MCR) for companies within Local Compliance, Large and Complex (LC).

15.14 The operational has involved:

- increased resource, internal reorganisations, revised working methods and better supporting technology;
- a change of behaviour in the form of a more aggressive pursuit of those undertaking tax avoidance arrangements.
- settlement programmes such as HRCP, Managing Complex Risk (MCR), CFC and EBT settlement initiatives.

15.15 The legislative has involved:

- the introduction of the disclosure regime in 2004 and subsequent tightening of the rules aimed at identifying avoidance arrangements at an earlier stage and counteracting the perceived abuse;
- the introduction of numerous targeted anti-avoidance provisions within new legislation.

Strategic initiatives

The moral dimension

15.16 Tax avoidance has never been popular with governments. However, in recent years both the previous Labour government and now the Conservative

15.16 *Tax avoidance investigations*

and Liberal Democrat coalition have signalled their commitment to crack down on tax avoidance with the introduction of a General Anti Avoidance Rule now a realistic prospect. HMRC and the government have over the last few years embarked upon a battle to win hearts and minds by seeking to make tax avoidance a moral issue and positioning itself on what it sees as the moral high ground. In so doing, HMRC has removed the gloves by using emotive statements in public pronouncements to paint a very black picture of anyone engaged in tax avoidance activity.

15.17 It was Dennis Healey who once said 'the difference between tax avoidance and tax evasion is the thickness of a prison wall'. This quote has been recycled by HMRC seemingly in an attempt to blur the distinction between tax avoidance and evasion, effectively tarring both with the same brush.

15.18 It is possible that this kind of rhetoric will influence a significant number of uninformed taxpayers and even practitioners from undertaking any form of avoidance, purely on the basis that they may perceive the risk as being too great. From HMRC's perspective if such comments achieve this aim, they are only likely to increase in frequency and intensity.

15.19 Whilst at a strategic level (in particular through the establishment of a Dispute Resolution Unit) HMRC is keen to promote a more collaborative approach to dispute resolution, this has yet to filter down to the majority of officers on the ground. Where avoidance is concerned the approach seems to be to make life as difficult as possible (unless the taxpayer's affairs are being dealt with as part of HMRC's special programme for companies with a number of outstanding high value avoidance issues).

15.20 Perhaps one of the most significant examples of HMRC's strategy to change behaviours is the announcement in the 2009 Budget of its intention to introduce a voluntary code of practice for the banking sector. A bank signing up to the code would in effect be agreeing not to participate in any tax-avoidance arrangements, whether in relation to their own affairs, as a promoter or providing finance for tax structured finance transactions. The Banking Code, accompanied by detailed guidance of expected behaviours, is now in place. Signatory banks are unlikely to be willing to act as counterparties to overt avoidance schemes

15.21 It is a matter for individual choice as to where taxpayers stand in terms of the arrangements they are prepared to contemplate (assuming of course they are legal). Comments regarding the morality of the arrangements, whilst part of the 'political agenda', have no place in the course of an enquiry. This somewhat confrontational approach will hopefully change as HMRC will be putting more emphasis on collaborative dispute resolution.

Litigation and settlement strategy

15.22 Until relatively recently, the uncertainty created by the lack of guidance and clear judicial precedent in relation to avoidance arguably suited both sides. HMRC liked the idea of uncertainty because it believed this discouraged many taxpayers from entering into arrangements where the

Tax avoidance investigations **15.24**

outcome was far from clear. Equally for taxpayers and their advisers, the uncertainty meant there was ample scope to negotiate a settlement with HMRC, which although it may not always have been for the full anticipated tax benefit of the planning, the outcome, nevertheless, typically represented a very good financial return on fees invested by the taxpayer.

15.23 In 2007 HMRC sought to change its previous approach in relation to negotiated settlements (which it considered tacitly encouraged avoidance due to a lack of a downside) by introducing a new policy known as the litigation and settlement strategy (LSS). This was re-issued in 12 July 2011 in order to refresh the strategy in the light of specific developments (e.g. changes to the Tribunal structure) and experience since its introduction. It also incorporates HMRC's latest thinking on resolving disputes cost effectively through collaborative working and attempts to clarify some of the misinterpretations of HMRC's key messages in the original document.

15.24 The key aims of the LSS in relation to disputes are as follows:

- resolve disputes consistently with HMRC's objectives of maximising revenues, reducing costs and improving customer experience;
- resolve disputes consistently with HMRC's considered view of the law;
- deal with each dispute on its own merits – i e 'Do not enter into package deals';
- settle all or nothing issues on all or nothing terms;
- where HMRC has a strong case seek full value from any settlement, or take the matter to litigation;
- not to seek low value settlements where HMRC is not prepared to litigate; rather the case should be dropped.

Whilst improving customer experience is an objective of HMRC, it remains to be seen whether the apparent emphasis on a more customer friendly collaborative approach will extend to the handling of avoidance cases.

The revised LSS is shorter than the original but is supplemented by guidance for HMRC staff on how to implement the principles of the LSS in their day to day working of enquiries.

The revised LSS reinforces the previous messages that HMRC will not compromise its view of the law in order to reach a settlement. It also remains committed to proceeding with litigation in cases where it believes it is likely to succeed and that litigation would be both effective and efficient. This caveat is a subtle but very important refinement of the previous LSS document which many within HMRC and externally interpreted as requiring HMRC to litigate in all cases where it believed it had a greater than 50% chance of success. HMRC has now clarified that the strength of opinion is only one factor to take into account. HMRC will no longer now base its approach solely on their initial view on the strength of its argument. It will be seen to test this view against the taxpayer's position before arriving at a conclusion. If both sides' estimate of success adds up to more than 100% then it is clear that one of the partners is over estimating their chance of success and HMRC wishes to explore this further before reaching a definitive view. This may provide scope for a negotiated settlement if the issue is not of an 'all or nothing' nature. In this

15.24 Tax avoidance investigations

respect the guidance also urges inspectors to explore whether the issue is truly of an 'all or nothing' nature, or whether there are a range of possible answers.

15.25 Clearly, the introduction of such a strategy has significant resource implications for HMRC. At the time LSS was introduced, HMRC's view was that in the early days the approach was likely to lead to a bulge of litigation activity but over the longer term this will tail off as the courts' decisions would lead to clearer lines in the sand. Alternatively, if HMRC lost the litigation, legislation could be introduced to counteract the effect of the court's decision in order to counter the avoidance arrangement. As a result, fewer taxpayers would wish to push unclear technical boundaries. Whilst there has been a significant amount of litigation since the introduction of the LSS, the cases have not established a clear line in the sand. Significant uncertainty remains as to the limit of purposive construction (see the case law summary below).

High Risk Corporate Programmes

The process typically starts with both sides committing to a mutually agreed target date for resolution of the enquiry and negotiation process. The target is intended to be stretching on both sides but achievable.

All open issues are identified, their status logged and a time tabled action plan (including key milestones) is agreed by both sides, together with a commitment to delivery dates and adherence to protocols.

The mutual commitment and delivery on turnaround times is a key element in the success of the process, and the resource required to deliver on timeframes should not be underestimated. However, the benefits referred to above are worth the effort.

The approach has the following key phases and actions:

Initial HMRC engagement, timetabling and protocol setting

- Board to Board meeting
- Agree mutual desire and commitment to work towards resolving issues via negotiated settlement.
- Agree scope and timetable, principles regarding information requests, method of exchanges, formats and roles and responsibilities of team members on both sides etc

Information gathering and agreed bundle of documents relied upon

- Assess outstanding HMRC information requests (if any); project manage provision; challenge HMRC request where applicable.
- Agree facts with HMRC.

Technical analysis and exchanges

- Drafting technical position papers and /or presentations in support of position adopted.
- Respond to HMRC technical analysis.
- Meet HMRC to clarify and resolve differences.
- Identify significant points of difference.

Dispute and negotiation phase

- Determine whether any basis for further negotiation and understand parameters.
- Obtain second opinion if necessary to reassess litigation prospects.
- Model scenarios and explore what may be mutually acceptable

Project settlement

- Agree mutually acceptable basis for settlement and wording of settlement terms
- In the event that any issue(s) have been excluded from the agreement commence formal proceedings to litigate.

The MCR process for businesses within LC is modelled on the HRCP approach and therefore has equivalent phases and actions.

Settlement initiatives

HMRC has recently adopted an approach of proposing an approach to settlement in situations where there are large numbers of taxpayers with the same or broadly similar tax issues involving planning arrangements and an impasse has been reached. Initiatives have included Lease Premium planning arrangements for employees and arrangements involving Employee Benefit Trust, the latter of which received a very lukewarm reception because its terms were considered too unattractive.

The most significant and creative of these settlement initiatives of seemingly intractable issues is HMRC's controlled Foreign Company (CFC) settlement initiative, launched in March of 2010. A significant number of the UK's largest companies with international operations have typically undertaken planning around their international financing arrangements to ensure they are not caught by the CFC regime, which in broad terms aims to tax the passive profits of UK controlled entities based in low tax jurisdictions. A significant number of companies have availed themselves of this settlement opportunity to clear these open issues, the most high profile being Vodafone which received considerable press coverage.

The proposal involves a company electing to pay a taxable dividend in settlement of potential CFC liabilities for earlier years on the basis that HMRC will apply the motive test CFC exemption for those years. As a settlement proposal it has some practical merit in the sense that the proportion of the dividend paid can be flexed significantly depending on the circumstances and strength or weakness of the taxpayer's position (in particular the level of substance the CFC has in the overseas territory) can take account of other tax attributes such as losses and typically gives a considerable interest saving. However, whilst the basis of the offer has some nexus with the CFC rules it is hardly the most robust technical basis. In reality it is a practical expedient which in many instances has enabled a seemingly intractable ("all or nothing") issue to be overcome.

15.26 *Tax avoidance investigations*

Operational initiatives

Background

15.26 In order to implement the strategic objective of clamping down on tax avoidance, HMRC continues to refine its operational effort both to focus resource on where it perceives the greatest risk to be and to improve the overall effectiveness of the resource so targeted. This has been most notable to date in the corporate sector where the policy of reallocating resources from low to high risk companies is being implemented in practice.

15.27 In the early years of the LSS signs were that HMRC was more intent on pursuing cases to litigation than before. More recent experience of avoidance enquiries into companies is that deals are firmly back on the table, particularly in instances where taxpayers have availed themselves of a number of tax-saving arrangements and have, as a result, been able to take advantage of one of HMRC's settlement initiatives. In these circumstances it has been possible to negotiate an overall settlement (which in many respects resembles the 'package deals' of old). This tends to involve trading one arrangement for another, as opposed to agreeing an arbitrary percentage disallowance on individual arrangements or across the board. However, there is also increasing evidence that HMRC is more inclined to negotiate a settlement in 'one-off' transactions providing an acceptable technical rationale can be found. In personal tax avoidance arrangements HMRC appears to be more committed to litigation, as in many of these cases a taxpayer will not have a portfolio of arrangements whereby trades can be done.

15.28 Other key changes being noted in practice include:

- a more rigorous approach to information gathering with ever wider requests for information and much tighter timeframes for compliance (though it appears that this may be tempered somewhat in the future, in order to being more focus to fact finding – see below.;
- greater coordination, team working and centralisation involving advice from specialist resources (including external sources);
- an increased threat of penalties where planning fails as a result of poor implementation.

Change of behaviour

15.29 As mentioned above, it is HMRC's stated desire to pursue tax avoiders and their advisers rigorously. HMRC's statement of purpose (its mission statement) says that it will be 'relentless in pursuing those who bend the rules'. This approach is likely to be reflected in the behaviour of officers tasked with investigating avoidance arrangements.

15.30 The desired changes in behaviour are being encouraged by a change in the performance measures of HMRC officers. HMRC officers are for the first time ever being targeted on tax yield in their performance measures. At one time this would have been politically unacceptable but now provides a driver for

HMRC officers to challenge avoidance arrangements with as much vigour as the law permits.

Internal organisation

15.31 HMRC has set extremely stretching targets in its compliance efforts to reduce the tax gap. The impact of this is reflected in a shift in resources in departments such as Specialist Investigations (SI), (formerly Special Civil Investigations (SCI)) where there has recently been greater emphasis on tackling avoidance arrangements, as opposed to cases of suspected serious fraud. This is because the former provides significantly more payback in terms of yield to resource ratio.

15.32 Since April 2006, SI has been organised in three streams: Delivery, Assurance and Business Relationships. The vast majority of investigation work is conducted in the Delivery stream. The Business Relationships stream is responsible for high level liaison with other HMRC Directorates such as the Large Business Service (LBS), High Net Worth Unit (for the top tier of wealthy individuals) (HNWU) and Anti-Avoidance Group (AAG). There are protocols in place covering interaction with these departments.

15.33 As discussed below SI has increasingly become involved in joint working cases with these departments but shares responsibility with divisions of Charities, Assets and Residence (CAR) for areas of general avoidance involving offshore arrangements. These include: residence or domicile status; the use of tax haven companies; the use of dual contract arrangements; the use of trusts and settlements; treaty shopping.

The Anti-Avoidance Group

15.34 As referred to above, as a result of the merger, HMRC set up a combined Anti-Avoidance Group comprising staff working on direct and indirect cases. The Anti Avoidance Group is arranged into three sections:

- intelligence, clearance and counteraction;
- policy; and
- investigations.

15.35 The intelligence group is responsible for the review and dissemination of disclosures. Clearance and counteraction handles applications for clearance in mergers and acquisitions, applying the long standing Transactions in Securities, purchase of own shares etc rules.

15.36 The policy group is responsible for monitoring the impact of avoidance arrangements including the disclosure regime and liaising with the Treasury and technical divisions to coordinate responses where necessary.

15.37 The investigations arm comprises what was formerly Special Investigations Section which investigated direct tax avoidance with teams dealing with VAT.

15.38 Tax avoidance investigations

15.38 Whilst the Anti Avoidance Group, in conjunction with the Solicitor's Office, has overall responsibility for arrangements which will be litigated, the actual allocation of cases identified through the disclosure regime is determined for day-to-day working by a committee to a number of departments such as the Large Business Services office (LBS), the HNWU and Specialist Investigations. The LBS and HNWU have responsibility for the taxpayer's affairs and therefore it can be seen that it makes sense for these departments to work the cases with central support from the Anti Avoidance Group.

15.39 Within the Anti Avoidance Group, schemes are allocated to project teams who are running a stable of similar arrangements (eg intellectual property, Forex, loan relationships, leasing etc). Often in practice, the exact dynamics of the various departmental interactions will come down to personalities and individual effectiveness.

15.40 For significant cross-border avoidance arrangements, the head office department 'CT International' retains full control of the case management.

15.41 What is less clear is the allocation of responsibilities between the Anti-Avoidance Group, SI, and teams within widely spread Local Compliance offices. In practice, SI's role, in addition to working some cases in its own right, is one of support to the LBS and network offices. This support involves assistance with the scope and nature of information requests and assisting with the review of the documentation obtained in order to establish the facts; it is also increasingly involved in a coordination and project management role. SI also often investigates mass market schemes across all customer segments. The LBS has its own Strategic Response Unit to project manage large corporate schemes.

Working methods

Case identification

15.42 There are two main ways by which HMRC identifies avoidance cases:

- disclosure: schemes or arrangements which have been disclosed under the disclosure rules;
- profiling: the process of identifying avoidance in cases not disclosed from characteristics identified in particular schemes.

15.43 Prior to the introduction of the disclosure legislation in 2004 (see below), neither the former Inland Revenue, nor Customs & Excise had excelled at identifying tax-avoidance arrangements undertaken by individuals and companies. Indeed, it was not uncommon for tax advisers to warn their clients to expect a rigorous investigation only to find that no enquiry was raised, notwithstanding clear disclosure of the arrangement in the relevant return.

15.44 The disclosure regime and improved risk assessment have changed this and it should now be the exception that any avoidance arrangement escapes the attention of HMRC. On the corporate side HMRC are using software to analyse results and identify indicators of avoidance arrangements through the impact on various ratios. On the personal tax side it is possible for the Anti

Avoidance Group to conduct searches of specific boxes on tax returns or white space entries to ensure that they have captured all examples of particular avoidance arrangements and exercise oversight to ensure they are dealt with appropriately. This reduces the discretion of network offices to ignore cases due to resource pressures or to enter into settlements which head office consider are inappropriate (see **15.24**).

15.45 Even where an avoidance arrangement has not been identified and challenged in the relevant enquiry period, it is not uncommon for HMRC to identify the arrangement in a subsequent year (possibly as a result of a change to, or unwind of the planning). In these circumstances, HMRC will usually seek to raise a discovery assessment or use its information powers to establish the facts to put it in a position to make a discovery assessment. In the absence of an enquiry or very full disclosure it is very difficult for taxpayers to achieve certainty that the benefit of the planning has been achieved without any prospect of the position being revisited within the time limits for assessment of the duty involved, normally now four or six years.

Profiling

15.46 Originally, profiling was ad hoc and relied on individual officers to identify instances of the particular arrangement they were working on using a combination of tax technical/accounting and IT resource.

15.47 The process is now more structured with a dedicated profiling unit within LBS (which sits within the Strategic Response Unit). The team's work involves taking an undisclosed scheme, establishing key footprints considered to be linked to the avoidance arrangement and devising a program to identify other cases from those characteristics (eg British Virgin Islands companies, partnership structures, guarantee companies etc). Once identified, these cases can then be subjected to more detailed scrutiny.

Team working and consistent approach

15.48 In challenging the planning, HMRC is likely to be much more rigorous and consistent in its approach to fact finding, decisions as to whether a particular case is litigated and, if not, the basis of settlement.

15.49 Out of the stable of cases being worked by the person in the Anti Avoidance Group for the particular scheme, one or more lead cases will typically be worked up with a view to a submission being made to the Solicitor's Office and ultimately counsel for a decision as to whether it is strong enough to warrant litigation. At any point in the process the decision could be made that, following legal advice, the case(s) is not sufficiently strong to litigate. If this happens, it is likely that another case would be found or alternatively, if the weakness is generic, a view is likely to be taken as to whether or not the amount at risk warrants legislation.

15.50 This decision-making process is aided by project management because the total tax at risk can be estimated with a fair degree of certainty and

15.50 *Tax avoidance investigations*

so a strong case can be made within HMRC as to what is at stake. Unless there is a fundamental principle at stake which HMRC cannot compromise (in which case HMRC will litigate simply to test the law and legislate if it is held by the courts to be defective from their perspective) the case should be dropped if it is not strong enough to litigate. There are understood to be internal governance procedures for such decisions for strategic litigation.

Embedding specialist department working methods into the network

15.51 Until relatively recently, projects targeting certain avoidance arrangements involving offshore arrangements were the remit of Specialist Investigations or Business International and were conducted by a relatively small number of individuals. Now there are larger numbers of officers both within Specialist Investigations and the network who are working on projects which have an avoidance/fraud crossover.

15.52 A notable example is a project conducted by various network offices involving targeting companies with offshore parents for enquiry. This might include scrutinising UK situs property transactions involving an offshore company or trust. Such action has taken the form of writing directly to the directors or conducting third party enquiries of the purchaser/vendors to establish with whom they negotiated. Such projects are the combination of the transfer of skills and experience from Specialist Investigations to the network (as those long-serving officers in SI complete their stint in that office) and an emphasis on a risk-based approach to the allocation of resources.

Legislative

15.53 In recent years there have been a number of targeted anti-avoidance measures and consideration of these provisions is beyond the scope of this chapter. However, by far the most significant legislation to be introduced has been the disclosure regime rules.

Disclosure rules

15.54 The Finance Act 2004 introduced a set of disclosure requirements that are imposed on promoters and users of certain tax schemes and arrangements. They were designed to enable HMRC to identify at a much earlier stage tax-avoidance schemes they were likely to find unacceptable, with a view to introducing swifter and more targeted legislation in response.

15.55 The original rules introduced by Finance Act 2004 covered employment-related schemes and schemes involving financial products. These were the high risk areas that HMRC had identified from known tax-saving schemes. From 1 August 2006 the scope of the rules were extended to cover a much wider range of transactions. The rules were extended further by FA 2007 to enable HMRC to raise enquiries into non-disclosure and to permit HMRC to require reasons to be given as to why a proposal or arrangement is not disclosable.

The rules have been further extended by FA 2010, Sch 17 and supporting regulations to compel promoters to provide lists of disclosable schemes implemented by clients from 1 January 2011.

15.56 In addition, FA 2007 brought in changes enabling HMRC to apply to the First Tier Tribunal for an order requiring the promoter to provide:

- specified information or documents in support of the stated reasons why an arrangement is not disclosable;
- specified information and/or documents if they are satisfied that HMRC has reasonable grounds for suspecting that the information or documents form part of the prescribed information or will support or explain the prescribed information.

15.57 As well as introducing information powers relating specifically to the disclosure rules, FA 2007 also introduced powers under which HMRC can apply to the First Tier Tribunal for an order that an arrangement is disclosable, if they are satisfied on the evidence that it is disclosable. HMRC can also apply to the Tribunal to deem an arrangement to be disclosable providing the Tribunal is satisfied that HMRC has reasonable grounds for suspecting that it is disclosable and has taken all reasonable steps to establish this. AAG is the only department that can conduct such enquiries and take any penalty action (see below).

15.58 Where practitioners consider the rules may be in point a more detailed review of the provisions will be required and in areas of doubt further advice should be sought.

15.59 The primary legislation set out at FA 2004, ss 306–319, provides the basic framework and definitions for the regime. The majority of the detail is found in secondary legislation.

15.60 The basic structure is based on the concept of a 'notifiable arrangement'. A notifiable arrangement is an arrangement:

- that falls within descriptions provided by the Treasury (in secondary legislation);
- that enables a person to obtain a tax advantage; and
- where the tax advantage is the main benefit of the arrangement.

15.61 A 'notifiable proposal' is a proposal for notifiable arrangements. For example, where a promoter tells a client about a notifiable arrangement, that is a notifiable proposal.

Promoter

15.62 A person is a promoter in relation to a notifiable proposal if, in the course of carrying on a business which involves the provision to others of services related to taxation or certain other services, he:

- has any responsibility for designing any notifiable proposal or arrangements except in excluded circumstances;

15.62 *Tax avoidance investigations*

- makes a notifiable proposal available to another person (for example, by marketing or promoting arrangements designed by another person); or
- has any responsibility for the organisation or management of the notifiable arrangement but only if they are connected with the design of the arrangement.

15.63 There are three exceptions relating to persons involved in the design of arrangements. They are intended to ensure only those directly involved in the arrangement are required to make a disclosure. The exceptions do not, however, exempt persons who are promoters by virtue of making a notifiable proposal available for implementation by others.

Penalties

15.64 Failure to comply with the above requirements attracts a maximum penalty of £5,000 together with a further maximum penalty of £600 each day for continued failure to disclose after the imposition of the initial penalty. Finance Act 2010 introduced the potential for a penalty of up to £1 million where the penalty under the existing provisions was inappropriately low.

15.65 In addition to the financial penalties there is reputational risk attached failure to comply with these disclosure requirements, as penalty proceedings will be heard before the Tax Tribunal.

THE EVOLUTION OF AVOIDANCE CASE LAW

Introduction

15.66 Whatever the rights, wrongs or the potential effectiveness of HMRC's campaign on the moral agenda, it is the courts that will ultimately decide the success or otherwise of a particular arrangement (assuming agreement cannot be reached with HMRC).

15.67 As stated at the outset, a detailed analysis of avoidance case law is beyond the scope of this chapter. However, given that it is the courts that are the ultimate arbiters of whether a particular arrangement is effective, it is essential that practitioners take a realistic (as opposed to 'rose-tinted') view of how the courts may react to a particular arrangement and whether it has the characteristics of an arrangement that is likely to be litigated by HMRC.

15.68 The difficulty in assessing the likely success of tax planning arrangements is that the courts appear to make what at first sight are contradictory decisions. In addition, the long lead time between the decision to enter into the planning arrangement and any litigation can result in views evolving considerably from when the planning was conceived and implemented to when its fate is ultimately decided in the courts (assuming a negotiated settlement cannot be reached).

15.69 The evolution of the courts' approach and thinking over time is currently demonstrated by the debate over the extent to which the courts will adopt a literal or purposive construction in their interpretation of the statute. The potted history below shows it is not easy to predict outcomes or determine a clear and consistent rationale for decision making.

A potted history

15.70 In answering issues of artificially (and to some extent morality), tax advisers in seeking to defend a client's right to plan their tax affairs so as to reduce their liability often rely on the classic dicta of Lord Tomlin in *Duke of Westminster v CIR* 19 TC 490:

> 'Every man is entitled if he can to order his affairs so that the tax attaching under the appropriate Acts is less than it otherwise would be. If he succeeds in ordering them so as to secure this result, then, however unappreciative the Commissioners of Inland Revenue or his fellow taxpayers may be of his ingenuity, he cannot be compelled to pay an increased tax.'

15.71 In a similar vein, the comments of Lord Clyde in *Ayrshire Pullman Motor Services and Ritchie v CIR* 14 TC 754 imply that the courts at the time perceived tax avoidance as something of a game between the taxpayer and the authorities. He commented:

> 'No man in this country is under the smallest obligation, moral or other, so to arrange his legal relations to his business or to his property so as to enable the Inland Revenue to put the largest possible shovel into his stores. The Inland Revenue is not slow – and quite rightly – to take every advantage which is open to it under the taxing statutes for the purpose of depleting the taxpayer's pocket. And the taxpayer is, in like manner, entitled to be astute to prevent, so far as he honestly can the depletion of his mean by the Revenue.'

15.72 The strict legalistic approach to statutory interpretation favoured in early decisions is perhaps best summed up by Rowlatt J in *Cape Brandy Syndicate v CIR* 1921 12 TC 358:

> 'In a taxing Act one has to look merely at what is clearly said. There is no room for any intendment. There is no equity about a tax. There is no presumption as to tax. Nothing is to be read in, nothing is to be implied. One can only look fairly at the language used.'

15.73 However, the explosion of highly artificial tax-avoidance arrangements during the 1970s ultimately led to the House of Lords case of *WT Ramsay Ltd v CIR* 54 TC 101. The case marked a watershed in judicial thinking in relation to avoidance arrangements. The taxpayer sought to avoid capital gains tax by the creation of a loss via a series of pre-ordained, self cancelling transactions which had no commercial purpose other than the avoidance of tax. It was accepted by the courts that all the transactions were genuine and not a sham.

15.74 Lord Templeman in the Court of Appeal, while finding for the Crown on the narrow technical point of whether a loan was a debt on a security, in his opening comments reflected how, in the writer's experience, many if not most

15.74 *Tax avoidance investigations*

officers would view arrangements of a circular nature as those described in *Ramsay*. It is so apt in this respect that the relevant passage has been included in full below:

> 'The facts set out in the case stated by the Special Commissioners demonstrate yet another circular game in which the taxpayer and a few hired performers act out a play; nothing happens save that the Houdini taxpayer appears to escape from the manacles of tax. The game is recognisable by four rules. First, the play is devised and scripted prior to performance. Secondly, real money and real documents are circulated and exchanged. Thirdly, the money is returned by the end of the performance. Fourthly, the financial position of the actors is the same at the end as it was at the beginning save that the taxpayer in the course of the performance pays the hired actors for their services. The object of the performance is to create the illusion that something has happened, that Hamlet has been killed and that Bottom did don an asses head, so that tax advantages can be claimed as if something had happened. The audience are informed that the actors reserve the right to walk out in the middle of the performance but in fact they are the creatures of the consultant who has sold and the taxpayer who has bought the play: the actors are never in a position to make a profit and there is no chance that they will go on strike. The critics are mistakenly informed that the play is based on a classic masterpiece called "The Duke of Westminster" but in that piece the old retainer entered the theatre with his salary and left with a genuine entitlement to his salary and to an additional annuity.'

15.75 The case was heard in the House of Lords where Lord Wilberforce set out four principles:

- A subject is only to be taxed on clear words, not upon 'intendment' or upon the 'equity' of an Act. Any taxing Act of Parliament is to be construed in accordance with this principle. What are 'clear words' is to be ascertained upon normal principles: these do not confine the courts to literal interpretation. They may, indeed should, be considered in the context and scheme of the relevant Act as a whole.
- A subject is entitled to arrange his affairs so as to reduce his liability to tax.
- It is for the Commissioners to find whether a document or transaction is a sham.
- If a document or transaction is genuine the court cannot go behind it to some supposed underlying substance.

15.76 Lord Wilberforce considered his decision fully respected the first three principles but did, however, make an important clarification of the fourth principle. In this respect he said that:

> 'This is a cardinal principle but it must not be overstated or overextended ... for the Commissioners ... It is wrong and an unnecessary self limitation, to regard themselves as precluded by their own finding that documents or transactions are not 'shams' from considering what the relevant transaction is. They are not, under the Westminster doctrine or any other authority,

bound to consider individually each separate step in a composite transaction intended to be carried out as a whole'.

15.77 Lord Wilberforce also went on to consider the argument that because the capital gains tax code did not contain a wide-ranging anti-avoidance measure such as what was then s 703, Taxes Act 1988 and because Parliament had never passed a general anti-avoidance rule, if loopholes remained in the capital gains tax system, these should be plugged by Parliament and not the courts. In response he stated:

> 'While the techniques of tax avoidance are technically improved, the courts are not obliged to stand still. The capital gains tax was created to operate in the real world not that of make belief ... it is a tax on gains, it is not a tax on arithmetical differences. To say that a loss which appears to arise at one stage in an individual process, and which is intended to be and is cancelled out by a later stage, so that at the end of what was bought as, and planned as, a single continuous operation is not such a loss as the legislation is dealing with, is in my opinion well ... within the judicial function.'

In this sense Lord Wilberforce was adopting a purposive interpretation of the legislation.

15.78 In the immediate aftermath of *Ramsay* it remained unclear whether its groundbreaking doctrine could be applied to schemes which were not 'circular' in their nature. Clarity, or so it seemed, arrived on this point in the case of *Furniss v Dawson* (1984) STC 153.

15.79 In *Furniss v Dawson* the *Ramsay* principle was applied to establish the true parties to a transaction and its true nature. A sale which was a practical certainty was arranged between the taxpayer (Mr Dawson) and a particular purchaser, Wood Bastow Holdings Limited, was held to be the true transaction and the inserted intermediary step of a sale solely for tax reasons to a wholly-owned creature company (Greenjacket Limited) was to be ignored. Brightman J stated:

> 'First there must be a preordained series of transactions; or, if one likes, one single composite transaction. Secondly, there must be steps inserted which have no commercial purpose apart from the avoidance of tax. If those two ingredients exist, the inserted steps are to be disregarded for fiscal purposes.'

15.80 By way of contrast in *Craven v White* 62 TC 1, which involved the same basic scheme as that which failed in *Furniss*, it was held that it was not sufficient that the inserted steps had a sole tax avoidance purpose for them to be ignored. The fundamental difference in the cases was that in *Craven v White* the inserted sale of shares to an intermediate company took place at a time when there was no preordained onwards sale to an ultimate purchaser.

15.81 In *Craven v White*, Lord Keith said:

> 'In my opinion both the transactions in the series can properly be regarded as preordained if, but only if, at the time when the first of them is entered into the taxpayer is in a position for all practical purposes to secure that the second also is entered into.'

15.82 *Tax avoidance investigations*

15.82 As a consequence of these cases the debate for many years often centred upon whether transactions with inserted steps were preordained or not.

15.83 Since 2001 a number of cases have been heard which again demonstrate the difficulty of achieving clarity as to where the goalposts lie in relation to tax planning and how difficult it can be to predict how the courts will react.

15.84 Lord Hoffmann in the case of *MacNiven v Westmoreland Investments Ltd* [2001] STC 237 attempted to bring clarity to over 20 years of tax-avoidance case law. He confirmed that *Ramsay* is a principle of statutory construction which does not provide a general 'substance over form' doctrine but

> '... was a recognition that the statutory language was intended to refer to commercial concepts, so that in the case of a concept such as a "disposal" the Court was required to take a view of the facts which transcended the juristic individuality of the various parts of a pre-planned series of transactions.'

15.85 Lord Hoffmann then went on to impose limitations to which commercial concepts could be applied to statutory language. He considered these limits were set by the purpose of the relevant statutory provision and the particular statutory language. Lord Hoffmann considered that there were many terms in the tax legislation which could not be construed in this way because they referred to purely legal concepts which have no broader commercial meaning. In these cases he considered that the *Ramsay* principle would have no application. However, his attempt to distinguish between commercial and legal concepts was subsequently found to be unsustainable as a general proposition (see *Barclays Mercantile Business Finance Ltd v Mawson* [2005] STC 1 (*BMBF*)).

15.86 In *BMBF* (and *CIR v Scottish Provident Institution* (*SPI*) released on the same day) the House of Lords took the unusual step of giving a combined judgment which was clearly intended to bring some clarity to the confusion which had arisen from Lord Hoffmann's introduction of the commercial/legal division of statutory language.

15.87 In *BMBF*, the House confirmed that it was necessary to consider carefully the particular statutory provision and identify its requirements before deciding whether circular payments or elements inserted for tax avoidance should be disregarded or treated as irrelevant for the purposes of the statute. However, this did not justify the assumption that the answer to this analysis could be determined by classifying all concepts as either 'commercial' or 'legal' in the first instance. The House of Lords summarised [para 32] the *Ramsay* principles as follows:

> 'The essence of the new approach was to give the statutory provision a purposive construction in order to determine the nature of the transaction to which it was intended to apply and then decide whether the actual transaction (which might involve considering the overall effect of a number of elements designed to operate together) answered to the statutory description. Of course this does not mean that the courts have to put their

reasoning into the straight jacket of first construing the statute in the abstract and then looking at the facts. It might be more convenient to analyse the facts and then ask whether they satisfy the relevant requirements of the statute.'

15.88 Their Lordships dismissed as a general proposition that any elements inserted into transactions without any commercial purpose were to be treated as having no significance. Instead a purposive approach involved two steps: 'First to decide, on a purposive construction, exactly what transaction will answer to the statutory description and secondly, to decide whether the transaction in question does so.' Their Lordships went on to quote from Riberio PJ in the Hong Kong appeal *Collector of Stamp Revenue v Arrowtown Assets Ltd*:

'The ultimate question is whether the relevant statutory provisions, construed purposively, were intended to apply the transaction viewed realistically.'

15.89 In applying this principle to BMBF's capital allowances claim, their Lordships appeared to have been swayed by the purpose of the capital allowances legislation in providing a tax deduction equivalent to accounting depreciation where the plant is used for the purpose of the trade. HMRC's claims that the funding arrangements were artificial and circular were dismissed as irrelevant or 'happenstances' which had no bearing on the creation of an entitlement to capital allowances. Moreover, the legislation was concerned with the acts of the lessor and said nothing about the lessee's position, in terms of how he should fund the rental payments.

15.90 By way of contrast, the loss claimed by Scottish Provident did not answer the statutory description. In this case, the arrangement had no other purpose than seeking to take advantage of the legislative transition from the old pre-derivative contracts regime to the new regime. The scheme involved Scottish Provident granting an option to buy gilts to the bank who devised the scheme at an 'off market' price in return for a large premium. This premium was not taxable under the old regime. Once the derivative contracts regime came into force, the option was exercised requiring Scottish Provident to sell the gilts at a loss, which was allowable for tax purposes under the new regime. Commercially the transactions cancelled each other out but in tax terms gave rise to an allowable loss and a non-taxable gain.

15.91 The Special Commissioners found as a fact that:

'There was a genuine commercial possibility and a real practical likelihood that the two options would be dealt with separately. Likewise, there was genuine commercial possibility and a real practical likelihood that the [Scottish Provident] option would not be exercised.'

15.92 The House of Lords recognised that it could not disturb this finding of fact but considered that a question of law was involved. The House of Lords concluded that the Commissioners had erred in law in concluding that a contingency which had been deliberately inserted in the documents to give a possibility that the transaction might not have happened prevented it from being construed as a composite transaction when that contingency did not in reality arise.

15.93 Tax avoidance investigations

15.93 The House of Lords considered that the question to be answered was whether the option gave an entitlement to gilts which would then enable it to be a qualifying contract as defined in the legislation. Despite the argument that the legislation in question was highly prescriptive, the House of Lords ruled that the statutory language was to be given a 'wide practical meaning' and required the court to have regard to the whole series of transactions which were intended to have 'a commercial unity'.

15.94 In both of the above cases the application of the facts to the legislation was crucial in reaching the respective decisions. In BMBF the taxpayer's evidence as to what constituted its 'ordinary trade of finance leasing' was important; in SPI the fact that a commercially irrelevant contingency was inserted to ensure there was no prospect of arguing that the transaction was pre-ordained weighed heavily against the taxpayer.

15.95 However, it would appear that the courts regard the issue of what constitutes a composite transaction to be a question of law as opposed to fact. The courts continue to deny the existence of judicially created law. HMRC, however, appears to consider the decision in SPI as strengthening of the *Ramsay* principle. This may well be the case with regard to schemes which have been entered into purely for tax-avoidance reasons with no commercial purpose. Irrespective of whether this is a principle of a statutory construction or judicially created law there remains a considerable degree of uncertainty as to what type of arrangement will, in the words of their Lordships in SPI, 'sail through the gap'.

15.96 There have been a significant number of cases since these two landmark House of Lords judgments, with decisions both for and against the taxpayer. HMRC has undoubtedly been encouraged by recent successes such as *Astall v HMRC* [2008] STC 2920, *Prudential plc v HMRC [2009] EWCA 1094 civ, HMRC v DCC Holdings (UK) Ltd [2010] UKSC 58 and HMRC v Tower M Cashback[2011] UKSC19* .. But there have been equally significant wins for the taxpayer in cases such as *HMRC v D'Arcy* [2008] STC 1329, HMRC v Mayes [2011] EWCA 407 civ and *HMRC v Bank of Ireland Britain Holdings Ltd* [2008] STC 398.

15.97 These latter three cases provide further recent evidence that the courts are prepared to find for the taxpayer, notwithstanding that the transaction in question was designed with the exploitation of a perceived loophole in the legislation in mind.

15.98 In *HMRC v D'Arcy* the taxpayer sought to take advantage of a mismatch between the tax legislation relating to the accrued income scheme and the manufactured interest payment regime in order to create a tax deduction with no corresponding charge. HMRC sought to argue that a purposive interpretation of the accrued income provisions should impose a charge on the taxpayer. However, the court found in favour of the taxpayer. Henderson J commented:

> 'The Revenue's real complaint, as it seems to me, is that the accrued income scheme does not throw up a charge to counterbalance the deduction

admittedly available to Mrs D'Arcy for her manufactured interest payment. But the accrued income scheme and the provisions relating to manufactured interest were enacted at different times and with different statutory purposes. They do not form part of a single unified code, and their separation is indeed emphasised by section 727A. In short, this is in my view one of those cases, which will inevitably occur from time to time in a tax system as complicated as ours, where a well-advised taxpayer has been able to take advantage of an unintended gap left by the interaction between two different sets of statutory provisions.'

15.99 Similarly, in *HMRC v Bank of Ireland Britain Holdings Ltd*, the taxpayer had entered into an arrangement (involving a tripartite repo) which exploited a mismatch between two sets of repo provisions (ss 730A and 737A TA 1988). The legislation in question had not envisaged a tripartite repo involving a non-resident interim holder. HMRC argued that the taxpayer's interpretation gave a bizarre result and suggested that:

'If the court is presented with two alternative constructions, the construction which gives a result in line with the policy of the Act should be preferred to a construction which gives a result so bizarre it could not possibly have been intended.'

15.100 The Court of Appeal, however, rejected such an approach. Lawrence Collins LJ acknowledged that the scheme had been devised to take advantage of a mismatch between two sets sections but considered there was no legitimate process of interpretation that would solve HMRC's problem.

15.101 In a similar vein, in *Coombes v HMRC* [2008] STC 2984, HMRC sought to tax the taxpayer as if he was the settlor by virtue of him having provided the funds to purchase the settled property. As a settlor, the taxpayer would have been subject to tax under s 86 TCGA 1992. HMRC contended that the arrangement adopted by the taxpayer effectively emasculated the anti-avoidance effect of s 86 TCGA 1992. However, Sir Donald Rattee, whilst acknowledging this point, commented:

'That may be, but that fact does not, of course, enable me to do violence to the actual provisions of sections 68 and 86 of, and Sch 5 to, the 1992 Act.'

15.102 From HMRC's perspective, the Court of Appeal case of *Astall v HMRC* [2009] EWCA 2494 appears to have further developed the concept of a 'commercially irrelevant contingency' which was introduced in SPI. The taxpayers had in separate transactions sought to create an income tax loss by using a discounted security; both admitted the transactions took place solely for tax avoidance purposes. The terms of the security were structured in such a way as to provide a 15% chance that the transaction would give rise to a gain on redemption. However, this contingency was considered to be commercially irrelevant to the security (given that it related to the dollar/sterling exchange rate when the security was in sterling) and as such was viewed as an insertion to *Ramsay*-proof the transaction.

15.103 Tax avoidance investigations

15.103 The Special Commissioner held that the conditions inserted to introduce uncertainty could be ignored under the *Ramsay* principle because they lacked reality. The Special Commissioner concluded:

> 'A purposive construction of the definition of relevant discounted security must have regard to real possibilities of redemption, not ones written into the document creating the security that the parties know, and any reasonable person having the knowledge available to the parties knows, will never occur'

15.104 Both the High Court and Court of Appeal concurred with the Special Commissioner's view. In the Court of Appeal, Arden LJ rejected counsel's argument for the taxpayer that regard should only be had to the terms of the security, not extraneous facts such as the likelihood of redemption. She considered paras 2 and 3 of Sch13 to the FA 1996 had to receive a purposive construction. That purpose was that there should be a real possibility of a deep gain if losses incurred on a relevant discount security were to be offsettable for income tax purposes. Interestingly, while in Arden LJ's view the process probably started with determining the purpose of the statutory provision, she considered that it may be necessary to refine that purpose as and when the facts are more closely defined. She felt that this may have been what Lord Hoffmann had in mind when he spoke in Privy Council judgment in *Carreras* of the need to find facts 'in the process of construction'. This is yet another reminder to advisors of the importance of the facts when considering how the courts are likely to view a particular avoidance transaction.

15.105 These cases emphasise the difficulty in determining where the line is in terms of success and failure with regard to tax avoidance. They also serve to highlight the importance that HMRC will attach to establishing every last piece of information relating to the transactions in question, in order to give what they will believe is the most realistic view of the transaction, taken as a whole.

Summary of current position

15.106 To sum up where we currently stand the following key points appear to have emerged from recent decisions:

- The *Ramsay* principle is confirmed as a purposive approach to statutory construction involving a consideration of what the legislator intended that its requirements would be.
- The legal/commercial dichotomy formulated by Lord Hoffmann in *MacNiven* is not an unreasonable generalisation but does not provide a substitute for what the statute actually means.
- The effect of a single composite transaction should be considered as it was intended to operate without regard to the existence of commercially irrelevant contingencies.
- There is no universal rule that transactions or elements of a transaction which have no commercial purpose should be disregarded in construing the transaction as a whole.
Lewison J in *Berry v HMRC* [2011] UKUT FTC/29/2010 gave a helpful

and up to date summary of the Ramsay principles with their judicial derivation at para 41

15.107 Put simply arrangements which involve a 'real' loss and 'real' risk are likely to be successful, notwithstanding the fact that tax savings played a part in how the transaction was structured, whereas those involving artificial losses and only the appearance of risk are more likely to fail. In addition, attempts to '*Ramsay* proof' a transaction by artificially creating an element of uncertainty are likely to undermine the chance of success before the courts. As would be expected, transactions with 'real' or 'genuine' legal and commercial consequences remain likely to be successful, irrespective of whether they contain a degree of circularity or tax-motivated elements within them. *Mayes*, *D'Arcy* and *Bank of Ireland* show that even without commercial loss or risk the more prescriptive (or closely articulated) the legislation in question is the less likely the courts will construe it purposively to defeat the arrangement.

The avoidance versus evasion distinction

15.108 It should go without saying that it is critical to keep on the 'right side of the line' between tax avoidance and evasion, the former being legal and the latter illegal. However, in recent years there have been attempts by HMRC and lobby groups to blur the distinction between tax evasion and fraud. There is, however, a very clear distinction.

15.109 A tax fraud will normally involve some pretence or deception; some form of dishonesty is necessary for tax avoidance to cross the line and constitute the criminal evasion. Offences range from the common law offence of 'cheat' (of the public revenue), to fraudulent evasion of tax Finance Act 2000, Fraud Act 2006, Forgery Act, Perjury Act offences and so on. On the back of these offences, money laundering offences will commonly follow. The effectiveness of avoidance schemes depends on the steps taken in them being real as distinct from a pretence or a sham. A sham is a pretence, something which pretends to be something it is not. A forged document is a sham. Actions deliberately purported to be conducted by one person, but in fact conducted by someone else, possibly in a different location, are sham transactions. There will be occasions where genuine mistakes are made in documents or misunderstandings over the precise demarcation of responsibilities or difficult interpretations, but deliberate attempts to mislead or conceal the true facts are dishonest actions with the perpetrators being liable to criminal proceedings. The possibility that a transaction could have happened as envisaged in the planning, but in fact did not, would not diminish the seriousness of the offence.

15.110 The case of *R v Charlton* [1996] STC 1418 demonstrates the potential difficulties involved. The crux of the fraud involved interposing a Jersey company between the overseas supplier of tyres and a UK-based purchaser. Originally tyres were purchased directly from the original supplier, but following the incorporation of the Jersey company, they were subsequently bought from that source at an inflated price. It was contended on behalf of the defendant that the Jersey company was properly incorporated and contracted with the overseas supplier for the purchase of the tyres, the scheme although unsuccessful (technically speaking) was not fraudulent. The accounts properly reflected the transactions which had occurred. The Revenue successfully contended the arrangement comprised a dishonest avoidance scheme.

15.111 The case was important as it lifted the corporate veil. The defence sought to argue that because the Jersey company was properly incorporated, transactions with that company did not cease to be real or bona fide simply because they were uncommercial. However, what seemed decisive in securing the defendants' conviction was the combination of the lack of commerciality of the transactions combined with the intention to keep the arrangements from the attention of the tax authorities, whilst the financial benefits accrued to the directors.

HMRC APPROACH TO WORKING AVOIDANCE ENQUIRIES

Introduction

15.112 Since HMRC announced its drive to crack down on avoidance arrangements, the approach to fact finding taken by officers has been much more intense, both in terms of scope and in significantly shorter time frames for compliance with information requests.

HMRC approach to fact finding

15.113 In the writer's experience, it is not uncommon for practitioners to be surprised by the extent of fact finding in what they may perceive to be a technical enquiry, as opposed to a full-blown investigation down to prime records of the business where some form of impropriety is alleged or implied.

15.114 As a rule of thumb, HMRC regards any technical enquiry as 80% fact finding and 20% technical analysis and this is typically borne out in practice.

15.115 So what are the facts and how does HMRC seek to establish them? Facts are established when they are proven; the means of proof is evidence. Evidence is essentially anything which tends to persuade someone that a particular factual position exists. The most common forms of evidence are oral and documentary.

15.116 The focus of any HMRC avoidance enquiry has in recent years been to initially obtain all the evidence that might conceivably have some relevance in relation to the enquiry.

15.117 In relation to tax planning entered into by companies, HMRC is now putting significant emphasis on reviewing transactions in real time. Until the introduction of new powers in Finance Act 2008, HMRC had to rely on the cooperation of the taxpayer for a real-time examination of a transaction. However, it is now possible for HMRC to require the taxpayer to provide information without the need for an enquiry where it becomes aware of a transaction. The changes in disclosure of Tax Avoidance Scheme rules referred to at **15.55** are likely to increase the probability of HMRC seeking to review transactions in real time as they become aware of scheme users sooner than before.

15.118 A potential change in direction may come about as a result of the guidance to inspectors accompanying the revised LSS. The guidance, driven by HMRC's desire to make the enquiries more collaborative and cost effective, promotes a more targeted approach to information requests than the previous widely drawn requests. The guidance advocates an approach that seeks to balance three factors:

(a) the need for HMRC to have a good understanding of the facts before it reaches firm conclusions on what it believes to be the right tax;

(b) the need for requests for information to be well targeted, confined to the relevant facts, and framed with a view to making the fact-finding process as cost effective as possible for both HMRC and the customer; and

(c) the need to ensure that tax avoidance is not accepted as successful unless HMRC is satisfied that the relevant tax planning has indeed been implemented as described.

However, the guidance is drafted to cover all disputes and also acknowledges that widely drawn requests will be appropriate in certain circumstances. These circumstances are likely to include tax avoidance arrangements, particularly in light of the comments at **15.149**. The evidence sought is invariably in two forms, documents and particulars (ie information). The documents requested are formal documentation, such as contracts, agreements, trust deeds and board minutes typically found in a transaction bible and informal documentation such as step plans, drafts, emails, and bank statements and accounting entries to evidence fund flows.

15.119 A standard information request in relation to a transaction will typically cover the following:

- all legal documents and board minutes;
- all communications including emails, notes of meeting, etc between the company and any other person concerning or referring directly or indirectly to the transaction (including with all advisers);
- opinions tax/accounting including 'details of substance of meetings, etc where no notes taken';
- all instructions to banks, engagement letters;
- all calculations, all bank statements, all bookkeeping entries;
- chronology of events and explanation of commercial rationale;
- reasons for the amendments of documents;
- requests to see privileged information.

15.120 HMRC is also paying much closer attention to the basis for claims to privilege over certain documents. HMRC will now typically make a request for the taxpayer to provide a statement of the following in relation to privileged documents:

- date of document;

15.120 *Tax avoidance investigations*

- details of sender/receiver;
- purpose of the document;
- reason why Legal Professional Privilege (LPP) applicable.
  So that HMRC can consider a challenge under the new LPP Dispute Regulations 2009, SI 1916 (under which from August 2009 the First Tier Tribunal can examine withheld material and direct disclosure if it decides that an item is not protected by LPP).

15.121 The time frame for responding to information requests is also typically becoming much shorter, especially where HMRC considers the transaction to be an avoidance arrangement.

15.122 The following quote is indicative of the attitude of officers dealing with avoidance arrangements.

> 'we would expect with a transaction of this nature that all necessary information would have been collated in anticipation of an enquiry'.

15.123 The more recent letters from HMRC put as much emphasis on explanations (under the heading 'particulars') as they do on documents, particularly around the consideration of commercial versus tax-related factors in undertaking a particular transaction.

15.124 Examples of requests include:

- an explanation setting out why the arrangements connected to the disclosed scheme were undertaken;
- an explanation setting out why the arrangements connected to the disclosed scheme can be considered commercial and would have been entered into by third parties;
- what commercial benefits arose from borrowing in this way;
- an explanation of the commercial reasons the arrangements were structured in the way they were;
- an explanation of the extent to which tax was a factor in the arrangement.

15.125 Even in cases where there is no purpose test, or *Ramsay* challenge (see below) but rather the outcome is dependent on the interpretation of specific sections within the statute, there will still be factual information relating to the implementation of the transaction which HMRC will consider relevant. This is because it is not uncommon for an avoidance arrangement to work technically but be ineffective as a result of an implementation failure because certain steps have not taken place as envisaged. HMRC will wish to check for any such failures in the course of an avoidance enquiry.

Requests for tax advice

15.126 The scope and nature of HMRC's information powers are considered in detail in **Chapter 11**. In relation to tax planning, access to tax advice provided by one or more advisers is typically a source of contention between HMRC and taxpayers as regards its relevance to the determination of a tax liability. HMRC's view is that tax advice will be potentially relevant to the taxpayer's liability where tax avoidance is involved because it may shed light on the taxpayer's motive for entering into the transaction.

15.127 In this respect, pre-implementation advice may make the tax benefits of a particular arrangement known to a taxpayer and, therefore, may potentially influence behaviour and, as a consequence, may be relevant in determining motive. On the other hand post-implementation advice, in the form of opinion as to the operation of particular sections of the legislation should not be relevant. Indeed, it is hard to understand why HMRC should wish to see it, since it could be presumed they are qualified to form their own view as to the interpretation of the law; Nevertheless, HMRC continues to press for such documents (see below).

Protection for tax advisers' papers

15.128 The issue of an officer's right to access from the taxpayer, advice covered by legal professional privilege was covered in the case of *R (on the application of Morgan Grenfell & Co Ltd) v Comrs of Income Tax* [2002] STC 786. Lord Hoffmann dismissed the Inland Revenue's contention that it was important for them to have access to the taxpayer's legal advice which was subject to legal professional privilege in those cases in which liability may turn upon the purpose with which he entered into a transaction.

15.129 He observed that there were many situations in both civil and criminal law in which liability depends upon the state of mind with which something was done. Apart from the exceptional case in which it appeared that the client had obtained the advice in furtherance of a crime, this was not sufficient reason for overriding legal professional privilege. Hoffmann considered 'the court must infer the purpose from the facts'. Consequently, tax advice which is covered by legal professional privilege is protected from disclosure.

15.130 With effect from 1 April 2009 (the date Sch 36 to the FA 2008 became operative) there is a statutory protection Sch 36(23) from disclosure for documents held by the client which are covered by legal professional privilege. It is also important to note that there is a statutory protection from disclosure for accountants' tax advice in respect of advice held by the advisor at Sch 36(25/26)..

15.131 However, where documents containing tax advice are in the hands of the taxpayer, then following the judgement in the recent Court of Appeal decision in Re *Prudential plc v Special Comr of Income Tax and anor* [2010] EWCA 1094 civ only advice from a legal advisor that may be subject to a claim to legal professional privilege (LPP) is protected from disclosure (subject to the relevance test being satisfied (see **15.147**). Prudential failed in its argument that in the modern context where skilled and professional advice on tax law is obtained from accountants, the long-established common law rules regarding LPP apply to the communications between client and accountant. The judge acknowledged the anomalous situation that although accountants and lawyers fulfilled exactly the same function in providing tax advice, it was only the latter's advice that was protected by LLP. He considered this point had been addressed by the Court of Appeal in respect of patent agents in *Wilden Pump*

15.131 *Tax avoidance investigations*

Engineering Co v Fusfeld [1985] FSR 159. It was acknowledged in that case that the patent lawyers provided legal advice but this did not justify extending the concept of LPP to any professional person who happened to provide legal advice in the course of their business.

15.132 Lloyd LJ also did not consider that policy and public interest considerations justified such an extension in the modern context. Other jurisdictions had generally not extended the common law protection to non lawyers and in the UK with ample opportunity Parliament had not extended LPP to advisers except as explained at **15.130** a limited right over an adviser's own records.

This decision was upheld by the Court of Appeal in October 2010, which also found itself bound by the judgment in *Wilden Pump Engineering Co*. However, the Court of Appeal went further, holding that even without this precedent they would still have concluded that it was not open to the court to hold that LPP applied outside the legal profession, except as a result of relevant statutory provisions.

15.133 As a consequence, all communications from the tax advisor other than a lawyer, which are in the possession or power of the taxpayer, are potentially disclosable. Given the importance of this principle and its application beyond tax to regulatory investigations generally the *Prudential* case is to be heard by the Supreme Court and with Human Rights argued in court reference to the European Court remains a possibility.

15.134 In addition to the question of whether the advice is protected by privilege, whether advice needs to be disclosed will also depend on whether it is potentially relevant to the taxpayer's liability.

HMRC's justification for requesting tax advice

15.135 So what support is there for HMRC's stance of seeking access to confidential tax advice in avoidance enquiries? HMRC considers that Special Commissioners cases such as *Marwood Homes* (see [1997] STC 37, [1998] STC 53 and [1999] STC 44) and the Special Commissioners ruling in SpC 647 which is the *Prudential* litigation (**15.131** and **15.132**) are supportive of its stance with regard to access to tax advice.

15.136 Whilst only Special Commissioners' decisions, it is easy to see why HMRC regard them as authority justifying their approach. It is, after all, the Special Commissioners who are the arbiters of fact and, therefore, arguably well placed to opine on whether HMRC's information requests can be justified from an evidential perspective.

15.137 *Marwood Homes* concerned the issue of whether transactions in securities giving rise to a tax advantage were carried out for bona fide commercial reasons and was first heard by Special Commissioners comprising the s 703 tribunal who found in favour of the taxpayer. The former Inland Revenue subsequently gave notice to the Special Commissioners requiring the appeal to be reheard by a tribunal constituted under s 706 which found in favour of the Inland Revenue.

15.138 Prior to the second hearing an order for discovery of documents was issued. The tribunal noted that, to a large extent, the difference in the conclusion they reached was attributable to the substantial amount of additional written material relevant to the issue they were provided with. This material had not been disclosed to the Inland Revenue and had not been produced as evidence before the Special Commissioners at the s 703 hearing.

15.139 In relation to the order for discovery, the Commissioners commented that:

> 'where [as here] the question of liability depends on the intentions of those responsible for implementing the transactions, the advice they acted on is crucial at every stages [sic] of the proceedings'.

15.140 In this respect the Commissioners appear to have been particularly influenced by the comments in communications and notes of meeting between the tax advisers and the taxpayer. These included references by the tax advisers to excluding the words 'some significant taxation savings' in a letter from the taxpayer company to its solicitors and references to 'beefing up' the commercial justification for the transactions in the necessary clearance applications to the Inland Revenue. They also appear to have been swayed to a considerable extent by the prevalence of the tax issues in the communications with the advisers.

15.141 The company's advisers maintained that the transaction was carried out for bone fide commercial reasons and the tax advantages were incidental to the commercial drivers.

15.142 Whilst the comments that the Commissioners noted were unhelpful to the taxpayers' cause, in the writer's view, the more significant point was that part of the steps undertaken to reorganise Marwood's two divisions could not (to the Commissioners' satisfaction) be rationally explained unless the requirement to obtain a tax advantage was taken into account. This was the ultimate nail in the taxpayer's case. In simple terms, there was nothing to 'beef up' commercially; had there been, the comments should have taken less significance. It is easy to overlook this aspect of the case and come away with the view that any comment in a document referring to a tax advantage is fatal. This is simply not the case; what is important is the context within which the comment and the tax advantage itself arise.

15.143 Nevertheless, the case is a useful indication of how the Commissioners are likely to approach the issue of access to documentation where the purpose for entering into a transaction is potentially relevant to the determination of the tax treatment. The Commissioners considered that, as a general principle, intention should be determined by looking at the transactions as a whole in their proper commercial context; the relevant intention being that which led to the implementation. A company's object in this respect was to be determined from the intentions of those who govern its policy. The Commissioners considered this might involve looking at intentions of directors, shareholders or, where appropriate, the company's professional advisers.

15.144 *Tax avoidance investigations*

15.144 The issue of the relevance of certain emails was also considered in the High Court case of *Prudential plc v Special Comr of Income Tax*. Before the Special Commissioners (case SpC647), it was contended on behalf of HMRC that the request was to enable HMRC to understand the relevant transactions, to see why they were entered into and, in their words, to see whether the statutory provisions, construed purposively, applied to the transactions as they actually were, viewed realistically.

15.145 On behalf of the taxpayer in relation to the relevance issue the point was made to the Special Commissioner that *R v A Special Comr, ex p Morgan Grenfell & Co Ltd* 74 TC 511 supported the company's claim. In particular, the view of Lord Hoffmann expressed at para 38 whereby he disagreed with the Revenue's argument that it was important for them to have access to legal advice in cases where the liability turns on the purpose for which a transaction was entered into, rather, the court must infer purpose from the facts.

15.146 The Crown argued *Morgan Grenfell* was solely about legal professional privilege and the case did not consider an extension to it. The Special Commissioner concurred with the Crown's view and considered that the taxpayer had misread the passage from *Morgan Grenfell*.

15.147 Before the High Court counsel for Prudential argued that in seeking disclosure of skilled advice on tax law given by accountants, HMRC were unlawfully departing from their earlier stance and practice. This was essentially the practice contained in 'Tax Bulletin 46' and 'Tax Bulletin 62' albeit that these had subsequently been withdrawn. The judge rejected the argument that there had been a departure, and pointed out that in many cases HMRC accept that pure legal advice will be irrelevant. Both Special Commissioner and High Court judge referred to certain emails which had been included in documents submitted to HMRC. The content of the emails included the following:

> 'As the preference is not to mention the declaration and payment of the dividend by PCAHL the 'outline proposal' element of the note is brief and just details the intention to issue the warrants to SNC … Just as a presentational point, we mention that the reasons for the issue of the warrants is to facilitate the winding up of PCAHL but we do not explain how the issue helps to achieve that – perhaps a point to gloss over …
>
> Please do NOT include reference to the dividend in the approvals note as that would give it an inevitability.
>
> As you know Robin has let us have a copy of the proposed steps to effect the payment of the charge by PGL. Myself and David have had discussions to try and 'put a little flesh in the bones' and as a result have numerous questions for PwC e.g., duration and terms of the warrant, are the Australian directors aware of the proposals, nature of the investment in the partnership – capital or debt –, does the partnership need a general partner, how does PCAHL reconcile the issue of the warrants which will include a provision that no dividends will be paid during the term of the warrant with the fact that it will propose to pay a dividend to PGL on the same day, etc, etc …'

The Special Commissioner considered the officer was 'entirely reasonable in his opinion that the documents sought contain or may contain information that shows the whole facts which are relevant to the tax liability of the subsidiary'. Similarly, in the High Court, the judge considered that the above extracts indicated that the content of the final transactional documents may not include all the facts. In the context of these particular emails it is perhaps not difficult to see why the Special Commissioner and High Court reached the conclusion they did in this instance.

In the High Court in *Prudential* Charles J (para 81) stressed that what HMRC sought was not pure legal advice on the meaning and effect of the relevant taxing provisions but information concerning the nature of the transactions and, in particular, what was and what was not pre-ordained..

However, the *Prudential* case should not be regarded as a general precedent that all tax advice is disclosable. It is implicit in the judgement that pure tax advice on the meaning and effect of the statute will not be relevant. Each situation will need to be considered on its own facts.

15.148 In considering the influence of advisers, HMRC's attitude appears to be that a person intends the natural consequences of his actions; so where a taxpayer incurs significant tax advisers' fees and a tax advantage is secured as a result of the advice, then from HMRC's perspective, it seems to follow that the main purpose is tax avoidance. Whilst this is clearly a gross over-simplification, it should also be borne in mind that there will generally be an onus on the taxpayer to displace this prima facie assumption, and particularly so where sections such as s 703 are at issue. In *Snell* Spc 532 the Tribunal held that if the adviser's purpose is to avoid tax and the client understands that then the arrangement will have that (tax avoidance) purpose. Tax advisers need to have this at the forefront of their mind when implementing tax-planning arrangements.

15.149 The courts recent emphasis on the legislation applying to the facts (viewed realistically) means that despite HMRC's general desire to adopt a more focussed approach to information requests, it remains to be seen whether information requests in relation to avoidance arrangements will be narrowed significantly, especially given the need to ensure arrangements have been implemented correctly. In this respect, the guidance accompanying the LSS suggests that HMRC may be willing to place reliance on an implementation review carried out by an experienced adviser. Indeed, recent experience is of HMRC seeking more documentation from third parties than ever before in order to build as complete a picture as possible of the transaction. As stated above, there remains protection for tax advice papers in the hands of tax advisers but there is no protection for other third parties, such as banks, where they are merely a counterparty to a transaction. If a third party obtains it own legal advice (to assure itself of its own position) LPP will apply in the normal way.

15.150 HMRC does, however, appear to have recognised that in certain instances, the amount of time involved in reviewing very extensive documentation may not be the most cost effective use of their time. Also, at the

15.150 *Tax avoidance investigations*

very least the guidance makes it clear that HMRC should be clear about the risk it is addressing (ie the technical concern) and how the information is relevant to address that risk.

Case batching

15.151 One recent development in certain tax-avoidance arrangements is that of case batching. This involves the Anti-Avoidance Group contacting advisers (or vice versa) with a view to securing their agreement to a sample-based approach to raising enquiries. The approach is reserved for highly generic schemes with near identical (or relatively straightforward) fact patterns. In such cases, whilst all taxpayers who have availed themselves of a particular generic arrangement will have an enquiry notice issued, only a sample will be looked at in detail.

15.152 The proposal is voluntary and individual taxpayers are free to opt out of the arrangement. The idea being that the sample will be representative of the arrangements as a whole and will save both time and cost for both sides. The advantage for those that agree to the arrangement is the ability to share the adviser's costs amongst all those taking part. Anyone not agreeing to enter the sample arrangement will have the arrangements looked at in detail in the usual way.

15.153 Examples of arrangements where such an approach has been adopted include personal tax planning involving relevant discounted securities and gilt strips, certain intellectual property planning and certain arrangements involving share or other asset-based payments to employees.

15.154 Whilst this approach has the practical advantage of convenience and a potential reduction in costs, there are dangers in making assumptions as to the uniformity of fact patterns. Decisions of the courts can differ in cases which appear on the face of it to have very similar facts. Tiny nuances can play an important part as to why certain decisions are reached.

HMRC's current technical approach in light of recent case law

15.155 What can the taxpayer or his advisor take from the recent decisions set above? *Scottish Provident Institution* appears to have resulted in HMRC putting significantly greater emphasis on purposive-based arguments. Only time will tell how this approach will pan out in the courts as the litigation and settlement strategy progresses, but taxpayers and their advisers can expect arguments to focus on this aspect in addition to any unallowable purpose considerations where these are in point.

Despite the courts rejecting the concept of economic equivalence, HMRC continues to adopt this approach albeit now under the guise of a purposive construction.

The increased threat of penalties

15.156 HMRC has made it clear that it will seek penalties where it believes the failure of an avoidance arrangement is the result of neglect (or from 1 April 2008 failing to take reasonable care).

15.157 Where a taxpayer has sought professional advice in relation to a particular arrangement, it should not generally be open to HMRC to charge a penalty should the advice ultimately prove to be wrong, either as a result of litigation or accepting HMRC's position, providing the position adopted was tenable. In relation to whether a scheme was disclosable the Special Commissioner in *Mercury* SpC 737 (2009) held that as Mercury took counsel's advice on the question of disclosure he would not penalise them if that advice turned out to be wrong. They had done all they could in seeking such advice.

15.158 However, where HMRC is able to establish that the advice was sought by the taxpayer was from a firm whose capability was clearly not commensurate with the technical complexity of the issue under consideration it is likely HMRC would seek to charge a penalty for failing to take reasonable care.

15.159 Similarly, where the planning is ineffective because of an implementation failure (for example, funds did not move as envisaged) HMRC will contend that the taxpayer has been negligent, or from 1 April 2008 has failed to take reasonable care.

HMRC's approach where fraud is suspected

15.160 Where it suspects that the taxpayer has acted fraudulently in implementing a planning arrangement the avoidance investigator will refer the matter elsewhere within HMRC where it may be decided another office should pursue the matter or whether a criminal investigation should be instigated. Examples of issues that would trigger such a referral are back-dating of documents or other forms of deliberate misrepresentation.

KEY IMPLICATIONS AND CONSIDERATIONS FOR THE ADVISOR

15.161 Those taxpayers undertaking avoidance arrangements can expect a far bumpier ride under HMRC's new strategy. Some of the impacts of the above changes will be obvious. Perhaps the most basic is that anyone undertaking avoidance can expect the arrangement to be identified and challenged in contrast to the past where it was not uncommon for planning to go completely unchallenged.

15.162 At the risk of stating the obvious, preparation is the key to achieving a successful outcome. Being prepared sounds easy but it is not uncommon for taxpayers and their advisers to be taken by surprise at some stage during an enquiry. The best preparation involves rigorous self challenge at every stage of

15.162 *Tax avoidance investigations*

the planning cycle from inception and implementation of the idea to defence against HMRC challenge. There are three key responses:

- thoroughly 'road testing' ideas and responses;
- being rigorous in execution;
- being proactive.

'Road testing' ideas and responses

15.163 Forewarned is forearmed. Counsel, when blessing an idea, will usually give an indication of the potential risks and possible challenges but this tends to focus on the theoretical. Road testing of the planning idea, its implementation and enquiry responses should also use insights based on practical experience of avoidance enquiries. It is important to know exactly what to expect from the enquiry in terms of information requests, the types of technical challenge and how they have been resolved. This enables any potential weaknesses in the planning to be addressed before it is potentially too late or identifies transactions which should not be undertaken because the risk of a successful challenge is too high.

15.164 It is essential that advisers in relation to any planning that they propose test at an early stage the strength of the fact pattern, particularly the commercial rationale (if this has a significant bearing on the analysis) from objective standpoint and do not merely accept at face value what they are being told or what they believe the position to be. The facts, particularly the rationale for entering into a transaction will be the subject of detailed scrutiny during the course of an enquiry and possibly during litigation in the form of cross-examination.

15.165 The same goes for responses during the course of an enquiry. It is a mistake to rush a reply, and responses should never be left to the last minute; the wrong response (especially at a key juncture) can be difficult to recover from and can be costly in terms of time, money or the ultimate outcome.

15.166 Recent tax cases have amply demonstrated that the courts take an 'unblinkered' approach when it comes to interpreting the facts. Where the evidence submitted (whether oral of documentary) is not sufficient to satisfy the finding of fact sought by the taxpayer, the fact-finding tribunal (formerly the Special Commissioners and now the First-tier Tribunal) will find their own version of the facts (even where this may involve a degree of speculation on their part).

15.167 A recent example of this was in the case of *Burns and Neil v Revenue & Customs Comrs* [2009] SPC 728. The case involved a Special Commissioner's decision on the bona fide defences under s 741 ICTA 1988 against a liability under s 739. In this case two daughters of a family resident and domiciled in Jersey transferred their interest in settled property (investment property in the UK) to two Jersey companies, one owned by each. The transfers satisfied the conditions for a liability on the transferors and the only issue was whether the bona fide commercial transaction defences applied. Witness evidence from the girls' mother was that she and her husband did not want their daughters to have the responsibility of managing the investments at the age of 18. This, together with the aim of protecting the girls from the aspirations and bad influence of unwelcome boyfriends, was given to be the reason for the transfer of the properties into companies of which the girls' parents would be directors. However, this was undermined by evidence from cross-examination which showed that the girls' parents were not involved in managing the companies, this had always been done by the girls' grandfather who had established the families wealth. Consequently, the Special Commissioner did not accept that separation of ownership was the reason for the transfer. Nor did the Commissioner accept the 'gold digger' explanation as this protection could have been undone by any boyfriend prevailing on the daughters to sack the directors as a route to the companies' assets.

15.168 Failing to identify and address potential weaknesses in contentions and supporting evidence early on can ultimately damage the likelihood of success, as it will be too late to deal with them once the Tribunal has made a finding of fact. Anticipating challenges (either from the Tribunal or HMRC) and having arguments and evidence to withstand them provides for a greater likelihood of success than focusing only on the taxpayer's contentions.

Rigour in execution

15.169 It is not uncommon for planners to focus on the idea itself and not give its implementation the attention it requires. It is important to plan well ahead and ensure that the implementation step plan leaves no stone unturned. Effective execution requires a comprehensive implementation blue print to cover every aspect of the planning from start to finish; nothing should be assumed or taken for granted. Strong processes and controls are necessary to ensure all required actions are performed timeously, documented appropriately and are readily available in a well-organised and 'audit ready' format in anticipation of HMRC requests.

15.170 The implementation programme should foresee any potential pitfalls and ensure that they are addressed. The step plan should assign the person responsible for each step with a date for completion and that person must evidence the fact that the required action has been completed. Whether the plan is on a simple Word or Excel document or more sophisticated planning tools such as Microsoft Project, ownership for implementation of each step in the planning is critical to ensuring success.

15.171 Preparing on the basis that the case may end up in litigation proceedings is a valuable discipline. The documentation should be maintained on the basis that it may need to be presented in court. As rule of thumb taxpayers and their advisors should not write anything they would not be happy being read out in court. This is not, however, to suggest that what is written should, in anyway, be misleading, as this could lead to criminal proceedings.

15.172 Statements of fact should be carefully researched before being documented, advisers should not rely on verbal confirmation alone, where necessary, independent documentary evidence should corroborate the facts.

15.173 Care must be taken to ensure that nothing is ever done which could be construed as misrepresentation of any factual information. Deliberate misrepresentation is dishonest conduct which potentially carries a criminal sanction. This includes the creation or destruction of documents with the intention to mislead the authorities.

15.174 Where the taxpayer's witness evidence is likely to be critical, this should be fully explained to the taxpayer at the outset. The taxpayer, company director or other key employees should be made aware of the possibility of the need for them to give evidence which may be subject to cross-examination in proceedings.

15.175 In anticipation of an HMRC challenge, documents should be categorised into those that are relevant, those that are covered by legal professional privilege, and those which are not relevant. In maintaining the demarcation between relevant and irrelevant documents it is important to try, as far as is practical, to separate factual information from opinions.

15.176 Where documents contain a mixture of fact and opinion it may be impossible to prevent disclosure of the opinion unless the parts of the document containing the opinion are redacted. Redaction is best avoided if possible as it is often viewed very unfavourably by HMRC, even though it is a legally recognised and a reasonable way of dealing with different types of material within the same document.

Adopting a proactive approach

15.177 HMRC has said that an enquiry typically comprises 80% fact finding and 20% technical argument. Taxpayers and their advisers can fall into the trap of viewing the enquiry as a one-sided affair with HMRC in the driving seat.

15.178 Assertion, questioning and challenge is just as much a matter for the taxpayer as it is for HMRC; when and how is a matter of judgement based on experience. However, a lack of pro-activity and a failure to focus on the key points can lead to missed opportunities to close an enquiry down or give false expectation to HMRC that digging in for the long haul will grind a taxpayer into whole or partial submission.

15.179 HMRC typically focuses on tax advice in order to seek to demonstrate that an arrangement is wholly tax motivated. This over emphasis on tax advice can, however, lead to a less than objective assessment of the commercial drivers behind a transaction and to HMRC confusing the form of a transaction with its purpose.

15.180 A transaction can have a commercial driver but be structured in a tax-efficient way. Thus, whilst the form of the transaction may be tax motivated it does not necessarily follow that the underlying purpose is tax driven and advisers should not be overly defensive in relation to the tax benefits of a particular arrangement. Any planning which saves significant amounts of tax will contain references to this benefit; it would be surprising if it were otherwise. What is important is that these tax benefits are not allowed to be taken out of context, especially in a way that appears to undermine a genuine commercial purpose for the transaction as a whole.

15.181 In addressing HMRC's contentions, a question can often be as, if not more, disarming than an assertion. HMRC is keener to ask questions than answer them. Nevertheless, taxpayers are entitled to a clear articulation of the case against them both in terms of factual and technical differences.

It can be difficult to elicit HMRC's detailed technical argument in advance of proceedings before the Tribunal. In some instances, it is not until skeleton arguments have been exchanged immediately prior to the hearing that a sufficiently full analysis is provided to properly understand HMRC's contentions.

This somewhat one-sided approach has recently been subject to internal review by HMRC following an internal report by Gabs Maclouf on how HMRC manages tax disputes. That report concluded that HMRC should be more transparent in articulating its position. In addition, experience to date from HMRC's pilot Alternative Dispute Resolution (ADR) is that many disputes reach an impasse because neither side has properly understood the questions to be answered. It is not uncommon for disputes to have been running for many years where neither party has been able to clearly articulate their position. This is clearly unacceptable for the client who is unnecessarily incurring significant additional costs.

15.182 From 1 April 2009, taxpayers have a legal right to have appealable tax decisions or assessments reviewed by another HMRC officer before appealing to the Tribunal. The impact of this legislation is likely to be less important for cases involving tax avoidance because these cases are already subject to internal review by subject-matter specialists and in many instances the Solicitors Office. As such, it is unlikely that another officer is likely to reach a different conclusion.

15.183 HMRC's 'conclusion of review letter' should provide a full and clear explanation of the reason for the officer's decision. A request for a review in relation to an appeal against an information notice may also be helpful in relation to assisting the taxpayer gain a better understand as to why HMRC is continuing to request further information. Given that the decision maker within HMRC is required to prepare a report for the review officer summarising:

- the decision;
- the facts;
- the relevant legislation and guidance;
- the decision maker's reasoning;
- the taxpayer's argument and evidence; and
- the decision maker's argument and evidence

this may help focus the officer's attention on why specific information is being requested.

15.184 In monitoring cases centrally, HMRC is not only looking to apply consistency, but also to identify what it regards as a representative case, in order that this may be litigated. Practitioners need to be aware that there is a potential

15.184 *Tax avoidance investigations*

for a case with an excellent fact pattern to be undermined by HMRC successfully litigating a case with a weaker fact pattern. Whilst in theory it should be possible to distinguish a case based on the facts in practice, the taxpayer is facing an uphill battle to overturn an existing decision albeit on slightly different facts. It is, therefore, important for practitioners to network in order to be aware of similar arrangements that may be heading for litigation, as the best policy may be for interested parties to seek to drive a more favourable case before the Tribunal judges.

Appendix 1

Supplementary Anti-Money Laundering Guidance for the Tax Practitioner

Guidance for those providing tax services in the United Kingdom, on the prevention of money laundering and the countering of terrorist financing.

This Guidance is issued by

- the Chartered Institute of Taxation,
- the Association of Taxation Technicians,
- the Institute of Chartered Accountants in England and Wales,
- the Association of Chartered Certified Accountants,
- the Chartered Institute of Management Accountants; and
- HM Revenue and Customs

as an Appendix to the anti-money laundering guidance released by the Consultative Committee of Accountancy Bodies (CCAB).

This supplementary Guidance is not stand alone Guidance; it must be read in conjunction with the CCAB's anti money laundering guidance (*please insert link to CCAB guidance on your websites*) to which this Guidance is an appendix. It focuses on the interaction between anti money laundering compliance and tax offences and covers the issues that a tax practitioner is most likely to encounter in practice.

The comments received on the exposure draft of this guidance have been considered and incorporated where appropriate. HM Treasury has approved this guidance. This means that the Courts must consider the content of the Guidance when determining whether an accountant's or tax practitioner's conduct gives rise to an offence under either the Proceeds of Crime Act 2002, Terrorism Act 2000 or the Money Laundering Regulations 2007.

Issued on 25 June 2009

Appendix 1

CONTENTS

1. About this supplementary guidance
2. How to use this supplementary guidance
3. Tax practitioners, MLR 2007 and POCA
4. Overview of the tax sector
5. What are the money laundering risks in the tax sector?
6. Tax offences
7. Reluctance to correct past errors
8. Intention to underpay tax
9. Tax evasion
10. Failure to obtain Treasury consent
11. Indirect tax
12. The privilege reporting exemption
13. Customer due diligence

Appendix 1: Money Laundering and disclosures to HMRC

Appendix 2: Examples of when the privilege reporting exemption might apply

Appendix 3: Examples of when the privilege reporting exemption is unlikely to apply

GLOSSARY AND INTERPRETATION

1.

CCAB	The Consultative Committee of Accountancy Bodies
CDD	Customer Due Diligence
CEMA	Customs and Excise Management Act 1979
HMRC	Her Majesty's Revenue and Customs
ICTA	Income and Corporation Taxes Act 1988
JMLSG	Joint Money Laundering Steering Group
MLR 2007	Money Laundering Regulations 2007
MLRO	Money Laundering Reporting Officer
POCA	Proceeds of Crime Act 2002
SAR	Suspicious Activity Report
SOCA	The Serious Organised Crime Agency
TMA	The Taxes Management Act 1970
UK	United Kingdom
VATA	Value Added Tax Act 1994

2. Words importing the masculine gender include the feminine, words in the singular include the plural and words in the plural include the singular.

Note: This guidance is incomplete on its own. It must be read in conjunction with the CCAB's Anti Money Laundering guidance.

Appendix 1

1. ABOUT THIS SUPPLEMENTARY GUIDANCE

1.1   This supplementary guidance has been developed by the Chartered Institute of Taxation, the Association of Taxation Technicians, the Association of Chartered Certified Accountants, the Institute of Chartered Accountants in England and Wales, the Chartered Institute of Management Accountants and HMRC for professionals providing tax services.

1.2   This supplementary guidance uses the descriptive term 'tax practitioner' for someone in business offering tax services. The MLR 2007 uses the term 'tax adviser' and defines a tax adviser as

> 'a firm or sole practitioner who by way of business provides advice about the tax affairs of other persons, when providing such services'.

The meaning of 'advice' is widely interpreted. For the purpose of this and the CCAB guidance, tax compliance services, ie assisting in the completion and submission of tax returns, is included within the term. It was considered that, for the purposes of this supplementary guidance, the term 'tax practitioner' minimises the risk of someone assuming that MLR 2007 does not apply to their business because they provide tax compliance services.

1.3   The term 'tax' covers all direct and indirect taxes including duties.

1.4   A tax practitioner providing tax advice privately on an unremunerated or voluntary basis (for example as an unpaid volunteer with the Citizens Advice Bureau) does not come within the scope of the MLR 2007 as he is not providing his services 'by way of business'. However tax advice given by way of business is within the scope of MLR 2007 even if it is provided to the client on a pro bono or unremunerated basis. See also paragraph 1.6 of the CCAB guidance.

1.5   The Treasury has approved this guidance. As noted in the CCAB's guidance approval means that the Courts must have regard to the guidance in deciding whether businesses or individuals affected by it have committed an offence under the MLR 2007 or ss 330–331 POCA or s21A of The Terrorism Act 2000..

2. HOW TO USE THIS SUPPLEMENTARY GUIDANCE

2.1   This supplementary guidance is for professionals providing tax services. It focuses on the interaction between anti money laundering compliance or countering terrorist financing and tax offences and those issues that the tax practitioner is most likely to encounter. It is not intended to be a comprehensive guide to tax offences. It is not stand alone guidance – it must be read in conjunction with the CCAB AML guidance. The broad interpretation of 'tax adviser' means that this guidance cannot cover every aspect of tax work but the principles set out in the CCAB guidance and in this guidance apply to all taxes and duties.

2.2   A tax practitioner must have a clear understanding of his obligations under the anti Money Laundering legislation. Detailed guidance is given in the CCAB guidance as follows: Section1 About this guidance

Appendix 1

Section 2   The offences
Section 3   Anti money laundering systems and controls
Section 4   The risk based approach to Customer Due Diligence
Section 5   Customer Due Diligence
Section 6   Internal reporting
Section 7   Role of MLRO and SAR reporting
Section 8   Consent
Section 9   Post SAR actions

2.3   Where a tax practitioner is uncertain of his obligations under the anti-money laundering legislation he should seek specialist help.

3. TAX PRACTITIONERS, MLR 2007 AND POCA

3.1   The obligations placed on a tax practitioner under MLR 2007 and POCA are covered in the CCAB guidance.

3.2   Paragraph 1.14 of that guidance sets out the role of the supervisory authorities and advises tax practitioners who are in business of the requirement to be supervised by a supervisory authority.

3.3   A tax practitioner should be aware of HMRC's responsibility under MLR 2007 to regulate trust and company service providers, which may impinge upon the work they undertake for their clients. However if the tax practitioner is supervised by another supervisory authority for other tax and accounting services, that supervisory authority can act as supervisor for the trust and company service work.

3.4   Whilst this supplementary guidance focuses on tax offences, a tax practitioner should be aware of the potential need to report to SOCA (or to his firm's MLRO where he is not a sole practitioner) where he knows or suspects or has reasonable grounds for knowing or suspecting, on the basis of information which came to him in the course of his work as a tax practitioner, that another person is engaged in money laundering. This means that where, in the course of his work, a tax practitioner has knowledge or suspicion of proceeds derived from any crime (ie not restricted to tax crimes) a report may be required.

3.5   In particular, a tax practitioner should also take proper care, under Section 328 POCA, to ensure he does not become concerned in an arrangement which he knows or suspects facilitates (by whatever means) the acquisition, retention, use or control of criminal property by or on behalf of another person when assisting clients.

4. OVERVIEW OF THE TAX SECTOR

4.1   Tax work covers a broad range of activities from routine compliance work to complex tax planning.
4.2   Tax compliance includes the processing and submission of returns to the tax authorities.
4.3   Tax planning looks at advising on and structuring tax affairs in a

Appendix 1

taxefficient manner. This can sometimes involve the use of trusts, offshore entities and tax favourable regimes.

5. WHAT ARE THE MONEY LAUNDERING RISKS IN THE TAX SECTOR?

5.1   The money laundering risk areas that a tax practitioner may encounter in practice include the following:

(a) Where a client's actions in respect of his tax affairs create proceeds of crime, for example:
- a client's refusal to correct errors (both for the past and on an ongoing basis); or
- a client's deliberate under declaration of profits/income/gain or deliberate overstatement of expenses/losses.

(b) Where during the course of dealing with a client's tax affairs a tax practitioner suspects or becomes aware that the client is holding proceeds of crime derived from criminal activity which may or may not be tax related.

5.2   The tax practitioner needs to be alert to the risk of assisting or facilitating the laundering of proceeds of crime whether through the evasion of taxes or otherwise. For example, where a client puts significant importance on maintaining the anonymity of beneficiaries or owners or in keeping confidential the structure of a complex plan ostensibly intended to minimise legally a tax liability, then the possibility that the funds involved are derived from the proceeds of crime should be kept in mind.

6. TAX OFFENCES

6.1   Introduction

6.1.1   There are a number of tax offences which can give rise to the proceeds of crime and SARs. These are discussed further below. When a tax practitioner has identified proceeds of crime, he (or his firm's MLRO where he is not a sole practitioner) should consider carefully whether the privilege reporting exemption applies before submitting a SAR. See section 12 below and section 7 of the CCAB guidance.

6.1.2   A tax practitioner is not required to be an expert in criminal law but would be expected to be aware of the boundaries between deliberate understatement or other tax evasion and simple cases of error or genuine differences in the interpretation of tax law and be able to identify conduct in relation to direct and indirect tax which is punishable by the criminal law. There will be no question of criminality where the client has adopted in good faith, honestly and without misstatement a technical position with which HMRC disagrees.

6.1.3   The main areas where offences may arise in direct tax are:

Appendix 1

- tax evasion, including making false returns (including supporting documents), accounts or financial statements or deliberate failure to submit returns;
- deliberate refusal to correct known errors; and less commonly
- failure to obtain consent under s765 ICTA

6.2 Taxes Management Act 1970 ('TMA') tax 'offences'

6.2.1 The TMA provides a civil penalty regime covering both fraudulent and negligent conduct. It is only fraudulent or dishonest conduct which is reportable under POCA. The money laundering legislation is only concerned with the proceeds of criminal conduct. Therefore, it is only that conduct which the law treats as criminal offences which can lead to money laundering issues.

6.2.2 Where conduct may attract a civil penalty under the TMA but may also, on the particular facts, amount to criminal conduct then the conduct is criminal. By way of example, only, knowingly assisting in the preparation of an incorrect return etc could give rise to a civil penalty under s99 TMA, but the conduct concerned would typically amount to a criminal offence (such as false accounting or cheating HMRC) as well. Any case where fraudulent conduct is suspected should be reported unless the privilege reporting exemption applies. See section 12 below and section 7 of CCAB guidance

6.3 Prosecution policy – the need to report

6.3.1 In the tax environment, there are many circumstances in which the tax authorities have a long and established practice of dealing with matters on a civil basis. A policy view is taken that this is a more cost effective approach and that the interest and penalties that can be charged on a civil basis constitute sufficient restitution and deterrent.

6.3.2 This is the case across direct tax and VAT where criminal prosecutions are very much the exception.

6.3.3 However, the practices or anticipated practices of HMRC are irrelevant to the reporting obligations under POCA. If a tax practitioner suspects that a criminal offence may have been committed, and that there may be or may have been proceeds, whether actual or prospective proceeds, then unless the privilege reporting exemption applies (see section 12 below and section 7 of the CCAB guidance), he is obliged to report to SOCA (or to his firm's MLRO where he is not a sole practitioner) irrespective of the fact that a criminal prosecution may in the member's view be highly unlikely in practice.

7. RELUCTANCE TO CORRECT PAST ERRORS

7.1 Innocent or negligent error – direct tax

7.1.1 It is not uncommon for tax practitioners to become aware of errors in or omissions in current or in past years from clients' tax returns or any calculationsor statements appertaining to any liability or an underpayment of tax, for example because a payment date has been missed. If the tax practitioner has no cause to doubt that these came about as a result of innocent mistake or negligence then he will not have formed a suspicion. However, in some cases, the tax practitioner may form a suspicion that the original irregularity was criminal in nature and should make a report unless the privilege reporting exemption applies (see section 12 below and section 7 of the CCAB guidance).

7.2 Innocent or negligent error – indirect tax

7.2.1 In the case of indirect tax, see section 11 below on handling the original error.

7.3 Unwillingness or refusal to disclose to the tax authorities

7.3.1 Where a client indicates that he is unwilling or refuses to disclose the matter to HMRC in order to avoid paying the tax due, the client appears to have formed criminal intent and hence the reporting obligation arises unless the privilege reporting exemption applies (see section 12 below and section 7 of the CCAB guidance). A tax practitioner will need to be careful in applying the privilege exemption when the client has expressed clear intention to evade taxes and needs to consider whether the crime/fraud exception applies. The tax practitioner should also consider whether he can continue to act and consult his professional body's guidance on such matters. This paragraph applies equally to potential clients for whom the tax practitioner has declined to act.

7.4 Adjusting subsequent returns

7.4.1 Where the law permits the correction of small errors by subsequent tax adjustments, and the original error was not attributable to any criminal conduct, then the adjustment itself will not give rise to the need to report, since no crime will have been committed. However, it should be noted that the legislation does apply to any conduct which constitutes the laundering of the proceeds of any criminal offence however small the amount involved.

8. INTENTION TO UNDERPAY TAX

8.1.1 A client may suggest that he will in the future underpay tax which would be tax evasion and a money laundering offence when it occurs.

8.1.2 A tax practitioner can and should apply his professional body's normal ethical guidance to persuade the client to comply with the law. Should the client's intention in this regard still remain in doubt, the tax practitioner should consider carefully whether he can commence or continue to act.

8.1.3 A SAR may well be required in such cases once there are proceeds of crime, depending upon the facts and circumstances and whether the

Appendix 1

privilegereporting exemption applies (see section 12 below and section 7 of the CCAB guidance). As in 7.3.1 above a tax practitioner will need to be careful in applying the privilege exemption when the client has expressed clear intention to evade taxes.

9. TAX EVASION

9.1 General

9.1.1 Where a tax practitioner knows or suspects, or has reasonable grounds for knowing or suspecting, that a client or other party is engaged in tax evasion in the UK or overseas, this will clearly amount to one or more of a number of possible criminal offences, such as theft, obtaining pecuniary advantage by fraud, false accounting, cheating HMRC, the offence of fraudulent evasion of income tax under s 144 Finance Act 2000 or a range of specific indirect tax offences (see section 11 below). Unless the privilege reporting exemption applies (see section 12 below and section 7 of the CCAB guidance) a tax practitioner should report the matter to SOCA (or to his firm's MLRO where he is not a sole practitioner) immediately.

9.1.2 If the suspected evasion is of taxes outside the UK, in circumstances which would be a criminal offence if the conduct occurred in the UK, this should also be reported immediately unless it is known to be lawful under the criminal law applying in that country and that conduct, if carried out in the UK, would attract a maximum sentence in the UK of less than twelve months, except as prescribed by order.

As in other cases, this is unless the privilege reporting exemption applies (see section 12 below and section 7 of the CCAB guidance). There are other very limited exceptions regarding the reporting of overseas criminal conduct; see 2.4 and 2.5 of CCAB guidance.

9.1.3 A tax practitioner can and should apply the principles set out in his professional body's normal ethical guidance to persuade the client to act properly. A tax practitioner will need to consider carefully whether he can continue to act if the client refuses to make a full disclosure to HMRC.

9.2 Civil Investigation of Fraud (CIF) Procedures

9.2.1 In circumstances where a potential or current client asks a member to act in the making of a CIF disclosure to HMRC a suspicion of tax evasion will often, but not always, arise.

9.2.2 A tax practitioner should be aware that notification to HMRC is not a substitute for a report to SOCA. Where appropriate a report must also be made to SOCA as soon as the tax practitioner has knowledge or suspicion or reasonable grounds for knowledge or suspicion that tax has intentionally not been paid when due. The tax practitioner (or his firm's MLRO where he is not a sole practitioner) should consider carefully whether the privilege reportingexemption applies (see section 12 below and section 7 of the CCAB guidance) before submitting a SAR.

9.2.3   There may be occasions where the tax practitioner does not hold sufficient information to make a detailed disclosure of his client's tax evasion to HMRC at the same time as he (or his firm's MLRO where he is not a sole practitioner) submits a SAR to SOCA. However the tax practitioner will be keen to protect his client's position by notifying HMRC of the tax evasion before SOCA does so that the case may be regarded as a voluntary disclosure. The practicalities of this situation are covered in a Question and Answer note agreed with HMRC attached as Appendix 1.

10. FAILURE TO OBTAIN TREASURY CONSENT – S765 ICTA

10.1.1   This section is relevant to members who deal with transactions by companies with international aspects – those transactions that may require consent relate to the creation or issuing or transferring of shares or debentures.

10.1.2   Under s766 ICTA 1988 companies, their officers and advisers may be guilty of criminal offences if a transaction requiring special consent under s765(1) takes place without such consent. The person needs to know that the actions were unlawful under s765(1) in order to be guilty of a criminal offence (s766(1)). In practice this is of limited assistance in cases of innocent oversight because s766(2) puts the burden of proof as to the person's state of knowledge on to the individual in the case of directors.

10.1.3   The next question is whether there are proceeds. If a client has undertaken a tax planning transaction for which Treasury consent was needed and would have been unlikely to have been granted, the tax not paid as a result of the planning would constitute proceeds from the crime. In other circumstances there may be no proceeds, but this will need to be considered on the facts. Where there are proceeds, the tax practitioner should finally consider whether the alleged offender knew or suspected that the proceeds arose from criminal conduct. The tax practitioner would usually advise the client that a criminal offence may have occurred, so that the client would then have the requisite knowledge.

10.1.4   When a tax practitioner realises that there has or may have been a breach of s765 ICTA, he (or his firm's MLRO where he is not a sole practitioner) will need to consider making a SAR based on the factors discussed above. He should also bear in mind whether the privilege reporting exemption applies (see section 12 below and section 7 of the CCAB guidance). The tax practitioner should also consider what other action is appropriate, for example, advising the client to notify HMRC.

Appendix 1

11. INDIRECT TAX

11.1 Overview

11.1.1   Where indirect tax is concerned, innocent or negligent errors may be criminal offences as strict liability is imposed by such as167 (3) CEMA which provides:

> 'If any person –
>
> (a) makes or signs, or causes to be made or signed, or delivers or causes to be delivered to the Commissioners or any officer, any declaration, notice, certificate or other document whatsoever; or
> (b) makes any statement in answer to any question put to him by an officer which he is required by or under any enactment to answer,
>
> being a document or statement produced or made for any purpose of any assigned matter, which is untrue in any material particular, then, without prejudice to subsection (4) below, he shall be liable on summary conviction to a penalty of level 4 on the standard scale'.

'Assigned matter' is defined in section 1 of CEMA as meaning 'any matter in relation to which the Commissioners are for the time being required in pursuance of any enactment to perform any duties'.

11.1.2   This broadly makes most errors, however innocent, criminal offences in VAT and all other indirect taxes. The fact that VAT matters are in practice handled under the civil penalties regime in most circumstances is irrelevant (see section 6.3 above) to the fact that there is an offence under s167(3) CEMA. However an innocent or negligent error will not fall to be classed as money laundering where the person making the error was not aware/did not suspect that they had committed a criminal offence.

11.1.3   Property is only criminal property for the purposes of POCA if it not only constitutes or represents benefit from criminal conduct, but the 'alleged offender knows or suspects that it constitutes or represents such a benefit' (s340(3) POCA). A client who has knowledge of s167 CEMA will 'know or suspect' that they are in receipt of funds once they become aware of the error or mistake so the normal SAR regime applies. There is no presumption that the client is aware of the strict liability offence in s167(3) and a practitioner does not have to investigate the client's knowledge, but should make a judgement based on his knowledge of the client. If a practitioner believes a report is necessary but that the client made an error or innocent mistake they should consider making reference to this opinion in any SAR they make.

11.1.4   Where the practitioner suspects that the irregularity may have amounted to tax evasion or tax fraud, the need to make a SAR should be considered on the usual basis and in the same way as for direct tax. There are large numbers of specific criminal offences in the indirect taxes legislation and these are outlined in paragraphs 11.2 and 11.3 below. However in essence they all amount to variations on tax evasion and involve some intent to avoid paying the correct amount of tax.

Appendix 1

11.1.5   Unwillingness or refusal to correct indirect tax errors should be treated as set out in 7.3 above.

11.2 Other offences applicable across indirect tax

11.2.1   There is a range of crimes in the Customs and Excise legislation, covering such areas as:

- the bribing of a Commissioner, officer or appointed or authorised person;
- the obstructing of an officer performing any duty, or similar conduct;
- production, signing etc of untrue documents and statements;
- the counterfeiting or falsifying of documents;
- obstructing, or failing to assist in, the inspection of a computer;
- the breaching of conditions applied in respect of relief from VAT conferred on specified classes of persons, such as members of visiting forces; and
- the failure to furnish a supplementary declaration under the Intrastat procedure.

In addition there is the common law offence of Cheating the Public Revenue.

11.2.2   There are a number of other offences relating to particular indirect taxes and excise duties, such as stamp duty and stamp duty land tax, alcohol, tobacco products and mineral oil duties, betting and gaming duty, aggregates levy etc. The legislation in respect of these duties, taxes and levies provides the offences specific to them.

11.2.3   As VAT is the indirect tax most commonly advised upon by tax practitioners further details about specific offences applicable to VAT is given in 11.3 below.

11.3 Specific offences applicable in VAT

11.3.1   **Fraudulent evasion of VAT (s 72(1) VATA)** A person who is knowingly concerned in, or is taking steps with a view to, the fraudulent evasion of VAT by him or any other person is liable under this offence. A person's conduct may amount to fraudulent evasion under this provision if he understates payments due to the Commissioners for a prescribed accounting period. In certain circumstances the over claiming of VAT (eg a refund in respect of bad debts) may also result in fraudulent evasion. If proceeds arose from such conduct, this would also constitute money laundering.

11.3.2   **Production, furnishing or sending of false documents and statements (s72(3) VATA)** This involves the production, furnishing or sending of a false document with the intent to deceive. In addition, it includes knowingly or recklessly making a false statement. If proceeds arose from such conduct, this would also constitute money laundering.

11.3.3   **Conduct which must have involved an offence (s72(8) VATA)** Where a person's conduct during any specified period must have involved

Appendix 1

thecommission by him of one or more of the offences listed above, then, regardless of whether the specifics of the offence(s) are known, he is guilty of an offence. The purpose of this provision is to cover cases where it can be proved that an offence has been committed during a period spanning a number of prescribed accounting periods, but it is not clear to what extent it was committed in any particular prescribed accounting period within the total period concerned. It is only one offence, even if it covers more than one period. If proceeds arose from such conduct, this would also constitute money laundering.

11.3.4 **The possession and dealing in goods on which VAT has been evaded (s72(10) VATA)** A person commits an offence, and is liable to penalties, if, having reason to believe that tax has been or will be evaded on them, he either acquires possession of any goods; deals with any goods; or accepts the supply of any services. If proceeds arose from such conduct, this would also constitute money laundering.

11.3.5 **Supplying of goods or service without providing security (s72(11) VATA)** A person who is required, under VAT Act 1994 Schedule 11 para 4(2), to give security for the further payment of VAT as a prerequisite for making taxable supplies and who makes those supplies without the provision of security, has committed an offence. If proceeds arose from such conduct, this would also constitute money laundering.

12. THE PRIVILEGE REPORTING EXEMPTION

12.1.1 A tax practitioner should be aware that the privilege reporting exemption does not apply to 'information or other matter which is communicated or given with the intention of furthering a criminal purpose'.

12.1.2 A tax practitioner should read this section in conjunction with paragraphs 7.26–7.46 of the CCAB guidance which covers the privilege reporting exemption and the crime/fraud exception in detail.

12.1.3 In summary a tax practitioner who is a professional legal adviser or a 'relevant professional adviser' who suspects or has reasonable grounds for knowing or suspecting that another person is engaged in money laundering is prohibited from making a money laundering report where the knowledge or suspicion comes to him in 'privileged circumstances'.

12.1.4 Relevant professional adviser is defined in s330(14) POCA as follows:

'an accountant, auditor or tax adviser who is a member of a professional body which is established for accountants, auditors or tax advisers (as the case may be) and which makes provision for

(a) testing of competence of those seeking admission to membership of such a body as a condition for such admission; and
(b) imposing and maintaining professional and ethical standards for its members as well as imposing sanctions for non-compliance with those standards.'

12.1.5 The legislation does not list the professional bodies which meet the criteria but the CCAB bodies, the Chartered Institute of Taxation and theAssociation of Taxation Technicians meet the criteria and hence their members may be considered to be 'relevant professional advisers'

12.1.6 Privileged circumstances is defined at s330 (10) POCA as

'Information or other matter comes to a professional legal adviser or other relevant professional adviser in privileged circumstances if it is communicated or given to him:

(a) by (or by a representative of) a client of his in connection with the giving by the adviser of legal advice to the client;
(b) by (or by a representative of) a person seeking legal advice from the adviser; or
(c) by a person in connection with legal proceedings or contemplated legal proceedings.'

12.1.7 The CCAB gives guidance on when the privilege reporting exemption might apply. The CIOT and ATT took Counsel's opinion on the privilege reporting exemption and how it might affect their members. This advice included examples of when the privilege reporting exemption might apply and is unlikely to apply. Those examples together with the CCAB's are attached as Appendices 2 and 3.

13. CUSTOMER DUE DILIGENCE (CDD)

13.1.1 Customer due diligence and beneficial ownership is considered in detail in Section 5 of the CCAB guidance and a tax practitioner should refer to that guidance in the first instance. A tax practitioner should have regard to the financial restrictions list issued by the government and its advisory notices against countries with material deficiencies in their anti-money laundering and counter terrorist financing regimes. See paragraphs 5.32, 5.44 and Glossary Annex B of the CCAB guidance for further details and HM Treasury's website at www.hmtreasury.gov.uk/documents/financial_services/sanctions/fin_sanctions_index.cfr

13.1.2 A tax practitioner may be called upon to advise another professional firm. Unless there is a clear agreement between the firms that the advising firm is intended to form a client relationship with the other firm's client, or unless the advising firm comes into contact with and/or enters into a dialogue with the other firm's client, the other firm is the client of the advising firm and accordingly must be made subject to CDD.

13.1.3 In cases where the advising firm's involvement is also with the other firm's client, then the other firm's client must also be made subject to CDD. It may be possible for the advising firm to rely on the other firm's CDD of the client but there are strict criteria which must be met; see paragraphs 5.33 – 5.41 of the CCAB guidance.

Appendix 1

APPENDIX 1: MONEY LAUNDERING AND DISCLOSURES TO HMRC: A QUESTIONS AND ANSWERS GUIDANCE NOTE

This note is an updated version of a note originally agreed between HMRC, the Association of Taxation Technicians and the Chartered Institute of Taxation.

Object of note

To provide guidance about the practical effect of the money laundering legislation on disclosures of tax evasion by tax practitioners.

Questions and answers

1. Will the money laundering requirements make any difference to HMRC's willingness to use Code of Practice 9 or in local offices their willingness to come to a settlement without prosecution?

HMRC have confirmed that the money laundering requirements will not affect enquiries under Code of Practice 9 or local office procedures.

2. Which government departments should I as a tax practitioner inform when I am approached by an individual who tells me that he wants to make a full disclosure of undeclared taxable income and/or gains?

Traditionally, you as a tax practitioner, having taken instructions and collected all necessary information from your client, will have informed the relevant office within HMRC, depending on the circumstances.

But if you have reasonable grounds for knowing or suspecting that your client has intentionally evaded tax then the money laundering laws will also apply. You or your Money Laundering Reporting Officer (MLRO) if you have one, will be obliged also to make a report to SOCA in the specified form unless the privilege reporting exemption applies. Where you have a MLRO, you must notify him or her and they will in turn consider whether a report should be made to SOCA. See Section 7 of the CCAB anti money laundering guidance regarding the need to appoint a MLRO where you do not have one.

3. Should I make a report to SOCA when I receive a CoP 9 enquiry letter from HMRC?

It is your knowledge or suspicion that counts rather than HMRC's suspicion. You should make up your own mind whether such a letter gives you grounds for making a report applying the criteria in Section 330 POCA 2002, ie do you know or suspect, or have reasonable grounds for knowing or suspecting, that the client is engaged in money laundering as defined at Chapter 2 of the CCAB anti money laundering guidance.

4. When should I make a report to SOCA?

The money laundering legislation says that SOCA must be told 'as soon as is practicable after the information or other matter' that gave rise to the knowledge or suspicion was received.

Appendix 1

5. It is possible that the potential client may not instruct me at all. Will HMRC monitor me as the tax practitioner named in the SOCA report to see if a disclosure emerges, and if so for how long?

HMRC recognize that the potential client may go elsewhere (or nowhere) for advice. They have said they have no intention of monitoring reputable practitioners after SOCA reports have been submitted.

6. Once I have told SOCA, what happens next assuming no other agency is involved?

SOCA will pass reports to a special intelligence unit within HMRC in the first instance. The unit will consider whether it is suitable for investigation towards criminal prosecution. If it is not, the case will either be considered for enquiry under a Civil Code of Practice or be referred to HMRC's Centre for Research and Intelligence in Llanishen, Cardiff. Where it is considered appropriate to pass intelligence on to relevant staff in taxpayer-facing offices neither the fact that the intelligence has come from SOCA, nor the identity of the original source of the intelligence, is disclosed.

7. Does the need to report to SOCA before I am ready to tell HMRC affect the timing of my providing information to HMRC about my client's undeclared income and or gains? Although I have made a report to SOCA when approached by a potential client with a tax disclosure to make, I may not immediately be able to approach HMRC because I will have to be formally instructed and the approach to HMRC approved by the client. Collecting and collating the information will inevitably take time especially where several individuals or entities are involved. How long will HMRC regard as a reasonable period before the approach is made while leaving the option of using CoP 9 open?

HMRC have confirmed that a delay would not jeopardise the CoP 9 approach where it would otherwise be available provided that the taxpayer is taking active steps to regularise their affairs. Doing nothing involves the risk that a CoP 9 enquiry may not be available and that prosecution may follow; or at least that penalty abatements are at risk.

One option, having obtained the client's permission, is to put down a marker by writing to HMRC, saying you have been instructed by a named client to act for them in coming to a settlement about undeclared income or gains. You would also provide a date by which you expect to be able to let HMRC have these details.

8. To which HMRC office should I send the marker letter?

9. How long a time period for providing the information would HMRC consider reasonable in my 'marker' notification?

Under these circumstances all letters should be sent to the Centre for Research and Intelligence, Ty Glas Road, Llanishen, Cardiff, CF4 5YF.

It will depend on the circumstances of each case but HMRC have indicated that they will take a reasonable approach.

Appendix 1

Your estimated timetable will obviously depend on your assessment of the likely complexity of your client's affairs.

10. What happens if I miss my self-imposed deadline set out in my marker letter?

HMRC appreciate that the information may be difficult to obtain. You should obviously inform HMRC if you wish to extend your self-imposed deadline. You will need to update HMRC from time to time to reassure them that the client is taking active steps to help you move matters forward.

11. What is the position where HMRC already had concerns about a taxpayer and the money laundering notification is the trigger for the raid or the launch of an investigation? HMRC may not be prepared to wait, possibly due to concerns that documents might be destroyed. Would a CoP 9 enquiry still be a possibility for my client if the normal conditions are met (for example if the raid does not indicate that my client is unsuitable for a CoP 9 enquiry)?

HMRC have informed us that receipt of a report from SOCA or your 'marker' notification will not necessarily make them deviate from their proposed course of action. HMRC will look at the SOCA report in context of all other information available to them regarding a case when prioritizing the cases for investigation.

12. Will HMRC wait for a reasonable period of time before launching an enquiry on receipt of a report from SOCA?

In the majority of cases, given the time it would take for SOCA to pass information to HMRC and for HMRC to consider what action to take, the time lag between the report to SOCA and the making of a voluntary disclosure to HMRC may not be an issue in practice. You should monitor the receipt of acknowledgements to track progress. If you are concerned you could consider the use of a marker letter as discussed above.

APPENDIX 2: EXAMPLES OF WHEN THE PRIVILEGE REPORTING EXEMPTION MIGHT APPLY

For the privilege reporting exemption to apply the information must come to a legal professional adviser or a relevant professional adviser in privileged circumstances. Whether the privilege reporting exemption applies will depend on the specific facts of the case. These examples are intended as general guidance only and are not a substitute for seeking legal advice in cases of doubt.

Examples included in the CCAB guidance

- advice on taxation matters, where the tax adviser is giving advice on the interpretation or application of any element of tax law and in the process is assisting a client to understand his tax position;
- advice on the legal aspects of a take-over bid, for example on points under the Companies Act legislation;

- advice on duties of directors under the Companies Act;
- advice to directors on legal issues relating to the Insolvency Act 1986, eg, on the legal aspects of wrongful trading; and
- advice on employment law.

Further examples based on advice given to the CIOT and ATT

- advice on how to order or structure a client's tax affairs in a tax efficient manner;
- advice on disclosure obligations to the tax authorities, including advice given in the context of compliance work on reporting requirements and situations where previously there may have been failure to disclose.
- Suspicions derived from pre-existing documents may be covered by the reporting exemption where those documents come to the tax practitioner in privileged circumstances. For example, if a client asked for tax advice on settling past tax under declarations and provided copies of bank statements or invoices or past tax returns in order that the tax adviser could advise, that information could be regarded as having come to the adviser in privileged circumstances.

Examples where relevant professional advisers might fall within privileged circumstances as regards litigation privilege include:

- assisting a client by taking witness statements from him or from third parties in respect of litigation;
- representing a client, as permitted, at a tax tribunal; and
- when instructed as an expert witness by a solicitor on behalf of a client in respect of litigation.

APPENDIX 3: EXAMPLES OF WHEN THE PRIVILEGE REPORTING EXEMPTION IS UNLIKELY TO APPLY

Examples included in the CCAB guidance

It should be noted that conducting audit work does not of itself give rise to privileged circumstances for this purpose, as the relevant professional adviser is neither providing legal advice, nor is he instructed in respect of litigation. Nor do routine book-keeping, accounts preparation or tax compliance assignments, though privileged circumstances may arise if the client requests or the adviser gives legal advice on an informal basis during the course of such an assignment

Further examples based on advice given to the CIOT and ATT

- Information uncovered during tax compliance work, for example

Appendix 1

spotting that personal expenditure had been claimed as a business expense in a previous year.
- Information uncovered during a tax due diligence assignment or other agreed upon procedures exercise which is for the purposes of producing an evaluation report or an assurance based opinion (other than an audit) to the client or a third party.
- Information provided by or communications received direct from any third party particularly if no advice has been sought in respect of the underlying detailed content by the client. For example, receipt of information or communications when acting as the client's tax agent.
- Information received about the client's or a third party's affairs which is outside the scope of the tax services in respect of which the adviser has been engaged.

Appendix 2

An Anti-Money Laundering Strategy for the Inland Revenue

1. **Background**
    1.1 What is money laundering
    1.2 The Inland Revenue's role within the Government's Anti-Money Laundering Strategy
2. **Roles and Responsibilities within Government**
3. **The Inland Revenue's prosecution policy**
    3.1 The Revenue's role as a prosecutor
    3.2 Roles and responsibilities within the Inland Revenue
    3.3 Professional Advisers
    3.4 International dimension
4. **Strategic Themes**
    4.1 Identification and countering of risks
    4.2 Maximising effective use of information provided to the Inland Revenue
    4.3 Effective management of provision of information to other organisations tackling money laundering
    4.4 Use of expertise
    4.5 Working with the private sector – consultation with practitioners
    4.6 Ensuring that the Inland Revenue is not being used as a means to launder money

1. BACKGROUND

1.1 What is money laundering?

Traditionally, money laundering has been viewed as the 'processing' of all illegal or 'dirty' money derived from the proceeds of any illegal activity (eg the

Appendix 2

proceeds of drug-dealing, smuggling, fraud, theft, tax evasion or handling of stolen goods). This takes place through a succession of transfers and deals until the source of illegally acquired funds is obscured and the money takes on the appearance of legitimate or 'clean' funds or assets.

Money laundering can be used as a means to disguise the nature of profits generated from many types of criminality. This criminality can be tax evasion and thereby of direct interest to the Inland Revenue. Or it can be other serious forms of criminality, such as dealings in drugs, alcohol, tobacco or people trafficking. These crimes are of interest to others such as Customs and the police, and the Inland Revenue will work with these bodies to ensure that effective and co-ordinated action is taken against those engaged in such activities. In some cases money laundering is used to disguise both tax evasion and other criminality, in which case the Revenue will work with others to investigate and prosecute, sharing information as necessary.

However, the Proceeds of Crime Act 2002 updates, expands and unifies the money laundering offences. The predicate offences, which trigger other money laundering offences, include all criminal acts, irrespective of where in the world they occur.

It is also a money laundering offence to make arrangements to facilitate the use, acquisition or retention of criminal property on behalf of another person. And the definition is extended so that in certain circumstances no process is needed at all to trigger a money laundering offence. All that is needed is the acquisition, use or even possession of criminal property for money laundering offences to apply. So the mere possession of the proceeds of tax evasion in someone's wallet is sufficient for money laundering to have taken place. The definition has clearly been extended some way beyond traditional views of what money laundering is like.

A recent government estimate suggested that annually around £25 billion of criminal money might be available for money laundering in the UK.

1.2 The Inland Revenue's role within the Government's Anti-Money Laundering Strategy:

The Inland Revenue has agreed its core role within the Government's wider anti-money laundering strategy to be:

an investigatory and prosecuting body in the laundering of the proceeds of tax, national insurance contributions or tax credit fraud

further, we have agreed within the detail of that strategy that:

Inland Revenue has a role in the detection and investigation of money laundering. Investigation and prosecution by the Revenue is directed at combating the laundering of the proceeds of tax, national insurance contributions or tax credit fraud, with particular emphasis on professionals who facilitate tax evasion. Where money laundering offences relate to wider criminality beyond tax evasion, the Revenue discloses this information to the appropriate law enforcing authority.

Appendix 2

So our agreed role is partly one of investigation and prosecution and partly one of enabling others in law enforcement to achieve their objectives in countering money laundering. We will disclose information to them if it is legally possible to do so and we seek to find ways to disclose rather than reasons not to.

The legislative gateway to allow for this is in the Anti-Terrorism (Crime and Security) Act 2001, section 19. It is Revenue policy to make such disclosures. It will do so in accordance with the Memoranda of Understanding agreed with other law enforcing organisations and with its published Code of Practice governing such disclosures.

Further, we will take a positive approach to sharing our particular expertise in financial investigation, which is a valuable resource, potentially of significant use to others countering money laundering. As a part of this commitment to sharing our expertise, we will consider the scope for seconding our staff to other organisations.

2. ROLES AND RESPONSIBILITIES WITHIN GOVERNMENT

The lead organisations within Government and their core responsibilities are:

a) HM Treasury leads for the UK in international bodies (e.g. FATF), issues the Money Laundering Regulations, and is responsible under the Proceeds of Crime Act for approving guidance notes produced by industry.

b) Home Office is responsible for the UK primary legislation setting out the criminal law on money laundering and terrorist financing.

c) The Financial Services Authority devises and enforces the Rules. It also has powers to bring criminal prosecutions for breaches of the Money Laundering Regulations (but not the primary money laundering law).

d) The Financial Intelligence Division of the National Criminal Intelligence Services (NCIS) is the Financial Intelligence Unit (FIU) for the United Kingdom. It is the central, national unit responsible for receiving, analysing and disseminating Suspicious Activity Reports (SARs) in the UK.

e) Police forces are responsible for investigating money laundering and terrorist financing cases. HM Customs and Excise is both an investigatory and prosecuting body for money laundering, drug trafficking, indirect tax fraud and a number of other assigned matters. Customs operates the supervision of MSBs and will supervise dealers in high value goods under the Money Laundering Regulations 2003.

f) CPS, SFO and Customs are all prosecuting authorities. SFO prosecute money laundering cases where the underlying predicate offence involves serious or complex fraud. Customs have prosecution powers in relation to drug trafficking and indirect tax fraud with the CPS dealing with other cases (and fraud/drug cases investigated by the police).

g) The Foreign and Commonwealth Office is responsible for providing technical assistance to priority countries, and helping to implement

Appendix 2

      international anti-money laundering standards through FATF-style regional bodies.

h)   The Money Laundering Advisory Committee (MLAC) provides a forum for key stakeholders to co-ordinate the AML regime and review its efficiency and effectiveness. It examines industry produced guidance notes and makes recommendations prior to submission for government approval.

i)   Joint Money Laundering Steering Group (JMLSG) prepares, publishes and promotes industry guidance on the prevention of money laundering for the financial services industry. It provides a forum for the sharing of information and represents the financial services industry in discussion with government and regulatory bodies.

3. THE INLAND REVENUE'S PROSECUTION POLICY

As described above, the Inland Revenue's involvement in tackling money laundering is limited to those cases in which tax evasion is a feature. The Proceeds of Crime Act 2002 creates a new mirror offence of money laundering when someone commits tax evasion, even in the absence of any transfer of movement of these funds.

So the Inland Revenue is interested in money laundering because of the underlying tax evasion which may exist. There are also instances whereby funds are moved or transferred and complex financial structures are created. The intention may be to disguise the true nature and source of money, which is in reality the proceeds of tax evasion. The Revenue has an important role to play in detecting and investigating any such arrangements.

The new offences of money laundering create further options under which to charge a tax evader. The commonly used charges for tax evasion are False Accounting or the common law offence of cheat. A new offence of being knowingly concerned in the fraudulent evasion of income tax was created in the Finance Act 2000.

Where these cases fit the Board's prosecutions policy, a criminal investigation may be carried out by the Special Compliance Office (SCO). Prosecutions are carried out in serious cases across the range of offences and in all the areas of law for which the Board are responsible. The Board operate a policy of selective prosecution intended to bolster their overall enforcement strategy. The focus is on cases where prosecution will do most to promote compliance with the law by deterring tax, contribution and tax credit fraud. So criminal sanctions are used in those cases which counter identified risks to the compliance base. This is an important theme of the emerging departmental compliance strategy.

An exemplary approach is adopted, with publicity given to successful cases, providing a message that no tax evader should feel immune from criminal prosecution. The exception is only in those cases in which taxpayers come forward, voluntarily and unprompted, and make a full disclose of their evasion.

The Board's criminal prosecution policy for money laundering offences will follow these same principles.

3.1 The Revenue's role as a prosecutor

Where there are mixed cases of tax evasion and other money laundering offences, the Revenue will investigate the matter to the extent that there is tax evasion and it will disclose the other matters to other organisation to investigate further.

The Revenue will support other parts of UK Government in their efforts to tackle crime. The Revenue is a law enforcing organisation and a prosecuting body in its own right in England and Wales. It will investigate and prosecute in cases of money laundering which involve tax evasion and will offer co-operation and assistance to others investigating and prosecuting other money laundering offences where the law, its Memoranda of Understanding and Codes of Practice enable it to do so.

The Revenue is a signatory to the Convention between prosecuting authorities agreed on 11th February 1998 and published through a response by the Attorney General to a Parliamentary Question on 8th April 1998. Within this Convention are principles agreed between prosecuting authorities about co-ordination and co-operation in the circumstances of two or more prosecuting authorities considering action against the same individual for related offences.

The Attorney General confirmed in his response that proceedings brought by the Crown Prosecution Service will ordinarily encompass charges relating to tax evasion only in circumstances where that is incidental to allegations of non-fiscal criminal conduct.

We have agreed with other prosecuting bodies about how we will treat cases of serious tax evasion and associated money laundering. In particular, we have reached agreement, in principle, with the Crown Prosecution Service, the Serious Fraud Office and the Financial Services Authority that in cases in which the only predicate offence is tax evasion, then the Inland Revenue and its Special Compliance Office will be the investigating body. The Board of Inland Revenue will be the prosecuting body and its published prosecution policy will remain unaffected.

But for those cases in which there is both tax evasion and some other criminality, these other prosecuting authorities can give no undertaking that they will not prosecute for the money laundering offences, irrespective of the approach taken by the Inland Revenue to the predicate tax evasion offences.

3.2 Roles and responsibilities within the Inland Revenue

CCP will be responsible for overall co-ordination of the Revenue policy and strategy on countering money laundering. It will work with others on the departmental Working Group to monitor developments, the management of risks and progress made.

SCO is the only part of the Inland Revenue which conducts criminal investigations and its staff are trained in the conduct of such investigations accordingly. So criminal investigations into acts of money laundering which are predicated by tax evasion are to be carried out by SCO. SCO's Anti-Money

Appendix 2

Laundering Unit is the focal point for such investigations and the delivery of other aspects of the Inland Revenue's anti-money laundering strategy, including the sharing of information and expertise.

SCO will work with the Inland Revenue Solicitor's Office, who prosecute offenders on behalf of the Board of Inland Revenue, which is a prosecuting body in its own right in England and Wales. Cases in Scotland and Northern Ireland are prepared for criminal prosecution and referred to the Procurator Fiscal and the Director of Public Prosecutions respectively, so that these bodies may consider whether they wish to proceed with a criminal prosecution.

SCO and the Solicitor's Office will work with policy administrators in Cross-Cutting Policy (CCP), who own the prosecution policy and maintain it on a delegated basis, on behalf of the Board of Inland Revenue. CCP has the role of signing Board's Orders to proceed with a criminal prosecution, having regard to investigation reports from SCO and legal advice from the Solicitor's Office. CCP applies a public interest test, as set out in the Code for Crown Prosecutors. Once this test is satisfied, CCP will issue a Board's Order. So each case involves three parts of the Inland Revenue. This tri-partite working has a proven track record, in ensuring a high standard of cases being put before the criminal courts.

3.3 Professional Advisers

The Inland Revenue will seek to prosecute accountants, tax advisers and other professionals who assist their clients, or who act in their own capacity, to evade tax through means of money laundering activities. Professionals are an important stakeholder in the process of ensuring that taxpayers pay the right tax at the right time and the Inland Revenue places great reliance on the integrity of these professionals who act on behalf of their clients.

The Financial Action Task Force on Money Laundering noted in its 2000/01 report that 'Lawyers, notaries, accountants and other professionals offering financial advice have become the common elements to complex money laundering schemes. The trend is mentioned by almost all FATF members'. The report goes onto note that one consequence of the continuing efforts of governments to combat money laundering is an increasing complexity of schemes being operated, increasing the need for the involvement of a professional adviser.

So advisers who enable tax evasion offences are key to the success of these crimes. It is appropriate for the revenue authorities to target them as 'centres of infection'.

The Proceeds of Crime Act 2002 requires certain reports from those in the regulated sector, which will include accountants, tax advisers and other professionals from March 2004. These reports are of their suspicions or knowledge of money laundering of their clients, which may include tax evasion offences. Reports should be sent to the National Criminal Intelligence Service as soon as is practicable after the suspicion or knowledge arises. Making a report is a defence against certain money laundering offences outlined earlier.

Appendix 2

When these professionals fail to make a report they commit an offence and may be the subject of a criminal investigation and a subsequent criminal prosecution. The Inland Revenue will take the lead in the investigation and prosecution if the predicate offence of the client is tax evasion and the adviser has failed to report this.

A further offence provided for in the Proceeds of Crime Act 2002 is one of tipping off. A professional adviser is not only obliged to report his or her knowledge or suspicions, but they must not inform the subject of the report that they have done so. Any action which prejudices a related criminal investigation is an offence of tipping off under this part of the Act.

For each of the offences outlined in this part of the strategy and in earlier sections, where the predicate offence is tax evasion, the Inland Revenue will take the lead in countering such offences. It will have regard to this strategy document and to its published prosecution policy in deciding which cases to purse criminally. SCO's dedicated anti-money laundering unit will take the lead within the Inland Revenue in conducting a criminal investigation.

3.4 International dimension

The UK has taken a leading role in promoting the strengthening of links between tax and anti-money laundering authorities. In May 1998, following a UK initiative, G7 Finance Ministers urged OECD to give particular attention to improving the availability of information to tax authorities in order to curb international tax evasion and avoidance. OECD proposed a two prong initiative:

- first, to ensure that financial institutions report all suspicious transactions to the money laundering authorities, including transactions which are (or believed to be) related to tax crimes. Work on this proposal was pursued by the Financial Action Task Force
- second, to increase the flow of information from money laundering authorities to tax authorities, nationally and internationally, without undermining the effectiveness of anti-money laundering systems. Work on this continues to be pursued by OECD's Committee of Fiscal affairs.

The UK, including the Inland Revenue, has actively participated in initiatives to take these two themes forward and will continue to do so. The aims have included sharing experiences, to enable representatives to share information on some of the mechanisms used for both money laundering and tax evasion.

4. STRATEGIC THEMES

4.1 Identification and countering of risks

In line with its broader strategic approach to achieving compliance, the Inland Revenue will identify the risks posed through money laundering. It will identify ways to counter these and it will allocate resources accordingly.

Appendix 2

4.2 Maximising effective use of information provided to the Inland Revenue

The revised definition of money laundering to include all acts of tax evasion which generate a financial gain, means that all information gained by the Inland Revenue for the purposes of tackling tax evasion also has usefulness in tackling money laundering offences. So the strategic use of information to tackle tax evasion is effectively mirrored by its use for counter-money laundering purposes. All information powers which are used to tackle tax evasion are relevant here.

A considerable volume of information about tax evasion is expected to be provided by accountants, auditors and tax advisers. This information will be directly relevant to the Revenue in its efforts to tackle tax evasion as it will necessarily concern the professional's knowledge or suspicions or their clients tax evasion.

The offence has been provided for in order for Government bodies to counter money laundering. But the commonality of the money laundering and tax evasion offences means that the Revenue will be able to receive and make use of reports which are purely to do with tax evasion offences.

The reports will be submitted to the National Criminal Intelligence Service (NCIS) in the first instance. NCIS will carry out checks using their other information sources and analytical techniques to identify links to any other wider criminality. NCIS have advised that these reports will carry valuable information about what those suspected of serious crimes are doing with their finances.

If NCIS are satisfied that no wider criminality is evident and that the suspected offences are limited to tax evasion, they will pass the information onto the Inland Revenue and Customs and Excise as appropriate. The revenue departments will work together to share this information and add value to each other's information wherever possible.

Special Compliance Office Intelligence Group will be the receiving point within the Inland Revenue for all information provided by NCIS. SCO will analyse the information and route appropriate cases to other parts of SCO. They will also sanitise the information before passing it onto others, so as not to readily identify the source of the report to NCIS. Failure to do so may result in some awkward circumstances between the Revenue, the adviser and the client. In some cases it may even involve personal safety risks. Similarly, the Service Delivery Support Financial Investigation Unit will receive un-sanitised information form SCO, but will sanitise it before sending it onto staff in the Revenue network.

Only trained and qualified staff will handle this information.

Appendix 2

4.3 Effective management of provision of information to other organisations tackling money laundering

Disclosures about money laundering offences to other investigating organisations will be via the gateway in the Anti-Terrorism (Crime and Security) Act 2001. Such disclosures are subject to agreed Memoranda of Understanding with other organisations and the published Code of Practice about how we will manage and operate these. All disclosures will be routed via a single point of contact within SCO.

4.4 Use of expertise

The Revenue has considerable expertise in specialist financial investigations, including the countering of money laundering and tax evasion, especially where complex and contrived structures have been used, including cases involving trusts, often located offshore.

The Revenue has seconded staff to several other organisations involved in countering fraud, including money laundering. We have staff working on these types of duties at the Home Office, Customs and Excise, the National Crime Squad, the National Criminal Intelligence Service, the Assets Recovery Agency and the Serious Fraud Office. It is our policy to make use of secondments, interchange and loans to provide the expertise of our staff to others, to open up lines of communications inter-departmentally and to benefit from the knowledge our staff bring back to the Revenue when they return.

4.5 Working with the private sector – consultation with practitioners

We recognise the value of working with the private sector in tackling money laundering and the value of the contribution this sector can make. There is clear commonality of objectives with the private sector in seeking to eliminate money laundering offences.

We will also consult with the private sector about how we will counter money laundering and seek their views about the impact our actions will have on legitimate trade.

4.6 Ensuring that the Inland Revenue is not being used as a means to launder money

A further dimension to tackling money laundering is to have robust internal controls to ensure that the Inland Revenue itself is not being used a means to launder money. A cheque or bank transfer from the Inland Revenue provides the launderer with a very high level of legitimacy for the funds which generated these.

Some of those laundering criminal money may take the view that the payment of 40% tax is a reasonable price to pay for legitimacy of funds. Revenue staff

Appendix 2

will need to be aware of this when dealing with sham 'front' companies or when receiving cash or cheques in settlement of tax debts.

Staff awareness at all relevant levels will be vital in countering these types of activity. SCO's anti-money laundering unit will have a leading role to play in developing such awareness.

Appendix 3

Criminal Finances Strategic Framework

CONTENTS PAGE

HMRC's Objectives
Business Areas
Powers
Cash Seizures and Forfeiture
Restraint and Confiscation
Civil Recovery and taxation (ARA)
Money Laundering
Money Service Businesses and High Value Dealers
Taxing Crime and the Criminal Taxes Unit
Next Steps
Abbreviations

PURPOSE

1. This strategic framework seeks to reinforce the recovery of proceeds of crime as a central tenet of HMRC's enforcement work and, in accordance with the Government's drive to improve performance in the field of asset recovery, to make the recovery of criminal finances a priority for HMRC.

2. Tackling criminal finances is a top priority for the UK Government, reiterated regularly by the most senior politicians. Parliament has strengthened the powers available to enable law enforcement agencies to recover the proceeds of crime, most recently in the Proceeds of Crime Act 2002 (POCA) and the Serious Organised Crime and Police Act 2005 (SOCAP). Expectations are high, and individual departments will need to deliver against an ever-increasing Government demand for tangible results. HMRC will assist the wider government in achieving this objective, translating these principles into an agenda for HMRC and, in accordance with the importance the wider government attaches to proceeds of crime recovery, ensure that this work is recognised and treated as a top priority within this Department.

Appendix 3

3. Recovering the proceeds of crime allows law enforcement agencies both to reduce the incentive for future illicit activity and to dent the criminal's capacity to engage in such pursuits. The crimes investigated by and committed against HMRC are primarily motivated by the prospect of financial gain, so removing the profit is seen as an effective method of reducing crime. The proceeds of crime are often used to fund further criminal activity, so recovering this money (thus disrupting the criminal cycle) is central to the reduction of crime and, consequently, the damage it inflicts on society.

4. HMRC's criminal finance strategic framework will act as an effective lever to promote asset recovery within the Department's regime-specific strategies, giving greater prominence to the use of confiscation, cash seizure, referral of cases to the Assets Recovery Agency (ARA) and other responses available under POCA and other legislation. It will ensure that the investigation of a predicate offence includes a financial element. Where fraud is investigated it will be expected that enquiries into a suspect's financial affairs will run concurrently with a view to obtaining a confiscation order upon conviction. And if there is evidence of money laundering, charges should be considered in addition to or (where appropriate) instead of the predicate offence.

5. Eliminating the financial benefits of crime is key to de-incentivising and reducing criminal activity, and it is for business areas across HMRC to ensure that their activities are fundamentally geared towards achievement of this. Regime-specific strategy owners will be responsible for leading the development of operational plans which will enable the Department to deliver the requirements of this strategic framework, and for setting the targets and performance indicators in accordance with which success may be measured.

CROSS-GOVERNMENT WORKING

6. Tackling the proceeds of crime is seen as an increasingly important aspect of law enforcement and a field in which Ministers are keen for performance to improve. The Home Secretary has emphasised the need for law enforcement agencies to maximise use of the new powers contained in SOCAP and, amid perceptions that performance is low relative to the potential volume of recoverable assets, the Prime Minister's Delivery Unit has completed a priority review of cross-governmental asset recovery. This has led to the establishment of new governance and performance arrangements and increased impetus being given to the importance and effectiveness of asset recovery work. It has also resulted (see paragraph 9) in Ministers setting new and very demanding targets for the period to 2009/10 and beyond. More recently, the Prime Minister's Strategy Unit has conducted a further study into the recovery of criminal proceeds. This document will be updated when Ministers have taken decisions on the recommendations and implementation plans have been formulated.. HMRC's strategic framework will contribute to this agenda, seeking to ensure that maximum advantage is taken of the available powers to ensure that criminals are denied the financial gain they presume to make by engaging in illicit activity.

Appendix 3

7. The Government's overall objective of reducing crime is supported by a multi-agency approach to depriving criminals of their assets. This work is driven forward by the recently-established Asset Recovery Board (ARB), supported by the Asset Recovery Working Group (ARWG). The latter was previously known as the Concerted Inter-agency Criminal Finances Action Group (CICFA). Previously overseen by HMRC, chairmanship of this group passed to the nascent SOCA in autumn 2005. ARB and ARWG partner departments and agencies are committed to the enhancement of asset recovery by mainstreaming such activity within their organisations and through bi- and multi-lateral capacity building.

8. HMRC is committed to the development of partnership working with SOCA, ARA, others in the law enforcement field and their Scottish and Northern Ireland equivalents. Working in partnership is often the most effective way of tackling organised crime, transcending conventional departmental boundaries in reflection of the shape and threat of organised crime, and ensuring that nothing falls between departmental 'cracks'.

9. Though there are no specific HMRC criminal finance PSA targets, action against criminal finances contributes directly to the closure of the tax gap, the key objective of HMRC PSA 1. Additionally, law enforcement and criminal justice agencies were collectively tasked to recover at least £100 million of criminal assets in 2005/6. The outturn for 2005/6 was £97 million, of which HMRC cases accounted for some £39.3 million. For 2006–7, Ministers agreed that law enforcement and criminal justice agencies collectively would need to increase the value of assets recovered by 25% to £125 million. The year-end outturn is expected to come very close to the target amount, with HMRC cases again generating a substantial contribution. Furthermore – and in the wake of the PMDU report – the target requirement for 2009/10 has been set at £250 million with significant further increases expected thereafter.

10. Arrangements for 2006/7 and 2007/8 mean that asset recovery agencies receive a proportion of the amount they recover. Maximising the asset recovery side of HMRC's law enforcement work will allow criminal monies to fund projects to strengthen law enforcement efforts, thus creating a 'virtuous circle' in which criminals effectively subsidise action against their own activities. CICFA (now ARWG) agreed the arrangements for implementing the scheme, while HMRC has developed its own method of ensuring receipts from the Asset Recovery Incentivisation Scheme (ARIS) are utilised most effectively [see paragraph 24 for more detail.]

11. HMRC has worked with other Government departments in developing this document to ensure HMRC's aims and objectives complement the wider Government agenda. In particular, we have worked closely with the Home Office to ensure we support that department's drive to reduce crime and the harm it causes society. Mainstreaming efforts to recover the proceeds of crime is central to the Home Office agenda and key to the activity of the Serious Organised Crime Agency (SOCA), which has a specialist Proceeds of Crime Department. HMRC has worked with SOCA to develop our stance against criminal finances, ensuring that it complements SOCA's Proceeds of Crime Blueprint and that our themes are congruent. The Department will continue to

Appendix 3

work together with SOCA in contributing and responding to Government initiatives and are committed, as are SOCA and the wider criminal justice community, to reducing harm by taking the profit out of crime.

12. HMRC has also worked closely with HM Treasury, who drafted the revised UK anti-money laundering and terrorist finance strategy (issued on 28 February 2007) in developing these aspects of our strategic framework. The UK is seen as an international leader in effective money laundering controls – the principles of HMRC's anti-money laundering regime will serve to reinforce and strengthen this position.

13. The next section of this document sets out what HMRC seeks to achieve by publication of this framework, and the subsequent one the responsibilities of the HMRC business areas that will deliver its requirements. Thereafter, the document is broken down into sections by regime. Each sets out the principles in accordance with which work should be carried out in order to deliver the objectives of both HMRC and the wider law enforcement community.

HMRC'S OBJECTIVES

14. In line with other agencies and the wider Governmental agenda, recovering the proceeds of crime is a priority for HMRC's enforcement and compliance work areas.

15. The criminal finance strategic framework complements HMRC's overarching strategy, in accordance with which enforcement and compliance work streams will work with others (such as ARA, SOCA, Treasury and the core Home Office) to deliver wider government objectives. HMRC will work to understand the evolving behaviours of those who seek to undermine the functions of the department, and use this knowledge to inform and improve efforts against such groups. In particular, we will continue to work with the Home Office and others to achieve a better understanding of the size and nature of the criminal economy and the potential impact of the various asset recovery and associated options.

16. This document seeks not to prescribe how operational business areas should operate in order to increase performance in the asset recovery arena, but to provide a high-level framework within which operational colleagues can design plans and set targets in accordance with which the Department will deliver. It will be incumbent upon these areas to convert the principles set out in this document into tangible results. The strategic framework therefore necessitates a response from business areas to provide the detail of how the Department will deliver the high-level requirements. This response is focused on four key objectives.

17. **Maximising seizures of cash and other negotiable instruments which result in forfeiture**. This will be achieved by

- developing strategic and tactical assessments of cash movements, creating clear channels of communication and intelligence flows between all stakeholders and fully exploiting financial opportunities

Appendix 3

across commodity areas through the establishment of a National Financial Intelligence Branch;
- mainstreaming detection activity by raising awareness of how cash movements impact on other strategies;
- quality interceptions at the frontier (and inland) by a workforce equipped with the appropriate skills and equipment (including detector dogs);
- maximising retention of seized cash by ensuring appropriate professional standards of interception, questioning and subsequent investigation;
- debriefing and evaluating cases, especially where cash is not seized or is returned, in order to improve the quality of seizures and increase the proportion retained;
- focusing on innovation and sharing of best practice and management information to maximise opportunities for detection and seizure; and
- developing a performance framework which clearly articulates the effectiveness of our activity and the contribution to overall delivery of the individual work areas.

18. **Maximising the value of criminal proceeds recovered through confiscation**. This will be achieved by

- ensuring that financial investigation with a view to confiscation is a feature of all criminal investigations; and
- seeking restraint orders at the earliest appropriate stage during the investigation of any acquisitive crime to preserve assets for confiscation following conviction.

19. **Using every opportunity to use tax laws to tax criminal profits, and civil proceedings to recover criminal proceeds.** This will be achieved by

- the newly-established Criminal Taxes Unit working in partnership with other agencies to identify and pursue, or pass on for action, cases which offer tax intervention opportunities against suspects, their businesses and associates;
- referring cases for civil recovery where criminal action has failed or is not appropriate but there is evidence of unlawful activity and the existence of assets derived therefrom; and
- recycling funds from the Asset Recovery Incentivisation Scheme into new and innovative measures to enhance our attack on criminal activity and related profits.

20. **Identifying opportunities to further undermine criminal financial gains by pursuing money laundering offences in addition (or as an alternative) to other offences**. This will be achieved by

- maximising intelligence flows related to HMRC assigned matters through our financial intelligence officers embedded within SOCA;
- further and proactively developing close relationships with key players
- regulatory bodies, international partners, compliance colleagues – in order to drive investigation efforts against targeted money launderers,

Appendix 3

- sharing information to the fullest extent possible within available gateways; and
- considering the potential for taking money laundering criminal action, especially in cases of serious fraud and for those in positions of responsibility.

21. Tackling criminal finances will assist the Department in meeting its public service agreement targets, particularly PSA objectives 1 and 3. Respectively, these objectives require HMRC to improve the extent to which individuals and businesses pay the amount of tax due and receive the credits and payments to which they are entitled, and strengthen frontier protection against threats to the security, social and economic integrity and environment of the United Kingdom in a way that balances the need to maintain the UK as a competitive location in which to do business.

22. This strategic framework will facilitate the reduction of the tax gap under PSA objective 1 by mainstreaming and prioritising the recovery of the proceeds of crime. It will also contribute to PSA objective 3, both by restricting the extent to which criminal finance is able to enter the UK economy and – by restricting the amount of criminal money leaving the UK – reducing the volume of illicit goods entering the country.

23. HMRC is committed to utilising POCA powers on confiscation, money laundering, cash seizure and investigative techniques wherever appropriate, and to ensuring that the principle of financial investigation alongside the investigation of predicate offences applies across all regimes. HMRC will develop and deploy non-traditional and innovative methods to most effectively deprive crime of the finance by which it is fuelled. We will work closely with the Proceeds of Crime Department in SOCA to place HMRC at the forefront of this work and will establish our own Criminal Taxes Unit to ensure that income deriving from criminal activity is taxed. More detail of this new measure can be found in paragraph 88 et seq.

24. In addition to depriving criminal circles of the profit upon which they thrive, asset recovery can generate funds which can be used to increase work on recovering the proceeds of crime, further emphasising the need for the Department to prioritise efforts in this field so as to maximise the benefit offered by the Asset Recovery Incentivisation Scheme (ARIS). The amount of money available to HMRC will be determined by the total value of receipts received by the Home Office in the financial years 2006–07 and 2007–08. Allocations will be based upon each agency's contribution to the total value of remittances from cash forfeiture orders, confiscation orders (including part-paid orders and interest), civil recovery and certain taxation cases.

25. HMRC cash forfeitures will secure the Department 50% of the amount remitted to the Home Office. Money raised by confiscation order receipts will be split into three equal portions to reflect the stages of investigation, prosecution and enforcement, so HMRC, RCPO and HM Courts Service (HMCS) confiscation order activity will result in a 3-way equal split of the 50% share where all three agencies are involved[1]. In cases referred to ARA by

Appendix 3

HMRC, the two agencies will equally split the 50% allocation of receipts achieved via ARA's civil recovery and direct tax functions.

1 This could be a four-way split if the case is undertaken jointly with, for example, SOCA or a local constabulary.

26. HMRC expects the scheme will generate between £12 and £15 million for the Department in 2006–7, of which approximately £5 million is expected to be set aside to fund three key projects[2]. HMRC has developed a set of criteria against which other receipts from the scheme will be allocated internally. Activities/projects for which bids are made will have to meet all the primary criteria, which demand that the activity for which funding is intended fits with both HMRC's PSA objectives and broader Government asset recovery objectives, contributes to the incentivisation fund or has a similar negative effect on criminal finance, and will result in the recovery of further proceeds of crime. In addition, some of the secondary criteria must be met – the work will need to be innovative, encourage integration of former Customs and Revenue areas, be project-based rather than adding to baseline of existing activities and/or make an indirect contribution to asset recovery, eg publicity or research type projects.

2 These projects already have an expectation of receiving funding and have been established accordingly. They are the Cash Forfeiture Litigation Team (CFLT), Document Exploitation facility (DOCEX) and the Anti Money Laundering Unit which were created and funded by the Recovered Assets Incentivisation Fund (RAIF). This was a scheme for which the Home Office provided £45m over three years for projects agreed by CICFA.

27. These criteria are designed to ensure that funding is not restricted only to those areas whose activities raise money for the scheme. Areas of the Department undertaking civil investigations are also eligible so as to ensure that we continue to pursue the most appropriate means of stripping the profit from crime. In some cases, the civil route may be the most suitable course of action and, as it allows a substantial amount of profit to be stripped from crime at relatively low cost, can represent good value for money for HMRC.

28. Bids for funding from HMRC's ARIS receipts will need to be underwritten by the relevant Deputy Director and submitted for consideration to a panel chaired by Criminal and Enforcement Policy (CEP).

29. With the introduction of the asset recovery incentivisation scheme, HMRC will have greater capacity to direct funds towards a wider range of important work directly or indirectly supporting our criminal finances activity than would otherwise have been feasible within Departmental resource constraints.

30. In summary, HMRC is committed to supporting and furthering the wider Governmental agenda of stripping the financial incentive from crime so as to reduce the harm caused by such activity. The criminal finance strategic framework will drive other departmental strategies and provide a structure within which operational plans may be constructed in order to ensure delivery of HMRC's objectives.

Appendix 3

BUSINESS AREAS

31. A number of operational business areas within HMRC will deliver the Department's objectives.

32. **Criminal Investigation** identifies recoverable tainted assets during the normal course of investigation and, as a result of specific asset targeting, sources further cases (including those for referral to the Assets Recovery Agency), provides intelligence on money flows, modus operandi etc and, as a result of their range of investigatory work, sources convictions for money laundering and other offences. Financial investigation work can be broken down into five integral parts:

- Use of high quality intelligence to identify money flows and non-compliant businesses as possible precursor indicators to criminal activities.
- Money laundering investigations where we aim to tackle the most complex systems, organisations and professionals, requiring specialist knowledge and training.
- The identification of money laundering activities through investigations into predicate crime.
- Civil seizure and forfeiture of crime related cash detected at the frontier or inland.
- The identification, restraint and confiscation of assets.

33. **Intelligence** provides high quality operational and tactical intelligence for Investigation, Detection and MSB/HVD assurance activity. It produces strategic intelligence to inform wider Departmental and HMG priorities. It acts as a catalyst for the deployment of departmental resources and works closely with other organisations to exchange information and intelligence, such as suspicious activity reports (SARs) from SOCA. Intelligence also receives debriefing information from colleagues in other operational business areas, and manages human intelligence sources. The overseas Fiscal Liaison Officer (FLO) network will work more closely with their host counterparts in order to better facilitate international financial intelligence flows.

34. **Detection** identifies and seizes cash (and other commodities) primarily at the frontier, and sources cases for other business areas to take forward. They also provide further intelligence (stimulated by the interception and its circumstances) that can build the case against suspicious travellers for the police or for Criminal Investigation, which will be undertaken in conjunction with Intelligence.

35. **Criminal Finance Litigation Team** works with case officers to ensure that all cases referred to it are processed through the courts as swiftly as possible. It also inputs such cases onto the Joint Asset Recovery Database (JARD), liaises with investigation and finance officers regarding remittances of forfeited cash and provides statistics on amounts forfeited and remitted.

36. **Assurance Activity** is mostly concerned with the regulation of Money Service Businesses (MSBs) and High Value Dealers (HVDs). Since 1 June 2002 all MSBs have been required to register with Customs/HMRC (unless

Appendix 3

they are already part of a firm regulated by the Financial Services Authority). The Money Laundering Regulations 2003 extended this requirement to high value dealers in cash. (In December 2007, HMRC's regulatory functions will be extended to include Accountancy Service Providers and Trust and Company Service Providers.) Assurance activity affords HMRC the opportunity to educate regulated bodies of their obligations under the regulations and to ensure their compliance, providing an additional means of preventing the use of these businesses for money laundering purposes. The process of assurance also generates intelligence.

37. The contribution made by all these areas needs measuring in order for the department to assess the progress of its efforts against criminal finances. A number of measures will facilitate this, and these are outlined in the 'activity' chapters below.

POWERS

38. Part 8 of the Proceeds of Crime Act contains the investigatory powers for use in criminal confiscation, money laundering and civil recovery. These provisions consolidate and extend the powers for which earlier legislation provided.

39. Four powers are available to HMRC for the purposes of investigating whether a person has benefited from criminal conduct and the extent or whereabouts of that benefit, and/or whether a person has committed a money laundering offence. All require the approval of a circuit judge or equivalent. These are:

- **Production Orders**, which permit officers to take away or be given access to material;
- **Search and seizure warrants**, which authorise entry to and search of the premises specified, and the seizure and retention of material that is likely to be of value to the investigation;
- **Account monitoring orders**, which require financial institutions to provide information relating to a specified account for a specified period; and
- **Customer information orders**, which require financial institutions to provide any information they hold that relates to the person specified in the order. They should supply enough information to allow the HMRC officer to obtain a Production Order.

40. Part 7 of POCA also requires banks and other businesses in the regulated sector to make a disclosure to SOCA where they have knowledge, suspicion or reasonable grounds to know or suspect that another person is engaged in money laundering. The requirement to report suspected money laundering applies to all crimes which give rise to criminal property, including tax evasion.

41. HMRC's recovery of the proceeds of crime is also assisted by the Money Laundering Regulations 2003, which completed the implementation of the Second EC Money Laundering Directive. Previously, the regulated sector included banks and other financial services but the Regulations extended the

Appendix 3

scope of anti-money laundering controls to a much wider range of firms and professions including accountants, auditors, tax advisors, lawyers, estate agents, casinos, and High Value Dealers (these are businesses that deal in goods and accept, or are prepared to accept, the equivalent of €15,000 or more in cash in a single transaction).

42. The Serious Organised Crime and Police Act 2005 gives law enforcement agencies a number of new powers with which to combat serious crime. Sections 76–81 provide for the making of Financial Reporting Orders (FROs). FROs are a new weapon in the armoury of law enforcement. Where the courts are satisfied that there would be a high risk of re-offending, they may impose these orders where certain 'trigger' offences have been committed. This enables the financial affairs of serious acquisitive criminals to be monitored from the point of sentence for up to 15 years (up to 20 years where an individual is imprisoned for life). The order will require offenders convicted of specified offences to make such reports of their income and assets as are set out by the Courts in the order. The 'trigger' offences originally included specified deception offences in the Theft Acts 1968 and 1978 and criminal lifestyle offences as specified in Schedule 2 of POCA 2002 but have recently been extended to further serious offences including tax and duty evasion and cheating the public revenue.

43. FROs can be an important tool in ensuring the future compliance of a convicted tax evader provided that one of the 'trigger' offences is engaged. If there is a risk of the offender committing tax evasion offences in the future, either during imprisonment or upon release, then the opportunity to secure an FRO should not be overlooked. In particular, this may point to the laying of charges under the Theft Act and/or for money laundering offences.

44. SOCAP also provides for the making of Disclosure Orders under s 62–66. These powers are exercisable by the Director of RCPO and any Revenue and Customs prosecutor delegated by him. The Director RCPO has decided that these powers should be used in appropriate serious cases of fraud. An offence should be considered as serious fraud if its commission has led either to actual or potential substantial financial loss or gain. A stand-alone offence which would not be considered serious fraud may be treated as such if it forms part of any conduct which could lead to actual or potential substantial financial loss.

45. This new power allows for an appropriate person (ie an officer of HMRC as delegated by the Director RCPO) to issue a Disclosure Order, where:

- there are reasonable grounds to suspect that an offence under s61 SOCAP has been committed;
- it appears that any person has information (whether or not this information is in a documentary form) that is relevant to the investigation of that offence and;
- there are grounds for believing that the information so provided by compliance with the Order is likely to be of substantial value (whether or not by itself) to the investigation.

46. Failure to comply with such an order is an offence punishable by imprisonment or a fine. Access to this power provides prosecutors and law

Appendix 3

enforcement agencies with another powerful tool in tackling fraudulent behavior and wider criminality.

CASH SEIZURES AND FORFEITURE

47. POCA Part 5 provides for the seizure and forfeiture of crime-related cash. HMRC and police officers may seize cash in amounts of £1000 or more if there are reasonable grounds to suspect that it is either the proceeds of, or is intended for use in, unlawful conduct. Upon application by HMRC/Police, a magistrates' court may authorise seized cash to be detained whilst its origin and intended use are investigated, and may order it to be forfeited permanently if satisfied to the civil standard of proof that the money is in fact associated with criminal activity.

48. It is a priority for HMRC to increase the amount of illicit cash seized and forfeited. As well as disincentivising further crime by reducing its profitability, this activity will allow HMRC to better contribute towards the wider Government's asset recovery targets (see paragraph 9). It is of primary importance to HMRC, therefore, to increase the amount of illicit cash seized and forfeited and – by improving detection and intelligence work on cash – reduce the amount of seized cash returned to travellers. HMRC needs to ensure that innocent travellers carrying legitimate cash are not inconvenienced by having their cash seized in error and returned, whilst at the same time more accurately targeting and appropriating criminal cash.

49. HMRC is committed to increasing the value of criminal money detected and seized both at the frontier and, where appropriate, inland. The Department will continue to deploy cash-dedicated teams at key high-risk locations, and flexibly direct cash resources towards identified high-risk areas. New methods of working amongst cash detection staff will be explored in order to maximise the detection and seizure of criminal cash, and an understanding of the importance of cash work will be engendered amongst non-cash Detection staff.

50. Intelligence will be better developed to identify high-level intervention opportunities and cash consolidation points both in the UK and overseas. Investigation will look to Intelligence to allow them to maximise the impact of inland detection powers, allowing seizures to be made both at the frontier and inland. Better use of analytical tools will be sought in order to tackle issues such as high returns of seized cash. This will generate a better understanding of why officers return a significant amount of the cash they seize and do not seize a sizeable portion of cash detected, and inform efforts to improve performance in this area.

51. Intelligence will identify and profile cash courier targets so as to improve cash seizure 'success rates', as cash will more often be seized from those who are already identified as a risk and are, as such, more likely to yield potentially forfeitable cash. Strategic and tactical assessments relating to the movement of illicit cash, including methods and routings (for import and export) and sources, will be improved to facilitate effective detection and seizure.

52. Better interaction between Detection and Investigation Teams and local offices when cash is seized can facilitate HMRC's recovery of the proceeds of

Appendix 3

crime. Explanations offered by individuals from whom cash has been seized at the frontier may be efficiently verified by checking with local compliance staff. Such information may assist officers in seeking to maintain a cash seizure or otherwise returning the funds. In all instances, the facts surrounding the cash detection may assist compliance staff when dealing with taxpayers' affairs. Where relevant gateways allow, HMRC will share this information with other organisations such as ARA or Police forces when appropriate to do so in order to disrupt criminal financial activity.

53. This practice will facilitate the identification of individuals who represent a potential threat to HMRC's regimes, better equipping HMRC to take appropriate action against suspicious or illicit activity. The information will need to be properly targeted, and careful management will be required to ensure it can be used effectively.

54. Although POCA does not stipulate that either forfeiture or confiscation should take precedence where cash is seized in the course of a criminal investigation, it is HMRC's policy to seek forfeiture rather than await confiscation, especially where forfeiture is uncontested. Forfeiture is HMRC's preferred course of action unless it has the potential to prejudice the criminal proceedings, in which circumstances the prosecutor and cash forfeiture lawyer will take a view as to the best way forward. In all cases, best practice is for the prosecutor and cash forfeiture lawyer to liaise at an early opportunity, and review the case as matters progress.

55. Progress made on the seizure and forfeiture of cash may be gauged by the number and value of cash seizures, and the amount forfeited.

RESTRAINT AND CONFISCATION

56. Confiscation represents a valuable tool in the fight against criminal money flows. Rather than simply relieving a convicted defendant of cash or assets obtained directly from the criminal conduct specified in the indictment, confiscation can in many circumstances strip out assets up to the level of the entire benefit assumed to have been generated by crime within the six years prior to the court order.

57. Under the procedures the court must first decide whether the convicted defendant has a criminal lifestyle (eg has committed one of the offences listed in POCA Schedule 2). If it decides that this is the case, the court will assume that all assets which have passed through the defendant's hands in the previous 6 years are derived from crime (and must therefore form part of the benefit calculation) unless the contrary can be demonstrated or there would be a serious risk of injustice. It will then order the defendant to pay a sum of money equal to the value of his or her benefit, or a smaller sum where less than the determined benefit is available for payment. Where a defendant can not be categorised as having a criminal lifestyle, a more limited form of confiscation applies and the benefit figure is calculated by reference to the particular offence(s) of which the person has been convicted.

Appendix 3

58. POCA Part 2 makes provision for confiscation and restraint in England and Wales. A confiscation order can be issued to a convicted defendant by the Crown Court. Application for a confiscation order may be made by the prosecutor, and the subsequent proceedings are conducted according to the civil standard of proof. Restraint orders are issued by the Crown Court to ensure that the assets of a convicted defendant are not dissipated before a confiscation order can be made or enforced. The prosecutor may apply for a restraint order where a criminal investigation has been started or where proceedings for an offence have commenced but have not been concluded.

59. Confiscation has a number of clear advantages for the law enforcement community. The benefit recovery aspect of confiscation orders could potentially (and frequently does) enable the recovery of significantly more than the value of the tax evaded/assets originally obtained by deception, increasing the department's contribution to the government's asset recovery targets while severely denting the criminal's capacity to continue with such conduct in the future and, in consequence, reducing the harm caused by crime. The potential scope of confiscation orders and the default sentence for non-payment also represent powerful deterrents against the commission of acquisitive crime.

60. Rigorous financial investigation with a view to confiscation should be a feature of all criminal investigations where initial enquiries indicate that recovery of assets is in prospect. Restraint should be sought (and at the earliest appropriate time) whenever significant assets are identified during a criminal investigation of any acquisitive crime in order to maximize the potential for asset recovery.

61. HMRC will make use of all appropriate powers to increase the measure of benefit for confiscation purposes where fresh evidence comes to light suggesting that the original measure was inadequate. The recoverable amount may also be increased or decreased following a change in the defendant's circumstances or the uncovering of assets that were not disclosed at the time the order was originally made. The financial investigation may be refreshed at any time for revisiting the available amount and within 6 years for revisiting the determined benefit.

62. The Proceeds of Crime Act facilitates the acquisition of a restraint order. Restraint orders can now be issued by any Crown Court and may be granted at the start of the investigation rather than at the point of charge or when charging is imminent, though there are some circumstances in which it will not be appropriate to seek a restraint order lest an individual becomes aware that he or she is being investigated.

63. HMRC will be able to measure productivity in this field by gauging the number of restraint orders, the value of assets restrained, the number of confiscation orders made, the value of those orders and the amount of money realised as a result of the enforcement of these orders.

Appendix 3

CIVIL RECOVERY AND TAXATION (ARA)

64. Part 5 of POCA enables ARA to recover (in civil proceedings in the High Court) assets which are or represent those obtained through unlawful conduct. ARA's cases are referred by law enforcement agencies or prosecution authorities and this represents another method by which HMRC (and the wider law enforcement community) may strip the profit from crime. Where criminal prosecution has either failed or been judged impossible, HMRC will maximise the opportunities offered by ARA and its powers by referring appropriate cases. To meet ARA's case referral criteria, recoverable property must have been identified and have an estimated valued of at least £10,000 and must include property other than cash or negotiable instruments. There must also be evidence of criminal conduct that is supported to the civil 'balance of probabilities' standard of proof.

65. Part 6 of POCA provides that ARA may use revenue functions to tax the proceeds of crime in cases which pass a 'suspicion of wider criminality' test, meaning that ARA cannot take on cases in which the only suspected irregularity is in the tax affairs of an individual or business. Such cases are proper to HMRC. HMRC does not refer direct tax cases directly, but the Director of ARA may choose to use these functions once a case has been referred.

66. Cases should only be referred to ARA when all HMRC's options have been considered and exhausted. There is a single point of contact for all referrals to ARA, who have been advised to accept only those cases which have been referred through this route. All requests by ARA for information or intelligence will be handled by the single point of contact in the Centre for the Exchange of Intelligence.

67. HMRC will be able to gauge the benefit of the civil recovery/taxation option by measuring the number and value of cases referred to ARA for civil recovery and gauging those in respect of which ARA make use of the available civil recovery and taxation functions.

MONEY LAUNDERING

68. The UK is seen as an international leader in effective money laundering controls, and HMRC seeks to ensure that its efforts in this sphere serve to further bolster that reputation.

69. Previous legislation (eg the Criminal Justice Act 1988 and the Drug Trafficking Act 1994) drew a distinction between the laundering of proceeds derived from drug trafficking and non-drugs related offences. POCA updated, expanded and unified the money laundering offences, making it easier for money launderers to be investigated and prosecuted by removing the requirement to identify the specific offences which generated the money or property.

70. The existing UK anti-money laundering regime consists of measures ranging from criminal provisions to punish money launderers and deprive them of the proceeds of this activity to reporting obligations upon the financial

Appendix 3

services industry and other areas of business. International standards are set by the Financial Action Task Force (FATF) and the EU makes directives, while POCA sets out reporting requirements and primary money laundering offences. HMRC's anti-money laundering efforts, which are supported also by the money laundering regulations (see paragraph 80 for more information), will support the Government's overarching strategy and give further credence to the UK's international standing in the effective control of money laundering.

71. HMRC operates a discerning approach to prosecution in respect of all offences within its remit. Where evidence of money laundering is uncovered during the course of the criminal investigation of a predicate offence, HMRC will ask the prosecutor to consider the addition of money laundering charges to the indictment in order to further dent an individual or gang's capacity to fund or commit future illegitimate activity. Equally, stand-alone money laundering prosecutions are valid where there is sufficient evidence to support charges under the Proceeds of Crime Act. There is no monetary threshold for prosecution.

72. Where the suspicion of money laundering mounts during a civil investigation, and there is evidence of other serious illegal activities which are not assigned matters, HMRC will consider disclosing this information to other agencies under statutory gateway provisions, either in the CRC Act or other legislation[3].

3 For example, the Serious Organised Crime and Police Act 2005.

73. HMRC will normally investigate money laundering cases criminally where the money flows (benefit) are derived from fraud against HMRC regimes. HMRC will also investigate cases that will identify and investigate those persons benefiting from fraud by providing the means to launder the proceeds of crime, with particular focus on advisers, accountants, solicitors and others acting in a 'professional' capacity who provide the means to put tainted money out of reach of law enforcement. The focus will be on cases where investigation and referral to RCPO will do most to promote compliance with the law and where HMRC can make a contribution to the over-arching HMG anti- money laundering strategy. HMRC will utilise all of the investigative powers in the Proceeds of Crime Act 2002 in the course of investigating money laundering. It will devote effort to counter the use of trusts, offshore mechanisms, internet banking and other devices in the cleansing of criminal monies and will refer appropriate cases to RCPO who will consider prosecution.

74. Intelligence, particularly financial intelligence, is key to the fight against money laundering. HMRC's Financial National Intelligence Branch has been reinforced and reorganised into one national branch under a single command, which will allow the department to more effectively exploit financial intelligence and opportunities across all areas by establishing specialist Financial Intelligence cells within commodity commands. This will further entrench the financial element within the different strategy areas and ensure that other strategies, such as alcohol or tobacco, are developed and implemented with clearer emphasis upon the recovery of the proceeds of crime.

Appendix 3

75. This unit will work closely with the SARs exploitation team at SOCA, which will have a single point of contact with HMRC, to ensure the rapid sharing of intelligence. Representation within SOCA will be enhanced through an embedded financial intelligence team to better exploit SARs-derived intelligence and manage the relationship with the Proceeds of Crime Directorate there.

76. With the creation of SOCA, HMRC will focus more on criminal money flows as they relate to HMRC responsibilities, and will work with SOCA to ensure financial intelligence relating to areas in which SOCA lead can be utilised to strip the profit out of these crimes. For example, although HMRC will no longer investigate drug trafficking proactively, it will have an interest in the taxable profits generated by this sort of activity, to which end financial intelligence arising from drug trafficking will be of use.

77. As HMG's strategy outlines, money laundering is an international phenomenon. All intelligence branches will include trained financial officers, and HMRC will ensure that overseas opportunities are better exploited by utilising the Fiscal Liaison Officer (FLO) network. Supported by HMRC's Financial National Intelligence Branch, they will pro-actively engage overseas host agencies in order to better facilitate the timely exchange of relevant information.

78. Financial Intelligence will seek to develop closer relationships with the FSA, other regulatory bodies and private companies to improve intelligence flow and sources. The existing MSB/HVD financial intelligence unit, a dedicated team, will be expanded to allow HMRC to maximise investigation opportunities and to support compliance with the regulations. It will identify and develop specific intelligence regarding non-compliant MSBs and HVDs and those engaged in money laundering in order to drive targeted investigation efforts.

79. Measuring the number of successful money laundering prosecutions and the value of consequent confiscation orders will enable HMRC to gauge its success in this area.

MONEY SERVICE BUSINESSES AND HIGH VALUE DEALERS

80. Supervision of money service businesses (MSBs) and high value dealers (HVDs) and, from December 2007, Accountancy Service Providers and Trust and Company Service Providers will assist in identifying and deterring money laundering activity across these sectors. Since 1 June 2002 all MSBs have been required to register with Customs/HMRC unless they are already part of a firm regulated by the Financial Services Authority, in which case they have to notify the FSA of their money service activities. The Money Laundering Regulations, which came into force in 2004, extended this requirement to HVDs in cash. These are businesses that deal in goods and accept, or are prepared to accept, the equivalent of €15,000 or more in cash in a single transaction. We welcome the extension of the regulated sector and the intelligence benefits that this will provide.

Appendix 3

81. All MSB and HVD businesses must register with HMRC. They must also pay an annual fee based on the number of premises through which they operate. The register comprises some 4,600 businesses operating through about 34,500 premises. Though the total number of businesses remains similar, there is a high turnover of registered businesses.

82. Under the Money Laundering Regulations 2003, businesses are required to have systems and controls in place to prevent money laundering and to enable them to identify and report suspicious activity to SOCA. Businesses must be controlled in such a way as to facilitate the identification of suspicious activity, the identities of customers must be confirmed and records must be held for five years. The regulations also provide that businesses must ensure staff are fully trained and appoint a nominated officer to report suspicious activity.

83. The regime will support the compliant but come down heavily upon businesses that shirk their responsibilities. HMRC will seek to inform the sectors of their responsibilities through quality guidance, and encourage co-operative working and improve best practice by holding regular trade forums and seminars. Non-compliance will be tackled with prompt and effective sanctions.

84. HMRC will work in partnership with the sectors to achieve strong anti-money laundering systems across the industry, maintain the integrity of the MSB sector via effective operation of a 'fit and proper' test (as required by the 3rd Money Laundering Directive) and assure compliance with the regulations through a risk-based visiting programme guided by a specialist intelligence unit.

85. Partnership working is key to the success of the regime. HMRC will consult with industry on any changes to our guidance, encourage industry to participate in this work and assist them to develop their own guidance. We will seek industry views on any forthcoming legal changes, advising Treasury and Home Office of their opinions, and encourage the growth of trade bodies so that representations may be made direct to policymakers. HMRC will maintain frequent and regular dialogue with trade associations and individual businesses to improve anti-money laundering activity across the sector. Quarterly MSB Forums will allow the sector to discuss issues and facilitate best practice, and annual regional seminars will keep small businesses appraised of forthcoming developments and allow them to discuss their concerns.

86. HMRC's activity will maintain the integrity of the MSB sector. We will develop an effective anti-money laundering 'fit and proper' test that enhances the reputation of the MSB sector's active compliance with the regulations. We will make the process as transparent as possible and allow for independent appeals. Intelligence resources, including the development of advanced data-matching techniques in conjunction with the UK Financial Intelligence Unit at SOCA, will be utilised to 'police the perimeter' and ensure that unregistered businesses do not pose unfair competition to the legitimate MSB sector. They will also be used to drive forward an awareness programme among other parts of HMRC and with agencies such as Police and Trading Standards to encourage the flow of information to enhance our risk profiles. We will continue to have early contact with each new registered business to confirm their understanding

Appendix 3

of the regulations and their responsibilities, thereafter visiting businesses according to perceived risk.

87.   HMRC will regularly review the assurance and penalties policy to ensure that criminal activity and non-compliance with the regulations is promptly identified and remedied. Robust sanctions (including civil penalties) will be imposed to tackle non-compliance and, where noncompliance is serious and repeated, it may attract criminal sanctions. Where criminal offences are identified, HMRC will take the appropriate action under POCA in conjunction with RCPO.

TAXING CRIME AND THE CRIMINAL TAXES UNIT

88.   The Criminal Taxes Unit (CTU) will focus both on closure of the tax gap under PSA1 and on minimising the harm caused by crime in accordance with the wider governmental harm reduction agenda.

89.   HMRC has been working with the Home Office and others in law enforcement to consider how direct taxation may be used as a means of taking some of the profit out of crime. It is intrinsic in the nature of their activity that many suspected criminals evade tax on the income, profits and gains derived from their activities, contributing to the tax gap. HMRC will use its tax powers to recover any unpaid taxes and bring these individuals and their businesses into the tax system, with the aim of increasing tax yields, disrupting criminal finances and reducing both the profitability of crime and the harm it causes.

90.   Central to the taxing crime agenda is the creation of a Criminal Taxes Unit. This is a multi-disciplinary team, comprising civil and criminal investigators with direct and indirect tax experience, receivables staff to handle and advise on collection and enforcement, specialist intelligence and potentially secondees from the Police.

91.   The team will develop HMRC's taxing crime capabilities and build our partnership with other agencies, for and with whom it will act as a central point of contact. The team will adopt a proactive approach to ensure that taxation is fully utilised as a weapon against crime. It will establish good working relationships with local forces and specialist units such as Financial Investigation Units, Regional Asset Recovery Teams and Fraud Units. Centrally, the team will develop the department's relationship with SOCA and will act as the liaison point for the use of direct tax for tackling crime with RCPO, SOCA, ARA, ACPO and other government department partners.

92.   Our broad approach will be to ensure that, in any given case, we identify tax intervention opportunities, both civil and criminal, that may be used against identified suspects, their businesses and associates. Working in partnership with wider law enforcement, we will seek to use taxation to disrupt criminal finances. In appropriate cases the CTU will instigate and advise upon criminal investigation opportunities for tax evasion with a view to referral to RCPO for consideration of prosecution and subsequent confiscation of assets.

93.   The Unit will manage information flows and select suitable cases for tax interventions. HMRC wishes to tap into the information that law enforcement

Appendix 3

financial investigators uncover about the financial activities of suspects, and ensure that this information is acted upon within the Unit or is brought to the attention of the tax inspector dealing with the suspect's tax affairs. The team will focus on all levels of criminality. It will liaise with the police to identify level 1 and 2 criminals who are not fulfilling their tax obligations, and robustly pursue unpaid tax, late payment and filing, interest, fines and tax penalties. The team will also tackle the taxation of level 3 criminality in liaison with SOCA and other law enforcers, and will help develop HMRC's interface with SOCA.

94. HMRC is already working successfully with the police on a number of investigations, has identified several instances where tax interventions have been effective, and delivered criminal charges for tax evasion in some cases. HMRC is committed to maximising the use of direct taxation to raise the stakes for criminals and those who benefit from their activities, including their families and professional advisers.

NEXT STEPS

95. This strategic framework document will act as an effective lever to promote the importance of asset recovery within other departmental strategies and provide a framework within which operational plans may be constructed in order to ensure delivery of HMRC's objectives. It is not the intention of this document to set out the ways in which operational business areas must operate in order to increase performance in the asset recovery arena. Rather, it provides a high-level framework within which operational colleagues will design plans and set targets in accordance with which the Department will deliver. These business areas will be responsible for converting the principles set out in this document into tangible results.

96. The Head of Criminal and Enforcement Policy within HMRC will chair an implementation steering committee which will oversee progress in delivery of the Criminal Finance Strategic Framework. All key HMRC stakeholders, such as Detection, Investigation, Intelligence, Central Compliance and ECOps will be represented on this group, which will ensure the desired impact upon other Departmental strategies and frameworks is being achieved. The group will report regularly to the Enforcement and Compliance Management Forum.

97. In the interests of sustained and relevant activity against criminal finances, it will be necessary to update this framework document from time to time. The frequency with which this is done will depend on wider developments (eg those arising from the report of the Prime Minister's Strategy Unit on asset recovery and the progress of the Serious Crime Bill, currently before Parliament) and agreed by the implementation steering committee.

Appendix 3

ABBREVIATIONS

ACPO:	Association of Chief Police Officers
AMLU:	Anti Money Laundering Unit ARA: Asset Recovery Board ARA: Assets Recovery Agency ARIS: Asset Recovery Incentivisation Scheme ARWG: Asset Recovery Working Group
CEP:	Criminal and Enforcement Policy CFLT: Criminal Finance Litigation Team CICFA: Concerted Inter-agency Criminal Finances Action Group CRC: Commissioners of Revenue and Customs [Act] 2005 CTU: Criminal Taxes Unit
DOCEX:	Document Exploitation Facility
ECMF:	Enforcement and Compliance Management Forum ECOps: Enforcement and Compliance Operations
FATF:	Financial Action Task Force FLO: Fiscal Liaison Officer FSA: Financial Services Authority
HMCS:	Her Majesty's Courts Service HMG: Her Majesty's Government HVD: High-Value Dealer
JARD:	Joint Asset Recovery Database
MLR:	Money Laundering Regulations MSB: Money Service Business
POCA:	Proceeds of Crime Act2002 PSA: Public Service Agreement
RCPO:	Revenue and Customs Prosecution Office
SARs:	Suspicious Activity Reports SOCA: Serious Organised Crime Agency SOCAP: Serious Organised Crime and Police Act 2005

Index

Accommodation benefits 13.115–13.117
Agency workers 13.79–13.81
Appeals
  alternative dispute resolution 11.28
  closure notices
    closure notice applications 11.38–11.39
    form of closure notice 11.40–11.42
    self-assessment closure procedure 11.36–11.37
  court jurisdiction
    European Court of Justice (ECJ) 11.125–11.135
    High Court 11.123–11.128
  to Court of Appeal 11.119–11.122
  direct taxes
    closure notices 11.38–11.42
    postponement of tax 11.45–11.46
    questions during enquiry 11.43–11.44
    right to appeal 11.35
    self-assessment closure procedure 11.36–11.37
  failure to notify 14.109
  First-tier Tribunal
    basic cases 11.59–11.62
    case management powers 11.67–11.72
    central processing centre 11.55
    complex cases 11.64–11.65, 11.95–11.97
    costs 11.90–11.92
    court of first instance 11.54
    decisions 11.84–11.86
    default paper cases 11.56–11.58
    exchange of documents 11.66
    hearings 11.77–11.79
    pre-2009 appeals 11.98
    review of decisions 11.87–11.89
    standard cases 11.63

Appeals – *contd*
  First-tier Tribunal – *contd*
    statements of case 11.66
    strike outs 11.73–11.76
    wasted costs 11.93–11.94
  indirect taxes
    internal review process 11.31–11.34
    right to appeal 11.30
  information notices pre-FA 2008 Sch 36
    alternative approaches 10A.34–10A.35
    failure to comply 10A.58
    procedure 1.65–1.67 10A.53–10A.56
    third parties 10A.36
    time limits 10A.37
  internal review process 11.49–11.53
  legal privilege protection 10.103
  National Insurance Contributions
    Class 4 appeals 5.89–5.92
    decisions of HMRC officers 5.69
    decisions under Pension Schemes Act 1993 5.86–5.88
    determination by TAX Tribunal 5.77
    further appeals to Upper Tribunal 5.82–5.85
    late appeals 5.76
    modernisation of system 5.45–5.48
    notice of appeal 5.70–5.74
    place of hearing 5.75
    publication of decisions 5.98–5.99
    questions referred to Minister before 1 April 1000 5.93–5.97
    settlement by agreement 5.78–5.81
  new penalty regime
    failure to pay tax 14.164–14.165

Index

Appeals – *contd*
  new penalty regime – *contd*
    overview 14.77
    reductions for disclosure 14.148
  new rules 11.01–11.02
  new tribunal system
    background to change 11.11–11.12
    Leggatt Inquiry 11.13–11.16
    statutory provisions 11.17
    summary of procedure 11.18–11.23
  overriding objective 11.24–11.27
  private or public hearings 11.80–11.83
  self-assessment enquiries
    closure notices 1.94
    information powers from 1 April 2009 1.82
    information powers prior to 1 April 2009 1.51, 1.69
    notice of self-assessment enquiry 1.16
  settlements 11.47–11.48
  tactical approaches 11.05–11.10
  Upper Tribunal
    appeals to Court of Appeal 11.119–11.122
    case management powers 11.113–11.115
    costs 11.118
    decisions 11.117
    direct referrals 11.101–11.102
    from First-tier Tribunal 11.103–11.109
    functions 11.99–11.100
    hearings 11.116
  VAT assessments 3.84–3.86
Aspect enquiries
  classification 1.02
  disclosure strategy to avoid enquiries 1.06
Assurance visits
  basis of selection 3.05–3.09
  bookings 3.13
  general questions 3.15–3.18
  information available to visiting officer 3.10–3.12
  preparations for
    commencement 3.48–3.52
    importance 3.48
    need for 'reasonable care' 3.56
    part of ongoing routine 3.53–3.54

Assurance visits – *contd*
  preparations for – *contd*
    senior monitoring and accounting 3.58–3.60
    underlying criteria 3.55
    review of VAT returns 3.19–3.32
    role of professional advisers 3.91

Auditing Practices Board 8.60

Benefits and reimbursed expenses
  accommodation 13.115–13.117
  assets used by employees 13.118
  benefits in kind 13.28–13.29
  cars 13.119–13.125
  commissions 13.127
  conferences 13.128–13.132
  discounts 13.127
  dispensations 13.89–13.92
  entertainment expenses 13.133–13.143
  errors and omissions 13.114
  gifts 13.144
  home telephones 13.161
  loans 13.145
  long-service awards 13.146
  mobile phones 13.147–13.148
  personal incidental expenses 13.149–13.151
  prizes 13.152
  relocation expenses 13.153–13.156
  scope
    assessable on all employees 13.98
    higher paid employees and directors 13.103–13.108
    NIC 13.99–13.102
    self-assessment 13.109
  scope of employer compliance checks 13.10
  social functions 13.157
  subsistence 13.158–13.159
  suggestion schemes 13.160
  third party benefits 13.162–13.164
  travel expenses 13.165–13.170
  value of benefits 13.110–13.113
  working rule agreements 13.93–13.97
Books and records
  see also Electronic records
  employer compliance checks
    record keeping requirements 13.07
    scope 9.63–9.86

462

Index

Books and records – *contd*
  information notices pre-FA 2008 Sch 36
    auditors' and tax advisers' documents 10.104–10.108
    destruction of documents 10A.39–10A.41
    documents and information distinguished 1.58–1.61
    power to call for documents 10A.47–10A.52
    protected documents 10A.24–10A.28
    requests for information or documents 10.15–10.20
    VAT 10A.61–10A.67
  information notices under FA 2008 Sch 36
    inspection of premises under FA 2008 Sch 36, 10.53–10.58
    in a person's 'possession' defined 10.73–10.78
    in a person's 'power' defined 10.79–10.86
  National Insurance Contributions 4.19–4.21
  new penalty regime 14.90–14.96
  opening letters 9.10
  self-assessment enquiries
    documents and information 1.58–1.62
    estimated profits 1.43
    flexibility across range of businesses 1.44
    'Hansard' procedure 1.12
    necessary records 1.41–1.42
    penalties 1.45
    reason for early meeting with HMRC 1.32
    retention period 1.40
    statutory requirements 1.39

Capital gains tax
  business inspections 1.86
  information powers 1.72
  new penalty regime 14.23 14.26
  record keeping requirements 1.44
  search and entry powers 3.62
  time limits for assessment and claims 1.92
Carelessness 14.36–14.41
Cars 13.119–13.125

Case management powers
  First-tier Tribunal 11.67–11.72
  Upper Tribunal 11.113–11.115
Casual workers 13.73–13.78
Category X notations 6.18–6.23
Chartered Institute of Taxation 8.59
Civil investigation of fraud (CIF)
  see also Self-assessment enquiries
  allocation of cases 1.12–1.13
  Code of Practice 9
    direct tax questions 2.56
    guarantee of no criminal investigation 2.34
    indirect tax questions 2.57
    meetings with HMRC 2.36–2.50
    publication of new code 2.33
    statement of HMRC approach 2.37
    trigger points 2.35
  financial thresholds 2.58
  need for specialist approach 2.65–2.74
  suspected serious fraud 2.09
Cleaners 13.86–13.87
Closure notices
  appeals
    closure notice applications 11.38–11.39
    form of closure notice 11.40–11.42
    self-assessment closure procedure 11.36–11.37
  self-assessment enquiries
    appeals 1.94
    applications for directions 1.92–1.93
    requirement for officer to form conclusion 1.95–1.96
    statutory requirements 1.91
Code of Practice 8
  direct tax investigations 7.06
  tax evasion schemes 2.59–2.64
  types of investigation 2.10
Code of Practice 9
  definitions of fraud 2.27–2.32
  direct tax investigations 7.06
  direct tax questions 2.56
  guarantee of no criminal investigation 2.34
  indirect tax questions 2.57
  meetings with HMRC 2.36
  publication of new code 2.33
  trigger points 2.35

463

Index

Code of Practice 9 – *contd*
  types of investigation 2.09
Commissions 13.127
Complex cases
  First-tier Tribunal
    classification 11.64–11.65
    costs 11.95–11.97
    referral to Upper Tribunal 11.101–11.102
  role of SI 2.02 2.06
Compliance checks *see* Employer compliance checks
Computer records *see* Electronic records
Conferences 13.128–13.132
Consultancy Committee of Accountancy Bodies 8.58
Corporation tax
  business inspections 1.86
  information powers 1.72
  new penalty regime 14.26
    failure to make returns 14.126–14.128
    failure to pay tax 14.156–14.157
    new concepts 14.71–14.73
    scope 14.24
  record keeping requirements 1.44
  search and entry powers 3.62
  time limits for assessment and claims 1.92
Costs
  alternative to appeal 11.28
  First-tier Tribunal
    complex cases 11.95–11.97
    general principles 11.90–11.92
    wasted costs 11.93–11.94
  Upper Tribunal 11.118
Credibility visits
  preparations for 3.57
  VAT 3.33–3.35
Credit cards 13.126
Criminal Investigation Directorate 7.16
Criminal investigations
  direct taxes
    background 7.01–7.02
    HMRC powers 7.14–7.16
    new regime 7.05–7.07
    organisation of HMRC 7.13
    prosecution policy 7.08–7.10
    published statistics 7.03–7.05
    trigger points 7.11–7.12

Criminal investigations – *contd*
  information powers
    PACE powers 10.117–10.127
    production orders 10.128–10.131
    safeguards 10.132
    SOCPA powers 10.133–10.137
    third party search and seizure 10.138–10.145
    TMA s 20A 10.114–10.116
  SI investigations 2.10–2.16
Cross-border activities
  criminal investigation powers 7.12
  identity of directors 1.96
  offshore disclosures
    Liechtenstein Disclosure Facility 14.178–14.183
    new penalty regime 14.170–14.177
  Proceeds of Crime Act 2002 8.32–8.37
  remittances by non-domiciled individuals 12.63
  VAT supplies
    assurance visits 3.10
    Intrastat visits 3.36–3.41
    mutual assistance and exchange of information 3.42–3.46

Dawn raids *see under* Search and entry powers 3.42–3.46
Debtor contact details 14.122–14.123
Direct taxes
  see also Capital gains tax; Corporation tax; Income tax; Inheritance tax; Self-assessment enquiries
  appeals
    closure notices 11.38–11.42
    postponement of tax 11.45–11.46
    questions during enquiry 11.43–11.44
    right to appeal 11.35
    self-assessment closure procedure 11.36–11.37
  Code of Practice 9 questions 2.56
  criminal investigations
    background 7.01–7.02
    HMRC powers 7.14–7.39
    new regime 7.05–7.07
    organisation of HMRC 7.13
    prosecution policy 7.08–7.10
    published statistics 7.03–7.05
    trigger points 7.11–7.12

Index

Direct taxes – *contd*
  employer compliance checks
    inclusion of all relevant
      employees and
      directors 13.63–13.64
Directors
  control of documents 1.49, 10.82
  COP 9 questions 2.56
  cross-border activities 1.96
  employer compliance checks
    benefits and reimbursed
      expenses 13.103–13.108
    inclusion of all relevant
      employees and
      directors 13.63–13.64
    special points 13.88
  meetings with HMRC 9.45–9.47, 9.73, 9.75–9.80
  new penalty regime 14.107–14.108
  NIC
    Category X notations 6.19
    corporate responsibility 5.06–5.07
    record keeping requirements 4.16–4.18
  s 20 information notices 1.71
  self-assessment enquiries 1.23
  signatory to VAT returns 3.58 3.60
Disclosure
  Code of Practice 9 2.49–2.53
  compliance projects 2.80–2.89
  new penalty regime
    computer records 14.89
    deliberate understatement of tax 14.55–14.59
    deliberate understatement with concealment 14.60–14.64
    failure to notify 14.102–14.103
    failure to notify under-assessment 14.51–14.54
    mitigated penalties 14.42–14.43
    offshore disclosures 14.170–14.183
    prompted and unprompted disclosure 14.44–14.45
    reductions for disclosure 14.140–14.150
    relevant factors of assessment 14.46–14.50
    special penalty reduction 14.65
    suspended penalties 14.67–14.69
    third party errors 14.70

Disclosure – *contd*
  new penalty regime – *contd*
    timing differences 14.66
    self-assessment enquiries
      information not normally provided 1.23
      opening letter requesting information 1.17–1.22
      relevance dependant on circumstances 1.24
      strategy to avoid enquiries 1.06–1.08
Discounts 13.127
Discovery powers
  assessment for closed years 1.98
  presumption of continuity 1.101–1.102
  procedure 1.100
  settlements 1.103–1.106
  time limits for assessment 1.99
Dismissals 13.35
Dispute resolution
  alternative to appeal 11.28
  information powers under FA 2008 Sch 36, 10.99–10.102
  legal privilege protection
    court applications 7.41
    independent Counsel 7.42
Documents *see* Books and records

Electronic records
  assurance visits for VAT
    computer accounts officers (CAOs) 3.24–3.27
    general information 3.16
  employer compliance checks 9.81
  information powers prior to 1 April 2009 1.57
  new penalty regime 14.89
Emoluments 13.05
Employees *see* Employer compliance checks; National Insurance Contributions (NIC)
Employer compliance checks
  areas liable for review 9.91–9.93
  benefits and reimbursed expenses
    accommodation 13.115–13.117
    assets used by employees 13.118
    cars 13.119–13.125
    commissions 13.127
    conferences 13.128–13.132

465

Index

Employer compliance checks – *contd*
 benefits and reimbursed expenses – *contd*
  credit cards 13.126
  discounts 13.127
  dispensations 13.89–13.92
  entertainment expenses 13.133–13.143
  errors and omissions 13.114
  gifts 13.144
  home telephones 13.161
  loans 13.145
  long-service awards 13.146
  mobile phones 13.147–13.148
  personal incidental expenses 13.149–13.151
  prizes 13.152
  relocation expenses 13.153–13.156
  scope 13.98–13.109
  social functions 13.157
  subsistence 13.158–13.159
  suggestion schemes 13.160
  third party benefits 13.162–13.164
  travel expenses 13.165–13.170
  value of benefits 13.110–13.113
  working rule agreements 13.93–13.97
 conduct during visit 9.88–9.90
 credit cards 13.126
 dedicated agency 13.01
 directors
  benefits and reimbursed expenses 13.103–13.108
  inclusion of all relevant employees and directors 13.63–13.64
  special points 13.88
 Finance Act 2008 Sch 36, 10.13
 liability for tax arising 13.171–13.174
 new penalty regime 14.90–14.96
 overview 13.02–13.04
 PAYE and NIC calculations
  agency workers 13.79–13.81
  casual workers 13.73–13.78
  cleaners 13.86–13.87
  employment and self-employment distinguished 13.65–13.72
  errors and omissions 13.48
  inclusion of all relevant employees and directors 13.63–13.64

Employer compliance checks – *contd*
 PAYE and NIC calculations – *contd*
  new employees 13.56
  one-man companies 13.82–13.84
  payroll giving schemes 13.59–13.60
  SSP and SMP rules 13.57–13.58
  students 13.85
  third party payments 13.61–13.62
  timing of taxable earnings 13.49–13.55
 PAYE and NIC issues
  benefits in kind 13.28–13.29
  continuing benefits after termination 13.38
  other termination issues 13.43
  payments in lieu of notice 13.33
  redundancies and dismissals 13.35
  relevant issues 13.12–13.19
  restrictive covenants 13.34
  retirement 13.36–13.37
  round sum allowances 13.21–13.22
  salary sacrifice arrangements 13.44–13.47
  service charges 13.26–13.27
  sick pay 13.23
  termination payments 13.30–13.32
  tips 13.24–13.25
 pre-planning checklist 9.87
 record keeping requirements 13.07
 scope 9.63–9.86
  additional aspects 13.08
  benefit rules 13.10
  emoluments 13.05
  National Insurance Contributions 13.06
  'payroll cleanse' 13.09
Entertainment expenses 13.133–13.143
Errors and omissions
 employer compliance checks
  benefits and reimbursed expenses 13.114
  PAYE and NIC calculations 13.48
 National Insurance Contributions 4.22–4.24
 new penalty regime
  defaults and errors 14.11–14.15
  third party errors 14.70
 notes of meetings 1.38
 previous penalty regime 14.78
 settlement negotiations 12.64–12.68

Index

European Court of Justice
  (ECJ) 11.125–11.135
Evasion *see* Tax evasion

Failure to make returns 14.126–14.128
Failure to notify
  appeals 14.109
  companies officers' liability 14.107–14.108
  penalties 14.99–14.101
  penalty reductions 14.105–14.106
  previous penalty regime 14.111–14.113
  quantification of disclosures 14.103–14.104
  reductions for disclosure 14.102
  statutory provisions 14.97–14.98
  suspended penalties 14.110
Failure to pay tax
  appeals 14.164–14.165
  corporation tax 14.156–14.157
  new penalty regime 14.151–14.152
  PAYE 14.158–14.161
  penalties 14.153–14.155
  special reductions 14.162
  suspended penalties 14.163
First-tier Tribunal
  appeals to Upper Tribunal 11.103–11.109
  case management powers 11.67–11.72
  central processing centre 11.55
  classification of cases
    basic cases 11.59–11.62
    complex cases 11.64–11.65
    default paper cases 11.56–11.58
    standard cases 11.63
  costs
    complex cases 11.95–11.97
    general principles 11.90–11.92
    wasted costs 11.93–11.94
  court of first instance 11.54
  decisions 11.84–11.86
  exchange of documents 11.66
  hearings 11.77–11.79
  information notices under FA 2008 Sch 36, 10.33–10.37
  judicial review jurisdiction 11.112
  pre-2009 appeals 11.98
  private or public hearings 11.80–11.83
  review of decisions 11.87–11.89
  statements of case 11.66

First-tier Tribunal – *contd*
  strike outs 11.73–11.76
Fraud
  see also Errors and omissions;
    Tax evasion
  Code of Practice 9
    definitions of fraud 2.27–2.32
    direct tax questions 2.56
    guarantee of no criminal investigation 2.34
    indirect tax questions 2.57
    meetings with HMRC 2.36
    publication of new code 2.33
    trigger points 2.35
    types of investigation 2.09
  financial thresholds 2.58
  National Insurance Contributions
    evasion of contributions 5.05
    incorrect returns 5.19–5.20
    penalties for Class 1A contributions 5.25–5.26
    penalties for Class 4 contributions 5.27–5.33
  prerequisite of SOCPA powers 7.36
  previous penalty regime 14.79
  self-assessment enquiries
    discovery powers 1.98
    'Hansard' procedure 1.12
  SI definitions
    Fraud Act 2006 2.21–2.23
    'Hansard' procedure 2.24–2.27
    HMRC Enquiry Manual 2.18–2.19
    importance 2.17
  SI investigations
    criminal investigations 2.10–2.16
    suspected serious fraud 2.09
  trials
    committal from magistrates' court 7.47
    lengthy preparations 7.46
    offences and penalties 7.49
    role of professional advisers 7.48

Gifts
  benefits and reimbursed expenses 13.144
  payroll giving schemes 13.59–13.60

'Hansard' procedure
  definitions of fraud 2.24–2.27
  self-assessment enquiries 1.12

Index

Hearings
  First-tier Tribunal 11.77–11.79
  Upper Tribunal 11.116
High Court 11.123–11.128
HMRC
  see also Information powers
  approach to money laundering
    developing role 8.67–8.69
    flow of intelligence 8.70–8.71
    guidelines 8.63–8.66
    new strategy 8.72–8.77
  compliance projects 2.80–2.89
  Criminal Division 7.13
  criminal investigation powers
    Criminal Investigation Directorate 7.16
    cross-border powers 7.15
    interviews 7.43–7.45
    intrusive surveillance 7.39
    overview 7.14
    production orders 7.24–7.36
    search and entry 7.17–7.23
  employer compliance checks
    areas liable for review 9.91–9.93
    conduct during visit 9.88–9.90
    pre-planning checklist 9.87
    scope 9.63–9.86
  merger of HMCE and IR 3.01
  negotiations
    accountancy costs 12.24–12.27
    advantages to HMRC 12.69–12.72
    automatic interest charges 12.09
    correspondence rather than meetings 12.96–12.99
    disadvantage of sub-standard offers 12.94–12.95
    early groundwork 12.05–12.07
    fee savings 12.31
    funding and time to pay 12.81–12.89
    grey areas 12.38–12.42
    identifying unresolved matters 12.74–12.76
    importance of rapport with officer 12.100–12.101
    innocent errors and excuses 12.64–12.68
    letters of offer 12.90–12.93
    litigation and settlements strategy (LSS) 12.43
    no published *de minimis* limit 12.08
    payment on account 12.18–12.21

HMRC – *contd*
  negotiations – *contd*
    penalty negotiations 12.10–12.17
    practitioner finality 12.33
    re-opening of claims and allowances 12.61–12.62
    recognition of best possible outcome 12.77–12.80
    reduction of investigation period 12.29
    relationship with client 12.102–12.109
    relevant skills 12.44–12.60
    remittances by non-domiciled individuals 12.63
    situations which are negotiable 12.34–12.37
    tax savings 12.32
    taxpayer finality 12.30
    VAT disclosure 12.22–12.23
    workload pressures on HMRC 12.73
  NIC powers 4.02
  settlement negotiations
    overview 12.01–12.04
  VAT powers
    search and entry 3.61–3.69
    surveillance 3.70–3.74
Home telephones 13.161
Human rights 7.10

Identity unknown notices 10.41–10.50
Income tax
  see also PAYE
  business inspections 1.86
  information powers 1.72
  new penalty regime
    failure to make returns 14.126–14.128
    new concepts 14.71–14.73
    scope 14.23 14.26
  record keeping requirements 1.44
  search and entry powers 3.62
  time limits for assessment and claims 1.92
Indirect taxes
  see also VAT
  appeals
    internal review process 11.31–11.34
    right to appeal 11.30
  Code of Practice 9 questions 2.57

Index

Indirect taxes – *contd*
  information powers pre-FA 2008 Sch 36
    information and documents 10A.61–10A.67
    search and entry 10A.68–10A.71
    statutory provisions 10A.59–10A.60
Information powers
  criminal investigations
    PACE powers 10.117–10.127
    production orders 10.128–10.131
    safeguards 10.132
    SOCPA powers 10.133–10.137
    third party search and seizure 10.138–10.145
    TMA s 20A 10.114–10.116
  Finance Act 2008 Sch 36
    auditors' and tax advisers' documents 10.104–10.108
    compliance checks 10.13
    identity unknown notices 10.41–10.50
    inspection of premises 10.51–10.71
    involved third party notices 10.38–10.40
    legal privilege protection 10.87–10.102
    penalties 10.109–10.113
    in a person's 'possession' defined 10.73–10.78
    in a person's 'power' defined 10.79–10.86
    requests for information or documents 10.15–10.20
    restrictions on use of powers 10.72
    role of First-tier Tribunal 10.33–10.37
    statutory provisions 10.14
    taxpayer notices 10.21–10.28
    third party notices 10.29–10.32
  new penalty regime 14.90–14.96
  new system 10.01–10.03
  NIC visits and investigations 4.17–4.18
  pre-2009 provisions
    appeals 10A.34–10A.37, 10A.53–10A.56
    consent from Commissioner of Tax 10A.12–10A.20
    indirect taxes 10A.59–10A.71

Information powers – *contd*
  pre-2009 provisions – *contd*
    legal privilege protection 10A.21–10A.23
    notice requirements 10A.07
    offences and penalties 10A.38–10A.43
    overview 10A.05–10A.06
    penalties for non-compliance 10A.57–10A.58
    power to call for documents 10A.47–10A.52
    precursor notices 10A.09–10A.11
    protected documents 10A.24–10A.28
    search and seizure powers 10A.44–10A.46
    statutory restrictions 10A.08
    third parties 10A.29–10A.33
    wide ranging provisions 10A.01–10A.04
  rationale for change 10.04–10.12
  self-assessment after 1 April 2009
    business inspections 1.86–1.89
    statutory requirements 1.72–1.85
    third party information 1.90
  self-assessment prior to 1 April 2009
    appeals 1.51
    documents and information distinguished 1.58–1.61
    effect of forcing estimate of profits 1.54
    electronic records 1.57
    examinations of relevance 1.52–1.53
    limitations on required information 1.47–1.50
    procedure under s 19A 1.63–1.71
    reasonableness of requirement 1.55–1.56 1.62
    statutory changes 1.46
VAT
  cross-border supplies 3.42–3.46
  general questions 3.15–3.18
  review of VAT returns 3.19–3.32
Inheritance tax
  appeals 11.128
  information powers 10.12 10.86
  inspection of premises 10.69
  new penalty regime
    defaults and errors 14.13

Index

Inheritance tax – *contd*
  new penalty regime – *contd*
    failure to make returns 14.126–14.128
    failure to pay 14.151
Inspection of premises
  business premises 10.52
  self-assessment enquiries
    best practice for clients 1.89
    HMRC internal instructions 1.88
    new statutory powers 1.86
    restrictions on HMRC 1.87
  statutory provisions 10.51
  third parties 10.67–10.68
  timing 10.59–10.63
  for valuation 10.69–10.71
  VAT provisions 10.64–10.66
  what can be inspected 10.53–10.58
Institute of Chartered Accountants 8.54–8.57
Interest
  automatic charge on settlement 12.09
  on National Insurance Contributions
    Class 2 and 4 contributions 5.42–5.44
    overdue contributions 5.34–5.39
    repaid contributions 5.40
    repayment and remission 5.41
Internal review process 11.31–11.34 11.49–11.53
'Intervention plans' 9.72
Intrastat visits 3.36–3.41
Intrusive surveillance 7.39

Joint Money Laundering Steering Group 8.61–8.62
Judicial review
  First-tier Tribunal jurisdiction 11.112
  notice of self-assessment enquiry 1.16
  Upper Tribunal jurisdiction 11.110–11.111
  VAT assessments 3.90

Keith Committee 7.11 10A.29–10A.30

Large Business Service 3.29–3.31
Legal privilege protection
  dispute resolution
    court applications 7.41
    independent Counsel 7.42

Legal privilege protection – *contd*
  information notices pre-FA 2008 Sch 36, 10A.21–10A.23
  information powers under FA 2008 Sch 36
    dispute resolution 10.99–10.102
    legal advice privilege 10.90–10.93
    legal profession privilege 10.87–10.89
    litigation privilege 10.94–10.98
    pending appeals 10.103
  search warrants 7.20
  statutory provisions 7.40
Leggatt Inquiry 11.13–11.16
Letters of offer 12.90–12.93
Liechtenstein Disclosure Facility 14.178–14.183
Litigation and settlements strategy (LSS) 12.43
Litigation privilege 10.94–10.98
Loans 13.145
Long-service awards 13.146

Meetings with HMRC
  see also Settlements
  agenda 9.40
  alternative questioning under oath 9.18–9.19
  co-operation
    abatements for co-operation 9.15–9.17
    general approach 9.20
  Code of Practice 9 2.36–2.50
  compliance officer's requirements 9.34–9.37
  conclusion of meeting 9.59
  conduct of meeting 9.53–9.58
  current approach 9.02–9.05
  employer compliance checks
    areas liable for review 9.91–9.93
    conduct during visit 9.88–9.90
    pre-planning checklist 9.87
    scope 9.63–9.86
  interviews
    completion of evidential jigsaw 7.43
    role of professional advisers 7.45
    statutory caution 7.44
  key areas 9.62
  location 9.48–9.52
  no powers of compulsion 9.13–9.14
  note-taking 9.60–9.61

Index

Meetings with HMRC – *contd*
　overcoming reluctance to
　　attend 9.12
　overview 9.94–9.97
　persons present 9.41–9.47
　preparations for
　　case reviews 9.22
　　checklist 9.38–9.39
　　client advice 9.26–9.33
　　identifying problem areas 9.23–9.25
　　role of compliance officers 9.21
　purpose 9.07–9.11
　scope 9.01 9.06
　self-assessment enquiries
　　importance to HMRC 1.25–1.28
　　location 1.29 1.34–1.35
　　notes of meetings 1.36–1.38
　　presence of client 1.31 1.33
　　understanding business records 1.32
　　voluntary terms 1.30
　settlement negotiations 12.96–12.99
Minimum wages 14.184–14.188
Mobile phones 13.147–13.148
Money laundering
　guidance for financial intermediaries
　　Auditing Practices Board 8.60
　　Chartered Institute of Taxation 8.59
　　Consultancy Committee of Accountancy Bodies 8.58
　　HMRC 8.63–8.66
　　Institute of Chartered Accountants 8.54–8.57
　　Joint Money Laundering Steering Group 8.61–8.62
　legislative provisions
　　EU Directives 8.17–8.20
　　Proceeds of Crime Act 2002 8.21–8.40
　relationship with tax evasion
　　conclusions 8.106–8.109
　　development of government thinking 8.41–8.53
　　overview 8.01–8.03
　　role of fiscal authorities 8.67–8.77
　role of professional advisers 8.86–8.105
　　developments in law and practice 8.86–8.105
　　risk to intermediaries 8.78–8.85

Multiple penalties 14.129

'Naming and shaming' 14.119–14.121
National Insurance Contributions (NIC)
　see also PAYE
　appeals
　　Class 4 appeals 5.89–5.92
　　decisions of HMRC officers 5.69
　　decisions under Pension Schemes Act 1993 5.86–5.88
　　determination by TAX Tribunal 5.77
　　further appeals to Upper Tribunal 5.82–5.85
　　late appeals 5.76
　　modernisation of system 5.45–5.48
　　notice of appeal 5.70–5.74
　　place of hearing 5.75
　　publication of decisions 5.98–5.99
　　questions referred to Minister before 1 April 1000 5.93–5.97
　　settlement by agreement 5.78–5.81
　compliance regime 4.03–4.04
　decisions of HMRC officers
　　notice of 5.59–5.68
　　subject matter 5.49–5.58
　employer compliance checks
　　agency workers 13.79–13.81
　　benefits and reimbursed expenses 13.99–13.102
　　benefits in kind 13.28–13.29
　　casual workers 13.73–13.78
　　cleaners 13.86–13.87
　　continuing benefits after termination 13.38
　　employment and self-employment distinguished 13.65–13.72
　　errors and omissions 13.48
　　inclusion of all relevant employees and directors 13.63–13.64
　　new employees 13.56
　　one-man companies 13.82–13.84
　　other termination issues 13.43
　　payments in lieu of notice 13.33
　　payroll giving schemes 13.59–13.60
　　redundancies and dismissals 13.35
　　relevant issues 13.12–13.19
　　restrictive covenants 13.34

471

Index

National Insurance Contributions (NIC) – *contd*
  employer compliance checks – *contd*
    retirement 13.36–13.37
    round sum allowances 13.21–13.22
    salary sacrifice arrangements 13.44–13.47
    scope 13.06
    service charges 13.26–13.27
    sick pay 13.23
    SSP and SMP rules 13.57–13.58
    students 13.85
    termination payments 13.30–13.32
    termination settlements 13.39–13.42
    third party payments 13.61–13.62
    timing of taxable earnings 13.49–13.55
    tips 13.24–13.25
  errors and omissions 4.22–4.24
  funding principles 6.05–6.08
  importance 4.01
  inspectorate powers 4.02
  interest
    Class 2 and 4 contributions 5.42–5.44
    overdue contributions 5.34–5.39
    repaid contributions 5.40
    repayment and remission 5.41
  new penalty regime 14.126–14.128
  offences and penalties
    amounts for Class 1A contributions 5.25–5.26
    amounts for Class 4 contributions 5.27–5.33
    bodies corporate 5.06–5.07
    contravention of regulations 5.03
    contributions 5.04–5.05
    failure to pay contributions 5.08–5.16
    false information delays and obstruction 5.02
    incorrect manner of payment 5.21
    incorrect returns 5.19–5.20
    interest 5.34–5.44
    late returns 5.17–5.18
  overview 6.01–6.04
  record keeping 4.19–4.21
  trigger points
    Category X notations 6.18–6.23
    complaints from employees 6.24–6.26

National Insurance Contributions (NIC) – *contd*
  trigger points – *contd*
    end-of-year returns 6.11–6.17
    failure to reply to correspondence 6.31
    international employers 6.33–6.36
    large employers 6.32
    luck 6.37
    national programmes 6.28–6.29
    overview 6.09–6.10
    regional initiatives 6.27
    routine visits 6.30
  visits and investigations
    choice of employers 4.06
    commencement 4.16
    five-year cycle 4.08
    future visits 4.27
    inspection reports 4.25–4.26
    length of visit 4.13
    location 4.14
    overview 6.38–6.39
    preparations for 4.15
    prior notification 4.09–4.12
    purposes of visit 4.07
    reasons for visits 4.05
    records to be made available 4.17–4.18
    targeting for yield 4.28–4.30
Negligence
  see also Errors and omissions
  National Insurance Contributions
    incorrect NIC returns 5.19–5.20
    penalties for Class 1A contributions 5.25–5.26
    penalties for Class 4 contributions 5.27–5.33
  previous penalty regime 14.79
  self-assessment enquiries 1.98
Negotiations *see under* Settlements
New employees 13.56
Notices
  information notices pre-FA 2008 Sch 36
    appeals 10A.34–10A.37
    consent from Commissioner of Tax 10A.09–10A.11
    legal privilege protection 10A.21–10A.23
    precursor notices 10A.09–10A.11

Index

Notices – *contd*
  information notices pre-FA 2008 – *contd*
    presumption of reasonableness 10A.07
    protected documents 10A.24–10A.28
    statutory restrictions 10A.08
    third parties 10A.29–10A.33
  information notices under FA 2008 Sch 36
    identity unknown notices 10.41–10.50
    involved third party notices 10.38–10.40
    role of First-tier Tribunal 10.33–10.37
    statutory provisions 10.15–10.20
    taxpayer notices 10.21–10.28
    third party notices 10.29–10.32
  self-assessment enquiries
    closure notices 1.91–1.93
    information powers from 1 April 2009 1.79–1.80
    notice of enquiry 1.15–1.16

Offences and penalties
  abatements for co-operation 9.15–9.17
  information notices pre-FA 2008 Sch 36
    destruction of documents 10A.39–10A.41
    failure to comply 10A.42–10A.43, 10A.57–10A.58
    transitional provisions 10A.38
  information powers under FA 2008 Sch 36 10.109–10.113
  National Insurance Contributions (NIC)
    amounts for Class 1A contributions 5.25–5.26
    amounts for Class 4 contributions 5.27–5.33
    bodies corporate 5.06–5.07
    contravention of regulations 5.03
    evasion of contributions 5.04–5.05
    failure to pay contributions 5.08–5.16
    false information delays and obstruction 5.02 5.08–5.16
    incorrect manner of payment 5.21

Offences and penalties – *contd*
  National Insurance Contributions (NIC) – *contd*
    incorrect returns 5.19–5.20
    interest 5.34–5.44
    late payment 5.22–5.24
    late returns 5.17–5.18
  negotiation following settlement 12.10–12.17
  new penalty regime
    amount of penalty 14.74–14.75, 14.130–14.139
    appeals 14.77
    capital gains tax 14.23, 14.26
    carelessness 14.36–14.41
    consultation documents 14.03–14.06
    corporation tax 14.24, 14.26
    debtor contact details 14.122–14.123
    defaults and errors 14.11–14.15
    degrees of culpability 14.27–14.28
    failure to make returns 14.126–14.128
    failure to pay tax 14.151–14.166
    HMRC handbooks and manuals 14.08–14.10
    income tax 14.23 14.26
    innocent errors and mistakes 14.29
    minimum wages 14.184–14.188
    multiple penalties 14.129
    'naming and shaming' 14.119–14.121
    new penalty concepts 14.71–14.73
    offshore disclosures 14.170–14.183
    overview 14.01–14.02
    potential lost revenue 14.16–14.20
    quality of disclosure 14.42–14.70
    reasonable excuses 14.30–14.35
    reductions for disclosure 14.140–14.150
    relevant inaccurate documents 14.21–14.22
    relevant legislation 14.07
    senior accounting officers 14.114–14.118
    statutory provisions 10.09
    suspended penalties 14.167–14.169
    time limits 14.76
    time limits for assessments 14.124–14.125

Index

Offences and penalties – *contd*
  new penalty regime – *contd*
    VAT 14.25–14.26
    no published *de minimis* limit 12.08
    outcome of trials 7.49
  previous penalty regime
    failure to notify 14.97–14.113, 14.111–14.113
    overview 14.78–14.87
    transitional rules 14.88
  Proceeds of Crime Act 2002
    acquisition use and possession 8.24
    arrangements 8.23
    concealing 8.22
    funds derived from foreign jurisdiction 8.32–8.37
    interpretation 8.25–8.31
    knowledge or suspicion 8.38–8.40
    relevant inaccurate documents 14.21–14.22
  self-assessment enquiries
    books and records 1.45
    information powers from 1 April 2009 1.83
    third party search and seizure 10.145
  VAT 3.56
Offshore disclosures
  Liechtenstein Disclosure Facility 14.178–14.183
  new penalty regime 14.170–14.177
Offshore Project Group 2.85–2.87, 7.07
Omissions *see* Errors and omissions
One-man companies 13.82–13.84
Opening letters
  client advice 9.26
  prelude to meetings 9.10
  self-assessment enquiries 1.17–1.24
Overriding objective 11.24–11.27

Partnerships
  COP 9 questions 2.56
  meetings with HMRC 9.45–9.47, 9.73, 9.75–9.80
  payments on account 12.21
PAYE
  see also National Insurance Contributions (NIC)
  business inspections 1.86 10.51
  decline in fraud 7.04
  employer compliance checks
    agency workers 13.79–13.81

PAYE – *contd*
  employer compliance checks – *contd*
    benefits in kind 13.28–13.29
    casual workers 13.73–13.78
    cleaners 13.86–13.87
    continuing benefits after termination 13.38
    employment and self-employment distinguished 13.65–13.72
    errors and omissions 13.48
    inclusion of all relevant employees and directors 13.63–13.64
    new employees 13.56
    one-man companies 13.82–13.84
    other termination issues 13.43
    payments in lieu of notice 13.33
    payroll giving schemes 13.59–13.60
    redundancies and dismissals 13.35
    relevant issues 13.12–13.19
    restrictive covenants 13.34
    retirement 13.36–13.37
    round sum allowances 13.21–13.22
    salary sacrifice arrangements 13.44–13.47
    service charges 13.26–13.27
    sick pay 13.23
    SSP and SMP rules 13.57–13.58
    students 13.85
    termination payments 13.30–13.32
    termination settlements 13.39–13.42
    third party payments 13.61–13.62
    timing of taxable earnings 13.49–13.55
    tips 13.24–13.25
  failure to pay tax 14.158–14.161
  information powers 1.72
  interest 5.34–5.44
  new criminal investigation regime 7.05
  new penalty regime 14.126–14.128
  record keeping requirements 1.44
  search and entry powers 3.62
  time limits for assessment and claims 1.92
Payments in lieu of notice 13.33
Payroll giving schemes 13.59–13.60
Penalties *see* Offences and penalties

Index

Personal incidental expenses 13.149–13.151
Prizes 13.152
Procedure
  information powers prior to 1 April 2009
    appeals 1.65–1.67, 1.69
    multiple notices 1.68
    s 20 notices 1.70–1.71
    time for compliance 1.63–1.64
  new tribunal system 11.18–11.23
  production orders 7.25
  self-assessment enquiries
    allocation of enquiries between offices 1.12–1.13
    helpful publications 1.14
    statutory and non-statutory procedure distinguished 1.09–1.11
Proceeds of Crime Act 2002
  consolidating Act 8.21
  offences
    acquisition use and possession 8.24
    arrangements 8.23
    concealing 8.22
    funds derived from foreign jurisdiction 8.32–8.37
    interpretation 8.25–8.31
    knowledge or suspicion 8.38–8.40
Production orders
  see also Search and entry powers
  compliance requirements 7.26–7.32
  general principles 10.128–10.131
  legal privilege protection
    court applications 7.41
    independent Counsel 7.42
    statutory provisions 7.40
  PACE Code of Practice 7.35
  pre-2009 provisions
    overview 10A.05–10A.06
  pre-conditions for application 7.33
  procedure 7.25
  requirement for serious fraud 7.36
  special procedure material 7.23
  statutory authority 7.24

Random enquiries 1.05
Records see Books and records
Redundancies 13.35
Reimbursed expenses see Benefits and reimbursed expenses

Relocation expenses 13.153–13.156
Restrictive covenants 13.34
Retirement 13.36–13.37
Revenue and Customs Prosecutions Office (RCPO) 7.04, 10.04
Round sum allowances 13.21–13.22

Salary sacrifice arrangements 13.44–13.47
Search and entry powers
  see also Production orders
  dealing with dawn raids 7.37–7.38
  employer compliance checks 9.67
  inspection of premises under FA 2008 Sch 36
    business premises 10.52
    statutory provisions 10.51
    third parties 10.67–10.68
    timing 10.59–10.63
    for valuation 10.69–10.71
    VAT provisions 10.64–10.66
    what can be inspected 10.53–10.58
  PACE Code of Practice 7.35
  PACE powers
    general principles 10.120–10.126
    key points 10.127
  pre-2009 provisions
    indirect taxes 10A.68–10A.71
    overview 10A.05–10A.06
    search and seizure powers 10A.44–10A.46
  pre-conditions for application of warrant 7.34
  requirement for serious fraud 7.36
  scope
    legal privilege protection 7.20
    premises 7.17–7.18
    relevant material 7.19
    special procedure material 7.21
  third parties 10.138–10.145
  VAT 3.61–3.69
  without warrant 7.22
Self-assessment enquiries
  accountancy costs 12.24
  appeals
    closure notice applications 11.38–11.39
    closure notices 11.36–11.42
    form of closure notice 11.40–11.42
  benefits and reimbursed expenses 13.109

Index

Self-assessment enquiries – *contd*
  books and records
    estimated profits 1.43
    flexibility across range of businesses 1.44
    necessary records 1.41–1.42
    penalties 1.45
    retention period 1.40
    statutory requirements 1.39
  classification 1.02–1.03
  closure notices
    appeals 1.94
    applications for directions 1.92–1.93
    requirement for officer to form conclusion 1.95–1.96
    statutory requirements 1.91
  commencement
    HMRC notice of enquiry 1.15–1.16
    opening letter and provision of information 1.17–1.24
  disclosure strategy to avoid enquiries 1.06–1.08
  discovery powers
    assessment for closed years 1.98
    presumption of continuity 1.101–1.102
    procedure 1.100
    settlements 1.103–1.106
    time limits for assessment 1.99
  essential element of system 1.01
  information powers from 1 April 2009
    business inspections 1.86–1.89
    statutory requirements 1.72–1.85
    third party information 1.90
  information powers prior to 1 April 2009
    appeals 1.51
    documents and information distinguished 1.58–1.61
    effect of forcing estimate of profits 1.54
    electronic records 1.57
    examinations of relevance 1.52–1.53
    limitations on required information 1.47–1.50
    procedure under s 19A 1.63–1.71
    reasonableness of requirement 1.55–1.56, 1.62
    statutory changes 1.46

Self-assessment enquiries – *contd*
  meetings with HMRC
    importance to HMRC 1.25–1.28
    location 1.29, 1.34–1.35
    notes of meetings 1.36–1.38
    presence of client 1.31, 1.33
    understanding business records 1.32
    voluntary terms 1.30
  pre-2009 provisions 10A.48
  procedure
    allocation of enquiries between offices 1.12–1.13
    helpful publications 1.14
    statutory and non-statutory procedure distinguished 1.09–1.11
  trigger points 1.04
Senior accounting officers 14.114–14.118
Service charges 13.26–13.27
Settlements
  see also Meetings with HMRC
  appeals 11.47–11.48
  employer compliance checks 13.39–13.42
  negotiations
    accountancy costs 12.24–12.27
    advantages to HMRC 12.69–12.72
    automatic interest charges 12.09
    correspondence rather than meetings 12.96–12.99
    disadvantage of sub-standard offers 12.94–12.95
    early groundwork 12.05–12.07
    fee savings 12.31
    funding and time to pay 12.81–12.89
    grey areas 12.38–12.42
    identifying unresolved matters 12.74–12.76
    importance of rapport with officer 12.100–12.101
    innocent errors and excuses 12.64–12.68
    letters of offer 12.90–12.93
    litigation and settlements strategy (LSS) 12.43
    no published *de minimis* limit 12.08
    overview 12.01–12.04
    payment on account 12.18–12.21
    penalty negotiations 12.10–12.17

Index

Settlements – *contd*
  negotiations – *contd*
    practitioner finality 12.33
    re-opening of claims and
      allowances 12.61–12.62
    recognition of best possible
      outcome 12.77–12.80
    reduction of investigation
      period 12.29
    relationship with client 12.102–12.109
    relevant skills 12.44–12.60
    remittances by non-domiciled individuals 12.63
    situations which are negotiable 12.34–12.37
    tax savings 12.32
    taxpayer finality 12.30
    VAT disclosure 12.22–12.23
    workload pressures on HMRC 12.73
  NIC appeals 5.78–5.81
  self-assessment enquiries
    discovery powers 1.103–1.106
    'Hansard' procedure 1.12
  tactical approaches 11.05–11.10
Sick pay 13.23
Social functions 13.157
Sole traders
  COP 9 questions 2.56
  payments on account 12.21
Special Investigations Office (SI
  allocation of cases 1.12
  Code of Practice 8 investigations
    tax evasion schemes 2.59–2.64
  Code of Practice 9 investigations
    definitions of fraud 2.27–2.32
    direct tax questions 2.56
    guarantee of no criminal investigation 2.34
    indirect tax questions 2.57
    meetings with HMRC 2.36
    publication of new code 2.33
    trigger points 2.35
    types of investigation 2.09
  definitions of fraud
    Code of Practice 9 2.27–2.32
    Fraud Act 2006 2.21–2.23
    'Hansard' procedure 2.24–2.27
    HMRC Enquiry Manual 2.18–2.19

Special Investigations Office (SI – *contd*
  definitions of fraud – *contd*
    importance 2.17
  directorate and assistants 2.07
  liaison points with other authorities 2.76–2.79
  need for specialist approach 2.65–2.74
  role
    large and complex cases 2.02 2.06
    relationship with other offices 2.03 2.05
    removal of prosecution teams 2.04
    successor to SCI 2.01
  types of investigation
    criminal investigations 2.10–2.16
    non-fraud cases 2.10
    suspected serious fraud 2.09
  use of qualified accountants 2.75
Special penalty reduction 14.65
Special procedure material
  production orders 7.23
  search and entry powers 7.21
SSP and SMP rules 13.57–13.58
Stamp duties
  appeals 11.35
  information powers 10.12
  inspection of premises 10.67, 10.69
  new penalty regime
    defaults and errors 14.13
    failure to make returns 14.126–14.128
    failure to pay 14.151
Students 13.85
Subsistence 13.158–13.159
Suggestion schemes 13.160
Surveillance powers
  criminal investigations 7.39
  VAT 3.36–3.41
Suspended penalties
  deferred payments 14.167–14.169
  failure to notify 14.110
  failure to pay tax 14.163
  new penalty regime 14.67–14.69

Tax Education, Enabling and Leverage teams (TEELs) 2.82
Tax evasion
  see also Fraud
  Code of Practice 8 investigations 2.59–2.64
  criminality 8.14–8.16

Index

Tax evasion – *contd*
  grey area for negotiation 12.41
  history 8.04–8.05
  increased government
    awareness 8.11–8.13
  published statistics 7.03–7.05
  relationship with money
    laundering
    conclusions 8.106–8.109
    development of government
      thinking 8.41–8.53
    overview 8.01–8.03
    role of fiscal authorities 8.67–8.77
  significance 8.06
  'untaxed economy' 8.07–8.10
Tax Health Plan 2.88
Taxpayer notices
  Finance Act 2008 Sch 36, 10.21–10.28
  role of First-tier Tribunal 10.33–10.37
Telephone expenses
  home telephones 13.161
  mobile phones 13.147–13.148
Termination of employment
  continuing benefits after
    termination 13.38
  other termination issues 13.43
  payments in lieu of notice 13.33
  redundancies and dismissals 13.35
  restrictive covenants 13.34
  retirement 13.36–13.37
  termination payments 13.30–13.32
Third parties
  employer compliance checks
    benefits and reimbursed
      expenses 13.162–13.164
    PAYE and NIC calculations 13.61–13.62
  information notices pre-FA
    2008 Sch 36
    appeals 10A.36
    reform of the law 10A.29–10A.33
  inspection of premises under
    FA 2008 Sch 36, 10.67–10.68
  new penalty regime
    approach to errors 14.70
    debtor contact details 14.122–14.123
  notices under FA 2008 Sch 36
    involved third party notices 10.38–10.40

Third parties – *contd*
  notices under FA 2008 – *contd*
    role of First-tier Tribunal 10.33–10.37
    statutory provisions 10.15
    third party notices 10.29–10.32
  previous penalty regime 14.81
  search and seizure powers 10.138–10.145
  self-assessment enquiries
    information powers from
      1 April 2009 1.90
    response to opening letters 1.23
Time limits
  appeals
    information notices pre-FA
      2008 Sch 36, 10A.37, 10A.53
    National Insurance
      Contributions 5.71, 5.76
  assessments 14.124–14.125
  new penalty regime 14.76
  self-assessment enquiries
    closure of 'enquiry window' 1.08
    discovery powers 1.99
    information powers from
      1 April 2009 1.81
    notice of enquiry 1.15
    retention period for books
      and records 1.40
Tips 13.26–13.27
Travel expenses 13.165–13.170
Trials
  committal from magistrates'
    court 7.47
  lengthy preparations 7.46
  offences and penalties 7.49
  role of professional advisers 7.48
Tribunals *see* First-tier Tribunal;
  Upper Tribunal
Trigger points
  Code of Practice 9 2.35
  criminal fraud investigations 2.14
  direct tax criminal
    investigations 7.11–7.12
  employer compliance checks 13.18
  NIC visits and investigations
    Category X notations 6.18–6.23
    complaints from employees 6.24–6.26
    end-of-year returns 6.11–6.17
    failure to reply to
      correspondence 6.31
    international employers 6.33–6.36

Index

Trigger points – *contd*
  NIC visits and investigations – *contd*
    large employers 6.32
    luck 6.37
    national programmes 6.28–6.29
    overview 6.09–6.10
    regional initiatives 6.27
    routine visits 6.30
  self-assessment enquiries 1.04

'Untaxed economy' 8.07–8.10

Upper Tribunal
  appeals from First-tier Tribunal 11.103–11.109
  appeals to Court of Appeal 11.119–11.122
  case management powers 11.113–11.115
  costs 11.118
  decisions 11.117
  direct referrals 11.101–11.102
  functions 11.99–11.100
  hearings 11.116
  judicial review jurisdiction 11.110–11.111

VAT
  accountancy costs 12.27
  assurance visits
    basis of selection 3.05–3.09
    bookings 3.13
    general questions 3.15–3.18
    information available to visiting officer 3.10–3.12
    preparations for 3.48–3.60
    review of VAT returns 3.19–3.32
    role of professional advisers 3.91
  business inspections 1.86 10.51
  credibility visits 3.33–3.35
  cross-border supplies
    Intrastat visits 3.36–3.41

VAT – *contd*
  cross-border supplies – *contd*
    mutual assistance and exchange of information 3.42–3.46
    trigger points for criminal investigations 7.12
  employer compliance checks 13.15
  information powers 1.72
  information powers pre-FA 2008 Sch 36
    information and documents 10A.61–10A.67
    statutory provisions 10A.59–10A.60
  inspection of premises under FA 2008 Sch 36, 10.64–10.66
  investigations 3.75–3.78
  merger of HMCE and IR 3.01
  National Advice Service (NAS) 3.04
  new penalty concepts 14.71–14.73
  new penalty regime 14.25–14.26
  penalty regime 5.13–5.33
  production orders 10.131
  record keeping requirements 1.44
  registration 3.02–3.03
  role of professional advisers
    appeals 3.84–3.86
    assurance visits 3.91
    business reviews 3.79–3.81
    complaints to adjudicator 3.87–3.89
    judicial review 3.90
    review of assessments 3.82–3.83
  search and entry powers 3.61–3.69, 3.62
  settlement negotiations 12.22–12.23
  specialist visits 3.47
  surveillance 3.70–3.74
  time limits for assessment and claims 1.92

Working rule agreements 13.93–13.97